ESSENTIALS OF LAWYERING SKILLS IN AFRICA

ESSENTIALS OF
LAWYERING SKILLS
IN AFRICA

Festus Emiri
Ernest Owusu-Dapaa
Ayuba Giwa

malthouse

Malthouse Press Limited

Lagos, Benin, Ibadan, Jos, Port-Harcourt, Zaria

First Published 2020
ISBN: 978-978-57643-5-2

Published and manufactured in Nigeria by

Malthouse Press Limited
43 Onitana Street, Off Stadium Hotel Road,
Off Western Avenue, Lagos Mainland
E-mail: malthouselagos@gmail.com
Facebook:@malthouselagos
Twitter:@malthouselagos
Istagram:@malthouselagos
Tel: 0802 600 3203

Distributors:

African Books Collective Ltd, Oxford, UK
Email: abc@africanbookscollective.com
Website: http://www.africanbookscollective.com

Dedication

Honourable Justice Charles Oluremi Jacobs, CJ (retired Chief Judge of Ogun State)

Acknowledgements

We graciously thank Chief Edwin Kiagbodo Clark, OFR, for his singular support to the production of this book in furtherance of the professorial chair in lawyering skills endowed by him, presently occupied by one of us. This is a commendable feat by Chief Clark in a clime where research funding for academics is a commodity in short supply.

We graciously thank our families for their sacrifice and support in writing this book:

Festus Emiri- to my wife, Nkoyo and children, Ovie, Efe and Dafe

Ernest Owusu-Dapaa -to my wife, Afia, and daughters Owusuwaa, Akua, Tiwaa

Ayuba Giwa - to my wife, Awushetu, and children Halim, Jubril and Jemila

Preface

The book has twenty-two chapters, divided into six parts for convenience.

Part I begins with preliminary matters of persuasion through the path of classic rhetoric; the place of technology in the practice of law; case management; case analysis; and legal reasoning.

Part II addresses core skills of writing, analysis and presentation, such as how to write persuasive judicial opinions, analysis government regulations; and make effective public presentations.

Part III interrogates features of good writing, particularly the observance of grammar rules and length of documents.

Part IV engages the skills of substantive persuasive advocacy and writing. It particularly focuses on strategies and techniques for effective lawyering, such as developing case theme, case theory, imaginative writing, use of demonstratives, and effective brief writing.

Part V addresses matters of literary allusions going to means and style of presentation, such as use of metaphor and other figures of speech.

Part VI examines the ethics and professional responsibilities negotiated by skills of persuasion and an afterword epilogue.

It is hoped that reading and applying some of the suggestions in this book will go a long way in making a lawyer more effective, skilful and a proper lawyer useful to the client and society.

Foreword

Continuous skills improvement is a imperative for lawyers and all those that have to deploy knowledge of the law in resolving one conundrum or the other. Indeed for colleagues in the legal fraternity most of the efforts during legal education are geared towards impartation of more of substantive and adjectival knowledge of law than the forensic and rhetorical skills needed for harnessing the problem solving resources of the law. The present book by Emiri, Owusu-Dapaa and Ayuba is imperative for providing the aid that enable lawyer and even law students to continuously develop and sharpen their skills.

Using twenty-two chapters the book explores diverse but intersecting themes relating to effective lawyering and advocacy skills. Preliminary matters of persuasion through the path of classic rhetoric; the place of technology in the practice of law; case management; case analysis; and legal reasoning are explore in the opening part of the book. Most of the lawyers of ten or more years standing at the bar had their legal education at the time during which internet and computer technology generally were not incorporated into legal education. Nevertheless, it cannot be doubted that electronic resources and various computer applications have become critical component of law practice and work of judges and magistrates. Speaking from the perspective of my Ghanaian judicial experience, for example, mention can readily be made of the Ghana law finder and other modes in which Laws of Ghana and Ghana Law Reports have been digitized for easy retrieval of information and researching the law. These electronic resources cannot be put effective use to enhance legal practice and judicial work unless one is imbued with the requisite skills. Moreover, as part of measures to expedite judicial processes and curtail backlog of cases that have been pending for long time, a discernible practice from our courts seem to be emphasis of written submission and Statement of Case. Thus, any scholarly effort that seeks to provide opportunity to refresh and continuously improve their written advocacy is worth celebrating.

It is therefore welcoming that the book addresses core skills of writing, analysis and presentation, such as how to write persuasive judicial opinions, analysis of government regulations; and make effective public presentations as well as strategies and techniques for effective lawyering, such as developing case theme, case theory, imaginative writing, use of demonstratives, and effective brief writing. In our present milieu where practitioners and professional law students are preoccupied with the quest to accumulate knowledge of what the current legal position of the law is, the authors have made a very useful contribution to legal academy as their books seek to address the deficit of legal skills oriented book written from perspective from authors acquainted with the common law as practised in African jurisdictions.

The ethics and professional responsibilities are also addressed in the closing chapters of the Book. The necessity of revisiting ethics and professional responsibilities cannot be over-emphasised particularly so when takes notice of current volume of complaints lodged with professional regulatory bodies like the General Legal Council in Ghana against lawyers for unprofessional or unethical behaviour against clients and other users of their service.

The Book is written in a language and style which are not only accessible but very interesting to read. I am quite sanguine that this book will be welcomed by lawyers, legal officers and law students in the common law world.

Professor Justice Sir Dennis Dominic Adjei (GIMPA)
Justice of Court of Appeal, Accra, Ghana and Former Dean, Faculty of Law, Ghana Institute of Management and Public Administration.

Table of Cases

Table of Contents

Chapter 1

Rhetoric Path: *Logos*, *Pathos* and *Ethos*

Introduction

Discussion about persuasion ordinarily begins with exploring the connection between persuasion and rhetoric because classical rhetoricians were the first documented persons who practiced the art of persuasion. Also, classical rhetorician theory of persuasion rooted in *logos*, *pathos* and *ethos* developed over 2,500 years ago remain the basic principles for structuring persuasive writing and advocacy.[1]

Some are of the view that rhetoric is misleading advocacy. In fact, rhetoric was associated with the antics of ancient courtroom tactics of Sophists advocates, some of whom were known for spurious lawsuits, who unfortunately were also among the teachers of rhetoric.[2] So, by the turn of the fifteenth century B.C., the Sophists created an impression where "sophistry" became associated with clever but false arguments. Thus, the disfavour that some philosophers like Plato attached to rhetoric followed the courtroom antics associated with the Sophists, who severed the once intimate association between law and rhetoric, "where to practice law meant to employ rhetoric."[3] This was however a mistaken conjunction. For in taking the disfavourable stance against rhetoric, those philosophers did not give enough thought to the intellectual heft rhetoric can and does bring to the practice of law. Associating rhetoric with manipulative use of language, a tool of persuasion, devoid of ethics was certain prejudicial, without grounding.[4]

---

[1]Michael R. Smith, *Advanced Legal Writing: Theories and Strategies in Persuasive Writing*, Aspen L. & Bus.2002 @ 11.

[2]Kristen Konrad Robbins, Philosophy v. Rhetoric in Legal Education: Understanding the Schism between Doctrinal and Legal Writing Faculty (2006) 3 *J. ALWD* 108.

[3] Laurie C. Kadoch, The Third Paradigm: Bring Legal Writing Out of the Box And Into the Mainstream: A Marriage of Doctrinal Subject Matter and Legal Writing Doctrine (2007) 13 *J. Leg. Writing* 55 @ 57-58

[4]Linda L. Berger, Studying and Teaching Law as Rhetoric: A Place to Stand (2010) 16 *J. Leg. Writing* 3 @ 3 (an article introducing students to rhetoric, making it possible for them to envision their role as lawyers as constructive, effective, and imaginative lawyers, grounded in law, language, and persuasive rationality states "The first of these [attacks on rhetoric], the attack from above, argues for a politics of reason whose indisputable truths can only be obscured by the rhetorician's passionate appeals. This is the position that Socrates defends. The second, the attack from below,

Aristotle on the other hand, took an opposing view. For him, rhetoric was a deeper activity. He referred to it as "a habit of the mind."[5]Some scholars are of the view that the schism between law and rhetoric, which is beneficial and has long existed to the present, (exacerbated by Langdell's scientific approach to law) is responsible for the loss "of a [once] coherent and all-encompassing approach to legal discourse," which connected the intellectual study of law with the intellectual practice of law.[6]

In fact, treating law as rhetoric goes beyond seeing rhetoric as a tool for persuasion. It goes deeper. It rather reveals how law is an interactive process of persuasion and argumentation used to resolve controversy. Thus rhetoric isn't a trick-game, using literary devices to cloak reasoning, but is an activity centred on perception, understanding, expression, integrating the study of effects of texts, composition process and perspective.[7] It is rather an activity that helps lawyers to become more aware of the effects of language in creating meaning, an awareness that makes them more rhetorically effective speakers and writers. Rhetoric beyond improving writing and advocacy skills, helps the lawyer to channel natural ability

---

insists that the rhetorician's invocation of truth and justice is a sham, a technique for gaining power whose success requires that its practitioners either fail to understand what they are doing or deliberately conceal it. This is the line of attack forcefully pressed by Callicles...Gorgias stands between these two, between Socrates and Callicles, and the question is, does he have any ground on which to stand? Does the craft of rhetoric have a separate and legitimate place in human life, in between pure reason and pure power?");Laurie C. Kadoch, So Help Me God: Reflections on Language, Thought and the Rules of Evidence Remembered (2007) 9 *Rutgers J.L. &Relig.*2 (available at http://org.law.rutgers.edu/publications/law-religion/forthcoming.shtml). See also, Kristen K. Robbins, Paradigm Lost: Recapturing Classical Rhetoric to Validate Legal Reasoning (2003) 27 V.*t. L. Rev*.. 483; Anthony T. Kronman, Rhetoric (1999) 67 *Univ.. Cin. L. Rev*.. 677; Jack L. Sammons, *The Radical Ethics of Legal Rhetoricians* (1997) 32 V.*al. U. L. Rev*.. 93 @ 93 ("[Legal rhetoric] is not unbridled because this particular form of rhetoric is located . . . within a particular rhetorical community with a particular rhetorical culture.").

[5]Francis J. Ranney, *Aristotle's Ethics and Legal Rhetoric* (Ashgate Pub. Co. 2005) @ 2 (providing insight into the source of the split paradigm of theory and practice, while drawing from Aristotle to explain the relationship between law and rhetoric as that between that theory and practice). See also, *Aristotle's Nicomachean Ethics,* Book VII.

[6]Kadoch above n. 4 @ 59 ("The ancient schism continues to have pro- found effects on the shape and substance of modern legal education.") The article also states that the absence of narrative in early English trials may be traced to the schism between rhetoric and law begun by Plato and other philosophers. See also, Michael H. Frost, *Introduction to Classical Legal Rhetoric: A Lost Heritage* 6 (Ashgate Pub. Co. 2005).

[7] The use of classical and new rhetoric is encouraged by scholars. See Michael R. Smith, *Advanced Legal Writing: Theories and Strategies in Persuasive Writing,* Aspen L. & Bus. 2002; Kirsten Konrad Robbins-Tiscione, *Rhetoric for Legal Writers: The Theory and Practice of Analysis and Persuasion* (West 2009);Michael H. Frost, *Introduction to Classical Legal Rhetoric: A Lost Heritage* (Ashgate 2005) (a collection of articles published between 1990 and 2003 used in analysis of legal interpretation and composition.).

to imagine and invent, and it may enable the lawyer to better listen to alternative views and to speak in the client's own voices.[8]

It is important to appreciate that rhetoric is itself embedded in the practice of law to help it attain truth as much as possible. In this respect, it can be likened to the practice of medicine, which seeks not "to make a man quite healthy, but to put him as far as may be on the road to health."[9]

Rhetoric Triangle

Judges and lawyers write the way they do using flexible organisational structures because they recognise that good writing must persuade. In doing so, they mimic ancient rhetoricians. Rhetoric refers to the "use of language for persuasive purposes."[10] In ancient Greece (around 450 BCE) classic rhetoric was acquired through rigor, systematic study in the art of persuading through advocacy and writing. Aristotle is reputed to be first and best known rhetorician.[11] Much as legal argumentation based on formal or informal models of logic constitutes the primary way to reason in law, it is obviously inadequate to fully capture persuasion.[12] Ancient rhetoricians unpacked persuasion through three paths: the concept of *logos*, *pathos*, and *ethos*.[13]

---

[8]Berger, above n. 4 @ 9.

[9]Aristotle, *The Rhetoric of Aristotle* 224, bk I, ch. I, 1355b, line 26 (Lane Cooper trans., D. Appleton & Co. 1932). The Rhetoric continues: "It is clear, then, that rhetoric is not bound up with a single definite class of subjects, but is as universal as dialectic; it is clear, also, that it is useful. It is clear, further, that its function is not simply to succeed in persuading, but rather to discover the means of coming as near such success as the circumstances of each particular case allow. In this it resembles all other arts. For example, it is not the function of medicine simply to make a man quite healthy, but to put him as far as may be on the road to health; it is possible to give excellent treatment even to those who can never enjoy sound health. Furthermore, it is plain that it is the function of one and the same art to discern the real and the apparent means of persuasion, just as it is the function of dialectic to discern the real and the apparent syllogism. What makes a man a "sophist" is not his faculty, but his moral purpose."

[10] Edward P.J. Corbett & Robert J. Connors, *Classical Rhetoric for the Modern Student,* 4th ed. PUP, 1999 @15.

[11]Aristotle, above n. 9 @ 7.

[12] Classical rhetoric reputed to have begun in the fifth century B.C.E. continued for nearly 1,000 years of the Greco-Roman history. It started with scholars like Socrates, followed by Plato, Aristotle, Cicero and Quintilian. See Aristotle, *The Rhetoric* (trans. W. Rhys Roberts, 1965) available at htpp://www.iastate.edu/honey1/Rhetoric/ (accessed Sep, 2016); Marcus Tullius Cicero, *De Inventione* (trans. H.M. Hubbell, 1949); Marcus Tullius Cicero, *De Oratore* (trans. E.W. Sutton, 1942); Marcus Fabius Quintilian, *Institutio Oratoria* (H.E. Butler, 1954). See Michael Frost, Introduction to Classical Rhetoric: A Lost Heritage (1999) 8 *S. Cal. Interdisc. L.J.* 613 (traces the history of rhetoric and argumentation to Corax of Syracuse). See also, Bernard Jackson, *Law, Fact and Narrative Coherence*, Deborah Charles Pub., 1988; Walter R. Fisher, *Human Communication as Narrative: Towards a Philosophy of Reason, Value, and Action*, U.S.C. 1989; Robert Burns, A Theory of the Trial, Princeton Univ. Press, 1999.

[13] Michael R. Smith, *Advanced Legal Writing: Theories and Strategies in Persuasive Writing,* Aspen Law & Bus., 2002 @ 22; Aristotle, *On Rhetoric* (transl. George A. Kennedy, Oxford Univ. Press, 1991);

Logos is persuasion accompanied through logical reasoning embodied in the content of the communication. It is the process of persuading through logical argument and reason. It is the primary method lawyers use in persuasion. This explains why primer learning of writing and advocacy embedded in legal methods tilts towards teaching strategies and techniques for persuasion through logos – the learning of IRAC organization schemata. Learning thus centres on skills of researching primary and secondary sources of legal precedent; skills of analysing legal issues; communicating legal analysis, and the like. Lawyers generally persuade using logos through substantive and logical argument, in the form of precedent (such as statute law, case-law and policy).

Pathos is persuasion accomplished through the emotional response of the audience to the communication. Pathos interrogates two aspects: emotional substance and medium mood control.

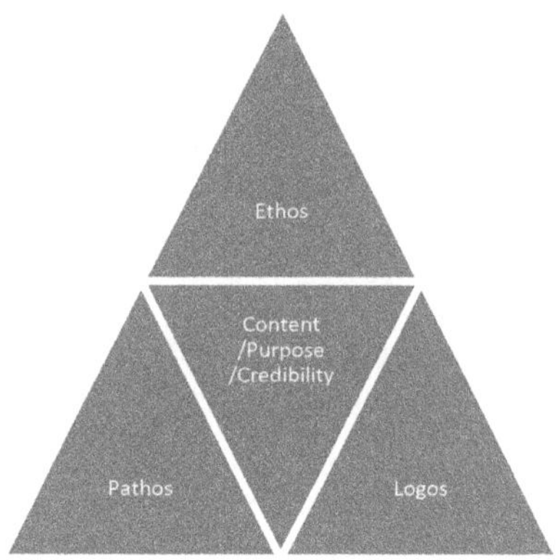

George A. Kennedy, *A New History of Classical Rhetoric,* Princeton Univ. Press, 1998; Stephen Toulmin, *The Use of Argument,* Cambridge Univ. Press, 1958. For detail discussion on a theory of persuasion, see J. Christopher Rideout, Storytelling, Narrative Rationality, and Legal Persuasion (2008) 14 *J. Legal Writing Inst.* 53 (in answer to the question 'what is it about narratives that make them persuasive in the law,' he stated that (1) narratives are innate ways of understanding and structuring human experience; this makes them inherently persuasive; (2) narrative models go beyond models of persuasion based on formal or informal logic, to encompass 'narrative rationality; (3) narratives embody several properties that are psychologically persuasive: (a) coherence (a formal property); correspondence (a formal property); (c) fidelity (a substantive property) Id @ 55. See also the interesting read, W. Lance Bennett & Martha S. Feldman, *Reconstructing Reality in the Courtroom: Justice and Judgment in American Culture*, Rutgers Univ. Press, 1981 (the social science researchers stating that American criminal trial is organized around storytelling).

Emotional substance aspect of pathos refers to the lawyer's effort to persuade by appeal to the audience's values and emotions.

The second aspect of pathos is medium mood control. It is persuasion through the medium (as opposed to the substance) of persuasion. For general advertising this is easily recognizable in the style in which an object is projected. Some project through commercial entertainment, other through fear, etc. in legal writing or advocacy, medium mode involves the stylistic strategies used by the lawyer to capture attention. If used in writing, it implicates the writer's style, as opposed to the substance of the argument.

An audience may be captured by the effective organization of document, its paragraphing etc. In advocacy, it could be the use of simple, understandable grammar, stylistic techniques, etc.

Ethos is persuasion through acquired through the credibility of the presenter. Classical rhetoricians recognize it as occupying the same square with logical arguments using logos. Ethos as persuasion accomplished through the perceived character or reputation of the speaker, refers to establishing and maintaining credibility in the eyes of the audience by showing intelligence, character and good will.[14]

The three pathways to persuasion (logos, pathos and ethos) are often depicted as the "rhetorical triangle", the three paths leading into one another. Logos affects the pathos in the audience and simultaneously affects the perception of the ethos of the author, the pathos of the audience affects how they perceive the ethos of the author and how they receive the logos of the argument.[15]

Aristotle for example, reminded advocates that the rhetorical pathways are fundamentally connected this way: a logical argument will not persuade an audience if the author is perceived as a baboon. Also, a respected author whose reputation is beyond question will not persuade if her argument is riddled with logical fallacies and flaws. Similarly, an ironclad argument delivered in a manner that antagonizes the audience or one in which the audience questions the integrity and credibility of the author will not persuade.[16]

Logos is taught as doctrinal lessons. Students are very familiar with its basic structure: 'think like a lawyer.' That IRAC already teaches them. So, they just

---

[14]Smith, above n. 13 @ 61.

[15]Michael Frost, Ethos, Pathos and Legal Audience (1994) 99 *Dick L. Rev.*. 85; Linda Levine & Kurt M. Saunders, Thinking Like a Rhetor (1993) 43 *J. Legal Educ.* 108. See also Michael Frost, Justice Scalia's Rhetoric of Dissent: A Greco-Roman Analysis of Scalia's Advocacy in the VMI Case (2002) 91 *KY. L.J.* 167.

[16]Michael D. Murray, Classical Rhetoric, Explanatory Synthesis and the TREAT Paradigm (Univ. Ill. L. & Econ.Working Paper No. 75, 2007), available at http://works.bepress.com/michael murray/9; Frost, above n. 15.

present that way as lawyers. Traditional legal pedagogy teaches legal analysis using logos. Pathos and ethos on the other hand, rarely are part of lawyers learning at the law school. They are thus skills that must be learnt and mastered. This is so because the essence of lawyering is persuasion. If the persuasion pathway is tripod, then effective lawyering must acquire the tripod skill pathway. A lawyer can learn persuasion through pathos and ethos by acquiring the narrative and storytelling skills, while the tension between logos, pathos and ethos offer lawyers an opportunity to reflect on professional responsibility and values.

New Rhetoric

Building on classical rhetoric, Phelps developed a new paradigm for the study of rhetoric, called the "new legal rhetoric", in 1986. New rhetoric shifts rhetoric focus from product to process.[17] According to Phelps this new paradigm is designed around five principal ideas:

(i) Writing is a process; the process is recursive rather than linear; pre-writing, writing, and revision are activities that overlap and intertwine;
(ii) Writing is rhetorically based; audience, purpose, and occasion (the components of the rhetorical situation);
(iii) The written product is evaluated by how well it fulfils the writer's intention and meets the audience's needs;
(iv) Writing is a disciplined creative activity that can be analysed and described; writing can be taught; [and]
(v) The teaching of writing is fruitfully informed by linguistic research into the composing process.

Employing the new paradigm for example, informs us that recursive writing requires the use of all the persuasive tools of classical rhetoric (logos, pathos and ethos) to produce a convincing story to an audience. New rhetoric interrogates the process of eliciting facts from the client, figuring out how to present and prioritize them, and then reducing it to writing to construction a coherent, credible story.[18] It involves developing the plot of the story and character, articulated the theme conveyed in an ascertainable narrative structure.[19]

---

[17]Theresa Godwin Phelps, The New Legal Rhetoric (1986) 40 *Southwestern. L.J.* 1089 @ 1094. See also, Peter Brooks & Paul Gewirtz, *Law's Stories: Narrative and Rhetoric in the Law* (Yale U. Press 1996); Donald M. Murray, *Teach Writing as a Process Not a Product, in Rhetoric and Composition: A Sourcebook for Teachers and Writers* (Richard L. Graves ed., Boynton/Cook 1984) @ 89; Michael R. Smith, Rhetoric Theory and Legal Writing: An Annotated Bibliography (2006) 3 *J. ALWD* 129.

[18]Stacy Caplow, Putting the "I" in Writing: Drafting an A/Effective Personal Statement to Tell a Winning Refugee Story (2008) 14 *Leg. Writing* 249.

[19]Caplow, above n. 18 @ 263(an article illustrating the recursive writing process is a conscious labouring one requiring the writer to elicit facts, measure the facts against other standards such as

Applied in the context of writing, new rhetoric is a composition theory. It see reading and writing as a process of creating knowledge, not merely a means for communicating it.[20] Thus the writer views the writing process as a thinking process, where the client's problem is reflected on and ideas are generated to address it. Writing is viewed not as a record of facts, thought and conclusions, but a product that meets the expectation of the reader and audience.

Legal Imagination and Lawyering

Legal imagination is significant to writing, reading and advocacy. Rhetoric of writing law requires the lawyer to imagine situations, roles, actors, and contingencies when drafting legal instruments. For example, when drafting a document the lawyer should be able to imagine surrounding facts that would guide the shape, content and structure of the legal document. White gives the example of drafting say a marital separation agreement. The lawyer must ask his or her client questions to determine the limits to a given situation. In other words, a person simply will not obtain everything he or she wants in a settlement; should ask the client to recognize that "essential fairness is important to both sides" and that such an agreement cannot resolve every issue or address every possible pitfall or shortcoming. He uses the agreement to further illustrate something fundamental. He states that the agreement does not simply stipulate rules the parties will either obey or disobey, but that it also creates roles for husband and wife. So, the process of imagining speakers, roles, situations, constituencies, and contingency becomes integral to writing any legal text (e.g., statute establishing an

---

historical facts and common sense, identify truthful and accurate language to convey facts and emotions in a recursive writing process); @ 261 the writer states that ("The New Rhetoric approach offers two important lessons for affidavit drafting. First, it recognizes that writing can be a long and interconnected chain of fact-gathering, thinking, composition, reflection, and rewriting leading to identifying themes, locating gaps and inaccuracies, and connecting facts and law. Building the facts one block at a time is a means of discerning the best legal theory, constructing a factual case that tells a "compelling story" within the boundaries of the legal elements, and building attorney- client relationships. Thus, the task of affidavit drafting serves multiple goals in addition to a finished product. Second, it is a process that is inextricably connected to a particular audience. Asylum officers and immigration judges, as noted above, often approach adjudication sceptically with an inclination to disbelieve the applicant."). For good use of new rhetoric in legal reasoning, writing and advocacy, see Binny Miller, Teaching Case Theory (2002) 9 *Clin. L. Rev.*. 293; Brian J. Foley & Ruth Anne Robbins, Fiction 101: A Primer for Lawyers on How to Use Fiction Writing Techniques to Write Persuasive Fact Sections (2001) 32 *Rutgers L.J.* 459; Binny Miller, Give Them Back Their Lives: Recognizing Client Narrative (1994) 93 *Mich. L. Rev.*. 485 (1994); Lucie White, Subordination, Rhetorical Survival Skills, and Sunday Shoes: Notes on the Gearing of Mrs. G. (1990) 38 *Buff. L. Rev.*. 1.

[20]Linda L. Berger,A Reflective Rhetorical Model: The Legal Writing Teacher as Reader and Writer(2000)6 *J. Leg. Writing* 57; Linda L. Berger, Applying New Rhetoric to Legal Discourse: The Ebb and Flow of Reader and Writer, Text and Context (1999) 49 *J. Leg. Educ.* 155; J. Christopher Rideout& Jill J. Ramsfield, Legal Writing: A Revised View (1994) 69 *Wash. L. Rev.*. 35, 52.

administrative agency, a Supreme Court opinion, or a business contract). From this reasoning the lawyer must imagine how the document will define the various actors it speaks about and what relation among them to create? The imagination will obviously require thinking whether the document will specify every contingency, or will rather use a general standards rule or not.[21] Thought must also be given to the choice of one over another. For example, it would be helpful for the lawyer to visualize if the legal document she prepares would continue to be regarded by the parties as relevant authority after the date of its making.[22]

What this illustrates is simple. The lawyer can only do a good job of drafting if she engages in the activity of dramatic imagination. She herself how the language used in a document would be read and understood by the audience, or abused. Thus writing drawing up legal documents must interrogate pertinent questions that give their document (whether transactional documents, legal memorandum or brief) the intended message sought to be conveyed.

White makes forceful the need for imagination as a lawyering skill when he state: "You are familiar, for example, with the ubiquitous personage of the law of torts, the Reasonable Man, and could write a story about him, I suppose: A Day in the Life of the Reasonable Man. Would such a story have any life or interest? Compare a similar effort on behalf of the Offeror, the Preferred Shareholder, or the Victim of Robbery. If you cannot imagine that a novel built around characters defined in that way would have any interest for you, how can legal talk about the same characters, the same events, have any interest?"[23]

Like the rhetoric of writing, the rhetoric of reading also invites imagination, because deriving meaning from any text requires the reader to imagine the world and its actors. Also, the act of reading necessitates imagining both the text and the context from which it is written.[24] A classic example is the rhetoric that attaches in reading the Constitution. The document only takes on real meaning when the reader imagines that it as a "set of authoritarian commands:" commanding as it does that it is supreme and that its provisions shall have binding effect on all authorities and persons in Nigeria.[25] But it has other interesting features that create competing possibilities as to how it should be interpreted. It is open to imagine that the framers created a document with certain ambiguities and

---

[21]Louis Kaplow, Rules versus Standards: An Economic Analysis (1992) 42 *Duke L.J.* 557 (discussing rule versus standard in law and economics).

[22] White, above n. 1 @ 40-41.

[23]James Boyd White, *The Legal Imagination* (Abridged Edition), Chicago: Univ. Chicago Press, 1985 @ 110.

[24]White, above n. 23 @ 42. See also Linda H. Edwards, The Convergence of Analogical and Dialectic Imaginations in Legal Discourse(1996) 20 *Legal Stud.* 7.

[25] See section 1 of the Constitution of the Federal Republic of Nigeria

uncertainty, in the confidence that other people, especially the judiciary would resolve them in the light of the language used and the exigencies of emerging future reality.[26]

What this mean is that a legal document, even the Constitution, when being read, can be imagined in multiple ways. Law can therefore be imagined as rhetoric.[27]

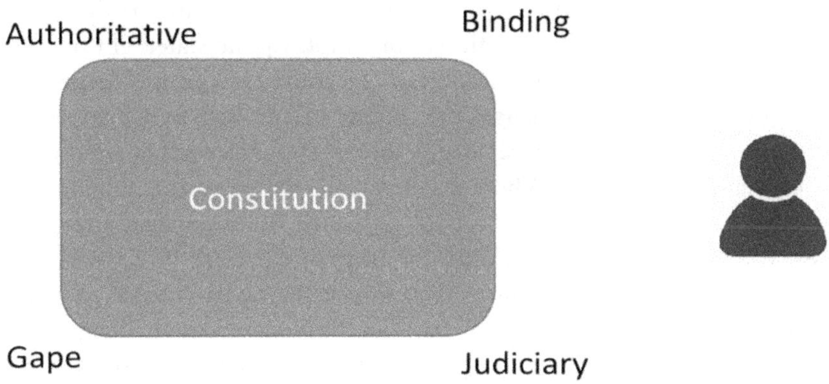

[26]See P. Amselek & N MacCormick, *Controversies about Law's Ontology*, Edinburgh: Edinburgh Univ. Press, 1991; Pierre Schlag, Hiding the Ball (1996) 71 *New York Univ. L. Rev*. 1681 (an article in ontology which examines the multitude of meanings that can be ascribed to authoritative legal sources) [it states for example that the United States Constitution has been interpreted as "what it *is,* whereas for others, it is what it *ought* to be. Indeed, there is a great deal of disagreement about how the "is" and the "ought" of the Constitution are related. Consider some of the professionally respectable possibilities: what the Constitution ought to be is of no bearing on what it is; what the Constitution ought to be ought to have no bearing on what it is; what the Constitution ought to be is of some bearing on what it is; what the Constitution ought to be is determinative of what it is; the Constitution is always already becoming what it ought to be; the Constitution is something that can never become what it ought to be]." Id. 1682.

[27]Narrative and legal storytelling provides an important dimension to imagining the law. The cultural and legal significance of narrative is related to how narrative helps to structure experience and constituting meaning for stories carry with it linguistic and intellectual ramifications. For example, a lawyer relates stories about other people and other situations in competition with other lawyers' stories with the understanding that each narrative lacks completeness. The competing stories therefore imply that the listener is driven to the edge of language and consciousness demand thinking, imagining and silence of the hearer where transformation and invention takes place for a new story to emerge, perhaps in a new language. The narrative manifests one's imagination/imagining, and it becomes important for engaging the rhetoric of writing and reading law. See James Boyd White, Telling Stories in the Law and in Ordinary Life: The *Oresteia* and 'Noon Wine.'" *Heracles Bow: Essays on the Rhetoric and Poetics of the Law.* Madison: The University of Wisconsin Press, 1985 @ 174

Learning Skills of Rhetoric Analysis

Mastering rhetoric is a skill effective lawyers must possess. Let us illustrate by an analysis of two cases decided by the Supreme Court on analogous contending questions. They are *Lagos State Government* v. *Ojukwu*[28] and *Group Danone* v. *Voltic Nig Ltd.*[29] Both cases fall within the question of whether a person in contempt of court can seek a judicial remedy while in contempt. In *Ojukwu's* case the court expressed the view that it is a very serious matter for anyone to flout a positive order of a court and proceed to taunt the court further by seeking a remedy from the court while still in contempt. [quote statement by the justices]. The *Voltic* case is not so different, but the court reached a different conclusion, stating that if a party challenges the validity of an order by way of appeal and so refuses to obey the order (technical contempt), such conduct would not amount to contempt. It stated: "Where a defendant challenges the validity of an order directed against her either by way of appeal or other application, she cannot be treated as being in contempt until the issue of the legality of the order is settled one way or the other" (stating that where the order disobeyed is one issued without jurisdiction or where the party in disobedience is challenging the validity of the order, the principle that a contemnor shall not be heard does not apply). "The court has concluded that to try a party for contempt who is challenging the validity of a lower court's order on appeal is improper because pending the determination of the validity of the order to punish the applicant could well turn out to be for an order without legal basis."

The Voltic decision on face reading will be strange to reasoning considering that contempt is based on acts that somehow affects the dignity of court in the administration of justice.[30] In Ojukwu the court took the position that disobeying an order was illegitimate as "no man can be judge in his own case . . . however righteous his motives." But in Voltic like the Ojukwu decision the court struggled with how far to protect contempt theory at a time of less social and cultural disruption. Both decisions show disagreement in reasoning. Voltic seemed irreconcilable with precedent. The Voltic opinions raise provocative and important rhetorical questions. Critical reading of the statements of facts in the

---

[28] (1986) NWLR (pt. 18)621 (1986) All N.L.R 233. See also *Agbor* v. *Metropolitan Police Commissioner* (1969) 1 WLR. 703 the court held that self-help amounts to breach of due process. See also *Okotie-Eboh* v. *DPP* (1962) 1 All NLR.353; *Attorney-General of Lagos State* v. *Attorney-General of the Federation* (2004) 9-12 SCM (pt. I) 82; *Saidu Garba* v. *FCSC* (1988) 7 SC (pt. II) 170; *Prof. Ajibayo Akinkugbe* v. *Ewulum Holdings Nigeria Limited* (2008) 4 SCNJ 404 (a landlord who resorts to self-help held to run foul of the law and liable to be assessed for damages).

[29] [2008] 3-4 SC 32

[30] *Odu* v. *Jolaoso* [2005] 3-4 SC 116.

majority and dissenting opinions may change the minds of anyone who believes that judicial opinions merely "state the facts".

Rhetoric analysis requires imagination of the setting for both decisions. Ojukwu was decided during the military era, while Voltic was during the nascent democracy. Exploration of background facts, such as social conditions during the military era, particularly "rights-abuses" and the struggle of the judiciary to protect its independence, can supply context to the decision. For instance, a pathos (appeals to the audience's values, beliefs, and emotions) analysis of Ojukwu can reveal to the lawyer much more than meets the eyes in the opinion. So too, is an analysis of Voltic. In Voltic, the majority opinion framed the complaint within the structure of pursuing legal rights, the complainants were referred to as trespassers and . . . The majority opinion mentions . . . all providing justification to sidestep Ojukwu as precedent.

But the minority opinion took the other route. It emphasized the legitimacy of the order appealed against and why it ought to have been obeyed before complain, by way of appeal.

Rhetoric analysis also demands that both decisions be compared using the other tools of classic rhetoric (analysis for *logos*, *pathos* and *ethos*). If and when completed, the lawyer would certainly have learnt that case analysis and the process of law is a rhetorical activity, in which lawyers interpret and compose legal texts. And if anything, that rhetoric is a way of thinking and imagining about how law works. Rhetoric analysis thus makes a lawyer more efficient and in fact, more ethical.

As a skill it centralizes critical reading and analysis of legal texts.[31] Following the suggestion of White, it beckons on the lawyer to:

(i) examine the inherited context underlying the legal text: the language or culture within which this writer works; the writer's role and background; how these affect the kind of language, authority, values, arguments, and materials the writer uses;

(ii) study the art of the text: how the writer uses, modifies, or rearranges the language or culture that is prevalent; the effect of the rearrangement; the internal and external coherence of the text;

(iii) description of the rhetorical community created by the text: what kind of person speaks in it; communicates to what audience; what voice is used in communication; what kind of response is being elicited by the communication; how does the reader fit in the interpretive community addressed.

---

[31] James Boyd White, Law as Rhetoric, Rhetoric as Law: The Arts of Cultural and Communal Life (1985) 52 *Univ. Chi. L. Rev.* 684 @ 701–702.

A lawyer who goes through this motion in reading legal text will no doubt get a better understanding of it, as it supplies a whole load of extra-legal information about an understanding of culture, history, and knowledge of language and law. This is how the activity of rhetoric interrogates the imagination.[32]

By reading, say the cases of Ojukwu and Voltic within the structure of logos only, it becomes clear to the lawyer that appeal to reason alone may not be enough to support persuasion in the sense of establishing belief in uncertain truths – how supposed contempt behaviour should be treated. A lawyer can thus appreciate that appeals based on the reason may well far from syllogism, but verge more as enthymeme, if not logical fallacy.

Ethical Concern about Rhetoric

Schism about rhetoric has hardly evaporated even in our time. At pains of repetition we will present a brief defence of rhetoric in the legal process. James Boyd White's *A Dialogue on the Ethics of Argument*, in which the writer (imagining) speaks as Socrates in dialogue with two young lawyers is what we use to interrogate the propriety of rhetoric in lawyering.[33]

The challenge posed by an imagined Socrates goes this way:

> By reason of your training and natural capacities you have what is commonly called a great power, the power of persuading those who have power of a different kind, political and economic power, to do what you wish them to do. . .
>
> Your professional aim is to present your case, whatever its merits, so that those with control over economic and political forces will decide for your client, and you most succeed when you most prevail. You use your mind, as we used to say of the Sophists, to make the weaker argument appear the stronger...[But] neither the

---

[32]Berger, above n. 4 @ 37.

[33]James Boyd White, *Reading Law and Reading Literature: Law as Language*, in *Heracles' Bow: Essays on the Rhetoric and Poetics of the Law,* Univ. Wis. Press, 1985 @ 215. See also Jack Sammons, A Symposium: The Theology of the Practice of Law, February 14, 2002 Roundtable Discussion (2002) 53 *Mercer L. Rev*.. 1087(The article providing further discussion of the ethics of rhetoric states: "[W]hen rhetoric is appropriately located within its own tradition it is never unbridled in the way we tend to think of it. It is almost always instead a craft with constitutive restraining rules located in a particular rhetorical culture that carries within it a certain understanding of the virtues and vices based upon ideals of character for both rhetoricians and for their particular audiences. . . . And, what is more, while rhetoric is not only about persuasion—the beauty of the argument on the other side can be appreciated—it is always about persuasion as opposed to force, isn't it?")

> power of money nor the power of persuasion is a good thing of itself; that depends upon whether it is used to advance or injure one's interest, and that is no concern of yours, with respect to your client or apparently to yourself.
>
> You say you are your client's friend, but you do not serve his interests; in truth you are not his friend...Likewise, you are no friend to the law . . .
>
> In all of this you are least of all friend to yourself . . . You never ask yourself in a serious way what fairness and justice require in a particular case, for to do that would not leave time for what you do.

White imagines the lawyers' responses in the dialogue as well. In one of them, he makes the case that practising law has a tendency "not to injure but to improve the character," a tendency "greatly affected by the nature of the ethical community that one establishes both with one's clients and with other lawyers and judges." He claims that Socrates misunderstands the lawyers' enterprise, which is to "preserve and improve a language of description, value, and reason—a culture of argument—without which it would be impossible even to ask the questions that you think are most important, questions about the nature of justice in general or about what is required in a particular case."[34]

The lawyer's answer gives insight to understanding the process in which the lawyer takes part, the lawyer's life can be justified in that she merely makes the best case she can out of the materials of her culture in addressing the judge. Effectiveness demands that she hones her skills by improving on her materials – which in this case demands exploring how social life and realities is interrogated through law.

This view provides an answer as well to ethical questions:

> While I am in a sense "insincere" when I say to a judge, for example, that "justice requires" or "the law requires" such and such result, this insincerity is a highly artificial one, for no one is deceived by it. . . . But at the same time I am implicitly saying something else, with respect to which I am by any standard being sincere: that the argument I make is the best one that my capacities and resources permit me to make on this side of the case.

[34]Berger, above n. 4.

There is therefore good reason to master rhetoric. It does not make a weak argument come strong. The adversarial system for testing truth will protects against any ethical problems that might otherwise be caused by rhetoric. Rhetoric can thus be viewed as a sword that can be used to advance and defend. It creates lawyer's consciousness that she is an intermediary between the abstract and the real - the conduit that brings words of law and words of life together. The skill of rhetoric provides a respite from the cold nature of law viewed as lifeless rules. It rather encourages a lawyer to experience law as a rhetorical activity, with opportunity to think professionally in constructing reality of present by reflecting on the past. Lawyers skilled in it read more critically, more reflectively and can present better. Reflective reading generates skills of to become more rhetorically effective advocates and writers. In addition to discovering the nuances of law, rhetoric helps shape a lawyer's skill to present legal arguments to accommodate diversity and individual circumstances that depart from the norm and the form.

Chapter 2

Technology and Legal Practice

Introduction

The place of technology in law is indisputable. Courts and process are increasingly being computerised. So too are legal research materials. Any lawyer without technology skills is not only analogue but will find practice space difficult to find. Proficiency in the use of computer and other forms of electronic technology is certainly a required core skill to function in the e-world of today. Recognizing the importance, *Best Practice* lists the use of technology among the core competency skill a lawyer ought to possess.[1]

The modern practice of law is evolving towards technology. Practice of law is increasingly digital. Many lawyers use computers in their offices and conduct legal research electronically. The Internet has fast become a critical source for factual research. Even in litigation, pleading and motions are now filed and served electronically.[2]Evidence is presented digitally and e-discovery is fast becoming a central part of practice.[3]

---

[1] Best Practice states that a lawyer should be able to effectively use "current technologies and strategies to store, retrieve and analyse information and to undertake factual and legal research." What this requires is that law schools should provide up to date law practice management curriculum that teaches their students to understand and manage technology in their practice as well as meet all the duties of professional responsibility interrogated by technology, such as the protection of client's digital information and the like. This certainly demands that lawyers and law schools must change the way they behave in a brave new world driven by data and technological change, and process management. Roy Stuckey et. al., *Best Practices for Legal Education: A Vision and a Roadmap,* 2007 (hereinafter called *Best Practices*) and generally, Association of American Law School, Conference on the Future of Law School Curriculum: Brochure (Seattle, 2011); William M. Sullivan, et al. eds. *Carnegie Fund for the Advancement of Teaching, Educating Lawyers: Preparation for the Profession of Law,* 2007 (hereinafter called the *Carnegie Report*) Foundation for the Advancement of Teaching, Preparation for the Professions Programme (PPP) 2007, Legal Education Report based on a survey of more than two hundred law faculties (schools) in the US and Canada in 1999. See also, Richard Susskind, *The End of Lawyers? Rethinking the Nature of Legal Services* (a book that urges lawyers to re-examine what present legal task and workloads can be undertaken differently-cheaper, quicker, efficiently, and with better predictability).

[2] See the directive of the National Judicial Council initiative on providing simple, fast and efficient communication between lawyers and the courts, directing that starting July 16, 2018, that it is mandatory that all Supreme Court processes shall be served by electronic means – legal mail. Lawyers are accordingly requested to use only legal email addresses obtainable from the Nigeria Bar Association. See http://www.nigerianbar.ng.

[3]David I. C. Thomson, *Law School 2.0: Legal Education for A Digital Age,* 2009; Gerald F. Hess, Blended Courses in Law School: The Best of Online and Face-to-Face Learning? (2013-2014) 45 *McGeorge L.*

Law libraries today are moving away from print materials to electronic holding. As a result there is an expected decline in the availability of print legal resources. Some have even suggested that in the near future print materials could become obsolete, as modern libraries are moving away from analogue holding. Many libraries are only updating electronic copes of their resources.[4]Even for the heavily used legal material sought for in the library - cases and statute, readers are beginning to prefer the electronic format. In fact, lawyers still show a preference for online sources in situations where print copies are equally available. The decline in preference for print text on shelves is understandable. They are bulky to carry; susceptible to dirt and dust. What is more, library-lending policy may not favour easy removability and convenience for readers. Print resources are thus becoming an endangered species.

The increased cost of print resources is likely going to drive out of libraries print resources in the near future, making them less available to legal academy, law firm, and government libraries. The new world of legal research is likely to be dominated by a variety of digital data and resources. With the passing of time, more and more lawyers going to buy into the world of electronic resources.[5]

The world is now being dominated by online, not traditional, print research.[6] The inevitable consequence is that law, which used to be the most book-centre profession, is becoming bookless. Every lawyer therefore who desires to remain relevant must learn to do online research for print materials may so become extinct with time.

Rev. 51 (an article suggesting that effective blended course design requires the teacher to integrate online and classroom instruction thoughtfully, seeking to maximize the advantages of both online and face- to-face learning); Kristen B. Gerdy et. al. Expanding Our Classroom Walls: Enhancing Teaching and Learning Through Technology, (2005) 11 *J. Legal Writing Inst.* 263; Catherine Dunham &Steven I. Friedland, Portable Learning for the 21st Century Law School: Designing a New Pedagogy for the Modern Global Context (2009) 26 *J. Marshall Comp. & Info. L. 371* (discussing the changing technological and legal environment and the need for teaching methods to align with it).

[4] Sanford N. Greenberg, Legal Research Training: Preparing Students for a Rapidly Changing Research Environment (2007) 13 *J. Legal Writing* 241 (an article based on a survey on the ascendency of online resources over print materials). But cf. Michelle M. Wu, Why Print and Electronic Resources Are Essential to the Academic Law Library (2005) 97 *Law Libr. J.* 233, 235, 247 (an article arguing that despite the preference for electronic resources by libraries and an apparent decrease in print subscriptions, that both print and electronic materials are necessary in a quality law library). See also, Paul E. Howard & Renee Y. Rastorfer, Do We Still Need Books? A Selected Annotated Bibliography (2005) 97 *Law Libr. J.* 257.

[5]Carol M. Bast & Ransford C. Pyle, Legal Research in the Computer Age: A Paradigm Shift? (2001) 93 *Law Lib. J.* 285.

[6] Ibid. Tracy L. McGaugh, Generation X in Law School: The Dying of the Light or the Dawn of a New Day? (2003) 9 *Legal Writing* 119 (an article which shows that the paradigm shift for online material by generation X persons – those born in modern time, is responsible for decline demand for traditional print resources).

The electronic space is being dominated by the likes of major commercial and non-commercial players, such as Westlaw, Lexis, Legalpedia, Compulaw, HeinOnline, LawPavilion and a host others. The Internet plays host to these websites, some of which are free and other fee paying.

Learning e-research however requires first mastery of the skills for conducting traditional print research, particularly skills interrogating techniques of how to conceptualize problems; how to access legal resources through an index or table of content; and know how to evaluate the credibility and authoritativeness of resources. These skills are necessary for e-competence research. This is because a lawyer who cannot conceptualize problem for example, will still find the e-research resource unhelpful. This is how ability to conduct print research constitute the foundation for competent online research.[7] Unquestionably, print-oriented research skills remain important even if online resources dominate the practice. It is the transferable print research that can assist a lawyer to conduct more efficiently research online.

This chapter is concerned with an understanding of how lawyers can learn and master the skill of electronic research in an age of informatics.[8]

Visual of law practice/office dominated with computers

---

[7]Molly Warner Lien, Technocentrism and the Soul of the Common Law Lawyer (1998) 48 *Am. U. L. Rev.* 85 (a paper encouraging young lawyers to first master print research skills that are transferable to online research). See also Lee F. Peoples, The Death of the Digest and the Pitfalls of Electronic Research: What Is the Modern Legal Researcher to Do? (2005) 97 *Law Libr. J.* 661 (an article that shows that familiarity with traditional print materials like the print digest enables online legal researcher to quickly locate online relevant area of rules interrogated by particular legal problem); Suzanne Ehrenberg & Kari Aamot, Integrating Print and Online Research Training: A Guide for the Wary (2007) 15 *Persps.* 119.

[8] Informatics refers to an analysis of the information flow for a given function, (in this case a legal function), legal technology (the mechanism that facilitates the legal flow of information), and the professional responsibility implications of both. In fact, it is the study of the structure and properties of information, and the application of technology to the organisation, storage and retrieval and dissemination of legal information.

Changing face of legal services market

The world's shrinking economy and rise in legal information technology are the invading armies of the market for legal services.[9] They foist a permanent downturn in the legal employment market. Present innovative technologies in the profession include platforms designed to help drive down legal costs for potential clients at all price points—from a simple consumer using LegalZoom.com to the sophisticated general counsel applying informatics techniques to lower his or her company's legal bill.[10]

Whether we like it or not, the legal profession like other white-collar jobs is increasingly been subject to automation. The bundle of skills associated with the practice of law falls on a continuum where a number of basic tasks have already been displaced by computation, automation, and soft artificial intelligence.[11]Faced with cost pressures, clients and law firms are leveraging legal information technology to either automate or semi-automate tasks previously performed by teams of lawyers.

We just must get it straight. Informatics, computing, and technology are certainly going to change both what it means to practice law and to "think like a lawyer." In fact, the most disruptive of these possible displacing technologies - quantitative legal prediction (QLP) - now stands on the horizon.

The march toward quantitative legal prediction will define much of the coming innovation in the legal services industry. The reason is simple. Every

---

[9]Daniel Martin Katz, Quantitative Legal Prediction – or – How I Learned to Stop Worrying and Start Preparing for the Data-Driven Future of the Legal Services Industry (2013) 62 *Emory L.J.* 909; Ibrahim Sule, E-Lawyering: Some Trends and Lessons from the USA (2011) 11 *NL & PJ* 14.

[10]LegalZoom, http://www.legalzoom.com/ (last visited September 23, 2018) (advertising low-cost, legal document creation).See also, David B. Wilkins, Team of Rivals? Toward a New Model of the Corporate Attorney–Client Relationship (2010) 78 *Fordham L. Rev.* 2067 (an article which states that some corporations in the United States are beginning to trim the number of law firm retained to provide legal services by creating preferred provider networks); Larry E. Ribstein, Delawyering the Corporation [2012] *Wis. L. Rev.* 305 (an article that discusses how the expanded role of corporate counsel and the use of new legal technologies is affecting the legal market).

[11] R. Susskind, *The End of Lawyers? Rethinking the Nature of Legal Services*, Oxford University Press, 2008 (the author considered one of the technology evangelists in the book predicts the "end of lawyers, asserting that entire profession may be driven into oblivion by the internet and what he called 'automation efficiencies'. In the learned writers view legal practice would be redefined by two forces – by a competitive market leaning towards the commoditization of legal services and by the prevalent development and inventions of new and 'disruptive legal technologies). No question about it. The end day of brick and mortar law office is in the wings. See Andrew L. Askew, iEthics: How Cloud Computing has Impacted the Rules of Professional Conduct (2012) 88 *North Dakota L. Rev.* 454, available on http://law.und.edu/_files/docs/ndlr/pdf/issues/88/2/88ndlr453.pdf accessed on September 23, 2018 (an article that states that the traditional brick- and-mortar law offices, crowded with dozens of shelves filled with legal reporters and digests, and countless file cabinets containing droves of confidential information will soon disappear). See also Sule, above n. 9.

single day lawyers and law firms are providing predictions to their clients regarding the likely impact of choices in business planning and transactional structures, as well as their prospects in litigation and the costs associated with its pursuit.

How are these predictions being generated? Precisely what data or model is being leveraged? Could a subset of these predictions be improved by various forms of outcome data drawn from a large number of "similar" instances? Simply put, the answer is yes. Quantitative legal prediction already plays a significant role in certain practice areas and this role is likely to increase as greater access to appropriate legal data becomes available.

Today's AI is soft AI because it attempts to mimic human intelligence in outcomes, but not in its underlying processes. It turns out that we still have only a very limited understanding of the human brain, and thus the direct artificial intelligence attempts to model its internal processes have borne little fruit. By contrast, for a certain class of problems, the outcome-based approach has been quite successful. These approaches generally place a black box around the internal dynamics used by human reasoners and instead model and predict the choices made by actors. Using large segments of observational data, today's soft AI is built upon modelling what people actually do, thereby allowing a machine to probabilistically emulate their behaviour.

Automation achievements

So much is being achieved by automation now. Let us consider just two examples of the invading imperialist – technology.

Aspirational spelling: We all as human reasoners learn the rules of spelling at an early age. We learn also the rules on grammar. From there we read and write prose, poetry, letters, memo and the like.

How has AI done in this respect mimicking human reasoning? From an algorithmic perspective, the difficult was how to mimic that behaviour. Historically, spelling and spell checking were "hard" problems and the "best" available solutions to the problems were only moderately successful. Many researchers and technology companies, including Microsoft, invested millions of dollars and countless hours trying to develop a robust, flexible, and scalable spell-checking algorithm. Big Data broke the logjam and pioneered what is the current approach to spell checking.

Google succeeded where others had previously failed by leveraging massive "click data" and more than three billion daily queries to harvest out probabilistically likely matches to commonly misspelled words. The key is to develop an approach that generates a series of often-correct answers to the specific problem. As individuals click through to specific answers, that data is harvested so that, in the aggregate, the program quickly begins to approximate. And today no one doubts that computers have mastered aspirational spelling.

Self-Driving: in 2012 the Google self-drive car was licensed in the State of Nevada and has completed more than 300,000 miles without causing an accident.

These are just some of the feats of automation, not to mention robotics and others.

Implications of automation to law

How does all of this translate to the future of lawyering? What do clients often ask? This! Do I have a case? What is my likely exposure to liability? How much is this going to cost to litigate? Are these documents relevant? What will happen if we leave this particular provision out of this contract? How can we best staff this particular legal matter to win? These are core questions often asked by clients.

Many lawyers earn their respective fees by generating informed responses to these and other related types of questions.

For many years, the answers to these questions have been the exclusive province of human assessment. Ability to give informed answers usually comes with the skill and experience of the lawyer. A seasoned lawyer can draw upon both extensive legal training as well as personal experience developed over years of law practice to advise. But you know like I do that the client pays for this. The advice can be expensive depending on the billing hours of the lawyer. Yet this expert advice isn't without probabilistic limitation. This is the entry point for quantitative legal prediction.

QLP-based technologies are designed to remedy or supplement the shortcomings of human reasoners. For example, human reasoners are limited in the scope of their observations. They only possess the observational data they have observed. While an experienced lawyer might be familiar with hundreds, if not thousands, of prior events, he or she is unlikely to have observed tens of thousands, hundreds of thousands, or millions of prior events. Thus, when answering the question, "Do I have a case?" an individual's particular understanding of likelihood might be driven by personal observations that are anecdotal, censored, or otherwise not indicative of the true distribution of outcomes. This is particularly problematic for rare events. The best way to remedy these and other related issues is to observe a large-scale and truly representative selection of the relevant event data, which the QLP now provides.

The rise of Big Data and soft artificial intelligence, however, has invigorated the formerly dormant field of legal prediction.

Building somewhat off their prior technical work, political scientists Andrew Martin and Kevin Quinn, together with legal scholars Theodore Ruger and Pauline Kim, set up a tournament for the 2002– 2003 Supreme Court Term. Like any Term of the Court, the issues presented were wide ranging and included controversial topics such as *Miranda* rights, affirmative action, state sovereign immunity, the First Amendment, sex offender registration, and three strikes laws.

The tournament pitted a classification tree (Method #1) against the predictions of elite lawyers and law professors (Method #2) with the straightforward task of determining the votes of individual United States Supreme Court Justices (affirm or reverse) in upcoming cases. Through the tournament, the goal was to observe both the relative and absolute performance of individuals and the machines. For many, the results were surprising: "[T]he machine did significantly better at predicting outcomes than did the experts. While the experts correctly forecast outcomes in 59.1% of cases, the machine got a full 75% right."[12]

The pattern is familiar—machines outperforming humans on a task that typically requires expert judgment (and this was about ten years ago).

QLP have been successfully used in patent cases. Even for stock exchange trading and prediction. While the human element has not been completely removed from finance, the rise of the quants displaced many of the status quo practices. The emphasis has shifted from human to machine judgment. Thus, on any given day, a majority of trades executed on the New York Stock Exchange are generated algorithmically.[13] Automation has also proved useful in e-discovery using sorting and coding.

QLP is indeed a revolution. It is very unlike the tools of empirical research. For it the tools of causal inference are not necessarily, for it uses the observables to build the model rather than using the model to assign causal weight to observables.

Legal Reasoning and Artificial Intelligence (AI)

While useful work has been done in this basic thrust, we are still far away from a machine that can engage in "hard" analogical reasoning. The more immediate question is whether it is possible to develop some sort of second- best or "soft" analogical reasoning technology designed to aid human reasoners in their efforts to develop more persuasive arguments. On this front, there is significant hope, and it is likely that advances will be driven by an iterative mix of data + model +

---

[12]Theodore W. Rugeret *al.,* Essay, The Supreme Court Forecasting Project: Legal and Political Science Approaches to Predicting Supreme Court Decision-making (2004) 104 *Colum. L. Rev.* 1150.

[13]Michael Mackenzie, High-Frequency Trading Under Scrutiny, *Financial Times* (July 28, 2009, 6:44 PM), http://www.ft.com/intl/cms/s/0/d5fa0660-7b95-11de-9772-00144feabdc0.html.

more data and so on. It will start with a more intelligent legal search and then will move up the intellectual value chain.

Analogical reasoning is at the core of how lawyers reason and how lawyers argue. The casebook method developed by Christopher Columbus Langdell is designed to tune the understanding of law students in an effort to help perfect their ability to reason by analogy. Through immersion, students are bombarded with analogy after analogy in case after case. Much like the inductive models, successful students are able to harvest, retrieve, and induce the relevant method of common law reasoning and develop the sort of clever arguments that others find persuasive. They can execute this task despite not fully understanding the underlying model of persuasion. Although an individual human reasoner cannot precisely identify the rules, it is quite clear that some phrases and analogies captivate the imagination.[14]

Consider three increasingly sophisticated forms of tools designed to guide a lawyer's legal reasoning: (1) People who cite *Case X* also cite *Case Y*; (2) Lawyers who argue *Principle X* also typically argue *Principle Y*; and (3) Given the mixture of argument and content in your brief, have you considered this argument and content, which is largely parallel (analogous) to your argument and content? On the spectrum of AI complexity, each of these models is increasingly sophisticated and would be hard to fully express and predict in a model alone. However, like many of the breakthroughs in commercialized artificial intelligence and in our feedback economy, it was not the model, but rather the click data, or the feedback effect that ultimately led to a transformative product. The key to getting that feedback (click data) is to express a plausible-enough model to maintain end user participation during a "burn in" period. This issue was faced in the move between the Music Genome Project (model) and Pandora (the commercialized product).

With the development of an elaborate and adaptive mapping of the case space, a number of potential technologies become possible. For example, to a greater degree of precision one should be able to predict the cases that lawyers should read in crafting their arguments (intelligent legal search), better predict relevant documents (e-discovery), and perhaps even suggest (predict) cases with analogous content or argumentation structure.

---

[14]Vincent Aleven, Using Background Knowledge in Case-Based Legal Reasoning: A Computational Model and an Intelligent Learning Environment (2003) 150 *Art. Intelligence & L.* 183; Layman E. Allen & C. Rudy Engholm, Normalized Legal Drafting and the Query Method (1978) 29 *J. Leg. Educ.* 380; Katie Atkinson et al., Computational Representation of Practical Argument (2006) 152 *Synthese* 157; Kevin W. Saunders, A Logic for the Analysis of Collateral Estoppel (1986) 12 *Rutgers Comp. & Tech. L.J.* 99; Adam Wyner, An Ontology in OWL for Legal Case-Based Reasoning (2008) 16 *Art. Intelligence & L.* 361 (2008); Edwina L. Rissland, Comment, Artificial Intelligence and Law: Stepping Stones to a Model of Legal Reasoning (1990) 99 *Yale L.J.* 1957.

All of these search-based technologies could improve and streamline the core task of legal argumentation undertaken by many lawyers. In addition, such information retrieval is also needed for the highest end prediction engine. In order to develop a case prediction engine, one needs to be able to "pre- predict" the set of cases that are sufficiently similar to the base case to be indexed for purposes of executing the actual prediction of case outcomes. In order to deliver optimal results, the retrieval or "pre-predicted" set of comparison cases needs to include cases that share an analogical structure to the reference case. Since analogy is so powerful in law, its development cannot be ignored when it comes to the question of selecting the comparison group of cases. Modelling this sort of analogical reasoning is nontrivial, but it is not impossible. Thus, it should be one of the most pressing goals of research in the legal informatics and artificial-intelligence-and-law community.

Online Legal Services

Technology competition challenge to lawyers technology is real.[15]Online legal services which made its debut in the 1990s in the United States of America in the form of simplistic databases of legal information (providing the public with text-based explanation of legal rights and simple standard draft and legal form contractual agreement) now is common place. Over time similar sites have been developed to make readily accessible standardised legal documents at relative low costs to viewers.[16] Some of the sites now provide more tailor specific information to viewers, such as legal advice and tailor-specific clauses to agreements, wills and other transactional planning. Some even extend to do "attorney-referrals" for services considered incongruent to render with use of technology.

Interestingly, these service providers combine technology with a business model that provide cheap, efficient and affordable legal services through two main strategies: commodification of legal services, and Unbundling of legal services

Commodification of legal services

This involves the standardization of legal services that are readily adaptable to technology and repackaging them for lower cost and efficient delivery, such as providing basic legal information and document for free or at reduced costs.

Unbundling of legal services

This entails breaking down legal services into component parts to allow for choice by viewers, such as . . .

---

[15]Chris Johnson, Leveraging Technology to Deliver Legal Services (2009) 23 *Harv. J. Law & Tech.* 259 (an article exploring the evolution and nature of online legal services).

[16]These companies include MyLawyer.com.inc; LegalDocs.com; WeThePeople ("WTP"); and USLegal.

Sometimes the services are customised beyond the automated system. Clients can submit request for specific documents, which is customised to their need. No matter the shape of services online service providers render, the bottom-line is that in majority of cases the providers and users are happy. The providers earn profit, the users enjoy services (value) at lower and sometimes more efficient costs. So, the system provides an alternative to hiring a lawyer - a cheap alternative to hiring a lawyer.

Aside questions bothering on professional responsibility implicated by online legal services, the profession must grapple with the associated challenges of information security, liability breaches of rules of unauthorised practice and accessing underserved markets.[17] Privacy and confidentiality are particularly important for transactional planning services, such as those connected with personal wills and estate planning.[18] The question of unauthorised practice is of heightening importance because only lawyers are permitted to render legal services. This mean that online providers will need to operate within a confine that does not bring them face to face with regulations prohibiting unauthorised practice. Some providers have sought to short-circuit this by expressing stating that what they provide is legal information as opposed to legal advice. While it is plausible to argue that "information" is concerned about informing users of the law and how to exercise their rights, and that "advise" on the other hand, tells what course of action to take in a given situation-an exclusive preserve of legal practitioners, both would certainly shade into the other in many respect.

While it beyond dispute that the biggest winners in online lawyering are the consumers of legal services who invariably benefit in lower cost and easy accessibility, it is plausible to construct a space for intuitive lawyers to also benefit even though online services offered though web-contract is generally considered disruptive of the traditional model of lawyering. The possible benefits are as follows:

(i) Since online lawyering is more likely to adversely affect solo and small practices that traditionally serve the low and moderate-income market clients, as it largely covers their core practice and business areas, lawyers can take

---

[17]Johnson, above n. 15.

[18]RPC Rules 17, 23, 50(3) and 54. See also, *Ndukwe* v. *LPDC* (2007) 5 NWLR (pt. 1026) 47 @48, Mohammed JSC; *Nigerian Bar Association* v. *Fobur* (2006) 13 NWLR (pt. 996) 196 @ 216, per Abdullahi Ibrahim, SAN, Chairman LPDC ("The relationship between a legal practitioner and his client is a fiduciary one and this implies that the legal practitioner must act with the utmost honesty and fairness to his client. Any form of dishonesty or fraud perpetrated against the client by the legal practitioner will amount to misconduct."); *Labode* v. *Otubu* (2001) 7 NWLR (pt. 712) 256 @ 282, per Onu, JSC.

advantage of online lawyering by setting up partnerships whose scope of businesses operates at a different business level. Large practice firms who do complex corporation matters usually operate outside the scope of online competition. So their business is not likely to be adversely affected by online competition.[19] There is therefore incentive for solo and small partnership to transform into large law firms.

(ii) Technology could provide opportunity for lawyer to buy into the evolving market, thereby improving their revenue base. In fact, the "lawyer-facing" side of the technology can be the very empowering bases for professionals to grow their practice. To illustrate, online website creates centralised platform for interaction between lawyers and clients in jurisdictions where advertisement for legal services is not proscribed.[20] Johnson states that such "symbiotic" can be used to introduce a centralised advertising platform for lawyers and clients. In fact, one online provider *USLegal* hopes to create a business model where lawyers in addition to their customised website will have a centralised one where they can meet with clients seeking specific services.[21] Such a leap will enable lawyers provide the human angle often absent in the provision of online services to clients. This way lawyers benefit from an expanded market, the clients are happy to get the human ouch to their problems.

(iii) By moving traditional staple of legal services into the e-market, lawyers are provided the opportunity to devote time and attention to more challenging, complex and stimulating problems more relevant to the legal process. The legal resource diversification and relocation online brings to professional services provides an opportunity for lawyers to buy into and harnessed technology for its good, rather than lawyers resorting to old fashion rules of professional ethics generally bars unauthorised practice. Technology drives the world, so whether lawyers like it or not, the profession stands powerless in the face of this invading imperial master. The sooner lawyers see, take hold and enjoyment the "doughnut," rather than debate about the propriety of its "hole" the better. Embracing technology is the only way our profession will remain relevant.

(iv) The thinking that online services would adversely affect traditional client patronage is sheer alarmism, not demonstrable. A recent survey in the U.S. suggests that about 26 per cent of persons with legal problems seek no remedy. They constitute what can be referred to as the "latent legal market" (those not

---

[19] This position could change with the emergence of quantitative legal prediction (qlp) machines in common use. See also, Ruger, above n. 12.

[20] RPC Rules 39 (3) proscribes advertisement by lawyers. Query? With the emergence of online lawyering should the rule not be relaxed?

[21] Johnson, above n. 15.

able to afford the cost of face-to-face lawyer services and so take no redress action).[22]In developing economies, the percentage is likely to be higher. It is this "latent market" that online technology primarily serves. So, why should traditional practice worry about the intrusion of technology, if not for sheer alarmism, unfounded fears? What is more, by online providers making legal services more available to these otherwise "no-worry" potential clients, technology is invariably expanding the space and market for legal services rather. It is not shrinking the market. Neither is it diverting business from lawyers.

(iv) Very fundamental, technology makes it easier for "potential clients" to find legal services. Lawyers, whether as solo or large firm practitioners should therefore consider business models that can deliver online legal services in the marketplace to remain competitive in our "e-era." The market is fast growing and is set to capture a large chuck of what traditional lawyering holds.

Effective lawyers must now seek to acquire requisite skills that would enable them function in the e-era; identify and develop business online business model practice; managee-research; operate virtual office; use latest technology to increase revenue base; create successful marketing strategies to deliver online services; understand professional responsibility components implicated in online practice; find more flexible and costs efficient ways to deliver legal service products.

Research skills preparatory to online research

It is plausible to think that since most lawyers are familiar with and use digital devices, online research will be a simple task not needing serious learning. Just knowing how to use the computer does not guarantee effective online legal research. In whether conducted by print-paper or online research, all research requires mastering certain skills for effectiveness.[23]

Four essential research skills must be mastered to effectively conduct research. They are: (i) an understand of the legal question to be addressed; (ii) finding solution to the problem through research using secondary sources; (iii) locating relevant research materials; and (iv) asking for help.[24]

---

[22]Ibid @ 279-80.

[23]Richard Buckingham, Thinking Like a Librarian: Tips for Better Legal Research (2010) 12 *T.M. Cooley Prac. & Clin. L.* 1 (an article providing four useful tips to legal researcher and suggest that a good legal researcher needs to think not just like a lawyer, but also like a librarian; in particular, a law librarian. It states that Law librarians make excellent legal researchers for two reasons: their knowledge of general (non-law specific) research techniques; and their knowledge of legal resources and law-related research tools and that by applying traditional research techniques to the legal field, law librarians are able to research more efficiently and effectively).

[24]Buckingham, above n. 23. These tips are merely general guide not meant to be exhaustive.

(i) Understanding the problem

It is important for the researcher to understand the nature of the problem or challenge the research is designed to address. The lawyer can get to know this by asking questions. For example, an associate assigned to write a memorandum for a senior partner would need to ask (clarifying and specific) questions about the facts of the legal challenge, the jurisdiction of the legal problem and the context for which the research is needed.[25]

(ii) Start with secondary sources

Generally, every researcher has the intuition to begin research from primary sources. The urge should be resisted.[26]It is suggested that research should begin with a trustworthy secondary sources for the following reasons: (a) secondary sources often provide citation to relevant authorities interrogated by the legal controversy. For example, if the research topic is one that intersects several primary law sources, say a question about a client wrongfully arrested and detained by the police, a researcher who resorts to primary sources first will need to research in at least three different primary sources – legislation, including materials like the Constitution; case-law precedents; and may be, police regulations on the subject-matter. But if the researcher chooses a trustworthy text (secondary source), say a good book on constitutional law, the reader is more likely to quickly see all the primary law sources cited in the chosen one publication. With that the researcher identifies the relevant information needed to address the problem; (b) secondary sources often provide guiding and explanatory information about the intended research area. It aids the researcher to understand the issues being researched by providing analysis and explanation not often available in primary source materials. So, instead of the researcher having to read and synthesis say a number of statute, case-law and regulation to determine the controlling precedent, secondary source gives the reader the finished product.[27]

---

[25]Kent C. Olson & Robert C. Berring, *Practical Approach to Legal Research,* 1988, 73.

[26]Morris L. Cohen & Kent C. Olson, *Legal Research in a Nutshell,* 9th ed. 2007, 15 ("It is generally best to begin research by going to a trustworthy secondary source - a legal treatise or a law review article."); William A. Hilyerd, Using the Law Library: A Guide for Educators Part IV: Secondary Sources to the Rescue (2005) 34 *J.L. & Educ.* 273 ("For individuals who are new to a given area of law, including attorneys who have never practiced in that area, secondary sources provide a quick method by which they can get a grasp on potential issues and pitfalls within that topic. If not for secondary sources, each legal problem would have to be researched by sifting through primary materials and that would be a truly daunting task. While not an impossible task, it would not be recommend-ed.") Id. @ 292. See also Patrick Meyer, Law Firm Legal Research Requirements for New Attorneys (2009) 101 *Law Libr. J.* 297 @ 303-304.

[27]Ibid @ 96.

Statute annotation, encyclopaedias, law review articles, and legal treatises are useful secondary sources.

(iii) Locate relevant materials

A library's bibliographic control is used by librarians to organise law materials available in the library for their use, location and identification. The catalogue record shows a book's title, author and call number. Thus, once the reader knows the citation of an item, finding it is easy. The library catalogue or index is used to locate the book. In like manner, an online researcher trying to find the relevant primary authority on a given issue may use a computer-assisted research tool, such as *Westlaw*, *CompuLaw* or *Legalpedia*. By simply running searches in full text databases of legal materials the researcher could locate the relevant material sought.

Just as knowing, say the title of a book can be an effective way to find materials, there may be times when the research can be carried out more efficient using bibliographic control tools of catalogues and indexes.[28] Similarly, a digital library's online search through public access catalogue can help identify books available in a library. For example, *WorldCat*, a free online union catalogue, gives researchers the opportunity to search more broadly and identify items in the collections of thousands of libraries around the world. To carry out proper online research a reader looking for primary source materials should use the library's online public access catalogue or say *WorldCat* by running keyword searches, which look in the title, contents and subject fields.

If the search produces what appears irrelevant, the reader can further review the subject headings to identify additional search terms that can be used in a new keyword search. The researcher can also use the call number to find related items, either by going to the shelves and browsing, or by searching the catalogue using the known call number.[29] Where however the keyword search returns too many results, the reader can prune the result to something manageable by limiting the

---

[28]A library catalogue is composed of bibliographic records that de- scribe the items in a library's collection. There is a record for each item in the collection, whether it is a treatise, periodical, code set, DVD, or some other type of research material. The record is divided into numerous fields, for example author, publisher, and call number. When librarians use a catalogue to *identify* items related to a given is- sue, they focus on the title, contents, and subject fields. On the other hand, "Index means 'to point to.' Indexes 'point to' information located somewhere else . . . Librarians use print indexes because some- times it is easier to find legal materials if a research tool points to them, rather than having to search for the materials themselves. A good index can be an especially useful tool because it will point to the same material in several ways (i.e., the same material will be indexed under more than one entry); use cross-references to direct the user to similar or related terms; be structured in a way that gives con- text to the terms used; and help the user find material based on the concept covered and not the specific words used.

[29] Buckingham, above n. 23 @ 20.

keyword search to the title field alone. This will reduce the number of results and improve the result quality. In this respect, a treatise with a researcher's search words in its title is likely to be more pointedly relevant.[30]

(iv) Seek help

If the researcher despite following the above three steps in the research finds it difficult to get satisfactory research result, it would be appropriate to seek help from other colleagues. These tips can advance the reader's research skills whether the research is on print-paper or online.

The process of accessing information through research as common to both research for secondary or primary materials online. Secondary source research requires a legal researcher to look for key terms in either the index or table of (book) contents; find the relevant article; read it to gain general knowledge of the subject; as well note the citation to primary legal authority. To find a statute, a researcher will similarly have to look in a key word index to find the statutory code citation, and look up the citation in the relevant code volume. To find a case, a researcher would also look up key terms in the index of a digest; find the relevant key number; find the entry for that key number; and obtain citations to case reporters where the case is located.[31]

The search engine is the vehicle through which material in online databases is accessed. While there are individual differences in search engines, the basic function is the same. The researcher enters search terms into a search box. The box using an algorithm to retrieve results matches the search item with what is in the database. Unlike print research where the materials come in an organized form, online research produces a large chuck of information not readily organized for the researcher use. The researcher therefore must take the pain to filter what is material from immaterial.[32]

However more important than knowing how to find materials online by clicking on keywords is learning the skills of intelligently using that is more critical. The lawyer must be able to specifically identify a legal source when she sees one and she must learn to question the nature of everything that turns up on the click. Even more fundamentally, she must understand exactly what authority governs a particular legal issue. This is far more critical than knowing how to navigating the various online platforms. Real legal research has two components: locating information and deciding what to do with it. It involves gathering and

---

[30] Ibid.

[31] Ellie Margolis & Kristen Murray, Using Information Literacy to Prepare Practice-Ready Graduates (2016) 39 *Univ. Hawai'i L. Rev.* 1 @ 9.

[32] Ibid.

analysis. The first is pretty easy to master once the lawyer can click using keyword search. The challenge is with analysing. For example, it is not sufficient using the goggle search or LawPavilion to gather relevant cases on say unlawful arrest and detention, the lawyer must be competent to analyse the cases gathered: carefully read the cases to understand the general rules; the controlling precedent applicable to her particular facts situation; assessing how other additional cases affect the controlling precedent; consider the policy considerations in the cases; implications of the reasoning for the fact pattern, etc.[33]

In this respect, traditionalist legal research theory holds important lessons for the new researcher who is still developing the knowledge base necessary to conduct thoughtful research. Traditionalist legal research theory provides a focused means of organizing information - from general background information to the specific rules that govern a particular legal issue. And organizing and categorizing legal authority are core skills that new researchers desperately need to master. So, it would be foolhardy to discount mastering traditional research skills because the "traditionalist" paradigm is grounded in some timeless concepts that can provide a lifeline for novice online researcher. It gives the researcher background knowledge in secondary sources, helping her to develop a foundational understanding of the topic and to identify terms of art. Also, when searching for case law, the traditional researcher consults legal digests to connect search terms to specific, recognized legal topics. This type of search strategy calls in aid more experienced researchers (the publications' legal editors) to identify the relevant universe of authorities recognizing that while keyword searches have a role to play, a topic search helps to define the relevant universe in ways that a keyword search simply cannot. So embracing certain traditional concepts can instil a sense of confidence in the completeness of the results. Therefore, we can confidently reason that while traditionalist theory was certainly born in the print era, it certainly advances online research.

Online Legal Research

As legal research software has evolved and legal content migrated online, it is now impossible to talk about legal research from a purely bibliographic perspective. The organization of legal materials in digital databases is getting further and further away from the world of books it once replicated. Instead of digests, indexes and other finding tools, lawyers conduct most of their research electronically, typing requests into a search box.[34]

---

[33]Ibid @ 130-133.

[34]Ellie Margolis & Kristen Murray, Using Information Literacy to Prepare Practice-Ready Graduates (2016) 39 *Univ. Hawai'i L. Rev.* 1 @ 9. Ellie Margolis, Is the Medium the Message? Unleashing the

Online research involves a lot of legal research skills: skills of reading, how to conceptualise problems, how to access legal resources through an index or table of content, how to evaluate the credibility and authoritativeness of resources organisation, storage, retrieval and dissemination of legal information, analysing, citation and many more. So, effective print-oriented research skills cannot be discounted as transferable skills to effectively do online research.

However, since legal resources are increasingly transforming from text-based materials to virtual materials it is imperative for lawyers to acquire in addition to traditional research skill, the online research skill.[35] Online research is especially challenging because data in the web is generally unstructured, poorly suited for research. It is information displayed to be read on screen may be unsuitable for the researcher who would want it in other ways. For instance, the researcher may want the unstructured material structured in a way that makes sense of the data or information for comparative purposes. Displaying two materials for reading at the same time could cause eye and cognitive fatigue. Doing so through screen read or print out may be laborious as well as complex and confusing. A simple example will do. Suppose, a researcher wants to examine how many times the Supreme Court is dispositive of appeals on procedure rather than substance in the past twenty years compared to prior twenty years before the time relevant to research, the researcher will have to do a lot of surfing the web, cutting and pasting to compare. All of this can quickly be done by understanding computer processing

---

Power of E-Communication in the Twenty-First Century (2015) 12 *Legal Comm. & Rhetoric: JALWD* 1 (an article analysing why the move to a digital medium should cause lawyers to consider changes in traditional approaches and to identify the changes in both writing and reading electronic texts that create the possibility of change).

[35] Paul Ohm, Computer Programming and the Law: A New Research Agenda (2009) 54 *Villanova L. Rev.* (an article showing how lawyers can access legal information trapped on the web, while proposing a new interdisciplinary research agenda to be known as computer programming and the like, similar to other interdisciplinary studies like law and economics). See also Ellie Margolis & Kristen Murray, Using Information Literacy to Prepare Practice-Ready Graduates (2016) 39 *Univ. Hawai'i L. Rev.* 1 (an article serving as an attempt to find a new way to think about how to prepare law students to be "practice-ready" for the legal research and writing tasks they will face as they enter law practice, and how to equip them with the skills they need to communicate with older generations of lawyers,while adapting to new and evolving technologies); Toree Randall, Meet Me in the Cloud: A Legal Research Strategy that Transcends Media (2014) 19 *J. Legal Writing Inst.* 127 (an article discussing a flexible legal research paradigm that de-emphasizes information gathering process and focuses instead on the importance of understanding and analysing legal authority. The learned writer is of the view that the very nature of information technology calls for an emphasis on substance rather than form and that legal research should de-emphasis the method and means of information gathering to the research and focus instead on the foundational knowledge necessary to accurately categorize the information and access its completeness).

which automatically structures the material through extractive devices like scraping or spidering – not common knowledge to an average computer user.[36]

Digital reading

Though it is not presently envisaged that we would completely give up paper documents for digital ones, the transition from paper-based documents to digital documents is bound to affect how lawyers read for research purpose. Legal reading is properly described as "active reading" because the purpose is to help the lawyer quickly reach at decision-making: to analyse the relevant law and apply it to legal controversy. So, lawyers and judges do not read in a linear, but recursive fashion.[37]

Active reading is the appropriate reading strategy for lawyers because lawyers are busy people by nature. They have to write memorandum and briefs, prepare oral arguments, etc. So, their goal in reading legal and non-legal materials is broadly strategic- to learn to educate themselves on problem-solving. Prior to the digital revolution lawyers read and wrote on paper. Now much of reading is digital. It is therefore plausible to think that the change from print reading to digital reading will be unproblematic and that receptive readings on digital devices feel the same like reading on paper.

Research however suggests that it is not so. Studies suggest that the device used in reading has a significant impact on how people engage and understand information read. According to one report "[a] page of online text viewed through a computer screen may seem similar to a page of printed text. But scrolling or clicking through a Web document involves physical actions and sensory stimuli very different from those involved in holding and turning the pages of a book."[38]

---

[36]Scraping allows the data in the web to be used in an endless number of new ways, such as graphing, tabling, etc. which is put into application managers like Microsoft Excel. On the other hand, spidering is a programme that visits Web sites and reads their pages and other information in order to create entries for a search engine index. The major search engines on the Web all have such a programme, which is also known as a "crawler" or a "bot". Scripts can also track websites over time, allowing researchers to study dynamic data, and helping them contend with the evanescent nature of the web.

[37] Active reading is associated with a broad set of cognitive skills and activities, such as thinking, learning, note taking, annotations, searching and skimming that enable an individual to achieve a deep level of comprehension of a document. See Mary B. Beazley, Writing for a Mind at Work: Appellate Advocacy and the Science of Digital Reading (2016) 54 *Duquesne L. Rev.* 415 @ 420 ("Active Reading contrasted with "receptive Reading," which is described as "the process of linearly progressing through the text without interruption)". Id. @ 420.

[38]Nicholas Carr, *The Shallows: What Internet is Doing to Our Brains*, W.W. Norton &Co. 2011 @ 90, cited in Beazley, above n. 31 @ 423.

This probably explains why some judges and lawyers still prefer to read on paper. Aside the online reading advantages of convenience, availability and the like, empirical evidence suggests that the brain seem to work better and be engaged better with paper for active reading.[39] Active readers' preference for print resources is connected with how reading device connects with the brain and ultimately cognition. Our comprehension is interestingly affected by how we touch and move around the document we read, its physical space and organization. This explains why active readers still show a preference for the paper-print.

Studies increasingly confirm that the brain connects better with print resources and that it is the format that advances cognition better for active readers.[40] Additionally, the reduced physical or visual cues of digital resources slow down cognition for active readers in three main ways: (a) it imposes on the reader more cognitive load burden; (b) it challenges the reader's ability to navigate between and among multiple documents; and (c) challenges the reader's ability to annotate while reading.

As an example of cognitive burden, simply consider how digital devices capture visual and cognitive resources of the reader. If the reader clicks a link or jump from search term to search team in a database, the system beams up new cognitive landscape often with no contextual cues to the information the reader is reading. Also, it could be challenging for active readers to achieve deep comprehension when navigating between want to navigate between documents when using digital resources. Active reader usually annotate by marking for relevance and importance of particular content. While skimming through print-paper the reader can easily annotate for quick reminders. Flexibility to achieve a similar feat online could pose annotation problems.

Recognizing these limitations inherent in digital reading would help the legal researcher to choose effective online materials and think ahead of how best to use the resources for deeper comprehension. For example, in choosing an online resources the lawyer may need to give priority to designed hardware and software that will promote the engagement of active readers with the text. Software that provides more visual cues, promoting reader's comprehension, creates

---

[39]Mary B. Beazley, Writing (and Reading) Appellate Briefs in the Digital Age (2004) 15 *J. App. Prac. &Process* 47, available in http://llaw-repository.ualr.edulappellatepracticeprocess/voll5/iss1/5 (an article which reveals that while most judges report that they do a significant amount of their reading on digital devices: desktops, laptops, tablets, and even phones, they would however prefer to read paper documents, and research among academics yields similar results).

[40] See Nicholas Chen *et al.*, Designing a Multi-Slate Reading Environment to Support Active Reading Activities, ACM Transactions On Computer-Human Interaction, Oct. 2012 @ 18, available in http://doi.acm.org/10.1145/2362364.2362366.

opportunities for neuro-spatial between reading material and reader. Such are the type of technological wares lawyers should strategically purchase for their practice. In this respect, lawyers preference should be for digital resources that provide structural cues for active readers, such those manufactured to make provision for headings, topic sentences, roadmap paragraphs and the like. They better suit the purpose of active readers.

How to teach technology skills to lawyers

The Best Practice suggests that the content of legal education must begin to recognise and introduce technology in legal education curriculum.[41] It states:

> If technology is not the future of legal education, it is at least part of the future. Proven and experimental uses of technology will continue to grow, and some components of legal education will be transformed by it. Distance learning is already becoming an accepted part of the landscape of legal education, and interactive computer programmes are allowing students to acquire knowledge and skills outside of the classroom setting.[42]

Technology can be employed to make legal instruction and evaluation more efficient and effective. But it can do more. Current technologies allow law professors to implement many of the best practices described in the *Best Practice* document. For example, course web pages can be used to disseminate instructional objectives; to encourage reflection by students' on the learning processes; to teach students strategies and techniques of active learning practices, such as posting graphic organizers or original mnemonics; to create an environment of cooperative learning, such as analyses of hypotheticals or development of student-authored practice exams; to increase student opportunities for practice and feedbacks, such as opportunities for more online multiple choice exams and short answer quizzes; etc. Likewise, PowerPoint, as technology can be used a tool for responding to students' diverse ways of learning by integrating visual movement and imagery into classroom teaching.

Other forms of technology being used in law schools include television, videotapes and DVDs, overhead projectors, digital recorders, electronic visual

---

[41] . Roy Stuckey et. al., *Best Practices for Legal Education: A Vision and a Roadmap,* 2007 (hereinafter called *Best Practices*) @ 117. See also, Kristin B. Gerdy, Jane H. Wise & Alison Craig, Expanding Our Classroom Walls: Enhancing Teaching and Learning Through Technology (2005) 11 *J. Leg. Writing* 263.

[42] Ibid.

presentation cameras, and classroom performance systems to name a few. Classroom performance systems use "clickers," in which each student is given a keypad to respond to in-class multiple choice questions. The software records and reports on the results as a tool for responding to students' diverse ways of learning and serves as a classroom assessment technique that informs the teachers whether the students are learning. It also informs the students whether their learning strategies are working productively. Another technological innovation is the use of recording systems that automatically make video and sound records of students' classroom answers and performances for subsequent review.

Digital technology is making it possible to record and broadcast classroom instruction over the internet, "podcasting." Some law schools are currently running free digital recording and blog accounts for podcasting of courses. It enables students to listen to classroom lectures or weekly summaries created by the instructor and because of the anytime, anywhere nature of podcasts, they can listen at times that are not necessarily dedicated to studying.

Technology has also been used by some innovative law schools to help prepare and deliver teaching materials and assessment tools. For example, there is a web-based platform called *Cyber Workbooks* that allows faculty to publish their course materials by integrating learning outcomes such as critical thinking, applied reasoning, and creative problem-solving.[43]

On the whole, technology in the classroom greatest unused role in in promoting learning outcomes is in helping students acquire core legal knowledge and understanding. Software programmes now exist that can generate myriad of formative assessments, quizzing students on substantive law principles and other subjects using hypothetical questions. The process of drill and practice enables students to know immediately if they are learning the assigned materials, thereby helping them to develop competencies and motivate them to learn better.

The doubting "Thomas" lawyers

Does the combination of Big Data and the "soft AI" revolution represent a fundamental transformation, rather than some sort of predictable, incremental change? It is pretty common for those with a vested interest in the status quo to argue that what they do is outside the possibility frontier. When an individual

[43]The *Cyber Workbooks* platform consists of an authoring tool for developing course modules with lessons, questions, and answers; a user website accessible by students with a user name and password; and an administrative site for generating reports and allowing faculty to evaluate course modules. The platform has built-in assessment features that will identify, measure, validate, and report on learning outcomes and identify student weaknesses, without any special training. The programme will time, grade, and record student responses to minimize faculty time and burden.

argues, "You cannot replace me with a machine," it is useful to begin by evaluating his or her basis for that belief. Do they have the requisite technical understanding to evaluate what is and is not possible? Typically, claims of this type represent more of a hope than a grounded analysis.

Remember, this is the age of robotics, AI, and the "race against the machine." Be wary of backward-looking statements such as, "That was already tried and did not work." The ground is rapidly shifting. Peril and possibility, as well as disruption, are fundamental features of our times.

Mistaking exponential change for linear change is a very common mistake. Indeed, our desire to linearize a nonlinear function is a well-studied cognitive bias. A classic prism through which the non-linear march of technological progress is sometimes described is the "chessboard" problem. There are many versions of this story, but it generally surrounds payment by a ruler to the local individual who invented the chessboard. Whether it be a Persian king or Indian leader, the basic thrust is as follows: The ruler was so pleased with the game of chess that he allowed the inventor of the game to name a prize for the invention. The inventor, who was both brilliant and wise, asked the king to provide him with one grain of rice for the first square on the chessboard, two grains for the second square, and four grains for the third square with continued doubling until payment was received for all 64 squares. The ruler quickly accepted the inventor's offer and was even offended that the inventor was asking for such a low price. The story ends with the inventor becoming the new leader because the promise yielded a pile of rice that was larger than the size of the tallest mountain.[44]

The ruler's fatal mistake was equating linear growth with exponential growth. In the early portions of the chessboard, the returns associated with each doubling are quite close. For example, assume that the ruler were to give 100 grains for each square. This function - *100x*—would yield the follow series: 100, 200, 300, 400, 500, 600, 700, 800, and so on. This would look quite similar to values such as 1, 2, 4, 8, 16, 32, 64, 128, 256, 512, 1024 (i.e., 2^0, 2^1, 2^2, 2^3, and so on). Eventually, the exponential function overtakes and rapidly passes the values returned by the linear function - 6400 versus 2grains on the final square alone.

Arguably we are transitioning to the second half of the chessboard where new technological possibilities are consistently presenting themselves. Each doubling of an already massive number is extremely significant because exponential increases initially look a lot like standard linear ones, but they're not.

[44]Wheat and Chessboard Problem, WIKIPEDIA, http://en.wikipedia.org/wiki/Wheat_and_chessboard_ problem (last modified Apr. 5, 2013).

As time goes by - as we move into the second half of the chessboard—exponential growth confounds our intuition and expectations.

That is what happens to doubting Thomas. Let me share with you some frightening scenario. In 1998, Kodak company had 170,000 employees and sold 85% of all photo paper worldwide. Today there is no Kodak. It has gone bankrupt. Why they ignored Steven Sasson the inventor of digital photography who worked form the company in 1975.[45]

AI is here to stay. We are n the fourth industrial revolution. Software will disrupt most traditional industries in the next ten years. Uber is just a software tool. It owns no car, and yet is the biggest taxi company in the world. Airbnb owns no property, but is the biggest hotel company in the world. Computers beat the best Go player in the world.

In the US young lawyers already are finding it hard to get jobs. Law school enrolment is on the decline. Why? IBM Watson gives legal advice (on basic legal stuff) within seconds, with 90 per cent accuracy compared with 70% human accuracy. So, there is likely to be 90 per cent fewer lawyer in the future, only specialists will remain. Watson already helps diagnose cancer four times more accurate than human physicians. Facebook facial recognition software recognizes faces better than humans. By 2030, computers will be more intelligent than humans. The list is endless. We all must brace up for real change.

For us lawyer, we must see competition coming from technology. Presently, simple legal transactions are being automated. For example, online dispute resolution (ODR) platforms like PayPal and eBay handled over 60 million civil cases in 2012. To date they have resolved over 400 million disputes. The happy thing about all of this is that unlike court disposition, all the results of ODR resolutions are available for study and for process fine-tuning. By use of data customer satisfaction and feedback is tracked. EBay even tweaks the system continually to maximize settlement, human involvement and customer satisfaction.[46]

ODR helps customers resolve disputes themselves in fast efficient ways. So, Big Data and machine learning can automate the handling of transactions, especially low-valve transaction at higher speed and lower cost than traditional litigation process that would have forced injurers to abandon their claims. Is this competition not real? Less and less judges, lawyers and court officials would be needed in the near future.

---

[45]Robert M. Goldman, Future Predictions at http://www.linkedin.com/pulse/future-prediction.

[46]Emeka Albert, Transforming the Rivers State Judiciary through Information and Communication Technology, lecture delivered at stakeholders forum on the Judiciary and Information Technology on May 31, 2018 at NBA House, Port-Harcourt.

Legal education and automation

The nature of business and the job market today gives technology a central role education. It would therefore be strange for a university classroom to look significantly the same as it was twenty years ago. Today's classroom should look hi-tech because e-learning and other instructional methods that focus on developing skills will be more prevalent. Technology itself has become a core skill for effective law practice. It is thus imperative that university education captures this component, which will likely shape the structure of present curriculum. For instance, teachers will likely incorporate more formative assessment into their courses to be facilitated by technology. Instructional models and materials changes are also envisaged.[47]

It is not the thinking (for now) that technology will replace the traditional university classroom, but it must play an integral role in the implementation of new teaching methods and means of assessment required for the transformation of education. Many students now use laptops and other forms of computer and are generally e-learner friendly. In fact, learning is enhanced and reinforced when verbal communication is combined with visual.

The use of technology in university education is not widespread in Nigeria. Though some faculties now have e-learning libraries, thanks to accreditation, there is minimal use of them in delivery of instruction. Online and computer-based learning conducted through a combination of software and hardware, and delivery of online content through the Internet is rare phenomena in most faculties.[48]

For example, a simple the *class web page technology* can be designed to introduce technology into the classroom. Developing a webpage for a course by the teacher for purpose of academic interaction with the class carries numerous advantages, namely: (i) it provides an efficient communication means with the class much more than any synopsis or lesson plan; (ii) in today's digital age where young people are addicted to computer gadgets rather than paper, e-communication enjoys special attraction of affordability and availability to more students; (iii) e-communication carries with it the advantages of flexibility, spontaneity and convenience not constrain by space and time; (iv) free the teacher's consulting hours with students, because with the webpage in place students will rarely bother the teacher with administrative questions; (v) promotes

---

[47]Stephen M. Johnson, Teaching for Tomorrow: Utilizing Technology to Implement the Reforms of MacCrate, Carnegie, and Best Practices (2013) 92 *Nebraska L. Rev.* 46.

[48] There is however global recognition of e-legal education in the form of computer, internet and distant education. See Peter B. Maggs & Thomas D. Morgan, Computer-Based Legal Education at the University of Illinois: A Report of Two Years' Experience (1975-1976) 27 *J. Leg. Educ.* 138; Alan Davidson, Electronic Legal Education (2003) 2 *J. Commonwealth L. & Leg.Educ.* 16.

easy delivery of course materials while expanding teaching material package; (vi) serves as repository of academic materials; (vi) helps the teacher to respond to varying student learning styles, as it helps the crop of students who learn more comfortably in electronic environment; (vii) and is an inexpensive method of delivering course materials.

A course webpage should be designed to be functional, not complex for navigation. Its menu should consist of items like, syllabus, lesson plan, synopsis, general, etc. - all functioning as hyperlinks. If permitted and available the hyperlink should include a menu link to other websites. For example, it can be linked to that of the courts. Its design should admit post of Microsoft Word, PDF files, PowerPoint presentation, and other modern formats. [49]

Much as technical assistance may be needed to maintain the page, the teacher could use software that facilitates direct, hands-on control, such as TWEN,[50] Blackboard,[51] ExamSoft,[52] Electronic BlueBook,[53] Extegrity[54] or Contribute, to edit or update the webpage and to streamline administration and grading.[55]

To prevent being caught pants-down all faculties and the academy must begin to prepare by moving the regulated norm in their teaching to a place where online schools cannot follow, such as extensive teaching of the many practical skills that require to be taught effectively, face-to-face, in-person interactions.[56] Time is ticking fast and late movers will find that complacency does not pay. Many entities thought impregnable to technology are now extinct. Given that current technology can deliver on efficient cost and convenience of most university disciplines creates the possibility that universities cannot remain an exception to technological imperative to adapt or die. The handwriting is very visible to the sighted.

Obviously, the training should be better tailored to the economic realities of the new legal labour market and many of those realities are being driven either directly or indirectly by technology. In order to ensure that there is more there,

---

[49]Katz & O'Neil, above n. 4 @ 60.

[50]See Twen Resources, Thomas Reuters Westlaw, https://lawschool.westlaw.com/shared/signon10.asp?path=%2ftwen%2fdefault.aspx (last visited March 1, 2017).

[51]See Blackboard, http://www.blackboard.com/ (last visited March 1, 20017).

[52]See ExamSoft Worldwide, http://www.examsoft.com/main/index.php (last visited March 1, 2017).

[53]See EBB Electronic Bluebook, Computest, http://electronicbluebook.com/ (last visited March 1, 2017).

[54]See Exam 4 Exam Software, Extegrity, http://www.exam4.com/ (last visited March 1, 2017).

[55]Katz & O'Neil, above n. 4, 60. See also, web management tools at http/www.lawschool.westlaw.com; http//www.blackboard.com; http/www.www.adobe.com/products/contribute.

[56]Michele R. Pistone& John J. Hoeffner, No Path but One: Law School Survival in an Age of Disruptive Technology (2013) 59 *Wayne L. Rev.* 193 @ 202.

some of the hothouse walls will have to come down. The future belongs to those institutions and individuals who act as though their livelihoods depend upon it—because in many cases they do.[57]

Conclusion

For white-collar professions such as law, medicine, or finance, the medium-term future centres on a mixture of humans and machines working together to more efficiently deliver the services than either could alone. However, with respect to the existing market for legal services, the total number of humans needed to service the current demand for legal services is simply going to decline. Without tapping previously untapped markets (and there is good reason to believe they can be tapped), law is an otherwise mature industry whose total labour market participation will likely never exceed its prior peak.

The future of legal space market is for innovators only.[58] Lawyer must develop skills to make them drivers of automation lawyering – yes, the generals of

---

[57] Larry E. Ribstein, Practicing Theory: Legal Education for the Twenty-First Century (2011) 96 *Iowa L. Rev.* 1649 @ 238 "Law school needs to transition from its liberal arts predisposition to a polytechnic research and teaching operation. From both a scholarship and training perspective, it is time to get serious about science, computation, data analytics and technology. [There is an] arbitrage opportunity in the market for legal education . . . for an institution(s) [to] move toward an "MIT School of Law."

[58] Tanina Rostain, The Emergence of Law Consultants (2006)75 *Fordham L. Rev.* 1397. See, Sule, above n.4. In addition, there are great opportunities for various legal entrepreneurs (whether or not they are lawyers) LegalZoom is a good example. It was revealed that the company had served almost two million customers in its 10 years of operations. In 2011 alone, the company claimed to fill 490,000 orders for online legal services. The company conspicuously states on its website that "over the past 12 years, over 2 million businesses and families have used LegalZoom for their wills, trademarks, LLCs and more". In 2012, LegalZoom formed partnership with one of the United Kingdom's legal services provider QualitySolicitors, in a deal to jointly offer online legal services in the United Kingdom including company formations and divorce documents. And in 2014 Permira which is one of the Europe's biggest private capital firm acquired $200 million outstanding equity of LegalZoom. In the US also due to the intense competition, a number of law firms submit to the whims of financial market where performance which is the main concern is rated by customers and law firms's equity are being sold like all other companies. It happened in Australia in 2007 when Slater & Gordon which is a personal injury law firm was listed on Australian Stock Exchange - it was the first law firm in the world listed. Slater & Gordon had more than 95 million shares on offer and another 12 million non-voting shares. Devoid of ethical concerns, public listing of law firm is a good thing to do. For example, Slater & Gordon had about 20 offices and around 400 staff. As of 2011, the firm had around 50 offices and service centres at different locations, with close to 1000 staff members. And this growth is of course connected with raising of additional funds through public listing of law firm's equity and through acquiring other smaller law firms. For example, in 2010 Slaters took over the Queensland's Trilby Misso for $57 million, "of which $40 million was raised through an additional capital raising offer". Slater & Gordon later acquired UK personal injury specialist law firm Russell Jones & Walker (RJW) for £53.8m. And several other law firms also followed quickly on the heels of Slater & Gordon in listing on the stock exchange, like Integrated Legal Holdings Limited (ILH) which was first listed in the same year Slaters was listed. ILH consisted of about four law firms - Argyle Lawyers, Civic Legal, Law Central and Talbot Olivier Lawyers. It should be noted however, ascertaining the actual worth of a law firm and its reputation

the invading army of technology. Law schools owe the profession a duty to start the training of technology-savvy lawyers.

professionally by a new client will now be challenging. The intense competition among publicly listed firms will make it difficult for clients to calculate reputation and goodwill of law firm. The prospectus will only provide some financial information, mainly about profit, rather than professional details about law firm. And even if there were some profit declines, the prospectus can forecast an increase.

Chapter 3

Case-Management Skills

Introduction

Case planning or management is a lexicon often associated with judges and the work they do. Judges have piles of cases so they need to plan how to structure their case load for efficient justice delivery. So, expeditious and efficient dispensation of justice is a common public yearning implicating judicial case management.[1] But lawyers also need to learn and practice case planning to manage their work. A client who briefs a lawyer certainly has some challenges for which she demands solution. Looked at from this perspective, a lawyer is a problem-solver. That being so, case planning ought to be a skill lawyers should possess.

Once briefed, a lawyer begins by identifying the applicable law to the facts scenario, hoping that the entire case will turn out well either at the negotiation, hearing or appeal stage, as the case may be. On taking instructions, it is expected that the lawyer would open a case file, start preparing letters or processes with a view to negotiation or litigation and the like.

The process of receiving client's instruction involves translating the client's social challenge into the world of law. The lawyer synthesizes the facts to fit legal remedy or defeat an entitlement.[2] We are all too familiar with this routine of

---

[1] For example, the U.S. State of California is reputed to be the U.S. largest court system, with over 500 locations, serving a population of over 37 people, with over 9 million cases. See http://www.courtinfo.ca.gov/reference/documents/factsheets/Calif Judicial Branch.pdf, accessed on 30 March 2018. For example, as part of its court case management reform in 2010, it instituted the California Court Case Management System (CCMS) Project as a strategic technology plan to transform the trial courts from a paper-based process, where interactions with the courts occur primarily through the mail or over the counter and response time is measured in days, to an electronic environment, where interactions occur via Internet or automated voice-response with improved servicing timeframes. By it 90% of court staff and judges transform the way cases are received, adjudicated, communicated and disposed. The idea is to significantly improve the quality of justice rendered in California's trial courts by providing attorneys, judges and litigants with visibility and access to case information across all California courts). See *Review of CCMS*, Feb. 28, 2010.

[2] The process of translating clients' instruction to generate or defeat legal obligations or remedies can be challenging to manage in some cases. For example, while most clients in matrimonial causes petitions speak moral language as instruction bases, lawyers are often more concerned with the general no-fault requirements of relevant statute to ground or defeat reliefs, a thing that could

client's instruction. Case planning however goes beyond the mundane routine. It involves more. It is a specific, special kind of problem-solving skill.

What Is Case-Management?

Case management however, involves much more the routine. It involves identifying the client's objectives, analysing facts of the case, possible causes of action and remedies, analysing the cast of character in the facts scenario, developing the case theory, selecting forum for negotiation or litigation, and formulating a work plan to carry these identified objectives to fruition. These are the main components of case planning.

In effect, the lawyer on taking up a brief must think through and strategize on defining the client's problem, identify possible solutions that meet the client's objective, construct a big, complete picture of the client's social world, the way in which the facts and the law fits within the context in which they occur. This is what implicates critical lawyering skills of constructing what happened to include the meaning of what happened to define the boundaries of what will happen.[3] It is

cause irritation for the client. On how case-management can help bridge the epistemic gap between client's reality and expectation, see Festus Emiri & Ayuba Giwa, Metaphoric Thinking About Law as Language and Lawyering as Translation: Reflection on Legal Clinic [2008] *Enugu State University of Technology Journal of Public Law* 15 (an article that reveals that it is the presence of the distortion that generally explains the epistemic gap between "what happened" and "what will happen." For clients the talk centres on the former, while the lawyer is concerned about the latter.)

[3]Critical lawyering. For discussion and application of client-centred, critical lawyering, see Lucie E. White, *Goldberg v Kelly* on the Paradox of Lawyering for the Poor (1990) 56 *Brook. L. Rev.* Clark D. Cunningham, Lawyer as Translator Representation as Text: Towards an Ethnography of Legal Discourse (1992) 77 *Cornell L. Rev.* 1298; Ruth A. Robbins, An Introduction to Applied Storytelling and to this Symposium (2008) 14 *J. Legal Writing Institute* 3; Lucie E. White, Subordination, Rhetorical Survival Skills, and Sunday Shoes: Notes on the Hearing of Mrs. G (1990) 38 *Buffalo L. Rev.* 1 (where the commentators using the story of Mrs. G welfare hearing application reveals that cultural images and long-established legal norms construct the subjectivity and speech of socially subordinate groups, like women, blacks etc., as inherently inferior to those of dominant groups. where the narrative was expanded beyond 'what happened' scope of whether the $592 received by the defendant as damages benefit from an accident, spent by her in buying Sunday shoes for her children, should count as money deductible from her social benefit. Her lawyer chose a narrative that concentrated on the meaning of what happened to vindicate and justify the receipt); Binny Miller, Give Them Back Their Lives: Recognising Client Narrative in Case Theory (1994) 93 *Mich. L. Rev.* 485 (showing how the practice of lawyering should be reconstructed to embrace a greater role for clients in constructing case theories. In using stories to recreate reality, critical theorist distinguishes 'what' happened from the 'meaning' of what happened, believing that by opening the client's world, the meaning of what happened can be better understood. The article tells the story of a black charged for disorderly conduct, resisting arrest, and assault and battery after he was stopped and wrongfully accused of shoplifting by three white security guards. The writer uses the scenario to raise provocative questions about the relevance of the client's experience in creating tension between the story and theory, in respect of stories serving as perfunctory reference for theoretical conclusions). See also, Peter Gabel & Paul Harris, Building Power and Breaking Images: Critical Theory and the Practice of Law (1982-83) 11 *N.Y.U. Rev. L &Soc. Change* 369; Lucie White, Mobilization on the Margins of the Lawsuit: Making Space for Clients to Speak (1987) 16 *N.Y.U. Rev.*

what makes germane and foundational a conscious development of the case theory - the conscious construction of the client's narrative compelling entitlement. Developing the theory furthers demands that the lawyer pays attention to the real big picture, in the sense of testing the possible persuasive degree of the client's theory of the case and imagination of how the opponent would seek to destroy the theory.

It is important to think through all of these and related matters in case planning because clients are not only interested in winning cases, they are also interested in timelines for winning and the nature of remedies they get vindicated. What is more, quality representation requires that lawyers make things happen for their clients according to plan. Since every step in the lawyer's plan influences ultimate outcome and could well alter outcome and perception, lawyers ought to pay considerable attention to case planning.[4]

Components of Good Case Management

The components of good case planning are as follows:

(i) Identify the client's objective

Identifying the client's objective is germane to client satisfaction. The client may a times not need litigation to settle a matter. There are times all she needs from the other party is just an acknowledgement of fault and possibly an apology.

The 1,000 widgets case is a good illustrative example.[5] Permit me to relate part of the story. A teacher reviews various doctrines in contract with his students saying: in a long-term instalment contract, the seller promises the buyer to deliver widgets at the rate of 1,000 per month. The first two deliveries were perfect, however the third is short of 10 widgets. So the buyer is incensed that he rejects deliveries and refuses to pay for the widgets already delivered. Most of the students laboured for contract principle that would force the buyer to pay for the widgets and make the buyer keep the contract. But an eight-year old who can with the mother to class raised his hand to answer. He said, "I'd say, I'm sorry."

Yes, experience shows that an apology may just be the key to dispute settlement otherwise unattainable. At times, all the injured party wants is an admission of wrong from the injurer. Even if an apology is insufficient to resolve a

---

L &Soc. Change 535; Jessica A. Rose, Rebellious or Regnant : Police Brutality Lawyering in New York City (2000) 28 *Fordham Urban L.J.* 619 (addresses current legal limitations in combating police brutality for subordinate groups and why and how the legal community must develop a more creative and rebellious methodology if it is to accomplish the goal of social transformation).

[4] Benchmark Institute, *Legal Services Practice Manual: Skills,* 2017

[5] Goldberg, Green & Sander, Saying You're Sorry in JW Breslin & JZ Rubin, *Negotiation Theory and Practice,* Camb, Mass: 1991 @ 141

dispute, it certainly reduces tension and eases the relationship between the parties that the issues separating them are resolved with dispatch.

What this tells is that there are times when what a client wants isn't just winning law suit. Clients could sometimes value psychological ephemerals, such as friendship, status and the like to instrumental victories measured in money or property terms. So, from the interview stage a lawyer should be quick to determine what the client's goal is. This may sometimes not be obvious from the interview because the client may just be confused as to what her goals are or should be. This is why probing beyond the client's expressed goal may be important.

Whatever is discerned as the client's objective, it should be an outcome that makes the client feel that she gets a fair deal and is not cheated.[6] Lee and Fox contain an account of how lawyers can show discernment in an interesting way. It is a pointed example of how to pay attention to client's desired outcome:[7] the example is a hypo problem in a contract law class. In a long instalment contract, the seller promises the buyer to deliver 1,000 widget a month. After the third month, the seller delivers only 990, a thing that incensed the buyer, who refuses to take the deliveries. Most of the students with knowledge in the various common theories may think about what doctrines could possibly force the buyer to pay for the widget for to do otherwise would be breach of contract. But the real solution may just be extra-legal, the mere words of the seller "I'm sorry." That could just do the magic. How? Cool the nerves of the buyer, sustain their business relationship, and solve the problem with dispatch and less transactional costs. This is what good case management requires.

(ii) Summarize the Facts

Once the objective is identified, the lawyer will need to keep track, best by writing, of the client's narrative. Opening a case file where the facts of the client's problem are summarized best does it. The summary should include vital information of what happened, the role played by the material parties, as to who did or said what, who are the key players in the narrative, and how the main players are related to the client. The summary should be a well-written summary of the facts that

---

[6] Carrie Menkel-Meadow, Towards Another View of Legal Negotiation: The Structure of Problem-Solving (1984) 31 *UCLA L. Rev.* 754 (list the following as good outcome checklist: (a) does the solution reflect the client's real needs, goals and objectives, in both short and long terms (b) does it promote the relationship the client desires with the other party? (c) has the solution been achieved at the lowest transactional costs relative to the result? 9d) is the solution achievable, or has it raised more problems that need to be solved) at 760

[7] Simon Lee & Marie Fox, 2nd ed. *Learning Legal Skills,* London: Blackstone Press, 1994, 144. The example is an excerpt from Goldberg, Green & Sander, Saying You're Sorry, in J W Breslin & J Z Rubin eds. *Negotiation Theory and Practice,* Cambridge, Mass., 1991, 141.

someone unfamiliar with the client's problem could grasp from the summary of the facts the problem, which necessitated briefing the lawyer as problem-solver.[8]

(iii) Identify and Classify the Legal Issues

Training in law necessitates classification.[9] Law like other disciplines relies heavily on categorization. For example, if D punches the face of P with her fists, it is not difficult for the lawyer to see the set of facts as triggering remedies in the tort of assault or criminal assault. Identifying the category to which the client's problem comes under aids the lawyer to quickly recognize the issues interrogated in the case. Once the particular areas of the law interrogated by the client's facts are identified, the lawyer is then enabled to do further research or elicit material facts relevant to success of the case.

(iv) List Possible Solutions

Having classified the problem and distilled the issues they raise the lawyer would next have to brainstorm on possible solutions. It is advisable to generate as many possible solutions from which the best qualities are chosen. In this respect quality breed quality and so the lawyer should not sheer away from even possible crazy possible solutions. Sometimes solutions possibilities transcend legal categories. An example of this can be gleaned from an English cases remedies scholar have over the years used to show the vanishing lines between rights and remedies in rem and rights *in personam*. It is *Lipkin Gorman* v. *Karpnale*.[10] At the trial court the plaintiff raised claims against the defendants for accessory to trust via the concept of "knowing assistance" and knowing assistance."[11] However, when it became obviously difficult to proceed on those count, the plaintiff at the House of Lords changed the claim to one for common law restitution founded on unjust enrichment to succeed in recovery.

---

[8] RPC

[9] Under the classical view, categories are metaphoric containers. Like containers, they operate according to a simple in/out structure. Each potential category member is evaluated according to at least one characteristic that defines category membership. If the potential category member possesses the necessary characteristic, category membership is granted. If not, the potential member is excluded. Classical category labels identify a characteristic shared by all category members. The classical theory of categories, which is the default view held by nearly everyone in our culture, is that categories have a fixed, stable, and objective structure." Mark Johnson, *Mind, Metaphor, Law* (2007) 58 *Mercer L. Rev.* 845, 848 (2007) (citing George Lakoof, *Women, Fire, and Dangerous Things: What Categories Reveal About the Mind*, 1987; Steven L. Winter, *A Clearing in the Forest: Law, Life, and Mind*, 2001.

[10] [1991] 2 AC 548 (where the writ of debt retains property flavour).

[11] For a discussion on the concept of accessories to trust, see Festus Emiri & Ayuba Giwa, *Equity and Trust in Nigeria*, Lagos: Malthouse Press, 2012 @ 344; Simon Gardner, Knowing Receipt and Knowing Assistance: Taking Stock (1996) 112 *LQR* 56. A similar tactic was employed in *Henderson* v. *Merrett Syndicates Ltd* [1995] 2 AC 145 (a case showing the complex interrelation of contract, equity and tort). See also, Geoffrey Samuel, Equity and the Legal Divisions (1986) 37 *NILQ* 211

In this respect, the lawyer should think of legal, extra-legal, statutory, administrative, social or economic strategies that can skilfully be complementary to whatever legal solution is workable to reach desired outcome.[12] It is helpful to list out all possible solutions to the client's problem, the client's fear and how to assuage the fears while pressing for a fair remedy for the client.

That was exactly what the lawyer did in the "Sunday Shoes" case.[13] The case was about the question if the $592 received by the defendant as damages benefit from an accident, spent by her in buying Sunday shoes for her children, should count as money deductible from her social benefit. An analysis of the case reveals that the lawyer noted the apprehension of Mrs. G who had to attend the department fraud appointment and signed the repayment contract when she had been told not to attend. That of course made it harder to contest the county claim. But that was reason for the lawyer to device additional strategy: attack both the payment contract and the underlying overpayment claim.[14] That she disregarded the advice from her lawyer certainly could provide further insight, as in the Sunday Shoes case, the fear of the poor client from retaliation from the county on her social benefit. But there was also another perspective not very glaring until the lawyer engages in further research or fact investigation. The lawyer did. This revealed to her the insurance received by Mrs. G under state regulation would disentitle her client for social benefit for about two months on the theory that the client's family could live for that time off of the insurance award. The discount of the insurance money from the client's welfare was a policy position of the then Reagan's administration to teach poor people the value of money and virtue of saving money. So, if the county did not recover the insurance money from Mrs. G, it would be sanctioned.[15] The pressure was on both, her client and the county. Looking at the big picture, estoppel was an available defence. Also available was the defence "life necessities" which permitted waiver for expenditure to avert a crisis situation. The client was certainly uncomfortable with the estoppel defence. It points fingers to the county and welfare officer who failed to warn her and she runs the risk of retaliation. The second option was then chosen.

What the story tells us is simple: when the lawyer takes a real look at the problem of the client with a view to fashion remedy, she could discover more than meets the eye from the client's story. Elucidating questions and investigation

---

[12] Those familiar with the holocaust litigations for reparation know well how the Jews combined the legal processes with political and economic strategies to overcome certain legal hurdles such as the trans-generational challenges having to do with statute of limitation and the like.

[13] Lucie E. White, Subordination, Rhetorical Survival Skills, and Sunday Shoes: Notes on the Hearing of Mrs. G (1990) 38 *Buffalo L. Rev.* 1.

[14] Id. @ 23-24.

[15] Id. @ 25.

could reveal latent power relationship and processes interrogated in the client's case. In fact, an understanding of these relationships could provide the lawyer further insight on how to identify possible, alternative solutions to the client's problem. For instance, ruminating on the client's problem whether the action taken against the client represents a policy position or change of policy could inform the lawyer whether an administrative hearing or litigation is an appropriate strategy to challenge a wrong. Understanding the wider context and seeing the big picture may suggest further research and fact investigation. Failing for example to examine the larger context within which problems arise can result in handling a case ineffectively to achieve the client's desired goal. In this respect, the lawyer should take advantage of say local expertise in finding out how institutions and systems function – knowledge of which could dictate possible, or alternative, non-conventional strategies and solutions.

It is therefore proper that in listing possible solutions, the lawyer would need to identify any further facts investigation or legal research and analysis to help arrive at suitable alternative remedies. Further factual investigation unquestionably helps in fashioning in alternative strategies in that could give perceptive not revealed in the client's brief. It is helpful for the lawyer to list out the possible sources of the information sought and the method to be deployed to receive it - the "what, source and how" of the information. Such information may be obtained by personal contacts or calls to say the administrative agency or employer of their usual practice.

A reading of the Sunday Shoes article can provide a guide as to how a skilled lawyer can go about steps of listing possible solutions and strategies in solving the client's problem.[16]

(v) Formulate Timelines

Having formulated possible solutions, the lawyer should move on to formulate timelines for carrying out and perfecting the client's instruction. A brief requires some sort of time sequencing, and the order and timing of events.[17] This requires interrogating the what, when and who of the case-what should be done to perfect the client's instruction, when the task should be undertaken, and who is responsible to drive it through. A timeline work plan is especially compelling if

[16]Lucie E. White, Subordination, Rhetorical Survival Skills, and Sunday Shoes: Notes on the Hearing of Mrs. G (1990) 38 *Buffalo L. Rev.* 1.

[17] Timeline for case management is different from trial timeline. Trial timeline gives the adjudicator an intuitive understanding of a case. It is designed to make a case clearer, showing the relative position of the events in the story it tells. See, A2L Consulting, *The Complex Civil Litigation Trial Guide*, 3rd ed. Washington DC, 2014 @ 111.

the lawyer works in consortium of lawyers. This reminds us to the popular saying that 'work left for everyone gets undone.'

(vi) Discuss Options with Client

It is important to discuss the possible options on remedies with the client to make constitutive of the process. In the Sunday Shoes case, after the lawyer mused on the two options open to fight the county, she invited the client and explained the advantages and possible drawback of each to Mrs. G. The estoppel story though good to tell, would likely cost them losing the case, and provoking the county ire. The hearing officer- though charged to be neutral-would surely identify with the county in the challenge to government power to evade the costs of its own mistake. The necessities story would force Mrs. G to grovel, but it would give both county and state what they wanted to hear-another "yes sir" welfare recipient.[18] The counsel being a poverty lawyer was familiar to the setting. Counsel explained the options to Mrs. G. in the ensuring discussion on the options Mrs. G asked that both possible options should be placed before the hearing - tell both stories.

But at the hearing Mrs. G abandoned the estoppel option when examined may be in not wanting to make the welfare officer, a fellow Black woman scapegoat, so her counsel abandoned the estoppel story. So, the necessities option was argued. Interestingly, because the options were discussed with Mrs. G before hearing and she had a voice in it, she was satisfied with how the case was conducted. She was elated after the hearing, asking her lawyer "how she had done at the hearing." The counsel thereon told Mrs. G that they could not be sure who would win. Even though the case was lost Mrs. G was satisfied with the conduct of the trial.[19] That is what happens when the client's voice is not muted in choice of remedy options.

(vii) Identify Character in the Case

It is important to identify the cast of the character in the case, as an artist or movie producer would ordinarily do in painting or directing a movie or play.[20] Counsel should therefore draw a list of the material witnesses for the case, identify their

---

[18] White, above n. 12 @ 27.

[19] Id. 32. An appeal was filed against the decision. Happily, the county chose to withdraw its overpayment clam against Mrs. G, necessitating a withdrawal of Mrs. G's appeal the matter settled. Id. 32. See also, Binny Miller, Give Them Back Their Lives: Recognising Client Narrative in Case Theory (1994) 93 *Mich. L. Rev.* 485.

[20] For parallel between movie/art and the litigation process, and what lawyers can learn from them, see, Martin Jay, Must Justice Be Blind? The Challenges of Images to the Law, in Costas Doziness & Lynda Neads, eds., *Law and Image*, Univ. Chicago Press, 1999, 21. See generally, James P. Eyster, Lawyer as Artist: Using Significant Moments and Obtuse Objects to Enhance Advocacy (2008) 14 *J. Legal Writing Inst.* 87 (a discussion of how to apply key techniques of the visual artists-the obtuse objet and significant moments to legal advocacy and their persuasive sting according to art history scholars, aestheticians, psychologists, and psycholinguists).

strength and weaknesses any additional information that is helpful in prosecuting the cause of action and developing the case theory.

(viii) Develop the Case-Theory

This is a crucial stage in case management. Case theory or the theory of the case is the "explanatory statement linking the case to the client's experience of the world. It serves as the lens for shaping reality, in the light of the law, to explain the facts, relationships, and circumstances of the client and other parties in the way that can best achieve the client's goals. The relevant reality combines the perspectives of the lawyer and the client with an eye toward the ultimate audience-the trier of facts."[21] Case theory provides the framework for trial preparation and ultimately the trial. It generally consists of two separate theories, a legal theory and a factual theory. The former is the 'legal framework developed by the lawyer from interpretation, analysis, and expansion of legal rules and standards,' while the latter is 'the party's story justifying relief under the legal theory.'[22]

The theory must be rooted in facts, containing three main components: (i) explaining the party's version of the facts; (ii) the unfavourable facts; (iii) and the disputed facts. It is also to be measured against its sufficiency and in terms of how well it responds to the likely theory of the opponent.[23]

The heighten importance of case theory is embedded in the fact that once it is chosen, it serves as the centrepiece for all strategic and tactical decisions in the case. It is primarily incorporated in the pleadings and any other application or process, such as those for discoveries, pre-trial, motions and the like. And of course, when trial begins, it shapes examination of witnesses and address by counsel.[24]

Since case theory describes how the lawyer would want the trier of facts to view the case, the theory must be based on the equities that appeal to the trier's sense of what constitutes fair or right. This connection is easier to draw if the theory is based on strong facts and inferences, which can be fairly drawn by ordinary people from the facts as, presented. In this respect, most persons can reason from cause to effect. So, a theory based on such premiss is clear understandable without more. Also, the theory is advanced when built on facts not subject to much, or any dispute. Theory is made more compelling to believe if

---

[21]Miller, above n. 17 @ 487.

[22] Marilyn J. Berger, John B. Mitchell & Ronald H. Clark, *Pretrial Advocacy: Planning, Analysis and Strategy*, 5th ed. Aspen Casebook, 2015

[23] Miller, above n. 17 @ 492-493

[24] Miller, above n.17 @ 495 (case theory is an elusive concept, sometimes mistaken by lawyers for 'narrow tactical decisions, case theory isn't the same thing as the theme of the case, for while the former being theory implies a linear, rational concept that drives the trier to a favourable conclusion, the latter while geared to the same result, mixes facts and emotion).

it is not inconsistent with incontestable facts. Whatever theory is chosen must be good enough to explain away unfavourable facts. This is material because it is rare to find a case where all the facts just sit in support of the client. So, if there are unfavourable facts, as there are bound to be, the theory must explain them their existence and show why they do not trump a favourable conclusion for the client.

When the trier, not one needing her to stretch imagination, bases on theory easy to imagine scenario theory of the case is easier to persuade. It is therefore important for the facts to be grounded in common sense experience, especially of the trier.[25] This can be very challenging for the lawyer, especially for those who practice poverty law or represent not-mainstream litigants. From the very way judges are selected, they are likely to belong to the middle-class, conservative segment of society. Therefore, drawing a felt connection between their experience and those in the same group can be challenging, but doable, by employing the narrative style of advocacy, paying attention to strategies of persuasion and the use of critical lawyering skills.[26]

(ix) Select the Forum

In mixed, hierarchical systems of law, the counsel is obligated to select the forum, considering factors such as the jurisdictional cause of action, resolution time, understanding of claim by trier, availability of suitable remedies, complexities of rules of practice and the like.

---

[25] On imagination see, James Boyd White, *Legal Imagination*, Boston: Little, Brown, 1973 ("Think of or read a law case, imagine the characters freed from the page and live in a storyland, and ask what their story would be like. You are familiar for example, with the ubiquitous personage of the law of torts, the Reasonable Man, and could write a story about him, I suppose: A Day in the Life of the Reasonable Man. If you cannot imagine that a novel built around characters defined in this way would have any interest for you, how can legal talk about such characters, the same events, have any interest?")

[26] For narrative strategies in creating felt connection, see Ruth A. Robbins, An Introduction to Applied Storytelling and to this Symposium (2008) 14 *J. Legal Writing Institute* 3; Kim Lane Scheppele, Forward: Telling Stories (1989) 87 *Michigan L.Rev.*2073; Steven L. Winter, The Cognitive Dimension of the *Agon*: Between Legal Power and Narrative Meaning (1989) 87 *Mich. L. Rev.* 2223. For persuasion strategies employing logos, pathos and ethos see, Michael R. Smith, *Advanced Legal Writing: Theories and Strategies in Persuasive Writing,* 3rd ed. Aspen Law & Bus. 2013; Aristotle, *On Rhetoric* (transl. George A. Kennedy, Oxford Univ. Press, 1991); George A. Kennedy, *A New History of Classical Rhetoric*, Princeton Univ. Press, 1998; Stephen Toulmin, *The Use of Argument,* Cambridge Univ. Press, 1958; Linda Levine & Kurt M. Saunders, Thinking Like a Rhetor (1993) 43 *J. Legal Educ.* 108; Michael Frost, Ethos, Pathos and Legal Audience (1994) 99 *Dick L. Rev.* 85; Michael Frost, Justice Scalia's Rhetoric of Dissent: A Greco-Roman Analysis of Scalia's Advocacy in the VMI Case (2002) 91 *KY. L.J.* 167 For reading on critical lawyering, see above n. 2. See also, Anthony V. Alfieri, The Antinomies of Poverty Law and a Theory of Dialogic Empowerment (1987-88) 16 *N.Y.U. Rev. L & Soc. Change* 659; Anthony V. Alfieri, Speak Out of Turn: The Story of Josephine V (1991) 4 *Geo. J. Legal Ethics* 619. Clark D. Cunningham, Lawyer as Translator Representation as Text: Towards an Ethnography of Legal Discourse (1992) 77 *Cornell L. Rev.* 1298; Lucie E. White, *Goldberg v Kelly* on the Paradox of Lawyering for the Poor (1990) 56 *Brook. L. Rev.*

(x) Final Checklist

The lawyer then rounds up case management by taking another look and notation of timelines, such as those concerned with identifying who will do what, a listing of support needed to accomplish the task and then, states the estimated completion dates.[27]

Visual of all case management check-list

Setting: Lawyer taking instruction from client
The Table has a checklist of case management

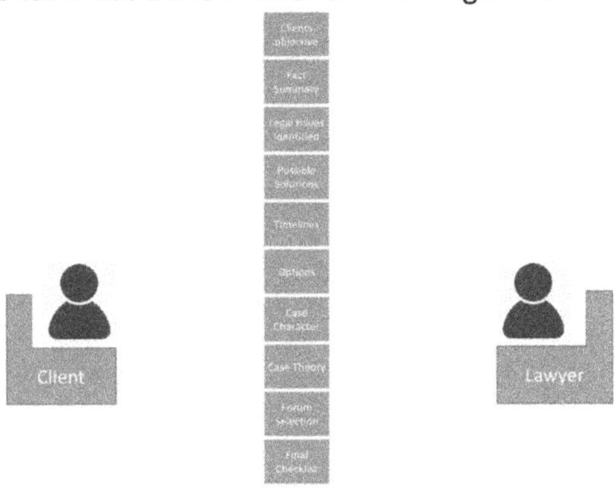

Conclusion

Following the steps above make for the requisite skills of case management that can helps further efficient service delivery. Just as proper judicial case management improves timeliness and efficiency of court docket, lawyers who effectively employ case management can better deliver efficient services and legal value to their clients.

[27] Above n. 3.

Chapter 4

Case Analysis Skills

Introduction

Analysis is simply a detailed examination of the elements or structure of a thing. lawyers by virtue of how they reason, rely primarily on precedent. Thus skilful analysis of precedent is an essential skill for advocacy. Effective advocacy requires more than the ability to read cases and analogically apply it to facts interrogated in legal disputes. Lawyers must also be able to pluck out of precedent nuances not apparently visible but material to making a precedent governing in particular situations.[1]

We will use the judgment of King Solomon to study case analysis skills. The story is known to many. It is recorded in the Holy Scriptures and some oriental books.[2] Its wisdom generally appeals to people across faith, race, culture and

---

[1] American Bar Association, Section of Legal Education and Admission to the Bar, Rules of Procedure for Approval of Law School, 2006-2007 [hereinafter referred to as ABA Standards] Standards 302(a)(2) and (a)(4) [stating that law schools must to provide all students instruction in the "legal analysis and reasoning" skills generally regarded as necessary for effective and responsible practice of law). See also, Roy Stuckey et. al., *Best Practices for Legal Education: A Vision and a Roadmap,* 2007 (hereinafter called *Best Practices*) @ 51-52; William M. Sullivan, et al. eds. *Carnegie Fund for the Advancement of Teaching, Educating Lawyers: Preparation for the Profession of Law,* 2007 (hereinafter called the *Carnegie Report*) Foundation for the Advancement of Teaching, Preparation for the Professions Program (PPP) 2007 @ 87 (stating that "[T]he primary focus of future lawyers' education is legal analysis. Learning to think like a lawyer is, accordingly, the main occupation of students' first phase in law school. But developing lawyers must at some point learn another set of demanding skills, all the while negotiating the complex transition from the stance of student . . . to that of apprentice practitioner.").

[2] Holy Bible, 1 Kings 3: 16-28. It is reputed to be a story which appears in many forms in at least twenty-two folk tales from many cultures. See, Ann Althouse, Beyond King Solomon's Harlots: Women in Evidence (1992) *S. Cal. L. Rev.* 1265, 1269. See also, Bertolt Brecht, *The Caucasian Chalk Circle*, 1947, a play in which a judge draws a circle and ask two mothers to pull a child over the line. The resulting tug-of-war causes pain to the child, and one woman, to spare the child this pain, let's go. The judge then awards the child to the woman who released her own claim for the sake of the child. It is said that Brecht based this play on a thirteenth century Chinese play, *The Circle of Chalk*, attributed to Li Hsing-Tao. Benet's Reader's Encyclopaedia, 3rd ed. 1987, cited in Althouse, id, 1269. Stefan H. Krieger & Richard K. Neumann, Jr., *Essential Lawyering Skills: Interviewing, Counselling, Negotiation, and Persuasive Fact Analysis* § 13.4, 164–165 (3d ed., Aspen L. & Bus. 2007).

background. It has long been accepted as a paradigmatic account of justice and of wisdom.

The thread is simple. Two women described as prostitutes come before the king, the first woman saying, "this woman and I live in one house, and I gave birth while was in the house. On the third day after I gave birth, this woman also gave birth. We were together, just two of us, there was no one else with us in the house. During the night this woman's son died, because she lay on him. So, she got up I the middle of the night and took my son from my side while your slave girl was asleep and laid him in her arms, and she laid her dead son in my arms. When I got up in the morning to nurse my son, I saw that he was dead. So, I examined him closely in the morning and saw that it was not my son whom I had given birth to." That would appear to be what moderns would term the statement of claim and pleadings for the plaintiff.

Rebuttal evidence was not absent. The other woman (referred to as "the second woman" in this article for purposes of clear distinction) said: "no my son is the living one, and your son is the dead one! Having joined issues, the first woman argued on her stand. Both kept arguing their case before the King, "no, your son is the dead one, and my son is the living one."

The parties didn't have the advantage of representation by lawyers. So, the King performed the role of examination and adjudicator. The King then said: bring me a sword," and when it was brought he sternly commanded, "cut the living child in two," and give both parties one half. That was the point when emotions ran high in the first woman who is reported at once to plead: "please my lord, give her the living child!" The King then sets in to pronounce judgment: "give the living child to the first woman."

The verdict is generally applauded as just, fair and ethically correct.[3] Many have given little or no thought so to whether plausible arguments could be

---

[3] 1 Kings 3: 28 relates that all who heard of the judgment came to be in awe of King Solomon, acknowledging the divine wisdom with him to execute justice. But cf. articles from the feminist perspective criticizing the judgment and its narrative discrimination. See, Ann Althouse, The Lying Woman, The Devious Prostitute, and the Stories from Evidence Casebooks (1994) 88 *Northwestern Univ. L. Rev.* 914; Ann Althouse, Beyond King Solomon's Harlots: Women in Evidence (1992) *S. Cal. L. Rev.* 1265 ("The text portrays women as mothers and whores, desperately attached to babies. These women fall into two categories. There are the bad ones who will lie and cheat to get their way. And there are the good ones who will selflessly sacrifice for the sake of others. The man occupies centre stage as the judge of women. He is the one who defines the categories and sorts the women into them. He is the one who receives the awe of the people he will rule.") Id. 1269; Marie Ashe, Abortion of Narrative: A Reading of the Judgment of Solomon (1991) 4 *Yale J.L. & Feminism* 81 (an article showing how adjudication accomplished by words and sword is directed against

advanced in favour of the second woman. That is why it will be of concern to us as case study in sharpening our skills of deep, keen, case analysis.

What is Legal Analysis?

Most persons are not in doubt that a good lawyer should be able to separate relevant from irrelevant facts, think logically and critically, evaluate knowledge, possess skills to analyse and solve problems, among other skills.[4] Many who side with the pedagogy of law stepped in liberal arts argue (with certain justification) that the humanities supply to the profession cutting knowledge required for interpreting and analysing texts, distinguishing facts from assertion, appraising doubtful arguments, and the like. Case or legal analysis undoubtedly is a core skill for lawyering.

Legal analysis is not a term of art with precise definition. But it is essentially captured as a process of perceiving and selecting traits of facts and analogizing and distinguishing it from prior decisions.[5] It is therefore, the simplification of a given legal scenario into component parts to see how it fits with stated rules, such as breaking complex perception and problems into discrete items and characteristics of law.[6]

The task here in analysing Solomon's judgment is not to question the correctness or otherwise of the judgment, but our simple task is to see how it could be possible to represent the second woman, if legal presentation were permitted in Solomon's court and yet present credible evidence that could have swung the case in her favour.[7]And, more importantly, how a theory of her case could have been constructed for possible appeal, if such window were open to her.

---

women). For general reading on feminist narrative in jurisprudence, see, Kathryn Abrams, Hearing the Call of Stories (1991) 79 Cal. L. Rev. 971.

4 On core lawyering skills see *Carnegie Report* (Legal Education Report based on a survey of more than two hundred law faculties (schools) in the US and Canada in 1999); *Best Practices;* Association of American Law School, Conference on the Future of Law School Curriculum: Brochure (Seattle, 2011).

5 M Minow, *Making All the Difference: Inclusion, Exclusion and American Law*, New York: Cornell Univ. Press, 1990, 1.

6 Ibid. (an article that uses the children's television show Sesame Street instruction pattern of animation, skits and songs to analyse the world as similar to legal analysis). See also S. Lee, Changing the Province of Jurisprudence, Inaugural lecture delivered at Queen's University, Belfast, 1990 (the author revealing how legal analyse is a perspective of the cathedral of law from an angle.)

7 For those who take offence at questioning scriptural account, we must however be reminded that the inquiry here isn't about it, and in any event, questioning under Jewish tradition is not impious as questioning is at the heart of Jewish piety, asking question constitutes an activity of being a Talmudic scholar.

Visual of King Solomon in judgment

Learning Analysis Skills through Practice

In one of the author's skills class where he teaches legal writing, reasoning, and research, he has found it useful to assign and make his students work with the Solomon's judgment. He employs it especially to help students' reason on syllogism associated with *IRAC* reasoning, and why enthymeme better explains legal conclusions in the face of evidential ambiguity and indeterminacy in law.[8] The class is requested to read the facts leading up to the Solomon's Judgment.[9] The assignment requires the students to read and to analyse Solomon's Judgment as a case and prepare a solution. When they are done, they review the statements of the parties as evidence before the judge, King Solomon. Students are asked to stand in his place and decide in accordance with the available evidence. They all agree that the baby should be given to the *real, true* mother- that is a position that better meets with justice of the case.

They are next asked what is the burden of proof required in the case, and whether they are satisfied with the evidence leading to the judgment? They are interrogated on what is the reasoning of King Solomon? What was his major

[8] Gerald F. Hess & Steven Friedland, *Techniques of Teaching Law,* Durham: Carolina Academic Press, 1999, 42.

[9] Holy Bible, 1 Kings 3: 16-27.

premise about *reality* in the case? Most of them agree that it is that the real mother would prefer to have her child alive, even in the hands of a stranger, rather than let it cut in two. It is understandable. A split would be death of the child.

In the role-play that follows, he asks them to act as lawyers for the second woman. He probes and trigger their reasoning asking them if there is any tangible evidence or law they can employ to overcome the orthodox position- that taken by wise King Solomon? Most of them can hardly think of any. The narrative of the first woman and the judgment by Solomon appear unassailable.

But for the teacher this is where to begin teaching legal analysis. For example, just raising a few puzzles does the trick. Questions such as, doesn't the story of the first woman imply that she saw the second woman's baby die? Is that not almost certainly false? Why does he say so? Think for once, if they were in different rooms (but in the same house), would she have seen the second woman lay on her baby? If so, could the second woman knowing so have dared to enter her room to change the babies? If we think that they were in the same room, then more questions, would she have let the first woman crush her own baby and then proceed to change the babies?

These questions are sufficient to trigger the critical skills of the students and that is exactly what we shall do in some details here. The students can then start an analysis which makes them think that it is after all possible that Solomon *may* have reached a wrong custody conclusion. They could in fact, reason that the possibility of guilt by the first woman rather than love for the baby would have influenced her to be willing to give up the baby. Some even start thinking and connecting procedural rights to legal conclusion and that even with a King as wise as Solomon, cross-examination can alter legal conclusion.

The teacher stimulates the analysis further, by saying, (assuming for purpose of argument) that you think Solomon reached a wrong conclusion, in awarding the baby not to the *true* mother, but the *better* mother, was that what Solomon set out to do? At this point the students come pointedly to see how society could be unsettled if the rule for awarding custody is on the basis of being the *better* parent. A floodgate of litigation gate would be open for those who want a child more than its parents. What is more, the possibility of a judge as wise as Solomon following a different rule (custody rule) from that which he claims to follow (identity rule) becomes a further teaching tool for selection of the ratio of a case.

He also use the judgment to interrogate questions of professional responsibility and ethics. He further ask them, how should lawyers deal with matters related to witness coaching, especially women seeking legal advice within the Solomon Judgment case square? With hindsight of our analysis, he ask, would you coach your witness if she were to appear before Solomon? What ethical dilemma does this present to you in lawyering? Just to move up a step further, he could just well ask, what they as judges would decide if both women have said, "Let her have the baby."[10]

The story lesson encourages the students to read carefully and analyse. Deciding, or nearly deciding that Solomon could have reached a wrong conclusion encourages them to read cases carefully and it emboldens them to challenge court decisions on appeal.

It is hoped that this simple story would have thought them some lawyering skills and values: how to critically analyse facts, how to ask questions, present arguments and avoid some ethical pitfalls.[11]

The [Il]Logic of Solomon's Judgment

Let us now add to the analysis with the hindsight of that skills class scenario. Let me start with the main plank of the case.

(i) Reasoning in Logic

One way lawyers reduce complexities of the social world, which generates controversies into simple, manageable legal formula and equation has been with the use of *IRAC* schemata. It is generally taken to be the signature pedagogy for legal analysis and reasoning.[12]

IRAC is extolled by the profession for its deductive reasoning potential, reasoning from the major to minor premise through syllogism. Reasoning in syllogism proceeds from the major premise, such as, "All humans are mortal," to the minor premise, "Socrates is a human," therefore making the conclusion logically correct: "Therefore Socrates is mortal." Lawyers extol syllogism because it closes on a science of reasoning and analysis associated with common sense and comprehension.[13]

---

[10]Hess &Friedland, above n. 7.

[11] See Shulamit Almog, Windows and Windows: Reflections on Law and Literature in the Digital Age (2007) 57 *Univ. Toronto L.J.* 755, where the learned writer uses Shakespeare's *Measure for Measure* to teach poetic justice in law and literature.

[12]Abiola O. Sanni, ed., *Introduction to Nigerian Legal Method*, Ile-Ife: Kuntel Pub. 1999, 54; Festus Emiri, Ayuba Giwa & Jonathan Ehusani, Revisiting the Traditional IRAC Organizational Structure of Legal Analysis: Towards a Multidisciplinary Approach (2017) *Nig. LJ* 1; Harold A. Lloyd, Plane Meaning and Thought: Real-World Semantics and Fictions of Originalism (2015) 24 *Southern Cal. Interdisciplinary L.J.* 657; Tracy Turner, Finding Consensus in Legal Writing Discourse Regarding Organizational Structure: A Review and Analysis of the Use of IRAC and its Progenies (2012) 9 *Legal Comm. & Rhetoric: JALWD* 351; Tracy Turner, Finding Consensus in Legal Writing Discourse Regarding Organizational Structure: A Review and Analysis of the Use of IRAC and its Progenies (2012) 9 *Legal Comm. & Rhetoric: JALWD* 351 at 359.

[13]Ibid.

Transposed to the Solomon's judgment, were the requirements of deductive logic satisfied?[14] No question about it, the position of the second woman is bound to raise feeling of disgust about her cruel response: "he will be neither mine nor yours! Let them cut him in two!" But deciding her fate based on that alone would be clearly unsatisfactory. So, can we search for reasonable ground for the decision in logic? It is plausible to simply state that the conclusion is logical. For no right-thinking mother will want her baby put to death, and for that matter in such graphically horrible way. Yes, Solomon exhibits a sense of logic in his testing of inconsistencies. The second woman's response is inconsistent with her claim of being mother that she earlier argued.

But is the conclusion resting on logic, such as "if she is the true mother, she will not say such a thing" (major premise), "if she did say such a thing as she did" (minor premise), "then she cannot be the true mother" (conclusion)?[15]

Was the major premise full proof? Don't we read and hear of mothers who abandon and sometimes throw away their babies? If so, then it is not without suspect to reason that it is possible that a real mother could wish the death of her baby. That being so, the syllogism associated with the judgment that equates maternal cruelty and maternal infanticide is nothing but a conclusion on probability.

Some could argue that the conclusion satisfied equity that the king after all decided on equitable grounds to give the baby to the better mother and that is just. Then we can probe further the perceived wisdom in the decision. Equity is not the basis on which the judgment appears unassailable and applauded. Deciding the question of who is the *better* mother isn't ingenious reason after all. Even a not so bright judge or person could have reached the right (custody) conclusion easily on those grounds also.

(ii) Enthymeme in Solomon's Judgment

There are two generally permitted logical structures for argumentation-deductive and inductive reasoning. Even at that, deductive reasoning admits of syllogism and enthymeme. Like syllogism, enthymeme begins with a major premise, followed by the minor premise. The difference between them being that in the former both premise (major and minor) is absolute certainty, making the

---

[14] James A. Gardner, *Legal Argument: The Structure and Language of Effective Advocacy*, 2nd ed., 1999; Anita Schnee, Logical Reasoning "Obviously" (1997) 3 *J. Legal Writing Inst.* 105; Kristen K. Robbins, Paradigm Lost: Recapturing Rhetoric to Validate Legal Reasoning (2003) 27 *VT L. Rev.* 483;

[15] The logic can also find justification in *modus tollens* as reasoning that whenever "one has two propositions, a conditional statement (if A, then B) and also the negation of the consequent (not-B), then one may affirm the negation of the antecedent (not-A)". See, L H LaRue, Solomon's Judgment: A Short Essay on Proof in (2004) 3 (1) *Law. Probability and Risk* 13 available in http://doi.org/10.1093/lpr/3.1.13 accessed March 10, 2017.

conclusion an absolute, irrefutable truth, while in the latter they are merely strong probabilities.

No one can seriously doubt that legal rules constructed from multiple sources, coloured by persuasive authorities, in context of facts indeterminacy should be a candidate for enthymeme. In fact, even Aristotle recognizing the indeterminate nature of law and facts in legal disputes was of the view that enthymeme constitutes a better model for legal reasoning.[16]

In enthymeme, a highly probable legal principle is applied to the specific facts of the case to produce a highly probably conclusion. This explains how law works in the real world, as we know it.[17] It appears to better explain the Solomon's judgment, like all judgments, rooted in enthymeme. Let us interrogate enthymeme in the judgment in the context of conclusiveness, completeness, consistency, credibility, and clarity.[18]

The probabilistic inconclusiveness of evidence in trial applies to the judgment. Whether it is admitted or not, using the fact of maternal infanticide as basis for cruelty and motherhood is not an exclusive phenomenon. Much as it is assumed that no woman the true mother would agree for her baby to be split in two, is a generalization, it is equally general to think that no woman (not the real mother) would say such a thing. So, it is neither here nor there. What is more, is it not plausible to think that the first woman's plea could have been motivated more of courage to stand against the king's perceived brutality than having to do with the question of true mother?

Completeness of the narrative is also suspect. For even though the first woman is on record saying both parties were in the house alone without stranger, it is conceivable to think that had neighbours. They were not living in isolation in a world of their own. So, if there were neighbours, as we would like to believe, could the neighbour's evidence not have helped to clarify matters, such as to identity and distinction between both babies, as neighbours who may have helped in delivering the babies, helped out in care-giving, etc. Would not such evidence if available be helpful? The account does not supply these details, so at best the evidence before the judge may well have been incomplete to justify the conclusion.

---

[16] Aristotle, *The Rhetoric,* Book 1, ch. 1 at 1355; Book 1, ch. 2 at 1356; Kristen K. Robbins-Tiscione, *Rhetoric for Legal Writers: The Theory and Practice of Analysis and Persuasion,* 2009; Michael D. Murray, Classical Rhetoric, Explanatory Synthesis and the TREAT Paradigm (Univ. Ill. L. & Econ. Working Paper No. 75, 2007), available at http://works.bepress.com/michael_murray/9.For the difference between syllogism and enthymeme and the supposed preference of the former to the latter; Linda L. Berger, Studying and Teaching "Law as Rhetoric": A Place to Stand (2010) 16 *J. Legal Writing Inst.* 3 at 50;

[17]Diane B. Kraft, CREAC in the Real World (2015) 63 *Clev. St. L. Rev.* 567.

[18]LaRue, above n. 15.

Aside this is the matter of consistency. Both women told inconsistent stories. Lawyers would say the second woman joined issues with the first. Most cases invariably implicate discordant notes, if the analyser pays sufficient attention to details. The evidence before the king was no different. The acclaimed wisdom of Solomon was made bright by how he dealt with the inconsistent testimonies of the two women.

But here again, giving that both women understand the gravity of the controversy, and that the first woman gives the answer that satisfies the king, is it not possible to explain the second woman's response as one in desperation having lost her case, something unconnected with the question of rightfulness of the baby? Can't a psychological motive be constructed for her cruel response or speech? Furthermore, watching the demeanour of the women, was it possible for the king to determine if the second woman's words were borne out of bitterness or despair? So, did the king judge her emotional state correctly?

Clarity of testimony, as an absence of ambiguity can hardly be tested in the Solomon's judgment because of the terse way the case is reported. A real trial envisages lengthy narrative by the parties, as each trying to describe the condition of her baby, the place the baby laid down, and the like. If this type of testimony had crept in they certainly would have introduced ambiguity into the case.

Conclusion

The exercise above can teach lawyers how to read more carefully and not take as given 'stock positions' revealed in judgments. Lawyers must develop and improve on the skills of critical analysis. Careful reading therefore helps the lawyer to see how court judgments transform ambiguity and indeterminacy into decidability, opening every legal conclusion to indictment of enthymeme.

Chapter 5

Legal Reasoning

Introduction

Legal reasoning can be described as the mental activity of marshalling one's premises, detecting logical connections and making inferences. It is a cognitive process of the mind and argumentation presented in form of premises and conclusion.[1]

Reasoning is innate to humans and this largely distinguishes us from other lower forms of life. We are all born with the ability to think. Animals on the other hand are not that endowed. But critical thinking or reasoning is not innate to humans. It requires a measure of hard work and training to be skilled in it.

Generally, philosophy is associated with critical reasoning or thinking. Ancient Greek philosophers like Plato, Aristotle and their contemporaries were reputed to excel in the art of formal logic. Philosophers then underwent training in formal logic and argumentation to acquire skills of reasoning. In effect, considerable time, training and hard work is necessary to acquire skills of critical reasoning.[2]

Legal reasoning is a genre of critical reasoning or thinking. It interrogates the skills needed to function as a professional lawyer. For example, it involves the skills of identify and articulates complex legal issues; applying legal reasoning and research to generate appropriate jurisprudential and practical responses to legal

[1] Brian N. Larson, *Law's Enterprise: Argumentation Schemes and Legal Analogy* (2018) @ 6.

[2] Steven J. Burton, *An Introduction to Law and Legal Reasoning*, 1995; Edward H. Levi, *An Introduction to Legal Reasoning,* 1948; Lloyd L. Weinreb, *Legal Reason: The Use of Analogy in Legal Argument,* 2005; Barbara A. Kalinowski, Logic Ab Initio: A Functional Approach to Improve Law Students' Critical Thinking Skills (2018) 22 *J. Legal Writing* 109; Ruggero J. Aldisert, Stephen Clowney& Jeremy D. Peterson, Logic for Law Students: How to Think Like a Lawyer (2007) 69 *Univ. Pittsburgh L. Rev.* 100; Brian N. Larson, *Law's Enterprise: Argumentation Schemes and Legal Analogy* (2018); Mary M. Ross, A Basis for Legal Reasoning: Logic on Appeal (2006) *J. Legal Writing*; Ruggero J. Aldisert, *Logic for Lawyers: A Guide to Clear Legal Thinking*, 28—29 (Nat'l Inst. for Trial Advocacy 3d Ed. 1997); Edwin W. Patterson, Logic in the Law (1942) 90 *U. Pa. L. Rev.* 875; Michael R. Smith, Rhetoric Theory and Legal Writing: An Annotated Bibliography (2006)3 *J. ALWD* 129 (2006) (listing dozens of scholarly works discussing logic and rhetoric in the discipline of legal writing); Richard D. Friedman, Logic and Elements (Symposium: Premises and Conclusions: Symbolic Logic for Legal Analysis) (1998) 73 *Notre Dame L. Rev.* 575; Ruggero J. Aldisert et al., Logic for Law Students: How to Think Like a Lawyer(2007) 69 *U. Pitt. L. Rev.* 1 @ 2; Charles Fried, The Artificial Reason of the Law, or: What Lawyers Know (1981) 60 *Tex. L. Rev.* 35.

issues; engagement in critical analysis and making reasoned and appropriate choices amongst alternatives; demonstration of sophisticated cognitive and creative skills in approaching legal issues and generating appropriate responses, and the like to controversies.[3] These are no mean skills. They certainly demand from lawyers' time expended in training and hard work. Those not so trained can hardly acquire the skills of legal reasoning. It is therefore not a surprise to hear Chief Justice Coke, CJ, tell the English King Edward that legal reasoning isn't just

[3] Over the years the profession has been concerned about the core skills lawyers ought to possess. The abysmal failure of legal education in this respect have engaged the profession. For example, in *Dawood Global Integrated Co. Ltd* v. *Gajere* (2017) LPELR 43369, Muyiwa Abiru, JCA stated: "This appeal is a complete abuse of the appellate court process. The facts are so elementary that even a kindergarten pupil should have no difficulty understanding them. It is appeals of this nature that makes this court question whether the authorities of the Nigerian Law School do a proper screening of the quality of people they pass and certify fit to be lawyers and to engage in the practice of law. This appeal also brings to fore the need of the Nigerian Bar Association to carry out and insist that lawyers who intend to practice law attend compulsory continuing legal education and to consistently rescreen and recertify people that can practice law." In a similar vein, the 1992 American Bar Association (ABA) Task Force on Law Schools and the Profession (the *MacCrate Report)*,the 2007 report of the Carnegie Foundation for the Advancement of Teaching on Legal Education (the Carnegie Report),and the 2007 report issued by Roy Stuckey and others on Best Practices for Legal Education (*Best Practices*) have all expressed concerns and identified the core skills of lawyers. See, Section on Legal Education and Admissions to the Bar, American Bar Association, Legal Education and Professional Development – An Educational Continuum, Report of the Task Force on Law Schools and the Profession: Narrowing the Gap, 1992, [hereinafter *McCrate Report)* The report's core set forth ten fundamental lawyering skills and four professional values that the Task Force believed every lawyer should acquire before assuming responsibility for the handling of a legal matter. The ten fundamental lawyering skills the report identified are: problem solving; legal analysis and reasoning; legal research; factual investigation; communication; counselling; negotiation; litigation and alternative dispute resolution procedures; organization and management of legal work; and recognizing and resolving ethical dilemmas. The four fundamental values are: provision of competent representation; striving to promote justice, fairness and morality; striving to improve the profession; and professional self-development. Also see, William M. Sullivan, et al. *Educating Lawyers: Preparation for the Profession of Law*, 2007 (*Carnegie Report*) which proposed an "integrative strategy" for legal education, identifying three apprenticeships—the cognitive, the practical and the ethical-social—that should be integrated to marshal all three apprenticeships "in support of the larger goal of training competent and committed practitioners." The first apprenticeship, the cognitive, "focuses the student on the knowledge and way of thinking of the profession." The second apprenticeship, the practical, schools' students in "the forms of expert practice shared by competent practitioners." The third apprenticeship, the ethical-social, "introduces students to the purposes and attitudes that are guided by the values for which the professional community is responsible). *The Best Practices for Legal Education: A Vision and a Road Map*, 2007, available at http://cleaweb.org/documents/bestpractices/best_practices-full.pdf (hereinafter Best Practices) also makes recommendations reminiscent of those in the *MacCrate and Carnegie Reports.* It states that the primary goal of legal education should be to develop competence defined as the ability to resolve legal problems effectively and responsibly; that law schools should integrate the teaching of theory, doctrine, and practice, and teach professionalism pervasively throughout all three years of law school; that law schools should employ context-based instruction; and that law schools should assess student learning through various methods of assessment, including multiple formative and summative assessments.

about every day reasoning but is rather the product of "long study and experience."[4]

Lawyers by training represent others. They make arguments before judges and other audience using legal analogy every day. It is common for lawyers to pray judges to grant their client's motion on the ground that their case is like earlier cases where the court grants the same type of motion or unlike earlier cases where the court denied motion. That explains why they spend considerable effort learning how to frame and formulate argument. Arguing by analogy is what is often meant as "thinking like a lawyer." Yes, the profession values rational consistency and logic.[5] Logic is therefore useful for lawyers, judges and scholars who seek a common template for assessing, critiquing and possibly attacking argument of others. This explains why lawyers are interested in argumentation – a series of propositional statements, called premises and conclusion.

General Note

Lawyers by reason of their profession work with rules and apply them to facts. These rules may be expressed or synthesized. Express rules are stated exactly by legislation. Lawyers only break them down to elements to apply them. To apply a rule, lawyers may use deductive or analogical reasoning. Generally, deductive reasoning is used for simpler rules; while analogical reasoning is used for more complex rules or rules with gaps.

Noteworthy of mention is that legal reasoning implicates two types of activities:

(i) the process of applying legal rules; and

(ii) the process of developing legal rules.

---

[4]See for example the reply of Chief Justice Edward Coke response to King James' claim to exercise jurisdiction personally. "[T]hen the King said, that he thought the law was founded upon reason, and that he and others had reason, as well as the Judges: to which it was answered by me, that true it was, that God had endowed His Majesty with excellent science, and great endowments of nature; but His Majesty was not learned in the laws of his realm of England, and causes which concern the life ... or fortunes of his subjects are not to be decided by natural reason but by the artificial reason and judgment of law, which law is an act which requires long study and experience ..." Prohibitions del Roy, 12 Co. 63, 64-65, 77 Eng. Rep. 1342, 1343 (K.B. x655), cited in Robert M. Cover, Nomos and Narrative (1983-84) 97 *Harv. L. Rev.* 4 @ 42 ft. nt. 120.

[5] Scott Brewer, Exemplary Reasoning: Semantics, Pragmatics, and the Rational Force of Legal Argument by Analogy (1996) 109 *Harv. L. Rev.* 923. But cf. Derrick Bell, Who's Afraid of Critical Race Theory (1995) *Univ. Ill. L. Rev.* 893 (an article suggesting that logic has little place in legal reasoning, that politics, not logic, drives the outcome of most cases). He stated at 899-900 that the law is "not a formal mechanism for determining outcomes in a neutral fashion - as traditional legal scholars maintain - but is rather a ramshackle ad hoc affair whose ill-fitting joints are soldered together by suspect rhetorical gestures, leaps of illogic, and special pleading tricked up as general rules all in a decidedly partisan agenda . . . ").

Applying Legal Rules

Legal rules can be applied to facts either by deductive or analogical reasoning. Deductive reasoning is usually suitable for applying simple rules, such as enacted rules. For example, if a simple rule states that a defendant will be criminally responsible if fake currency is found in her possession, deductive reasoning will be an appropriate reasoning technique to determine responsibility. All that is required is to construct the major premise as prohibiting possession of fake currency. If the defendant has it in her possession (minor premise), then she is liable (conclusion). Formal reasoning of this sort has the "rule" given to the reasoner as true. The minor premise is the factual situation. The conclusion is simply a combination of the given rule and specific facts. This is what makes it congenial for analysis of statutory rules.

On the other hand, analogical reasoning is a technique suitable for analysis complex rules, such as common law rules. Common law rules are general developed to make clearer the application of enacted or statutory rules. They are generally synthesized from cases and so may be complex in application. For example, if a driving rule states that a driver should not drive in a reckless manner, the stipulation will require the court to determine what reckless driving is. It could require the breakdown of the elements of the enacted rule and then how it applies to factual situations. This process of synthesizing is what makes the rule complex. The paradigm example of the rule on negligence requires an analysis of the three elements (duty of care, standard of care and remoteness of injury) to specific fact situation to determine whether negligence is raised. Analysing *Australian Knitting* case[6] requires that the reasoner to draw certain similarities or comparison between underwear in the *Knitting* case and beer in opaque bottle in *Donoghue* v. *Stevenson*[7] to determine if the three elements are raised to determine negligence in the *Knitting* case. This therefore involves comparing things that appear different to show their commonness.

Developing Legal Rules

Where however the legal rule is not given or expressed and has to be developed, lawyers use inductive reasoning to develop one. The rule is developed through a process of observation or "inductive reasoning." To do this, reasoning proceeds from observing the specific to the general to develop the general rule, rather than from the general to the specific. It is the method used to "mine" rules of a common law where there is no express rule. For example, to develop the modern

[6] *Grant* v. *Australia Knitting Mills Ltd* [1936] AC 85

[7] [1932] AC 562 (HL)

law of restitution as the third branch of the law of obligations lawyers had to mine its doctrines from quasi-contract cases.[8]

It is a model of reasoning from observing multiple particulars to create a general principle (major premise). It is founded on observation of general characteristics of things from which a general rule can be formulated. The number of specifics observed however does not guarantee the truthfulness or reliability of the general rule constructed.

Relationship between Reasoning and Logic

Ancient philosophers like Plato and his contemporaries practiced formal logic as the basis for reasoning. By emphasizing the form or structure of an argument came to conclusion whether the substance of an argument is true or false. Because these ancient philosophers were megacognitive thinkers they spent considerable time thinking about how the form or substance of an argument reveals its truth or falsity and ultimately its reliability. The legal profession recognising that the basis for legal reasoning, including the use of precedent to mine principles of law, were merely variations of deductive and inductive reasoning (which themselves are the building blocks of logic) thus introduced logic to the profession as the foundation for legal reasoning. Logic for the profession coincided with the quest for empiricism that swept the world of scholarship in the late twentieth century.

When law schools were being invented to replace the apprenticeship system in Anglo-American legal education, most university-based training were designed and implemented along the lines of case method for study of common law jurisprudence in a structured way.[9] For example, Christopher Columbus Langdell

---

[8] Festus Emiri, *The Law of Restitution in Nigeria*, Lagos: Malthouse Press, 2012; Graham Virgo, *The Principles of the Law of Restitution*, Oxford: Clarendon Press, 1998; Andrew Burrows, *Understanding the Law of Obligation: Essays on Contract, Tort and Restitution* (1998); Graham Virgo, *The Principles of the Law of Restitution*, Oxford: Clarendon Press, 1998; Peter Birks, *An Introduction to the Law of Restitution*, Oxford: Clarendon Press, 1985.

[9] For example, it has been suggested that that the German scientific method of legal education influenced The German university system, then at its apex, strongly influenced Harvard's president, Charles Eliot, and his law school dean, Christopher Columbus Langdell, in the design and implementation of the case method for study of common law jurisprudence in a structured way, together with the Socratic method of questioning in class. See Laura I. Appleman, The Rise of the Modern American Law School: How Professionalization, German Scholarship, and Legal Reform Shaped Our System of Legal Education (2005) 39 *New England L. Rev.* 251 (an article that shows that legal historians generally agree that, from the time of Dean Langdell's introduction of the case method at Harvard Law School in the 1870s, education in the American law school classroom has focused largely on the techniques of case analysis, the use of Socratic dialogue, and an emphasis on the skills of advocacy or adversarial lawyering). See also Josef Redlich, *The Common Law and the Case Method in American University Law Schools: A Report to the Carnegie Foundation for the Advancement of Teaching*, Bulletin No.8, 1914 @12. (hereinafter *The Redlich Report*) which states that "according to Langdell and his pupils, the law...should be acquired methodically from the original material of all principles and doctrines of the common law...by the individual, purely

who was Dean of Law at Harvard University has been described as the father of the case-method, a pedagogy that emphasises that the library should be at the heart of the law school and that legal education is like scientific research where principles of law are mined from reading cases.[10] The Langdell scientific model of legal instruction ushered in the late 1800s unfortunately is still the prevalent pedagogy despite its many shortcomings.[11] This notwithstanding, logic remains central in legal reasoning, especially in the context of "thinking like a lawyer". This is a skill that involves critical thinking, that of employing logic to construct valid arguments. Lawyers believe that logic provides correct answers to controversy and that logic is what provides correct answers through the application of abstract principles of law to cases. As a tool, it provides the profession a common vocabulary to identity valid argument, identify deficiencies in legal analysis and conclusion. This is what makes logic the lifeblood of law.[12]Litigation lawyers use logic to structure their client cases. Transactional

personal, intellectual labour on the part of the student". But cf. Byron D. Cooper, The Integration of Theory, Doctrine, and Practice in Legal Education, in Pamela Lysaght *et al.* eds. *Erasing Lines: integrating the Law School Curriculum*, 2002, 51 @ 62-63 (Christopher Columbus Langdell's claim that the content of legal education must be scientific to be worthy of study in a university. John Dewey traced the origins of the dualism of theory and practice to the distinction drawn in Near Eastern cultures between higher and lower kinds of knowledge for purposes of social status. This distinction was unfortunately perpetrated by the Greeks, who confined experiential knowledge to the artisan and trader classes and hindered the development of scientific knowledge for more than one and a half millennia. Whether arising from a desire for social status or respectability within the university or from some other cause, the determined separation of theory from practice has severely limited the scope of modern legal education. see [hereinafter erasing Lines] (citations and emphases omitted).

[10] In the 1880s when Langdell published the first modern casebook, the model was premised on the view that law is an autonomous discipline, complete, formal and conceptually ordered system that satisfies legal norms of objectivity and consistency. Above, see *Redlich Report* @ 12

[11] Bruce A. Kimball, 'The Proliferation of Case Method Teaching in American Law Schools: Mr.Langdell's Emblematic "Abomination," 1890-1915' (2006) 46 *History of Education Quarterly* 192 at 194; M.H. Sam Jacobson, A Primer on Learning Styles: Reaching Every Student (2001) 25 *Seatele U.L. Rev.* 139 (an article that suggest that the traditional heuristic for reasoning by analogy using IRAC is unhelpful for many learners because what constitute application is uncertain); J.T. Dillon, Chase and the Socratic Method of Teaching Law (1980) 30 *J. Legal Educ.* 528; Jerome Frank, A Plea for Lawyer-Schools(1947) 56 *Yale L.J.* 1303. See Mark Bartholomew, Legal Separation: The Relationship Between the Law School and the Central University in the Late Nineteenth Century (2003)57 *J. Legal Educ.* 368, 378 (a paper which states that the Socratic dialogue and case method introduced into the law school curriculum by Christopher Columbus Langdell in the 1870s was not primarily to prepare his students for practice, because law schools of the time were intended to complement apprenticeships, not replace them. So, Langdell's objective was to engage in the "scientific" study of law by distilling its principles from the study of cases which was the professors job. But even at this he was wrong both about the usefulness of the case method for discovering the basic principles of law and about the similarities of his approach to German scientific inquiry because later academics, like William Keener, were more sophisticated and saw the law as more complex, with an infinite variety of principles).See generally *MacCrate Report*.

[12] But cf. Oliver Wendell Holmes who said that "[t]he life of the law has not been logic, it has been experience." Oliver Wendell Holmes, Jr., *Common Law*, 1881 @1. Oliver Wendell Holmes, The Path

lawyers construct transactions following logical order traced in law and facts. Judges call upon logic rules to reach conclusions. Law teachers demand (through *IRACian* syllogism) that their student must think like a lawyer.[13] Unquestionably, a lawyer skilled in the logic of critical reasoning is more likely to argue more effectively than one who is not.[14] Lawyers are expected to present logical legal arguments. Interestingly, the etymology of logic is from the Greek word "logos" meaning notoriously large number of things, including words, speech, argument, reason, etc. This explains why some logicians insist that a logical argument should be one reducible to mathematical certainty by converting it into formal, symbolic logic or at least to a deductive syllogism.[15]

It is however useful to make a distinction between logical types and logical form in legal reasoning. Types generally describe the known patterns of legal argumentation marked out as deduction, analogy and induction; while forms demonstrate the relation between the truth of an argument's premises and the truth of its conclusion.[16]

Methods of Legal Reasoning

There are a handful of ideas relevant to legal reasoning. Traditionally, logicians separate the world of logical reasoning into two categories: deductive and inductive. Both models of reasoning are applicable to law. Lawyers generally use deductive reasoning and analogical reasoning in the process of rule application, while inductive reasoning is used for developing rules. Deductive reasoning is the prevalent method of reasoning in law. By unempirical count, it can be suggested that the majority of cases decided in law follow the deductive reasoning method. This reasoning model according to Aristotle is based on the act of proving a conclusion by means of two other propositions. The legal profession however uses analogy to solve cases where the rules are complex or the rules have gaps making them not easily susceptible to apply using deductive reasoning. This is often the technique used to solve problems not controlled by precedent. Reasoning by

---

of the Law, (1897) 10 *Harv. L. Rev.* 457 @ 167 of *The Essential Holmes* (Richard A. Posner ed., 1992). This notwithstanding, it has been suggested that the overarching writings of Holmes are comparable to the methods of deduction employed by Sherlock Holmes. See John H. Watson, M.D., A Case of Deduction, Or, Upon the First Meeting of Sherlock Holmes and Oliver Wendell Holmes, Jr. (2002) 24 *U. Ark. Little Rock L. Rev.* 855, n.1

[13]Tracy Turner, Flexible IRAC: A Best Practice Guide (2015) 20 *J. Legal Writing Inst.* 233 .

[14]Ruggero J. Aldisert, *Logic for Lawyers: A Guide to Clear Legal Thinking*, 3rd ed. Nat'l. Inst.For Trial Advo.1997 (hereinafter called "Logic"); Edwin W. Patterson, *Logic in the Law*, 90 *U. Pa. L. Rev.* 875 (1942). See also Ruggero J. Aldisert, *Winning on Appeal: Better Briefs and Oral Argument,* 2nd ed. 2003.

[15]Dukor, Larson @ 12.

[16]Brewer, above n. 5 @ 942.

analogy is a form of inductive reasoning in that like inductive reasoning it is used to develop a rule.

Visual relationship between reason and logic

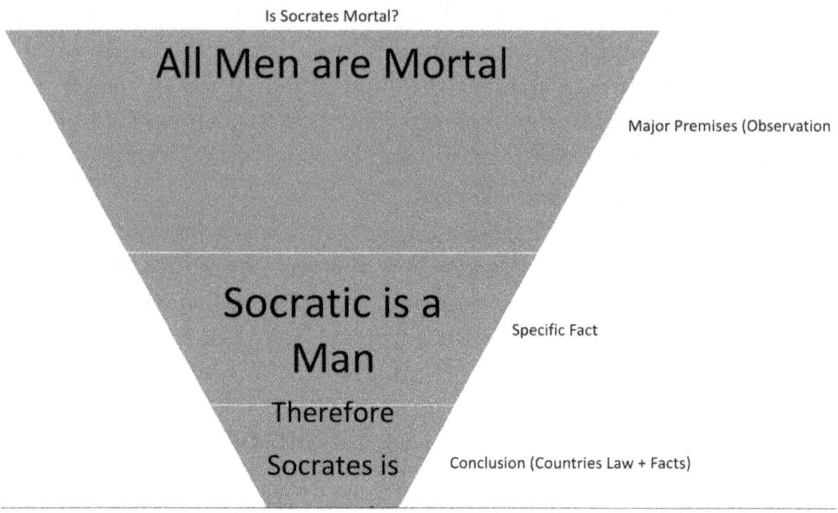

Deductive Reasoning

A valid deduction provides the strongest proof of the truth of an argument. It is the commonest logic principle to learn and coincidentally, the lawyer's most fundamental skill. As a process of reflective thinking or art of the mind, it moves from general truth to specific conclusion. It involves the relationship between two propositions, which helps to affirm or understand a third proposition.[17]It is a reasoning in which the conclusion is compelled by known facts. It involves two propositions if true, taken together affirms the third proposition. The classical tool of deductive reasoning is the syllogism.[18]

The paradigm example being: "All men are mortal. Socrates is a man. Therefore, Socrates is mortal." According to the traditional jargon, the syllogism's three parts are called the major premise, the minor premise, and the conclusion. The major premise states a broad and generally applicable truth. In this example, "All men are mortal." The minor premise states a specific and usually more narrowly applicable fact: "Socrates is a man." The conclusion then draws upon

---

[17]Maduabuchi Dukor, *Symbolic Logic*

[18] There are three basic types of syllogisms: (i) conditional syllogism (e.g. if A is true then B is true (if A then B); (ii) categorical syllogism (e.g. if A is in C (and B is in A) then B is in C; (iii) disjunctive syllogism (e.g. if A is true, then B must be false (A or B). See Aldisert, Logic, above n. 9 @ 145.

these premises and offers a new insight that is known to be true based on the premises: "Socrates is a mortal."

The reliability of a syllogism comes from the objective certainty that the conclusion is entailed from the truth of the first two propositions or premises. Logicians test the reliability of a syllogism by analysing the patterns of the terms within each proposition. Following this each of the three propositions is analysed in two categories: the subject term (e.g. "all humans") and a predicate term ("are mortal). The specific idea contained in each of these terms appears twice in the syllogism. The major term appears in the major proposition or premise and in the conclusion. The minor term appears in the minor proposition or premise but not in the conclusion. The middle term appears in the major and minor premises but not the conclusion.[19]

Using our paradigm example, it would thus be:

(i) "Mortal" is the major term

(ii) "Human" is the middle term

(iii) "Socrates" is the minor term.[20]

"<u>All humans</u> are mortal <u>Middle Term</u>, Major Term

Socrates is a <u>human</u>. Minor Term, <u>Middle Term</u>
Therefore, Socrates is mortal. Minor Term, Major Term

Each term can further be described as "distributed" or "undistributed." A subject term is distributed if it represents all members of the class and is undistributed if it represents only part of a class. A predicate term is distributed if it is a negative statement and undistributed if it is a positive statement. Only certain patterns of distributed and undistributed terms can be valid syllogistic forms.

Syllogism is a major reasoning tool employed by lawyers. In the legal context, the syllogism involves taking a legal premise (e.g. an enacted or judicially created "rule") and applying it to a factual premise (the facts of a case) to reach an objectively result (the conclusion).

---

[19]Kalinowski, above n. 2.

[20] Even though the example is classic of syllogism extolled for certainty it nonetheless shows the emptiness of deductive reasoning for the conclusion cannot state more than is said in the premises. It simply makes explicit some consequences which is contained implicitly in the premises. To that extent it unwraps the conclusion that was wrapped up in the premises. See Hans Reichenbach, *The Rise of Scientific Philosophy*, 1951, Berkeley: Univ. of California Press, 1951 @ 37.

Legal syllogism is overt reasoning. The structure promotes consistency and clarity. An example of categorical syllogism in criminal law would follow this pattern:

Major premise: (*doing* something which violates the law);

Minor premise: (the defendant *did* the something which violates the law);

Conclusion: (the defendant violates the law and criminally responsible)

Since syllogism is useful in preventing analytical errors, lawyers are therefore able to quickly debunk weak opponent's argument and judges' conclusion that do not follow structured reasoning. This is what makes reasoning skill critical to lawyering. Formal logic structure allows lawyers to comparatively analyse legal argument, by comparing and contrasting it to valid or invalid structures and reach conclusive logical decisions about validity or invalidity of the form of the argument.

Aside categorical syllogism, another helpful reasoning structure is the conditional (or hypothetical) syllogism. This takes an "if-then" form. The "if" term is known as the "antecedent" and the "then" term is known as the "consequent". To be valid, a conditional syllogism must take one of two forms. One such form, known as *modus ponens*.

If A is true, then B;

B, therefore A.

The syllogism is valid when the antecedent is "affirmed" as existing or being true. For example, if a land document is not evidenced in writing, then it is unenforceable.

If the minor premise of a conditional syllogism negates the consequent of the major premise, the form is called *modus tollens*.

If *A*, then *B*;

Not *B*, then therefore not *A*.

This basic principle of syllogism is particularly attractive in that what is true of the universe is true of the particular and it is straightforward.[21] This makes it the predominate way to reason, write and advocate in law. Most legal rules can be stated in the form of a valid deductive form: whenever the operative facts then the normative consequence.

For all its power, the basic principle of the syllogism is surprisingly straightforward: What is true of the universal is true of the particular. A clear,

---

[21] Note however that the simple syllogism used here on "Socrates" does not account for some rather complex syllogism such as the hypothetical syllogism (the "if-then" statement), or the disjunctive proposition (the "either-or" statement) etc. See, Richard Posner, *The Problem of Jurisprudence*, 1990, 38 (on the usefulness and strength of syllogism in legal reasoning).

well- constructed syllogism ensures each conclusion is well-supported by the first two propositions.

Learning Syllogism

While some lawyers can instinctively think logical, other need to learn it through patience and practice.[22]This can be learned by first shaping a legal issue in the form of a syllogism. The starting point is learning to state the general rule of law or widely-known legal rule that governs the case as the major premise. Next, is to frame the minor premise by describing the key facts of the legal problem at hand. Finally, is the drawing up of the conclusion by examining how the major premise about the law applies to the minor premise about the facts. The pattern would be like this:

Major premise: the 1999 Constitution prohibits unlawful arrest and detention save an arrest and detention with warrant.

Minor premise: the plaintiff was arrested and detained without warrant.

Conclusion: the unlawful arrest and detention is forbidden by the 1999 Constitution.

Much as this construction appears on face value to be simple, constructing sound syllogism is tasking. It requires thorough research of statute, precedent or other legal material to determine and state the major premise. Additionally, the lawyer must be sufficiently knowledgeable about the facts of the case to isolate key facts material to law (minor premise). It only when these two propositions are known that a conclusion becomes valid.

Judge Aldisert generic prosecutors' template can be useful in horning the skill. It goes like this:

> Major premise: [Doing something] [violates the law]
> Minor premise: [The defendant] [did something]
> Conclusion: [The defendant] [violated the law][23]

The prosecutor's model can serve as a useful template for most legal problems. Using it will help reduce an argument to its most essential parts. In addition to providing a useful template, the above example reflects the fact that the three parts of a syllogism—the two premises and conclusion—are themselves built from three units. Logicians call these units "terms." Two terms appear in each statement: the "major term" in the major premise and conclusion, the "minor term" in the minor premise and conclusion, and the "middle term" in the

---

[22]Aldisert, Clowney & Peterson, above n. 2.

[23]Aldisert, above n. 1 @ 6.Antonin Scalia, The Rule of Law as the Law of Rules (1989) 56 *Univ. Chi. L. Rev.* 1175.

major and minor premises but not in the conclusion. Notice that the middle term covers a broad range of facts, and that, if the conclusion is to be valid, the minor term must be a fact that is included within the middle term. Although the jargon can get confusing, the basic idea is not hard to grasp: Each statement in a syllogism must relate to the other two.

But syllogism is not always apparent in legal writing or argument. Sometimes it is obscure, and some effort is required to discern it by digging beyond the surface to see its underlining structure. In fact, the absence of syllogism is no evidence that a particular writing or argument is windy, illogical or sloppy. That syllogism follows the general IRAC model of argument does not make it the only tenable and reliable method to reason.[24] Interspersed forms of writing and arguments that mix both law and facts (major and minor premises), especially in the narrative style, can also be powerful persuasion technique.[25] The important thing is for lawyers to learn how to parse statements by reading between the lines to see the deep structure of syllogism as they rearranging sentences and rephrasing statements to match up with the syllogistic basic form.

For example, though the statement of Justice Blackmun in *Roe* v. *Wade* that "this right of privacy, whether it be founded in the Fourteenth Amendment's concept of personal liberty and restrictions upon state action, as we feel it is, or, as the District Court determined, in the Ninth Amendment's reservation of rights to the people, is broad enough to encompass a woman's decision whether or not to terminate her pregnancy,"[26] is difficult to pigeonhole within our two premises structure to reach valid conclusion, a lawyer can impose an implicit syllogism on it by re-characterising it this way:

Major premise:

Minor premise: A woman's decision to terminate her pregnancy is protected by the right of privacy.

Conclusion: Therefore, a woman's decision whether to terminate her pregnancy is protected by the Fourteenth or Ninth Amendment.

So, even though the statement of Justice Blackmun appears fluid, the skilful reader can impose syllogism on it by rearranging the statement (as some writer do not mention all the parts of syllogism leaving the reader to discern it) into the two premises and conclusion.

---

[24]Festus Emiri, Ayuba Giwa & Jonathan Ehusani, Revisiting the Traditional IRAC Organizational Structure of Legal Analysis: Towards a Multidisciplinary Approach (2017) *Nig. LJ* 1.

[25]Narrative style and the interspersed brief.

[26] (1973) 410 US 113 @153 (state significance of case on woman's right to abortion)

Enthymeme

Logicians recognising that not all valid arguments are founded on syllogism as not all parts of the syllogism are expressly named. Such statements are enthymeme. It has been suggested that enthymemes are used for efficiency, usually where the audience shares a cognitive model with the writer.[27]For instance, if a premise or conclusion is obvious, then a writer can save her precious words try to make a less obvious point.

A contract law teacher might find it cumbersome to commend Kwame by saying, "Good contract law students make great transactional lawyers (major premise); Kwame is a good contact student (minor premise); Kwame will be a great transactional lawyer (conclusion)." Though in real term the expression contains the indicia of syllogism, the teacher may think it too lengthy a way to commend Kwame to her contract class. Rather than take such windy route of commendation she could just say "Kwame will be a great transactional lawyer because he is good in contract law." The expression omits the major premise because it is generally understood that her contract class know that a good grasp of contract law sets the foundation for transactional lawyering. The teacher and her class share what can be termed a common or shared-cultural schemata or an idealised cognitive model (ICM).[28] So, there is hardly a need to express statement with all the ingredients of syllogism.

Sometimes, legal writing and arguments proceed on the basis of enthymeme because they are addressed to an educated audience. For example, in *Felix Amadi* v. *INEC*[29] where the Supreme Court said that "the provisions of section 285 (7) do not deny an appellant the right to fair hearing, just like every statute of limitation. It merely gives all parties and the court a time frame within which parties are to exercise their right to fair hearing in the relevant appeal."

The major premise is that the Constitution is the overriding law in Nigeria. The minor premise is that section 285 (7) does not conflict or compete with the right to fair hearing. The conclusion being that the appellant who fails to exercise the right to fair hearing within the 60 days window for election matters is doomed.

Noteworthy of mention, the court left out an important minor premise: it never stated that the right to fair hearing conflicts with the 60-day bar. But the Supreme Court can hardly be faulted in not being explicit on this. The parties and

---

[27]Aldisert, Clowney & Peterson, above n. 2 @ 106.

[28]Steven L. Winter, Transcendental Nonsense and Metaphoric Reasoning, and the Cognitive Stakes For Law (1989) 137 *Univ. Pa. L. Rev.* 1105.

[29] Suit No. SC/476/2012 delivered on Friday, February 3, 2012, per Walter S. N. Onnoghen, JSC (a case in which the claimant stated that the mandatory 60 days prescribed by s. 285 (7) of the 1999 Constitution for the hearing of an election appeal amounts to a denial of the right to fair hearing)

legal audience recognise that is avoiding needless words. All a skilful lawyer does here is to recognise the enthymeme to develop the statement into a full-fledged syllogism.

Poly-Syllogism

It is also possible to have a pill of syllogism, as where there are a series of syllogisms in which the conclusion of one syllogism supplies a premise of the next syllogism. Logicians refer to this as poly-syllogism. Typically, poly-syllogisms are used because more than one logical step is needed to reach the desired conclusion. A paradigm example would be:

All men are mortal. "Socrates is a man." Therefore, Socrates is mortal.
All mortals can die. Socrates is mortal. Therefore, Socrates can die.
People who can die are not gods. Socrates can die. Therefore, Socrates is not a god.[30]

Skilled lawyers therefore learn how to identify enthymemes and poly-syllogism in arguments.

Flawed or Bogus Syllogism

As a general rule, if the premises of a syllogism are properly structured the conclusion would be entailed. This is why lawyers must be quick to scrutinise arguments masquerading as syllogism when they are indeed flawed or bogus syllogism. A typical example would be:

Major premise: Some men are tall.
Minor premise: Socrates is a man.
Conclusion: Therefore, Socrates is tall.

True, this looks like a syllogism, but it is not. It is flawed syllogism because knowing that *some* men are tall isn't enough for you to conclude that a particular man is tall. He might fall into the group of other men about whom we know nothing about. These persons may be tall or short.

Interestingly, this type of non-syllogism has been common in judicial pronouncements where judicial officers adopted primitive generalisations to hold down people considered inferior on grounds of races, tribe, sex, sexual orientation, religion and the like.

Feminist are very familiar with. About 150 years ago, Justice Barker of the United States in *Bradwell* v. *Illinois,* adopted the discredited *separate but equal* sphere doctrine stating: "the civil law, as nature herself, has always recognised a

---

[30]Aldisert, Clowney & Peterson, above n. 2 @ 108.

wide difference in the respective sphere and destinies of man and woman. Man is, or should be, woman's protector and defender. The natural and proper timidity and delicacy which belong to the female sex evidently unfits it for many of the occupation of civil life. The constitution of family organisation, which is founded on the divine ordinance as well as the nature of things, indicated the domestic sphere as that which properly belongs to the domain and functions of womanhood."[31]

No question about it. This is flawed syllogism.

Major premise: that nature has reserved serious business of law for men only.
Minor premise: Bradwell is a female aspiring to become a barrister in Illinois.
Conclusion: Since the legal profession is made for the strong she cannot be admitted to the Bar.

Such bogus syllogism was also applied to people of black race in the United States. The U.S. Supreme Court in the Dred Scott case made a similar pronouncement.[32] The dissenting opinion noted that the Court's ruling relied on a bad syllogism, simplified here:

Major Premise: At the time of the adoption of the Constitution, *some* states considered members of the black race to be inferior and incapable of citizenship and of suing in federal court.
Minor Premise: Dred Scott's ancestors at the time of the Constitution were members of the black race.
Conclusion: Therefore, Dred Scott's ancestors were considered to be inferior and incapable of citizenship and of suing in federal court.[33]

An easy way to spot bogus syllogism is the presence of words like "some", "certain", "a", "one", "this", "that", "sometimes", "many", "occasionally", "once", or "somewhere".[34] The presence of those phrases in a statement more often than not spells bogus syllogism and so lawyers should keep an eye on them. To remain

---

[31](1873) 83 US (16 Wall) 130 @ 135. See also *In Re French* (1905) 37 NBR 359, where the New Brunswick court decided that women are not eligible for admission as barristers. Tuck J. at 361-362, declared that he had no sympathy for women who wanted to compete with men. He said: 'Better let them attend to their legitimate business.' For critique of case, see Festus Emiri, Law in Context: Feminism (2003) 1 *Legal Science Review* @ 55. See also Hilaire Barnett, *Sourcebook on Feminist Jurisprudence*, London: Cavendish Pub, 1997.

[32] (1857) 60 US 393; The case decided by the US Supreme Court on March 6, 1857, ruled (7-2) that a slave, Dred Scott, who had resided in a free state and territory where slavery was prohibited was not thereby entitled to his freedom. It held that an African-American could never be a citizen of the United States.

[33]Aldisert, Clowney & Peterson, above n. 2 @ 109.

[34] Ibid.

ever skilful in argumentation lawyers must always remember to scrutinise the basis structure of syllogism to see if it applies to arguments. This dictates that they scrupulously test to determine that behind every syllogism is that what is true of the universal is also true of the specific. Deductive reasoning proceeds from the general to the particular. So, where the general is suspect, the particular is more likely to be bogus and flawed.

This is important because some bogus syllogism is difficult to spot. Experience, learning and familiarity with the major premise often help to identify bogus syllogism. For example, a statement that

> Trawlerlong line fishing is tough business (major premise); Jack a longline trawler fisher is strong (minor premise); so, Jack is a superman (conclusion)...

may not altogether be valid. Familiarity with the business of ocean trawler business of longline fishing can be helpful to the lawyer to determine the truth-value of the major premise. What is more, knowing that the longline fishing business is tough does not warrant a conclusion that all engaged in the business are endowed with strength. It must be kept in mind that in syllogism one can only draw a conclusion about the particular (superman) after one can validly say it is part of the universal (the business is tough).

This being so, a correct syllogism would look like this:

Major Premise: only the very strong can get involved in longline fishing. [General statement about a class]

Minor Premise: Jack is involved in longline fishing [Statement that an individual belongs to the class]

Conclusion: Jack is strong. [Conclusion that the individual has properties common to other members of the class]

Also, it should be remembered that just because two things share a common property does not mean they also share a second property. So, the statement that "All lawyers are fit and proper persons, and Owusu is a fit and proper person," does not mean that Owusu is a lawyer. Owusu can be a lawyer or a non-lawyer. That lawyers are fit and proper does not entail that all fit and proper persons must be lawyers.

Undoubtedly, there are many type of flawed syllogism and it can be challenging to identify them all. Notwithstanding, logicians provide us a guide to map valid from invalid syllogism.[35] They tell us that letters "A" and "E" often describes universal propositions (major premise). "A" as an indefinite article is affirmative, while "E" negates. "I" and "O" describe particular propositions. "I" being affirmative, and "O" negative.

Logicians would describe the three propositions in paradigm example as "All men are mortal" syllogism as "All."

Therefore, for the major premise to be valid, it must be either "A" or "E." No valid major premise comes out of an "I" or "O," because they describe particular proposition, what can be termed minor premise. Thus the "IAA" structure form, for example, cannot be a valid syllogism. All minor premise and conclusion must be either an "I" or an "O". Once a tentative syllogism does not meet these requirements, the lawyer should suspect that something is wrong with the syllogism.[36]

This being so, lawyers must be skilful and critical readers. Particular attention must be paid to read written documents or listen to argument. The place of good research to determine correct major premise and minor premise is critical.[37] Bad reasoning can seem persuasive at first glance and logical fallacies can be challenging to spot in briefs, memos, and court opinions because of the dense writing and complex fact patterns. Yet the effort is worthwhile. The ability to detect and avoid logical missteps will improve a lawyer's writing and thinking ability.

Limitations of syllogism

Much as deduction is the standard of legal reasoning, too much premium should not be placed on it in legal argument. This is because deduction only operates on its premises but does not provide the premises. Even Aristotle recognised this shortcoming with syllogism when he admitted that stating the truth of a major premise could be challenging because it is sometimes near impossible to perceive what is universal in every case. Universal description is often itself a product of observation, experience and seeing, which is a form of inductiveness.[38]

---

[35] S. Morris Engel, *With Good Reason: An Introduction to Informal Fallacies*, 1994 @ 89, cited in Aldisert, Clowney & Peterson, above n. 2 @ 110 n. 24.

[36] Aldisert, Clowney & Peterson, above n. 2 @ 110

[37] Geoffrey Samuel, Can the Common Law Be Mapped? (2005) 55 *Univ. Toronto LJ* 271.

[38] Aristotle, *Posterior Analytics*, ch. 31 @ 43. See Posner, above 17. See also Hans Reichenbach, *The Rise of Scientific Philosophy*, 1951, Berkeley: Univ. of California Press, 1951 @ 37 (where the author argues that logical deduction cannot create independent results as it is merely an instrument of connection: it derives conclusions from given axioms but cannot inform us about the truth of the axioms).

This is particularly so with legal reasoning for two reasons: the difficulty of stating the major premise with correctness; and the difficulty of applying legal-categorical labels to actual instances.

Let us for instance consider cases having to do with a competent patient refusal of a treatment choice by her doctor. If a patient is ill for instance, and the doctor recommends say a particular treatment choice the patent rejects, it can be classified as suicidal. But it is also possible to categorize it as a proper exercise of right to personal autonomy. The way and manner the facts are classified will determine how the major premise is constructed. From the same facts scenario, the general rule could be stated either as: "suicide is prohibited" or as "every person of full age and capacity has a right to personal liberty and choice of medical treatment."

If one adopts the later position then the major premise will draw on facts like a distinction between the right to die and the right to choose how to live.[39]

So, in facts situation like this the construction of the major premise requires first that we observe the facts scenario and classify them, all products of experience, thereby drawing on inductive reasoning to make standard arguments using syllogism.

Important note on logic and enthymeme

The major premise in syllogism is the legal rule. But what this is can be problematic for many reasons. Rules are not objects out there in the world for capture. Worse still, in legal analysis, they can just be in a state of flux. Identifying them is not as simple as the application of syllogism could seem to suggest. This is especially so for the common law, a system that function more at the level of facts than the abstract.[40] For example, because the common law system operates at an inductive level it would likely make fundamental distinction between types of persons and things and words used in legislation.[41] That being so, a court decision such as in *Donoghue* v. *Stevenson*[42] concerning injury caused by a defective bottle of ginger beer containing decomposed snail, may not necessarily apply to other defective products. So, formulating the rule emerging from the case could be problematic. Would we for instance, reason that the rule would apply or be relevant for damages inflicted by say a defective wall or damages caused by an old

[39] *Okonkwo* v. *MDPDT* (2001) 6 NWLR (pt. 710) 1; [2001] 3 SC 76; [2001] All NLR 305, per Ayoola, JSC (lead judgment).

[40] Geoffrey Samuel, Can the Common Law Be Mapped? (2005) 55 *Univ. Toronto LJ* 271.

[41] Geoffrey Samuel, *Law of Obligations and Legal Remedies,* 2nd ed., London: Cavendish Pub., 2001. See also Cass R. Sunstein, Incomplete Theorised Arguments (1995) 108 *Harv. L. Rev.* 1733.

[42] [1932] AC 562 (HL)

tree, even though all these items can be properly described as "things". That is difficult to say with certainty.

That explains why even four years after the invention of the negligence rule in *Donoghue* it was unclear if the rule (formulated from the facts of injury caused by the defective bottle of ginger) would apply to defective pair of underpants. Not surprising counsel for the defendant in *Grant* v. *Australia Knitting Mills Ltd.*[43] argued that a rule fashioned for ginger beer bottle should not apply to an article of clothing because beer and clothing are different entities. Though the Privy Council rejected the argument, it does not detract from the fact that a system, which operates at the level of facts is bound to draw distinction between "things" and "persons," and so a rule may just well mean many things to different persons depending on how they construct the relevant ratio emerging from given facts. What the rule of negligence is from *Donoghue* v. *Stevenson* is therefore a matter of fitting the facts to law. It is plausible to construct several rules from the case. That is why it was not illogical for defendant to argue in *Australian Knitting* that the *Donoghue* ratio did not apply (as major premise) to the set of facts in the instant case.

Undoubtedly, syllogism is unable to tell how the major premise (the rule) is constructed. That explains why the defendant could characterise and constructed *Donoghue* in the new fact-situation as inapplicable to the *Australian Knitting* case. This is understandable, especially in the context that common lawyers reason inductively.[44]

An understanding of what "rule" implies exacerbates the situation. Legal rules can be divided into two -the general rule and the precedent (which decides the facts-specify application to the abstract rule). That in a way explains why the defendant's argument (though dismissed by the court) in the *Australian Knitting* could count as valid legal reasoning and analysis.[45]

---

[43] [1936] AC 85

[44] Geoffrey Samuel, above n. 19. In fact, one hallmark of the common law legal system is that it is under theorised, in the sense that a court decision is not an instantiation of an explicit theory for resolving similar matters. Cass R. Sunstein, Incomplete Theorised Arguments (1995) 108 *Harv. L. Rev.* 1733. (an article that states that since the incremental work of judges is accomplished by merely fitting new facts into existing precedent without necessarily articulating broad theory in the area that is in issue or dispute, the ultimate implication leaves unfilled theoretical gaps until the court is presented in future by facts pattern that demand gap-filling decisions).

[45] See Laura P. Graham, Why-RAC? Revisiting the Traditional Paradigm for Writing About Legal Analysis (2015) 63 *Kansas L. Rev.* 681 at 683 (an article that suggest that IRANian syllogism in legal writing should replace the "R" with "GP," "G" being the general rule and "P" the precedent that decides specific facts situation. Such a stance will convert IRAC to IGPAC); Barbara Blumenfeld, Why IRAC Should Be IGPAC, *The Second Draft* (Legal Writing Institute, Tacoma, Washington, Nov. 1995, 3.

Skilled lawyers recognise the flux nature of the major premise being constructed from precedent. They know that amateurs who linearly reason in simplistic dualism of right and wrong would be quick to find determinate legal rule, but does not make it the controlling rule or major premise. With skills and intellectual development lawyers transform to the multiplicity stage, where they read in between the lines of precedents (statute or case law) and can begin to formulate controlling rule as largely unknown. At this skill stage, the lawyer sees rules as indeterminate, amenable to diverse interpretation. Yes, "rule" takes on the meaning of "general rule" and precedent. More skilled lawyers even go past the multiplicity stage into contextual relativism, a stage where they gradually see for the first lawyers as readers of precedents are themselves legitimate source of knowledge and that former knowledge-iconoclasts (statute, case-law and legal texts) are also fellow knowledge and truth-seekers of what "legal rules" are.[46]

Thus, the "rule" is formulated from the given facts scenario, precedent and policy all synthesised. So, a legal rule may not just be something out in the world capable of summarising in one way and one way only. It can be susceptible to different analysis. Legal reasoning can thus be a difficult task of choosing between competing and sometimes conflicting rules. Thus, to the extent that syllogism suggests and encourages its users to narrowly construct the major premise as certain and determinate it discourages evaluation of competing rules-a necessary skill for lawyers.[47]

Although a sceptic position to reasoning, some commentators even dispute the proposition that there is anything clearly marked as rules, to warrant an "R" within the paradigm. They question whether judicial decisions are founded on rules. Maintaining such a stance for instance, Sinclair posits that rules can be formulated in many ways to fit several opinions, none of which can lay validity to superiority.[48] The learned writer presses the point by an analogy. Assuming ordinary people can read and understand cases and distil rules therefrom, he argues that lawyers would be amazed at the different interpretations they will put on cases. Perhaps corroborative of his position is the thinking that lawyers do not

---

[46] For a parallel on students' development analogically applicable to lawyering, see Paula Lustbader, Construction Sites, Building Types, and Bridging Gaps: A Cognitive Theory of the Learning Progression of Law Students (1997) 33 *Willamette L. Rev.* 317. See also Gerald F. Hess & Steven Friedland, *Techniques for Teaching Law*, Durham, North Carolina, Caroline Academic Press, 1999, 7.

[47] Marion W. Benfield, Jr., Thoughts on IRAC, The *Second Draft* (Legal Writing Institute, Tacoma, Washington, Nov. 1995, 17. See also Ronald Dworkin in *Taking Rights Seriously*, 2nd ed. Cambridge, 1978 @ 23 (where the learned writer states that legal norms are in two categories-rules and principles. While the former is applicable in an all-or-nothing fashion, the latter are best described as value-maximising norms, i.e. they aim at promoting certain legal values). This mentality could explain why common lawyers trained in Anglo-American legal system would treat a statute as not intended to introduce new legal principles.

[48] Michael Sinclair, What Is the "R" in IRAC (2003) 19 *N.Y.L. Sch. J. Hum. Rts.* 87.

extract rules from a single case but rather from a series of them. That being so, a science of law which constructs principle from them should be seen as a process of synthesizing, which ordinarily admits of rule pluralism.

Example

Let us drive home the point by comparing some decisions of the Supreme Court on the question of finality.[49] In *Akinsanya* v. *United Bank of Africa Ltd* the court was faced with the issue of whether the appeal was an interlocutory or final appeal.[50] This issue is material for many reasons. For instance, the Constitution stipulates different time for an interlocutory and final appeal. Every interlocutory appeal must be lodged within 14 days to be competent. For a final appeal the time bar is 90 days.

In the *Akinsanya* case, the appeal was lodged after 14 days, but within 90 days to an order decreed by the Court of Appeal.[51] The matter originated before the Lagos High Court as a dispute between the plaintiff and the defendant relating to payments by the defendant in pursuance of an irrevocable letter of credit. The trial court dismissed the claim. On appeal to the Court of Appeal, the court *suo moto* raised the issue of jurisdiction; whether the Lagos High Court had jurisdiction to hear the matter, it been an admiralty matter that should go to the Federal High Court and not a state high court, as the Lagos High Court. On this it held that the Lagos High Court had no jurisdiction over the suit it being an admiralty matter that should have gone to the Federal High Court. The defendant appealed the judgment on the question of jurisdiction to the Supreme Court. The appeal was filed after 14 days but within 90 days. The question before the Supreme Court had to do with the competence of the appeal- whether it was filed within time. If the decision is interlocutory, an appeal after 14 days will certainly

---

[49] *Compagnie Generale Geophysique* v. *Alhaji Musa* LER [2017] SC 310/2008, per Mohammad, JSC; *Igunbor* v. *Afolabi* (2001) 11 NWLR (pt. 723) 148 @ 165; *Western Steel* v. *Iron & Steel Workers Union* (1986) 3 NWLR (pt. 30) 617; (1987) 1 NWLR (pt. 49) 284; *Akinsanya* v. *UBA* (1986) NSCC (vol. 16) 147, per Kayode Eso, JSC, (1986) 4 NWLR (pt. 35) 273, [1986] 7 SC 233; *Sken-Consult* v. *Ukey* (1981) 21 SC 6; *Adeyemi* v. *Awobokun (1968) 2 All NLR 318; Bozson* v. *Altrincham Urban District Council* (1903) 1 KB 547 @ 548, ("in my opinion a final order that puts to an end to the dispute between the parties and finally disposes of the rights of the parties. An order is final where the court orders something to be done in answer to the enquires, without any further reference to itself or any other court of co-ordinate jurisdiction."); *Salaman* v. *Warner* (1891*);* Right v issue; Order made (correct); Nature of proceeding; Right of the parties determined; Logic- Salaman; Experience- Bozson.

[50] *Akinsanya* v. *UBA* (1986) NSCC (vol. 16) 147; (1986) 2 NSCC 968, (1986) 4 NWLR (pt. 35) 273.

[51] See for example, section 31(2)(*a*) of the Supreme Court Act, 1960 (Nigeria) provides that the periods prescribed for the giving of notice of appeal or notice of application for leave to appeal applicable to

(*a*) an appeal in a civil case shall be fourteen days in an appeal against an interlocutory decision and three months in an appeal against a final decision.

be incompetent. But if it is final, then the appeal lodge within the 90 days was competent. In this case the appeal was enter after 14 days but within 90 days. So the material question was whether the decision of the Court of Appeal on the jurisdiction of the Lagos High Court was final or interlocutory order.[52]

What the governing rule on "finality" is not a thing of much controversy. The major premise is that "a final order or judgment at law is one which brings to an end the rights of the parties in the action, in that it disposes of the subject matter of the controversy or determines the litigation as to the parties on the merits."[53] But constructing the major premise this way without more leaves unsettled and controversial how the precedent should fit facts scenario (minor premise).

Stating the governing rule this simple can be unhelpful, without a synthesizing it from previous cases. Just stating the finality rule the way it is does not tell us whether the term "final" is referable to the subject matter of dispute between the parties or whether it is a function of the order the court makes. It does not tell us whether "finality" can apply to matters determined interlocutory or whether it only relates to final decisions on merit. Yes, whether finality applies to both rulings and judgments of courts. In fact, it leaves doubtful how "final" to be construed in particularities, particularly in varied cases having to do with orders of court on *rights* of parties in controversy and *issues* before the court.

For instance, it can be problematic to use the simple unsynthesized finality rule to determine the question whether a ruling on an issue of jurisdiction raised *in limine* is final or interlocutory. It can be reasoned that the question of jurisdiction of court touches only the competence of the court and that it does not raise any issue touching the rights of the parties in the subject matter of the litigation or dispute, and so it is not final.[54]

Possible construction of the synthesis rule would require certain particularization as so whether "final" is a function of (either or both) examining the *nature of the order* or the *nature of the proceedings* resulting from the order. Interestingly, in the *Akinsanya* case the Supreme Court had to determine the "rule" on finality by synthesizing it from an analysis of cases. The court noted that there are two English decisions on the subject, interpreted differently. The two decisions adopted different rules.[55] *Salaman* adopts the nature of the application or proceedings test, while *Bozsson* adopts the nature of the *order* test.

---

[52]Ibid.

[53]*Igunbor* v. *Afolabi* (2001) 11 NWLR (pt. 723) 148 @ 165, per Karibi-Whyte, JSC. See also *Alor* v. *Ngene* (2007) 17 NWLR (pt. 162) 163 @ 175-177.

[54]See *Western Steel Works Ltd and another* v. *Iron* and *Steel Workers Union* (1986) 3 N.W.L.R. (pt. 30) 617 @ 625, Obaseki JSC.

[55]*Bozson* v. *Altrnicham UDC* test [1903] 1 QB 547; *Salaman* v. *Warner* test [1891] 1 QB

In *Bozson* v. *Altrinchim UDC* the court stated that an order will be treated as final only if it finally disposes of the rights of the parties. That is, it is an order which would not bring the matter back to court that makes the order.[56] On the other hand, the *Salaman* v. *Warner* the court took the position that finality depends on examining the nature of the application before the court and not the nature of the order made by the court. In *Bozsson* the test rest on whether the *order* as made finally dispose of the rights of the parties? If it does then it is a final order, but if it does not it is an interlocutory order. *Salaman* however states that an order is an interlocutory order unless it is made on an application of such a character that *whatever order* had been made finally disposes of the matter in dispute. Thus, while the former one looks at the nature of the order, the later looks at the nature of the application that triggers the order made. *Salaman* is said to be founded on experience and practice, but *Bozson* on logic.[57]

To formulate the rule on finality, the Supreme Court in the *Akinsanya* case, the court had to trace the practice in England and Malaysia to settle for a preference for the rule in *Bozson*, that it is the nature of the order (not nature of proceedings) that determines whether an order is interlocutory or final. Thus, what determines finality is a product of considering whether the order finally determines the rights of the parties in the issue before the court. A final order brings to an end the rights of the parties in the action, in that it disposes of the subject matter of the controversy or determines the litigation as to all parties on the merit. If the decision determines the rights of the parties as to a particular issue disputed, it is final even if it arises from an interlocutory application.

It thus synthezised the rule on finality adopting the *Bozson* test of the nature of the order stating that in the *Akinsanya* case the Court of Appeal, having determined that the trial court had no jurisdiction, had nothing further to determine in regard to the rights of the parties, was *final.*

The example illustrates that governing rule sometimes require particularisation for it to be the major premise that settles the controversy. It would therefore not be out of place to construct a general rule separate from the precedent that ought to apply in particular. The possible inadequacy of the general rule would throw up the following questions: (i) would the rights of the parties in the instant appeal be finally determined if the trial court (Lagos High Court) had no jurisdiction to deal with the subject matter or put in conversely, if the trial court was incompetent to deal with the subject matter, are the rights of the parties still subsisting; (ii) as the Court of Appeal has decided that the High Court was incompetent and devoid of jurisdiction, would that be the end of the

---

[56] *Omonuwa* v. *Oshodin* recognises the test as good reasoning though critical of it.
[57] *Salter Rex & Co.* v. *Ghosh* [1971] 2 Q.B. 597, per Lord Denning.

matter for the parties; (iii) does the *Omonuwa* decision operate to give finality to the decision of the Court of Appeal on the jurisdiction decision over which the appeal is raised; (iv) assuming for purposes of argument that the Court of Appeal decided that the Lagos High Court was vested with jurisdiction would the appeal have been interlocutory or final?

The Supreme Court in its wisdom thought that the simplistic notion of "final" as 'a decision where there is nothing else or nothing more for the court to do with the case in that it becomes *functus officio*"[58] is not all that is helpful to state the rule. To resolve the challenge the court sought to interpret and synergise two English decisions to shed light on the finality rule.[59]

Illustrating how this works, Karibi-Whyte, JSC in *Igunbor* v. *Afolabi*[60] stated extensively that: "To determine whether an order is interlocutory or final requires an examination of the nature of the order *made*, rather than the nature of the *proceedings* resulting in the order. Thus, what is material is to consider whether the order finally determines the rights of the parties in the issue before the court. A final order brings to an end the rights of the parties in the action, in that it disposes of the subject matter of the controversy or determines the litigation as to all parties on the merit. If the decision determines the rights of the parties as to a particular issue disputed, it is final even if it arises from an interlocutory application. "For example, an order of committal for contempt arising in the course of proceedings in an action is a final order."[61]

So, in the *Igunbor's* case where in furtherance of an interlocutory application the court ordered persons to be joined, the order determines the rights of the parties in the application, and it is final, in that the order does not require something else to be done by itself or any other court of coordinate jurisdiction.

Thus constructing the general rule in deductive reasoning is not as scientific as some imagine.

Analogical Reasoning

Analogical reasoning is often used for the application of complex rules or rules containing gaps. It is a form of reasoning suitable for solving nasty hypotheticals. It is the everyday kind of reasoning technique people use and or most persons are

---

[58] Per Niki Tobi, JSC in *Alor* v. *Ngene* (2007) 17 NWLR (pt. 162) 163 @ 179 – 190.

[59]Akinsanya @ 9, per Kayode Eso, JSC, ("...the problem that would arise is where the decision is final or interlocutory. I think an answer to all of these will depend on how the court applies – the *Bozson* v. *Altrnicham UDC* test [1903] 1 QB 547 or the *Salaman* v. *Warner* test [1891] 1 QB or has *Omonuwa* v. *Oshodin* propounded another test, and if so, what is it...the ratio in *Omonuwa* v. *Oshodin* did not touch the age distinction, settled in this country, between final and interlocutory decisions, in courts of first instance.")

[60]*Igunbor* v. *Afolabi* (2001) 11 NWLR (pt. 723) 148

[61]Ibid., @ 165, per Karibi-Whyte, JSC. See also, *Adeyemi* v. *Awobokun* [1968] 2 All NLR 318.

familiar with. Essentially, analogy is a process of drawing similarities between things that appear different. Informal analogies (used in everyday decision-making) such as, "I own a Toyota Corolla that doesn't overheat in the Lagos traffic, so I conclude that my friend's Toyota Corolla will not overheat." Lawyers and lay persons are also familiar with formal analogies of the "Sun is to Day as Moon is to night."

This type of reasoning has a simple structure:

(i) A has characteristic Y;
(ii) B has characteristic Y;
(iii) A also has characteristic Z;
(iv) Because A and B both have Y, we conclude that B also shares characteristic Z.

Lawyers employ analogy in rule application by to determine whether a controlling precedent applies to new legal issues raised.[62] The process involves comparing a current case to an older one with others to predict how the court will decide a new case. It is the effort of lawyers and judges to classify or evaluate operative facts in an instant case with reference to precedent, to determine whether a particular legal consequence should apply. It is rooted in the thinking that treating like cases alike.

Analogical reasoning is frequent used in legal arguments to resolve problems of classification, whether one situation comes within the meaning of a rule, or is used to evaluate a legal problem. For example, if a court has to determine how to interpret the legal standard of "fair use" in copyright, the court will have to consider previous precedent of how the rule has been applied and then analogically compare or contrast the facts with the present case.[63]

---

[62]Lloyd L. Weinreb, *Legal Reasoning: The Use of Analogy in Legal Argument,* 2005 ("[T]he use of analogy is at the very centre of legal reasoning, so much so that it is regarded as an identifying characteristic not only of legal reasoning itself but also of legal education."); Richard A. Posner, *The Problems of Jurisprudence,* 1990 @ 86 Legal "analogy is the principal candidate for a method that will set lawyers apart from everyday reasoners."); Edward Levi, *An Introduction to Legal Reasoning,* 1949 @ 9 (the learned author states that analogical reasoning involves three distinct steps; establishing the similarities between the two cases; mining the legal rule embedded in the first case; and then applying the mined rule in the case to the second case); Cass R. Sunstein, On Analogical Reasoning (1993) 106 *Harv. L. Rev.* 741; Grant Lamond, Precedent and Analogy in Legal Reasoningin Edward N. Zaita, ed. *The Stanford Encyclopaedia of Philosophy,* 2016 @ 1; http://plato.stanford.edu/archives/spr2016/entries/legal-reas-prec/ (last visited September 23, 2018); Scott Brewer, Exemplary Reasoning: Semantics, Pragmatics, and the Rational Force of Legal Argument by Analogy (1996) 109 *Harv. L. Rev.* 923; Frederick Schauer & Barbara A. Spellman, Analogy, Expertise, and Experience (2017) 84 *U. Chi. L. Rev.* 246; Scott Brewer, Exemplary Reasoning, Semantics, Pragmatics, and the Rational Force of Legal Argument by Analogy (1996) 109 *Harv. L. Rev.* 921.

[63]Neil MacCormick, *Rhetoric and the Rule of Law: A Theory of Legal Reasoning,* 2005 @ 41. But cf. Fabrizio Macagno & Douglas Walton, Argument from Analogy in Law, the Classical Tradition, and Recent Theories (2005) 42 *Phi. & Rhet.* 154 @ 155 (Legal "analogy is used to apply general legal rules to cases not directly falling under the classifications of the rule.").

Some scholars have suggested that classification or evaluation problems determine whether operative facts are present in the entities compared calling for the application of some normative consequences.[64] The process is described as "(dis)analogising."[65] It can also be described as 'argument from example' or 'argument from illustration.'

Visual on analogical reasoning

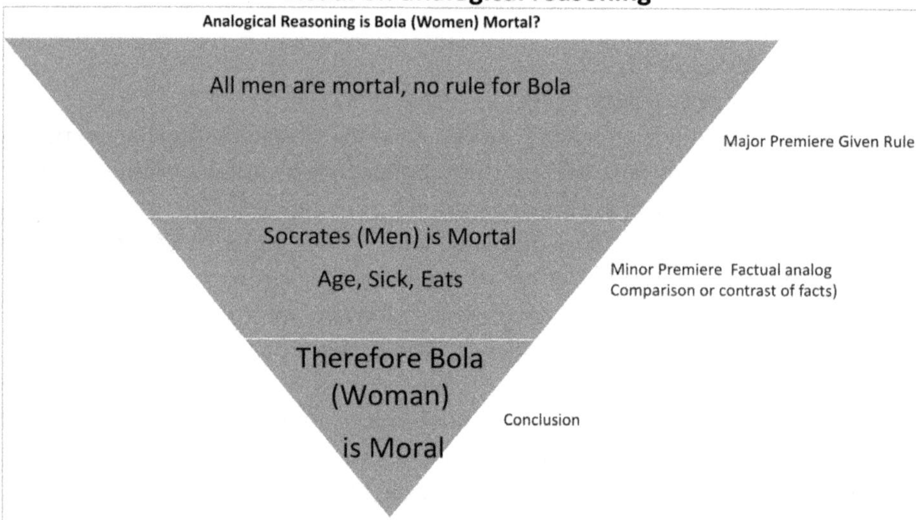

Analogy can sometimes go beyond classification and evaluation problems, such as when it is used to transfer information and procedures from one domain or entity to another. It is then used to transfers information from the source to another, the target. So, scientists might use the flowing of water in pipes - a source domain that the audience understands from direct personal experience - as an analogy for the flow of electricity - a target domain of which most have no direct personal experience. But for these properly to be called 'analogies', the source and target come from different domains.[66]

Analogical reasoning is unlike deductive reasoning which employs two propositions to arrive at a conclusion – reasoning from universal to the particular. It is also different from inductive generalisation where large rules emanate from a number of specific examples. Analogy by contrast makes one-to-one comparison

[64] See for example, MacCormick, above n. 49 @ 1
[65] Larson, above n. 1 @ 10.
[66] Ibid.

between dissimilar events that require no generalisation or reliance on universal rules. It is a process of reasoning from the particular to the particular.[67]

A good example would be a scenario close to the Hart open-ended proposition.[68] Suppose, a lawyer has to defend a defendant charged for driving a scooter without a helmet. If there is no controlling statute governing the situation and there exist two precedents (one states that motorcyclists must wear helmet and the other that bicycle riders don't require helmet) that could influence the trier's conclusion, our lawyer friend would need to employ some analogical reasoning to get a favourable judgment for her client. The question would be whether a scooter is like a motorbike or a bicycle? Which more appropriately should apply to the scooter case? Without a clear universal rule susceptible to syllogism or an inductive generalisation, the lawyer is put in a position where she has to draw similarities between things that appear different. Yes, between motorcycles or bicycles on one hand and scooter on the other hand. She must resort to analogy showing why the scooter is more like a bicycle and not like a motorcycle to convince the trier why a helmet is not a requirement for the scooter rider. To do this, she may well suggest that the scooter is similar to a fast bicycle; that scooters can travel fast and far like motorcycles; that unlike motorcycles scooters are not permitted to ride on the freeway, etc. The process of drawing these comparisons and explaining why they are important is the heart of reasoning by analogy. The idea is to find enough similarities between the new case and old precedent to convince a judge that the outcomes must be the same.

Therefore, to draw an analogy between two entities in reasoning is to show that in certain respects they are similar and that the legal consequence attached to one set of particular facts may apply to a different set of particular facts because of the similarities in the two sets. Because a successful analogy is drawn by demonstrating the resemblances or similarities in the facts, the degree of similarity is always the crucial element. So, it may be argued that a partial resemblance between two entities is equal to a substantial or exact correspondence.

Analogy as a reasoning tool thus, proceeds on the basis of finding similarity between two things that are dissimilar. It requires identifying how the compared cases are similar or differ, employing relevance as standard for comparison.[69] In this respect it is difficult if not impossible to devise a mathematical equation of how similarities or differences should exist between the compared objects to make

---

[67]Sunstein

[68]HLA Hart, *The Concept of Law*, 1997 @ 126 (ordinance prohibiting operating a vehicle in a municipal park). A similar example to the Hart's is the ordinance requiring dogs in the park to be leashed. See Kent Greenawalt, *Law and Objectivity*, 1992 @ 42.

[69] Relevance here means assigning similarities or differences that are material to determining the governing precedent. See

it material to analogical reasoning. While in some case a single instance of similarity or difference would do, in other cases myriads of concurring or contrasting difference is what is required.[70] The strength of an analogy does not depend on numbers or a mechanical application of a rule but is essentially a matter of judgment.

Using our scooter case, it is possible for the prosecution to counter stating that the scooter is more a motorcycle for it shares similarities of say quick-starting, petrol-powered engine, etc., which of the two arguments the trier finds more persuasive is then a matter of judgment.

So, the effort to treat like cases alike can be a "hard question".[71]

It is important to pay attention to analogical reasoning to spot if it contains illogical fallacies. In this respect familiarity with these three criteria may prove useful: (i) the acceptability of the analogy will vary proportionally with the number of circumstances that have been analysed; (ii) the acceptability will depend upon the number of positive resemblances (similarities) and negative resemblances (dissimilarities); or (iii) the acceptability will be influenced by the relevance of the purported analogies.

Spotting relevance for purposes similarities or dissimilarities is a crucial skill to master. It helps to spot analogies that are not strong. Learning to master the skill requires practice. So, if a lawyer is faced with a legal analysis not amenable to syllogism but must find an argument she should learn to probe the boundaries of the particular legal issues; study the seeming controlling precedents carefully; absorb its details; compare the two cases; lay out possible similarities; determine the strength and relevance of the similarities if it outweighs the relevant differences; and then marshal points why the outcome of the case should be the same. The more practice a lawyer does working with analogies, the more skilled she becomes in articulating similarities or differences that are relevant.[72]

For example, a skilled lawyer would have no challenge spotting the weakness of the following analogy:

> "Bayelsa State junior secondary football team were champions last year in the national junior secondary football competition. Team members came from junior schools A, B, C and D. This year the State has again recruited new players from junior schools A, B, C and D. Therefore, Bayelsa State team will be the champions this year."

---

[70]Brewer, above n. 75.
[71] Ronald Dworkin, *Law's Empire*, (see chapter on hard cases)'
[72] Irving M. Copi & Keith Burgess-Jackson, *Informal Logic*, 1996 @ 119.

A skilled lawyer would ask, is the resemblance relevant in analogical reasoning? Is the resemblance or similarities (players from the same junior secondary schools) striking? Does it help us get to the conclusion sought to be drawn? If one good player came from a particular school, does that mean that another player is likely to be similarly good? Probably not, unless the school is extremely unusual and has only good footballers. More likely, what we have here is an analogy based on irrelevant similarities, and such an analogy is of no use at all.

Inductive Reasoning: Generalisation

Much as deductive reasoning and its adherence to syllogism is central to legal reasoning and lawyers are constantly spending time worrying how to pigeonhole facts of the case into arguments of the "Socrates is Mortal" type of syllogism, there are instances of cases that be so easily resolved because the law on the subject matter is unsettled and there is no binding precedent to supply the major premise for the use of syllogism. This is where inductive reasoning becomes helpful. Inductive reasoning is a form of logic, which uses observation to create general principles which is applied to small events.[73]It is a model that of reasoning from multiple particulars to create a general principle (major premise). For instance, if

Visual inductive reasoning

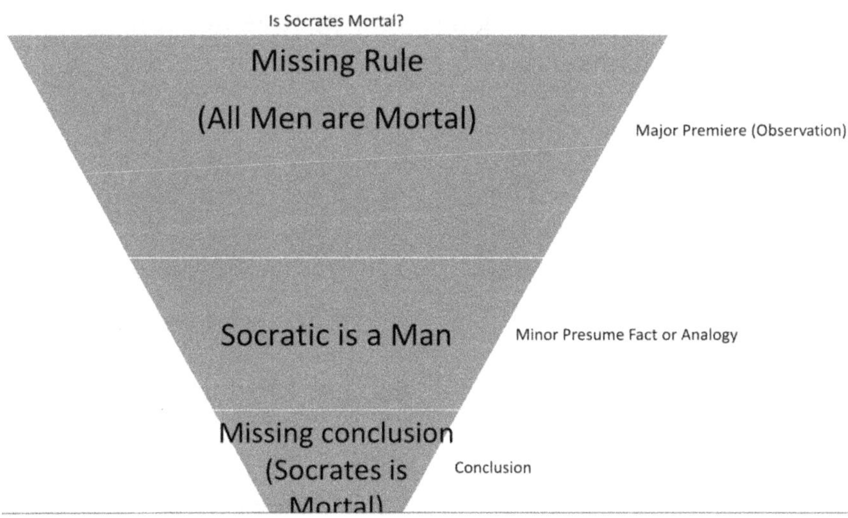

we were to use our paradigmatic example for classical syllogism to know how mortal men are i.e. to determine whether all men are mortal without the

---

[73] Dan Hunter, No Wilderness of Single Instances: Inductive Inference in Law (1998) 48 *J. Leg. Educ.* 365.

advantage of our deductive statement “all men are mortal,” the only way we can arrive at the knowledge of the mortality of man would be through inductive reasoning. We would have to observe man, what we know about particular men and their mortality. We probably know of many men who have died. From this particular we can then arrive at a generalisation that “all men are mortal.” We reason that since things in the world happen with a degree of regularity and predictability the general rule is applicably derivable from the particular. If what happened yesterday is likely to happen again today, we may use past experience to guide our future conduct. That is how inductive reasoning works.

Logicians divide logical reasoning into two categories: inductive and deductive. Inductive reasoning is based on generalizing from our existing knowledge or experience. The premises "of an inductive argument are not offered as conclusive evidence for the truth of their conclusions, but as evidence for the likelihood or reasonable probability of the conclusion's truth." Inductive reasoning generally takes one of two forms, inductive generalization or reasoning by analogy.[74]

It contrasts with deductive reasoning which applies a mechanical and exact syllogism because inductive reasoning is logic of probabilities and generalities, not certainties. It yields workable rules, but not proven truths.[75]

Synthesizing a rule: Inductive Reasoning
Move From Specifics to the General

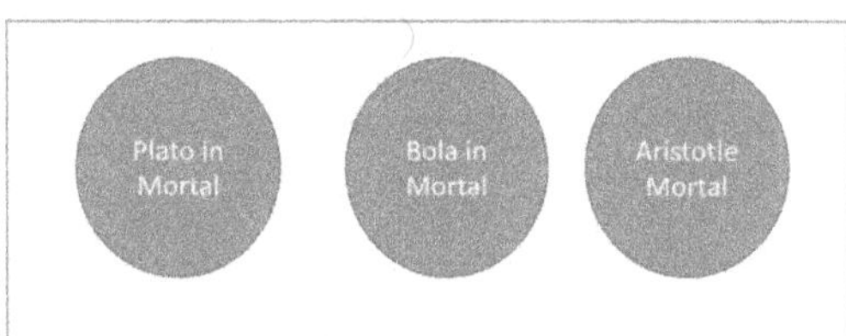

All Men are Mortal

Francis Bacon is reputed to have clearly seen the indispensability of inductive inferences for scientific method. He saw that reason alone does not have any predictable capacity: for it is built on reason combined with observation. The

---

[74]Massarron Ross, above n. 2 @; David Kelley, *The Art of Reasoning*, 1998 @ 453.

[75]Aldisert, Clowney & Peterson, above n. 2 @ 111. See Copi @ 57 (on the fundamental differences between deductive and inductive reasoning)

predictive methods of reason are contained in the logical operations by means of which we construct an order into observational material and derive conclusions. Prediction is arrived through the instruments of logical derivation. So, if logical derivation is to serve predictive purposes, it cannot be restricted to deductive logic. It must include methods of inductive logic. For example, the statement "All men are mortal. Socrates is a man. Therefore, Socrates is mortal" is empty. The premises analytically imply the conclusion and it does not add anything to it. In contrast, the inference "All men so far observed are mortal, therefore Socrates is mortal": is one where the conclusion is not contained in the premise. It refers to mortals not yet observed and extends to them a property of observed mortals. The truth of the conclusion is not guaranteed. It is possible some are not.

But despite the drawback, it is taken as satisfactory when some other things than mortality are interrogated. The risk of error is not sufficient reason not to take it as establishing general truth. Inductive inference belongs to the theory of probability because observable facts can make a theory only probable. Inductive logic isn't empty. Its inferences lead to conclusions not contained in the premises. The conclusion that "Socrates is mortal" is not logically committed to the premise that all men so far observed are mortal. The conclusion may be false while the premise is true.[76]

Reasoning by analogy constitutes the most familiar form of legal reasoning in the common law legal system. It generally proceeds based on a theory of probabilities. For example, it goes like this: I have a Honda car that is fuel efficient, so I assume that your Honda would also be fuel efficient. The logical structure is simple: (i) A has characteristic Y; (ii) B shares that characteristic; (iii) A also has characteristic Z; (iv) Because A and B share characteristic Y, we conclude what isn't known, that B shares characteristic Z as well. This form of reasoning pervades daily life and law. This reasoning does not guarantee truth about conclusions. It focuses on the particulars and is developed from concrete controversies.[77]

Inductive reasoning is a sort of bottom - top thinking because ideas are developed from details. Principles are created which operates at a low or intermediate level of abstraction. For instance, when we say the state cannot ban civil demonstration, we invariably are implying that the state has no constitutional power to prevent lawful assembly and association without showing that in the

[76]Cass R. Sunstein, On Analogical Reasoning (1993) 106 *Harv. L Rev.* 741 @ 747]

[77] Even though Holmes is of the view that common law court decides a case first and determines the principle latter, the position is hardly supportable because legal reasoning must somehow be raised from some rough commitment to principles (values) that form the underlying basis for fitting facts. See Oliver W. Holmes, Jr., Codes and the Arrangement of Law (1870) 5 *Am. L. Rev.* 1 reprinted in (1931) 44 *Harv. L. Rev.* 725.

instant case such demonstration poses imminent and clear harm. This is a principle, and it does involve a certain degree of abstraction from the particular case (legitimacy of civil demonstration), but it does not entail any high-level theory about the purpose of the free assembly and association provision of the Constitution or what is considered the proper relation between the citizen and state.[78]

The presence of probability in inductive reasoning does not make it less useful in legal reasoning. It is the useful tool to turn to where there is no controlling precedent (statute or case law) to provide the major premise necessary for syllogism.

Let us consider some restitution cases verging on the principle of restitution for acquisitive wrongs, particularly those on the murder of testator by an intended beneficiary.[79]

For example, it is a well-established general principle that a criminal shall not benefit from the benefit of her crime. So, if a person kills another in order to benefit under the deceased will or intestacy he will be disallowed from enjoying the benefit of the will or intestacy. It can however be queried if this principle ought to be part of restitution law – a subject concerned with the prevention of benefit or an enrichment, rather than with the transfer of benefit.[80]

Syllogism would certainly provide an incomplete answer to the research. How do the pioneer English scholars on restitution, Goff and Jones, answer the question? Using what would better be referred to as inductive reasoning they argue that it is appropriate to pigeonhole it within restitution law because both the denial of benefit and transfer of benefit are motivated by the same policy consideration, namely that no criminal shall be allowed to profit from her crime. Since the same policy consideration ought to apply regardless of the time of transfer of benefit whether before or after the defendant obtains the proceeds of crime it is only proper to discuss this notion in a restitution work of this kind.[81]

---

[78] It is unlike deductive reasoning which resembles top - bottom thinking. Legal problems are solved in terms of some general theory. Law is made to operate at a high level of abstraction. General theories are applied to the concrete, disregarding the fact that people are disturbed by particular outcomes that seem counterintuitive but compelled by general theory. Analogy plays no role in deductive reasoning. Even when it does as some commentators posit, its role is quite different from a system that is basically inductive. See Katja Langenburher, Argument by Analogy in European Law (1998) *Camb. L. J.* 481 (an article which discusses the role analogy plays in the deductive legal system).

[79] Festus Emiri, *Law of Restitution in Nigeria*, Lagos: Malthouse Press, ch. 21.

[80] Burrows, *The Law of Restitution* p. 380

[81] Goff & Jones, *The Law of Restitution* @ 802; Virgo, *The Principles of the Law of Restitution* pp. 570-571. *Cleaver* v. *Mutual Reserve Fund Life Association* [1892] 1 QB 147 at 156, per Fry, L.J. (no system of jurisprudence can with reason include amongst the rights which it enforces rights directly resulting to the person asserting them from the crimes of that person)." See also *Beresford* v. *Royal*

Another example of the limitation of deductive syllogism under the forfeiture rule relates to how the Wills Act should be interpreted to determine whether a defendant who kills the testator should be allowed to benefit from the will. The Act does not make express provision disentitling killer. So, it could be challenging to state whether a killer should enjoy succession rights under the will. If the answer is that the defendant should not, then the next challenge. Who should benefit in the event of the disentitlement? An inductive reasoning would suggest that the killer should not benefit but that the benefit should go to those who have succession right to the killer's estate, since the successor's rights is not created by the commission of the crime but rather takes root from the laws of succession, and the law does not prevent the rights of succession.[82]But it can plausibly be argued as it was done in *Re Callaway*, that the property should go *bona vacantia* to the state.[83] This being so, the difficult facts situation is analysable under three possible solutions, namely; (i) that the legal title does not pass to the criminal (ii) that the legal title passes and he may retain it in spite of the crime or (iii) that the legal title passes to the criminal, but equity will treat the criminal as a constructive trustee of the title because of the unconscionable mode of its acquisition.[84]

This being so, inductive reasoning is a model that does not yield exact answers because constructing a general rule requires an assemblage of sufficient number of examples before formulating it. Lawyers must therefore be careful not to anoint isolated instances as sufficient basis for generalisation for as a thumb rule the more examples observed the stronger the argument for generalisation.[85]

Even at that large numbers can prove untrue and unreliable. Aldisert gives a very good example using an American presidential election. In 1936, *Literary Digest* magazine conducted a massive polling effort to predict the outcome of the Presidential election between Alf Landon and Franklin Roosevelt. The *Digest*

Insurance Co Ltd [1938] AC 586 at 590, per Lord Atkin (I think that the principle is that a man is not to be allowed to have recourse to a court of justice to claim a benefit from his crime whether under a contract or a gift... The absolute rule is that the courts will not recognise a benefit accruing to a criminal from his crime). *Re K (deceased)* [1986] Ch. 180; Fry LJ in *Cleaver* case [1892] 1 QB 147 at 156; Lord Wright in *Berresford* v. *Royal Insurance Co Ltd* [1937] 2 KB 197 at 220. See Lord Denning in *Hardy* v. *Motor Insurer's Bureau* [1964] 2 QB 745 at 760; *The Amicable Society for a Perpetual Life Assurance Office* v. *Bolland* (1830) 4 Blight (NS) 194; 5 ER 770. See also statutory enactment in England which codifies the public policy rule of forfeiture into a statute. See s.1 of Forfeiture Act (UK), 1982.

[82] *Re Peacock* [1957] Ch310; *Re Sigsworth* [1935] Ch. 89

[83] [1956] Ch. 559.

[84] Ames, Can A Murderer Acquire Title by His Crime and Keep It, cited by Youdan, above n.60 @ 253

[85] Hasty generalisation in inductive reasoning is often referred to as converse accident. See S. Morris Engel, With Good Reason: An Introduction to Informal Fallacies, 1994 @ 137, cited in Aldisert, Clowney & Peterson, above n. 1 @ 113 n. 33.

polled well over two million people, and the vast majority indicated they would vote for Landon (keep in mind that modern news organizations base their polls on the responses of 1,000 people). In the actual election, however, Roosevelt won 523 electoral votes and Landon received only eight. How did *Literary Digest* get it so wrong when it had crafted its rule from a massive number of particular examples? It seems the Digest focused its polling efforts on car owners—an unrepresentative group of the American public in 1936.[86] A similar prediction greeted the Hilary Clinton and Donald Trump presidential predictions.[87]

The lesson here is this: the strength of an inductive argument rests not only on the number of examples used to create the generalization, but also on the representativeness of the sample size. A skilled lawyer therefore must recognise that it is possible to puncture an opponent's argument based on inductive reasoning by attacking the particulars used in constructing the general rule.

Notwithstanding its shortcomings, the inductive generalisation remains a vital tool because the ability to shape persuasive legal arguments when no clear precedent exists.

Visual deductive, analogy, inductive reasoning and lawyering

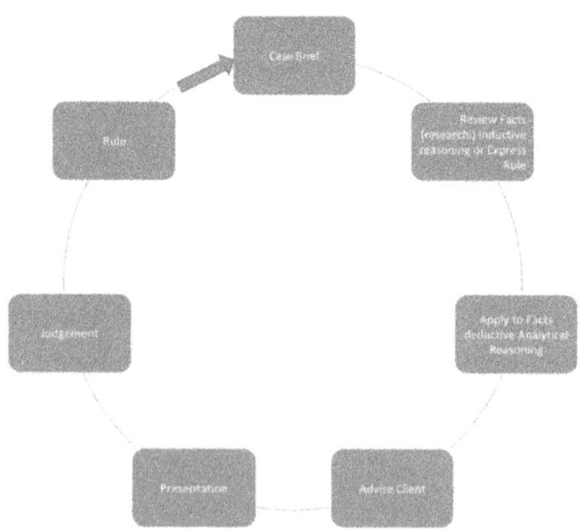

Conclusion

No question about it, that logic is the lifeblood of the law and that understanding its basic logical forms is a core skill for lawyering. Lawyers must therefore ensure that their argument proceeds on sure premises at all times to avoid an opponent

[86]Aldisert, Clowney & Peterson, above n. 1 @ 114.

[87] See general polls prior to the U.S presidential election in 201`6.

deflating the balloon of their argument. But skilled lawyers must go beyond constructing true premises and logic. They must recognise the place rhetoric also plays in persuasion.[88] This notwithstanding, learning to reason like a logician is an indispensable tool for lawyering because an argument that is correctly reasoned may be wrong, but an argument that is incorrectly reasoned can never be right.[89]

[88]Derrick Bell, Who's Afraid of Critical Race Theory (1995) *Univ. Ill. L. Rev.* 893. See articles on rhetoric, legal realism. *United States* v. *Jannotti* (1982) 673 F. 2d 579 @ 612 (3d Cir.) per Judge Aldisert "[w]e judges come to our robes bearing the stigmata of our respective experiences." Also state Holmes statement.

[89]Aldisert, Clowney & Peterson, above n. 1 @ 114

PART II

Chapter 6

Legal Memorandum

Introduction

Internal memoranda are written by one lawyer to another for the purpose of communicating law and legal analysis and meant to serve as the basis for legal advice. They are crucial part of the practice of law.[1] Memoranda are usually written by lawyers for the purpose of analysing legal issue, to offer prediction on the outcome of legal issue, and to provide a basis for proposed action. It is therefore a lawyer's tool of assessing the possible arguments and predicting the outcomes in a legal matter.

A legal memorandum is a means that allows lawyers to reason through the law and facts, to construct and create arguments and advice, and to document or convey that analysis from one lawyer to another. Accordingly, its comprehensive form includes sections on the question presented, a brief answer, the facts, a discussion of the facts and legal principles applicable and then the conclusion.

By its very nature, the memorandum is an objective or predictive piece of writing, meant to report rather than persuade. Thus, the writer's purpose is to communicate to a senior lawyer the writer's professional opinion as to how the dispute will be resolved and the rationale for the resolution.

It is first taught as a necessary skill in legal writing. After students master the objective or predictive writing, they are moved to the next stage - persuasive writing as the second segment of legal writing where they learn advocacy, which usually involves writing persuasive briefs and presenting oral argument before a

---

[1] Kirsten K. Davis, The Reports of My Death are Exaggerated: Reading and Writing Objective Legal Memoranda in a Mobile Computing Age (2014) 92 *Oregon L. Rev.* 471. For general reading on legal memorandum, see Teresa J. Reid Rambo & Leanne J. Pflaum, *Legal Writing Design: A Guide to Great Briefs and Memo*, 2nd ed. Durham: Carolina Academy Press, 2013; John Bronsteen, Writing A Legal Memo, 2006 @ 132 (stating that the tone of a legal memorandum should be "objective and dispassionate". To be sure, a good memorandum should inform the reader whether the facts of the case are likely to have an emotional impact on the jury or the judge, so that the lawyer or client reading the memo can make a rational assessment of potential damages. But it is not the purpose of an advisory memo to stir the passions of the *reader* through the use of pathos; that is likely to be counterproductive if the goal is to enable the decision-maker to calmly and rationally assess the options. So while a memo does need to evaluate the potential role pathos will play in a case, it does not itself need to connect with its intended audience at an emotional level).

mock appellate court. While legal memorandum teaches how to analyse, persuasive writing on the other hand teaches how to convince.

A memorandum is like a brief. A memorandum states the legal issues, describes authorities, and applies those authorities in analysing the facts. The brief also has similar feature, but it is framed as an argument. In a brief, the author argues her approach for resolving the legal matter, rather than presenting a neutral analysis. Thus, while pathos is a requirement for the legal brief as primarily a tool of persuasion, it is generally not as useful where the central purpose of the document is merely to convey information rather than to persuade, as in an office memorandum.[2]

Today the world is gradually moving away from paper to paperless communication. Some scholars have therefore suggested that the trend of moving from paper communication to electronic communication will put memo in the back stage of legal practice.[3] Much as this is no doubt a threat to the place of memo in the legal practice, it would appear that the assertion is more wrong than right. This is because legal memo remains central to lawyering experience and is an era of practice that relies on core lawyering competencies, especially that of research, understanding of law, application of law to facts, and conveying that analysis in writing. Memorandum writing is therefore like an intersection interrogating how a lawyer understands her client's case and can apply law to its resolution, which often sets the stage for subsequent activities on behalf of the client. Thus, unless a lawyer fully understands the relationship between memo writing and competency, she is likely to discount the value of memo as a core lawyering skill. Skills of reasoning, analysis, communication and research are undoubtedly essential tools of lawyering.

While not disputing that e-communication brings pressure to bear on the place of memo in practice, this chapter seeks to explain the task of reading and writing legal memos in today's intensely technological world and assess the value

---

[2] Rambo & Pflaum, above n. 1.

[3] See Kristen Konrad Robbins-Tiscione, The Rhetoric of Email in Law Practice (2015) 92 *Oregon L. Rev.* 525; KristenKonrad Robbins-Tiscione, From Snail Mail to Email: The Traditional Legal Memorandum in the Twenty-First Century (2008) 58 *J. Legal Educ.* 32; Kristen Robbins-Tiscione, Ding Dong! The Memo is Dead. Which Old Memo? The Traditional Memo, Second Draft (Legal Writing Inst., Macon, Ga.), Spring 2011, at 6 (quoting survey participant who said "[m]ost of my legal research is communicated by e-mail and that the days of memo is dead); Kristen Konrad Robbins-Tiscione, From Snail Mail to E-Mail: The Traditional Legal Memorandum in the Twenty-First Century (2008) 58 *J. Legal Educ.* 32 (a finding that traditional legal memorandum has become nearly obsolete, in favour of substantive email as preferred method for communicating with clients); Ellie Margolis, Is the Medium the Message? Unleashing the Power of E-Communication in the Twenty-First Century (2015) 12 *Legal Comm. & Rhetoric: JALWD* 1; Terry Jean Seligmann, Why Is a Legal Memorandum Like an Onion? - A Student's Guide to Reviewing and Editing (2004) 56 *Mercer L. Rev.* 729. But cf. Davis, above n. 1.

of the objective legal memorandum for competent lawyering as it examines how the crafting of memo relates to lawyer competence.[4] Since the essential structure of memo remains unchanged whether it is e-mail memo and the traditional informal memo, this chapter will concentrate on how lawyers should write and read competent legal memorandum.

Partner asking an associate to draw up memo

History of memorandum

Memorandum writing has a relatively recent history in legal writing, just like legal writing is also recent. While the ability of law schools to teach legal skills, such as writing, had been questioned since law school's inception in the mid-1800s by lawyers like Judge Jerome Frank and many others, the first references to legal writing as a separate subject matter, apart from bibliographic instruction, appeared in the late 1940s in the United States. One of the first bar journal articles about legal memo writing appeared in 1956.[5] The article traces the origins of the legal memo to law firms in the "big cities". It states that a junior in such big offices

---

[4]Bryan A. Garner, Sense and Sensibility: A Primer on Preparing Research Memos (2010) 38 *Student Law* 12; John C. Kleefeld, Write Me A Memo (2010) *Canada Legal Educ. Ann. Rev.* 217; Terry Jean Seligmann, Why Is a Legal Memorandum Like an Onion? - A Student's Guide to Reviewing and Editing (2004) 56 *Mercer L. Rev.* 729.

[5]F. Trowbridge vom Baur, *How to Look Up Law and Write Legal Memoranda*, Prac. Law. Dec. 1956 @ 27–28 cited in Davis, above n. 1 @ 473 ft. nt. 4. See also F. Trowbridge vomBaur ,*The Practical Lawyer's Manual on Memoranda of Law*, Ali-Aba, 1970; Robert Stevens, *Law School: Legal Education in America from the 1850S to the 1980S*, 1983 @ 214; Marjorie D. Rombauer, First-Year Legal Research and Writing: Then and Now (1972) 25 *J. Legal Educ.* 538; Theodore Voorhees, Legal Research and Memoranda (1964) 36 *N.Y. St. B.J.* 222.

is usually required to prepare law memoranda for use of the senior partners. Writing the memoranda meant that the junior was to prepare an easily read, accurate and useful memorandum. Juniors learn through strenuous effort and errors how to write well as they give legal advice to seniors. The more complicated or important the problem, the greater the need for a first-rate memorandum of law.

The structure of the memoranda was general streamlined. It followed a structure like this: the facts, question presented, short answer or summary, and discussion.

It is undoubtedly serious business because it interrogates the competence of the junior to give good advice through process of careful reasoning and deliberation. So, to the young lawyer it is clear what skills are demanded. Thinking like a lawyer in full accord with standards of thoroughness, precision, and judgment is certainly required to write useful memoranda.

Soon thereafter, memoranda became a staple for law practice as firms growing recognized the importance of juniors to help and advice on areas of law considered complex. Associates were required to come up with answers to questions and give the reasons backing the answer in terms of advocacy.

In the 1970s texts stating instructions on how to write good and useful memoranda started appearing.[6] Memoranda metamorphosed to become both practice writing and advisory writing. While the former is directed toward analysing a particular legal problem for the purpose of predicting a probable solution or stating the basis for suggested advice, the later includes client letters, informing readers of conclusions and the reasons therefore and gives advice.[7]

Legal memorandum in the computer era

A lawyer's ability to construct and convey competent legal advice by means of traditional legal memoranda is significantly being impacted on by rapidly advancing communication and composition technology. Lawyers are reading and writing in ways not contemplated many years ago when the practice of memo developed. This shift to computers no doubt affects the way lawyers and judges read and write legal documents.

---

[6]See Marjorie D. Rombauer, *Legal Analysis and Research*, 1970 (a book that describes legal memoranda as critical writing that analyses and discusses a problem in a manner that is exploratory, unaffected by personal goals or desires). See also, Mary S. Lawrence, An Interview with Marjorie Rombauer (2001) 9 *J. Leg. Writing* 19.

[7] Some legal writing scholars are however of the view that memoranda should be confined to only practice writing, meant only for other lawyers. In their view if the audience of document includes a client that removes it from the confines of objective legal memoranda because it would then bear properties different from those of an objective memorandum. See Rombauer, above n. 5 @ 111.

The advent of computers, and most recently, mobile technology, has altered the way lawyers communicate. In fact, the advent of predictive artificial intelligence into the equation likely to automate much of practice will impact on the status of memo.[8] These changes would certainly act as constraints on the way lawyers respond to and communicate about the legal situations confronting them. What is more, the pressure on time today makes it challenging to stick to traditional memo writing styles. Yes, as "non-traditional," electronic modes of writing and reading grow, and the preferences of lawyers (and clients) in today's legal market change, the usefulness of the traditional legal memo comes under attack.[9]

While of these constitute fertile grounds to suggest that memo is out-dated or is an inefficient way for conveying legal analysis, such arguments are erroneous for conflating substance with form. The structure of memo and content remain substantially the same whether the mode for communication is paper or electronic. The commitment to traditional legal memorandum remains appealing for many reasons:

(i)Just because lawyers might want "shorter" memos, on-screen or otherwise, this does not mean that shorter memos are suitable for either legal readers or legal writers.

Even though some suggest that new communication media requires that memos must be written to meet the demands for easier and "quicker" reading and invariably demands that they be transmitted by e-mail or read on a screen, such a demand (if true) overlooks how writing the traditional legal memo is essential to the advice-giving process. Legal memo writing is an inter-subjective, deliberative, and a rhetorical act that leads to advice-giving, which plays an important role in ensuring that lawyers have met their duty to give competent advice.[10]

Short-form electronic writing run the risk of giving readers what they should not want - poorly thought-through legal analysis. In other words, a memo, whether electronic, formal, informal, or streamlined, should use the

---

[8]Richard Susskind, *The End of Lawyers: Rethinking the Nature of Legal Services*, Oxford, 2008 @ 1. (stating that "many aspects . . . of the way we practise law . . . can and should be enhanced or even replaced by computer technology"; noting that "[c]ommoditatization and IT will shape and characterize twenty-first century

[9] Tiscione (argues that substantive e-mail and informal memos should be favoured over a traditional memo, because their elements are "organic" whereas the elements of the traditional memo are "static". And, she concludes that traditional memoranda are a "dying breed" and will be replaced by informal memoranda and substantive e- mail).

[10] See RPC

number of words and paragraphs necessary to convey a solid, well-thought-out legal analysis.

(ii) On-screen is not a new legal writing category for objective memos.

Email or computer writing is not a new category of memorandum. The fact that the reader reads not on paper but on a screen doesn't make reading that fundamentally different. Reading is flexible enough to other features. So, on the screen reading is simply one of the genres of reading. Conveying legal analyses in e-mail correspondence is simply a technologically spurred extension of long standing diversity in law office communications.

Because flexibility has always been a feature of the traditional memorandum, however, the notion that a different category of legal memo has emerged is incorrect. That readers may somewhat differently read and comprehend on-screen texts, does not suggest that the basic tenets for structuring comprehensible documents have changed simply because readers will read those documents on the screen. In fact, the classic organizational structures that have been available to legal writers for decades are even more powerful when used to draft documents for electronic media. If anything, contemporary media demands a return to classic techniques to improve reader speed, comprehension, and satisfaction.

Importance of the legal memorandum

The place of legal memorandum in law practice remains relevant despite some readers' preference for shorter and easier reading of legal analysis. Readers preference does not mean that they would be happy to receive legal analysis that is less than competent and deliberate. A legal memo, whether transmitted by paper, e-mail, or otherwise, does more than simply convey law and analysis that existed prior to the act of writing. Rather, a memo is a present process by which law and fact come into being through the deliberative and interpretive acts of the writer. As a rhetorical process constitutive of the law and analysis it conveys, a memo's objective analysis is paradoxically the product of inter-subjectivity, which is the act of meaning-making that occurs between writer, reader, text, and context.

Not only is memo writing the product of inter-subjectivity, it is also a core component of the advice-giving function and lawyer competence. As both a creative and ethical task, memo writing is fraught with the dangers associated with bias and intuitive decision making. Yet, the deliberation that can occur through writing acts as a check on cognitive bias and fallacies of reasoning. It provides a space where legal writers can be sceptics of their own thinking and doubt their own conclusions in an effort to shore up the accuracy and precision of their analyses.

To the extent that memorandum interrogating the lawyers' skill of competent advice-giving and the ethical obligation to be truthful in advice-giving, lawyers must undertake reasonable research to make reasoned informed judgments. Lawyers are expected to make an "intelligent evaluation of the case" and to "examine the law and facts relevant to the representation." This includes "analysis of precedent, the evaluation of evidence," "inquiry into and analysis of the factual and legal elements of the problem," and, perhaps most fundamentally, "determining what kind of legal problems a situation may involve."

In legal memoranda, lawyers are expected to give advice that reflects "independent professional judgment – a process that calls for honest assessment, even when the reader of the memo might disagree with the advice or the analysis in the memo. Accordingly, the lawyer must address unpleasant facts and alternatives that a client may be disinclined to confront. This includes carefully considering both sides of the legal and factual story they seek to advance.

At the core of competency and the advice-giving function is what this author calls the duty to doubt.[11] The duty to doubt requires that for a lawyer to be competent in advice giving, the lawyer must approach the task with an attitude of scepticism, curiosity, and challenge. The lawyer's motivation must be to treat the law and the facts as open as possible. A duty to doubt requires careful, painstaking examination of legal issues, the law, and the facts.

The basis for good legal advice, such as that contained in a legal memorandum, is essentially an objective assessment, which might be defined as the ability to take multiple perspectives on the same set of events. In the context of legal judgment, multiple authors have pointed out that objectivity is not about "neutrality." Rather, objectivity involves the ability to recognize, understand, and account for differences in perspectives and the values that underlie them. It requires that the writer, who is essentially performing as a critic of the law, the facts, and the way in which the facts intersect with the law, approach the question with a fair and open mind, with a detached curiosity, all while keeping in mind the lawyer's duty to find the best possible outcomes for the client.

Importantly, at the heart of memo writing is the process of decision-making. The lawyer must recognize that as the memo writers she is conveying decisions about what law is applicable, what facts are meaningful, what arguments are viable, and what advice is appropriate. This is what implicates the obligation to be ethical, reasoned, fair and open-minded.

Finally, the act of writing the legal memo is important because it creates an opportunity for the legal reader to reflect upon what is written. Without

[11]Davis, above n. 1.

preserving legal analysis in writing, the audience lacks the same opportunity to consider and question the analysis. Reading is a form of engagement between writer and reader; the memo itself is a place for the reader to engage in invention, to assess what is written and to add to it, question it, or revise it. Reading a memo is therefore a creative act.

What has changed is the media on which lawyers read and write legal memos. Does the use of electronic media require a new approach to the substance or form of the legal memo? Are electronically delivered memos a new category of legal writing? The next section dispels the myth of this category change and argues that the traditional approaches to memo writing are exactly what legal readers need for reading legal memos on new media.

Conclusion

While a memorandum written in the "comprehensive" style is arguably best for legal thinking, it is the complexity of the question presented, and *not* the type of media that should dictate the structure of the memo.

The legal memorandum is important as a heuristic device for writing. If one sees a memo as merely restating what can be "found" in the law and what can be logically deduced from what has been found, then it is easy to see how the memo, in its comprehensive form, may be unnecessary. But, as Joel Cornwell notes, a memo is not simply an "algorithmic exercise"; rather, memos are a place to be "creative and educative," and are the product of writers who "use language . . . to reach new formulations of the positions" and perpetually remake the law. The memo, no matter its technological medium, is essential to competent lawyering. The memo's formalism forces well-developed deliberation that leads to creative problem-solving and advice-giving. It provides a rhetorical "space between" for knowledge construction; the memo itself is the construction of legal advice, not just the recording of it.

Accordingly, the legal writer needs to evaluate the *context* of a given document in order to determine whether elegant writing is appropriate for that document. For example, in the context of a typical office memorandum, the principal goal is to convey information in an expeditious manner in order to help the client or the senior lawyer make wise decisions. Generally, the client is not interested in funding a literary work and does not want to spend extra money to enable a lawyer to produce a memorandum that is elegant. Therefore, in that context, elegance must give way to more practical considerations, such as cost.

Chapter 7

Writing Technique

Introduction

Legal writing demand lawyers to evaluate the strength of their client's case and effectively communicate it by keeping focus on three basic elements, the "who", the "why" and the "how". As a form of writing it is serious business, its heightened importance deriving from the critical impact it can have on the lives and destinies of the people who are the subject of it. Because legal writing is a core skill lawyers must possess, faculties of law give it its deserved importance. Usually, it forms part of the first lessons students receive in a legal method class on admission. One of the things they are quickly taught is to start 'think like a lawyer'. Thinking as a lawyer is often associated with students becoming familiar with the organizational schemata known as *IRAC*, suggested to help them think and write logical. While this paper recognizes that the *IRAC* structure can be helpful in imposing a logical grammar for lawyers to understand themselves and explain law to outsiders, it disagrees with it being used as the paradigm and the primary method for organizing writing because it is an approach that funnels human disputes into a single rule-based approach leaving little or no room for recognizing the complexities of human interaction which generate disputes. The paper therefore seeks to open legal analysis and reasoning beyond rigid rule-based rule in a manner which admits alternative analysis in the light of social realities, by encouraging the profession, especially teachers of legal method and legal writing to reassess the foundation of *IRAC*, ceasing to cling to it as paradigm for successful legal and brief writing. It concludes by urging that *IRAC* and its *cousins* should be treated as illustrative of basic framework for legal reasoning and analysis in a manner that admits of other styles incorporating analysis that melds facts and experience with legal rules.

Writing Deficiency

A survey of recruiters of fresh lawyers in the United States reveals that legal writing deficiency is one of the five basic skills lacking in new lawyers.[1] This

[1]Bryant G. Garth & Joanne Martin, Law School and the Construction of Competence (1993) 43 *J. Legal Educ.* 469. Cite the US survey. For the position in Nigeria, see Augustine Alegeh, in Olanrewaju Onadeko, et al., *Legal Education in Nigeria*: Challenges and Next Steps, Abuja: CLE, 151

observation is also representative of the situation in Nigeria. In our country concerns have been expressed by the bar and bench about the competence and character of "new wigs," especially their communication skills. This is particularly worrisome considering that lawyers are constantly required to communicate with others either in the form of memorandum or processes connected with resolution of disputes. That being so, lawyers are expected to deploy persuasive writing to convince deciding authorities to resolve disputes in favor of their clients. Legal writing is therefore a form of writing which demands lawyers to evaluate the strength of their client's case and effectively communicate it, focusing on the three basic elements of *who*, *why* and *how*.[2] The "who" being the audience, the "why" representing the purpose of communication, and the "how" being the manner or style of writing. It is serious business, its heightened importance deriving from the critical impact the communication can have on the lives and destinies of the people who are the subject of it.[3]

Recognizing the importance of legal writing as a core skill, faculties of law give it its deserved importance. Usually, it forma part of the first lessons students receive in a legal method class on admission.[4] One of the things they are quickly taught is to start 'thinking like a lawyer.' Thinking as a lawyer is often associated with students becoming familiar with the organizational schemata known as *IRAC*. It is said that analysis and reasoning using the schemata helps then to think and write logical.[5] The importance of *IRAC* is elevated to a paradigm for analysis, reasoning and writing, further reified by teachers telling them that good grades in law are entailed with an ability to master the lawyers' scientific way of reasoning: the *IRAC* schemata for organizing legal analysis and reasoning. The students naturally thus settle for IRAC as key to success in the legal profession.[6]

The IRAC Schemata

IRAC (Issue, Rule, Application, and Conclusion) constitutes the building block for exams and writing in the faculties of law, snowballing eventually into the legal profession. Students are generally happy to master *IRAC* because it allows them to reduce complexities of the social world, which generates controversies into

---

[2] Teresa J. Reid Rambo & Leanne Pflaum, *Legal Writing by Design: A Guide to Great Briefs and Memo*, 2nd ed. NC, Durham: Carolina Acad. Press, 2013, xiii.

[3] Rambo & Pflaum, above n. 2 at xii.

[4] Legal method is a core course under the BMAS scheme and it is suggested in the guideline as a pre-law core subject. See BMAS Guide.

[5] Garth & Martin, above n. 1. Cite other articles on core skills demanded of lawyers.

[6] The precise origin of IRAC is largely unknown, but it as been suggested that it likely originated as a simple mnemonic for teaching legal analysis. It certainly was not intended as an organizational paradigm for legal writing. See Laura P. Graham, Why-RAC? Revisiting the Traditional Paradigm for Writing About Legal Analysis (2015) 63 *Kansas L. Rev.* 681 at 706.

simple, manageable legal formula and equation. They are proud to tell other not so fortunate to gain law admission about their new organizational tool that can be logically deployed to even every day analysis of events in the social world. The paradigm they reason enables them to seamlessly join the elite group of learned people. This is what translates *IRAC* to become the signature pedagogy for legal analysis and reasoning.[7] Over time this practice of reasoning and writing fossilizes.

IRAC is extolled by the profession for its deductive reasoning potential, reasoning from the major to minor premise through syllogism. Reasoning in syllogism proceeds from the major premise, such as, "All humans are mortal," to the minor premise, "Socrates is a human," therefore making the conclusion logically correct: "Therefore Socrates is mortal." Transposed to *IRAC*, having framed the issue as question for determination, the rule requires stating the broad statement of general applicability "All humans are mortal," as representing the *R* (rule). It is from this that the minor premise is constructed. The minor premise or narrow statement of particular applicability, "Socrates is a human," translates to *A* (applicability of the rule to facts). A combination of both premises makes "Therefore Socrates is mortal," the *C* (conclusion) logically correct.[8] So you can see why lawyers extol the rule. It is stepped in deduction reasoning by syllogism, which closes on a science of reasoning and analysis associated with common sense and comprehension.[9] What is more, members of the legal community think that

---

[7]Abiola O. Sanni, ed., *Introduction to Nigerian Legal Method*, Ile-Ife: Kuntel Pub. 1999, 54. Generally, Nigerian universities teach writing as part of the subject legal method and research methodology. Legal writing as a distinct course in the curriculum is however taught in U.S. as a distinct subject. See generally, Tracy Turner, Flexible IRAC: A Best Practice Guide (2015) 20 *J. Legal Writing Inst.* 233; The IRAC Formula, http://www.lawnerds.com/guide/irac.html (visited) and courses in legal writing. The US has courses in legal writing in many of its universities. The first legal writing conference was held in 1984 and the Legal Writing Institute was established in 1986. Since then the Institute has established the journal of the Legal Writing Institute. Noteworthy, some teachers of legal writing advice that writing should begin with conclusion not issue, especially for persuasive writing, arguing that such a pattern follow more the way human ground meaning from experience. See Tracy Turner, Finding Consensus in Legal Writing Discourse Regarding Organizational Structure: A Review and Analysis of the Use of IRAC and its Progenies (2012) 9 *Legal Comm. & Rhetoric:JALWD* 351 at 359; Harold A. Lloyd, Plane Meaning and Thought: Real-World Semantics and Fictions of Originalism (2015) 24 *Southern Cal. Interdisciplinary L. J.* 657 ("judges, lawyers, and clients want to begin with conclusion. Unlike readers of mystery novels, judges, lawyers, and clients do not consider matters spoiled if they get the ending first ... These audience demands therefore require that IRAC be modified to begin with a conclusion." Id 673). See also Harold A. Lloyd, Crushing Animals and Crushing Funerals: The Semiotics of Free Expression (2012) 12 *First Amend. L. Rev.* 237.

[8] James A. Gardner, *Legal Argument: The Structure and Language of Effective Advocacy*, 2nd ed., 1999.

[9] Anita Schnee, Logical Reasoning "Obviously" (1997) 3 *J. Legal Writing Inst.* 105; Kristen K. Robbins, Paradigm Lost: Recapturing Rhetoric to Validate Legal Reasoning (2003) 27 *VT L. Rev.* 483; Tracy Turner, Finding Consensus in Legal Writing Discourse Regarding Organizational Structure: A

this form of syllogistic reasoning is best suited for the profession that professes to adjudicate controversies without bias.

But not all of us are fans of these organizational schemata. While we recognize that the *IRAC* structure can be helpful in imposing a logical grammar for lawyers to understand themselves and explain law to outsiders, we disagree with it being used as the paradigm and the primary method for organizing writing. [10] Often, any simplistic method of synthesizing the complex to manageable comprehension can be *Procrustean*, masking subtleties and peculiarities not overt to the mind. That is why some of us suggest that students should not see analysis of human disputes from a single rule-based approach leaving little or no room for recognizing complicated and hard cases requiring a multidisciplinary approach to problem-solving.[11] This paper therefore seeks to open legal analysis and reasoning beyond rigid rule-based rule in a manner, which admits alternative analysis in the light of historical, political, and economic contexts. We encourage the profession, especially teachers of legal method and legal writing to reassess the foundation of IRAC, by ceasing to cling to it as paradigm for successful legal and brief writing. We rather urge that the rule and its *cousins* should be treated as illustrative of basic framework for legal reasoning and analysis in a manner that admits of other styles incorporating analysis that melds facts and experience with legal rules.[12]

Review and Analysis of the Use of IRAC and its Progenies (2012) 9 *Legal Comm. & Rhetoric: JALWD* 351.

[10] For example, even though some commentators think that IRAC is a basic way of organizing winning briefs, they urge the use of narrative style for making brief persuasive. See Karin Ciano, A Briefreader's Guide to Brief-writing, Fed. Law., Jan-Feb. 2012, at 43, cited in Diane B. Kraft, CREAC in the Real World (2015) 63 *Clev. St. L. Rev.* 567 at 573 n. 36.

[11] Clyde H. Hamilton, Effective Appellate Brief Writing (1999) 50 *S.C. L. Rev.* 581 at 587 (commentator did not include the IRAC method in the list of factors that make a good brief); Jane K. Gionfriddo et al., A Methodology for Mentoring Writing in Law Practice: Using Textual Clues to Provide Effective and Efficient Feedback (2009) 27 *Quinnipiac L. Rev.* 171.

[12] Legal writing teachers have suggested a range of IRAC cousins to include acronym like CREAC (conclusion, rule, explanation of rule, analysis and conclusion), CRAC (conclusion, rule, analysis and conclusion); CRExAC (conclusion, rule of law, explanation of rule, application of facts to the rules and connection-conclusion); RIRAC (reference, issue(s), rule(s), application, and conclusion) etc. See also, Phillip C. Kissam, The Decline of Law School Professionalism (1986) 134 *U. Pa. L. Rev.* 251 ("the study and practice of law would be improved by a more contextual approach that places a greater emphasis on both the application of law to concrete situations and the understanding of how law serves or fails to serve conflicting social values. This approach would improve professional education by initiating future practitioners into the uncertainties, complexities and value conflict of the 'practice situation.'") Id at 254.

Chapter Content

In this chapter we will examine the limitations and sometimes-harmful effects of *IRAC* to writing skills in stratifying analysis under the single *IRAC* jacket. We navigate this part essentially using the 1995 Washington Report of legal writing teachers conference as reference. We shall thereafter review why the legal profession, especially teachers, continues to cling to *IRAC* as signatory pedagogy for writing despite its recognized limitations and criticisms, by suggesting that the paradigm aligns with logic and the general Socratic pedagogy of law school training. Our discussion will be further deepened as we examine why good legal writing often departs from the IRAC style, because good writing centralizes facts than the *IRAC* rule-based form. We employ illustrative example of writing forms in the real world to enable the reader appreciate that good writing need not be located within the *IRAC* square to qualify as good. We further show that good brief writing and judicial opinion are generally non-*IRACian*, because judges and brief writers seek to persuade like ancient rhetoricians through the three triangular paths of logo, pathos and ethos. The chapter compares the *IRAC* and non-*IRAC* structure for writing and persuasion by using illustrative examples drawn from the basic components of lawyering-transactional lawyering, regulatory practice and litigation, it shows how non-*IRACian* style, incorporating narrative elements further the client's theory of the case better than the IRAC structure. It essentially shows how non-*IRAC* writing can expand and open otherwise closed doors for robust legal reasoning and analysis. The lawyer will also find suggested ways and means writing experts can teach the subject using flexible organizational techniques to produce future great brief or judicial opinion writers. It includes empirical examples of how some teachers have helped their students to develop analytical minds that transcends the simplistic, dogmatic and rule-centred *IRAC* structure. The conclusion is modest. While admitting that *IRAC* can be a good learning formula for starters, teachers must help their students outgrow the template remembering that *IRAC* conceived primarily as an analytical tool must not be converted into a writing formula that stupefies reasoning in society.

Limitations of the IRAC Method

Since the emergence of legal writing as a discipline, writing teachers have been critical of the use of *IRAC* as template for writing for two basic reasons: the limitation of the rule as a tool for analysing complexities in law and for the suffocating influence it can exert on the architecture of legal reasoning.[13] It is reasoned that a strait-jacket rule-based tool can fossilizes students reasoning, preventing them from the flexibility and creativity legal analysis requires.

This is what prompted legal writing teachers in 1995 to make topical an examination of the advantages and disadvantages of *IRAC* at the Legal Writing Institute conference in Washington.[14] The Report issued after the conference indicated clearly that writing professors acknowledge the value of *IRAC*, but are split on the danger of using it without flexibility.[15] One group think the template truncates and restricts the architecture of legal reasoning, while the other urges for its usefulness as standard template for legal analysis with certain modification.[16] We shall navigate the criticism of the rule essentially from the Second Draft, the report issued at the conclusion of the 1995 deliberations.

---

[13] For general reading on a critique of the IRAC paradigm for legal writing, see, Terri LeClercq, The Success-And Failure-of IRAC (1987) 50 *Tex. B.J.* 222; Jane K. Gionfriddo, Dangerous! Our Focus Should Be Analysis, Not Formulas Like IRAC, The Second Draft Nov. 1995 of the Legal Writing Institute, Tacoma, Wash, at 2; Wilson R. Huhn, Teaching Legal Analysis Using a Pluralistic Model of Law (2000-2001) 36 *Gonz. L. Rev.* 433; Helen A. Anderson, Changing Fashion in Advocacy: 100 Years of Brief-Writing Advice (2010) 11 *J. App. Prac. & Process* 1 (judges expect legal analysis to go beyond atomistic logic); Christine M. Venter, Analyse This: Using Taxonomies to "Scaffold" Students' Legal Thinking and Writing Skills (2006) 57 *Mercer L. Rev.* 621; Jennifer Sheppard, Once Upon a Time, Happily Ever After, and in a Galaxy Far, Far Away: Using Narrative to Fill the Cognitive Gap Left by Overreliance on Pure Logic in Appellate Briefs and Motion Memoranda (2009) 46 *Willamette L. Rev.* 255;; Kristen K. Robbins-Tiscione, A Call to Combine Rhetorical Theory and Practice in the Legal Writing Classroom (2011) 50 *Washburn L.J.* 319; Soma R. Kedia, Redirecting the Scope of First-Year Writing Courses: Towards a New Paradigm of Teaching Legal Writing (2010) 87 *U. Det. Mercy L. Rev.* 147; George D. Gopen, IRAC, REA, Where We Are Now, and Where We Should Be Going in the Teaching of Legal Writing (2011) 17 *J. Legal Writing Inst.* xvii (keynote address at Capital Area Legal Writing Conference, Feb. 26, 2011- "there is not and cannot be a single structure that is the right answer to the question of how argumentative thought is best conveyed from the mind of a writer to the mind of a reader. ... These organizational structures [CRAC, CREAC, MIRAT, IDAR, ILAC, TREACC, CruPAC, ISAAC, CRRACC, BARAC etc.] are both necessary and dangerous, both supporting and defeating. As with any good idea or good invention, they can all be used for harm as well as good," id xviii); Laura P. Graham, Why-RAC? Revisiting the Traditional Paradigm for Writing About Legal Analysis (2015) 63 *Kansas L. Rev.* 681. But cf. generally, Lurene Contento, Demystifying IRAC and Its Kin: Giving Students the Basic to Write "Like a Lawyer," *The Second Draft*, Nov. 1995 of the Legal Writing Institute, Tacoma, Wash; Tracy Turner, Flexible IRAC: A Best Practice Guide (2015) 20 *J. Legal Writing Inst.* 233 (recommends the syllogistic IRAC reasoning, while suggesting the best guide for teachers use of the rule, such as the one-sequence IRAC; the alternating IRAC; IRAC by paragraph; the IRAC sentence; and the narrative add-ons which mixes facts into the "I" of IRAC).

[14] See generally The Value of IRAC, *The Second Draft* (Legal Writing Institute, Tacoma, Washington, Nov. 1995).

[15] Above n. 14 at 1.

[16] For critique of the rule see, Jane K. Gionfriddo, Dangerous! Our Focus Should Be Analysis, Not Formulas Like IRAC, *The Second Draft* Nov. 1995 of the Legal Writing Institute, Tacoma, Wash, at 2. For flexibility of the rule see, Tracy Turner, Flexible IRAC: A Best Practice Guide (2015) 20 *J. Legal Writing Inst.* 233.

Critique of the *IRAC* Template

1. Issue (I)

There is no question about it. Before a student formulates the "I" she must have done some preliminary analysis. This is to be expected. If asked what "I"is of *IRAC* in a fact scenario where say C is knocked down his bicycle by D, a driver on the highway, she can only formulate the issue from preconceived knowledge of the question (Q), the entire relevant facts and rules (fr) and the relevant facts and rules (FR) governing the formulation of "I." in truth, "I" is only formulated when the student has done all the research and analysis of the controversy and is ready to report a conclusion.[17]

So in this fact scenario, the student has to draw on "what question arise here." She recognizes that the frame is one within the bracket of accident. Next, she proceeds to reflect on the possible relevant facts and rules. Reflection on facts would require her to know the nature of the highway, whether it is a busy one, whether the driver skidded off his own section of the road etc. Reflection on relevant rules possibly informs her that it is a matter connected with either (criminal) dangerous driving or (tortious) liability in negligence. Finally, she uses the relevant facts and rules to plot what will resemble a prima facie conclusion, which she calls issue. That being so, *IRAC* must account for these preliminary matters that enter the cognitive mind in formulating the "I" presently omitted in the *IRAC* template. This explains why one contributor to the Report suggested that there is the need to expand *IRAC* into an acronym like '(QfrFR)+IRAC,' if it must retain its explanatory power as an accurate formula for organizing legal analysis.[18]

Implicit in this (that preliminary analysis is what triggers the "I"), it follows that legal analysis stands on its head, upside down, because, the "I" is itself at worse an answer (conclusion). As one commentator puts it "assuming that "I" correctly understand . . . the legal problem solving process, then analysis of a

---

[17] Framing the issue as a thesis however has its attraction, e.g. "the defendant will be liable for negligence because the defective product manufactured by the defendant caused the plaintiff injury." See Michael D. Murray, Classical Rhetoric, Explanatory Synthesis and the TREAT Paradigm (Univ. Ill. L. & Econ. Working Paper No. 75, 2007), available at http://works.bepress.com/michael_murray/9 ("Presenting the thesis on the issue first brings to the front the most important part of the discussion: the answer to the legal question posed by the issue. Readers of all types-judges and law clerks... -will appreciate not having to wait for the answer.")

[18] Dennis R. Honabach, IRAC or (QfrFR)+IRAC, *The Second Draft* (Legal Writing Institute, Tacoma, Washington, Nov. 1995, 8.

question raised by a legal problem should begin with the answer to that question."[19]

2. Rule

What is meant by "R" in the IRAC template can be problematic for many reasons. Rules are not objects out there in the world for capture. In legal analysis, they can just be in a state of flux. Identifying them is not as simple as the *IRAC* formula would have us think. For example, a system that function at the level of facts, such as inductive common law would likely make fundamental distinction between types of persons and things and words used in legislation.[20] That being so, a court decision such as in *Donoghue* v. *Stevenson*[21] concerning injury caused by a defective bottle of ginger beer containing decomposed snail, may not necessarily apply to other defective products. So formulating the rule emerging from the case could be problematic. Would we for instance, reason that the rule would apply or be relevant for damages inflicted by say a defective wall or damages caused by an old tree, even though all these items can be properly described as "things" difficult to say with certainty.

That explains why even four years after the invention of the negligence rule in *Donoghue* it was unclear if the injury caused by the defective bottle of ginger could be extended to injury caused by a defective pair of underpants. Not surprising counsel for the defendant in *Grant* v. *Australia Knitting Mills Ltd*,[22] argued that a rule fashioned for ginger beer bottle should not apply to an article of clothing because beer and clothing are different objects. Though the Privy Council rejected the argument, it does not detract from the fact that a system that operates at the level of facts is bound to draw distinction between "things" and "persons," and so a rule may just well mean many things to different persons depending on how they construct the relevant ratio emerging from given facts. What the rule of negligence is from *Donoghue* v. *Stevenson* is therefore a matter of fitting the facts to law. It is plausible to construct several rules from the case. That why it was not

---

[19] Kim Cauthorn, Keep on TRRACING, *The Second Draft* (Legal Writing Institute, Tacoma, Washington, Nov. 1995, 4. The learned scholar recommend that rather than retain the IRAC acronym, it should be replaced the "I" with "T" (for thesis). See id at 5; Laura P. Graham, above n. 6. See also Tracy Turner, Finding Consensus in Legal Writing Discourse Regarding Organizational Structure: A Review and Analysis of the Use of IRAC and its Progenies (2012) 9 *Legal Comm. & Rhetoric: JALWD* 351 at 359 (survey of writing whether legal writing should start with issue or conclusion). But cf. Tracy Turner, Flexible IRAC: A Best Practice Guide (2015) 20 *J. Legal Writing Inst.* 233 n. 2 (where the learned writer states that in her paper she treats "issue as synonymous with thesis or conclusion."

[20] Geoffrey Samuel, *Law of Obligations and Legal Remedies*, 2nd ed., London: Cavendish Pub., 2001.

[21] [1932] AC 562 (HL)

[22] [1936] AC 85

illogical for defendant to argue in *Australian Knitting* that the *Donoghue* ratio did not apply to the set of facts in the instant case.

While the *IRAC* "R" represents the general premise in the deductive reasoning paradigm, it could admit of fact specific examples about how the premise is constructed. That explains the basis for which the defence constructed *Donoghue* in the new fact-situation in the *Australian Knitting* case. This is understandable, especially in the context that common lawyers reason inductively.[23] That being so, the acronym "R" can be divided into two parts-the general rule and the precedent (which decides the facts-specify application to the abstract rule). That is the only way the defence argument (though dismissed by the court) in the *Australian Knitting* could count as valid analysis, though overruled by the Privy Council. Some commentators have therefore suggested that "R" should be rather replaced and represented as "GP," "G" being the general rule and "P" the precedent that decides specific facts situation. Such a stance will convert *IRAC* to *IGPAC*.[24] The rule states the law that governs the legal issue. But rule explanation presents principles of interpretation derived from case and secondary authorities to show how a rule or sub-rule applies in actual situation. Both are simply referred to as rule in *IRAC*, when they in fact, implicate different types of analysis. The latter involves using inductive reasoning to derive genus principles of how a rule is to be interpreted and applied. These principles derive from factual elements, policies, or themes found in the cases and other authorities that are relevant to the interpretation of the rule. To therefore refer to both as one, as "R" does in the *IRAC* paradigm is misleading.

Furthermore, it must be recognized that "R" can make a difference on how students write. Because they think that "R" is always determinate, they are given to linear analysis of the "R" which they mathematically apply to arrive at a legal answer. But legal educators know that this kind of modular reasoning does not properly align with the intellectual development of students. No sooner after being taught *IRAC*, they see "R" from the perspective of dualism-right/wrong, true/false, good/bad etc. At this elementary stage, they can see the "R" as clear as sun in midday. But as they progress in learning they get transformed to the multiplicity stage, where they see the "R" as "R" or unknown. They realize that it

---

[23]Geoffrey Samuel, above n. 20. In fact, one hallmark of the common law legal system is that it is under theorised, in the sense that a court decision is not an instantiation of an explicit theory for resolving similar matters. Cass R. Sunstein, Incomplete Theorised Arguments (1995) 108 *Harv. L. Rev.* 1733. (discussion that because the incremental work of judges is accomplished by merely fitting new facts into existing precedent without necessarily articulating broad theory in the area that is in issue or dispute, the implication of this is that gaps are left unfilled until presented by facts pattern that demand gap-filling decisions).

[24] See Barbara Blumenfeld, Why IRAC Should Be IGPAC, *The Second Draft* (Legal Writing Institute, Tacoma, Washington, Nov. 1995, 3; Laura P. Graham, above n. 6.

is important to know *how* to think rather than *what* they think.[25] They progress from multiplicity to contextual relativism, where they gradually sees for the first time that they too can be a legitimate source of knowledge and that former knowledge-iconoclasts, such as their teachers, who analyse statute, case-law and legal texts to them are also fellow knowledge/truth-seekers, who likely possess more experience in the adventure. At this stage of their development, they begin to recognise that "R" is principle of law on which they can evaluate arguments in any given setting, and that the principle or "R" in a case is facts, precedent, and policy synthesis, not a determinate given. So "R" may not just be something out in the world capable of summarising in one way and one way only. It can be susceptible to different analysis.

It is no wonder therefore that a theoretical level some contributors think that the *IRAC* rule stupefies reasoning and analysis. They critique the "R" for encouraging students to assume that there is a rule clearly set forth by the facts so that all they need to do is apply the rule to get right answers in law, when in truth analysis requires making the difficult choice of choosing between competing and sometimes conflicting rules. Thus, to the extent that teachers use *IRAC*, it encourages students to keep a narrow perspective of law, when indeed writing ought to encourage evaluation of competing rules-a necessary skill for lawyers.[26]

Although a sceptic position to reasoning, some commentators even dispute the proposition that there is anything clearly marked as rules, to warrant an "R" within the paradigm. They question whether judicial decisions are founded on rules. Maintaining such a stance for instance, Sinclair posits that there are many ways rules can be formulated to fit an opinion, none of which can lay validity to superiority.[27] The learned writer presses the point by an analogy. Assuming ordinary people can read and understand cases and distil rules therefrom, he states that lawyers would be amazed at the different interpretations they will put on cases. Perhaps corroborative of his position is the thinking that lawyers do not extract rules from a single case but rather from a series of them. That being so, a

---

[25] Gerald F. Hess & Steven Friedland, *Techniques for Teaching Law*, Durham, North Carolina, Caroline Academic Press, 1999, 7. See also Paula Lustbader, Construction Sites, Building Types, and Bridging Gaps: A Cognitive Theory of the Learning Progression of Law Students (1997) 33 *Willamette L. Rev.* 317.

[26] Laura P. Graham, above n. 6 at 684; Marion W. Benfield, Jr., Thoughts on IRAC, The *Second Draft* (Legal Writing Institute, Tacoma, Washington, Nov. 1995, 17. According to Ronald Dworkin in *Taking Rights Seriously*, 2nd ed. Cambridge, 1978, p. 23, legal norms are in two categories-rules and principles. While the former are applicable in an all-or-nothing fashion, the latter are best described as value-maximising norms, i.e. they aim at promoting certain legal values. It is therefore not surprising why common lawyers trained in Anglo-American legal system would treat a statute as not intended to introduce new legal principles.

[27] Michael Sinclair, What is the "R" in IRAC (2003) 19 *N.Y.L. Sch. J. Hum. Rts.* 87.

science of law which constructs a principle from them should be seen as a process of synthesizing, which ordinarily admits of rule pluralism.[28]

3. Application (A)

The "A" is justified in *IRAC* as rooted in deductive syllogism. This form of reasoning that relies of the certainty of the major and minor premises is said to yield truth about the conclusion. If that were the case, then our "A" would certainly be problematic in yielding truth value using the *IRAC* rule. Teachers agree at a minimum that if the issues are even correctly framed, in the application section, students may not agree as to how the rules sit with the facts application. For instance, while students may agree that a given rule prohibits say murder (major premise), they are bound to defer on whether doctor assisted suicide or euthanasia should be classed as murder (minor premise). That being the case, it is hard to justify the certainty of conclusion, a position which implicates appeal to syllogism as bases for justifying *IRAC*. So in the theoretic sense, *IRAC* is less prevailing as deductive reasoning. The scope of ambiguity in the "A" weakens the algorithmic of *IRAC* transforming legal analysis into a model fit for enthymeme. There are no clear major and minor premise. Therefore, legal conclusion is stepped in enthymeme, mere probabilities of truth. Nothing more.[29]

If that puts legal analysis in the mould of enthymeme, then legal analysis is inductive reasoning (reasoning by analogy) pretending to be scientific deductive reasoning.[30] What this tells us is that the "A" is not simply an analysis of facts

---

[28]Murray, above n. 17.

[29] Logicians generally recognise two logical structure for argument: the deductive and inductive. The deductive comprises of syllogism and enthymeme. The latter is more suited for legal arguments. See Steven J. Burton, *An Introduction to Law and Legal Reasoning*, 1995; Ruggero J. Aldisert, Stephen Clowney & Jeremy D. Peterson, Logic for Law Students: How to Think Like a Lawyer (2007) 69 *Univ. Pittsburgh L. Rev.* 100;See also Murray, above n. 17 ("Given the uncertainties of the law, where legal rules are constructed from multiple controlling authorities and, in certain instances, coloured by persuasive authorities, and where facts might be uncertain or subject to multiple credible interpretations, the model of enthymeme with its anticipation of uncertainty, is the better model. Aristotle recognizes that in legal discourse (continuous discourse), the enthymeme is preferred)."

[30]Cass R. Sunstein, On Analogical Reasoning (1993) 106 *Harv. L.R.* 741 at 747; Burton, *An Introduction to Law and Legal Reasoning*, Boston & Toronto, 1985. Reasoning by analogy constitutes the most familiar form of legal reasoning in the common law legal system. It general proceeds based on a theory of probabilities. For example, it goes like this: I have a Honda car that is fuel efficient, so I assume that your Honda would also be fuel efficient. The logical structure is simple: (i) A has characteristic Y; (ii) B shares that characteristic; (iii) A also has characteristic Z; (iv) Because A and B share characteristic Y, we conclude what isn't known, that B shares characteristic Z as well. This form of reasoning pervades daily life and law. This reasoning does not guarantee truth about conclusions. It focuses on the particulars, and is developed from concrete controversies. It is a bottom-top thinking because ideas are developed from details. Principles are created which operates at a low or intermediate level of abstraction. For instance, when we say the state cannot ban civil demonstration, we invariably are implying that the state has no constitutional power to prevent lawful assembly and association without showing that in the instant case such

tied to some absolute correct rules. Legal writing is therefore contextual and expansive to a large extent which includes not just analysis but also counter-analysis and policy analysis.

4. Conclusion (C)

The "C" is actually the beginning point. Legal writing begins with it, then move backwards from there. When faced with legal questions, lawyers instinctively first reach a conclusion and thereafter try to make the analysis fit.[31] But the *IRAC* rule as against the customary instinctiveness. It encourages suspending conclusion in pretence of promoting the objective character of law, especially in adjudication.

That notwithstanding, the "C" component has a way of stupefying reasoning in that it tends to make students think that deductive reasoning must produce right answers and conclusions. According to Seymour, "when *IRACian* students make up their mind how the law applies to the facts, they can undervalue opposing views. *IRAC* pushes students towards answers rather than arguments. *IRAC* is sleek and efficient, once issue emerges, conclusion ever beckons."[32]

These are some of the critique of the *IRAC* paradigm, which triggers suggestion for revisiting it as a writing style.

Why Some Writing Teachers and Lawyers Continue to Cling to *IRAC*

Despite recognizing the limitations of the *IRAC* template, some writing teachers cling to it because of the thinking that deductive reasoning (one that moves from the general to the particular) is good basis for legal analysis in reducing complex to the simple.[33] Relying on deductive syllogism, a number of other versions of the rule-based *IRAC* paradigm have been invented. They include acronym like *CREAC* and many others.[34] Some have suggested other *IRAC* acronyms to fill the gaps of deficiency of *IRAC* to better capture the supposed different methods of

---

demonstration poses imminent and clear harm. This is a principle, and it does involve a certain degree of abstraction from the particular case (legitimacy of civil demonstration), but it does not entail any high-level theory about the purpose of the free assembly and association provision of the Constitution or what is considered the proper relation between the citizen and state.

31 Kristen K. Robbins-Tiscione, *Rhetoric for Legal Writers: The Theory and Practice of Analysis and Persuasion,* 2009. According to Justice Holmes, the common law court decides a case first and determines the principles afterwards. Oliver W. Holmes, Jr., Codes and the Arrangement of Law (1870) 5 *Am. L. Rev.* 1 reprinted in (1931) 44 *Harv. L. Rev.* 725. But that hardly be the factual position, because legal reasoning must somehow be raised from some rough commitment to principles (values) that form the underlying basis for fitting facts.

32 Thomas H. Seymour, Between IRAC and a Hard Place, *The Second Draft* (Legal Writing Institute, Tacoma, Washington, Nov. 1995) 14.

33 James A. Gardner, *Legal Argument: The Structure and Language of Effective Advocacy,* 1st ed., 1993, 6; Teresa J. Reid Rambo & Leanne J. Pflaum, above n. 2; Anita Schnee, above n. 9.

34 See Gopen, above n. 13.

analysis in law. As revealed in the preceding section this have sometimes led legal writing teachers to suggest acronyms like '(QfrFR)+I*RAC,' IGPAC, CREAC, TREAT, CREXAC, CRAC, CRuPAC,* and other similar formulations to better capture the multifaceted dimensions legal writing requires.[35] All of these *IRAC* cousins, like its progeny are rooted in the philosophy that it is best to teach students to reason as syllogistically as possible, and that a rule-based approach enables law to remain an autonomous discipline, divorced from mundane bias. It is the general thinking that anything short of *IRAC* syllogism implicates enthymeme; a thing lawyers' must avoid in keeping law the envy of other disciplines.[36] The beauty of the paradigm and its cousins is extolled for its capacity to project argumentation within scientific boundaries to produce logically accepted conclusions.

But herein lurks the danger of the so-called scientific analysis. Following deductive syllogism, the first task is to frame the general rule before applying it to the facts. We must first begin with "All humans are mortal." The facts, "Socrates is a human," is therefore made relevant only as defined by the rule. The paradigm does not permit placing the facts before the rule. So the facts relevant are simply those conscripted by the rule. One scholar captures this way: "no paradigm recognizes a place for inclusion of facts within the analysis-other than the limited facts that may be part of the initial conclusion-before the rule is stated and explained, much like no effective syllogism puts the minor premise before the major premise."[37] That being so, the minor premise is confined to the structure only permitted by the major premise. Only facts within the confines of the framed question (issue) for determination can get ventilated.

For those of us who subscribe to the thinking that law must account for peoples' experience and reality, syllogism must be construed expansive. After all, there are two generally permitted logical structures for argumentation-deductive and inductive reasoning. Even at that, deductive reasoning admits of syllogism and enthymeme. Both syllogism and enthymeme begin with major premise, followed by the minor premise. The difference between them being that in the former both premise (major and minor) are absolute certainty, making the

---

[35] See for example Richard K. Neumann, Jr., *Legal Reasoning and Legal Writing: Structure, Strategy and Style*, 5th ed., Aspen Pub., 2005; Charles R. Calleros, *Legal Method and Writing*, 5th ed., Aspen Pub, 2006; Michael D. Murray & Christy H. DeSanctis, *Legal Research and Writing*, Found Press, 2006, 95-112; Mary B. Beazley, *A Practical Guide to Appellate Advocacy*, 2nd ed., Aspen Pub, 2006, 61-76; Brian Foley &Ruth A. Robbins, Fiction 101: A Primer for Lawyers on How to Use Fiction Writing Techniques to Write Persuasive Facts Section (2001) 32 *Rutgers L.J.* 459 at 462.

[36] For the difference between syllogism and enthymeme and the supposed preference of the former to the latter, see Robbins-Tiscione, above n. 31; Linda L. Berger, Studying and Teaching "Law as Rhetoric": A Place to Stand (2010) 16 *J. Legal Writing Inst.* 3 at 50; Kraft, above n. 10.

[37] Kraft, above n. 10.

conclusion an absolute, irrefutable truth. This kind of reasoning should be a suspect candidate in legal analysis. No one can seriously doubt that legal rules constructed from multiple sources, coloured by persuasive authorities, in context of facts indeterminacy should be a candidate for enthymeme. In fact, even Aristotle recognizing the indeterminate nature of law and facts in legal disputes was of the view that enthymeme constitutes a better model for legal reasoning.[38] In enthymeme, a highly probable legal principle is applied to the specific facts of the case to produce a highly probably conclusion. This explains how law works in the real world as we know it.

But adherents of *IRAC* just remain glued to it standard pedagogy for analysis. While some admit that it imposes an architectural restrain of the edifice of legal reasoning they are reluctance to discard it because it adherents argue (may be rightly so) that the organizational paradigm is useful to teach starters the rudiments of legal analysis, especially in helping them grasp doctrinal analysis, thinking as a lawyer.[39]

Recognizing the place of legal writing in the law academy, writing professors in the United States in 1984 organized a writing conference, which led to the establishment of the Legal Writing Institute in 1986. The goal of the Institute has been to encourage a broader understanding of legal writing and the teaching of it. To further the goal, the Institute established the Journal of Legal Writing Institute in 1988 to showcase the developing discipline of legal writing.[40] Since emerging as

---

38 Murray, above n. 17; Aristotle, *The Rhetoric,* Book 1, ch. 1 at 1355; Book 1, ch. 2 at 1356.

39 It is recognized that legal training involves doctrine, skills and ethics. See tilt towards professionalism in Reports. William M. Sullivan, et al. eds. *Carnegie Fund for the Advancement of Teaching, Educating Lawyers: Preparation for the Profession of Law,* 2007 (hereinafter called the *Carnegie Report*) Foundation for the Advancement of Teaching, Preparation for the Professions Program (PPP) 2007, Legal Education Report based on a survey of more than two hundred law faculties (schools) in the US and Canada in 1999; H.R. Cort & J.L. Sammons, The Search for Good Lawyering: A Concept and Model for Lawyering Competencies (1980) 29 *Cleveland State L. Rev.* 397; James R. Maxeiner, Educating Lawyers Now and Then: Two Carnegie Critiques of the Common Law and Case Method (2007) 35 *International J. Leg. Info.* 1; John B. Garvey & Anne F. Zinkin, Making Law Students Client-Ready: A New Model in Legal Education (2009) 1 *Duke Forum Law & Soc. Change* 101; Karen Tokarz, *et al.,* Legal Education at a Crossroad: Innovation, Integration, and Pluralism Required (2014) 43 *Washington Univ. J Law & Policy* 11. See also Robert MacCrate in forward to *Best Practices* said: "The central message in both Best Practices and in the contemporaneous Carnegie Report is that law schools should broaden the range of lessons they teach, reducing doctrinal education that uses the Socratic dialogue and case method: integrate the teaching of knowledge, skills and values, and not treat them as separate subjects in separate courses: and give greater attention to instruction in professionalism." Roy Stuckey et. al., *Best Practices for Legal Education: A Vision and a Roadmap,* 2007 (hereinafter called *Best Practices*) and generally, Association of American Law School, Conference on the Future of Law School Curriculum: Brochure (Seattle, 2011).

40 See webpage of the Institute. For a history of legal writing as a discipline see Mary S. Lawrence, The Legal Writing Institute the Beginning: Extraordinary Vision, Extraordinary Accomplishment (2005) 11 *Legal Writing* 213.

a discipline, writing teachers have been critical of the use of *IRAC* as template for two basic reasons: the limitation of the rule as a tool for analysing complexities in law and for its suffocating influence it can exert on the architecture of legal reasoning.[41]

While many agree that deductive syllogism is a useful way for organizing legal analysis and that it is signature template for writing, legal writing teachers and the profession demands re-assessment of the paradigm to make lawyering robust by giving attention to pluralistic and multidisciplinary reasoning not rooted in rule-based analysis. Strong critics of *IRAC* have been storytelling teacher, who argue that *IRAC* banishes from courts the real forces that generate disputes between parties.[42]

Because *IRAC* does not teach students who would become members of the legal profession flexibility and creativity in their analysis, writing teachers have been concerned about how they can collectively improve the writing skills of students. In 1995, for instance, they gathered in Washington to examine the

---

[41] For general reading on a critique of the IRAC paradigm for legal writing, see, Terri LeClercq, The Success-And Failure-of IRAC (1987) 50 *Tex. B.J.* 222; Jane K. Gionfriddo, Dangerous! Our Focus Should Be Analysis, Not Formulas Like IRAC, The Second Draft Nov. 1995 of the Legal Writing Institute, Tacoma, Wash, at 2; Wilson R. Huhn, Teaching Legal Analysis Using a Pluralistic Model of Law (2000-2001) 36 *Gonz. L. Rev.* 433; Christine M. Venter, Analyse This: Using Taxonomies to "Scaffold" Students' Legal Thinking and Writing Skills (2006) 57 *Mercer L. Rev.* 621; Kristen K. Robbins-Tiscione, A Call to Combine Rhetorical Theory and Practice in the Legal Writing Classroom (2011) 50 *Washburn L.J.* 319; Kedia, above n. 13; Jennifer Sheppard, Once Upon a Time, Happily Ever After, and in a Galaxy Far, Far Away: Using Narrative to Fill the Cognitive Gap Left by Overreliance on Pure Logic in Appellate Briefs and Motion Memoranda (2009) 46 *Willamette L. Rev.* 255; Helen A. Anderson, Changing Fashion in Advocacy: 100 Years of Brief-Writing Advice (2010) 11 *J. App. Prac. & Process* 1 (judges expect legal analysis to go beyond atomistic logic); George D. Gopen, IRAC, REA, Where We Are Now, and Where We Should Be Going in the Teaching of Legal Writing (2011) 17 *J. Legal Writing Inst.* xvii (keynote address at Capital Area Legal Writing Conference, Feb. 26, 2011- "there is not and cannot be a single structure that is the right answer to the question of how argumentative thought is best conveyed from the mind of a writer to the mind of a reader. ... These organizational structures [CRAC, CREAC, MIRAT, IDAR, ILAC, TREACC, CruPAC, ISAAC, CRRACC, BARAC etc.] are both necessary and dangerous, both supporting and defeating. As with any good idea or good invention, they can all be used for harm as well as good," id xviii);; Laura P. Graham, Why-RAC? Revisiting the Traditional Paradigm for Writing About Legal Analysis (2015) 63 *Kansas L. Rev.* 681. But cf. generally, Tracy Turner, Flexible IRAC: A Best Practice Guide (2015) 20 *J. Legal Writing Inst.* 233 (recommends the syllogistic IRAC reasoning, while suggesting the best guide for teachers use of the rule, such as the one-sequence IRAC; the alternating IRAC; IRAC by paragraph; the IRAC sentence; and the narrative add-ons which mixes facts into the "I" of IRAC); Lurene Contento, Demystifying IRAC and Its Kin: Giving Students the Basic to Write "Like a Lawyer," *The Second Draft*, Nov. 1995 of the Legal Writing Institute, Tacoma, Wash.

[42] Kenneth D. Chestek, Judging by the Numbers: An Empirical Study of the Power of Story (2010) 7 *J. Ass'n. Legal Writing Directors* 1 (study found that judges were more persuaded by narrative briefs than they were with rule-based logical briefs). See also Festus Emiri, Mainstreaming an Interdisciplinary Approach to Legal Education: Imperatives for Nigeria's Development [2015] *Proceeding of NALT*, 1.

advantages and disadvantages of the *IRAC* template.[43] Their Report revealed that writing professors generally acknowledge the value of IRAC rule but are split on the danger of using *IRAC* without flexibility.[44] One group think the template truncates and restricts the architecture of legal reasoning, while the other urge for its continuing use with modification to make it amenable to different types of analysis as the facts of a case admits.[45]

A survey of teaching methodology in Nigeria however indicates that despite the criticism of *IRAC* it remain the dominant pedagogy in faculties of law, and even brief writing.[46] The reason is not farfetched. One scholar suggests that this is because "there are not many alternatives from which to choose" given legal writing's fairly recent emergence as part of the law school curriculum.[47] The emergence of law clinics in many faculties is however indicative that legal writing is here to stay and that a review of *IRAC* as a writing style is in the wings.

IRAC and the Legal Profession

It is plausible to reason that if *IRAC* exhibits all the flaws said to attach to it as a writing style and yet teachers still cling to it, then it must be in part because practicing lawyers also use a similar thought thread in writing briefs. But it is not true. The most daunting criticism of *IRAC* does not really emerge from the legal academy and legal writing teachers, but it comes from legal practitioners and judges who call for better writing.[48] Complain by judges and senior lawyers over the writing skills of new lawyers is indicative of the harm caused by strict adherence to IRAC pedagogy in our teaching of law.[49] Trial and appellate judges prefer briefs that combine rule explanation with application to client's facts, especially in cases with complexity requiring depth of analysis. The flexible organizational style is most suitable for facts-intensive litigation. An integrated flexible organizational structure encourages centrality of facts and the client's

---

[43] See generally The Value of IRAC, *The Second Draft* (Legal Writing Institute, Tacoma, Washington, Nov. 1995. (Legal Writing Institute Conference), above n. 14.

[44] Above n. 14 at 1.

[45] For critique of the rule see, Gionfriddo, above n. 16.For flexibility of the rule see, Turner, above n. 7.

[46] Refer to the Nigerian Law School handbook and briefs filed at appellate courts.

[47] Kedia, above n. 13.

[48] For legal academy critique of IRAC, see the 1995 *Second Draft,* devoted to examine IRAC as a model for legal writing. Above n. 14.

[49] For complain of Nigerian judges and lawyers, see. See also the *MacCrate Report,* above n. 38; The *Carnegie Report,* above n. 14; Amy Vorenberg & Margaret S. McCabe, Practice Writing: Responding to the Needs of the Bench and Bar in the First-Year Writing Programs (2009) 2 *Phoenix L. Rev.* 1 (sample of trial judges in several U.S states indicates that they expressed reservations about IRAC as a good organizational structure for organizing writing. In fact, when asked, "Do you find IRAC effective or do you prefer organization that combines rule explanation with application to client's facts?' several judges preferred the latter); Graham, above n. 6 at 704; Kedia, above n. 13.

theory of the case, a thing extremely difficult to achieve with the rule-based IRAC paradigm.[50]

IRAC is particularly unhelpful to judges in deciding cases where the legal issues are fairly settled and frequently before the courts. For example, applications for interlocutory injunctions pending final determination of cases and those for stay of execution pending appeal are staple diet in our courts. Movants of such applications would be generally unhelpful to the courts by adopting the rule-based approach in persuading judges to exercise the court's discretion in their clients favour by citing the rule as expounded in say, *Kotoye* v. *CBN*[51] for injunction and *Vaswani Trading Co.* v. *Savalakh*[52] and *Kigo (Nig) Ltd* v. *Holman*[53] for stay of execution and then lacing them with the facts constricted by the syllogism of *IRAC.* Judges know enough of the rules expounded in the cases. What will help them in the exercise of their discretion to grant or refuse an application would be facts construction of applicants' case-theory creating compelling reasons for the orders sought. Yes, the compelling facts-intensive stories which fit a constructed theory of the case. So what is likely to be more useful to them in a brief seeking the material relief may well turn on how the movant matches the rules with the specific narrative of the client to create compelling persuasion for the orders sought. Good brief writing demands an organizational structure that is deep and flexible, combining rule application to the facts specifics of the client to create the client's theory of the case to persuade the court.[54] Rather than stick to a rigid *IRAC* structure, good brief writer goes

---

[50]Vorenberg & McCabe survey contains an interesting finding. They provided the judges survey with three students briefs written by their students. Two of the briefs were organized around IRAC, one was not. Most of the judges preferred the brief that was flexible combining rule explanation with client's facts in the same paragraph and section. Vorenberg & McCabe, above n. 49 at 14. See also, Ruminations From the Bench: Brief Writing and Oral Argument in the Fifth Circuit (1995) 70 *Tul. L. Rev.* 187.

[51][1989] All NLR 76. See especially the judgment of Nnaemeka-Agu, JSC stating that the important issues in the application for interlocutory injunction are (i) that there is a real possibility, not a probability, of success at the trial-that there is a serious question to be tried; (ii) balance of convenience favours the grant (iii) that damages cannot be adequate compensation; (iv) and conduct of the parties.

[52] [1972] All NLR 922, per Coker, JSC.

[53] [1980] NSCC 204, per Kayode Eso, JSC.

[54] For discussion on client's theory of the case and its persuasiveness, see Lucie E. White, Subordination, Rhetorical Survival Skills, and Sunday Shoes: Notes on the Hearing of Mrs. G (1990) 38 *Buffalo L. Rev.* 1 (where the commentators using the story of Mrs. G welfare hearing application reveals that cultural images and long-established legal norms construct the subjectivity and speech of socially subordinate groups, like women, blacks etc., as inherently inferior to those of dominant groups). See also Derrick Bell, *And We Are Not Saved*, 1987 (for critical race theory perspective); Anthony V. Alfieri, The Antinomies of Poverty Law and a Theory of Dialogic Empowerment (1987-88) 16 *N.Y.U. Rev. L & Soc. Change* 659; Patricia J. Williams, *The Alchemy of Race and Rights*, 1991 (literary and legal theory); Kathryn Abrams, Hearing the Call of Stories (1991) 79 *Cal. L. Rev.* 971 (feminist theory); Clark D. Cunningham, The Lawyer as Translator, Representation as Text:

beyond sheer deductive syllogism, combining inductive, problem-solving techniques with it to persuade.

A survey of good briefs filed in courts can give a representative idea of the virility or otherwise of the *IRAC* organizational paradigm. Good brief writers do not think that an organizational structure like *IRAC* is necessary for good brief writing.[55] In one such survey conducted by Kraft of briefs filed in the US Supreme Court, the US Circuit Courts of Appeal, and the Kentucky Supreme Court between 1989 and 2013, he found that while most briefs included elements of conclusion, rule, rule explanation, rule application, and conclusion (*CREAC*), the trend showed a general departure from the strict rule, explanation and application (*R-E-A*) template.[56] In the learned writer's view, most of the briefs rather followed three patterns: (i) they included facts before rule or rule explanation; (ii) they included the rule in a separate section, and started subsequent sections with a discussion of facts, and (iii) they interspersed rule explanation with rule application.

Let us illustrate with two examples of how the flexible style have been used by judges in judicial opinion and lawyers in good brief writing.

1. Judicial Opinion Writing

We have chosen to use the judgment of Peter Gibson J in *Baden* v. *Societe Generale pour Favorise le Developpement du Commerce et d l'Industrie en France SA*,[57] as a good judicial opinion for some reasons. Aside the fact that it is a brilliant writing, it is a fact-intensive, complex case that took 108 hearing days to be concluded. *Baden* was a case about a complex transnational financial scheme

---

Towards an Ethnography of Legal Discourse (1992) 77 *Cornell L. Rev.* 1298 (ethnography discourse); Binny Miller, Give Them Back Their Lives: Recognising Client Narrative in Case Theory (1994) 93 *Mich. L. Rev.* 485 (showing how the practice of lawyering should be reconstructed to embrace a greater role for clients in constructing case theories) [hereinafter referred to as 'Give Them Back']; Edward D. Ohlbaum, Basic Instinct: Case Theory and Courtroom Performance (1993) 66 *Temp. L. Rev.* 1; Binny Miller, Teaching Case Theory (2002) 9 *Clinical L. Rev.* 293.

[56] Kraft, above n. 10.

[57] [1992] 4 All ER 161. This is a case often used by one of the writers of this paper, Festus Emiri, to teach his students writing style in legal method and the concept of *knowing assistance* and *knowing receipt* liability of strangers in trust classes. For similar great style of judicial opinion see the lead judgment of Nnaemeka-Agu in *Kotoye* v. *CBN* [1989] All NLR 76 at 84; *Kigo (Nig) Ltd* v. *Holman Bros. (Nig) Ltd* [1980] NSCC 204, per Kayode Eso, JSC, where His Lordship used dramatic language like "this was the beginning of the drama which eventually culminated in the instant application in this court." Id at 206 lines 28-29; "the next stage in this interesting drama was set on 14th April, 1980." Id at 207 line 6. "Now, it has been necessary to state all these facts antecedent to the present application, before this court, to stay further proceedings before the High Court of Kano, and refer to the activities of learned counsel for the Third Party in the trial court for the reason that the jurisdiction of the court to entertain an application for the stay sought in the instant application is discretionary." Id at 208 lines 1-5.

was designed to defraud investors. His Lordship's style summarized in the judgment followed a pattern of introducing the facts before rule and rule explanation and thereafter interspersing rule explanation with rule application.

The learned judge started the introduction by narrating the background to the dispute this way:

> A decade or more after the troubles affecting the financial complex known as IOS exited the attention of the financial world, disputes arising from those troubles are still not resolved. In this action the plaintiffs seek to recover a sum a little in excess of $US4m from the defendant (SG), a major French bank which carries on a banking business in, *inter alia*, the City of London. SG has held that sum in an account designated as a trust account by its customer, Bahamas Commonwealth Bank Ltd (BCB).

It is from the background that the court went on to describe in detail the complex history and nature of the facts under the subhead/title, history. In the history section, His Lordship catalogues the IOS complex, the dollar funds, the acquisition and reorganization of IOS, change of the investment policies, the transactions that followed, all leading to the Security and Exchange Commission (SEC) proceedings, and SG's involvement and what led to the litigation. It is after this detailed narrative that His Lordship then resorted to the next section, applicable rule.

Noteworthy of mention, the court in laying the background for the dispute using the narrative style above gave life to the dispute by context, stating that the litigation is a fallout from the OIS financial scam. The court did not follow the a contextual style of some judicial opinion writings that would have simply started by just describing the plaintiff's claim, stating for example that "the claim of the plaintiff is for…The plaintiff filed and served his statement of claim …" type of run.

Rather the learned judge used a narrative form of writing, interspersing the facts with law in the rule and rule explanation sections to make the conclusion clear understandable. His Lordship started by first setting out in the introduction a narrative background to the dispute, then proceeding from there to give a background to the claim under the section of history, before stating the before stating the rule and rule explanation and thereafter interspersing rule explanation with rule application is what set the stage to understand the claim of the plaintiff. It is a style very flexible, fact laden and persuasive, not in any way *IRACian*.

2. Good Brief Writing

Good brief writers also employ a similar flexible style.

Let us consider the brief filed by the respondent in response to an appeal seeking to set-aside the judgment granted the respondent by the lower court in *Atlantic Airline* v. *Musa*.[58] The facts of the case had to do with the retention of the respondent by the appellant to provide it professional legal services. At the end of the service in 2010 the respondent delivered a detailed bill for his professional services, under section 16 of the Legal Practitioners Act for the sum of N5m. Unfortunately, the bill was not honoured and remained unpaid for four years. It was also not disputed by the appellant. On the strength of it, the respondent applied to the trial court to place the claim under the undefended list from where the respondent sought summary judgment in 2015. On the day the respondent moved for judgment at the trial court, the appellant raised objection to the court's jurisdiction to entertained the suit and also filed an affidavit of intention to defend the suit as provided under the undefended list procedure Order 10 of Gongola State (Civil Procedure) Rules, 2000.

It was the case of the appellant that the judgment obtained by the respondent should be set aside on appeal on the ground that the trial judge erred in law when he entered judgment against the appellant under the undefended list procedure of Order 10 of the Gongola State (Civil Procedure) Rules, 2000, without availing them fair hearing as guaranteed in section 36 of the Constitution of the Federal Republic of Nigeria, by failing to consider its pending applications before entering summary judgment in the respondent's favour.

The respondent reply brief did not follow the IRAC pattern. Rather it simply used a flexible organizational style where facts were interspersed with thesis, rule, rule explanation and legal conclusions that combined elements of logos, pathos and ethos.

For example, in the very beginning of the brief, it drew a taxonomical line between the complaint of the appellant and what is not complained about to enable the court narrow the confines of the appeal. It thereafter states the rule, explains the rule as applied to the legal principle and just intersperse the facts of the case with the applicable principles through inductive reasoning. It began like this:

This brief is in reply to the appellant's brief filed on 15 January 2015 in expatiation of the grounds of appeal filed against the decision of the trial court of the High Court of Gongola State, sitting in Yanbura. The said decision of the court was delivered on 3 January 2015 and is found at pages 40-49 of the records of proceedings.

---

[58] An imaginary case constructed from an appellate brief filed before the Calabar Division of the Court of Appeal.

The respondent who is a senior lawyer was retained by the appellant to provide it with legal services. In 2000, the respondent delivered a detailed bill for his professional services under section 16 of the Legal Practitioners Act, to the appellant for ₦5m.

After 41 months when the appellant did not contest or dispute any aspect of the said bill, nor paid the bill, after series of demands, the respondent brought an action under the undefended list procedure for his unpaid professional fees. Etc.

It then goes on to state as follows:

> The appellant has urged Your Lordships to resolve the issue as to whether having regard to section 36 of the 1999 Constitution the learned trial judge erred in law when he entered judgment against the appellant without availing them fair hearing.
>
> The appellant has neither contended that Order 10 of the High Court of Gongola State (Civil Procedure) Rules is unconstitutional or offends section 36 of the Constitution.
>
> The appellant has also not complained that the trial judge failed to apply the said Order 10 rule to the facts of case at the trial stage.
>
> The hearing under Order 10 procedure does not cease to be fair where a representation is made by an affected party in accordance with the established procedure for the undefended list. See *CRPIC Ltd* v. *Obongha* (2001) 45 FWLR 353 at 368.
>
> The court can even dispense with any counsel's address before entering judgment in the undefended list procedure of Order 10. *Eneji* v. *Internationals Ltd* (2001) 50 FWLR 765 at 775. See also *Chrisdon Industries Ltd* v. *AIB Ltd* (2002) 128 FWLR 355, where the court held that the provision for showing notice of intention to defend under the undefended list procedure does not require call for argument or hearing an address of counsel. It is the exclusive preserve of the trial court. The movant and defence counsel need not be heard.

It is trite law that an allegation of denial of fair hearing has to be clearly particularized to enable issues to be joined. However, in an apparent effort to justify the claim for breach the appellant has supplied what it would wish the court to take as amounting to breach of fair hearing in his grounds of appeal at pages 100-105 of the record of proceedings as follows: (It then list the facts stated in the pages).

From the records, this was an action commenced under the undefended list procedure. In order to sustain an argument of breach of section 36 of the

Constitution, such a breach must of necessity be founded on the undefended list procedure under which this action was commenced.

It is logical to conclude that the appellant complain is limited to the fact that the appellant was not served with hearing notice for the proceedings of 5th January 2015 and that there were pending applications that were not heard. We submit that in order to sustain an argument for breach of constitutional fair hearing (s.36 of the Constitution) the learned trial judge must have deviated from following the undefended list procedure of Order 10. There is no allegation that the learned trial judge breached any of the stipulations in Order 10 to reach the judgment complained of by the appellant. See *Ekulo Farms Ltd* v. *UBN Plc* (*below*).

There is no allegation that the trial court failed to take into account the materials provided by the appellant: the application for objection to the court's jurisdiction and its notice of intention to defend. The appellant has not disputed that where the court finds that the notice does not disclose a defence on merits, the court is at liberty to enter judgment without more. Accordingly, the appellant's argument about pending applications is grossly misplaced and ought to be discounted.

It is also necessary to consider the antecedent of the case in order to show that even though the trial judge needed not consider anything beyond the notice of intention to defend, the judge still out of abundance of caution, considered more than what the law requires. (It then catalogues the facts in a narrative style).

In *Ekulo Farms Ltd* v. *UBN Ltd* [2006] 4 SC 1, the Supreme Court outlined in broad terms the procedure for the undefended list in the following paraphrased words: (states the paraphrased words).

> In the circumstance, we urge this court to hold that no breach of fair hearing right has been breached and that the suit was properly decided under the undefended list by the learned trial judge.

What the brief sections above does is an articulation of the facts leading to the appeal, state the relevant question for determination, state the governing rule the court should apply, explains how the rule has been expounded by precedent (by citing the best possible authorities), relate how both the broad and narrow issues meld with the instant facts of the appeal using both inductive and analogical reasons to justify a favourable decision for the respondent. Noteworthy of mention, the rule application section freely interspersed the rule, rule explanation and facts together, drawing inferences and prima facie interim conclusions, before the omnibus conclusion.

The question then is why do good writers use the flexible organisational style, not *IRAC*? Good writers use the flexible style because it is reader-friendly to communicate.[59] Judicial opinion writing and brief writing do not structure their writing using the *IRAC* or *CREAC* paradigm in crafting legal arguments; they merely use elements of the structure. They especially show marked deviation in the "R-A" component of the *IRAC* rule or "R-E-A" component in the *CREAC* rule. The reason for this isn't just a matter of style, or preference. It is deeper. The styles chosen are in part informed by judicial preference to "let the facts do the talking."[60] A brief laced with story is likely to be more persuasive than one that rigidly follows the IRAC template. That explains why most would rather resort to either one or a combination of the three trends emergent in good brief writing: include facts before rule or rule explanation; include the rule in a separate section and start subsequent section with a discussion of facts; and intersperse rule explanation and rule application.

So while beginners in legal writing may need to start with *IRAC*, legal writing teachers should progressively inculcate the flexible style to create potentials for good brief writers.[61] Generally, good brief writers differ from students' writer in that their writing go beyond the parameters of the formalist analysis using the *IRAC* organisational structure. They rather emphasize facts through storytelling and narrative. It is by teaching our students to write like lawyers that they become great advocates who recognise that law is concerned about real people and the stories that generate controversies located beyond mere form of description of the contending parties as plaintiff and defendant. Students need to be taught that *IRAC* is a mere beginner guide to deductive reasoning, and that the rule is merely a primer and no more. It serves only to raise their thinking ability to think as lawyers. But that is the far it goes. To the extent that lawyering demands acquisition of lawyering skills and values, they will need to master a flexible organisation structure that brings the experience of their client's story to the courtroom.[62] It only when we as teachers instruct our students to master the

---

[59]Kraft, above n. 10.

[60] Susan H. Kosse & David T. Butle Richie, How Judges, Practitioners, and Legal Writing Teachers Access the Writing Skills of New Law Graduates: A Comparative Study (2003) 53 *J. Legal Educ.* 80. See also Symposium, Legal Storytelling (1989) 87 *Mich. L. Rev.* 2073; Symposium, Lawyers as Storytellers & Storytellers as Lawyers: An Interdisciplinary Symposium Exploring the Use of Storytelling in the Practice of Law (1994) 18 *VT. L. Rev.* 565. In fact, judicial writings follow a similar pattern.

[61] Helen A. Anderson, Changing Fashions in Advocacy: 100 Years of Brief-Writing Advise (2010) 11 *J. App. Prac. &Process* 1; Richard A. Posner, Judicial Opinions and Appellate Advocacy in Federal Courts-One Judge's View (2013) 51 *Duq. L. Rev.* 3; Kenneth D. Chestek, The Life of the Law Has Not Been Logic: It Has Been Story (2014) 1 *Savannah L. Rev.* 21.

[62] See George G. Gopen, Keynote Address at the Capital Area Legal Writing Conference, Feb. 26, 2011, in IRAC, REA, Where We Are Now, and Where We Should Be Going in the Teaching of Legal Writing

flexible organisational structure of legal writing that we can say we have given them the required arsenal to transform them from amateur students writers to great brief writers, effective advocates for their clients responding to judges expectations. This is a must-do because students must learn that in the real world many legal questions cannot be evaluated under straightjacket formalistic rules and application.

Good Writing Entails Persuasion

Judges and lawyers write the way they do using flexible organisational structures because they recognise that good writing must persuade. This way, they merely mimic ancient rhetoricians. Traditional models of legal argumentation based on formal or informal models of logic are increasingly considered to be inadequate for fully describing the persuasiveness of legal argumentation. [63] Ancient rhetoricians unpacked the goal of persuasion as following three paths: the concept of *logos*, *pathos*, and *ethos*.[64] *Logos* (persuasion accompanied through logical

---

(2011) 17 *J. Legal Writing Inst.* xvii at xviii (there is not and cannot be a single structure that is the right answer to the question of how argumentative thought is best conveyed from the mind of a writer to the mind of the reader). See generally, *The Carnegie Report*, above n. 38; *The Best Practice*, above n. 38. What is more, the word *client* derives from the Latin verb *cluere*, which according to Lucie White mean to "be named, hear oneself named." It was a word that grew from the ancient Roman practice of naming persons under the patronage of patricians as *clientem* because they were known by the name of their patrons. It is in this sense that lawyering is the practice of speaking for the client and therefore ought to be client-centred and client-empowering. See Clark D. Cunningham, above n. 54; Lucie E. White, Goldberg v Kelly on the Paradox of Lawyering for the Poor (1990) 56 *Brook. L. Rev.* 861 at 862 n. 2. Ruth A. Robbins, An Introduction to Applied Storytelling and to this Symposium (2008) 14 *J. Legal Writing Institute* 3. Law and literature is strong current in the legal academy. Robert McPeake, Fitting Stories into Professional Legal Education-The Missing Ingredient (2007) 41 *L. Teacher Intl' J. Leg.Educ.* 303 (ways of teaching storytelling as a lawyering skill). Generally, three are three strands of the scholarship. The first examines legal issues and representations of lawyers that appear in literary works. The second uses the tools of literary theory to analysis judicial decisions and legislative enactments. The third strand focuses on the transformative power of stories. See Paul Gewirtz, Narrative and Rhetoric in Law, in Peter Brooks & Paul Gewirtz, eds., *Law Stories: Narrative and Rhetoric in Law*, 1996.

[63] Classical rhetoric reputed to have began in the fifth century B.C.E. continued for nearly 1,000 years of the Greco-Roman history. It started with scholars like Socrates, followed by Plato, Aristotle, Cicero and Quintilian. See Aristotle, *The Rhetoric* (trans. W. Rhys Roberts, 1965) available at htpp://www.iastate.edu/honey1/Rhetoric/ (accessed Sep, 2016); Marcus Tullius Cicero, *De Inventione* (trans. H.M. Hubbell, 1949); Marcus Tullius Cicero, *De Oratore* (trans. E.W. Sutton, 1942); Marcus Fabius Quintilian, *Institutio Oratoria* (H.E. Butler, 1954). See Michael Frost, Introduction to Classical Rhetoric: A Lost Heritage (1999) 8 *S. Cal. Interdisc. L.J.* 613 (traces the history of rhetoric and argumentation to Corax of Syracuse). See also, Bernard Jackson, *Law, Fact and Narrative Coherence*, Deborah Charles Pub., 1988; Walter R. Fisher, *Human Communication as Narrative: Towards a Philosophy of Reason, Value, and Action*, U.S.C. 1989; Robert Burns, *A Theory of the Trial*, Princeton Univ. Press, 1999.

[64] Michael R. Smith, *Advanced Legal Writing: Theories and Strategies in Persuasive Writing*, Aspen Law & Bus., 2002, 22; Aristotle, *On Rhetoric* (transl. George A. Kennedy, Oxford Univ. Press, 1991); George A. Kennedy, *A New History of Classical Rhetoric*, Princeton Univ. Press, 1998; Stephen Toulmin, *The Use of Argument*, Cambridge Univ. Press, 1958. For detail discussion on a theory of

reasoning embodied in the content of the communication) is the process of persuading using substance and logical argument, such as statute law, case-law and policy. *Pathos* (persuasion accomplished through the emotional response of the audience to the communication) on the other hand is persuasion through emotive argument. *Ethos* (persuasion accomplished through the perceived character or reputation of the speaker) refers to establishing and maintaining credibility in the eyes of the audience by showing intelligence, character and good will.[65] The three paths are often depicted as the "rhetorical triangle:" the three paths leading into one another. *Logos* affects the pathos of the audience and simultaneously affects the perception of the ethos of the author, while the pathos of the audience affects how they perceive the ethos of the author and how they receive the logos of the argument.[66]

Aristotle for example, reminded advocates that the rhetorical pathways are fundamentally pragmatic this way: a logical argument will not persuade an audience if the author is perceived as a baboon. Also, a respected author whose reputation is beyond question will not persuade if her argument is riddled with logical fallacies and flaws. Similarly, an ironclad argument delivered in a manner that antagonizes the audience or one in which the audience questions the integrity and credibility of the author will not persuade.[67]

Logos is taught as doctrinal lessons. Students are very familiar with its basic structure: 'think like a lawyer.' That IRAC already teaches them. Traditional legal pedagogy makes it staple legal classroom diet. Pathos and ethos are not usual dietary prescriptions there. The reasons for this are numerous. Logos it is said is what stands out legal argument from other forms of argument. It is what makes law rational and a near science. The knowledge of law and training in logos is what makes law a distinct profession, what makes legal training unique. Yes, it has

---

persuasion, see J. Christopher Rideout, Storytelling, Narrative Rationality, and Legal Persuasion (2008) 14 *J. Legal Writing Inst.* 53 (in answer to the question 'what is it about narratives that make them persuasive in the law,' he stated that (1) narratives are innate ways of understanding and structuring human experience; this makes them inherently persuasive; (2) narrative models go beyond models of persuasion based on formal or informal logic, to encompass 'narrative rationality; ' (3) narratives embody several properties that are psychologically persuasive: (a) coherence (a formal property); correspondence (a formal property); (c) fidelity (a substantive property) Id at 55. See also the interesting read, W. Lance Bennett & Martha S. Feldman, *Reconstructing Reality in the Courtroom: Justice and Judgment in American Culture*, Rutgers Univ. Press, 1981 (the social science researchers states that American criminal trial is organized around storytelling).

[65]Smith, above n. 64.

[66]Linda Levine & Kurt M. Saunders, Thinking Like a Rhetor (1993) 43 *J. Legal Educ.* 108; Michael Frost, Ethos, Pathos and Legal Audience (1994) 99 *Dick L. Rev.* 85. See also Michael Frost, Justice Scalia's Rhetoric of Dissent: A Greco-Roman Analysis of Scalia's Advocacy in the VMI Case (2002) 91 *KY. L.J.* 167.

[67]Murray, above n. 17; Frost, above n. 66.

been suggested that the female embodiment of 'justice' found in law institutions and offices is always blindfolded because we do not want justice to see anything.[68] No one would seriously doubt this stance. Instructively, appellate judges focus more on *logos*. But that is the much it can go. Since lawyering is about persuasion, then attention must necessarily be paid to *pathos* and *ethos*. What is more, to the extent that legal practice focuses on all three aspects of persuasion, legal writing teachers must encourage their students to write recursively than sticking to the linear *IRAC* style. Teaching persuasion through the non-rational factors of *pathos* and *ethos* can be achieved by storytelling, while the tension between *logos, pathos* and *ethos* offer teachers opportunity to teach values. There is no question about it: overemphasizing of doctrine at the expense of skills and professional responsibility undermines professionalism and does not train students for the practice of law.[69] To see human conflict through the prism of legal abstraction only cannot help society to challenge the complexity of human conflict.

Facts and narrative reasoning are important components of *pathos*. Accordingly, good writers are encouraged to tell stories in all section of the brief, especially in the argument (*confirmatio*) section of legal documents, the introduction (*exordium*) section, the statement of facts (*narratio*) section, and the conclusion (*peroratio*) section to stress the facts of the case in such a way as to fully engage the emotions of the audience.[70]

Using the respondent brief in *Atlantic Airline* v. *Musa* in Part IV section 2 above, how did the brief writer employ the three elements of persuasion?

The introduction narrates the facts generating the appeal against a judgment in his favour, affording him the opportunity to make an emotional appeal

---

[68] Martin Jay, Must Justice Be Blind? The Challenges of Images to the Law, in Costas Douzinas& Lynda Neads, eds., *Law and Image*, Univ. Chicago Press, 1999, 21. See generally, James P. Eyster, Lawyer as Artist: Using Significant Moments and Obtuse Objects to Enhance Advocacy (2008) 14 *J. Legal Writing Inst.* 87 (a discussion of how to apply key techniques of the visual artists-the obtuse objet and significant moments to legal advocacy and their persuasive sting according to art history scholars, aestheticians, psychologists, and psycholinguists). For a discussion on the mental structures (rationality) that raise human cognition, see George Lakoff, *Women, Fire, and Dangerous Things: What Categories Reveal about the Mind*, Univ. Chicago Press, 1987.

[69] The first chapter of the *Carnegie Report* (79-81) which identifies and describes the traditional pedagogy of legal education, analogizing it with the concept borrowed from linguistics, describes its four structures: the surface structure, the deep structure, the tacit structure and the shadow structure. The surface structure is that commonly observable in class. The teacher using the Socratic method takes the students through the cases asking a series of questions. The deep structure is the essence of the first. Here the students are encouraged to think like lawyer. The tacit structure is that the student's personal sense of morality is not necessary in resolving legal conflicts. The shadow structure is about clinical training of students to act as lawyers. See above n. 8. The Report states that the weakness of legal education occurs primarily in the tacit and shadow structures. See Mark Yates, The Carnegie Effect: Elevating Practical Training Over Liberal Education in Curricular Reform (2011) 17 *J. Legal Writing Inst.* 233 at 235-236.

[70] Murray, above n. 17.

(pathos) for the appeal court to confirm the trial court's judgment. It also uses logos by stating the rule that governed the resolution of the dispute at the lower court, the undefended list procedure of Order 10 of the Gongola High Court Rules. The statement of the case/facts is a full narrative consisting of logos, pathos and ethos. In it the brief-writer seeks to bring the dispute within the context of the Legal Practitioners Act that provides the legal standard for the demand for professional services (logos). The writer then demonstrates that the bill forwarded to the appellant was not contested or disputes, neither was the bill paid despite repeated demands (pathos). The credibility and reputation of the respondent is bolstered by waiting for upwards of 41 months before commencing an action for recovery (ethos). Next, is the question for determination section. The section supplies the enthymeme relevant to resolve the appeal (logos). Noteworthy however, the section is not couched as a thesis which would have supplied the appeal court a front answer (ethos).[71] In the rule section, the brief-writer provides the legal standard to govern the issue, by supplying the general major premise for the enthymeme [or what some may prefer to call the deductive syllogism] (*logos*). In this section also the writer demonstrates his skills in researching the law that the complain of the appellant is not about how the undefended list procedure plays out in litigation, thereby bring to fore his grounding as respected researcher who has distilled the substance of the appeal (*ethos*). The section on rule explanation combines all the three forms of persuasion. In explaining how the undefended list procedure has been interpreted and applied based on inductive reasoning, the writer applies logos. By further demonstrating how the courts have analysed and synthesized in factual situations over time the rule on undefended list procedure, he induces the reader emotionally to apply the rules in the instant case in the respondent's favour. The brilliant synthesizing of the cases for the judges so that they have no need to do the research themselves is credibility plus for the writer (*ethos*). The rule application/facts section is in fact employs several levels of logos, pathos and ethos, as the brief-writer intersperse rule, rule explanation, stories and conclusion into one mould and square. The minor premise for the enthymeme on the issue of alleged breach is analysed (*logos*). He uses the narrative reasoning to make the necessary emotive appeal (*pathos*), while the proper intersperse of the facts with the rules of precedent establishes the writers 'reputation as a good brief-writer in the eyes of the judges (*ethos*). The section on conclusion is it. It reaches a conclusion on the enthymeme (*logos*) and

[71] Framing question for determination in the form of thesis is not a common practice with Nigerian lawyers, but it enjoys the advantage of supplying an interim conclusion, which is pleasing to impatient readers. See Murray, above n. 17.

indicates to the reader that the discussion has come to an end, the enthymeme properly applied (*ethos*).

Any lawyer reading the brief will readily see that even though the brief does not follow the *IRAC* structure, it is a good brief. All its content follows an agreed-upon analytical elements, intelligent by lawyers and judges modest count, of a good brief. It articulates the rule, explains it and any ambiguities thereto, stating how the rule should apply in the instant case. Noteworthy of mention, it uses the intersperse style of argumentation. Facts and the rules are argued together in all material sections from introduction to conclusion, thereby adopting the three pathways of persuasion, logos, pathos and ethos, without necessarily following a rigid rule-based *IRAC* formula that keeps the components tightly separated from one another. The brief writer constructs her own schemata for communicating legal analysis in a manner within the bracket of grammar understandable to the legal community and readers.

This is the kind of brief-writing style that our students need to learn about. That legal writing requires a variety of ways to communicate the facts of any given case, and that style can differ depending on the type of analysis required (whether it is a facts-intensive case or rule-intensive litigation). For example, if an analysis requires discussion on policy, such as is usually the case in regulatory practice, rule explanation may be heavier with lighter facts/scientific articulation. If on the other hand, it is a matter having to do with say, custody or matters of asylum or matrimonial proceedings, which require intensive-facts litigation, stories will be heavier than rule explanation.[72]

Recognizing that legal reasoning often rest on probabilities is what should encourage legal writing teachers to model analysis in ways that incorporates logos, pathos and ethos in writing assignments, a project greatly helped by the indeterminacy thesis of facts and language.[73]

Comparing the Persuasive Power of *IRAC* with the Flexible (Non-*IRAC*) Styles of Writing

All of this talk will be unhelpful if we fail to compare the persuasiveness of *IRAC* and non-*IRAC* structure of legal writing, using writing analogy drawn from non-flexible and flexible, contextual styles. First let us illustrate the point from a variety of employment perspective requiring legal writing. Legal employment was

---

[72] For illustrative brief writing of fact-intensive cases, see for example, Miller, above n. 54; White, above n. 54; Stacy Caplow, Putting the "I" in Writing: Drafting an A/Effective Personal Statement to Tell a Winning Refuge Story (2008) 14 *J. Legal Writing Inst.* 249 (the use of pathos in asylum law).

[73] For example, see Michael D. Murray, above n. 64. See also, Festus Emiri & Ayuba Giwa, Metaphoric Thinking About Law as Language and Lawyering as Translation: Reflection on Legal Clinic [2008] *Enugu State University of Technology Journal of Public Law* 15.

traditional thought to fall within two categories: litigation and transactional lawyering. With the growth of regulation in the modern state, we may now add regulatory practice, as a new area of legal practice.[74] In regulatory practice, lawyers spend time advising clients about the nature and scope of their obligations under various regulatory regimes, ranging from employment, banking, telecommunication, food and drug, health care, immigration, tax, transportation and a host many others; while representing their clients before government regulators, whether in drafting comments in response to notices of proposed rulemaking or in agency-level enforcement proceedings. On the government side, regulatory lawyers focus on writing legislation, developing regulations, drafting guidance documents, and pursuing enforcement actions. We have therefore chosen to discuss the persuasive viability of the *IRAC* and non-*IRAC* organizational structure in legal writing within the three categories: transactional lawyering, regulatory practice and litigation practice.

1. Transactional Documents

Let us first consider transactional legal writing. How can lawyers be more persuasive in drafting transactional documents? Does the linear, stock-position writing or the flexible, narrative technique more properly persuade and communicate?[75] What analogical lessons can be learnt from this comparison that can be transposed to the linear IRAC and flexible non-IRAC techniques of writing? It is generally reasoned that the inflexible, copied from precedent style of writing or drafting is what matters in transactional documents. Contextual, flexible, story like style should have no place in drafting transactional document. Such reasoning is rooted in the thinking that documents are essentially expository texts, designed to inform rather than relay a story. For example, in a simple conveyance, all the document needs tell (so it is erroneously thought) to state that the seller desires to sell at a given price and the buyer is interested in the purchase. The usual conveyancing clause relating to property description, covenants and the like are added to complete documentation.

Storytelling teachers however know better. We say that the fact that documents are essentially expository should not ordinarily abyss the narrative style in their drafting. It is flawed reasoning to think that stories enjoy a lesser

[74] Kristin E. Hickman, Designing a Broader Regulatory Practice Curriculum, *RegBlog*, Penn Programme on Regulation, Aug. 15, 2016.

[75] Susan M. Chesler& Karen J. Sneddon, Once Upon a Transaction: Narrative Techniques and Drafting (2016) 68 *Oklahoma L. Rev.* 263

place of prominence in transactional lawyering.[76] The reason isn't farfetched. Think for once. Every transaction is in truth a story. It is the stories that give life to transactions. It is it that metamorphoses to become the basis of agreements and the ultimate clauses of documents executed by the parties. Think for once, is a conveyance not a story of negotiation, title investigation, and the purchase agreement? If it is, then it is plausible to imagine that the ability of lawyers to visualise and conceptualise transactions as stories benefits the negotiation, drafting, implementation, interpretation, and the ultimate enforceability of the transaction document.[77]

Let us consider how good lawyering requires contextualising transactional documents in areas where there is stock-story perception.[78] The existence of adverse stock story should discourage linear drafting style without effort to customize the document to reflect the client's specific goals. One such areas highlighted by Chesler and Sneddon, is premarital (prenuptial) agreement. Medieval history tells us that these were agreements specifically designed for protection of women at a time when they enjoyed no property rights. They were essentially conceived to detail financial and non-financial responsibilities in the economic alliances between families created by marriage. Courts were however reluctant in enforcing them because they were thought of as encouraging divorces. That is the stock story behind premarital agreements.[79] It is also the thinking that since most premarital agreements were widely used by the rich, then such

---

[76]Chesler & Sneddon, above n. 75 (The learned writers drawing analogical on narrative techniques highlight the use of stock stories, plot and narrative movement, character, point of view, narrative setting, themes, and motifs across a spectrum of transactional documents).

[77]Chesler & Sneddon, above n. 75 at 268 ("narrative techniques further the attorney-client relationship by promoting a closer examination of individual client goals and designing documents to further those goals").

[78] Stock stories are conventional story type stripped of essential details but they carry cognitive models easily inferred by those who hear or perceive them. For example, it is easy to stereotype a man on dreadlocks wearing jean as a Rastafarian. Such automatic identification may prevent audience engagement with contrary narrative experience. For reading on stock story and cognition see, Vicki Schultz, Telling Stories About Women and Work: Judicial Interpretation of Sex Segregation in the Workplace in Title VII Cases Raising the Lack of Interest Argument (1990) 103 *Harv. L. Rev.* 1749; Mary Chiarella, Silence in Court: The Devaluation of the Stories of Nurses in the Narratives of Health Law (2000) 7 *Nursing Inquiry* 191 (the stock story of nurses as caregivers to patients, handmaiden of doctors or ministering angels, undermines the status of nurses which translated to a framework that devalues their professional opinion); Stephen Paskey, The Law Is Made of Stories (2014) 11 *Legal Comm. & Rhetoric: JALWD* 51 at 69.

[79] For a history and jurisprudence of premarital agreements, see Baker, History of English Law, *Snell's Equity*; Judith Younger, Perspectives on Ante-nuptial Agreements (1988) 40 *Rutgers L. Rev.* 1059; Brian Bix, Bargaining in the Shadow of Love: The Enforcement of Premarital Agreements and How We Think About Marriage (1998) 40 *WM & Mary L. Rev.* 145; J. Thomas Oldman, With All My Worldly Goods I Thee Endow, or Maybe Not: A Re-evaluation of the Uniform Premarital Agreement Act After Three Decades (2001) 19 *Duke J. Gender L. & Pol'y* 83.

agreements is limited to high-net-worth individuals or families. That is the stock character of ante nuptial agreements.

Faced with this stock position, how would students stewed in the *IRAC* linear writing style draft a premarital agreement for a client? The natural drafting technique after receiving client's instruction would be to take a precedent book, copy and paste with a few modifications. That being the case, they would have done nothing to thinker the stock story surrounding the type of agreement. In the event of litigation arising from the document, the interpreting authority is deprived the narrative benefits the client's specific needs so its implementation, interpretation, and the ultimate enforceability of the transaction document may just well follow the usual run of reluctance by the court to enforce.

All of that can change by simply using a recursive, storytelling writing technique that tells a story. Employing, say the narrative style, enables the drafter to take deliberate steps to thinker and reframe the document in a way that can supplant stock position. After all, what is wrong to clarify financial aspects of marriage that will eventually end in death or divorce? The learned writers give a few examples of how the document can be contextualized to displace stock story misunderstandings. One simple way suggested is to modify the standard acontextual premarital recital. The standard draft would look like this:

A. Marriage is intended soon between the parties.
B. Each party desires, before entering into the marriage, to know just what the rights of property are to be in each other's estate.

Standard draft

No question about it. The recital is accurate. But it misses context.[80] So it falls within the mould of stock story surrounding premarital agreements. To avoid the stock-position label, the recital could well be reframed this way:

A. Each party acknowledges and stipulates the purpose of this Agreement is not to promote or procure a divorce or dissolution of marriage, but to provide for marital tranquillity by agreeing on the property and support rights of each other at commencement of marriage.

B. The parties have determined that the marriage between them shall have a better chance of success if the rights and claims that accrue to each of them as a result of their marriage are determined and finalized by this Agreement.

Contextualised draft

This latter writing technique says it all. It contextualizes the party's

[80]Chesler & Sneddon, above n. 75 at 273.

intention, supplants the stock position, eliminates ambiguity, reframes the narrative by highlighting the party's specific goals. Deliberate use of this narrative non-IRAC paradigm as in the example above, puts the clients on the centre burner and leverages their presence to further their intention.[81]

2. Regulatory legal writing

It can no longer be seriously doubted that regulation is now part of modern society. Virtually no part of society or our lives is untouched by regulation. Government is gradually turning modern societies to regulatory states. There is virtually no part of our lives unregulated by the state. The state regulates education, food, movement, businesses, etc. It regulates who can vote, how to vote, what we eat, listen to or hear from the radio or television, and many others. It is not uncommon to hear individuals, groups and businesses that rail under legislation and regulations which threaten their existence and concerns question the ambits of the powers of the state. It is therefore important to legally analysis the range of activities covered in the modern state by growing legislation and regulation, especially in the context of whether the regulatory state is effectively mitigating the economic and non-economic problems regulation addresses. Yes, from communication fees, grazing, food safety, financial institutions to welfare and education, government reels out one form of regulation or the other.[82] The key to regulatory law is rooted in the philosophy that legal rules are nothing but responses to market failure.[83]

---

[81] On furthering other narrative techniques in transactional drafting, see Chesler & Sneddon, above n. 75. See also Frank L McGuane, Jr. & Kathleen A. Hogan, Drafting the Agreement Not to Encourage Dissolution, in *Colorado Prac., Family Law & Practice*, chapter 39.7, Drafting the Agreement-Not to Encourage Dissolution, 2nd ed. 2012, cited in Chesler & Sneddon, Id at 273 n. 45 (narrative in ante nuptial agreement); Joseph M. Williams & Gregory G. Colomb, Telling Clear Stories: A Principle of Revision that Demands a Good Character (1996) 5 *Persp. Teaching Legal Res. & Writing* 14 (on descriptive information about the parties in the background or recital section of agreements to provide three dimensional reference to the parties, such as on which includes (i) the human character of the parties, say (ii) seller and (iii) buyer rather than the two-dimensional reference of only seller and buyer).

[82] For literature on regulatory law, see Sidney A. Shapiro & Joseph P. Tomain, *Regulatory Law and Policy*, 1993; Stephen Breyer, *Regulation and Its Reform*, 1984; Samuel Peltzman, Towards a More General Theory of Regulation (1976) 19 *J. L. & Econ.* 211; Sidney A. Shapiro, Keeping the Baby and Throwing Out the Bathwater: Justice Breyer's Critique of Regulation (1995) 8 *Admin. L.J. Am. Univ.* 721; John Manning & Matthew, Legislation and Regulation; Lisa, Edward Rubin & Kevin Stack, *The Regulatory State*; Geoffrey P. Miller, *The Law of Governance, Risk Management and Compliance* (focus on risk definition, assessment, and management, which requires the identification of risk and ex ante preventive action); See also Penn Programme on Regulation at the University of Pennsylvania, *RegBlog*, especially *RegBlog* five-part series, Innovations in Teaching Regulatory Law, Aug. 15, 2016. Generally, after the financial thunderstorms between 2007 and 2009 in the U.S. compliance and regulatory programmes sprouted like mushrooms in both the U.S and around the world.

[83] Joseph P. Tomain& Sidney A. Shapiro, Analysing Government Regulation (1997) 49 *Admin. L. Rev.* 376 at 402 ("The presence of ... market failure serves as a justification for the government to enter

How can narratives be interspersed with regulation to persuade. Let us imagine that the government of Layanda, a pastoral and agrarian country seeks to acquire land from farmers to be used as ranches for pastoral purposes because of constant clashes between nomadic herdsmen and farmers over grazing land. Assuming a lawyer is hired to oppose the legislative proposal before Parliament, how can she structure persuasive writing in this regards? An integrated technique using *logos, pathos* and *ethos* stands the chance more of persuading than a non-narrative rule-based approach.

She may need to draft the letter using the section technique, beginning with the narrative section, using *pathos.* This section would ordinarily employ the storytelling technique - a narrative plot telling how farmer come unto their land, how land is reified and connected with ancestralship, why farming is an integral part of the lives of her clients, transcending property-personhood dichotomy, how her clients stable agrarian living, culture, tradition and existence is troubled by herdsmen, what efforts have been put in place to peacefully resolve the troubles, how it has failed to resolve the trouble, and why their ancestral rights (as protagonists) should be protected in the face of two invading antagonists, the herdsmen, with implicit support of the state; why it should be of concern in a modern democratic state; and the moral justification for preventing taking.[84]

It is after a narrative of this sort that the lawyer can then resort to *logos*, sometimes mixing it with *pathos* and *ethos* to create effect, in the section on rules, rules explanation, interpretation of law, policy and application. The section on rules could begin by asking the rhetoric question of 'why government regulate activities?' from there the argument could build up to rule explanation. The state regulates for two main reasons: (i) for economic or (ii) non-economic (social) reasons. But in all cases to correct market failure.[85] The reason for this is because

---

and fix a market in order to achieve better allocative efficiency. . ..regulation is unnecessary in the absence of efficiency defects.")

[84] This type of dramatic introduction aligns with literary theory and can be persuasive to the reader. For illustration of its usefulness of pathos in persuasion, see Elyse Pepper, The Case for "Thinking Like a Filmmaker:" Using Lars von Trier's Dogville as a Model for Writing a Statement of Facts (2008) 14 *J. Legal Writing Inst.* 171; Stacy Caplow, above n. 72 (the use of pathos in asylum law).

[85] For literature analysis of the economic justification for regulation see, Sidney A. Shapiro & Joseph O. Tomain, *Regulatory Law and Policy: Cases and Materials,* LexisNexis, 1993; Stephen G. Breyer & Richard B. Stewart, *Administrative Law and Regulatory Policy: Problems Text and Cases,* 3rd ed., Aspen Pub., 1992, 5-11, (7th ed. 2015); Richard Posner, *Economic Analysis of Law,* 4th ed., 1992, 367-368; Joseph P. Tomain & Sidney A. Shapiro, Analysing Government Regulation (1997) *Admin. L. Rev.* 377. It must be noted however that not every market failure invites an ex ante regulatory solution. A great deal of market failures are addressed directly by courts through common-law or statutory remedies that award damages ex post to injured persons. Thus, regulation would be necessary if a market fails, and courts are unable to address the problem with the remedial ambits of law. See also George J. Stigler, The Theory of Economic (1971) 2 *Bell J. Econ. & Mgmt. Sci.* 3; Richard A. Posner, Theories of Economic Regulation (1974) 5 *Bell J. Econ. & Mgmt. Sci.* 335; Samuel

legal economists have long believed that the invisible hand of the market creates allocative efficiency and distributive gains.[86] Under an economic justification, an absence of market failure makes it unnecessary for government to regulate, such as change the assignment of rights and obligations, which the bill proposes.[87] However, since markets can sometimes be defective (which is referred to as 'market failure') there will be justification for government to regulate market to create the necessary allocative efficiency. For social justification, the analysis starts from the premise that government is necessitated by a people who set up a political structure on certain core values (generally referred to in economics are 'market inalienable') on how they wish to be organised.[88] If markets therefore operate in such manner that discounts the values, the government will be justified in intervening to correct the defects by conforming market operation to those

---

Peltzman, Towards a More General Theory of Regulation (1976) 19 *J. Law & Econ.*211; Benjamin H. Barton, Why Do We Regulate Lawyers? An Economic Analysis of the Justification for Entry and Conduct Regulation (2001) 33 *Ariz. St. L.J.* 429.

[86] Adam Smith, *Wealth of the Nation*. Global demand for deregulation is grounded on the assumption that free market is better than government regulation. See Herbert Hovenkamp, *Enterprise and American Law: 1836-1937*, Cambridge, Massachusetts: Harvard Univ. Press, 1991; Cass R. Sunstein, *After the Rights Revolution, Preconceiving the Regulatory State*, 1990. See also for example Elizabeth Landes and Richard Posner, The Economics of Baby Shortage, (1987) 7 *J. Leg. St.* 323 (advocates an adoption market for babies). But cf. Frankel & Miller, The Inapplicability of Market Theory to Adoption (1986) 67 *Boston Univ. L. Rev.* 99; Prichard, A Market for Babies? (1984) 34 *Univ. Toronto L.J.* 341.

[87] Ronald Coase, The Problem of Social Cost (1960) 3 *J. Law & Econ.* 1; see reprinted in Ronald Coase, *The Firm, the Market, and the Law,* Chicago Univ. Press, 1988. The paper is reputed to be the most cited law paper in the world. See Fred R. Shapiro, The Most Cited Law Review Article Revisited (1996) 71 *Chi.-Kent L. Rev.* 751. See also, W.N. Landes & Richard Posner, The Influence of Economics on Law: A Quantitative Study (1993) 36 *J. of Law & Econs. 385,* (on recent study which suggest that the major American law journals cite articles using the economic approach more than articles using other approach in legal scholarship).

[88] Market inalienable follows commodification argument that certain kind of activities are of intrinsic value that a market valuation of them is inappropriate in that it distorts significantly their tangibility. Inappropriateness of market principles to such values has often rested on lines of property-personhood dichotomy and incommensurability hypothesis. See *Hegel's Philosophy of Rights*, London: Oxford Univ. Press, translated by T.M. Knox, 1952, s.44) cited in Neil Neil Duxbury, Do Markets Degrade? (1996) 59 *MLR* 331. For further reading on incommensurability in philosophical literature see, Joseph Raz, Mixing Values, *Proceedings of the Aristotelian Society* 83; J. Griffin, Mixing Values, (1991) 65 *Proceedings of the Aristotelian Society* 65; J. Griffin, Are There Incommensurable Values? (1977) 7 *Philosophy & Public Affairs* 39; Joseph Raz, *The Morality of Freedom*, Oxford: Clarendon Press, 1986, 339-340; Margaret Radin, *Reinterpreting Property*, Chicago: Univ. of Chicago Press, 1993; Brian Bix, *Law, Language and Legal Determinacy,* Oxford: Clarendon Press, 1993, 96; Cass Sunstein, Incommensurability and Valuation in Law (1994) 92 *Michigan L. Rev.* 779, Anderson, *Value in Ethics and Economics,* Cambridge, Mass: Harvard Univ. Press, 150. But cf. Schnably, Property and Pragmatism: A Critique of Radin's Theory of Property and Personhood (1993) 45 *Stanford L. Rev.* 347. Neil Duxbury, Law, Markets and Valuation (1995) 61 *Brooklyn L. Rev.* 657; Guido Calabresi & Douglas Melamed, Property Rules, Liability Rules and Inalienability: One View of the Cathedral (1972) 85 *Harv. Law Rev.* 1089; Festus Emiri, A Market Approach to Vocational Legal Education in Nigeria in *Trajectory of Nigerian Law: Underneath is Festschrift of Dean Smith* (ed.) Ibidapo-Obe, Lagos: Lagos Univ. Press, 2015, 144.

values. In effect, law can be used to also constrain markets. From this paradigm, regulation is unnecessary in the absence of efficiency defects.[89]

Honourable Parliamentarians, the difference between economic and social justification for regulation can be liken to that between *efficiency* and *equity*. While both can be strong currents in any political system, trumping one another, both cannot be ignored in regulatory.[90]

Economic regulation addresses three types of market failures: (i) natural monopoly; (ii) excessive competition; (iii) and economic rents. Regulatory prescriptions for correction are either by price control or entry and exit controls.

On the other hand, non-economic reasons for regulation address four market failures: negative externalities, asymmetric information, scarcity and public goods. Government response to this market failure is with the tools of regulatory or allocative controls.

Why is a discussion on the justificatory bases for regulation and the tools of regulation necessary? Simply this. To prevent what Justice Breyer has termed regulatory mismatches.[91]

The next section could then be termed "the bill and justificatory analysis."

In this section the writer situates the analysis in the context of the bill, by analysing why and how it possibly sits outside of or in the regulatory square in section 2 above. An intersperse discussion employing the triangular persuasion techniques will come to fuller play here.

For example, the writer could employ the Coase theorem regulating basic assignment of rights in the context of incompatible-users right, analogically extending it to the herdsmen-farmers incompatible land use, to show that forced taking in the form of compulsory acquisition power vested in the proposed commission does not align with economic logic.[92]

---

[89]Tomain & Shapiro, above n. 78.

[90] Arthur A. Leff, Economic Analysis of Law: Some Realism about Nominalism (1974) 60 *Virginia L. Rev.* 451 (a critique of pure economic analysis to legal and social questions in reaction to the first publication of Richard A. Posner's, *Economic Analysis of Law* book).

[91] Stephen Breyer, *Regulation and its Reform*, Cambridge, MA: Harvard Univ. Press, 1982, 191-368; Stephen Breyer, Analysing Regulatory Failure: Mismatches, Less Restrictive Alternatives and Reform (1979) 92 *Harv. L. Rev.* 549 at 586-604.

[92]Coase theorem is the most celebrated application of the concept of opportunity cost. See Ronald H. Coase, The Problem of Social Cost, (1960) 3 *Law & Economics* 1, see reprint in Coase, *The Firm, the Market, and the Law,* Chicago Univ. Press, 1988. See also Ronald Coase, The Nature of the Firm (1937) 4 *Economica*386. The theorem posits that under conditions of rational cooperation, full information and zero transactional costs, parties will negotiate around inefficiencies to allocate rights in order to establish optimal level of resource deployment. See also George Stigler, Economics: The Imperial Science? (1984) 86 *Scand. J. Econ* 301 at 304. Economists also think so of law. Efficiency in a legal situation arises if a right is given to a party willing to pay more for it. This explains why if the Coasean market is unavailable courts are urged to imagine what the parties would have agreed to in a hypothetical Coasean market. Since the right to a resource will have been

In this section the writer would be required to use the form of narrative that brings to fore, character development like a fiction writer, so that the reader can quickly spot the protagonist worthy of sympathy against the antagonist. The persuasive, skilled writer is here required to provide proof of each character in the trouble by piling objective detail, arranged in such a way to evoke emotional response by the reader. Again, argument using logos, pathos and ethos. The persuasive writer can then launch more missiles against the bill by drawing on the specific narrative of her client, regulatory justification, arguments showing why the bill does not come within the framework justification for economic or non-economic reasons and conclude.

No question about it. An argument that employs the three dimensions of rhetoric would be more convincing to Parliament than the linear inflexible writing style.

3. Litigation (brief) writing

We shall unashamedly use the scenario of Chestek to navigate the richness of flexible organizational structure over the usual non-flexible style. We have chosen to draw on the scenario used by the learned writer for many reasons.[93] (List the reasons)

The essence of the appellate brief is a story of adoption by a homosexual parent resisted by the state.[94] It is the story of Margaret Rubin, who is devastated by the loss of her homosexual partner, Francie Kohler, and the attempt of the legal system to take away her son from her, on the grounds that the marriage is not recognized by the *lex fori*, Old York, the residence of the parties. The gist of the matter is that both couple married of ten years and had a son, Johnnie, through *in vitro* fertilization (IVF). The marriage was entered into in Vermont, a state that

---

secured by the party willing to pay most for it, court are expected to mimic by auctioning entitlements to those who value them most - judged by each litigant's willingness to pay. See Jules Coleman, Economics and the Law: A Critical Review of the Foundations of the Economic Approach to Law (1984) 94 *Ethics* 649, Richard Posner, *Economic Analysis of Law*,8th ed., 2011. But cf. David Campbell, 'Ayer versus Coase; An Attempt to Recover the Issue of Equality in Law and Economics,' (1994) 21 *J. Law &* Society 434, for critique of law and economics pure materialistic theory of rights. But economists defend its position on the grounds that the term 'efficiency' when used to denote allocation of resources in which value is maximised does not extend to ethical criterion as basis for social decision-making. See Richard Posner, p. 16. But cf. Richard Posner, *The Problem of Jurisprudence*, Harvard Univ. Press, 1990, 375 (where learned writer doubted efficiency as an overreaching normative basis for law) and Guido Calabresi, *The Costs of Accidents: A Legal and Economic Analysis,* New Haven: Yale Univ. Press, 1970, 17-18 (argues that while efficiency should not be disregarded the legal system should draw a balance between consequentialist and principle-based ethics).

[93] Kenneth D. Chestek, The Plot Thickens: The Appellate Brief as Story (2008) 14 *J. Legal Writing Inst.* 127. For other great stories on how lawyers have written persuasive briefs, see....

[94] This story is fictional, product of a modified moot court problem from Indianapolis School of Law, Indiana University in 2004. See Chestek, above n. 93 at 128 n. 1.

permits the union of gay and lesbian couples. So what Margaret and Francie did was to leave Old York, a state that does not approve of lesbian marriage to marry in Vermont, a state that recognizes lesbian marriages. In fact, the Old York Supreme Court refuses to recognize the validity of Vermont gay marriages.

On the death of Francie, Margaret wanted to adopt Johnnie and continue to raise him. But Margaret's mother who has always been opposed to the lesbian marriage resisted the adoption. She asked the Old York State to declare Johnnie a dependent child and place him in a foster home because under the law Margaret has no legal claim to guardianship. The law does not recognize lesbian marriages. What is more, the state adoption prohibits homosexuals from adoption. That is the stage plotted in the story.

Faced with this fact-intensive situation what style of writing would be more persuasive to convince a court to permit Margaret to adopt Johnnie, a flexible or non-flexible analysis? What would be the shape of the IRAC argument here for Margaret? You can imagine it going this way: a review of the constitutionality of the Old York State adoption law. It will be dry and simply abstract with little or no power to convince. The technique will leave little room to dramatize the humanness of Margaret.

It can read this way:

1. Section on Introduction

This is an application by Margaret Rubin to adopt Johnnie, her son, against the wish of Francie Kohler's mother asking that Johnnie be declared a dependent child, placing him in a foster home. Margaret married Francie in 2000, ten year ago in Vermont, a state that permits gay and lesbian marriages. In the couple desire to mature and raise a child, they decided to go through IVF, which help give birth to Johnnie in 2003.

The couple and their son lived happily thereafter in Old York until Francie was killed in a car-pedestrian accident, necessitating the present application by Margaret to adopt Johnnie with a view of continuing his care under her superintendence. It is this application that Francie's mother is opposed to.

2. Section on Issue(s) for Determination

The main issue that arises for determination in this case is whether it is constitutional for the Old York statute to deny Margaret adoption rights over Johnnie, her child or put otherwise, whether Margaret should be entitled to succeed in her application for adoption under the adoption statute of Old York State.

3. Section on Rule

Section 19-67-2 provides that the following persons are eligible to adopt: (1) a husband and wife together, or (2) an adult who is not married. Subsection (B) however states that "homosexuals are not eligible to adopt under the statute.

Noteworthy of mention, subsection (B) was not in the original legislation. It was only added after a highly publicized incident of a prominent musician was convicted for sexually abusing an adopted child. See *State* v. *Smith* (1985) 489 O.Y. 142.

This said prohibition violates the constitution of the United States, especially the protected rights to privacy; right to family integrity; due process right and it discriminates homosexual rights to equal treatment.

(The remaining part of the section would then go on to relate how it does in specifics of say the Fourteenth Amendment, Due Process Clause (Amend. XIV, cl.3), Equal Protection Clause (Amend XIV, cl. 4) and the like)

It will end by asking the court to declare the Old York statute unconstitutional, especially when it is not narrowly tailored to serve a "compelling state interest."

4. Section on Application of Rules

This section would ordinarily synthesize the facts of the case with the rules asking the court to scrutinize the state legislation in the context of the constitution and the peculiar facts of Margaret.

5. Section on Conclusion

This section will pray the court to overturn the state legislation and declare Margaret eligible for adoption of Johnnie.

That is how an *IRAC* brief is likely to be structured. If in the brief-writer's opinion the brief involves multiple issues and sub-issues than the one issue plotted in this paper, then the writer will simply do a brief with multiple syllogisms. The writer may have to repeat the IRAC structure in multiple sections and sub-section, which ordinarily would involve rule, application and conclusion being repeated. To say the least, that can make the brief burdensome and a monotonous read.[95] Whether the single issue or multiple issues brief *IRAC* style is

[95] See Chestek, above n 93. But cf. Tracy Turner, Flexible IRAC: A Best Practice Guide (2015) 20 *J. Legal Writing Inst.* 233 (where the learned writer seeks to free IRAC from the its shackles by creating a best practice guide to it. The article argues that IRAC core syllogistic reasoning is still the template for good writing. See for example, outside the one-sequence IRAC, the writer makes useful suggestions on how to apply (i) "alternating IRAC" (IRARARAC)-places each application paragraph right after the corresponding rule paragraph so that a principle of law is applied as soon as it is introduced; (ii) "IRAC by paragraph" (IRACIRAIRAC)-an IRAC structure which bring each R and A together into a paragraph and add a topic sentence to unite them; (iii) "IRAC sentence"-an assertion about the legal impact of a fact followed by a parenthetical citation that proves the

used, the structure above certainly feels linear, mechanical and abstract. A heavy reliance on *logos*, with little of *pathos* and *ethos*.[96]

The *IRAC* brief plotted above has noticeable features: (i) It is rule-based. The U.S. Constitution is analysed and applied to the state legislation as possible topics for court scrutiny to determine if it is rational in the context of legitimate state interest; (ii) It is deeply rooted in rules, with little space for human narrative. The issue for determination is what sets the stage for the proper level of scrutiny. Invariably, the "R" becomes confined to a pure question of law, previous decisions of court measuring the application of the constitution to matters of rights; and (iii) Operating under the *logos* bracket of *IRAC* leaves little room to personalize the story of Margaret. A brief written in that style will hardly persuade. Such a mechanical attack on the statute will hardly persuade a court usually more interested in preserving the status of legislation.

A non-*IRAC* structure that plays the human drama of the case is more likely to help overcome the statutory barriers. Consciously thinking about the case as one requiring human elements of character, conflict, theme, and point of view can add the missing link. The learned writer suggests that employing the style of fictional writing can do the magic.[97] The transformational appellant brief written to the Supreme Court of Old York State is compelling that we have chosen to highlight some material sections of the brief to illustrated the persuasiveness of narrative structured briefs in especially facts-intensive legal writing. Its flow using narrative style would follow an organizational structure like this:

1. Section on Argument

Exposition (foundational law regarding standard of review, road map, legal conflict revealed)

A. Rising Action

i) First sub-plot (due process claim)-legal setting explained

Right to privacy and family integrity

---

asserted impact; (iv) "narrative add-ons: mixing facts into the I of IRAC"-adding a narrative element to IRAC by using the facts of the case to introduce and set the stage for each RA sequence to engage and persuade the reader. See also, Laura P. Graham, Why-RAC? Revisiting the Traditional Paradigm for Writing About Legal Analysis (2015) 63 *Kansas L. Rev.* 681 at 693 (where the writer suggests a fresh view of IRAC that recognizes its value as a basic analytical framework but loosens its grip on students as legal writers).

96 Chestek, above n. 93 at 163.

97 Fiction writer and film producers often plot stories using the structure of setting, conflict, character, point of view/voice, theme, plot, introduction/exposition, complicated incidents/rising action, climax, resolution/falling action, denouement and conclusion. See Anthony G. Amsterdam & Jerome S. Bruner, *Minding the Law*, Harv. Univ. Press, 2000, 20; Chestek, above n. 87; Elyse Pepper, The Case for Thinking Like a Filmmaker: Using Lars von Trier's Dogville as a Model for Writing a Statement of Facts (2008) 14 *J. Legal Writing Inst.* 171; James P. Eyster, Lawyer as Artist: Using Significant Moments and Obtuse Objects to Enhance Advocacy (2008) 14 *J. Legal Writing Inst.* 87

ii) Second sub-plot (equal protection claim)-legal setting explained Suspect classification and quasi-suspect classification

{CLIMAX (the factual and legal settings are complete, the conflict is apparent, the protagonists are at maximum peril)}

B. Falling action

i) Safe escape from peril tested (strict/intermediate scrutiny)

ii) Risky escape from peril tested (rational basis review)

C. Conclusion (denouement)

How does it all play out in the narrative constructed? Let us do an abstract of a few personalization highlighted by the learned writer. The facts section is very revealing. It goes like this:

> Margaret and Francie only wanted a child.
>
> Having committed themselves to each other emotionally and legally, they decided, as do many committed couples, that they wanted to raise a family. But the state of Old York told them that they were unfit parents, simply because they loved each other. Without knowing anything about the depth and sincerity of Margaret and Francie commitment to each other, and without any individualized investigation into their fitness as parents, the state categorically declared that they, along with all other gay and lesbian citizens, were unfit to adopt and raise children.

Facts

It then goes on to narrate how the couple devoted to their dream travelled to Vermont to legalize their relationship; how they attempted without success to seek agencies approval to adopt; how they then resorted to IVF which eventually produced Johnnie; what adjustment they made in their personal lives to create a happy family life and conducive environment for raising their child; how Francie got killed in an accident; the bond between Margaret and Johnnie; etc.

This narrative plot brings to fore the human elements of character (the story of a loving family, the kind law should promote, the hurdle erected by the state which prevents them to marry and raise a family, how they as protagonist scaled the pillars of hurdle erected by the state as antagonist, by the couple resort to travel to Vermont for their marriage and modern reproductive technology to raise a family). This is no doubt a great introduction preluding the beginning of the "rising action" of the story plot.

The rising action is the sudden intestate death of Francie, the couple not having planed and arranged their affairs. This absence is what introduces another antagonist to the scene, the mother of Francie, who now seeks a custodial regime over Johnnie. The rising action is part of the facts section which provides the setting for a discussion of the legal section, the relevant rules that govern the resolution of the facts situation.

Since the statute prohibits lesbian adoption, the strategy most likely to persuade will be to create at least a plausible reason to preserve the stable family life for Margaret and Johnnie, by showing the irrationality of disrupting a stable, loving home, and putting Johnnie in a state facility most probably devoid of love and attention. Here the writer gives a history of the unreasonableness of the prohibition, showing that it is adopted out of animus towards homosexuals without individualization perspective and consideration of the "best interest" of the child analysis and further that it is not one within the protected state legitimate interest.

No question about it. This narrative non-*IRAC* organization structure is more persuasive and compelling for being client-centred. The article happily tells that the brief written in the narrative form was successful as the Supreme Court of Old York held in favour of Margaret. The lesson from the narrative brief is that thinking about lawyering as storytelling gives us the opportunity to look behind and between black letter rules, which possibly reveals facts, language, structure and ideas that go beyond abstract stipulations of statute and opinion of courts.[98] Narrative style briefs help lawyers to wrestle with the law, to have it fit into their client's lived realities and experience, rather than funnelling their realities into what they think law requires. This is a hallmark of good legal writing.[99]

VII. How to Teaching Robust Legal Writing Skills

The rest of this paper will be devoted to what teachers can do to free their students from the shackles of *IRAC*. The paradigm no doubt can be a helpful tool for beginners of legal writing, who are faced with how to synthesis human complexities into logical form of reasoning. The basic quarrel with it is its inflexibility in capturing and evaluating legal questions by sheer rule-based formula.

How have some teachers been able to recreate flexible writing styles? Some commentators however think that *IRAC* should not be sacrificed for client's centeredness, urging that both are not necessarily adverse concepts.[100] Turner for example, argues that teachers can re-create flexible I*RAC* to capture complex

---

[98] Carolyn Grose, Storytelling Across the Curriculum: From Margin to Centre, from Clinic to Classroom (2010) 7 *J. Ass'n Legal Writing Directors* 37. On the need to develop case theory with the client at the centre, see cite from simulation paper.

[99] Carolyn Grose, Of Victims, Villains and Fairy Godmothers: Regnant Tales of Predatory Lending (2010) 2 *Northeastern Univ. L.J.* 97.

[100] Tracy Turner, above n. 95 (demonstrates who IRAC can be adapted to integrate narrative details often discouraged by rigid adherence to IRAC).

analysis without discarding *IRAC*. Her argument is that the paradigm is useful in legal writing if teachers can identify its variants under a common vocabulary that can be tailor-specific to the facts in controversy. So rather than abandon IRAC, she argues for its more sophisticated adaptations.[101] Let us examine her thesis in the context of a multidisciplinary approach.

In a bid to save *IRAC* the learned articulates four adaptation of the rule that should align it with fact centred lawyering: (i) one sequence *IRAC* (IRRRAAAC); (ii) alternating *IRAC* (IRACARAC); (iii) IRAC by paragraph (IRA-IRA-IRA-C); and; (iv) the IRAC sentence.[102] Even at this, she recognizes that the four flexible adaptation of *IRAC* will be limited in injecting narrative elements within them. To cure the supposed deficiency, she suggests what can be called *narrative add-ons* in mixing facts with the "I" of *IRAC*. The technique requires that the narrative element to *IRAC* should use the facts of the case to introduce and set the stage for each "RA" sequence.[103] The addition of narratives makes brief more persuasive.[104] Narrative introduction to the "R-A" sequence fits naturally more in the *IRAC* by paragraph structure (iii); than the other *IRAC* structures (i), (ii) and (iv).[105] These notwithstanding, the thesis paragraph in all the four flexible *IRAC* can be used to weld facts to the law to escape the monotony of a universal, rigid *IRAC* structure. She therefore encourages an incremental approach to organizational writing techniques starting with *IRAC* and then moving on as the students mature to the variety of *IRAC* models that incorporates narrative elements in a creative, self-reliant way.[106] That is itself a useful suggestion, but the flexible Chestek brief in "The Plot Thickens" referred to in Part VII section 3 above hardly follows any of the Turner's suggested style.[107]

---

[101]Turner, above n. 95. See also Tracy Turner, Finding Consensus in Legal Writing Discourse Regarding Organizational Structure: A Review and Analysis of the Use of IRAC and Its Progenies (2012) 9 *Legal Comm. & Rhetoric: JALWD* 351 (listing forty articles that discuss the benefit of IRAC, stating that the various acronyms formulated as alternatives to IRAC show no marked departure from the core concept of IRAC).

[102]Turner, above n. 95 at 237.

[103]Id at 258.

[104] Kenneth D. Chestek, Judging by the Numbers: An Empirical Study of the Power of Story (2010) 7 *J. ALWD* 8 ("a brief that relies purely on a logos-based argument will be lifeless, just as a single strand of the DNA molecule is incomplete. Winding in a solid story-based argument will bring the brief to life.)" Id at 18. See also Linda Edwards, Convergence of Analogical of Analogical and Dialectic Imagination in Legal Discourse (1996) 20 *Legal Stud. F.* 13.

[105]Turner, above n. 95 at 262 and 264.

[106]Turner, above n. 95 at 273 ("The faculty advisor of our moot court team has told me that the IRAC modifications are helpful to transitioning students from first-year course to moot court brief writing: rigidly IRAC-ed briefs do not tend to win competitions.)"

[107]Chestek, above n 93. See also the judicial opinion in *Baden, Kotoye* v. *CBN* [1989] All NLR 76; *Kigo* v. *Holman* [1980] NSCC 204, per Kayode Esho, JSC.

Learning Non-IRAC Writing Schemata

May be we should let our readers see how we teach narrative elements using non-*IRAC* structure in our legal methods and writing class. We often use the *Speluncean Explorers* as our teaching case. It is an imaginative case written by Fuller in 1949.[108] Largely taking the form of a fictional judgment, it presents the case involving five explorers who were caved in following a landslide in a cave. They learn via radio communication that without food they would likely to starve to death before rescue. On this basis they decide through throwing of a dice who should be killed and eaten for nourishment until rescue come their way. After the four survivors are rescued, they are charged and found guilty of the murder of the fifth explorer.

The appeal court offers five judicial responses to the facts whether they should be found guilty of breaching the law. Two judges affirm the conviction, two other overturn the conviction. The fifth judge is unable to reach a conclusion, so recuses himself. Since the court's decision is a tie, the original conviction stands.

We have used the *Speluncean* case over the years to teach our students how to analyse legal problems without necessarily following an *IRAC* style so that they can reason on basis gravitational organization scheme congruent with great brief writers' style and techniques. Immediately after mentioning the *IRAC* style, without emphasis that it is paradigmatic, we assign our students the *Speluncean* case to read and write their brief either in support of an affirmation of the four explorers conviction or in acquittal. We only forward to them the judgment of Truepenny, CJ, which states the facts of the case, the applicable law and His Lordship's judgment that the facts are suitable for executive clemency to mitigate the rigors of law.

After assigning the students to read the case, we ask that they also read the Criminal Code provision on unlawful homicide of murder.[109] Their writing assignment on murder takes this form:

1. Read the facts in the Speluncean's case.
2. Read the law on murder in Nigeria, especially section 316 that define the ingredients of the offence.
3. As you read the case, make note of facts which suggest that the four explorers can prima facie be tried for murder of Whetmore.

---

[108]It is based on an article by legal philosopher Lon L. Fuller, first published in the *Boner City* in 1949. The five possible solutions were delivered by judges sitting on the fictional "Supreme Court of Newgarth" in the year 4300. See Lon L. Fuller, The Case of the Speluncean Explorers (1949) 62 *Harv. L. Rev.*

[109]Criminal Code Act, s. 316 (definition of murder), Cap LFN 2004.

4. Identify and note what broad issues for determination you think the court ought to resolve.
5. Read the case and law again, this time noting what you consider to be the narrow issues that flow from the broad issues that need to be resolved by the court.
6. As you read the case again, identify what policy matters can impact on the construction of the narrow questions for determination.
7. Using legal imagination, common sense and your experience about cave exploration, if any, reconstruct what narrow questions and facts you consider more significant in resolving the broad question you identify in step 4.
8. What facts will you use in resolving the narrow questions and how do you think this merges with the applicable rule.
9. Based on your reformulated narrow issue and step 7, write a brief of argument to the court how the issue you identify should be resolved.

Most of our students after following steps 1 and 2 come up to think that a prima facie indictment can be raised for a murder trial of the four explorers. From there they generally frame the broad issue for determination to be "whether or not the killing of Whetmore by the four defendants amount to murder under section 316 of the Criminal Code Act?" [Refer to this as "I" of the IRAC]

However, after rereading the case (step 5) they formulate some narrow issues which they suggest are helpful in defining and explaining the broad issue. [Refer to as rule explanation] Some at this point narrow the issues to questions such as "are the facts of this case not sufficiently peculiar to warrant the law permitting a discretion with respect to the penalty?" do not the extreme condition the defendants found themselves not qualify as self-defence; should the law on murder, a positive legislation trump the law of nature; what is the effect of law of contract entered into by all the explorers on the law of murder; does the extra-territorial place where the killing took place within the contemplation of the law on murder? Following steps 7 and 8 enables our students to identify more narrow issues such as the absurdity in sentencing the defendants to death remembering that saving them cost the state ten heroic workmen; etc.

By the time our students arrive at step 9 their brief is robust. The briefs are returned to them and the four other judgments delivered by Foster, Tatting, Keen and Handy, JJ of the Supreme Court of Newgarth are handed over to them to study.

The next writing class is used to draw out lesson on legal analysis and reasoning. They find that by noting and drawing the broad issues for determination in step 4 they have articulated the "I" of *IRAC*, step 5 helps them intersperse narrative construct with possible narrow issues. They at this stage are deepening reasoning in a way that issues connect with rule explanation and the facts of the case (something close to the *narrative add-ons* in the "R-A" sequence of the Tracy's flexible *IRAC* by paragraph structure. Steps 7 and 8 relate to more narratives and the conclusion (analogue to "A-C" of *IRAC*). As we review the judgments delivered by the other four judges, which they compare to their written briefs, they see that their briefs and the judicial opinion they have read in the case do not necessarily follow *IRAC*, but they all share what can be termed "gravitational or intellectual elements" of rules of law, explanation of the rules, and application of the rules to facts. We only mention to them about *IRAC* so that they know it is a style of analysis stepped in syllogism generally useful as primer in analysing simply disputes. This way they are not trained to be "knowledge-builders or legal creators" (who project client-cantered lawyering and client's theory of the case), rather than "knowledge-tellers or legal technicians" (who must funnel their client's reality to rules).[110]

What the examples above drives home is the point that *IRAC* can be useful in organizing thought process, especially for beginners and those slow in creative writing, but it is incapable of accounting for all the nuances of legal analysis and writing which reflects the complexities of human disagreements. That being so, writing teachers should help their students develop the flexible style of writing with gravitational fidelity for clear understandable. Since law and facts remain indeterminate, writing styles must recognize the importance of the three pillars of classical rhetoric-*logos*, *ethos*, and *pathos*, as a slavish adherence to *IRAC* and similar formulations sucks the life out of human conflicts.[111]

Graham also has suggested how teachers can help their students learn the flexible writing style without necessarily clinging to *IRAC*. His example is interesting. He states that he does it by deliberately incorporation of pre-writing

---

[110] See Paula Lustbader, Construction Sites, Building Types, and Bridging Gaps: A Cognitive Theory of the Learning Progression of Law Students (1997) 33 *Willamette L. Rev.* 314; Graham, above n at 708.

[111] Laura P. Graham, above n. 6 at 693. See also Chestek, above n. 93 (emphasizing the storytelling dimension in writing as critique of the IRAC paradigmatic structure, the commentator stated: "'I' refers to the legal issue under consideration. No people in there. The same goes for 'R,' the rule . . . 'A' has a bit of promise, if you take 'A' to mean application, but even then, people are just objects upon which the rule operates. And if you take 'A' to mean analysis, that is just more processing of the legal rule. The 'C,' or conclusion, is then just the legal conclusion that follows logically from the previous pieces. Law, law, law. Where did the people go in this process? Law, and the legal system, should be about people. It decides disputes between people and provides people with neutral rules conduct in civilized society. It is a tool to enrich and order peoples' lives. So why do legal briefs focus so much o the abstract law and overlook the people?" id at 129-130; Bret Rappaport, Tapping the Human Adaptive Origins of Storytelling by Requiring Legal Writing Students to Read a Novel in Order to Appreciate How Character, Setting, Plot, Theme, and Tone (CSPTT) Are as Important as IRAC (2008) 25 *T.M. Cooley L. Rev.* 267

into his writing class.[112] The learned scholar says he rarely mentions *IRAC* when teaching pre-writing strategies, although the teaching techniques used does cover the four components of *IRAC*.[113] His strategy has been useful in preparing his students to recognize the flexible nature of legal writing which incorporates lawyers "agreed-upon analytical elements," such as rule articulation, citation and explanation of best possible authority for the rule, possible ambiguities of the rule and how the rule has been applied in the past, and how the rule should be analogically applied to the present case, how the facts persuade a conclusion in favour of the client etc. without mentioning the *IRAC* formula. The theory of agreed-upon analytical elements or what is termed "intellectual location" works like the underlying grammar for legal discourse and writing. We expect a well written memorandum or brief to feature and give attention to those common nuances. And that is what good brief writers do.

We would like to conclude this section with the admonition of Chestek on writing technique: "I do not contend that *IRAC* and its brethren are inherently bad. *IRAC* clearly has a place in legal writing; it is a very useful tool for explaining and examining logical pieces of the legal puzzle that every case presents. But its utility is limited to small scale organization and legal reasoning; when used to create the superstructure of a brief, it can lead to formulaic writing devoid of personal stories that form the conflict being presented in court. In short, *IRAC* is a building block-merely one type of material that a writer can use to construct a solid brief. My premise here is that what the writer builds with these blocks, the client's story, should be organized as a narrative."[114]

Conclusion

It cannot be seriously doubted that *IRAC* provides an intellectual framework of synthesizing legal reasoning by making law's complexity more manageable and that it allows lawyers to communicate with each other on common grounds in analysing social realities in a principled, rational manner. It can be termed the grammar structure of legal discourse. But that is the much it does. It is however harmful to treat it as the only way to good legal writing. Recognizing this fact should motivate teachers to help their students outgrow the amateur, basic analytical skills underlined in *IRAC* and its other cousins to more flexible writing techniques for analysing complex, sophisticated social realities and experiences in the social world. They must heed the warning: there is not and cannot be a single structure on how legal argumentative thought is best communicated. *IRAC* can be

---

112 See Graham, above 6 at 706.

113 Ibid., at 707.

114 Chestek, above n 93 at 132.

useful, but it is just one building block in the architectural edifice of legal analysis, and legal writing teachers should not overemphasize it to the detriments of the kaleidoscope and mosaic nature of legal analysis and reasoning. The Greek mythology of the *Procrustean bed* is enough caution for those who want to train great brief-writers.[115]

A final word! Good writing uses reflective techniques and approaches the writing process recursively by adopting specific rhetorical strategies for deep legal analysis.[116] IRAC is only a useful tool at the preliminary stage of the legal development of our students. And even at that, a rigid insistence on it as the organizational tool for writing can be dangerous. As teachers our goal should be to help them move quickly to complex analysis by drawing on other methods of organizing writing that better promotes our students' cognitive growth as useful members of the legal discourse community.[117] The writer's focus must be reader-centred with communicative purpose as objective. The non-*IRAC* narrative style is what best suits this objective in legal writing and it should be encouraged by legal writing teachers to broaden the imagination of would-be-lawyers to the social realities and sometimes conflict and complex commitments negotiated through the prism of law and the legal system.

IRAC was conceived primarily as an analytical tool, it must not be converted into a writing formula!

[115] The Procrustean bed symbolizes a standard that is enforced uniformly without regard to individuality. It derives from the Greek mythical giant Procrustes or the mode of torture practiced by him. According to George Gopen, Procrustean lived off the road from Athens to Eleusis. Each evening he offered hospitality to travellers on the road. While the food and wine he offered his guest were fine, the sleeping arrangement was not. The guest was required to fit perfectly to the iron bed he constructed. If the guest was taller than the bed, he would cut off the guest feet and legs to fit into the bed. The obvious effect is that the guest will die. See George G. Gopen, Keynote Address at the Capital Area Legal Writing Conference, Feb. 26, 2011, in IRAC, REA, Where We Are Now, and Where We Should Be Going in the Teaching of Legal Writing (2011) 17 *J. Legal Writing Inst.* xix

[116] Paula Lustbader, Construction Sites, Building Types, and Bridging Gaps: A Cognitive Theory of the Learning Progression of Law Students (1997) 33 *Willamette L. Rev.* 317 (identifies four stages in the legal development of law students-the technician, drafter, designer and creator stages).

[117]Graham, above n. 6 at 704.

Chapter 8

Judicial Writing

Introduction

By the very nature of the work judges do they are obligated to write. Judges write judicial opinions, especially in the form of rulings and judgments. Such opinions could be bench rulings and judgment. Judges write regularly and for many reasons. So, good writing is a core skill judicial officer must possess. Judges however write not simply to decree results in individual cases or announce applicable law to controversies, but also for other reasons.[1]

Judicial writing is an important skill judges (and those who assist them, such as judicial assistance, judicial clerks, etc.) must master because it is the major link between the court and the public. It is through judicial opinion that the court communicates with litigants, lawyers, other courts, and the society.[2]

No matter what is the status of the court, its pronouncement ultimately declares what the law is. Therefore, judge owes society a duty to communicate their opinion clearly.As Justice Benjamin Cardozo put it, "there can be little doubt that in matters of literary style the sovereign virtue for the judge is clearness."[3]

In fact, the use of language is crucial in any legal system. Lawmakers use language to make the law. Courts use it to state grounds for decisions. Language is the medium through which law is communicated and acts. The nature of this

---

[1] Patricia M. Wald, (extra-judicial), Rhetoric of Results and the Result of Rhetoric: Judicial Writing (1995) 62 *Univ. Chi. L. Rev.* 1371 (an article that explores rationale for judicial decision-making at appellate courts, stating how judges and their words matter.) For general reading on judicial writing, Ruggero J. Aldisert, *Opinion Writing,* 2nd ed. Author House, 2009 (The book divided into four parts, dealing with theoretical concepts underlying an judicial opinion; its anatomy; writing style; and opinion writing checklists); Joyce J. George, *Judicial Opinion Writing Handbook,* 5th ed. William S. Hein & Co. 2007; Ruggero J. Aldisert *et al.*, Opinion Writing and Opinion Readers (2009) 31 *Cardozo L. Rev.* 1; Symposium,*Judicial Opinion Writing* (1995) 62 *Univ. Chi. L. Rev.* 1363; Richard A. Posner, Judges' Writing Styles (And Do They Matter?) (1995) 62 *Univ. Chi. L. Rev.* 1421; Gerald Lebovits *et al.* Ethical Judicial Opinion Writing (2008) 21 *Geo. J. Leg. Ethics* 237 (an article discussing style and substance of judicial opinion writing through the lens of judicial ethics. The authors posit that opinion writing helps shape the public's perception of the judiciary, and therefore, judges must follow the highest ethical standards in writing opinions).

[2]*Judicial Writing Manual*, 1991, published under the authority of the Chief Justice of the United States, Judge J. Clifford Wallace. See forward by William W. Schwatzer.

[3] Benjamin Cardozo, *Law and Literature*, 1931, reprinted in Law and Literature and Other Essays and Addresses, Fred B. Rothman & Co. 1999 @ 7.

medium invariably has a bearing on what purpose can be achieved or furthered in law. So for litigants, lawyers and society, language holds a special fascination. Judges must therefore master this skill of communication.

It is therefore not sufficient for judges to write opinions that are correct, their opinion must also be seen as fair, reasonable and must be easily understandable. This is what places an onerous burden on judges to explain as well as persuade with their writing as their opinion can reveal the depth of their thinking.

Judicial opinions serve three main functions:

(i) It communicates a court's conclusions and the reasons for them to the parties and their lawyers;

(ii) When published, it announces the law to other lawyers, judges, academics, and the interested public;

(iii) Its preparation imposes intellectual discipline on the author, requiring the judge to clarify her reasoning and assess the sufficiency of precedential support.[4]

A good opinion should fairly, clearly, and accurately state the significant facts and relevant rules of law and demonstrate by its analysis the reasonableness of its conclusions. Misstating significant facts or authorities is a mark of carelessness or worse and it undermines the opinion's authority and integrity. Unclear or ambiguous writing reflects the author's lack of clear thinking and defeats the opinion's purpose.

This chapter is designed to horn judges' skill of critically thinking about their writing. No question about it, judges write often and fairly are masters of what their opinion ought to contain and exclude. Even at that they may still need some reminders on how to write well. The chapter encourages judges to take ownership of their writing. It does not pretend to be a benchmark discussion on skills for writing style, but it is a stimulant for evaluation.

---

[4] Judicial Writing @ Abner J. Mikva, For Whom Judges Write (1988) 61 *S. Cal. L. Rev.* 1357.

Visual of judge sitting in court

History of judicial writing

Judicial writing has been a part of common law adjudication for many years. It is suggested that as a tradition took its rooted from the Roman tradition.[5] Early Roman legal process was administered by two divisions: the *praetor* or magistrate on one hand, and the *iudex*, a lay judge. On receipt of parties' pleadings in a lawsuit, the praetor drafted the pleading into a formula, which instructed the *iudex* on how to decide the case. The formula was more like what would be termed the modern writ, and the instruction it contained can be described as a modern jury instruction communicated by a judge to the jury, although the instruction left the *iudex* to decide both law and fact. The *iudex* decided the case without written record. It was the jurists, a class of learned statesmen who had no official role in the adjudicating process, were the writers. They took it upon themselves not only to advice both litigants and praetors, but they published treatise (which were like commentaries) describing the resolution of real and hypothetical problems. Basically that was the beginning of law reporting and judicial writing.

Judicial writing in England has its origin in the pleas rolls and Year Books in the thirteenth century. During this period the county and King's courts kept plea rolls that were clerk's records describing the pleadings and the outcomes of the

[5]Barry Nicholas, *An Introduction to Roman Law,* Oxford Univ. Press, 1962 @19-35.

cases determined by the court.[6] The Year Books which appeared later in the last decade of the thirteenth century were chronological reports, of unknown authorship, containing rough transcriptions of court proceedings. Because they included the arguments made by the lawyers and the reasoning offered by the judge, they were not as terse as the plea rolls and so could be likened to our modern law report.[7]

The advent of print introduced law reporting by court reporters rather than the judges, though Lord Coke took it upon himself to report his judgments and those of other judges. By judicial practice at the end of the eighteenth century, judges routinely "authorized" certain reports by looking over the draft reports of their decisions prior to publication. This explains why some of the English reports still carry the inscription "published under the authority of the Chief Judge of England."[8]

Why do judge write opinion

Opinion writing is serious business. It requires a judge to consider and reflect deeply on the facts of the case, written briefs of counsels and their argument, confer with colleagues (if in appellate level), do research, organize thoughts and material, before even beginning the process of tentative writing that could lead to a final draft/decision. Each step further demands recalling facts and law interrogated in the process and an estimation of justice and morality. The process brings to play the characters and the plot of the case taking on a life of its own from which the judge like a skilled novelist draws irresistible conclusion.

Judicial opinion by its very nature announces broad commandments of what the law requires. Because adjudication presupposes impartiality, judges' opinion should show to the readers that their decisions are correct and unbiased. They therefore should structure their opinion in a way that it explains the rationale to educate the reader of the correctness of the conclusion. It is however plausible to think that embedded in explanation is also a desire to justify the decision. This being so, court decisions are crafted for purposes related to persuasion.

Judges write opinion to also tell society, especially the powerful that the operating ethos is a democracy is the rule of law, that ordinary people have a right to expect that the law will apply to all citizens alike. Yes, that the law would and is

---

[6]Wald, above n. 1 @ 1371 n. 1. See Theodore F.T. Plucknett, *A Concise History of Common Law,* 2nd ed. Law Co-op, 1936 @ 230.

[7]Plucknett, above n. 6 @239.

[8] See All England Law Report. In the United States of America, many states by the eighteenth century adopted the statutory requirement that judges write their opinion. See Wald, above n. 1 @ 1371.

interpreted the same way for all by a system of precedent and hierarchy consistent interpretation and application of law is guaranteed.[9]

Aside these altruistic reasons for writing, judges may also write for other mundane reasons. An ambitious judge may write in the hope of promotion to a higher judicial position in a political system that promotes merit. Some other write for personal gratification - to be cited as *locus classicus* or authority by lawyers and students. And for those who were academics before taking judicial appointment, there could be the temptation to communicate their intellectual processes and products to the world. And according to a judge (writing extra-judicial) judges who are "refugees from the world of politics and public affairs write to persuade their colleagues and the public that they are moving law in the right direction.[10]

It is plausible to think that if law reporters stick to the essence of publishing law reports – reporting only pungent cases (i.e. cases which introduce, or appear to introduce, a new principle or a new rule of law, or that modify an existing principle, or which settles, or materially tend to settle, a question upon which the law is doubtful or all cases which for any reason are peculiarly instructive) the pressure on judges to write lengthy opinions would be minimised.[11]

Style of writing

Generally there are two styles of judicial writing: the pure and the impure.[12] Pure judicial writing is impersonal, formal, ostensibly correct, and lofty. It takes the positivist scientific posture of formalist jurisprudence. On the other hand, the impure style is characteristically direct, informal, dramatic, and frank, akin to pragmatist jurisprudence.

Due to time pressure and the number of opinion judges write it is not uncommon for judges over time to plagiarise self and their styles soon begin to reveal personalised boilerplate. This is understandable. Judges generally have less time for elegant prose and rhetoric. Litigants want judgment not fanciful written judgments for them to quickly get on with their lives. Those who write know from experience that writing can become a chore over time if a person engages in it as a profession or hobby. Times could come when writers experience drought in writing imagination and then writing flow can become mere rout. Judges are not immune from similar experience. They don't have the luxury of stopping to write

---

[9]Waldt, above n. 1 @ 1371

[10]Ibid.

[11] See the basis for case reporting by the 1865 non-profit Incorporated Council of Law Reporting for England & Wales (ICLR). ICLR reports are cited with approval all over the United Kingdom. See Lord Judge CJ, Practice Direction (Citation of Authorities) [2012] 1 WLR 780.

[12]Richard A. Posner, Judges' Writing Styles (And Do They Matter?)(1995) 62 *U. Chi. L. Rev.* 1421.

as long as they are on the bench. So, it is possible that their drought period would reveal more boilerplate opinion. What is more, since the issues that confront a judge over time takes on a regular genre it is plausible that in an era of computers a judge can easily recognise similar facts pattern for which she can apply some level of writing automation.

The National Judicial Council has a minimum benchmark for judicial opinion a judge ought to write annually.[13] The pressure can remove the luxury of a judge spending much time on prose. A conceivable victim of the pressure can be less liveliness and originality of prose.[14]

Importantly, the style of a judges writing is revelatory of the personality of the judge. Some enliven their opinion from insight gathered from other disciplines, personal views and experience. Judge Jerome Frank is an example of a judge who drew on other disciplines for insight to concrete legal problems. Richard Posner was famous in this respect, especially in drawing insight from economics.

Some even adopt special form of writing to drive home their opinion. For example, it is said that Justice Scalia uses conceptual phrases sarcastically, always set out in capital letters. He peppers his opinion with caustic references by use of phrases like: to the 'Powers That Be" and the "Land of the Free."[15] Wald states that one judge, in their appeal court uses so much italics that the other members of the panel referred to the opinion as the "Neon Lights" judge.[16]

It is however expected that the rise of plain language movement in law and literature would shape judicial writing.[17]

Though Posner identifies two styles of writing, judges traditionally write opinions in an impersonal tone.[18]It explains why phrases like "this court", "his lordship", etc., appears in judicial opinion. The impersonal style is often used to

---

[13]See directive from NJC.

[14] Check out NJC directive.

[15]Wald, above n. 1 @ 1415.

[16]Ibid.

[17]Plain language movement is a movement led by an influential group of legal scholars, judges, and practitioners who seek to advance clarity in legal writing by purging it of cumbersome sentence constructions and empty legal jargon. For plain English movement impact in law see, the seminal work of David Mellinkoff, *The Language of Law*, Boston: Little Brown & Co. 1963, which gives rise to the Plain Language Movement in law. See also, Joseph Kimble, *Lifting the Fog of Legalese: Essay on Plain Language,* 2006; Judith D. Fischer, Why George Orwell's Ideas About Language Still Matter for Lawyers (2007) 68 *Mont. L. Rev.* 129; Joseph Kimble, Writing for Dollars, Writing to Please (1996-97) 6 *Scribes J. Legal Writing* 1. See also Bryan A. Garner, *Garner's Modern English Usage*, 4th ed. 2016; Richard Wydick, *Plain English for Lawyers*, 5th ed. 2005; Joseph Kimble, Drafting Examples from the Proposed New Federal Rules of Evidence, *Mich. B.J.* Aug. 2009 @ 52; Sept. 2009 @ 46; Oct. 2009 @ 54; Nov. 2009 @ 50; Joseph Kimble, Lessons in Drafting from the New Federal Rules of Civil Procedure (2008-2009)12 *Scribes J. Legal Writing* 25.

[18]Posner, above n. 9.

advance the neutral arbitral status of judges in the administration of justice. It is also designed to advance the notion that the court is a corporate body involved in declaring what the law is between parties. It further advances the notion of an interpreter, declarer and commander of what the law is.

Lawyers are familiar with the style and so consider it unethical to address judges personal. Traditionally, they address the office of the judge not her person. The third person language is thus deemed appropriate in addressing judges.

Of late, however, a practice has developed that see some judges speak in the first person language, setting forth bits of their own experience or views. The trend in storytelling and rhetoric encourages the practice. This is usually noticeable for judges who humanize the law - jettisoning the IRACian model of reasoning for an organizing schema that largely intersperses facts and legal analysis with experience.

Judges are advised to avoid the characteristics of bad writing. The text by Strunk and White or any good communication text can be used as primer to guide judges on what to avoid in writing.[19]Generally, judges should avoid being wordy, verbose, poor organisation, cryptic analysis, pomposity and humour, etc. They are encouraged to follow standard guide for good writing, such as eliminating unnecessary words, write in plain English, etc.[20]

Some writing may require the use of footnotes. Footnote conveys information that would disrupt the flow of the opinion if included in the text. They are used in judicial writing to convey information, such as the text of a statute or material from the record that supports the language of the opinion but is not immediately necessary to understand it. The court can also acknowledge and briefly dispose of tangential issues using footnote.

Some judges have a practice of placing all citations in footnotes, leaving the text entirely for discussion. This is a question of style. But it is important to note that footnotes should not be inserted as a matter of judge's preference or as a repository for information that the writer does not know what to do with. Conscious of the tendency to overuse footnotes, some now strive to eliminate or at least reduce the number of footnotes in their opinions.[21]

Good writing requires editing. Judges are therefore advised to read every paragraph of their opinion carefully, not sliding over text because it is familiar. In editing an opinion it would be necessary for a judge to consider questions such as: Have I said precisely what I intended to say? Is there a better way to say it? Does

---

[19] William Strunk, *The Element of Style*. Reading of chapters – in this book could also be a useful guide.

[20]Ibid.

[21]Mikva, Goodbye to Footnotes (1985) 56 *U. Colo. L. Rev.* 647. For proper footnote citation style see OSCOLA; A Uniform System of Citation (the "Blue Book") and the University of Chicago Manual of Legal Citation (the "Maroon Book") cited @ 24.

the thought flow clearly and logically? Will the reader understand it?[22] Considering these questions would be useful in producing drafts that sufficiently persuade.

A judge would find it useful to use as writing aids the following materials: a dictionary, a thesaurus, a citation manual, and a reference manual.[23]Being also with the style used by other judges contained in law reports can be a good way to master the art of good writing.

Collegiate judicial writing

Appellate opinions represent the collective decision of several judges or the panel. The judge assigned by the panel who writes the opinion must therefore take into account the thinking of the other judges of the panel or en bane court and incorporate the group's thinking into the opinion's rationale. In some cases, several judges participate in preparing an opinion. In that case, the opinion is jointly written or the other judges' comment on drafts prepared by the judge assigned to write the opinion. When the opinion does not represent the thinking of all of the members of the court, some judges may choose to prepare concurring or dissenting opinions.[24]

In collegial writing, usually the author of a majority opinion in an appellate tribunal writes the judgment for the court. If the court is composed of three judges, a least one other judge must concur in the opinion to give it precedential value.[25] Where however, the two judges only agree on a conclusion or result but not on the same underlying reason or rationale, they would issue a *per curiam* type of judgment. Each individual judge would give her reason.

Considerable planning and coordination is required when a panel chooses to issue a joint opinion. The reason for this is simple. So that it is readable and coherent final opinion. It is good practice to then have a post-argument conference to discuss the assignment of opinion parts, their interdependence, and

---

[22]For techniques of critical (recursive) editing see Anne Enquist & Laurel Currie Oates, *Just Writing: Grammar, Punctuation, and Style for the Legal Writer,* 2nd ed. Aspen, 2005,§ 1.4–1.6, 15–21 (useful discussion of revising, editing, and proofreading); Christopher M. Anzidei, The Revision Process in Legal Writing: Seeing Better to Write Better (2002) 8 *Leg. Writing* 23 @ 43–45; Terri LeClercq, Revision before Editing (1986) 49 *Tex. B.J.* 838.

[23]Bryan A. Garner, *The Redbook: A Manual on Legal Style* § 23 (2d ed. Thomson West 2006) (In his book, Bryan Garner not only addresses legal writing style in terms of mechanics, grammar, usage, and editing, but also covers preparing legal documents such as judicial opinions).

[24] Garner, above n. 23 @ 27.

[25] For example, s. 234 of the 1999 Constitution (Nigeria) provides that the Supreme Court shall be duly constituted if it consists of not less than five Justices of the Supreme Court; and s. 247 provides that the Court of Appeal shall be duly constituted if it consists of not less than three Justices of the Court of Appeal.

joint assumptions or factual predicates. The sequence of sections may need to be determined to avoid confusion and repetition of basic facts or legal analyses.

Generally, one judge on the panel must assume coordinating authority and circulate an outline and summary of the proposed sections before writing begins. One judge, usually the coordinating judge, must also take responsibility for writing the introduction and conclusion, covering all sections. The introduction is usually brief and confined to a statement of the proceedings leading to the court challenge. The facts in detail are better presented as needed in the individual sections.

After the authors have drafted and approved the various sections, the coordinating judge should assume authority to make non-substantive changes to avoid duplication or gross stylistic differences. Law clerks can then take up the responsibility of ensuring uniform citation and heading format.

Joint opinion is a desirable practice where cases before a panel increasingly become complex and time-consuming. The practice can help avoid delay and tying up one judge for too long. With careful planning, it is possible to maintain high standards of writing for these opinions.

Judges circulate draft opinions to other judges on a panel or en banc court to ensure that the opinion reflects the rationale of the judges in the majority. When commenting on an opinion written by another judge, it is always appropriate to comment on the substance of an opinion, but inappropriate to comment on matters of style. When the distinction between substance and style is fuzzy, comments are appropriate if the matter in question seems to speak for the court and thus might send a message that does not represent the view of the other members.

Separate concurring opinion is appropriate where it is intended to define with greater precision the scope of an opinion or otherwise inform the parties and other audiences of what the writer believes are important points. Thus, judges may issue concurrences where there are two argued grounds for a decision, the majority justifies its decision on one of those grounds, and other judges believe the alternative grounds should be stated. Concurrences may also serve to indicate to parties in future cases how far the court is willing to go down a road, and where the road ends. A concurring opinion should not be written simply to add a point of view or personal statement that does not further either the decisional or educational value of the opinion. A judge thinking of writing a separate concurring opinion should therefore ask herself: Am I writing this for myself or for the good of the court? If the answer tilts to the former, it would be best to drop the idea of writing a concurring opinion.

Judges should include in their concurring opinions a statement of reasons why they are concurring specially. The point is not to present an alternative opinion of the court, but to indicate the point of departure from the majority and to further define the contours of the opinion. Concurrences should not rehash the facts and legal principles on which the majority based its decision, except to the extent that differences in the factual findings and legal conclusions are significant to the concurring point of view. The arguments should be principled and the tone should be instructive but not pedantic.

The jurisprudential politics of collegiate judicial writing is often tested if an appellate court is composed of strong-minded characters of different political and personal philosophies.[26] To downplay possible conflicting opinion it is advisable that when the judges on the panel agree on most but not all of the issues in a case, the opinion writer should strive to fashion a rationale that does not even discuss the disputed matter, or chooses to bury it in a coverall phrase like "other issues raised by the appellant do not merit further discussion." In such cases, the writer for a precarious majority would have exhibited that she takes the feelings of other members into consideration and does not wish to start other panel members down the road of a special concurrence or partial dissent, least the whole compromise gets unravel. So, the writer may just sacrifice full treatment of all non-frivolous issues properly before the court.[27]

Recognizing that the different temperament of judges in a collegiate court can get ventilated by disparate viewpoints and could be the cause friction that can damage to the court's reputation, a presiding judge or the most senior judge would need skills of managing her other colleagues. For example, if the majority agrees on a conclusion with different rationale, the panel can find a compromise alternative reason to support the majority conclusion. In such a case the compromise alternative rationale can be garnered from that chosen by a majority of the judges even if it is not the writer's preferred one. But once a majority is assured for a rationale, further compromises to secure more votes or unanimity may comfortably be rejected.

Judges assigned to write the majority opinion come under judicial pressure to state with care the facts of the case and narrow their decision to resolving only the case, avoiding generalities or making many pronouncements on matters considered obiter. As is to be expected, the desire to have the opinion accepted to other members of the panel, it is the course of wisdom for the opinion writer to sacrifice much of her own rhetorical preferences to what a judge termed "hard-pressed suggestions" of her colleagues. Accordingly, it is advised that rhetoric be

---

[26] See Lord Denning books and his dissent judgments.

[27]Wald, above n. 1 @ 1377.

hostage of majority judicial politics. Rhetoric should be reserved for only minority, dissent opinion.[28]

Most of the considerations applicable to dissenting opinions also apply to concurrences. ***Dissenting opinion*** is rare. But when it does arise, it can be a frustrating a thing most appellate courts would assiduously want to avoid. For anything it is smack of personality incompatibility and could sends conflicting signals to the bar or the public as to how the court internally works.[29]

Not wanting to send such negative signals therefore makes for compromise by judges who may choose to drop their preferred reason and rhetoric to gain a full concurrence from other members of the panel.

Dissenting opinions serve several purposes. They may help to attract en banc or certiorari review and to isolate and refine the issues for further appeal. They may attract legislative action to correct possible shortcomings in the law. Dissenting opinions may also help to narrow the scope of a decision by pointing out the possible dangers of the position that the majority has taken or by sending signals to other judges and to the bar as to the limits of a particular decision and its effect on similar cases in the future. In these ways, dissenting opinions can serve useful functions in communicating important information to an opinion's audiences and aiding the growth of the law.

Dissenting opinions are written at a potential cost. A dissent that strikes a strident or preachy note may contribute to divisiveness and ill feelings on the court, may undermine the authority of the opinion and of the court as an institution, and may create confusion. Whether to dissent may depend on the nature of the case and the principle at issue. Dissents generally should not be written when the principle at issue is settled and the decision has little significance outside the specific case. Cases that involve emerging legal principles or statutory interpretation in areas that will affect future activities of the bar, the public, and the government are more likely to warrant dissenting opinions than cases of limited application. The issue should be significant enough that the judge's "fever is aroused," as one judge said, but the motivation should be to further the development of the law rather than to vent personal feelings. Judges considering whether to dissent should ask themselves whether the likely benefits outweigh the potential costs.

If a judge decides that writing a dissent will serve a useful purpose, it should be written as carefully and responsibly as the opinion of the court. Rarely should a judge dissent without opinion; doing so communicates no information to the

---

[28]Wald, above n. 1 @ 1379.

[29] Garner, above n. 23 @ 28.

opinion's readers. The argument should focus on the critical principles and distinguish the dissenter's rationale from that of the majority. But it is one thing to state the points of disagreement forcefully and effectively, and another to engage in argument or advocacy. A dissenting opinion should not simply slash at the majority opinion or its author. Personal attacks, offensive language, and condescending tone should not be used; although some judges believe that moral outrage and restrained indignation may sometimes be appropriate.

Unfortunately, a less mature majority can be caustic with the minority rhetorical outlet, especially if cordiality is in short supply among members. Judicial opinion can be used subtly to settle old scores. Skilful readers of law report can easily know by some identity marks, such the majority opinion calling the minority opinion judge by name. On the other hand, friendly fire can be disguised in impersonal terms like "the dissent opinion of my learned brother."

Sometimes also an appellate court's opinion can reveal their attitude to the particular judge of the lower court whose judgment is being reviewed. Generally, appellate judges are soft in their criticism of judges who have a reputation of care and sound judgments. But their anger is known to blaze against lower judges on the other extreme. It has been suggested that aside rhetoric appellate judges' perception of the legal ability of the trial judge counts heavily. Accordingly, if they consider her capable and generally astute, they will try harder to uphold her, especially in close cases.[30] Even the competent, reputational lower judge clearly errs appellate judges are known to treat it as understandable mistake, while uncharitable to those identified as less competent.

A similar feeling influences to some extent how judicial opinion rhetoric is employed on counsels. Judges sometimes express their intolerance of lawyers' errors in uncharitable form, especially for those with a reputation of less care and competence. These are often expressed as side comments, but it could become really damaging when contained in judicial opinion or reported in pages of law report.[31]

---

[30]Wald, above n. 1 @ 1380.

[31] For example, the Court of Appeal in *Ezemba* v. *Ibeneme* (2000) 10 NWLR (pt. 674), per Ubaezonu, JCA, castigating a senior counsel in an appeal stated: "This otherwise simple matter has been made difficult in many respects. But first, let me deal with the appellant's brief. The brief was prepared in the chambers of a Senior Advocate of Nigeria and stamped and signed by him. He filed 13 grounds of appeal in a case which turned on the quantity of goods actually supplied by the respondent to the appellate. I know of no case which however complex cannot be disposed of on 4, 5 or 6 grounds of appeal. The idea of making every small slip of a judge a ground of appeal is not the best thing to do. ... I now come to an equally serious problem in the appellant's brief. Having formulated one issue on 13 grounds of appeal, learned Senior Advocate of Nigeria after arguing the issue, proceeded to set out in seriatim and argue 13 grounds of appeal in his brief. I was so distressed. ... Could it be that by the end of the 20th century, a learned Senior Advocate of Nigeria does not know that he has only to argue the issues formulated by him, not the grounds of appeal?

Appellate construction of facts

The general rule is that an appellate court does not review facts from the lower court. Rules of procedure make extensive provision validating the position.[32] But nothing can be further from the truth than it. It is erroneous to think that an appellate court has no fact-finding authority. One fallacy of IRAC reasoning in syllogism is the lawyers (including judges) arrive at legal conclusions in a neutral, consistent and determined way. When an appellate judge sits down to write judgment, she first unconsciously conjures up a conclusion from which a narrative is formulated to justify the legal conclusion.

A simply scenario on how issues are formulated by the court would do. No issues are formulated without certain preliminaries. Suppose the fact scenario of a case where this: D knocks C down his bicycle, a driver on the highway. For the judge to formulate the issue, she has to draw on preconceived knowledge of the question (Q), the entire relevant facts and rules (fr) and the relevant facts and rules (FR) governing the formulation of the issue. The framework quickly helps the judge to recognise that the case-frame is one within the bracket of accident. Next, she proceeds to reflect on the possible relevant facts and rules. Reflection on facts would require her to know the nature of the highway, whether it is a busy one, whether the driver skidded off his own section of the road etc. Reflection on relevant rules possibly informs her that it is a matter connected with either (criminal) dangerous driving or (tortious) liability in negligence. Finally, she uses the relevant facts and rules to plot what will resemble a prima facie conclusion, which she calls issue. So, simply stating that issues are formulated without taking into account these preliminary matters that enter the cognitive mind in formulating it is nothing but a ruse. This explains why some scholars have suggested that IRAC syllogism should be expanded into an acronym like '(QfrFR)+IRAC,' if it must retain its explanatory power as an accurate formula for organising legal analysis.[33]

---

[32] Cite rules of procedure. But cf. *Ibitokun* v. *Strabag Construction Nig. Ltd* (2010) per Muhammad, JSC (where the appellate court exercises its general powers and steps into the shoes of the lower court below it, to do all that the court below ought to have done but which it failed to do, including re-evaluation of evidence, as in this case, the appellate court can make such valid decisions or orders which the court below it ought to have made."

[33] Dennis R. Honabach, IRAC or (QfrFR)+IRAC, *The Second Draft* (Legal Writing Institute, Tacoma, Washington, Nov. 1995, 8; Kim Cauthorn, Keep on TRRACING, *The Second Draft* (Legal Writing Institute, Tacoma, Washington, Nov. 1995, 4. The learned scholar recommend that rather than retain the IRAC acronym, it should be replaced the "I" with "T" (for thesis). See id at 5; Laura P. Graham, Why-RAC? Revisiting the Traditional Paradigm for Writing About Legal Analysis (2015) 63 *Kansas L. Rev.* 681 at 683 n. 11. See also Tracy Turner, Finding Consensus in Legal Writing Discourse Regarding Organizational Structure: A Review and Analysis of the Use of IRAC and its Progenies (2012) 9 *Legal Comm. & Rhetoric: JALWD* 351 at 359 (survey of writing whether legal writing should start with issue or conclusion). But cf. Tracy Turner, Flexible IRAC: A Best Practice

An appellate court's opinion on facts is often atomistic. Only one account of the facts is taken, unless there is a dissenting opinion. In an era of rhetoric and storytelling making important legal construction of facts, judges have sometimes engaged in the task of interpreting facts from the perceptive of characterisation, recasting, and the like. Gone are the days when it was fashionable to think that facts are immutable. If anything is learnt from Whyte, it is that facts can be as indeterminable as are legal rules.[34]An appellate court can choose to adopt a formal, impersonal construction of facts or take a human side of a story.

A good example of the two extremes is illustrated in the opinion of Judge Silberman (majority opinion) contrasted with that of Judge Wald (minority opinion) in the gay midshipman case of *Steffan* v. *Perry*.[35] The case was about a dismissed sailor and applicable Navy regulations. The facts were recounted by the majority as a normal dismissal case having to do with equal protection provision. It makes important rules applicable on enrolment in the Naval Academy on homosexuals.

But the facts taken from the same record by the dissenting opinion aligned the case much more closely to the category of cases that state the cherished American traditions of individual liberty and the rule of law forbidding the government to punish mere thoughts or to infer a likelihood of prohibited conduct therefrom.

Judge Wade stated:

> For the government to penalize a person for acknowledging his sexual orientation runs deeply against our constitutional grain. It has, we believe, no precedent or place in our national traditions, which spring from a profound respect for the freedom to think and to be what one chooses and to announce it to the world. The majority's ingenious plays on presumptions and inferences cannot disguise the injustice that lies at the heart of this case. In years to come, we will look back with dismay at these unconstitutional attempts to enforce silence upon individuals of homosexual orientation, in the military and out. Pragmatism should not be

---

Guide (2015) 20 *J. Legal Writing Inst.* 233 n. 2 (where the learned writer states that in her paper she treats "issue as synonymous with thesis or conclusion."

[34]James Boyd White, *The Legal Imagination* (Abridged Edition), Chicago: Univ. Chicago Press, 1985.

[35]41 F3d (DC Cir. 1994) (en banc), cited in Wald, above n. 1 @ 1386.

allowed to trump principle or the soul of a nation will wither. We respectfully dissent.[36]

It humanizes the facts framed around the outstanding performance of Steffan at the Academy, downplaying the Academy rules.[37]

Joseph Steffan, a former Navy midshipman who admitted to being a homosexual, appeals from the judgment of the district court sustaining the constitutionality of the regulations pursuant to which he was discharged from the Naval Academy. Midshipmen enrolled in the Naval Academy are subject to at least two sets of regulations relevant to homosexuality: the Naval Academy's own regulations and the Directives of the Department of Defence applicable to the armed forces generally. They generally state that homosexuality is incompatible with military service. Joseph Steffan enrolled in the Naval Academy in 1983 and successfully completed three of his four years of training, consistently being ranked near the top of his class. During the fall of his senior year, Steffan confided in two fellow midshipmen that he was a homosexual. One of the two reported Steffan's conversation to Academy officials and on the basis of this report the Naval Investigative Service began an investigation of Steffan's homosexuality. Steffan was informed of that inquiry by a fellow midshipman in March 1987. When questioned by Naval investigators, Steffan "invoked his right to remain silent," but did confide his homosexuality to a chaplain in the Academy. Subsequently, in a meeting with the Commandant of the Academy, Steffan stated that he was a homosexual.

Reconstructing facts on appeal (whether in dissent opinion or not) is often a function of how judges seek to determine relevant or controlling precedent. If a panel seeks to distinguish what would otherwise be a controlling precedent, it could recast and re-characterise the facts of the case to show why the precedent is unhelpful. This play has been more pronounced in political matters, especially in electoral litigation. Let us examine just one of them – *Buhari* v. *INEC*.[38] The main complain of the petitioner was that the Presidential election conducted in Nigeria in 2007 was fraught with substantial irregularities to render the process void. The primary question for determination in the case turned on the interpretation of s. 146 (1) of the Electoral Act, 2006; namely on whom the Act places the burden of proof of election irregularities, whether on the petitioner or respondent.[39] The

[36]Ibid., @ 721, per Wald, J.

[37]Ibid., @ 701-705.

[38]*Buhari* v. *INEC* [2008] 12 SC (pt.I) I.

[39] S. 164 (1) states: "an election shall not be liable to be invalidated by reason of non-compliance with the provisions of this Act if it appears to the Election Tribunal or Court that the election was

argument of the petitioner was that once substantial irregularities is established by him, it will be unnecessary to further burden him to show that the irregularities have substantially affected the result of the election to void it. The respondents argued that an entailment does not necessary result between irregularities and the result of election, and that both burden of proof rest with the petitioner. By a split decision of 4-3, the majority held that the onus falls on the petitioner, and since it was not discharged, the election of the respondent President of Nigeria was upheld. The majority relied on *Buhari* v. *Obasanjo* as controlling precedent.[40]

But the minority thought otherwise. Employing purposive reading of the Act it was of the view that the controlling precedent should be *Swem* v. *Dzungwe,*[41] a case that states that only the first of the two burden should be borne by the petitioner. For instance, Oguntade JSC (dissenting), stated that once the petitioner calls credible evidence to show non-compliance which compromises the principles of the Act, he should succeed without more. His Lordship reasoned that the Act does not condoned non-compliance with the provisions of the Act and electoral guidelines. In His Lordship's opinion the burden of proving resultant effect of non-compliance should properly rest the respondent responsible for conducting the election, in this case, the Independent National Electoral Commission (INEC),. His Lordship appears to capture justification for placing the burden on the respondent this way: given the fact that law must be obeyed, it is sufficient for the petitioner to give evidence of non-compliance, and if the evidence is satisfactory, he should be entitled to judgment without more, unless the respondent can show that irregularities are not substantial in nature or do not contravene the principles of the Act, and in addition that it does not materially affect the election result. Anything otherwise will lead to approaching the matter on the basis that law is not meant to be obeyed.[42]

There is no question about it. Storytelling techniques can be skilfully used by an appellate court to short circuit the legal constrain prohibiting reopening of decided facts by the lower court. Appellate judges can enlarge the scope of judicial discretion to tweak facts as long as they can reasonably mould the facts and law to tell a coherent story. In fact, to the extent that the court can pick and choose from the record as to what the controlling "facts" of the case are to that extent the coast for facts interpretation is large.

---

conducted substantially in accordance with the principles of this Act and that the non compliance did not affect substantially the result of the election."

[40]*Buhari* v. *Obasanjo* (2005) 13 NWLR (pt. 941) 1. See also *Hanma* v. *Modibbo* (2004) 16 NWLR (pt. 90) 487

[41]*Swem* v. *Dzungwe* [1960] 2 NMLR 297, [1960] 1SCNLR 111.

[42]*Buhari* v. *INEC* [2008] 12 SC (pt. I) I at , per Oguntade JSC.

Even at that, it is unethical for appellate judges to recast facts in skewed ways, such as leaving out important facts from the records, citing incomplete excerpts from testimony, conspicuously downplaying evidence going in the other direction in generalized summaries or footnotes.[43] The heighten importance of this is embedded in the fact that (conscious or unconscious) misinterpretation of facts is not easily discoverable to an opinion reader, unless a dissent judgment points it out. This being so, it can be damaging to the administration of justice, with adverse consequences for the losing litigant left without remedy. Misinterpretation of facts is unlike misinterpretation of precedent or even questionable interpretation of statute, which are easily discoverable by skilful reading and research.

The practice developed over the years is that case records are stored away in court archive, away from public view. So, it is only the most persistent inquirer that can likely track down any suspect factual assertions in an opinion purportedly taken from the record.[44]The situation is made more precarious because the likelihood of a review on appeal over an alleged factual misstatement in the opinion is nil. The higher the court, the more likely it sees its function as purely one of reviewing errors of law not facts. Invariably then, errors of facts would likely escape judicial scrutiny. Spotlight or hints given bout such facts by a colleague judge in her different interpretation could be the only chance providing an opportunity to review the facts. Purposeful misrepresentation of the record is rare in judicial circle, though not unknown.

While it is generally stated that judges do not go beyond records before them, in realty this is not true in practice. A record is at best a narrative of what transpires in the lower court. It ordinarily would be coloured by gaps in cognitive models.[45] Every writer knows that rewriting involves gap filling, some elaboration, and the like. For example, the lower court may do a good job evaluating the facts but a poor job explaining its holding based on the facts, it may not then be out of place for the appellate court to fill the gap by drawing on experience or scientific findings to justify the conclusion. For instance, an appeal court can draw on scientific evidence to clarify to readers the difference between two conditions, each of which may cause a stroke, if the lower court does not properly explain its holding using the piece of evidence before it.

---

[43]Wald, above n. 1 @ 1389.

[44]Ibid.

[45]Steven L. Winter, Transcendental Nonsense and Metaphoric Reasoning, And The Cognitive Stakes For Law (1989) 137 *Univ. Pa. L. Rev.* 1105; Ronald Chen & Jon Hanson, Categorically Biased: The Influence of Knowledge Structures on Law and Legal Theory (2004) 77 *S. Cal. L. Rev.* 1106 @ 1131–1218 (an article describing how categories and schemas are critical building blocks of the human cognitive process).

Aside instances like this, an appellate court can also draw on its experience as gap-fillers to recast facts. Judges live in society. So, a judge is expected to understand how the law of gravity works for instance. Therefore, if the record states something manifestly implausible, a judge can discount that piece of evidence.

It is a recognised fact that every appeal calls into question a benchmark for review.[46]It is the standard of review that often determines the outcome of an appeal. Thus, an appeal court is always engaged in guessing whether the trial court on its finding is "clearly erroneous," leading to a miscarriage of justice. Miscarriage of justice simply implies that a court arrives at a conclusion no reasonable person would arrive at based on the available evidence in the record.[47]Not even slip or error is reviewable.[48]The benchmark review standard is also another leeway appellate courts can expand their coast of fact recast. The announced standard can skilfully be used to makes relevant certain facts while discounting others, thus bringing into the facts patrimony indeterminism.

An appellate court reviewing a judgment of the lower court can do three things: affirm the lower court's decision; overturn the lower court's decision; or hear the appeal as de novo and enter judgment as it deems fit.[49]

Writing separate opinion

Generally, when there is no dissent/minority opinion appellate judges choose not to write separate opinion but merely concur. However, in rare cases some judges may still choose to write a separate opinion even where there is no dissenting judgment. An appellate judge can decide to write a separate judgment when she concurs or dissent. There are many reasons why a judge may choose to write separately. A dissenting judge may choose the path to as a means to publicly distance herself from her colleagues, especially if they are unable of convince her of their logic. Much as a dissenting judge recognizes that a dissenting opinion has less precedential value she may still insist on the position to highlight deep disagreement with the majority.

The dissenting opinion of Oguntade JSC (and the other two justices) in *Buhari* v. *INEC* is one good example. The judges choose to highlight the purpose of the provisions of the Electoral Act and electoral guidelines. In His Lordship's opinion the burden of proving resultant effect of non-compliance should properly rest the respondent responsible for conducting the election, in this case, the

---

[46] Rules of court and statute generally state that the standard for review is that the lower court's judgment must lead to a miscarriage of justice. Cite them.

[47]Cases on miscarriage of justice meaning.

[48] See above n. 16, *Ezemba* v. *Ibeneme* (2000) 10 NWLR (pt. 674), per Ubaezonu, JCA.

[49] Cite rules of court.

Independent National Electoral Commission (INEC).

In practice most judges are reluctant to write dissenting opinion. But non-conformist judges are known to write many. Brilliant and famous jurist like English judge Lord Denning, American judge Brandeis, Holmes, Jerome Frank, Scalia and Nigerian judge Kayode Eso, Oguntade[50] amongst a host of others were known for their dissent opinion. Dissent judgments have proved helpful to legal development as it could point out better alternatives to the majority's result or reasoning, or dangers in the development of the law, which while not earth shaking, are nonetheless worth noting. In this respect Lord Denning when in the House of Lords between 1957 and 1962 was reputed to write many dissenting opinions. For example in *Rahimtoola* v. *Nizam of Hyderabad*[51] where the House had to decide on a matter of international law, and the principle that the House is bound by the doctrine of *stare decisis* (if a previous judgment was wrong nobody except Parliament could change it), Lord Denning dissented. It was about a sum of £1,000,000 in the Westminster Bank in London. It had been placed there by the Nizam of Hyderabad. It was claimed by the Government of Pakistan. The question was whether Pakistan could claim sovereign immunity. In a dissent judgment, His Lordship stated that when sovereign states engaged in commercial transactions, they should not be entitled to claim immunity. He stated:

> I have considered some questions and authorities which were not mentioned by counsel. I am sure they gave all the help they could and I have only gone into it further because the law on this subject is of great consequence and, as applied at present, it is held by many to be unsatisfactory. I venture to think that if there is one place where it should be reconsidered on principle — without being tied to particular precedents of a period that is past — it is here in this House: and if there is one time for it to be done, it is now, when the opportunity offers, before the law gets any more enmeshed in its own net. This I have tried to do. Whatever the outcome, I hope I may say, as Holt CJ once did after he had done much research on his own: "I have stirred these points, which wiser heads in time may settle.

Even though Lord Denning was rebuke by Viscount Simonds (and other Law Lords join in it) His Lordship's position was helpful twenty years later in deciding

---

[50] *Buhari* v. *INEC* [2008] 12 SC (pt. I) I at , per Oguntade JSC.

[51] [1958] AC 379.

Trendtex v. *Central Bank of Nigeria.*[52]

Judges may also choose to write a separate judgment even if there is concurrence with the majority opinion. Though such opinion is not as scratchy as a dissent, it certainly is indicative of self-indulgent, single-minded. On the other hand, such a separate opinion could go to affirm that the majority decision is well supported and grounded. A judge may choose separate opinion in concurrence that agrees with a decision but for a different reason used by the majority. The strategy can be used to set forth reasons supporting the result the majority did not see fit to offer, or at least offer prominently enough. In that case, the separate opinion serves to emphasis, as it were the decision of the majority. Some judges have used it to warn that additional concerns in future cases may bring about different results. Also a judge could use it to underscore her own limited interpretation of the majority opinion as a precaution against too broad a future interpretation.

Judicial clerkship

A judge's relationship with her law clerks also affects the rhetoric of their opinion. It is a known ill-kept secret that clerks often do early drafts of opinion for judges, and following general human subtleties judges merely edit for prose correction and adopt them as the court opinion. This is more the case where the clerk is competent and the relationship judge and clerk is symbiotic. It is not uncommon for the judge instructing her clerk to do a first draft to discuss the proposed reason and framework of the case with the clerk.[53]

Law clerks can provide substantial assistance to the judge faced with writing an opinion. Especially in a time of burgeoning dockets, their help is crucial. Discussions with law clerks are helpful in planning the opinion and developing the outline. The opportunity to test one's thoughts in vigorous exchanges with the clerks is invaluable. This will continue to be a useful exercise throughout the writing process as the judge and the law clerks discuss and criticize the opinion as it develops, ferreting out error and ambiguity, striving for precision, and polishing the final product.[54]

---

[52] [1977] QB 529.

[53] Clerk contribution to judicial opinion writing has been criticised on many grounds. State some. Human weakness is likely not to change what appears okay. So, the one who wields the pen on the first draft often controls the last draft. See generally, Mary L. Dunnewold *et al., Judicial Clerkships: A Practical Guide,* Carolina Academic Press, 2010; Sylvan A. Sobel, ed. *Law Clerk Handbook: A Handbook for Law Clerks to Federal Judges,* 2nd ed., Fed. Jud.Ctr. 2007, (available at http://www.fjc.gov/public/pdf.nsf/lookup/lawclh bk.pdf/$file/lawclhbk.pdf); George Rose Smith, A Primer of Opinion Writing for Law Clerks (1973) 26 *Vand. L. Rev.* 1203; F. Frederick G. Hamley, Sample Instructions to Law Clerks (1973) 26 *Vand. L. Rev.* 1241.

[54] Judicial Manual @ 10.

In the writing process itself, judges use their law clerks in different ways. Some limit the clerks to performing research, preparing bench memos, and editing, cite-checking, and commenting on the judge's drafts. Some assign the writing of the first draft to a law clerk in routine cases only; others have clerks write drafts in even the most complex cases, having found that working from a draft, even a rough draft, makes the task of writing the opinion easier. A clerk assigned to write the first draft should use an outline developed by or with the judge, and should understand the scope, organization, and probable outcome of the opinion. Many judges, having found that it takes more time to work with a clerk's draft, write their own draft, then polish it into the final product. Some judges invite the law clerk to rewrite the judge's first draft before the judge returns to it for preparation of the final version.

The process the judge uses depends on his or her own work habits and style and on the capabilities of the particular law clerk. The judge must always remember, however, that the law clerk usually is fresh out of law school, with little practical experience. Even a distinguished academic record does not qualify a law clerk to practice the craft of judging, to draw the fine line between reversible and harmless error, to make the sometimes delicate assessment of the effect of precedent, and to recognize subtle distinctions in the applicable law. It is the unusual law clerk who has perfected a writing style that makes for a satisfactory opinion. Law clerks' fact statements, analysis, and conclusions may require major revisions. Judges should not simply be editors - no matter how capable the clerk, the opinion must always be the judge's work.[55]

Preparing to write

Judges must give conscious thought to the writing process. Writing an opinion is serious responsibility. As previously stated it serves three primary purposes. Judicial writing communicates a court's conclusions and the reasons for them to the parties and their lawyers; when published, it announces the law to other lawyers, judges, academics, and the interested public; its preparation imposes intellectual discipline on the author, requiring the judge to clarify her reasoning and assess the sufficiency of precedential support.

Because written decisions serve both case-deciding and law-making functions, a judge should think through the process to determine first what purpose is intended to be served by an opinion. If it is an opinion intended only for the parties, such as a bench opinion on says a preliminary objection in trial

[55]Judicial Manual @ 11.

that is not likely to be published, it should be less elaborate. Elaborate opinion should be reserved for decision intended to serve as precedent.

There are three main types of judicial opinions: *judgments*, *rulings*, *summary orders.*

Judgments are complete-dress opinions delivered at the end of litigation. It therefore requires structured discussion of the facts, legal principles, and governing authorities to arrive at a decision, which lays the matter to rest as between the parties and their privies. The significance or number of the issues presented, the novelty of the question, and the complexity of the facts are among the factors that determine whether an opinion requires full-dress treatment.

Rulings on the other hand are judicial opinions declared on preliminary matters pending the final disposition of a case. They include court decision on motions and applications filed either before or during or after hearing of a case. Usually they are in the form of summary orders that simply state the disposition of an application, sometimes with a brief statement of findings and conclusions, but often with little or no explanation. Depending on its complexity, most judges would dispose off them during bench hearing. In other instances the court may deem it necessary to elaborate if the ruling can be dispositive of the case in its entirety or would substantially affect the materiality of the litigation.

Summary orders are uncommon for courts of record. They are often a type of opinion reserved for inferior courts and tribunals, such as magistrates and area courts. They simply dispose of the case, sometimes with a brief statement of findings and conclusions, but often with little or no explanation. Summary orders are usually unpublished.

This being so, a judge who is saddled with the responsibility of writing a judicial opinion should first identify the type of opinion the case deserves. Next, she should consider the complexity of the facts and nature of the issues, the intended audience, and whether the opinion will be published.

Facts and issues

The scope of an opinion is often related to the complexity of the facts and the nature of the legal issues interrogated in a case. If the facts are complex, a judge would want to set them out in a clear, understandable form. Some judges acquire simplification by setting out the facts in chronological order. It may even require that technical terms be explained. It is also important to determine whether the facts interrogate an area of law where precedent is fairly settled or not. If the precedents are clear and the material facts are not complicated, the scope of the opinion will be limited. But, as the controlling law becomes more uncertain or the material facts more complex, the need for exposition and analysis to explain the reasons for the court's decision increases.

Some cases that present complex fact patterns may require lengthy discussion of the facts even though the applicable law may be simple. Others raising novel legal issues may require extended analysis of law and policy.

The scope of an opinion will be influenced by how well developed the law is in the area. Judges should consider whether the issue has previously been decided authoritatively and whether another opinion would aid in the development or explanation of the law. They should ask whether their opinion would say something that has not been said before. If the subject matter has been thoroughly aired in prior opinions, there would be no need to do an elaborate opinion that traces the origin and rationale for the rule. Such should be reserved for complex areas of law, especially where the controlling precedent is unclear or unsettled.

When, however, an opinion is written for an area of law emerging, such as say restitution law, cyber law, medical ethics and the like, or is one likely to lay down a new rule or modifying an old one, the writer must think not only about the rationale of the decision but also about the impact it will have as precedent. The judge would need to be discuss and analyse the existing precedents or analogous precedents in the area are, what they dictate as to road signs for new direction the law and the possible effect of the decision would have on existing law and society.[56]

The wisdom of detailed elaboration here is that it gives the opinion precedential value and it can help shape legal development. For example, in introducing the defence of change of position into English law of restitution (a defence that have long existed in many jurisdictions that recognize restitution or unjust enrichment law), Lord Goff had to state clearly the scope of the defence and how it is different (and should not be confused) with estoppel. His Lordship in *Lipkin Gorman* v. *Karpnale* thus stated:

> Where an innocent defendant's position is so changed that he will suffer an injustice if called upon to repay or to repay in full, the injustice of requiring him so to repay outweighs the injustice of denying the plaintiff restitution. If the plaintiff pays money to the defendant under a mistake of fact, and the defendant then, acting in good faith, pays the money or part of it to a charity, it is unjust to require the defendant to make restitution to the extent that he has changed his position. Likewise, on facts such as these in the

[56]Judicial Manual @ 4.

present case, if a thief steals my money and pays it to a third party who gives it away to charity, the third party should have a good defence to an action for money had and received. In other words, bona fide change of position should of itself be a good defence in such cases as these.

I am most anxious that, in recognising this defence to action of restitution, nothing should be said at this stage to inhibit the development of the defence on a case by case basis, in the usual way. It is of course, plain that the defence is not open to one who has changed his position in bad faith, as where the defendant has paid away the money with knowledge of the facts entitling the plaintiff to restitution and it is commonly accepted that the defence should not be open to a wrongdoer...I wish to stress however, that the mere fact that the defendant has spent the money, in whole or part, does not in itself render it inequitable that he should be called upon to repay, because the expenditure might in any event have been incurred by him in the ordinary course of things. I fear that the mistaken assumption that mere expenditure of money may be regarded as amounting to a change of position for present purposes has led in the past to opposition to some to recognition of a defence which in fact is likely to be available only on comparatively rare occasions. In this connection I have particularly in mind the speech of Lord Simonds in Ministry of Health v. Simpson (1950) 2 All ER 1137 at 1147 (1951) AC 251, 276.

I wish to add two further footnotes. The defence of change of position is akin to the defence of bona fide purchase but we cannot simply say that bona fide purchase is a specie of change of position. This is because change of position will only avail a defendant to the extent that his position has been changed, whereas, where bona fide purchase is invoked, no inquiry is made (in most cases) into the adequacy of consideration. Even so the recognition of change of position as a defence should be doubly beneficial. ...

It will enable a more generous approach to be taken to the recognition of the right to restitution in the knowledge that the defence is, in appropriate cases, available, and while recognising the different functions of property law and in equity, there may also

> in due course develop a more consistent approach to tracing claims in which common defences are recognised as available to such claims, whether advanced at law or in equity.[57]

No question about it, the dictum above is a clear, detailed statement of the law, creating and delineating the boundaries of the new rule introduced. Lord Goff also took time to review, analyse the relevant body of precedent and reservations on the law, citing the fears expressed by Lord Simonds in *Ministry of Health* v. *Simpson.*

This type of judicial opinion is then able to serve as good precedent because its detailed reasoning reveals the thinking that has gone into it.

Audience

The recipients of an opinion are usually the litigants and their counsels. They are the ones immediately concerned and affected by the court's opinion. It is therefore expected that they are the primary audience of judicial writing. To the extent an opinion is addressed to the parties, it should provide them with a fair and accurate statement of facts in controversy before the court, what the court decided, and the reasons for the decision.

This being so, they really are not persons who desire a detail explanation of the facts. They are familiar with it. But it may be advisable to set out in details the facts if they are complex and likely disputable. The parties may also not be interested in an extensive exploration of the law, other than what is needed to give the losing party a clear explanation for the result.

But an opinion is not only of interest to the parties and their counsel. Court opinions serve to inform others besides the parties. Therefore, opinions intended to inform other audiences may require additional factual development and legal analysis. How much analysis is required, and how detailed it must be, depends on the subject matter and the probable audience.

Where the area of law interrogated by the facts of a case are arcane, such as patent, antitrust law, etc. it may be useful for the judge to do an elaborate writing containing a discussion of the factual and legal background while avoiding legalese or technical language to aid comprehension by the uninitiated.[58]

No matter what audience an opinion is set at address, it must be clear, understandable. The intending audience must easily understand the expressed words in an opinion and the structure of the words. This is important so the direction in an opinion is taken seriously and complied with. An opinion setting

---

[57] [1991] 2 AC 548 at 581

[58] Judicial Manual @ 5.

guidelines for a trial court to follow, remanding a case must tell the lower court, stating legal rationale, policy foundation, directive of court to litigants and their counsel must be clear.

A skilful judge would endeavour to write clearly, setting out the statement of facts and legal analysis adequate to explain the decision to the parties that would also be sufficient for a higher court to understand the basis for the decision. An elaborate explanation would be necessary for complex cases to inform the parties and may be a higher court, in case of an appeal. But judges should generally avoid a situation where their opinion takes the form of a brief or become a vehicle for advocacy. Such style of writing could create impartiality suspicion.

Though most members of the public are hardly interested in reading judicial opinion, if an opinion is one of public interest, a judge should endeavour to write it in an elaborate way, that is easily understood to ensure it is not misunderstood.

Publication

In advanced jurisdictions where law reporting not stepped in commercialism, not all decisions of court are published. In fact, the objective of most law report societies and rules of court require a benchmark for cases that get published.[59]The

[59] See above n . 11. See also adopted rules or internal operating procedures or other policies concerning publication and non-publication of opinions in the United States such as Stienstra, Unpublished Dispositions: Problems of Access and Use in the Courts of Appeals (Federal Judicial Centre 1985); D.C. Circuit Rule 14(b) on what is publishable. It directs that only opinion that meet the criteria below would be publishable, namely: (i) with regard to a substantial issue it resolves, it is a case of first impression or the first case to present the issue in this Court; (ii) it alters, modifies, or significantly clarifies a rule of law previously announced by the Court; (iii) it calls attention to an existing rule of law that appears to have been generally overlooked; (iv) it criticizes or questions existing law; (v) it resolves an apparent conflict in decisions within the circuit or creates a conflict with another circuit; (vi) it reverses a published agency or district court decision, or affirms a decision of the district court upon grounds different from those set forth in the district court's published opinion; or (vii) it warrants publication in light of other factors that give it general public interest. See Judicial Manual @ 6-7 which states that Similar criteria are included in 1st Cir. R. 36.2(a); 4th Cir. I.o.P . 36.3; 5th Cir. R. 47.5.1; 6th Cir. R. 24(a); 7th Cir. R. 53(c)(1); 8th Cir. Plan for Publication of Opinions 9f 4; and 9th Cir. R. 36-2. Other circuits have more general guidelines, giving judges latitude to decide whether to publish. The standard in the Third Circuit, for example, is that "[a]n opinion is published when it has precedential or institutional value." 3d Cir. I.o.P. chap. 5.5.1.*See also* 11th Cir. R. 36-1, I.o.P. 3 ("Opinions that the panel believes to have no precedential value are not published"); Fed. Cir. R. 47.8(c) ("Unpublished opinions...are those unanimously determined by the panel as not adding significantly or usefully to the body of law and not having precedential value"). The Second Circuit permits disposition "in open court or by summary order" of "cases in which decision is unanimous and each judge of the panel believes that no jurisprudential purpose would be served by a written opinion ...." 2d Cir. R. 0.23. Otherwise, written opinions, including *per curiam* opinions, are published. *See also* 10th Cir. R. 36.1 (permitting disposition without opinion where "the case involves application of no new points of law that would make the decision of value as a precedent"). In the district courts, the decision to publish in the West Reporter System is entirely in the judge's discretion. Because decisions of district judges are merely persuasive authority-i.e., they are not binding precedent even in their own districts-publication should be the exception.

practice of just commercializing law report to contain as is done in Nigeria of virtually all Court of Appeal and Supreme Court report is therefore either novel or unprofessional.

An opinion should only be published if it meets the criteria of --- or such other criteria deemed proper. This can well be an area where the courts can also regulate commercial publication by setting out in their internal rules proper criteria for publication. Such rules it is suggested should require that unless the decision involves a novel or complex issue or a matter of public importance and thus may be useful to attorneys and judges or be of interest to the public they should not be published. The court can archive unpublished opinions. Such archived unpublished opinion could then be published later by reporters and styled "unpublished" opinions. The court it is suggested should then have no control over this, as is the practice in other jurisdictions. But those published under authority of the court must meet the laid down criteria.

Because unpublished decisions are written primarily for the parties, they will require little or no elaboration of the facts and law. The determination as to whether a disposition should be published or unpublished should be made as soon as possible, so that the judge who writes the opinion will not spend an undue amount of time on it if publication is not warranted.[60]

Final stage of preparing to write

When the judge has thought through the facts and issues, the audience of the opinion and the prospect of the opinion being published, it would then be time to think through what she want her opinion to say or decide and how it should be presented. The material facts would then be assembled, the issues formulated, the applicable law identified, and the appropriate nature and scope of remedy identified. The case is then broken into these components to begin the writing process. At this stage a judge likely reaches tentative conclusions.[61] When the writing does start however the judge should avoid fixation of original position in the first draft.

The writing process

Outlines

It is helpful to start the writing process with an outline. An outline helps a writer to organize thoughts, making eventual writing easy. In getting this ready the writer needs to have a fixed objective in mind and the steps needed to achieve it.

---

[60] See n. 56 @ 7.

[61] Writing should however be a recursive process. Citation. Judge Roger Traynor, Some Open Questions on the Work of State Appellate Courts (1957)24 U. Chi. L. Rev. 211 (an articles which encourage a recursive style of writing).

An outline may take a variety of forms: a formal, written outline prepared by the judge or law clerk; a rough sketch of important facts, issues, and points to discuss that the judge enlarges in the course of writing. It could even points noted by the judge during argument by counsel or a brief checklist; or perhaps only a mental framework. Whatever the form, the point is that judges, like all other good writers, must organize their thoughts before starting to write.

It is important to keep an outline simple because its purpose is to recall ideas that will form the road signs for the court opinion. it may be useful to write out in an outline a few sentences for use as an introduction. But by all means, its focus should be on ideas, not words. In putting the ideas down it would be beneficial to state them in short sentences. The few main point the judge plans to develop in the opinion should be made to clearly stand out. This can be done by italicizing, marking them in colours or writing them in capital letters. Under each main point should be put the list of ideas planned to be developed. For example, it would be useful to make a note of important facts, controlling precedents, legal analysis, illustrations, significant quotations, and the like. The outline should be extensive enough to cover the opinion to be delivered by the judge. The outline will be easier to use if it is neat.

A good time to prepare an outline is shortly after the conference at which the case is discussed and the opinion assigned, when the writer's own ideas and those of the other judges are fresh in mind. In addition to organizing the writer's thinking, the outline serves as an informal record of the discussion at the conference.[62]

Materials to review

The judge's is under obligation to read through the evidence before the court. They constitute the materials for review, and if the evidence is audio-recorded, to listen to it before beginning to draft an opinion. It is advisable to review the relevant material before beginning a draft to refresh one's memory of the significant issues and the arguments made.

Organizing and Writing the Opinion

In organizing and writing the opinion, the judge should clearly identify the relevant facts, the issues presented, and apply the governing precedent/law to produce a clear, well-reasoned decision. As a guide it would be useful to consider the following steps to meet the requirements:

---

[62]Judicial Manual @ 9.

Structure

A well-reasoned judicial opinion should contain five elements: (i) an introductory statement of the nature and procedural posture of the case; (ii) a statement of the issues to be decided; (iii) a description of the material facts; (iv) a discussion of the governing legal principles and the resolution of the issues; and (v) the disposition and necessary instructions. This is only a suggested organization structure as the style of an opinion may vary from case to case.

Undoubtedly, a clear and logical organization of the opinion will help the reader understand it. Accordingly, proper use of paragraphs, headings and subheadings, numbering as Roman numerals, or other means of disclosing the organization to the reader can be particularly helpful, especially where the opinion is long and the subject matter complex. The use of these markers, as it were, would serve as road signs for the reader. They also help to organize the writer's thoughts and test the logic of the opinion. And for collegiate judicial writing, it enables a judge who wishes not to join some part of the opinion to identify it. This organizational style can also assist in the indexing and classification of opinions and their retrieval by researchers.[63]

Elements of an opinion

The introduction

The purpose of an introduction is to prepare the mind of the reader to receive and be familiar with the case. An effective introduction helps the audience to understand the real significance of the opinion. It orients the reader to the case. It should therefore state briefly what the case is about, the legal subject matter, and the result.

Some judges have found it helpful to include the following in the introduction:

(i) The parties description: the parties should be identified, if not in the introduction then early in the opinion, preferably by name, and that identification should be used consistently throughout. The use of legal descriptions, such as "appellant", "appellee", "movant", etc. tends to confuse, especially in multi-party cases;

(ii) The procedural and jurisdictional status: the basis for the court's jurisdiction, relevant prior proceedings (if any), and how the case got before the court;

(iii) The issue: the issue or issues to be decided, unless they are so complex that they are better treated in a separate section.

[63]Judicial Manual @ 13.

The American practice of summarizing the holding at the outset can be useful in that it saves the reader's time, particularly researchers who will be able to determine immediately whether to read the rest of the opinion. Providing a terse summary of the holding at the start of the opinion also helps the writer to state it precisely and succinctly.

This way the final version of the introduction may be best written after the opinion is completed, when the judge has refined the issues, the conclusions, and the supporting analysis.[64]

However, some judges prefer to place the holding and conclusion at the end, believing that an opinion will be more persuasive if the reader must work through it before learning the outcome.

Statement of issues

The statement of issues is the mathematical formula for resolving legal controversies.[65] It is cornerstone of the opinion because how the issues are formulated determines which facts are material and what legal principles govern. In formulating issues, judges are not bound to follow counsels' analysis. Issues should be framed by the judges independently from the facts presented, even if this differs from how the lawyers state them. But it is important to state that the court is not bound to address every issue raised by counsel if resolution of the issue is not material to the outcome of the case.[66] Accordingly, the judge should refrain from considering academic issues or hypotheticals.

The statement of issues should be brief. Generally, two or three issues would be sufficient to dispose off a case. Some judges prefer to identify the issues before the statement of facts. Some other however choose the reverse. This is largely a matter of style. Stating the issues first is a preferred style because it makes the statement of facts more meaningful to the reader, helping the reader to focus on material facts.[67] This notwithstanding, the reverse style of keeping it after the

---

[64] This writing style no doubt aligns with the type of expanded IRAC syllogism described as '(QfrFR)+IRAC.' See n. 24.

[65] The statement of issues should not be confused with recitals of the parties' contentions. Lengthy statements of the parties' contentions, occasionally found in opinions, are not a substitute for analysis and reasoning and should be avoided.

[66] *Ishaya Bamaiyi* v. *State* (2001) FWLR (pt. 46) 956; [2001] 4 SC (pt. 1) 18, per Uwaifo, JSC; *State* v.*Ajie* (2000) 11 NWLR (pt. 678) 434 @ 448, per Onu, JSC ("The general rule is that a court has a duty to pronounce on all material issues raised before it. But the result of a court ... not complying with the general rule depends on the facts and circumstances of each case.")

[67] See the observations of Judge Frederick G. Hamley of the Ninth Circuit in Section of Judicial Administration, American Bar Association, Internal Operating Procedures of Appellate Courts, 1961 @ 30 ("A preliminary statement of the question, even in general terms, enables one to read the factual statement with discernment. It also aids the writer of the opinion in confining the factual statement to that which *is* essential)." Cited in Judicial Manual @ 14.

statement of facts can prove helpful in cases it may be difficult to state the issues clearly unless the reader is familiar with the material facts. This may be true, for example, where the issue is procedural and requires an explanation of the setting.

Facts

A judge is saddled with the responsibility of setting out the relevant facts in a controversy. Only the facts that are necessary to explain the decision should be included in an opinion. Background facts would be in some cases to give context of a decision and explaining its rationale. And opinions that are likely to be read by audiences other than the parties may require lengthier fact statements to provide the context for the decision and delineate its scope.

Much as a judge would like to state only the material facts at the outset to avoid repetition when discussing a particular issue, it is advisable to limit the historical elaboration at the outset if discussing particular issues would later require further elaboration of facts. To avoid this sort of clumsy situation, some judges would rather intersperse the facts and legal principle throughout their writing.

It is important to note that excessive factual detail can be distracting. For example, mention of too many dates can confuse the reader. They should be avoided unless material to the decision or helpful to its understanding. On the other hand, while brevity and simplicity are always desirable, they are secondary to the need for a full and fair statement. Facts significant to the losing side should not be ignored.[68]

Facts which are not material to the decision but can add colour or fun is dangerous, because a losing party can hold on to them as basis for the court arriving at an unfavourable decision, when in truth they may not have influenced the decision making. Moreover, this style of writing - though appealing to the author - may be seen by the parties as trivializing the case. It must therefore be a style approached with caution.

Above all, the statement of facts must be accurate. The writer should not assume that the facts recited in the parties' briefs are stated correctly. There is no substitute for checking fact references against the record. No matter how good the lawyers, the judge may find that the record facts differ from the way they are stated in the briefs. If time does not permit the judge to read the entire record personally, a law clerk should be assigned that task with instructions to mark all the relevant parts for the judge to review.[69]

[68]Judicial Manual @ 15.
[69]Judicial Manual @ 16.

Discussion of legal principles

The discussion of the applicable legal principles demonstrates the reason for the decision. The discussion of the legal principles should persuade the reader of the correctness of the result by the power of its reasoning, not by advocacy or argument.

The judge must consider and deal with arguably contrary authority and opposing argument, and must confront the issues squarely and deal with them forthrightly. Although the opinion need not address every case and contention, the opinion must sufficient demonstrate to the losing party that the essentials of its position have been fully considered.

To ensure that the principles are well thought out, a judge's discussion of the legal principles should contain statements showing that the follow were properly considered:

(i)Standard of review: The opinion should specify the controlling standard of review at the outset of the discussion of legal principles. Unless the reader is told whether review is under the de novo, the clearly erroneous, or the abuse of discretion standard, the meaning of the decision may be obscure. Specifying the standard of review, moreover, disciplines the writer's analysis. For example, it would be apposite to mention that the standard of proof applied for criminal litigation is proof beyond reasonable doubt.

(ii)Order of discussion: The opinion should contain something like an organizational chart. For example, matters that are fundamental, such as those that go to jurisdiction should be addressed first. Accordingly, general dispositive issues should be discussed first to quickly acquaint the reader with whether the case has a legal basis or not. However, it must be pointed out that the order in which those issues are taken up and discussed is a matter of personal style.

(iii)Which issues to address: As a general rule, an opinion should not range beyond the issues presented.[70]A judge should address only the issues that need to be resolved to decide the case. If the court determines that an issue not raised by the parties is dispositive and should be addressed - even though the parties have not properly preserved and presented it - the court should notify counsel and provide an opportunity to brief it. The simple logic of this is that a dispositive issue determines the life of an action and most rules and practice of court require that a dispositive issue can be raised at any time, during or after

---

[70]This is borne out of the principle that the court should not grant a relief not sought by a party. Cite cases to show that the court is not a Father Christmas.

trial, even on appeal.[71] It is therefore the course of wisdom for a judge to call on counsel to address her on dispositive issues even no party presents it as an issue for determination.

Issues not necessary to the decision but seriously urged by the losing party should be discussed only, to the extent necessary to show that they have been considered. The line between what is and is not necessary to the decision, however, is not always clear. Occasionally, a full explanation of the rationale for a decision may be enhanced by discussion of matters not strictly a part of the holding. Moreover, considerations of economy and efficiency may argue in favour of addressing issues not necessary to the decision if the court can by so doing provide useful guidance for the lower court on remand. In doing so, however, judges must be careful not to prejudge issues that are not before them and to avoid advisory opinions and unnecessary expressions of views that may tie the court's hands in a future case.[72]

(iv) ***Alternative holdings***: There are instances where a court's decision is supportable on alternative, separate and independent grounds. Some judges therefore make it a practice to state in their opinion the grounds. This is not a practice to encourage because when a decision is hinged on separate and independent grounds it discounts the precedential value of the decision.[73]

This notwithstanding, if an opinion is likely to have little impact as precedent, there is no reason why the court should not base its decision on alternative grounds, without giving one precedence over the other.

(v) Case citations: Generally, the court applies the most recent legal authority as basis for supporting a legal principle. The practice of citing several authorities on well settled legal principles should be avoided. Such string citations and dissertations on the history of the rule add nothing when the matter is fairly settled. It only gives the impression of a judge wanting to impress people about her erudition. Where however an opinion breaks new ground; or alters, modifies, or significantly clarifies a rule of law previously announced by the court; or calls attention to an existing rule of law that appears to have been generally overlooked; or criticizes or questions existing law; or resolves an apparent conflict in decisions within the circuit or creates a conflict with another circuit; or reverses a published agency or other court's decision, or affirms a decision of other court's upon

---

[71]See *Oloba* v. *Akereja* (1988) 3 NWLR (pt. 84) 508, per Fabiyi, JSC; *Madukolu* v. *Nkemdilim* [1962] SCNLR 341 both supporting the proposition that jurisdiction is the life wire to any adjudication)

[72]Judicial Manual @ 17.

[73]See Bernard E. Witkin, *Manual on Appellate Court Opinions*, 1977 @ 81 (the learned professor argues that the practice of inserting "even if" or "assuming" should be avoided in judicial opinions and he suggests that rather than use those words the judge should dispose of the case first and later state the substantial ground of the opinion last) cited in @ 17.

grounds different from those set forth in the court's published opinion; or warrants publication in light of other factors that give it general public interest, it would be useful for the court to marshal existing authority and analyse the evolution of the law sufficiently to support the new rule.

(vi) Secondary sources: Because the common law legal tradition relies heavily on case-law (and statute) as primary source for legal principles, it is would be imprudent for a judge to cite copiously secondary sources as basis for a legal principle. Accordingly, secondary sources (legal and non-legal), such as law review articles, treatises, texts, should be sparingly. They should be used to serve a purpose. A judge may cite secondary sources to support the reasoning of the opinion. Some authors are so well respected in their fields that, in the absence of a case on point, their words are persuasive. It would not be out of place to cite such works. For example, the works of Professor Peter Birks has been widely cited by courts to develop the law of restitution in England and other jurisdictions.

Court also cites public documents or other published works that shed light on relevant historical or policy considerations.

(vii) Quotations: While judges often cite or paraphrase from precedent, it would be helpful to quote from precedent if the point is germane to a decision. It makes the reasoning of the court more persuasive and informative than merely citing or paraphrasing it. The impact of a quote, however, is inversely proportional to its length. Quote briefly, and only when the language makes an important point.

While quotes should be short, they must also be fair. They must be taken out of context to mislead.

(viii) Avoiding advocacy: In justifying a decision it could sometimes be necessary for the judge to explain why a contrary argument is rejected. In doing so however, the judge must avoid the temptation to turn the court's reasoning to advocacy. The court's opinion should not be masked as an argument between the judge and the counsel, or other judges on the court, or the court below. The opinion should only explain why the contrary argument is rejected. It need not be a point-by-point refutation of the contrary argument. Neither should the language revealed in the opinion assume an adversarial tone. Judicial writing is not the place for emotive language and personal feelings. Thus a judge should avoid using adjectives and adverbs unless they convey information material to the decision.

(ix) Treatment of the court below: Appellate opinions can and should correct trial court errors and provide guidance on remand without embroidering on the circumstances or criticizing the court below. An appellate opinion need not attack a trial court's wisdom, judgment, or even its attitude in order to reverse its decision. And it should avoid unnecessary criticism, such as for having failed to consider authority or resting on improper motives.[74]

Concluding paragraph

Disposition of a case is the most important part of the conclusion. The dispositive declarations and orders must be clear, understandable. A judge should avoid making dispositive orders that require further clarification by subsequent litigation or applications. The court must not speak in riddles.

For example, where an appellate court state that "the case is remanded for further proceedings consistent with the opinion," it would only have succeeded in creating uncertainty. The lower court is made to fathom what the appellate court's opinion is. Opinions must spell out clearly what the lower courts or agencies are expected to do without, however, trespassing on what remains entrusted to their discretion. Thus, even where an abuse of discretion is found, the appellate court's decision is on the law, and the lower court or agency on remand retains the authority to exercise its discretion properly.

Summary disposition

A summary disposition may be appropriate in cases where only the parties and their lawyers are interested in the result, the facts are not complex, and the precedents are clear. It may take the form of a one-sentence order or a brief memorandum.[75]

Bench rulings

Judges rare issue bench rulings. When they do, such rulings are often couched in a one-line order, the reasons having been expressed orally. The practice saves much time and holds down the backlog of submissions.

Also on occasion, a judge may orally announce a ruling, or proposed ruling, and state that an opinion will follow at a later date. Appellate courts occasionally do. The practice presents obvious hazards: with the case more or less decided, the pressure is off and the judge may have trouble getting around to writing the opinion. Moreover, the judge may later find it difficult to write an opinion in a way consistent with the earlier oral ruling and might even arrive at a different result.

[74]Judicial Manual @ 18.
[75]Judicial Manual @ 19.

Chapter 9

Government Regulatory Analysis*

Introduction

This chapter is concerned about how lawyers can acquire the skills for understanding and analysing regulation particularly in the face growing ubiquity of government regulation in the public and private space of citizen's life. The analysis reveals why knowledge and application of administrative law as analytical tool are palpably deficient in understanding the regulatory state and the regulatory process which interrogates law, politics and policy in a common patrimony. It welcomes the lexicon of regulatory law as providing the normative and descriptive theory for analysing the regulatory process. It posits that it is plausible to analyse regulation with a vocabulary common as that used by the profession to mine ratio, concepts and justification from case law. We will therefore identify patterns of regulatory justification and the appropriate responses that explain government regulation. Using the regulatory mantra of match and mismatch as mantra for benchmarking regulation, we shall see how it helps pursue the modest prescription agenda for understanding the emerging of a common regulatory grammar that can be deployed to analyse complex legal disputes involving regulations.

One skill lawyers are familiar with is that of case analysis. Talks like this are the *ratio decidendi* or *obiter dictum* of the case is common vocabulary.[1] Lawyers know how to analyse case law. Primer books on legal method are replete with how it is done. Mining case law requires identifying the relevant facts, the issues thereto, the holding and reasoning for the holding of the court, which provides common lawyers with a common vocabulary in presenting legal arguments on principle. Common lawyers are home with the skill. The bulk of the common law

---

* Oghenemaro Festus Emiri is a Professor of Jurisprudence, Dean of The Rhetor Place Legal Academy, Lekki-Lagos & EK Clark Distinguished Professor of Lawyering Skills, Edwin Clark University, Kiagbodo, Warri & Ernest Owusu-Dappa, PhD, Head of Commercial Law, Kwame Nkrumah University, Kumasi, Ghana.

[1] See Simon Lee & Marie Fox, *Learning Legal Skills*, 2nd ed. London: Blackstone Press, 1994.

legal system is case law.[2] But that was at the early stages of the tradition. Today, the landscape of the tradition is fast being dominated by policy, regulation and legislation.[3] While rules for interpreting statute and legislation is not strange to lawyers, the skills for analysing them to determine match and mismatch is by no means easy.[4] This paper proposes a methodology to study government policy and regulation in a way and manner that parallels case analysis. It is designed to show that just as case study yields an understanding of the legal system, the institutions of law, its surface and deep structure of law, so too does an analysis of regulation shed light on an understanding of the types of regulations and institutions government ought to use in creating market efficiency.[5] When lawyers are skilled in regulatory analysis they acquire the tools for not only analysing government regulation, but also the ability to understand and evaluate better the allocative goals of the common law tradition, while providing lawyers an understanding of the nature of regulatory process.[6] This skill equips members of the bar to contribute meaningfully in policy debates on the economic, political and institutional dimensions of the regulatory state.

Why Regulatory Analysis Skill is Important

Just as it is right to think that we inhabit the *nomos* (normative sphere) governed by the laws empire.[7] More of the defining space of law is now regulatory. The state

---

[2]KotzZweigert & H. Kotz, *An Introduction to Comparative Law* (translated by T. Weir ed., 1977); Castan Tobenas, Contemporary Legal Systems of the Western World (1988) 25 *Comp. Juridical Rev.* 105; Lord Goff, The Future of the Common Law, (The Wilberforce Lecture 1997) (1997) 46 *ICLQ* 745.

[3]R. Jagtenberg, E. Oruici, and A.J. de Roo (eds.) *Transfrontier Mobility of Law*, 1995; Pierre Legrand, Against a European Civil Code (1997) 60 *MLR* 44; J. Bell, English Law and French Law- Not So Different? (1995) 48 *CLP* 63; Lord Goff of Chieveley, above n. 2 (where speaking from the perspective of reading and experience, the learned Law Lord thinks that the differences between the common law and civil law traditions is to be found rather in form than in substance, and more in procedure and method of legal reasoning).

[4] Stephen Breyer, *Regulation and its Reform*, Cambridge, MA: Harvard Univ. Press, 1982, 191-368.

[5]Joseph P. Tomain& Sidney A. Shapiro, Analysing Government Regulation (1997) 49 *Admin. L. Rev.* 377.

[6]Richard A. Posner, The Economic Approach to Law in A Ogus & C E Veljanovski, *Readings in the Economics of Law and Regulation,* Oxford: Clarendon Press, 1984, 43-6 (an article where the author reveals that efficiency is synonymous with justice, especially distributive justice defined crudely as the proper degree of economic inequality, and that injustice commonly describes wasting resources).

[7]Robert Cover, Nomos and Narrative (1983) 97 *Harv. L. Rev.* 4 For Supreme Court decisions, the narratives are stories not only about the case at hand, but also about who we are or wish to be as a community. In addition, Supreme Court decisions them- selves offer arguments for their own validity—including an implicit argument based on the underlying narratives; Richard K. Sherwin, Nomos and Cinema (2001) 48 *U.C.L.A. L. Rev.* 1519, 1520 (storytelling capabilities of these films along with their "[p]opular images of lawyers, criminals, and the legal system help people to understand, or think they understand, the reality these images depict; Ronald Dworkin, *Laws*

regulates virtually every sphere of public and a large part of private life. In public areas government regulates what counts as crime. It regulates education, health, communication, the environment and many others. Even in areas considered private, government regulates what we eat, wear, talk about, and many more. It has been suggested that there is virtually no part of society or of our lives untouched by government through regulation. The many concerns expressed on de-regulation and liberalisation are somewhat triggered by the wish of citizens to get government "off their back" especially in matters concerning business and economy.

Visual of government regulation

Working in an environment of regulation demands that lawyers at least possess skills for analysing whether particular regulation makes sense in the face of so many regulations being chunked out by government and its agencies. Regulatory skills enable professionals to evaluate the cost and benefit of regulation, and properly address the question whether the regulatory state is effective in mitigating the economic and social problems regulation addresses. Importantly, whether the right tool of regulation is used to address societal problems, to avoid what has been described as "regulatory mismatch."[8]

Empire.

[8]Above n. 5.

Prior Analytical Tool

Matters of an analysis of regulation have for ages been of interest to the profession, it been analysed through the prism of constitutional cum administrative law concern with process reforms, such as those of proper executive oversight or methods of statutory interpretation. Coming from this bias, lawyers have basically deployed administrative law skills to posit and promote provisions for greater executive control of agency powers to curb, as it were, excessive and oppressive government regulations. Lawyers have also resorted to use of statutory interpretation rules like the golden rule, the mischief rule, and the several refinements of the interpretation principles to curtain excessive or abusive regulations.[9]

Good as these skill tools can be in helping to check ubiquitousness of government regulations it falls short of providing a template for addressing and articulating substantive answers on regulation, substantive answers concerning what should be the substantive objectives and civilised norms of the regulatory state, which carry social significance. What is more, the administrative law model being atomistic, and law skewed, is unable to provide the needed multi-disciplinary understanding about government regulation which link and brings together interplay of how law, policy, and politics influence regulatory decisions of government.

Administrative law is unable to provide answers to questions about the regulatory state and regulatory process because administrative law interrogates procedural and formalistic questions, such as what branch of government has power to act in a particular case, scope of judicial review, whether a particular prescribed process is followed, etc. Much as these are matters with political and policy implications, the formalism of administrative law prevents an evaluation of what should count as good or bad policy, or what ought to be the ideal political landscape for government. These substantive matters having a bearing on the political and policymaking process, uncovering as it were of political influences and policy arguments underlying regulatory process admixed with the law, is what regulatory analysis skill gives the lawyer as arsenal in debating the regulatory process.

Thus, it basically defines the functions of institutions, the nature and scope of their jurisdiction, control mechanisms, ambits of statutory and regulatory interpretation and the like. These are not matters of substance, which can hardly account for an understanding of substantive policies and politics that inform the

[9] See for example, *Attorney-General of Bendel State* v. *Attorney-General of the Federation* (1982) 3 NCLR 1.

regulatory process.[10] Administrative law rather deals with formal, legal rules, on powers of control of government making it incongruent to interrogate variables, which bring into a common patrimony policy, politics and law. The first two variables distance administrative law from regulatory studies. Lawyers just imagine that their presence makes the field of study messy and complex for legal analysis. But it should not be so. The function of theory is to provide a form of "constellation to connect the stars." A proper theory or methodology elucidates complexities, untangling various strands of a phenomenon to clear understanding.[11]

There is therefore a need to devise a multi-disciplinary methodology to study and understand government regulation, which parallels what lawyers do in case analysis. This skill is what yields an understanding of the modern regulatory state and the nature of the regulatory process.[12] This analytical skill is what equips lawyers to logically debate, and question policy, institutional and political dimensions of the regulatory state.

Why Regulatory Analysis

The inability of administrative law to bridge between "process" (the formal concern of administrative law) and "substance and normative" attributes of the regulatory state and process is what gives birth to regulatory scholarship, a subject that is able to look within the formality of law and outside of law to address the content and values of the regulatory state. However, because the skills interrogated in analysing regulation is largely multi-disciplinary (as is presently the case with law on safety and environment), lawyers would have to come to terms with the substantive implications of law implicated by politics and policy from political science and economics respectively.[13]

The epistemic basis for regulatory analysis has not been easy to propound. Economic scholars have used self-interest as justificatory basis for understanding the regulatory process, which mixes law, politics and policy. Their descriptive theory has ranged between public interest, public choice, organisational and institutional hypothesis.[14] Of all of these however make central the public choice

---

[10] Robert L. Rabin, Administrative Law in Transition: A Discipline in Search of an Organising Principle (1977) 72 *Northwestern Univ. L. Rev.* 120

[11] Kris Franklin, Theory Saved My Life (2005) 8 *N.Y. City L. Rev.* 599, 601

[12]Above n. 5.

[13] Sidney A. Shapiro & Joseph O. Tomain, *Regulatory Law and Policy: Cases and Materials,* LexisNexis, 1993.

[14] James G. March &Johian P. Olsen, Rediscovering Institutions: The Organisational Basis of Politics, London: Free Press, 1989; Samuel Peltzman, Toward a More General Theory of Regulation (1976) 19 *J.L. & Econ.* 211; Richard A. Posner, Theories of Economic Regulation (1974) 5 *Bell J. Econ.& Mgmt. Sci.* 335; George J. Stigler, The Theory of Economic Regulation (1971) 2 *Bell J. Econ. & Mgmt.*

theory. Public choice is based on the assumption that rational actors will maximise their utility. It uses a market-like model to analyse regulation. In the theory, business groups are expected to prevail over the general citizenry because they have significant economic incentive to be more politically active in affecting legislative actions. There is no question about the truism of the hypothesis. Corporations like Shell, Dangote, MTN, Nigerian Breweries, Guinness, etc. acting in organised, self-interest can influence regulation in ways and manner the general citizens cannot. But that does itself provide an undisputable proof that the explanatory basis for regulation is public choice theory. Evidence abounds of regulations (in health, environment, safety, product liability, etc.) that are directed against business interest, which they have not been able to stop. This being so, while the theory can predict that business groups will prevail because of their deep pockets and political influence, the outcome can sometimes (often) be other way round. Therefore, as a theory, it is deficient it that it does not account for the influence of ideas or policy consideration in regulatory process not rooted in its self-interest underpin.

This is what necessitates a shift from an interest proposition to a value proposition as epistemological foundation for understanding the regulatory state and process.[15] The shift is thus a movement from procedure to substance, from a constellation of lobby to reason, a basis that somewhat veils the otherwise linkage between policy argument and regulatory outcome. This is because ideas that provide the linkage is not easily observable, unlike concrete matter out there. So, in the final analysis, while lobby and interest do have a place in regulation, sound policy argument, which aligns with social norms concerning the appropriate role of the state in society, appears to prevail as propeller of the regulatory state and process. This is especially the case in legislative era that posits that weighing the competing rationale of cost and benefit circumscribes much of government dealing in modern democracy. This is what makes less prevailing the public choice theory as the potential explanatory basis for regulatory analysis. This is what explains why when policy arguments are raised as to how best to reduce say

Sci. 3 (1971); all cited in Shapiro, n. 5 at 390 ft. 54. See also, Daniel Sokol, Explaining the Importance of Public Choice for Law (2011) *Mich. L. Rev.* 1030 (an article which shows how public choice helps to understand the dynamics of behaviour, and that as an economic tool it provides an understanding of political science, in that it addresses opportunities for and constraints on behaviour in public life in a manner akin to how economics does in private life (the market). Public choice also assumes rational actors who maximize their utility.

[15] Martin Shapiro, Of Interest and Values: The New Politics and the New Political Science in Marc K. Landy & Martin A. Levin, eds. *The New Politics of Public Policy*, John Hopkins Univ. Press, 1995, 3. (the book teaches the value of ideas in the post-utilitarian America as underlying regulation notably in education, immigration, and tax reform, rather than the public choice theory that places business as prevailing against citizens.

environmental pollution, or automobile injuries on our roads, government agencies seek to either defend regulation on policy grounds as within their statutory mandates or as consistent with the role of government in society, both of which are grounded in the substantive nature and scope of the regulatory state.

Since regulation is an admixture of law, politics and policy, it is less susceptible of a theory of self-interest promoted by public choice and so, it shades more into a complex world of study of political behaviour. It is therefore not readily analysable with the formal rules and procedure-sided bent of administrative law, but some other tool that can explain how the three components mix to trigger regulation in the regulatory state. There is therefore a need to study regulation within a theory with explanatory powers and methodology as lawyers do in mining case law to understand the theory of the legal system and legal principles deducible from them. The former intricately implicates the question of how to determine if the regulatory state is effective in mitigating the economic and social problems regulation addresses, while the later demands a methodology for analysing regulation.

Methodology for Analysing Regulatory

In an interesting seminal paper, the learned regulatory writers Tomian and Shapiro, have suggested a methodology that works like that which lawyers have long employed in grounding theories and principles of law over the ages.[16]Dean of Harvard Law School, Christopher Columbus Langdell, is reputed to have introduced the formal methodological approach to legal education rooted in the Socratic style of teaching in the nineteenth century as a clear demarcation from apprenticeship.[17] (state his view about the science of law and how this now provides the basis for case analysis - see Bix on Jurisprudence). Analysing cases have been useful in the development of classification and reasoning in law, without which the profession would have been faced with a mass of incomprehensible mass of particulars. This explains why lawyers must then design a systematic methodology for analysing regulation, so that a common regulatory vocabulary would be available to the profession.

Using a similar scientific method, regulatory analysis can reveal the basic principles and structure of public law and even provide insight into the justification or otherwise of regulatory policy (whether regulation addresses the challenges it seeks to address). There can be no question about it, a suitable regulatory methodology must be one that can provide an analytical pattern for identifying a template for understanding regulation across board, whether in the

---

[16]Above n. 5 at 398.
[17]Bix, Jurisprudence.

motor industry or the environment or any other sphere where the state regulates activities.[18]

Drawing on a similar scientific method for analysing case which generally follows the IRAC style, the learned writers have suggested the following four step analysis, but I suggest a five-component step for analysis, namely: (i) fact analysis/market situation; (ii) legal issues/policy issues; (iii) application/policy argument; (iv) holding/resolution; (iv) ratio/ratio.[19]

The workability of the structure can be amazing. Stage (i) in case analysis informs lawyers about the relevant facts in a controversy. Just as facts set the stage or scenario for adjudication, regulatory law takes as its starting point the economic or social challenges sought to be addressed by regulation. Because regulatory law is basically rooted in an economic analysis of law, the starting point can best be referred to as the market situation.[20]

Next, like case law, where lawyers distil issues from facts, regulatory analysis makes material the question of policy issues that are implicates by the prevailing economic and social challenges that require address by regulation.

Once the issues are identified, the analysis enters stage (iii) which is marching of the facts/market situation to the legal/policy issues to justify conclusion, which is the holding of court or the resolution of the regulatory challenge.

The final stage, which is distilling the ratio interrogates whether the method applied sufficiently addresses or dispose of the controversy or the issues requiring redress. The table would thus follow this pattern:

---

[18] For a discussion on justificatory category, see Peter Jaffey, Classification and Unjust Enrichment (2004) 67 *Mod. L. Rev.* 1012 (a discussion on the explanatory basis of the concept of unjust enrichment law and analyses the subject within the prism of analogical or theoretical reasoning as grounding the justification of a category as fundamental). The learned writer for example states that if the underlying claim for contract is say enforceable promise, then a theory of the subject must explain the common structure in contract controversies such as what type of contracts are enforceable, what should be decided if an agreement does not provide for a contingency that arises, what sort of remedies should be available for breach, etc. It is the ability of the theory to provide a uniform framework for treatment of claims that gives it justificatory basis. See also, N. MacCormick, *Legal Reasoning and Legal Theory* (Oxford: Oxford University Press, rev. ed., 1994) ch. 7; C. R. Sunstein, 'On Analogical Reasoning' (1992) 106 *Harv. L. Rev.* 741 E. Sherwin, A Defence of Analogical Reasoning in Law (1999) 66 *Univ. of Chicago L. Rev.* 1179.

[19]Above n.5.

[20] Most regulatory scholars are legal economists who take as given that the market is a better driver of development than control. See the invisible hand theory of Adam Smith. State contrary position which seem to justify the label of an economic analysis of law as neo-capitalism and a resurrection of utilitarianism

Case Analysis	Regulatory Analysis
Fact Analysis: what facts are relevant in the controversy?	Market Analysis: what is the economic or social challenge sought to be addressed?
Legal Issues: what legal issues do the facts interrogate?	Policy Issues: what is the philosophy of government interrogated by the economic or social problem sought to be addressed?
Application: how do the facts meld with the legal issues to provide justification for resolution?	Policy Argument: how do the market analysis meld with the philosophy of government?
Holding: how does the applicable rule of law dispose the controversy?	Resolution: what regulatory method best addresses the problem caused by the economic or social dysfunction addressed?
Ratio: an assessment of the justificatory basis for the holding and its further application to advance justice.	Ratio: assessing the efficacy and political correctness of the regulatory method chosen and its capacity to advance the fundamental philosophy of government.

The table analysis serves as a coherent template to understand government regulation in a way and manner that lawyers can deploy a common analytical language to explain regulation in diverse sphere, no matter where they apply - in environment, health, scientific, automobile industries, etc. With this skill, lawyers can deploy policy arguments that are appropriate to their area of practice. For example, lawyers skilled in regulatory analysis are thus better equipped to contribute in on-going debates on programmes of deregulation and other regulatory reform in the country.

Visual illustration of regulatory analysis

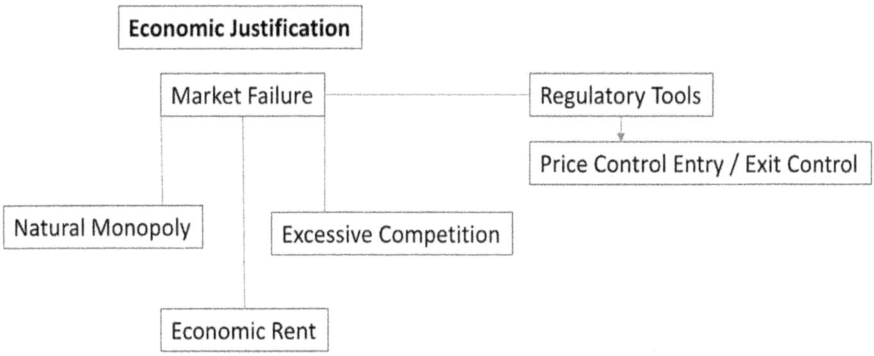

Explanatory Basis for Regulation

This brings us to the question, why should government regulate? Many reasons can be advanced for regulation. Reasons for regulation can range from politics, social, ethnic etc. The kaleidoscopic answers generated simply reveals different perception to how most person view the modern state. Most legal economists, and a number of economists and political scientists generally favour do not favour ex ante regulation. In fact, they moot for deregulation.[21]

Legal economists however posit that the state regulates for the singular reason to correct market failure (economic and non-economic).[22] The reason for this is obvious. Economists have long believed that the invisible hand of the market creates allocative efficiency and distributive gains.[23] Economists analyse society first from a preference for markets as a form of social ordering. Since markets can sometimes be defective for many reasons, it is the presence of 'market failure' that serves as justification for government to regulate a market to create the necessary allocative efficiency. From this paradigm, regulation is only necessary to promote efficiency.[24]

---

[21] Global demand for deregulation is grounded on the assumption that free market is better than government regulation. See Herbert Hovenkamp, *Enterprise and American Law*, 1991; Cass R. Sunstein, *After the Rights Revolution, Preconceiving the Regulatory State*, 1990. For readings on professional call for deregulating the legal profession, see Deborah L. Rhode, Policing the Professional Monopoly: A Constitutional and Empirical Analysis of Unauthorised Practice Prohibition (1981) 34 *Stan. L. Rev.* 1; Barlow F. Christensen, The Unauthorised Practice of Law: Do Fences Really Make Good Neighbours-Or Even Good Sense? (1980) 5 *Law & Social Inquiry* 159; Derek A. Denckla, Non-lawyers and the Unauthorised Practice of Law: An Overview of the Legal and Ethical Parameters (1999) 67 *Fordham L. Rev.* 2581.

[22] For literature analysis of the economic justification for regulation see, Sidney A. Shapiro & Joseph O. Tomain, *Regulatory Law and Policy: Cases and Materials*, LexisNexis, 1993; Stephen G. Breyer & Richard B. Stewart, *Administrative Law and Regulatory Policy: Problems Text and Cases*, 3rd ed., Aspen Pub., 1992, 5-11, (7th ed. 2015); Richard Posner, *Economic Analysis of Law*, 8th ed. NY: Aspen, 2011, 489; Joseph P. Tomain & Sidney A. Shapiro, Analysing Government Regulation (1997) *Admin. L. Rev.* 377; Richard A. Posner, The Social Costs of Monopoly and Regulation (1975) J. Pol. Econ. 807. It must be noted however that not every market failure invites an *ex ante* regulatory solution. A great deal of market failure is addressed directly by courts through common-law or statutory remedies that award damages *ex post* to injured persons. Thus, regulation would be necessary if a market fails, and courts are unable to address the problem within the remedial ambits of law. See also Richard A. Posner, Theories of Economic Regulation (1974) 5 *Bell J. Econ. & Mgmt. Sci.* 335; George J. Stigler, The Theory of Economic (1971) 2 *Bell J. Econ. & Mgmt. Sci.* 3; Samuel Peltzman, Towards a More General Theory of Regulation (1976) 19 *J. Law & Econ.*211; Benjamin H. Barton, Why Do We Regulate Lawyers? An Economic Analysis of the Justification for Entry and Conduct Regulation (2001) 33 *Ariz. St. L.J.* 429.

[23] Adam Smith, *Wealth of the Nation*. Global demand for deregulation is grounded on the assumption that free market is better than government regulation. See Herbert Hovenkamp, *Enterprise and American Law: 1836-1937*, Cambridge, Massachusetts: Harvard Univ. Press, 1991; Cass R. Sunstein, *After the Rights Revolution, Preconceiving the Regulatory State*, 1990.

[24]Above n. 22.

Thus, an absence of market failure makes it unnecessary for government to regulate, such as change the assignment of rights and obligations.[25] Where however, the reason for regulation is social, in that market promotes values inconsistent with core social values, the analysis for justification starts from the premise that government is necessitated by a people who set up a political structure on certain core values (generally referred to in economics are 'market inalienable')[26] on how they wish to be organised. If markets therefore operate in such manner that discounts these values, government will be justified in intervening to correct the defects by regulating market operation to maximise the values. In this respect, law is used to constrain markets. So, the difference between economic and social justification for regulation can be liken to that between efficiency and equity. While both can be strong currents in any political system, trumping one another, both cannot be ignored in regulatory scholarship.[27]

Let us now consider economic justification for regulation. Economic regulation addresses three market failures, namely: (i) natural monopoly, (ii) excessive competition and (iii) economic rents. Two regulatory tools are deemed appropriate to correct the failures natural monopoly, excessive competition and

---

[25] Ronald Coase, The Problem of Social Cost (1960) 3 *J. Law & Econ.* 1; see reprinted in Ronald Coase, *The Firm, the Market, and the Law,* Chicago Univ. Press, 1988. The paper is reputed to be the most cited law paper in the world. See Fred R. Shapiro, The Most Cited Law Review Article Revisited (1996) 71 *Chi.-Kent L. Rev.* 751. See also, W.N. Landes & Richard Posner, The Influence of Economics on Law: A Quantitative Study (1993) 36 *J. of Law & Econs. 385,* (on recent study which suggest that the major American law journals cite articles using the economic approach more than articles using other approach in legal scholarship).

[26] Market inalienable follows commodification argument that certain kind of activities are of intrinsic value that a market valuation of them is inappropriate in that it distorts significantly their tangibility. Inappropriateness of market principles to such values has often rested on lines of property-personhood dichotomy and incommensurability hypothesis. See *Hegel's Philosophy of Rights*, London: Oxford Univ. Press, translated by T.M. Knox, 1952, s.44) cited in Neil Neil Duxbury, Do Markets Degrade? (1996) 59 *Mod. L. Rev.* 331. For further reading on incommensurability in philosophical literature see, Joseph Raz, Mixing Values, *Proceedings of the Aristotelian Society* 83; J. Griffin, Mixing Values, (1991) 65 *Proceedings of the Aristotelian Society* 65; J. Griffin, Are There Incommensurable Values? (1977) 7 *Philosophy & Public Affairs* 39; Joseph Raz, *The Morality of Freedom*, Oxford: Clarendon Press, 1986, 339-340; Cass Sunstein, Incommensurability and Valuation in Law (1994) 92 *Michigan L. Rev.* 779; Anderson, *Value in Ethics and Economics,* Cambridge, Mass: Harvard Univ. Press, 150; Margaret Radin, *Reinterpreting Property*, Chicago: Univ. of Chicago Press, 1993; Brian Bix, *Law, Language and Legal Determinacy,* Oxford: Clarendon Press, 1993, 96. But cf. Schnably, Property and Pragmatism: A Critique of Radin's Theory of Property and Personhood (1993) 45 *Stanford L. Rev.* 347. Neil Duxbury, Law, Markets and Valuation (1995) 61 *Brooklyn L. Rev.* 657; Guido Calabresi & Douglas Melamed, Property Rules, Liability Rules and Inalienability: One View of the Cathedral (1972) 85 *Harv. Law Rev.* 1089; Festus Emiri, A Market Approach to Vocational Legal Education in Nigeria in *Trajectory of Nigerian Law: Underneath is Festschrift of Dean Smith* (ed. Ibidapo-Obe, Lagos: Lagos Univ. Press, 2015, 144.

[27] Arthur A. Leff, Economic Analysis of Law: Some Realism about Nominalism (1974) 60 *Virginia L. Rev.* 451 (a critique of pure economic analysis to legal and social questions in reaction to the first publication of Richard A. Posner's, *Economic Analysis of Law* book).

economic rents create. They are the regulatory tools of price control or entry or exit controls.

Visual on regulatory basis

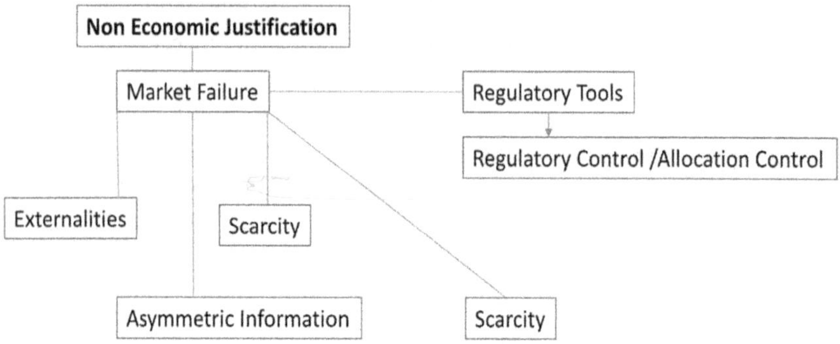

(i) Natural monopoly

Generally, the regulation of public utilities, such as provision of water, housing, electricity other social services is based on the concept of natural monopoly. Because monopoly leads to reduced output and higher prices, governments have traditionally responded with regulation of price control and in some cases with entry and exit control. For example, in Nigeria while the government through regulation grants the status of monopoly to electricity distributors like the Port Harcourt Distribution Company (PHDC) and other licensed distributors, the price of electricity to consumers is regulated by NERC.[28] Government also through an auction system controls entry and exit to the electricity market. This can therefore be likened to a government utility market, controlled by regulatory tools of price control or entry or exit control.

(ii) Excessive competition

The presence of excessive competition in an industry no doubt can create a real perfect market situation. But inherent in such competition can be lurking dangers for buyers of the industry's goods or services. Excessive competitors could lead industrial players to cut prices as strategy for remaining in business to the point where others would be run out of the market or a lowering of the quality of industrial products or services to stay in the market. Both scenarios can be detrimental to the economy and the people. This is more the case where the process triggers low quality services or a failure to observe minimum safety to users. In Nigeria for example, in the early 2000 when such cutthroat competition

[28]NERC Act.

affected adversely safety concerns in the aviation industry, the government was forced to employ entry and exit regulation to stop the slide into unsafe aviation by legislating that all airlines with single carriers should exit the market.[29]

(iii) Economic rents

Economic rent describes a situation where providers of goods and services sell products or services in short supply to earn make excessive profit. There is no question about it that such a situation is no different from a normal market where prices vacillate on the pendulum of demand and supply. This notwithstanding, government is justified to regulate such rents with a view to promote fairness in the market. One area that readily comes within this bracket is the supply for urban housing. For example, Lagos State by regulation in 2010 sought to stabilise the housing market and protect the poor by regulating rental prices for residential houses.[30] In areas as this the appropriate regulatory tool is either price control or entry or exit controls. That explains why some governments have regulatory control of licensing mortgage housing/banking businesses, while others have sought merely to control residential housing rents.[31]

Visual on regulatory match for market failure

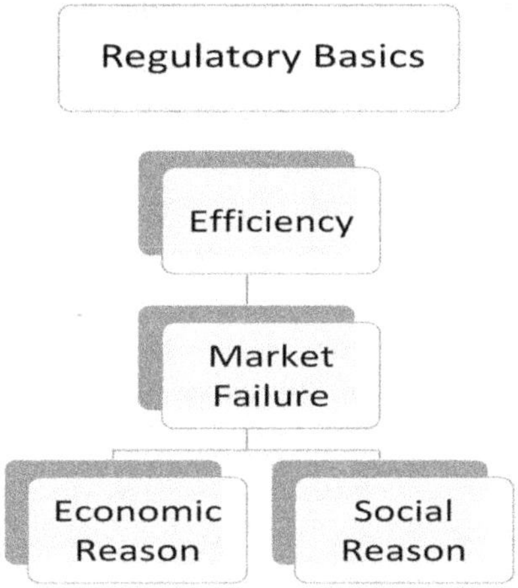

[29] See national policy on aviation.
[30] See Lagos State Tenancy Law, 2011.
[31] Rent control however can sometimes have negative impact on general housing needs, as in cases where it drives investments away from the sector. See for an economic analysis, Richard A. Epstein, Rent Control and the Theory of Efficient Regulation (1988) 54 *Brooklyn L. Rev.* 741. But cf. Margaret J. Radin, Reinterpreting Property, 1993, 87; J. Mandel, Does Rent Control Hurt Tenants? A Reply to Epstein (1989) 54 *Brooklyn L. Rev.* 1267.

Non-Economic Justification for regulations

Let us now turn attention to non-economic justification for regulation. The sphere (social regulation) addresses four market failures: (i) negative externalities; (ii) asymmetric information; (iii) scarcity; and (iv) public goods. In these four areas, government response to market failure is with the tools of regulatory or allocative controls.

(i) Externalities

A classic example of a negative externality is pollution that affects persons who live within the neighbourhood of emission from a cement factory.[32] A polluting company generally sells its products to customers at a price that covers production costs which ordinarily does not include the societal cost of production arising from its pollution. Control of negative externality could find expression through tort jurisprudence or regulation. If the legal system chooses to complement tort with regulation, the appropriate tool of control enters the equation. Governments have shown readiness to regulate negative externalities by specifying preventive actions injurers must take and degrees of precaution. For example, infuriated by incessant accidents caused by trucks and commercial transporters, the FRSC have proposed speed regulation and speed monitoring meters to those classes of vehicles.[33] Aside regulatory control of negative externalities, governments have also used allocative control, especially in pollution cases. The presence of carbon auctioning is a good example of using allocative control.[34]

---

[32] Pollution is the paradigmatic example that illustrates externality. Externality often arises from issues connected with conflict and cooperation in the use of property, as when the use of property by a person affects (positively or negatively) the welfare of others. One party's action is said to create an externality, if it affects with a probability, the wellbeing of others, in comparison to some standard of reference. An example, of negative externality, would be the case of a textile mill that discharges effluent, such as dye into a body of water. The harm (externality) reduces the utility of others who use the water. Salutary behaviours are a good example of positive externality, such where one person spraying to kill mosquitoes in his property also rids his neighbours of the pests. For classical discussion on externality, see Ronald H. Coase, The Problem of Social Cost (1960) 3:1 *J. Law & Econ.* 44; Steven Shavell, *Foundations of Economic Analysis of Law,* Cambridge, Mass: Harvard Univ. Press, 2004, 77. Generally, litigation or private bargain or regulation is used (in economic language, to internalise) to handle problems of negative externality.

[33] On forms of regulation justified as responses to externalities, see Daniel C. Esty, Towards Optimal Environmental Governance (1999) 74 *N.Y.U. L. Rev.* 113 (externalities and the environment); Jon D. Hanson & Kyle D. Louge, The Cost of Cigarettes: The Economic Case for Ex Post Incentive-Based Regulation (1998) 107 *Yale L.J.* 1163 (externalities and the cigarette market).

[34] See generally, the cap-and-trade system for greenhouse emission allowance See Peter Cramton, Tradeable Carbon Permit Auctions (2002) 30 *Energy Pol'y.* 333.

(ii) Asymmetric information

It has been suggested that regulation addressing information asymmetric is controversial, even though the regulatory method is not. In a situation where consumers can be adversely affected by lack of sufficient information about products, government regulation can be in the form of regulation requiring manufacturers to disclose information to consumers, as by proper labelling and description of content. It may require sellers' to even obtain a licence with minimum standard requirement before a product or service is offered to buyers. While the first option is regulatory control in that it enhances the buyers' capacity to make product choices, the second is more of allocative control, which limits products entry into the market. Food and drug control in Nigeria through government agencies like NAFDAC, SON, etc., are classical illustrations of the two regulatory tools.[35] NAFDAC certification for foods and drugs has been used to prevent harm to the public that can arise from inadequate information about products.

(iii) Scarcity

While pure economic theory suggests that there are no limits to what can be traded and that products should be generally treated as fungible, a society may choose to block certain exchanges for moral or equitable reasons.[36] For example, sale of body spare parts and sale of babies are prohibited. So, too are trading in say animals considered endangered species. Where market transaction is prohibited, the government can regulate limited dealing in the prohibited areas through an alternate method of allocation, such as lottery, auction, queue or allocation according to a public interest standard to those counted worthy of them. Again, appropriate regulation is by mean of regulatory or allocative controls.[37]

(iv) Public goods

Public goods in a society can range from education, housing, medical care and the like. Private market for these things considered public goods might be priced beyond the reach of many. A situation could also arise where these products are under-produced to the public resulting in a price system that some cannot pay for. No doubt it is generally accepted that government should pay for public goods, the debate however has to do with the size of government funding, especially in the wake of paucity of government funds. This is an area where

---

[35]National Agency for Food and Drug Administration and Control Act, 1992; Standard Organisation of Nigeria Act, 1990.

[36] See above n. 26.

[37] See organ allocation for transplant purposes in the USA.

government will be justified in intervening either through regulation or allocative control.

Visual on regulatory match for non-economic justification

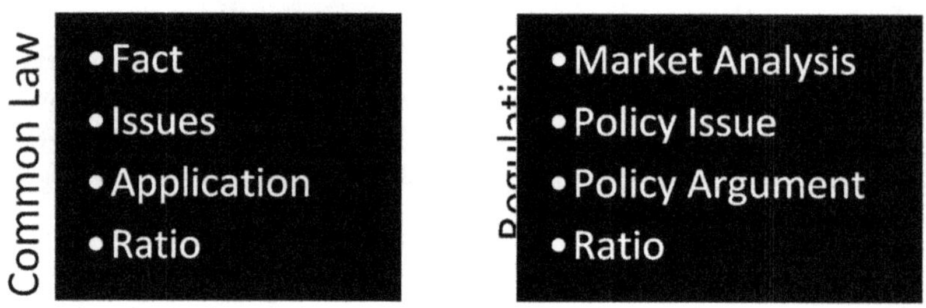

Conclusion

Why is a discussion on the methodology for understanding regulation and the appropriate tools of regulation necessary? Simply! Not only does it enable the lawyers to understand the regulatory state and contribute in debates about regulation, it helps to answer the question whether government has chosen the most effective method of regulation a particular economic or social problem, for if regulatory does not fit the justification, it would not address the problem and a situation of regulatory mismatch would arise, to use the term of Justice Breyer.[38]

At this point we would like to make some preliminary comment to clarify regulatory mismatch to ground the skill of the lawyer. Professor Stephen Breyer (now Justice of the United States Supreme Court) in his seminal work on regulation, generally referred to as the *regulatory manifesto* states this simple axiom for creating and implementing regulatory programme: determine the objectives, examine the alternative methods of obtaining the objectives, and choose the best methods for doing so. The best possible method being that which is the "least restrictive alternative". By his analysis the least restrictive is the intervention that preserves the greatest degree of contractual freedom consistent with eliminating the particular market failure in issue.[39] The manifesto therefore

[38] Stephen Breyer, *Regulation and its Reform*, Cambridge, MA: Harvard Univ. Press, 1982, 191-368; Stephen Breyer, Analysing Regulatory Failure: Mismatches, Less Restrictive Alternatives and Reform (1979) 92 *Harv. L. Rev.* 549 at 586-604.

[39] Stephen Breyer, *Regulation and Its Reform*, 1982. See also, Joseph P. Tomain & Sidney A. Shapiro, Analysing Government Regulation (1997) 49 *Admin. L. Rev.* 377; Thomas A. Lambert, Avoiding

challenges regulators to void regulatory mismatch by urging them to narrowly tailor regulation to respond to the particular market failure targeted.[40] So, by applying the methodology and tools skilled analysts considering market failure situations can determine what the appropriate policy tool to address the challenge is.

That being so, a mismatch occurs when the regulator adopts a regulation that is too broad to address the problem it sets out to correct. For example, if a market suffers from information asymmetry, a regulation, which bans the sale of the product, will be a mismatch. What would be required instead would be regulation that addresses the information problem, such as one requiring seller to provide adequate information to prospective buyers before selling the product.

Discussion on regulatory analysis suggests that there are certain common denominators that explain the relationship between law, politics and policy in the regulatory process and that an analysis of regulation has conceptual and practical consequences. Conceptually it marks the boundaries between traditional administrative law formal analysis of the regulatory state and normative and substantive regulatory law.[41] For while the concerns of the former has been with matters such as issues of rule-following (procedure) and accountability of administrative decision-making, the latter is concerned about explaining the

---

Regulatory Mismatch in the Workplace: An Informational Approach to Workplace Safety Regulation (2003) 82 *Nebraska L. Rev.* 1006.

[40]Tomain& Shapiro, above n. 5 at 402 ("The presence of ... market failure serves as a justification for the government to enter and fix a market in order to achieve better allocative efficiency. . ..regulation is unnecessary in the absence of efficiency defects."). It has been suggested that movement away from stringent command-and-control, end-of-pipe regulations towards flexible pollution control strategies worldwide, especially in the U.S. is evidence that regulation is progressing in the direction of the manifesto. See Lambert, above n. 4 at 1100. For literature on a market approach to environmental law, see Cass R. Sunstein, Endogenous Preferences, Environmental Law; Paradoxes of the Regulatory State (1990) 57 *U. Chi. L. Rev.* 407; Bruce Ackerman, Reforming Environmental Law: Democratic Case for Market Incentives (1987-1988) 13 *Colum. J. Envtl. L.* 171.

[41] Above n. 5 at 412-14 (the learned writers list the scholarly benefits of regulatory scholarship to include (i) providing a rich research agenda of technical and theoretical questions faced by government for scholars, such as exploring questions about the synergies and unintended consequences of mixing and matching regulatory goals and tools; (ii) providing a better understanding of institutional behaviourism, such as patterns of conflict among institutions, e.g. whether regulation should be administered through entitlements, thereby moving it from the bench to the legislature; (iii) providing insight to the political environment of regulation, such as how the regulatory state affects processes of democratic self-governance, how markets in government regulation are susceptible to same abuses of unorganised groups, matters of regulatory capture, etc.; (iv) could provide a research agenda to examine the normative dimensions to say define economic and noneconomic goals of the regulatory state; (v) produce rich interdisciplinary understanding of the regulatory state by bringing together the fields of law, economics, political science and history to construct a descriptive and more predictable model of regulatory behaviour which brings together).

interaction of law, politics and policy, raising issues at the heart of the regulatory state, as to what are the proper goals and tools of the modern state.

Practically, regulatory analysis helps to identify patterns of regulatory justification and the appropriate responses, thereby providing the necessary underpinning of regulatory debates, even when the percentage component of politics and policy mixture with law that generates regulation is unclear. But by providing the profession with identifiable justification and responses, lawyers with the aid of the theory can thus bring in policy argument on their clients' behalf in complex legal disputes involving legislation and policy analysis skills. Once the skill is mastered, 'the lawyer-policy analyst is better able to interact with legislatures and regulatory agencies, advise clients on strategy, advocate positions and mediate among conflicting interests and institutions.'[42]

[42]Ibid at 413.

Chapter 10

Opening Statement Presentation

Introduction

It is common parlance to hear people say that "the first impression is always a lasting impression." This is true for many things and it generally confirms what cognitivists term "confirmation bias" – a trend that reveals that most people decide on emotions, for illogical reasons and only confirm their decision on supposed rational grounds.[1] This is also true of decision-makers, judges and jurors. Several studies in cognition reveal that more than 80 per cent of decision-makers make up their mind about a case during the opening statement. So, winning or losing a case, or persuading a decision-maker on your presentation depends much on the opening statement.

The opening statement is one of the most important component of a trial. It is the lens through which most decision-makers focus. It is the framework through which a client's case is quickly understood. So, it must be kept, rousing the interest of the audience in the message.

Its importance is perhaps heightened as it provides the lens through which decision-makers view a presentation or trial. Like every reading lens the clearer the better for readability, understanding and persuasion. What is more, following general sequencing of importance in real life to put first more important things, it is tempting to think that the primacy of opening statement is critical to persuasion.

Effective Opening Statement

As a general rule, it is not the place for counsel to argue. It is rather serves as a preview of the case. Since it provides the framework to understand a case, lawyers

---

[1]Psychologist are of the view that confirmation bias plays a critical role in belief and that as a general rule decision-makers are not prone to objectivity. That when people make choices they are often follow a preference and subsequently evaluate information to confirm the leaning. Malcom Gladwell, *Blink: The Power of Thinking Without Thinking,* 2005; Ryan H. Flax, *The Opening Statement Toolkit,* A2L Consulting, Washington, 2015 text. See also Kathryn M. Stanchi, The Power of Priming in Legal Advocacy: Using Science of First Impression to Persuade the Reader (2010) 98 *Oregon L. Rev.* 305 (an article that teaches legal advocates about the sometimes nuanced and surprising ways in which the reader's first impressions can be shaped to the client's advantage, primarily by a process called "priming" - a process in which a person's response to later information is influenced by exposure to prior information)

must learn how to use it effectively. A legal consulting service law firm in its toolkit illustrates very graphic why this is so by this simple example of the person of Steve:

1. "Steve is smart, diligent, critical, impulsive and jealous."

and

2. "Steve is jealous, impulsive, critical, diligent and smart."[2]

No question about it, both sentences (1 and 2) contain exactly 8 syllables, all identical, but rearranged differently. A reading of the first creates good impression in the reader's mind as to who Steve is. Most will maybe want of think of Steve here as describing the person of Steve Jobs, famous for his computing skills.[3]This isn't surprising. A man of that repute is associated with being smart, diligent critical and impulsive. They are characteristics of successful inventors. So, when the phase "jealous" is added to those characteristics they conjure in the mind a person intolerant to unfaithfulness.

But the reverse is the case with the second description. By putting first, the word "jealous" in the description of Steve, a negative impression of the person is brought to the fore. The reader quickly associates jealous not with intolerance of unfaithfulness, but rather associates the word with negatives like 'hostile to a rival' or one obsessed with guarding possession or territory.' Coming from this perspective most would then discount the virtues of impulsive, critical, diligent and smart. It is now hard to think that the second opening words describe the much-loved Steve Jobs.

This is exactly how the opening statement serves as lens to any presentation. This is the same way it works in advocacy and writing. For a claimant, the opening statement is the lasting impression opportunity to nail the claim firmly to the stake. It is where the theme of the case must be highlighted in strong, clear understandable manner. It must then be quickly followed by a brief narrative of the wrong sought to be vindicated. The claimant has to do so because decision-makers would likely work from the hypothesis presented to them in the opening statement, which they merely use to interpret and understand subsequent facts presented. But for the defendant, the opening statement is a "dagger" opportunity. It should be used to ties apart the substance of the claim.[4]Once it

---

[2] Flax, above n. 1, 1-2.

[3] Steve Jobs is known for inventing the Apple Computer.

[4] See, Steve Johansen & Ruth Anne Robbins, Art-iculating the Analysis: Systemizing the Decision to Use Visuals as Legal Reasoning (2015) 20 *J. Legal Writing* 57 (an article stating that as legal writing moves towards a more digital medium, lawyers should learn to incorporate visual persuasion in

cuts off the throat of the claim, death follows immediately. The defence must go for the jugular because decision-makers by virtue of our adversarial legal system care about blame apportionment and are happy to arrive there through the quickest route.

Opening statement for lawyers (whether representing the claimant or defendant in trial or proponent or antagonist in presentation) should be used to warm-up and suck into the attention of the decision-maker. This is important because for the reason that it is natural for people to take sides in controversy.[5] And for decision-makers, it is a must anyway. So, it is best to get the decision-maker on your side early in the controversy. It helps in ensuring victory as the decision-maker is likely to apply confirmation bias to fill in the missing link to create a favourable story on your behalf.

It is the first-line audience contact that should be used to tell the decision-maker why she should care to listen or read and award a favourable judgment. Skilful lawyers recognise the time conscious link of opening statement and are quick to use the introduction to rouse interest. It is suggested that the "90 second rule" is the key to it, for generally within the space of 90 seconds of meeting a new person or reading a text or listening to a presentation, most persons decide whether it is worth reading or listening. Newscasters and film directors know this well. The highlights presentations are short, clear and pass a lot of information across quickly. Just listening or watching tells whether it is worth waiting to hear or watch the accompanying details.[6] Lawyers should learn from them. The introductory 90 seconds make or tear down.

The reason for this is simple. We are often inclined to pay more attention to first impression and discount subsequent information that contradicts the impression. Psychologists suggest that subsequent information is not weighed as

---

their writing. The article contains an illustrative visual brief written in 2011 by Cuban's lawyer to a motion for summary judgment. The four-page motion described as a "dagger brief" is available at http://www.scribd.com/doc/58470086/2011-06- 22-WC-Mavs-and-Radical-Mavs-Mngt-MSJ. For comments on the brief, see, Rachel M. Zahorsky, Texas Lawyer Honoured for Unconventional Brief(2012)*A.B.A. J.* Jan. 5, http://www.abajournal.com/news/article/texas lawyer honoured for unconventional brief.

5 Even as mundane as an activity as watching a match it is natural to take sides even if a person is not a fan of the contending teams.

6 On what lawyers can learn from newscasters and filmmakers, see generally, Elyse Pepper, The Case for "Thinking Like a Filmmaker": Using Lars von Trier's *Dogville* as a Model for Writing a Statement of Facts (2008) 14 *J. Legal Writing* 171 (suggesting that students can learn storytelling techniques from pop culture by recognising that film makers are also advocates for outcomes based on narrative clues told throughout the movie); Philip N. Meyer, Visual Literacy and the Legal Culture: Reading Film as Text in the Law School Setting (1993) 17 *Leg. Stud. Forum* 73 (an article which urges that like filmmakers, lawyers tell imagistic narratives constructed upon aesthetic principles . . . that control the formulation of plot-structure in commercial cinema and so the profession can learn from visual storytellers working the same popular cultural turf).

much as the first and that this is rather an unconscious thing because reliance on first impression is a kind of mental shortcut we take automatically.[7]

Decision-makers, especially judges are happy to take sides after the opening statement (and closing statement) as it makes their job easy. No matter how experienced a judge is, every litigation is somewhat confusing. The facts, applicable principles, balance of interest between the parties, the appropriate remedy and dispositive direction, etc., can confuse a judge. So, she would be happy from the very onset if an opening statement aids her in formulating a framework to understand the often-divergent stories the parties would present. After all, the reason for every litigation is rooted in some form of unconscionability of a sort, like anger, frustration, betrayal, lying, stealing, covetousness, etc. Getting through the maze of facts that lock them and understanding them can be challenging to the decision-maker. Thus, when an opening statement is clear, simple and attention rousing, the decision-maker is right on your start from the blast of the whistle.

Very importantly, remember that *how* you present is as good as *what* you present. Not only must the opening statement be well prepared, rehearsed and strong, it must be delivered like a newscaster.[8] The how includes those qualities that make a person likable (especially in public presentation), such as a warm smile, correct pronunciation, proper pausing, sense stress, emphasising the theme suitable volume, modulation, proper gestures, visual contact, good personal appearance, brief story of the case, and the like.

Place of Opening Statement

Where to place an opening statement in public presentation is fairly known – the introductory part of a presentation. Even at that great care should be put into how to make it a great presentation.[9] The secret of great opening statement is unlocked when it starts unconventional. Conventional opening presentation follows the weak, uninspiring schemata of what, how and why. When for example, a salesperson is called upon to make a presentation or a speaker is invited to address

---

[7]Daniel G. Linz &Steven Penrod, Increasing Attorney Persuasiveness in the Courtroom (1984) 8 *Law & Psychol. Rev.* 1 @ 9; Kathryn M. Stanchi, The Science of Persuasion: An Initial Exploration, [2006] *Mich. St. L. Rev.* 411.

[8] Flax, above n. 1, 69 ("High-calibre newscasters are an interesting group. They inform, they teach, and they persuade us. They use visuals in a way that complements what they are saying quite seamlessly. Their attire is impeccable, they look the part, and their delivery feels more like a conversation than a lecture. Somehow, they confidentially speak to an audience who can't talk back to them, and yet they manage to build a relationship with that audience. If you think about this description, it sounds a lot like a litigator)."

[9]Kenneth J. Lopez, *How to Make Great Presentations in or Out of the Courtroom*, A2L Consulting, 2013.

an audience why a certain action should be taken, it is common to hear the opening words like this:

> "Good morning ladies and gentlemen. I am XYZ, a salesperson for ABC Limited, manufacturers of D brand of cars. It is my pleasure to speak with you this morning as a group.
>
> ABC is the foremost auto manufacturer of good cars in Nigeria. If you want a durable, comfortable car made for our road, you will be happy to choose from the brand of our cars. They are efficient on gas and smooth to drive. I urge you to make it D brand purchase."

No question about it. The speaker would have presented some reasons why the audience should consider buying D brand cars. Accurate as the presentation may seem, it is nonetheless flat. This is because it is a conventional style presentation. It begins with the "what" –ABC Limited does. They are car manufacturers. it moves on to the "how" –the cars are well manufactured. It ends with the "why" –compelling reason to choose D brand of cars.

But the presentation would have been stronger if it followed the reverse path – why, how and what. Something like this:

> "Owning a great car is magical. It gives a sense of safety and comfort on wheels. For an automobile that delivers both with gas efficiency, turn to D brand of cars. Your car will reward your choice preference.
>
> I am XYZ, I am a proud salesperson for the foremost car manufacturer ABC Limited."

This latter presentation uses an unconventional style which is strong. It starts with a strong statement of belief (why) – the reason why people desire a good car. It then moves on to action (how) how the belief that people desire good cars is put into action by ABC Limited manufacturing cars that deliver comfort, safety and efficiency. It ultimately ends with the benefit (what) the audience need to do so that they get all the goodness D brand offers.

It is after this that the presenter introduces herself to the audience.

So, what a great opening statement does is more like creating a common ground for discussion with the audience.

(i) Belief/Why - It starts from the common accepted premise – people like good cars that deliver safety, comfort and efficiency. Most in the audience readily agree.

(ii) Action/How - Once this captures their attention they naturally would like to hear how these are factored by ABC Limited into the D brand of cars.

(iii) Benefit/What – It tells the audience what is the best choice that matches with the believe system of what a good car offers.

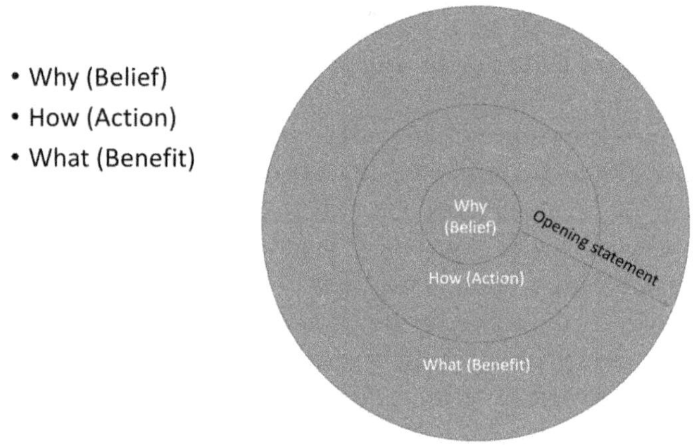

The presenter can then go on to tell details of the belief, action and benefit in the body of the presentation.

This path trajectory is amenable also to brief writing. For example, in a fundamental rights enforcement claim presented sometimes before brief writing became a requirement for advocacy in many courts in Nigeria, the counsel started the opening statement this way:

> "My Lord, the question presented interrogates the question whether the Respondent can resort of self-help and the use of public criminal enforcement tactics to enforce alleged breach of pure, commercial agreement.
>
> Every day across the country thousands of people (usually less powerful and disadvantaged) are subject to abuse of their rights by powerful persons who resort to self-help to enforce perceived grievances. While some of these right violations are challenged by the right-holders, a vast majority are glossed over.

> Also, common is the practice of stronger parties in private contract resorting to use of criminal enforcement mechanism to seek redress for contractual breaches without recourse to due process.
>
> This case concerns whether such tactics are proper in a civilized, democratic country in the light of the Constitution and our jurisprudence.
>
> My Lord, the stakes are high: Nigerians look to the court as the defender, protector and promoter of rights guaranteed under the Constitution. Because the core purpose of personal rights guaranteed under the Constitution safeguards personal freedom and business integrity from undue, unlawful interference, this honourable court should hold that even when contractual breaches occur between parties dealing in commercial setting, no party shall be entitled to use self-help or re-characterize the relationship of business as crime with a view to privatize public enforcement without due process. The Applicants therefore respectfully request the honourable court to protect their fundamental rights and preserve the purity of due process in the country."[10]

This kind of opening statement is likely to persuade a decision-maker as it follows the - belief – action –benefit.

Where to place an opening statement could pose a strategic challenge to a lawyer considering the nature of legal documents, whether in a letter or memo or brief. For a brief, the early sections (such as the statement of facts, the question presented and summary of argument sections) will be a good place to make strong opening statements. A skilful lawyer would in these sections prime the reader to visualise the case in a particular way by pushing forward the theme of the case to evoke the necessary emotions.

The petitioner's brief filed before the United Supreme Court in a Californian appeal case of *David Leon Riley* v. *State of California* is illustrative of how priming an opening statement is a good persuasion tool.[11]

In the opening sections, the attorney was careful to highlight the theme of the case– doing so particularly in respect of (i) the question presented; (ii) the

---

[10]See applicants brief filed in *Alhaji Shittu* v. *Lagos State Government*, (unreported) suit no. before the Federal High Court, Lagos.

[11] See American Bar Association www.supremecourtpreview.org, case No. 13-132 (a appeal for a writ of certiorari). A copy of the brief is in the appendix of the book. It is simply a sample and not a model. See appendix 1.

summary of the argument presented; (iii) the constitutional provision interrogated in the appeal; (iv) the introductory section; and (v) in the section on the statement of facts, even interspersing it with relevant law on the subject.

The relevant excepts are as follows:

> Question presented
>
> "Whether evidence admitted at petitioner's trial (namely, certain digital photographs and videos) was obtained in a search of petitioner's cell phone that violated petitioner's Fourth Amendment rights."

Notably, even the table of content is used to prime the opening statement. It is arranged in such a way that it both persuades and sucks in favourable emotion for the appellant's case. The table is not just arranged a pointer to what each section in the brief is and the material pages where they can be found. Rather it is used to skilfully draw attention to the facts intersperse with legal application to pointedly show the path why a favourable verdict should be entered for the client. It reads like this (the pages are removed):

> "TABLE OF CONTENTS
>
> QUESTION PRESENTED
>
> TABLE OF AUTHORITIES
>
> BRIEF FOR PETITIONER
>
> OPINIONS BELOW
>
> JURISDICTION
>
> RELEVANT CONSTITUTIONAL PROVISION
>
> INTRODUCTION
>
> STATEMENT OF THE CASE
>
> SUMMARY OF ARGUMENT
>
> ARGUMENT
>
> I. The Search Of The Digital Contents Of Petitioner's Smart Phone Exceeded The Bounds Of A Legitimate Search Incident To Arrest

The Search Was Unnecessary To Serve Any Legitimate Governmental Interest

Digital Data Does Not Threaten Officer Safety

Once Seized, It Is Unnecessary To Search A Smart Phone Without A Warrant To Preserve Evidence

The Degree of Intrusiveness Of The Search Of Petitioner's Phone Rendered The Search Unreasonable

1. Smart Phones Hold Extraordinary Amounts Of Sensitive Personal Information

2. Smart Phones Hold Information That Implicates First Amendment Concerns

C. Limiting Searches Of Smart Phones To Situations In Which Officers Believe Such Phones Contain Evidence Of The Crime Of Arrest Would Not Solve The Constitutional Problems Inherent In Such Searches

II. The Search Of Petitioner's Phone At The Stationhouse Was Too Remote From His Arrest To Qualify As A Search Incident To Arrest

CONCLUSION"

It will be observed that after listing the content of what the brief is as presented following the order of table of authorities, the brief for petitioner; opinion below; jurisdiction; relevant constitutional provision; introduction; statement of case; it then goes on to list the summary of argument as captured this way:

"a. The Search of The Digital Contents of Petitioner's Smart Phone Exceeded The Bounds Of A Legitimate Search Incident To Arrest (page)

The Search Was Unnecessary to Serve Any Legitimate Governmental Interest (page)

Digital Data Does Not Threaten Officer Safety (page)

Once Seized, It Is Unnecessary to Search A Smart Phone Without A Warrant to Preserve Evidence (page)

> The Degree of Intrusiveness of The Search of Petitioner's Phone Rendered the Search Unreasonable (page)
>
> Smart Phones Hold Extraordinary Amounts of Sensitive Personal Information (page)
>
> 2. Smart Phones Hold Information That Implicates First Amendment Concerns (page)
>
> Limiting Searches of Smart Phones to Situations in Which Officers Believe Such Phones Contain Evidence of The Crime Of Arrest Would Not Solve the Constitutional Problems Inherent in Such Searches (page)
>
> The Search of Petitioner's Phone at The Stationhouse Was Too Remote from His Arrest to Qualify as A Search Incident to Arrest (page)"

It is after this that the conclusion comes in. This style is conscious to create the necessary pathos and ethos.

Further highlighting the opening statement are the sections on the relevant constitutional provision and introductory section, as shown below:

> "Relevant Constitutional Provision
>
> The Fourth Amendment states in relevant part: "The right of the people to be secure in their persons, houses, papers, and effects, against unreasonable searches and seizures, shall not be violated, and no Warrants shall issue, but upon probable cause."
>
> Introduction
>
> "Every day across the country, thousands of people are arrested – a reality that results in over twelve million people being arrested each year,a majority of whom are never convicted of any crime.
>
> Surell Brady, Arrests Without Prosecution and the Fourth Amendment (2000) 59 Md. L. Rev. 1 @ 3.
>
> While some of these arrests arise from felony investigations, the vast majority are for alleged misdemeanours such as driving under the influence, simple assault, or petty theft. In California, for

example, about two-thirds of adult arrests are for misdemeanours; in New York, almost three-fourths are for misdemeanours.

What is more, in California as in most other states, the police may – and sometimes do – arrest people for traffic and other "fine only" infractions such as jaywalking, littering, or riding a bicycle the wrong direction on a residential street.

People v. McKay, 41 P.3d 59, 62-63 (Cal. 2002); Tobe v. City of Santa Ana, 892 P.2d 1145, 1178 (Cal. 1995); see also Atwater v. City of Lago Vista, 532 U.S. 318, 354-55 (2001).

Indeed, given that "very few drivers can traverse any appreciable distance without violating some traffic regulation . . . it is apparent that virtually everyone who ventures out onto the public streets and highways may then, with little effort by the police, be placed in a position where he is subject to a full search."

Wayne R. LaFave, Search and Seizure § 5.2(e), at 156 (5th ed. 2012) (internal quotation marks and citation omitted).

According to the California Supreme Court, every time the police effectuate one of these arrests and searches, officers may not only seize and secure any smart phone the arrestee is carrying but also may rummage through the digital contents of the device.

See People v. Diaz, 244 P.3d 501 (Cal. 2011) (reprinted at Pet. App. 25a-65a).

Furthermore, the police may undertake such warrantless examinations not only briefly at the scene of arrest but also later at the police station after booking the arrestee. Diaz, Pet. App. 33a.

This case concerns whether granting such a new police entitlement comports with the Fourth Amendment. The stakes are high: Americans use smart phones to generate and store a vast array of their most sensitive thoughts, communications and expressive material. Because the core purpose of the Fourth Amendment has always been to safeguard such personal and professional information from exploratory searches, this Court should hold that even when officers seize smart phones incident to lawful arrests, they may not search the phones' digital contents without first obtaining a warrant."

There is no question about it. This sort of opening statement invites the Supreme Court justices to side with the petition. Also, skilful is the way the attorney coloured the reader's perception in the section on statement of facts as the attorney intersperse legal rules and other material with facts to give meaning to the rules interrogated.

Elements of Opening Statement

The essential elements of an effective opening statement are:

(i) Case Theme

An opening with a strong theme and brief story of a presentation is useful to capture the attention of the audience. The theme is what the decision maker remembers most of the time. It constitutes the thread used to understand the case. Think for once reading a book without a theme. Unquestionable, the book will not make an interesting read. A captivating book theme could even be the reason why a reader chooses a book for reading.

That is why conscious effort should be put in selecting a theme because to some extent it is what influences how the audience would view and feel about the story and the parties involved.[12] It is important for the chosen theme to evoke emotion favourable to the client. For example, in the *Riley's* case the theme can range from, say "rights are sacrosanct," "search must serve government legitimate interest," "phone digital content is personal," etc. all designed to draw the court's attention to prevalence of police abuse of rights or unchallenged rights violation by many poor citizens, or the like depending on the card the lawyer wants to play. If the lawyer for instance, wants to plat the card that this is one right violation that should be commended because the client is, say poor but unhappy with her rights violation, the theme could well stress "bravery," highlighting it by saying something like this: "every day across the country thousands of people (usually less powerful and disadvantaged) are subject to abuse of their rights by powerful persons who resort to self-help to enforce perceived grievances. While some of these right violations are challenged by the right-holders, a vast majority are glossed over" and then telling that this is an exception as the poor citizen now challenges the powerful in instituting the action. This kind of statement that quickly follows the theme will likely evoke favourable emotions in favour of the

---

[12] Richard K. Neumann, *Legal Reasoning and Legal Writing: Structure, Strategy and Style*, 6th ed. 2009, 291.

right-holder. In fact, by reminding the court that "the stakes are high: Nigerians look to the court as the defender, protector and promoter of rights guaranteed under the Constitution," the court is quickly reminded that the architecture for safeguarding personal freedom from undue, unlawful interference, is a sacred duty it owes society. So, the theme could well be "no to self-help".[13]

Every theme should be the summary sentence that describes the case. For example, in a wrongful dismissal claim based on, say discrimination of the claimant, the theme could be "repeated, unfair treatment motivated by sexism." It is suggested that the theme should be couched as a one summary sentence devoid of legalese.[14]

In drawing it up the lawyer should consciously think about the parties, why they are contending, the parties' motivation, what do they seek to vindicate in court. For example, in the unfair dismissal claim on grounds of sexual harassment (discrimination), it could be useful to frame the theme as "he can't stand to take no for an answer." Defence counsel who seeks to say that dismissal is grounded on indiscipline could then dagger the claimant's statement by framing its opening statement theme like this: "refusal to take correction." It is suggested that whatever theme is chosen it should be one that resonates with common life experience (that the judge can relate with) that can evoke the necessary emotions. Importantly, theme must be borne out of the evidence in the case.[15]

(ii) Brief story of the case

Every good theme should be immediately followed by a brief story of the wrong that triggers the litigation. While it is tempting to tell story in a chronological style, skilful lawyers do not sacrifice time sequence for what persuades. Chronological ordering may sometimes not present an uninteresting version of a case. What is more, following the human tendency (of first impression being lasting) it is plausible for the judge to think that the first facts related as the story of the case are the most important facts. So, what is said first matters and they could be construed as the important fact. These important facts may not synchronize with a chronological recitation of the facts. So, the lawyer must structure a story in a manner that it is compelling without being slavish to chronology.

A good story should have a logical beginning, a body, a climax, and an ending. To make the story compelling however, the lawyer should not just place the events in the order (beginning –body – climax – ending) in which they occur.

---

[13]See above n. 10.

[14] See www.americanbar.org/labor/2003

[15] Ibid.

She should consciously select which of them best convey the emotion and the theme of the case.

Stories are not told for the fun of it. It is critical for a story to use sensory language for it to evoke emotions.[16] In this respect, it is advisable to paint a picture of the scene and the character.[17] It is critical in organising a story to keep it simple, to employ metaphors and analogies easily understandable, and if possible use word pictures to convey concreteness.

Again, like couching a theme, the brief story in the opening statement should be devoid of legalese. Legalese chokes the humanity out of the story, reducing it to legal essentials.[18] Stories must relate to daily experiences in the real world we live. So, it would be mistaken to turn say a story of a broken promise into a breach of contract lawsuit, or a story about the tragic loss of a loved one into a survivor's seeking damages for wrongful death.[19] While it is true that the both claims above are essentially legal, yet about breach of contract and for wrongful death, when the story is so framed as purely legal claims, it has the effect of choking the humanity in the facts presentation.

(iii) Personalize Your Client

The opening is an opportunity to persuade the decision-maker to like your client. So, the lawyer should use it to explain the client's motivations for the suit or application and to give the decision-maker reasons to feel camaraderie with the client. It requires that the client is represented as an individual claimant.

One way to do so is to mention the name of the client, rather than just describing the client as "the plaintiff." For example in a personal injury case between *Robert H. Bork* v. *The Yale Club of New York*, the narrative states in part:[20]

"Paragraph 2. Plaintiff Robert H. Bork is a resident and citizen of Virginia. He was injured while visiting the Yale Club in New York, New York, to give a speech at an event there on June 6, 2006.

Paragraph 6. On the evening of June 6, 2006, the New Criterion magazine held an event (the "New Criterion event") at the Yale Club. The New Criterion invited Mr. Bork, among other guests, to deliver remarks at the event.

Paragraph 9. When it was his turn to deliver remarks to the audience, Mr. Bork approached the dais. Because of the unreasonable height of the dais, without

---

[16]Stanchi, above n. 7.

[17]See discussion in chapter 16 (narrative and storytelling techniques).

[18]Flax, above n. 1, 6.

[19] For example, *Bello* v. *Attorney-General*

[20]See chapter 16 (narrative and storytelling techniques).

stairs or a handrail, Mr. Bork fell backwards as he attempted to mount the dais, striking his left leg on the side of the dais and striking his head on a heat register.

Paragraph 10. As a result of the fall, a large haematoma formed on Mr. Bork's lower left leg, which later burst. The injury required surgery, extended medical treatment, and months of physical therapy.

Paragraph 11. Mr. Bork suffered excruciating pain as a result of this in- jury and was largely immobile during the months in which he received physical therapy, preventing him from working his typical schedule before the injury. The months of relative inactivity weakened Mr. Bork's legs so that he still requires a cane for stability. In addition, Mr. Bork continues to have a limp as a result of this injury."

One thing is clear in the narrative brief above. The lawyer personalises her client, making the judge feel the concreteness of the person known as Mr. Bork who suffered personal injury. Mr. Bork is not simply described with the legalese of "the plaintiff".

The pathos effect of it is that it sends a compelling message to the decision-maker that the client is real, a person with integrity pressing a just cause, rather than some abstract thing out there seeking to make easy money. When the client is personalised the decision-maker more likely sees the client's injury as real harm, just and fair to trigger appropriate relief.

Obviously, a lawyer representing an individual against a corporation will have an easier task personalizing the client. For example, in one such litigation by a group of indigenous landholders against eminent domain exercised by government against their ancestral land for the benefit of certain powerful corporations, the brief opening statement was couched this way:

> Every day across the country hundreds of people (usually less powerful and disadvantaged) are subject to abuse of their rights by powerful persons who resort to means less than civilised and proper to breach rights of Nigerians. Sometimes, these powerful individuals and corporations act in conscious support and approval by government which subscribes to protect, promote and advance rights of its people. While a vast majority of these right violations are glossed over and not vindicated by the right-holders for many reasons not unconnected with the size of right-holders pocket, some are challenged, as in this case. When dared to be challenged,

right-violators usually cloak justification vide procedural landmines as protective cover.[21]

This is not to mean that a "management-side" lawyer cannot personalize her client as well. A "corporate-side" lawyer can equally do a good job personalising her client. That will require conscious effort of focusing on the ethical goals of the corporation or drawing attention on how the corporation runs. For example, rather than reflecting on the corporation itself, a management-side lawyer can focus on the people who constitute the corporation – the relevant supervisors, the human resources, representative, or the company's ownership structure.

For example, in a mortgage bank case where the defendant-banker was accused of making bad loans, counsel can create familiarity by saying the following:

"Who are bankers? Some think they are people who like to make money from the misfortunate of their customers. That smells like greed. That's how they make money. When they make good loans, they make money. When they make bad loans, they lose money. If as the claimant seeks to say, the defendant structured this loan as a bad one, if true would have to mean, they are not trying to make money. When was the last time you heard of bankers not trying to make money? It makes no sense.[22]

Another way familiarity can be created with the decision-maker is to mention in the corporate brief names of individuals in the corporation and their roles in the controversy. This way the decision-maker can envision and is made to put on the imaginary scale of justice the actions of "people versus people," rather than "people versus corporation". Once the judge can see the "people versus people" version in the litigation, the case changes from that of a single, sympathetic plaintiff standing against a huge, faceless corporation – like a David and Goliath - scenario.[23] A counsel representing Goliath should send a message in the opening statement that makes it okay to find for her client or against David.

---

[21]Above n. 10.

[22]Great Presentations, A2L @ 29.

[23] See for example, Stacy Caplow, Putting the "I" in Writing: Drafting an Effective Personal Statement to Tell an/a Winning Refugee Story (2008) 14 *J. Leg. Writing* 249 (structuring a refugee or asylum case as a brave individual struggle for freedom and democracy against tyranny); *Essar Oilfields*

(iv) Distinguish between Theme and Story

The heighten importance of theme is prevailing because studies suggest that theme is critical to remembering – memory and retention. It is what helps the audience tie in the details of a story, helping to put together the pieces of details into a composite picture. So, if any blank exists in a story-line the theme help fills the gap.[24]

But the theme should not be confused with the story. A theme is like a quick tag-line, something that resonates to tie the story. For example, some readers can quickly tie in the tag, "the real thing" as corporate slogan that once described the Coca-Cola drink or "the difference is clear", as slogan to describe the 7up soda drink. Such a slogan is like the theme of a case. It functions to keep remembrance and spark interest.

The theme of a case must be kept distinct from the story of the case. Both are different.[25] The fundamental differences are as follows:

(i) a theme is an attention-getter, while a story is an attention-keeper;

(ii) while a theme provides a reason to be interested in what the counsel is saying, a story provides the emotional connection requiring the audience to care about the case;

(iii) a theme explains, but a story motivates;

(iv) while a theme sounds much like the persuader is being a lawyer, the story sound like the persuader is being human; and

(v) while most lawyers are likely to know to use themes, many lawyers fail to use stories.

Generally, themes are used by lawyers in opening and closing statements. But it is also strategic to mention it repeatedly in the body of the brief. It is suggested that the theme should be particularly highlighted in the beginning and concluding parts of a brief to serve as reminders and to emphasize.

Storytelling on the other hand, is an activity that should be visible throughout the brief or trial, interspersed with legal principles.[26] Empirical evidence strongly suggests that decision-makers are persuaded and they remember briefs where the stories are interspersed with law and policy. Effective briefs are structured as stories interspersed with law.

Services v Norscot Rig Management PVT [2016] EWHC 2361 (Comm.) (discussing the propriety of recovery of money spent by litigation funder providing access to justice for claimants who have been mistreated by bigger and richer defendants)

[24] Kathryn M. Stanchi, The Power of Priming in Legal Advocacy: Using Science of First Impression to Persuade the Reader (2010) 98 *Oregon L. Rev.* 305 @ 312.

[25] See page 34 of opening statement.

[26] Festus Emiri, Ayuba Giwa & Jonathan Ehusani, Revisiting the Traditional IRAC Organizational Structure of Legal Analysis: Towards a Multidisciplinary Approach (2017) *Nig. LJ* 1.

It is important to recognize while stories have many characters with understandable motives, themes provide little in the way of character development. Stories follow the progression of theme, character, motive, conflict, resolution, message and consequence.

(v) Priming and Impression

Decorators such as painters and restorers recognise the value of primer. Teachers also do. Primer books used for teaching children how to read and understand basics. Primer books are also used for adult learning. For adult learning, primers are structured as small introductory books, simplifying otherwise complex subject. Most are designed as short informational piece of writing.

Just as a primer makes clear and attractive its subject matter, so too does priming of an opening statement aid persuasion. Opening statement priming process here refers to a process by which a person's response to later information is influenced by exposure to prior information.[27]

Cognitive psychology suggests that the priming process is strongly constitutive of knowledge. Priming affects how we feel, react, respond and know.[28] For example, if the brain is primed to think of money as an object, if the perceiver enters a room containing money and other things, most likely the perceiver will only remember seeing money even though the room has several other objects. Subconsciously, the mind just works that way – seeing and remembering that the room contains money.

---

[27]Stanchi, above n. 24 @ 306.

[28] Shaun B. Spencer, Words Count: The Empirical Relationship Between Brief Writing and Summary Judgment (2018) 22 *J. Legal Writing* (an article exploring and measuring the statistical relationship between brief readability and case outcome, stating that even though judges may be reluctant to suggest that the quality of a lawyer's writing can influence the outcome of a case because such a claim would conflict with the notion that judges resolve cases based on the facts and law, rather than on the advocate's quality, there is abundant evidence that readability of brief does influence case outcomes); Ruth A. Robbins, Painting with Print: Incorporating Concepts of Typographic and Layout Design into the Text of Legal Writing Documents (2004) 2 *JALWD* 109 (an article on some of the "whys" behind font and layout principles in documents, analysing some common myths about the visual design of legal briefs and concludes with a synthesized list of suggestions for lawyers to use in their documents. It shows how textual effects influences logos, pathos and ethos). For detail reading on how particular style of writing influences outcome (not readability). See also, Richard K. Neumann, Jr., *Legal Reasoning and Legal Writing: Structure, Strategy and Style,* 6th ed. Aspen Publishers 2009, 360 (suggesting that briefs be oxygenated by breathing life into the facts through telling compelling story about people||); Kenneth D. Chestek, Judging by the Numbers: An Empirical Study of the Power of Story(2010)7 *J. ALWD* 1 (storytelling/narrative style); Sean Flammer, Persuading Judges: An Empirical Analysis of Writing Style, Persuasion, and the Use of Plain English(2010)16 *J. Leg. Writing* 183 (plain English); Robert W. Benson & Joan B. Kessler, An Empirical Study of Persuasion and Credibility in Appellate Brief Writing (1987) 20 *Loy. L.A. L. Rev.* 301 (plain English versus legalese).

Since priming is like a seed planted in the brain that germinates to define how new information is interpreted, the opening statement should be used to highlight favourable information that the decision-maker would see and remember. If the statement is contained in a written brief, priming would dictate what information to highlight in the introductory part. Priming would also compel paying attention to style of writing and textual or layout design.[29]

(vi) Case Weakness

The opening statement should not ignore the weakness of the case. Every case no matter how well put together will have some weaknesses. A counsel who glosses over her case weakness will lose credibility in the eyes of the decision-maker. It is therefore better to handle weakness in the opening statement in a way that takes away the bite from the opponent.[30] This can be done by bringing out the weakness in as positive as possible. Such a stance creates credibility (ethos) and lessens the negative impact of the weakness.[31] One fine way to go about it is to identify the weakness as the opponent's strongest point and then explain why the point is of no significance to the decision. However, if the negative information is not raised by the opponent it may be strategic to mention it in the opening statement.

(vii) No argument

As a general rule, counsel may not argue in the opening statement. Rather, the opening statement should serve as a preview of the anticipated testimony, exhibits, and other evidence.

A good lawyer should think of the opening statement like a newscaster, who simply highlights the news in a way designed to provide general information, provoking further interest in the anticipated detail news to follow. A good

---

[29]Ruth Anne Robbins, Painting with Print: Incorporating Concepts of Typographic and Layout Design into the Text of Legal Writing Documents (2004) 2 *J. AWLD* 108 (explaining why an—argument must be presented in a visually effective manner so the reader can more easily understand the argument and retain more of the material). See also, Mathew Butterick, *Typography For Lawyers,* 2010 (explaining how typographic style affects clarity and persuasion in legal writing and providing a primer on how lawyers can use typography effectively).

[30]Robin Slocum, *Legal Reasoning, Writing, and Persuasive Argument,* 2nd ed. Matthew Bender & Co. 2006, 462-71 (urging the creation of appealing stories that emphasizes positive facts about the lawyer's clients and de-emphasizes negative facts).

[31] Jeanne M. Kaiser, When the Truth and the Story Collide: What Legal Writers Can Learn from the Experience of Non-Fiction Writers about the Limits of Storytelling (2010) 16 *J. Legal Writing* 163 (an article extoling the professional responsibility to be factual in the context of the ability to tell a captivating tale that does not ignore the skilful use of logical argument to the case, showing how the two strands of narrative and logical argument - related to each other like a twisting double helix that forms a lawyer's theory of the case).

opening statement is like the kind of preview you see in the inside jacket of a novel. It introduces a novel. It does not confuse the prospective reader with an overly detailed chronology of events; it does not bore the reader with a recitation of the characters' names in the order they will appear in the book; and it does not command the reader to feel a certain way about the story contained in its pages. Instead, the jacket text captures the essence of the book in a way that gives the reader a general sense of the book's theme, in a way that entices the reader to proceed further, and leaves the reader to make her judgment regarding the final meaning of the story. That is the way decision-makers should be left at the end of the opening statement – with an understanding of the case's theme, an eagerness to learn more, and an appreciation for the ultimate judgment they will be asked to make.

Conclusion

There is hardly any rule of court that prohibits opening statement in civil or criminal trial in Nigeria. How to structure opening statement is part of the curriculum of study at the Law School. It is designed to teach students how to prepare their case in a manner that is persuasive. Since every brief, whether designed as oral advocacy or written brief of argument or letter certainly should have an introductory part, it follows that an effective opening statement is useful for persuasion.

PART III

Chapter 11

Rules of Good Writing

Introduction

Lawyers spend a lot of their time preparing and drafting legal memorandum and briefs. This explains why there is so much legal literature devoted to how lawyers should write effectively.[1] Legal writing is part of law curriculum for law schools and faculties, usually embedded in the first year course of legal methods.[2]

The shift from extensive advocacy in court to what has been termed "front-loading" by rules of court puts effective writing in the centre-burner of lawyering. Unfortunately, judges, clients and lawyers and even law teachers are increasingly complaining about the quality of how lawyers and law students communicate.[3]

---

[1] Cite a few Nigerian texts. For example, Wolters Kluwer lists 68 textbooks and study aids in its legal research and writing category, http://www.wklegaledu.com/web-catalog/law-school/legal-research-and-writing (last visited Sept. 30, 2017). Carolina Academic Press lists 83 titles in its legal writing category. http://www.cap-press.com/ms/41/Legal-Writing (last visited Sept. 30, 2017).Almas Kahn, A Compendium of Legal Writing Sources (2011) 50 *Washburn L.J.* 395 (an article providing a compendium of legal writing articles).Peter Tiersma, *Legal Language.* Chicago: University of Chicago Press, 1999.

[2]Linda L. Berger, Linda H. Edwards, & Terrill Pollman, The Past, Presence, and Future of Legal Writing Scholarship: Rhetoric, Voice, and Community (2010) 16 *Leg. Writing* 537 (citing sourcebook on legal writing programs); Terence Collins & Darryl Hattenhauer, Law and Language: A Selected, Annotated Bibliography on Legal Writing (1983) 33 *J. Legal Educ.* 141; George D. Gopen & Kary D. Smout, Legal Writing: A Bibliography (1991) 1 Leg. Writing 93; James R. Elkins, The Things They Carry into Legal Writing (and Legal Education) (1998) 22 *Legal Stud. Forum* 749; Kathryn Stanchi, Persuasion: An Annotated Bibliography (2009) 6 *JALWD* 75; Carrie W. Teitcher, Legal Writing Beyond Memos and Briefs: An Annotated Bibliography (2008) 5 *J. ALWD* 133; Terrill Pollman& Linda H. Edwards, Scholarship by Legal Writing Professors: New Voices in the Legal Academy (2005) 11 *Leg. Writing:* 3; Michael R. Smith, The Next Frontier: Exploring the Substance of Legal Writing (2004) 2 *JALWD* 1; David S. Romantz, The Truth About Cats and Dogs: Legal Writing Courses and the Law School Curriculum (2003) 52 *U. Kan. L. Rev..* 105 (tracing the evolution of legal writing instruction in law schools back to moot court exercises during Langdell's tenure at Harvard Law School). In the United States legal writing is a stand-alone course taught in the first year. See 2017-2018 *ABA Standards and Rules of Procedure for Approv.al of Law Schools,* Standard 303(a)(2) (requiring a school's program of legal education to include "one writing experience in the first year and at least one additional writing experience after the first year"), https://www.americanbar.org/groups/legal_education/resources/standards.html (last visited Sept. 30, 2017).

[3]Unfortunately, in a comprehensive study of lawyers, judges, and legal writing professors, 94% agreed that there are problems with the quality of legal writing today, and 57.3% said that they did not think new lawyers write well. Susan Hanley Kosse & David T. Butle Ritchie, How Judges, Practitioners, and Legal Writing Teachers Assess the Writing Skills of New Law Graduates: A

This chapter is designed to hone the skill of effective writing. It generally examines the fundamental qualities of good legal writing and the various tools legal writers can use to make their writing clear, concise, and engaging. It marks out what legal writing encompasses. Legal writing includes documents that are expository writing that lawyers, judges, and related professionals (e.g., judicial clerks) produce in the course of their work. The prototypical examples of such writing are legal memoranda, letters, briefs, motions, and judicial opinions. In the context of this chapter it does not include academic legal writing or transactional drafting (e.g. contracts), although much of what is discussed in this chapter could apply to transactional drafting, especially in the context of expository writing.

Nature of legal writing

Legal writing is a specialized type of writing. It is technical writing – because it is directed at a particular audience for a discrete purpose.[4] In this case, legal writing aims to inform and to persuade. Like most technical writing it shares the ten distinctive attributes: it is designed for a technical subject; it has a purpose; it has an objective; it conveys information/facts/data; it is impersonal; it is concise; it is directed; it is performed with a particular style and in a particular format; it is archival; it cites contributions of others.[5] Because legal writing is built upon the law, citing and conveying (ideally in a concise manner) various legal authorities with a very specific purpose and objective to inform, persuade, or both it is directed at a particular audience, unlike fictional writing. It is an audience that shares two basic characteristics: the legal reader is impatient and is hypercritical.[6]

Comparative Study (2003) 53 *J. Legal Educ.* 80. Of course, even without evidence that good writing is positively associated with favourable outcomes, lawyers have other important reasons to write well, such as preserving one's professional reputation, conserving judicial resources, and promoting the image of the profession. See, e.g., Amy Vorenberg & Margaret Sova McCabe, Practice Writing: Responding to the Needs of the Bench and Bar in First-Year Writing Programs, (2009) 2 *Phoenix L. Rev.*. 1 @ 10 (reporting that judges and practitioners surveyed "raised the concern that poor writing reflects negatively on the profession"); id. @ 20-21 (judges reported on how legal writers can be helpful, and unhelpful, to the court); id. @ 21 ("Several judges noted that both excellent and sloppy work stand out, resulting in appropriate professional reputations for the authors."); Harry T. Edwards, The Growing Disjunction Between Legal Education and the Legal Profession (1993) 91 *Mich. L. Rev.*. 34.

[4]Darlene Smith-Worthington & Sue Jefferson, *Technical Writing for Success,* 3rd ed. 2010 (technical writing is uncommon writing).

[5] See Kenneth G. Budinski, Engineers' Guide to Technical Writing, 2001 @ 4 cited in Michael J. Higdon, The Legal Reader: An Expose (2013) 43 *New Mexico L. Rev.*. 77 @ 80. See also Jeffrey H. Mills, Write On (1990) 76 *Amer. Bar Ass'n. J.* 92 (an article which states that legal writing is inherently technical writing).

[6]Michael J. Higdon, The Legal Reader: An Expose (2013) 43 *New Mexico L. Rev.*. 77 @ 83. For example, judges complain about the amount of reading they have to do. See William P. Statsky & R. John Wernet, Jr. *Case Analysis and Fundamentals of Legal Writing*, 1994 @ 158 ("Judges, for example, are extremely busy. They may have numerous cases before them. Many judges complain about the overwhelming amount of reading they must do."). Richard K. Neumann, *Legal Reasoning and Legal*

This being so, legal writing is a serious business. In fact, communicating with the legal reader can be a tricky enterprise. The writer must craft a document that is internally consistent and extremely thorough. Further, the writer must ensure that every question (including those the reader may not even encounter until she actually reads the document) is answered fully in a way that is not only persuasive, but also objective and realistic. At the same time, however, this thorough document should ideally be one that the reader can breeze through, having to read it only once to have each and every one of her questions answered and, at the same time, never leaving her in suspense as to where the writer is going and never distracting her with irrelevant material. In simpler terms, the document must be thorough and exhaustive, yet succinct and to the point. Few would argue that this is quite a difficult balance to strike for the legal writer.[7]

Legal writing is not an academic exercise. It consists of two main parts: objective legal analysis and persuasive legal analysis.[8] A lawyer desirous of competence in writing persuasive argument and orally arguing a persuasive legal argument must master the basic skills of: (i) reading and comprehending applicable law; (ii) preparing a complete legal analysis, such as an objective legal memorandum; (iii) organizing a logic legal analysis using some version of an IRAC model; (iv) rough-drafting to communicate succinctly a logical, effective progression of ideas; (v) revising and editing to achieve straightforward writing that conforms to all writing, grammar, and professional standards; (vi) citing authorities using correct standards and formatting; (vii) adopting the appropriate tone and style for the product's purpose and intended audience; (ix) completing writing projects on time.[9]

It is not uncommon for non-lawyers to denounce the way lawyers communicate in writing. They described lawyers writing with adjectives like - wordy, abstruse, and generally unintelligent for the reading public. Even members of the profession do. For example, a law professor once said that "to write as a lawyer is to choose a perspective that can cheapen language and force us to relate to a narrow world of rules, not people," and another practicing lawyer states that "legal writing is one of those rare creatures, like the rat and the cockroach, that would attract little sympathy even as an endangered species."[10] No wonder why

---

Writing: Structure, Strategy and Style, 5th ed. 2005 (noting that "lawyers and judges are busy people who do not have time to wade through poor writing.") id 54, ("The reader is aggressively skeptical and will search for any gap or weakness in your analysis.") id. 52; Jill J. Ramsfield, *The Law as Architecture: Building Legal Documents*, 2000 @ 24 (most legal readers read in bad faith).

[7]Michael J. Higdon, The Legal Reader: An Expose (2013) 43 *New Mexico L. Rev.*. 77 @ 120.

[8] Amy Vorenberg, *Strategies and Techniques for Teaching Legal Analysis and Writing*, New York: Wolters Kluwer Law & Business, 2012 @ 2.

[9]Vorenberg, above n. 4 @ 3.

[10]Stark, Why Lawyers Can't Write (1984) 97 *Harv.. L. Rev.*.1389 @ 1393;Hyland, A Defense of Legal

some lawyers not only call for reform of legal writing but also have embraced the plain English movement in legal writing.[11]

Why do lawyers write in the world of their own? One reason for this is that lawyers write from a narrow perspective that focuses on rules rather than people. [12] It is also because legal writers often fail to recognize that their communication should essentially be conversational – designed to solve problems and discover answers to questions.[13]

Some scholars suggest that all writing involves four basic components: (i) the writer; (ii) the reader; (iii) the language; (iv) the reality.[14] Therefore, it is the aim of a particular writing that determines how the writer chooses to communicate. So, writing is considered effective if it aligns with the purpose set out as its objective by the writer. One that places emphasis on the writer would be expressive, e.g. a journal or diary. If language is the object, literary writing would be appropriate. If on the other hand the emphasis is on the reader, persuasive writing would be the better style. Where however the emphasis is on reality, then an exploratory, scientific or informative writing would be appropriate.

The template certainly shows that much of legal writing ought to come within the bracket of writing designed for the reader and for reality. For example, brief writing is designed to persuade triers and decision-makers to reach favourable conclusions, so it necessarily has to be persuasive if it must qualify as effective, good writing. The writing's purpose is to bring about a change in the reader, to get the reader to act in a certain way, to persuade. On the other hand, the objective legal memorandum designed for reality should propose solution,

---

Writing (1986) 135 *U. Pa. L. Rev*..599 @ 600, both cited in Teresa G. Phelps, The New Rhetoric (1986) 40 *Southwestern L.J.* 1089. See generally, Peter Tiesma, The Origin of Legal Language in Lawrence Solan& Peter Tiersma, eds. *Oxford Handbook of Language and Law*, Oxford, 2010 (an article which explores how lawyers develop a language that is entirely different from ordinary speech and why the profession uses language that contains a substantial amount of technical vocabulary and a number of distinct (often archaic) features that makes it difficult for the lay public to understand, even though they are spoken or written in a variety of ordinary language).

[11] For plain English movement impact in law see, the seminal work of David Mellinkoff, *The Language of Law*, Boston: Little Brown & Co. 1963, which gives rise to the Plain Language Movement in law. See also, Joseph Kimble, *Lifting the Fog of Legalese: Essay on Plain Language,* 2006; Judith D. Fischer, Why George Orwell's Ideas About Language Still Matter for Lawyers (2007) 68 *Mont. L. Rev*.. 129; Joseph Kimble, Writing for Dollars, Writing to Please (1996-97) 6 *Scribes J. Legal Writing* 1. Plain language movement is a movement led by an influential group of legal scholars, judges, and practitioners who seek to advance clarity in legal writing by purging it of cumbersome sentence constructions and empty legal jargon. Proponents of the movement apply this prescription broadly to legislative and transactional drafting, as well as to expository legal writing. For example of its use in expository text, see Wayne Schiess, The Art of Consumer Drafting (2007) 11 *Scribes J. Legal Writing* 1.

[12] Stark, above n. 4.

[13] Phelps, above n. 6.

[14] Phelps, above n. @ 1091

diagnose, define, inform and explore to be effective writing. The writing seeks to represent the reality, the thing outside. Its purpose is to inform rather than to persuade; clarity and accuracy are its hallmarks. The reader serves a relatively passive role, merely receiving information. Thus, even though legal writing is professional writing, it must meet with its specific and definable objective and audience for it to qualify as effective, good writing. Good writing has no place for the discount adjectives of being wordy, abstruse and unintelligent. Good writing is simply a document which helps the decision-maker, whether is a client or a judge to make the decisions she need to make in the course of her professional duties.[15]

What constitutes Good Writing

It is tempting to be prescriptive of what constitutes good writing. Some scholar claim that so-and-so are the rules which dictate what good writing ought to be. Much as such a prescription can be intuitive, it runs the risk of being inflexible and unnecessarily being an overestimation. General guideline can prove more useful because rules of composition are really nothing more than conventional generalizations about the best way to write effectively.[16]

As previously stated the baseline for determining whether a document is well written has a significant bearing with the purpose of the writing.[17]The writer's purpose provides guidance as to what it means for a legal document to be well written. This is a reasonable benchmark because the legal writer does not write in a vacuum. She writes to accomplish some specific objective. If it is an objective legal memorandum, to inform, and if it is a brief of argument, to persuade.

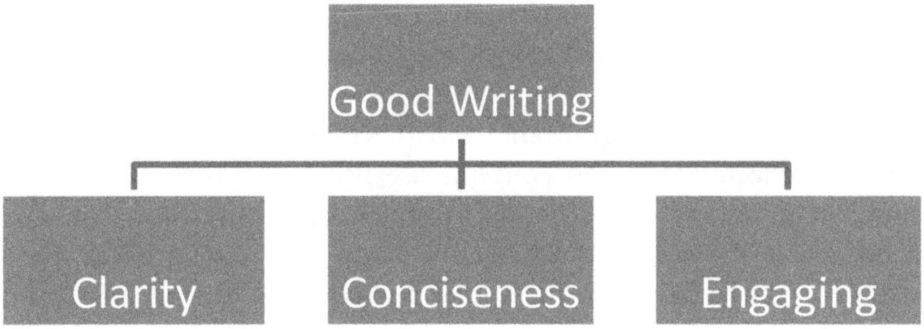

[15]Mark Osbeck, "What is "Good Legal Writing" and Why Does it Matter? (2012) 4 *Drexel L. Rev*..417.

[16] Charles Calleros, *Legal Method and Writing*, 5th ed. 2006 (noting that even the much of specific guidelines prescribed as simply geared to help writers produce clear, concise and engaging documents).

[17]Phelps, above n. 6. See also Stanley Fish, *How to Write a Sentence: And How to Read One*, 2011 @ 37 (People write or speak sentences in order to produce an effect, and the success of a sentence is measured by the degree to which the desired effect has been achieved).

Much as this proposition has its appeal, it can be circular reasoning. Aim or objective should not be the only basis for judging good writing. That a document meets its purpose does not account for that counts for whether a document is well written. By all mean the "purpose" proposition conflates an understanding of the words "effective" and "well." A document can be effective (in the sense of achieving the writer's objective) even if it not well written to qualify as good writing. The converse is also a truism. Phelps uses this simple example: or instance, a brief that takes advantage of a judge's known predilections or prejudices can be an effective document, even though it is poorly written; so too can a brief that is deliberately unclear.

Cases of this type of document that readily come to mind is an example of an opposition brief written by a lawyer to force the calling of evidence to an application to enter summary judgment on affidavit evidence only.[18] The opposing lawyer with a weak defence could through murky writing deliberately tries to obscure the material facts in hopes of creating conflict and confusion to render summary judgment inappropriate for the proceedings. If the court then concludes that there is need to call oral evidence to determine the material fact in dispute, the opposing lawyer would have succeeded in defeating the purpose of the summary practice. She would have written an effective brief no doubt. Yes, the brief meets the writer's objective, but no one doubts that such a brief should be treated as a well-written brief. So, even though it may count as effective litigation tactics, it surely falls short of being well written to qualify as a good brief.[19] Therefore, it is certainly possible for a document to be poorly written, even if the document advances the writer's purpose.

Conversely, a well-written document may not advance the writer's purpose. For example, weak brief (with weak legal arguments unlikely to persuade the court), may be well written.

Thus, while there is significant overlap between a well-written document and one that is effective, the two concepts are not coextensive. Some well-written documents do not achieve the writer's purpose, and conversely, some documents that do enable the writer to achieve the writer's purpose are not well written. Consequently, what it means for a legal document to be well written cannot be explained only by reference to the purpose of the writer.[20]

---

[18] Generally, the court would only decide a matter on affidavit evidence if the issues are not joined in the sense that the affidavits of parties is not in conflict requiring the court to request oral evidence to resolve the conflicts.

[19] Such unethical practice implicates the RPC. State the rule. A lawyer shall not knowingly make a false statement of law or fact to a tribunal

[20] Phelps, above n. 6 @ 425.

It is therefore suggested that the concept of good writing should take into account both the *objective* of the writer and the *needs* or interests of the reading audience. While the former is a judgment of the reader; the latter is a judgment of the audience.

In the context of legal writing (especially briefs), the lawyers and judges are the intended audience with particular needs and interests. They read legal documents to extract information from them to reach professional decision. For example, a partner in a law firm reads an associate's memo to obtain information concerning the law and its application to the facts. This in turn helps the partner decide how to advise the client, or how to approach a strategic decision the lawyer needs to make with respect to a case or a transaction. Likewise, a judge reads a lawyer's brief in order to obtain information about the case and in order to understand the parties arguments. This in turn helps the judge decide how to rule on a motion. And similarly, a lawyer reads a judicial opinion in order to obtain information about the law and how it is likely to be interpreted or applied in a future case. This information in turn helps the lawyer decide how best to make an argument, structure a transaction, or advise a client as to a proposed course of action.

So, for the legal community, a document would qualify as good writing if it facilitates the reader's decision-making. And thus, the legal reader will regard a document as well written if and only if the writing facilitates that decision-making. Good legal writing, therefore, is best understood as writing that helps legal actors make decisions in the course of their professional duties.

A legal document that satisfies the objective of the writer and need of the audience is generally expected to exhibit three fundamental features: (i) clarity, (ii) conciseness, and (iii) the ability to engage the reader.

Clarity

Clarity is the first and most fundamental ingredient of good writing. Justice Benjamin Cardozo states that it is the "sovereign" requirement.[21]Likewise, most contemporary commentators on legal writing exalt clarity above all else. When a lawyer or judge picks up a document to read, she seeks to understand the argument to arrive at a conclusion. Accordingly, the document must be easy to understand. This is what makes clarity the most significant quality of good writing. The writer's message must be clear. It is only when a document is clear that it is easy to comprehend the writer's message and be used to reach decisions.

---

[21] Benjamin Cardozo, *Law and Literature*, 1931, reprinted in *Law and Literature and Other Essays and Addresses*, Fred B. Rothman & Co. 1999 @ 7. Antonin Scalia & Bryan A. Garner, *Making Your Case: The Art of Persuading Judges*, 2008 @ 107.

The task of accomplishing clarity is by no means an easy one. Some scholars are of the view that clear writing come by following rules of grammar and proper punctuation,[22] and the like. There is no question that failure to follow such rules would reveal that a writer is sloppy, careless, and that major diversion contributes to making a document less clear, but it must be recognized that an insistence on following the rules may be putting the importance of grammar too high in the clarity equation.[23] The simple reason for the assertion that even though grammar rules do matter they may not be so fundamental is the recognition that language rules are flexible. Yes, there are certain-agreed rules governing every language for people to enjoy shared meaning, but it would be stating the proposition too high to suggest that the rules are shared watertight, accepting of no disagreements. Linguists disagree on a periphery of minor rules. For English language the periphery includes debate about the proper use of rules like those on ending a sentence with a preposition, or requiring that commas and periods be placed inside quotation marks, and the likes. In fact, it is plausible to think of instances where ignoring some of these minor rules can contribute to clarity. What detract from clarity is rather major disregard of major rules of language, such as deviation from core grammar rules, syntax and semantics.[24] For example, it would be challenging to follow a writer who consistently misuses verbs, or writes sentences in clumsy ways. Such writing would by no means be clear.

---

[22]See Lillian Hardwick, Classical Persuasion through Grammar and Punctuation (2006) 3 *JALWD* 75 (an article that discusses how errors in grammar and punctuation create interference with communication and persuasion between legal author and audience) id. @ 88 ("Grammar refers to the structure of a language, whether oral or written. Pieces of the structure have assigned names (noun, verb, adjective) that conveniently describe how the various pieces fit together. Idiom is a grammatical term for the knowledge that dictates that particular words can fit into the structural slots. For example, "live" and "leave" are both transitive verbs, which means they can take direct objects. However, they are not interchangeable in the same structure for all sentences. We can say "leave me," but it is not idiomatic to say "live me." In this sense, word choice is a part of grammar. Otherwise, word choice is generally a matter of stylistic choice, not grammatical rules. Punctuation applies only to written language. It has evolved as a convention for the same reason grammar has: so that we can have reliable cues for communication. The rules of punctuation are designed to permit a level of understanding as similar as possible to spoken language. These rules have changed very little over time. Although minor modifications have appeared from time to time, it is not difficult to describe a uniform set of consistent punctuation rules with reliable explanations)."

[23] See Lillian B. Hardwick, Classical Persuasion Through Grammar and Punctuation (2006) 3 *J. Ass'n. Legal Writing Directors* 75; John C. Dernbach *et al. A Practical Guide to Legal Writing and Legal Method,* 3rd ed. 2006 @ 75 (where the learned writers state errors in grammar, punctuation, and spelling suggest that the writer is sloppy and careless); Richard K. Neumann, *Legal Reasoning and Legal Writing*, 6th ed. 2009 @ 240 (stating that correct punctuation and grammar make writing clearer and easier to understand).

[24] John Bronsteen, *Writing A Legal Memo*, 2006 @ 36.

An excellent way to write clear is to use plain English.[25] The use of short, simple words also aids clarity.[26] Avoiding legalese also contributes to clarity.[27] Let us consider a few good examples of these features.

Justice Benjamin Cardozo's description of the facts in his famous opinion in *Palsgraf* v. *Long Island Railroad Co.* provides a good example of simple, concrete writing. His description of the facts leading to the plaintiff's injuries is in this lucid form:

> Plaintiff was standing on a platform of defendant's railroad after buying a ticket to go to Rockaway Beach. A train stopped at the station, bound for another place. Two men ran forward to catch it. One of the men reached the platform of the car without mishap, though the train was already moving. The other man, carrying a package, jumped aboard the car, but seemed unsteady as if about to fall. A guard on the car, who had held the door open, reached forward to help him in, and another guard on the platform pushed him from behind. In this act, the package was dislodged, and fell upon the rails. It was a package of small size, about fifteen inches long, and was covered by a newspaper. In fact it contained fireworks, but there was nothing in its appearance to give notice of its contents. The fireworks when they fell exploded. The shock of the explosion threw down some scales at the other end of the platform, many feet away. The scales struck the plaintiff, causing injuries for which she sues.[28]

The rather complex facts are made clear to the reader by use of ordinary, plain language by a series of simple words. Even though this factual scenario is fairly complicated, Cardozo makes it easy to follow – it begins with a concrete subject, followed by a verb that expresses a specific action.

---

[25] See generally n. 7 on plain English movement. See also Bryan A. Garner, *Garner's Modern English Usage*, 4th ed. 2016; Richard Wydick, *Plain English for Lawyers*, 5th ed. 2005; Joseph Kimble, Drafting Examples from the Proposed New Federal Rules of Evidence, *Mich. B.J.* Aug. 2009 @ 52; Sept. 2009 @ 46; Oct. 2009 @ 54; Nov. 2009 @ 50; Joseph Kimble, Lessons in Drafting from the New Federal Rules of Civil Procedure (2008-2009)12 *Scribes J. Legal Writing* 25. But cf. Soha Turfler, Language Ideology and the Plain-Language Movement (2015) 12 *Legal Comm. & Rhetoric: JALWD* 195 (an article where the learned writer describes the plain English movement as resting on three "ideologies" and she undertakes to "discuss how each ideology perpetuates discriminatory norms and practices). See reply to the criticism of the three ideologies by Joseph Kimble, A Curious Criticism of Plain Language (2016) 13 *Legal Comm. & Rhetoric: JALWD* 181. See also, Joseph Kimble, Answering the Critics of Plain Language (1994-95) 5 *Scribes J. Legal Writing* 51.

[26] Bronsteen, above n. 19 @ 33.

[27] Nancy L. Schultz & Louis J. Sirico, *Legal Writing and Other Lawyering Skills*, 5th ed. 2010 @ 90.

[28] 162 N.E. 99, 99 (N.Y. 1928).

While it is true that the Plain Language Movement can contribute to the cause of clarity, it has been suggested that clarity in this respect can also come with costs - inhibiting the precision of legal writing. There is no question about it. Certain legal terminologies carry precision very challenging to express in ordinary language. Conveying them in ordinary, simple, plain language can even lead to ambiguity. This isn't peculiar to the legal profession. For example, if a doctor were to seek help from say a consultant gynaecologist about treatment options for her patient suffering bleeding from the uterus it would be unhelpful to simple say: the patient before me is bleeding from the uterus. Specific, technical description as "my patient is suffering from" would be more helpful for purposes of clarity.

The same applies in law. There would be instances where plain language suffers limitation of conveying clarity.[29] This being so, the use of legalese does have a place also in promoting clarity. Plain language advocates also admit that the use of technical terms may sometimes be necessary for precision.[30] But as a rule, legalese should not be used if it is unnecessary.

It is therefore important that a insistence on plain language must take into consideration the audience of the reader. For what constitute good writing that is clear must take into consideration the reader and the context of the writing - such as the reader's vocabulary and language proficiency. It is best for instance, not to use words that constantly send the reader to the dictionary. But then, if the reader is a wordsmith, then a level of aesthetics would not be out of place.

In the final analysis, therefore, a general prescription to use plain language is helpful only if it is understood to be shorthand for a more nuanced rule, such as the following: When you use distinctive technical or legal terms, consider whether the terms add any value beyond their ordinary- language equivalents. If not, use the ordinary term. If so, then consider the nature of the audience to determine whether the increased precision resulting from the technical term outweighs any loss of clarity that may result from using a term that may not be familiar to all members of the intended audience.[31]

---

[29]Rabeea Assy, Can the Law Speak Directly to Its Subjects? The Limitation of Plain Language (2011) 38 *J. L. & Soc'y.* 376 (arguing that there is an inevitable linguistic gap between technical legal terms and ordinary language terms because the former are closely tied up with a body of theories, doctrines, principles, and rules that the speaker must have some understanding of in order to use legal language effectively), available at http://ssrn.com/abstract=1906372. See also Jeffrey Barnes, The Continuing Debate (2006) 27 *Stat. L. Rev.*. 83; David Crump, Against Plain English: The Case for a Functional Approach to Legal Document Preparation (2001-2) 33 *Rutgers L.J.* 713; Brian Hunt, Plain Language in Legislative Drafting: Is It Really the Answer? (2002) 23 *Stat. L. Rev.*.24.

[30]Joseph Kimble, Answering the Critics of Plain Language, 5 *Scribes J. Legal Writing* 51 @ 54; Garner @ 663.

[31]Phelps, above n. 6 @ 434.

Outside these rules of grammar there are other prescriptions suggested by legal writers that advance clarity. One such prominent prescription is that "a sentence should contain no unnecessary words, no unnecessary paragraph, for the same reason that a drawing should have no unnecessary lines and a machine no unnecessary parts."[32] It is also important in writing to use repetition to make writing clearer and to use a particular term consistently to avoid causing confusion in the mind of the reader.

The good writing rules are many. These include the following: not overusing negatives, avoiding noun strings and nominalizations, and preferring the active voice. Much of these are well documented in the *Element of Style*, a great English language text that advances clarity. [33] While writing scholars agree that organization of a document contributes to clarity, lawyers generally use an IRACian model for professional writing.

Conclusively then it would be safe to say that there is no simple prescription for clarity. Clarity is dependent on a number of different factors, and it is context-dependent. The legal writer must consider carefully the purpose of the writing, as well as the needs, interests, and background knowledge of the intended audience when deciding what is appropriate for a particular document. But it is important for the legal writer to keep in mind that clarity is the paramount goal of legal writing, since readers can only make effective use of a document to aid their professional decision-making if they understand the writer‘s message.

Conciseness

The second fundamental quality of good legal writing is conciseness. Conciseness is not synonymous with brevity. A concise document is not necessarily brief. It is rather efficient because it is succinct, without superfluous words, while laced with an appropriate level of detail to render the document understandable.

What constitutes the appropriate level of detail for any given document depends on the context. Often, it is simply not possible to explain a complex idea with the same degree of economy as one can express a simple idea. A motion *in limine* on a minor point of evidence and a complicated appellate brief on an important matter of constitutional law may both be written in a concise fashion, even though the appellate brief is much longer and more detailed than the motion *in limine*. The difference in length and detail is appropriate not only because of the relative complexity of the issues, but also because the appellate court has more time to give a careful reading to each brief.

---

[32] William Strunk, *The Element of Style*

[33]Ibid.

The interests and needs of the intended audience are paramount here: the appellate judges likely have more time and a greater inclination to read a more detailed and nuanced brief than a trial judge with a crowded docket. Concise writing, therefore, is often brief, but it is always efficient. Within any given context, the writing makes its points in the most economical way.[34]

Phelps offers an excerpt from Judge Richard Posner's dissent in *Jordan* v. *Duff & Phelps, Inc.* as a good example of conciseness.[35]

> A corporate employee at will quit, owning shares that he had agreed to sell back to the corporation at book value. The agreement was explicit that his status as a shareholder conferred no job rights on him. Nevertheless the court holds that the corporation had, as a matter of law, a duty, enforce- able by proceedings under Rule 10b-5 of the Securities Exchange Act, to volunteer to the employee information about the corporation's prospects that might have led him to change his mind about quitting, although as an employee at will he had no right to change his mind. I disagree with this holding. The terms of the stockholder agreement show that there was no duty of disclosure, and since there was no duty there was no violation of Rule 10b-5.

In this very short paragraph, Posner effectively describes the following: (i) the essential facts, (ii) the majority's position, and (iii) the basis for his dissent. This is expected of a judge who is the foremost advocate of economic efficiency.[36] No words were wasted.

A document exhibits conciseness if it follows the prescription of Strunk and White: "A sentence should contain no unnecessary words, a paragraph no unnecessary sentences, for the same reason that a drawing should have no unnecessary lines, and a machine no unnecessary parts."[37]

One way to write concise is to omit needless words. Particularly for legal writers it demands that needless legalese should be cut out of a document. Clutter phrases should also be removed. A lawyer should therefore train to look for common clutter words, like "of" and "it is" and remove them from the document.

A good way to be razor-sharp concise is to learn to stripe a sentence to its pieces, reworking it with the aim of becoming a sentence-builder and crafting. To master the craft, the lawyer should start from this foundation: work through from

---

[34]Phelps, above n. 6 @ 438.

[35] 815 F.2d 429, 444 (7th Cir. 1987).

[36] Richard Posner, *Economic Analysis of Law*

[37] Above n.8 @ 23.

the idea sought to be conveyed to the audience. With this idea in hand, the lawyer can tear apart a non-concise sentence and build it with purpose – a sort of content-word editing.[38] It is helpful to go about it this way: first jot down the crucial words that must appear in the sentence. Then underline a couple of key words that the audience need to keep in mind – the ideas that the writer cannot afford to miss out. From there the writer can start the sentence rebuilding to deliver the ideas.

An example would do. Suppose a lawyer wants to rework the paragraph that reads: "The Uniform Trade Secret Act, *inter alia*, generally provides a definition of trade secret as follows: any piece of information or document has intrinsic value such that it derives value from not being known."

The central idea being conveyed is "what is a trade secret." To achieve conciseness it would be important to underline the key words that convey that content. Once the key words are underlined, we can have a shot at conciseness – to convey only key ideas. The key words here are "trade secret," "information," "value from," and "not being known." With this in mind the sentence can then be rephrased as follows:

"A trade secret is information made valuable by its secrecy."

Or

"Information that derives value from its secrecy is a trade secret."

All we have done here is reduce the sentence to a manageable few words that convey the idea. This is what it means to be concise. Content-word editing is a good first step try to sentence-crafting.

Concise document is good writing because it is less complex, and easier to digest. Conciseness also contributes to make writing engaging.[39] Readers generally tend to lose interest reading unnecessarily long text.

A legal reader has limited time to devote to a document and a limited attention span. A concise piece that makes its point efficiently and with an appropriate level of detail does not waste the reader's time and takes full advantage of this limited window of opportunity. Conciseness may not be essential to all types of writing, but it is essential in the context of legal writing because the reader of legal writing has no time to spare and either will resent

---

[38] For techniques of critical (recursive) editing see Anne Enquist & Laurel Currie Oates, *Just Writing: Grammar, Punctuation, and Style for the Legal Writer*, 2nd ed. Aspen, 2005,§ 1.4–1.6, 15–21 (useful discussion of revising, editing, and proofreading); Christopher M. Anzidei, The Revision Process in Legal Writing: Seeing Better to Write Better (2002) 8 *Leg. Writing* 23 @ 43–45; Terri LeClercq, Revision before Editing (1986) 49 *Tex. B.J.* 838.

[39]Neumann, above n. 18 @ 217.

inflated verbiage or will simply refuse to read it. So, conciseness is fundamental to good legal writing because it helps readers make effective use of their limited time, which invariably promotes efficient decision-making by allowing legal actors to devote the appropriate amount of time to each of their decisions, rather than spending an excessive amount of time on one decision and having to short-change another as a result.[40]

Occasionally conciseness can be achieved only by eliminating qualifiers from a sentence that make the sentence slightly more accurate but that are not essential. And sometimes conciseness can be achieved only by eliminating details that make a paragraph slightly more thorough. In these situations, the legal writer needs to make a judgment call as to whether being a bit more accurate or thorough justifies lengthening and increasing the working parts of the document. While there are no simple rules of thumb to guide the legal writer in making these decisions, the legal writer should keep in mind the important role conciseness plays in facilitating the reader's professional decision-making when attempting to strike the appropriate balance.

Engaging

Good legal writing must be engaging. On the importance of engaging the reader Lord Denning, the importance of engaging the reader as follows:

> "No matter how sound your reasoning, if it is presented in a dull and turgid setting, your hearers—or your readers—will turn aside. They will not stop to listen. They will flick over the pages. But if it is presented in a lively and attractive setting, they will sit up and take notice. They will listen as if spellbound. They will read you with engrossment."[41]

Even if a document were clear and concise, it would only keep the reader's attention if it were engaging. Phelps gives the following example of a document that is both clear and concise, but misses out being engaging.

> "Our client is Bill Smith. Smith has filed a lawsuit in federal court. It is a personal injury case. Smith was watching a softball game. Smith got hit with a softball. He was injured. He suffered a concussion. Smith received treatment at Methodist hospital. He now

---

[40]Phelps, above n. 6 @ 440. See also Nelson P. Miller, Why Prolixity Does Not Produce Clarity: Francis Lieber on Plain Language (2007) 11 *Scribes J. Legal Writing* 107, 108 (2007)

[41]Garner, above n. @ 39 (quoting Lord Denning, MR, *The Family Story*, 1981 @ 216.

seeks damages. He claims to have mental and physical injuries. Smith doesn't know if he is entitled to damages for mental injuries. He wants us to find out. This memo addresses that issue."[42]

Unquestionable, the paragraph is clear and concise, but it is more of a drab. It sounds flat, without colour, and is monotonous a read.

The paragraph when compared to the engaging excerpt from Justice Louis Brandeis (concurring judgment) in *Whitney* v. *California* is clear. His Lordship stated:

> "Those who won our independence by revolution were not cowards. They did not fear political change. They did not exalt order at the cost of liberty. To courageous, self-reliant men, with confidence in the power of free and fearless reasoning applied through the processes of popular government, no danger flowing from speech can be deemed clear and present, unless the incidence of the evil apprehended is so imminent that it may befall before there is opportunity for full discussion. If there be time to expose through discussion the falsehood and fallacies, to avert the evil by the processes of education, the remedy to be applied is more speech, not enforced silence. Only an emergency can justify repression. Such must be the rule if authority is to be reconciled with freedom. Such, in my opinion, is the command of the Constitution.[43]

The Brandeis and the other excerpts above are all unquestionably clear and concise. But they also command the reader's attention. They are all crisp and powerful, and compelling the reader to keep reading. Their effect is contagious in that they all encourage the reader to engage with the material either by agreeing with it or disagreeing with it or re- constituting the content into the reader's own ideas, etc. They stimulate thinking.

It is said that engaging writing is the quality that separates truly good legal writing from merely competent legal writing.[44] Engaging writing makes the reader's job easier, just as clarity and conciseness make the reader's job easier. Writing that does not engage the reader's attention makes it more difficult for the reader to glean necessary information from a document because it makes the

---

[42] Above n. 8 @ 442.
[43] 274 U.S. 357 @ 337 (1927).
[44] Phelps @ 443.

reading process more laborious. And that in turn hinders the reader's ability to make professional decisions based upon the document.

There are various tools that advance engagement. One such simple tool is variety. The writer‘s use of varied sentence structures, can make the text more engaging. Writing that is overly repetitive in its syntax gets tedious; conversely, writing that has appropriate variation in the length and pattern of the sentences, with smooth transitions between sentences, has a natural flow that helps to maintain the reader‘s interest, in the same way that variation in speech patterns (such as pausing, modulation, sense stress, etc.) enlivens conversation. And the same holds true with respect to individual words: using a more expressive vocabulary adds interest to writing.

Other more abstract factors such as writing style also determine whether the writing will engage the reader. A document that is casual or artificial hardly resonates with the reader. The reason is that the voice of the reader comes out not authentic. Legal writing is more of an interpretive process than a compositional one. Therefore, the central task for the lawyer from this point of view is to give herself a voice of her own, a voice that at once expresses her own mind at work in its best way and speaks as a lawyer, a voice at once individual and professional.[45]

Consider, for example, Justice Holmes‘s infamous pronouncement in favour of forced sterilization in *Buck* v. *Bell* unquestionably reveals his voice. He said:

> It is better for all the world, if instead of waiting to execute degenerate offspring for crime, or to let them starve for their imbecility, society can prevent those who are manifestly un- fit from continuing their kind. The principle that sustains compulsory vaccination is broad enough to cover cutting the Fallopian tubes. Three generations of imbeciles are enough.[46]

Yes, the reasoning is to a large extent objectionable, but that does not distract from a projection of Holmes's strong character. His voice certainly stands out clear in the judgment.

In *Military Governor of Lagos State* v. *Ojukwu,* no one could doubt the voices of the judges.[47] Justice Kayode Eso, JSC in lambasting the illegal act of the military resorting to self-help stated:

---

[45]James B. White, *The Legal Imagination*, abr. ed. 1985, xv. The writer's voice implies the personality of the writer revealed through the document – the real person behind the document. See J. Christopher Rideout, Voice, Self, and Persona in Legal Writing (2009) 15 *Legal Writing* 67 (providing a brief history of the concept of voice and describing the difficulties in defining the concept).

[46]274 U.S. 200, 207 (1927).

[47][1986] NLR 233; (1986) NWLR (pt. 18) 621.

By virtue of the Constitution (Suspension Modification) Decree 1984 No. 1 a good number of the provisions of the Constitution were suspended. Indeed, what was left was what had been permitted by the Federal Military Government to exist. All the provisions relating to the Judiciary were saved. Section 6 of the Constitution, the most important provision, in so far as the institution known as the Judiciary is concerned, which vests in courts the judicial powers of the Federation was left extant. The Military Government had the power and still has to put an end to the existence of that provision, It has not done so, and that must have been advisedly for it does intend that the rule of law should pervade. It is the clearest indication against rule by Tyranny, by sheer force of arms against a presumption subjecting the nation to the rule of might as against rule of right.

That being the case, it behoves of every organ of the Military Government to make it clear at all times, albeit as the presumption is always that of rule by might of the military, to assume a perennial onus of demonstrating a rebuttal of this onus.

With the contempt of the Court of Appeal by the Applicants still subsisting, it would he inequitable for this Court to give a consideration to the application of the Applicants. Let the Lagos State Government purge itself of this serious contempt, of this apparent violation of the Constitution even as amended by Decree No. 1 of 1984 before coming to seek the favour of the Court.

Another very important matter emanating from the act of the applicants. They have no right to take the matter into their own hands once the court was seised of it. The essence of rule of law is that it should never operate under the rule of force or fear. To use force to effect an act and while under the marshal of that force, seek the court's equity, is an attempt to infuse timidity into court and operate a sabotage of the cherished rule of law. It must never be.

Obaseki, JSC (concurring) also stated:

> I will be doing injustice to the cause of the rule of law if I grant this application and allow the eviction of the respondent to stand...More relevant to the case in hand, the rule of law means that disputes as to the legality of acts of government are to be decided by judges who are wholly independent of the executive. See Wade on Administrative Law 5th Edition p. 22-27. That is the position in this country where the judiciary has been made independent of the executive by the Constitution of the Federal Republic of Nigeria 1979 as amended by Decree No. 1 of 1984 and No. 17 of 1985. The judiciary cannot shirk its sacred responsibility to the nation to maintain the rule of law. It is both in the interest of the government and all persons in Nigeria. The law should be even handed between the government and citizens.

There is no question about it. The distinct voice of the personalities of Eso and Obaseki, JJSC, sound out from the judgment.

It must be noted however that much as a document should project the writer's voice, legal writing it must be admitted must temperate the writer's voice within the bounds of professional responsibility and ethics.[48]

Occasionally, however, the legal writer like a novelist can choose a voice not personal to the writer to effectively convey a message in the character the writer wants the reader to identify with. Chief Justice Roberts's amusing dissent in *Pennsylvania* v. *Dunlap*, for example, illustrates this technique. In his recitation of the facts, he cleverly employs the point of view as well as the voice of the arresting officer in order to help the reader appreciate the officer's perspective on whether there was probable cause to make an arrest:

> North Philly, May 4, 2001. Officer Sean Devlin, Narcotics Strike Force, was working the morning shift. Undercover surveillance. The neighbourhood? Tough as a three-dollar steak. Devlin knew. Five years on the beat, nine months with the Strike Force. He'd made fifteen, twenty drug busts in the neighbourhood. Devlin spotted him: a lone man on the street corner. Another approached. Quick exchange of words. Cash handed over; small objects handed back. Each man then quickly on his own way. Devlin knew the guy wasn't buying bus to- kens. He radioed a description and Officer Stein

[48]RPC.

picked up the buyer. Sure enough: three bags of crack in the guy's pocket. Head downtown and book him. Just another day at the office.[49]

This use of other person's voice model notwithstanding, it is advisable for a writer to speak in her voice for it is the voice natural to the writer rather than mimicking the voice of others.

Humour is another great tool for advancing engaging writing. An appropriate use of it makes reading an interesting experience. It can be particularly effective in delivering an unpopular message. Consider, for example, Judge Cardozo's opinion in *Murphy* v. *Steeplechase Amusement Company.* There, the New York Court of Appeals held that the assumption-of-risk doctrine prevented recovery by a young man injured on an amusement-park ride that was aptly named "the Flopper". Justice Cardozo expressed the rationale for the decision as follows:

> One who takes part in such a sport accepts the dangers that inhere in it so far as they are obvious and necessary, just as a fencer accepts the risk of a thrust by his antagonist or a spectator at a ball game the chance of contact with the ball. The antics of the clown are not the paces of the cloistered cleric. The rough and boisterous joke, the horseplay of the crowd, evokes its own guffaws, but they are not the pleasures of tranquillity. The plaintiff was not seeking a retreat for meditation. Visitors were tumbling about the belt to the merriment of onlookers when he made his choice to join them. He took the chance of a like fate, with whatever dam- age to his body might ensue from such a fall. The timorous may stay at home.[50]

His Lordship by using a dry, tongue-in-cheek tone to suggest that a vigorous young man who elects to jump on a ride called 'the Flopper' might reasonably expect to be flopped about, Cardozo makes the application of an otherwise harsh doctrine seem more palatable to the reader. The mildly humorous tone disarms the reader's natural sympathies for the injured plaintiff and invites the reader to conclude that the plaintiff voluntarily assumed the risk of injury.

---

[49] 555 U.S 964 (2008) (Roberts, J., dissenting), denying cert. to *Commonwealth* v. *Dunlap*, 941 A.2d 671 (Pa. 2007).

[50] 166 N.E. 173 (N.Y. 1929). For a good overview of the effective use of humour in judicial opinions, see Thomas E. Baker, A Review of Corpus Juris Humorous (1993) 24 *Texas L. Rev*.. 869.

Humour must however be used with caution. Its use can backfire. Some could think it a way of trivializing serious matters. It is for this reason that some consider it inappropriate for legal writing, especially judicial opinion.[51] Its use can also disengage the reader from the text. The same can be said of illustrations.

Another important component of engaging writing is the writer‘s ability to tell a compelling story – what is now known as legal narrative or storytelling.[52] After all, law is all about events and experience of those who are the subject of legal writing. Legal memoranda and briefs stewed with narrative have engaging power in bringing lived experience to bear in law.

Here again, Lord Denning is a master. See how he describes the facts in *Miller* v. *Jackson*, a case concerning some rather simple allegations of negligence and nuisance:

> In summertime village cricket is the delight of everyone. Nearly every village has its own cricket field where the young men play and the old men watch. In the village of Lintz in County Durham they have their own ground, where they have played these last 70 years. They tend it well. The cricket area is well rolled and mown. The outfield is kept short. It has a club house for the players and seats for the onlookers. The village team plays there on Saturdays and Sundays. They belong to a league, competing with the neighbouring villages. On other evenings after work they practice while the light lasts. Yet now after these 70 years a judge of the High Court has ordered that they must not play there anymore. He has issued an injunction to stop them. He has done it at the instance of a newcomer who is no lover of cricket. This newcomer has built, or has had built for him, a house on the edge of the cricket ground which four years ago was a field where cattle grazed. The animals did not mind the cricket. But now this adjoining field has been turned into a housing estate. The newcomer bought one of the houses on the edge of the cricket ground. No doubt the open space was a selling point. Now he complains that when a batsman

---

[51]See Marshall Rudolph, Note, Judicial Humor: A Laughing Matter? (1989) 41 *Hastings L. J.* 175 @ 179 (lamenting the excessive and inappropriate use of humor in judicial opinions). 129.See, e.g., Michael D. Murray & Christy H. Desanctis, *Legal Writing and Analysis,* 2009 @ 266 (—The law is too serious of a business for humour).

[52] See Boyd White, Legal Imagination. See Kenneth D. Chestek, The Plot Thickens: The Appellate Brief as Story (2008) 14 *Legal Writing* 127 ("Law, and the legal system, should be about people . . . It is a tool to en- rich and order peoples' lives. So why do legal briefs focus so much on the abstract law and overlook the people?.") Id. @ 130.

> hits a six the ball has been known to land in his garden, or on or near his house. His wife has got so upset about it that they always go out at weekends. They do not go into the garden when cricket is being played. And the judge, much against his will, has felt that he must order the cricket to be stopped: with the consequence, I suppose, that the Lintz Cricket Club will disappear. The cricket ground will be turned to some other use. I expect for more houses or a factory. The young men will turn to other things instead of cricket. The whole village will be much the poorer. And all this because of a newcomer who has just bought a house there next to the cricket ground.[53]

In one long paragraph composed almost entirely of simple, plain sentences, Lord Denning is able to spin a very compelling narrative. It provides the reader with all the essential facts. But it does so in a way that is highly persuasive as well as engaging. The narrative sets up an almost archetypal conflict between happy villagers and a troublesome interloper that practically begs for resolution in favour of maintaining the villagers' traditional ways.

Judge Learned Hand's opinion in *Sheldon* v. *Metro-Goldwyn Pictures Corp.* provides another good example of effective storytelling.[54] In that opinion, the court awarded injunctive relief as well as compensatory damages to the authors of a play who had brought a copyright infringement action against a movie producer. Judge Hand's opinion first tells the historical story that provides the basis for the plot in both the play and the movie: the story of a young woman named Madeleine Smith who faced trial in Scotland in 1857 for allegedly poisoning her lover with a cup of arsenic-laden hot chocolate. The opinion then goes into significant detail comparing the specific plots and dramatic techniques of the play and the movie. It also discusses the plot of a contemporaneous novel - again based upon the story of Madeleine Smith - which the defendant movie-producer claimed the movie was based upon. (The movie-producer had purchased the rights to the novel but not the play.) After summarizing all three stories in a lively manner worthy of a novelist, and demonstrating the significant overlap among them, Judge Hand succinctly concludes, - if the picture was not an infringement of the play, there can be none short of taking the dialogue.

Unfortunately, storytelling ability like Judge Hand's and Lord Denning's is uncommon in legal writing. And far too many legal writers disregard storytelling

---

[53][1977] Q.B. 966, 976 (Eng.).

[54]135. 81 F.2d 49 (2d Cir. 1936).

altogether, merely reciting factual material in a cut-and-dry, mechanical way, as if the - facts were simply data points rather than stories about real people. But in doing so, these writers lose a powerful persuasive tool. A growing body of literature indicates that most people, including judges, make decisions more readily on the basis of stories that they can relate to their own experiences than they do through argument, statistics, or logic. As the Denning and Hand opinions illustrate, effective storytelling enhances the reader‘s receptivity to the writer‘s message. And thus a document that effectively blends legal analysis with narrative will be more engaging and persuasive than a document that focuses solely on legal arguments and the dry recitations of facts.[55]

Other tools that skilful writers use to engage readers have their roots in classical rhetoric.[56] One such tool is what classical rhetoricians called pathos, which refers to the writer's ability to connect with the reader at an emotional level, thereby increasing the reader's level of engagement by making the reader more receptive to the writer's message.[57]

The writer‘s choice of language can also influence the reader's emotional response. By employing emotive words that resonate with the reader's deeply held feelings and values, the writer can make the reader more sympathetic to the writer's message. This technique plays an important role in making Justice Brandeis's concurrence in *Whitney* v. *California* so powerful. Brandeis's references to the founding fathers as - courageous, self-reliant men and as -

---

[55]Phelps, above n. 6 @451. Kenneth D. Chestek, Judging by the Numbers: An Empirical Study of the Power of Story (2010) 7 *J. Ass'n. Legal Writing Directors* 1 @ 19-22 (presenting empirical evidence that judges prefer briefs that stress narrative); Linda H. Edwards, The Convergence of Analogical and Dialectic Imaginations in Legal Discourse (1996) 20 *J. Legal Stud.* 7, 28–40 (arguing that narrative is an essential component of our thinking about legal rules and principles); Elizabeth Fajans & Mary R. Falk, Untold Stories: Restoring Narrative to Pleading Practice (2009) 15 *J. Legal Writing* 3 @ 15–46 (arguing that storytelling can enhance the effectiveness of pleadings such as complaints); Brian J. Foley & Ruth Anne Robbins, Fiction 101: A Primer For Lawyers on How to Use Fiction Writing Techniques to Write Persuasive Fact Sections, (2010) 32 *Rutgers L.J.* 459 (discussing the benefits of storytelling for persuasion and explaining how to incorporate the techniques of fiction writing to tell stories in briefs). For a good overview of the scholarly literature on storytelling and the reasons why people are persuaded through stories, see J. Christopher Rideout, Storytelling, Narrative Rationality, and Legal Persuasion (2008) 14 *J. Legal Writing* 53.

[56] See discussion in chapter -.

[57]Aristotle, probably the principal architect of classical rhetoric, described rhetoric as - the faculty of observing in any given case the available means of persuasion. Aristotle, (c. 335–30, B.C.E.), *Rhetoric,* reprinted in *Poetics and Rhetoric,* (W. Rhys Roberts trans., Barnes & Noble classics ed., 2005 @ 93, 105). He then identified ethos, logos, and pathos as the three essential - modes of persuasion. Id. @ 104–09. In simple terms, ethos involves establishing credibility with the audience, logos involves persuasion through the use of rational argument, and pathos involves persuasion through the writer's ability to influence the emotions of the audience. For a general overview of these concepts, see Michael R. Smith, *Advanced Legal Writing: Theories and Strategies,* 2nd ed. 2008 @ 34, 94-101 (explaining how and why narrative techniques make the reader more receptive to the writer's message).

[t]hose who won our independence by revolution, and his liberal use of emotive words such as - free men, - liberty, and – democracy, serve to engage and persuade the reader by evoking feelings of patriotism and civic duty.[58]

The use of those words creates and inspires fellow feeling of community between the writer and the reader by calling attention to their shared heritage and shared political values.

Other subtle ways of employing pathos include the use of certain narrative myths, such as metaphors, and archetypes that resonate with the reader, such as the story of a hero on an epic journey or quest.

Like most tools of engagement with the reader, the use of pathos must be within professional bounds of ethics.[59]

Finally, in order for a legal document to be appropriately engaging, it is important that the document strike a proper tone.[60] This is a difficult concept to define, but essentially it involves making sure that the subject matter of the document and writing style are in sync, so that they reinforce each other‘s effect on the reader. For example, it would be appropriate for a debt demand notice to be serious to make the debtor think of the consequences of failing to repay a debt. So, it would be enough for the letter of demand to be clear, and concise, its tone must strike a tone of repercussion in the debtor.[61]

Clarity and engagement are both fundamental qualities of good legal writing, yet at times these qualities may conflict. When they do, the skilful legal writer needs to find an appropriate balance. For example, if repetition would promote clarity but make the document less engaging, the writer may choose a style less repetitive. Balance is especially helpful in presenting facts. For example, while clarity demands that facts should be presented in a chronological manner – in the sequence in which they happen, the writer may choose to present them in a non-linear manner say as a story to emphasis certain facts material to the writing.[62] Deciding how to balance clarity with engaging requires careful evaluation of the context of the document, its purpose, needs, interest and the background knowledge of the reader.

---

[58]274 U.S. 357, 372–80 (1927) (Brandeis, J., concurring).

[59]RPC.

[60]Bret Rappaport, Using the Elements of Rhythm, Flow, and Tone to Create a More Effective and Persuasive Acoustic Experience in Legal Writing (2010) 16 *J. Legal Writing* 65 @ 99–107.

[61]Bronsteen, above n. @ 132 (the tone of a legal memorandum should be objective and dispassionate. It is therefore inappropriate for it stir up the passion of the reader through use of pathos)

[62] See A2L. Phelps, above 6 @ 447.

The place of elegance in good writing

Much as clarity, conciseness and engagement are fundamental to good writing, the value of aesthetics cannot be discounted in advancing the cause of good writing. Aesthetic is about beauty. An artistic flair to a document can go a long way in facilitating decision-making by the reader.[63]

Elegance contribution to good writing does reside in its functionality. Rather, elegance adds value to writing for the same reason that beauty is valuable in any human endeavour: it gives expression to mankind's essential creative nature.[64]

Just as a piece of furniture is not considered museum-worthy merely because of its functional qualities; so too with writing: great writing transcends its functional purpose and exhibits an artistry not found in ordinary writing.

True not much of prose should be exhibited in legal documents given the context in which they are generated: for lawyers and judges write documents to aid professional decision-making, not to entertain audiences or create great works of literature, even at that elegance does have a place in good legal writing.

Let us illustrate the point with the opinions below.

The first is Justice Jackson's opinion in *West Virginia Board of Education* v. *Barnette.*[65] In that case, the Court upheld an injunction preventing enforcement of a state regulation requiring school children to salute the American flag. Writing for the majority, Justice Jackson paints a stark picture of the dangers inherent in state-coerced nationalism and the repression of dissenting views:

> Struggles to coerce uniformity of sentiment in support of some end thought essential to their time and country have been waged by many good as well as evil men. Nationalism is a relatively recent phenomenon but at other times and places the ends have been

---

[63]Marcus Tullius Cicero, (c. 55 BCE) On the Character of the Orator, in *On Oratory and Orators,* trans J.S. Watson, 1878 ("said of great oratory - one thing there will certainly be, which those who speak well will exhibit as their own; a graceful and elegant style, distinguished by a peculiar artifice and polish.") Id. @ 19. Unquestionably, a similar quality should be exhibited by great writing. See .Steven D. Jamar, Aristotle Teaches Persuasion: The Psychic Connection (2001-02) 8 *Scribes J. Leg. Writing* 61 (an articles that connects oratory with skills of writing).

[64]George Santayana, *The Sense of* Beauty, 1955 ("In all products of human industry we notice the keenness with which the eye is attracted to the mere appearance of things: great sacrifices of time and labour are made to it in the most vulgar manufactures; nor does man select his dwelling, his clothes, or his companions without reference to their effect on his aesthetic senses. Of late we have even learned that the forms of many animals are due to the survival by sexual selection of the colours and forms most at- tractive to the eye. There must therefore be in our nature a very radical and widespread tendency to observe beauty, and to value it. No account of the principles of the mind can be at all adequate that passes over so conspicuous a faculty.") Id. @ 5-6." Cited in Phelps, above n. 6 @ 458.

[65]319 U.S. 624 (1943).

> racial or territorial security...and particular plans for saving souls. As first and moderate methods to attain unity have failed, those bent on its accomplishment must resort to an ever-increasing severity. As governmental pressure toward unity becomes greater, so strife becomes more bitter as to whose unity it shall be. Probably no deeper division of our people could proceed from any provocation than from finding it necessary to choose what doctrine and whose program public educational officials shall compel youth to unite in embracing. Ultimate futility of such attempts to compel coherence is the lesson of every such effort from the Roman drive to stamp out Christianity as a disturber of its pagan unity, the Inquisition, as a means to religious and dynastic unity, the Siberian exiles as a means to Russian unity, down to the fast failing efforts of our present totalitarian enemies. Those who begin coercive elimination of dissent soon find themselves exterminating dissenters. Compulsory unification of opinion achieves only the unanimity of the graveyard."[66]

In *Nagle* v. *Feilden*,[67] where a lady who trained horses was refused licence by the Jockey Club because she was a woman, relying on their Rule giving them discretion to grant or refuse licence, Lord Denning struck down the refusal saying:

> ...If we were here considering a social club, it would be necessary for the plaintiff to show a contract. If a man applies to join a social club and is black-balled, he has no cause of action: because the members have made no contract with him. They can do as they like. They can admit or refuse him, as they please. But we are not considering a social club. We are considering an association which exercises a virtual monopoly in an important field of human activity. By refusing or withdrawing a licence, the stewards can put a man out of business. This is a great power. If it is abused, can the courts give redress? That is the question.
>
> It was urged before us that the members of a trading or professional association were like a social club. They had, it was said, an unrestricted power to admit, or refuse to admit, any person

[66]Id. @ 640–41.
[67][1966] 2 QB 633.

whom they chose: and that this was established by a case in 1825 concerning the Inns of Court. In *R* v. *The Benchers of Lincoln's Inn*, Bayley J said: "They make their own rules as to the admission of members; and even if they act capriciously upon the subject this court can give no remedy in such a case, because in fact there has been no violation of any right.

I venture to question this statement, notwithstanding the eminence of the judge from whom it fell. The common law of England has for centuries recognised that a man has a right to work at his trade or profession without being unjustly excluded from it. He is not to be shut out from it at the whim of those having the governance of it. If they make a rule which enables them to reject his application arbitrarily or capriciously, not reasonably, that rule is bad. It is against public policy. The courts will not give effect to it...We cannot, of course, decide the matter today. All I say is that there is sufficient foundation for the principle for the case to go to trial. We live in days when many trading or professional associations operate "closed shops". No person can work at his trade or profession except by their permission. They can deprive him of his livelihood. When a man is wrongly rejected or ousted by one of these associations, has he no remedy? I think he may well have, even though he can show no contract. The courts have power to grant him a declaration that his rejection and ouster was invalid and an injunction requiring the association to rectify their error. He may not be able to get damages unless he can show a contract or a tort. But he may get a declaration and injunction...All through the centuries courts have given themselves jurisdiction by means of fictions; but we are mature enough, I hope, to do away with them. The true ground of jurisdiction in all these cases is a man's right to work. I have said before, and I repeat it now, that a man's right to work at his trade or profession is just as important to him as, perhaps more important than, his rights of property.

Just as the courts will intervene to protect his rights of property, they will also intervene to protect his right to work. In this case the plaintiff alleges that the stewards of the Jockey Club make a practice of refusing any woman trainer who applies for a licence.

> She is refused because she is a woman, and for no other reason. The practice is so uniform that it amounts to an unwritten rule. The only way she can get round it is to get her head lad to apply. The licence is granted to him, not to her. It seems to me that this unwritten rule may well be said to be arbitrary and capricious. It is not as if the training of horses could be regarded as an unsuitable occupation for a woman, like that of a jockey or speedway-rider. It is an occupation in which women can and do engage in most successfully. It may not be a "vocation" within the Sex Disqualification (Removal) Act 1919, but still it is an occupation which women can do as well as men: and there would seem to be no reason why they should be excluded from it.

In informed consent cases and Oputa in Ojukwu case as other examples.

These judges are all widely regarded as exceptional writers. And the excerpts set out above unquestionably exemplify writing that is clear, concise, and engaging. But what sets these opinions apart as models of great legal writing is the elegant manner in which they are written. They have a literary quality that is lacking in ordinary documents - even those that are considered very well written. Even if you do not agree with one or more of the results, you find yourself wanting to read the language of the opinions more than once, not because you don't understand it the first time, but because you want to pause and admire the craftsmanship invested in the writing. This is how elegance advances good writing.[68]

Legal writing is a creative endeavour and creativity by its very nature opens up possibility of artistry and elegance. Furthermore, elegance may make writing more persuasive.

Whether elegance would be appropriate for a particular piece of writing would depend on the context of a given document. For example, it would be inappropriate to use it for an objective memorandum. This notwithstanding, a lawyer should not consciously stunt a natural aptitude for elegant prose if the context of the document does not detract from it.

Conclusion

This Article has argued that readers judge a document to be well written if the writing advances the readers' purpose in reading the document. In the case of

---

[68] See Richard A. Posner, *Law and* Literature, 3rd ed. 2009 (a text that comprehensively discusses the relationship between legal opinions and literature).

legal readers, that purpose is to glean information that will help the reader make professional decisions. Thus, good legal writing is writing that facilitates professional decision-making by making it easier for legal readers to obtain information from legal documents. The cause is advanced by a document that exhibits clarity, is concise and engaging. But great writing particularly interrogates the fundamental quality of elegance. That is what distinguishes the great legal writing from the good legal writing. In all, the chooser must consider context. It determines how the writer should balance among competing interests when the writer‘s various goals conflict.

Chapter 12

Brevity

Introduction

There is the popular saying that "lawyers do it in brief". The saying underscores the thinking that there is value in brevity, either in writing or in advocacy. Brevity is the quality of saying much with less text or words. Brevity persuades because it makes a presentation graphic, containing not more words than is required. Little wonder, judges are heard to say 'please tell me just what I need to arrive at a decision and no more.'[1] Judges are persuaded by clear, concise writing and distracted by writings that rambles or contain convoluted argument.

Some Mistaken Conception about Brevity

Brevity though synonymous with words like concise, terse, succinct and the like, encompasses more. It does not connote shortness. Neither is its proper measure determined by length of words, paragraphs or sentence. Its goal is clarity. That being so, the writer or persuader must strive to maintain a balance between obscurity and the substance of the argument. This delicate balance must not be missed if the persuader intends to drive home the heart of her argument.

For example, if the persuader intends to show, say the length of a wrongful conduct of a defendant germane to the client's case, it may be useful to indicate the time frame in days rather than weeks. Take for instance this: if the claim is for damages resulting from the defendant's false imprisonment of the plaintiff for *two weeks*, it may be more graphic to tell the decision-maker that the plaintiff was imprisoned for *fourteen days*. This shows that brevity is not synonymous with simplicity of expression or sheer length of words.

Lawyers sometimes think that the length of a brief or argument determines its persuasiveness, and so are lengthy in their presentation. Contrary to it is the

---

[1]Antonin Scalia & Bryan A. Garner, *Making Your Case: The Art of Persuading Judges,* Thomas West, 2008 ("long and flabby brief, far from getting a judge to spend more time with your case, will probably have just the opposite effect.") Id 98; Leonard I. Garth, How to Appeal to an Appellate Judge (1994) 21 *Litig.*20 ("If brevity were not important, we would not have called briefs 'briefs' in the first place.") Id 24; Judge Stephen J. Dwyer et al., How to Write, Edit, and Review Persuasive Briefs: Seven Guidelines from One Judge and Two Lawyers (2008) 31 *Seattle U. L. Rev.* 417, 422 ("A good brief is focused, concise, and persuasive."); Kristen K. Robbins, The Inside Scoop: What Federal Judges Really Think About the Way Lawyers Write (2002) 8 J. *Legal Writing* 257.

case. Lengthy presentation bores the decision-maker, gives an impression of non-clarity of thought.

Several surveys of decision-makers reveal that they prefer short, to-the-point briefs or arguments.[2] In fact, excessive length may hurt. Judges have limited time to devote to each case and so would appreciate briefs that save their precious time.

Lessons from Abraham Lincoln

It has been suggested that one lawyer who mastered brevity and was very effective in persuasion both in the courtroom and in public presentation was President Abraham Lincoln.[3] We can learn a few lessons about how he presented.

Oseid list some of the lessons great presenters, particularly lawyers, can learn from Lincoln, who was himself a great persuader in courts, politics and public service in America:

(i) He was brevity conscious

Lincoln worked at developing the skills of logical tightness of his arguments or speeches. It is said that he carefully sorted out his points and tighten his logic and his phrasing. He wrote, rewrote and edited his speeches.[4]

Some make the mistake of thinking that persuasive argumentation comes naturally. While that may be the case for a few exceptional persons, the Lincoln

---

[2]Flammer, Persuading Judges: An Empirical Analysis of Writing Style, Persuasion, and the Use of Plain English (2010) 16 *J. Legal Writing* 183; See for example, survey conducted by Robbins in 2000 of judges' opinion on brief length in the federal courts in the United States- Kristen K. Robbins, The Inside Scoop: What Federal Judges Really Think About the Way Lawyers Write (2002) 8 *Leg. Writing* 257 (brevity and clarity are essential to persuasiveness). I am not aware of any survey in Nigeria or Ghana, but I am confident that an empirical survey in both countries should yield a result not different from that of Robbins. In fact, the Supreme Court in Nigeria continues to frown at verbose briefs. If anything, a brief must address the real and crucial issues in controversy. See *Onifade* v. *Olayiwola* (1990) 7 NWLR (pt. 161) 130, *Okoye* v. *Nigerian Construction & Furniture Co. Ltd.* (1991) 6 NWLR (pt. 199) 501; *Shittu* v. *Fashawe* [2005] 7 SC (pt. II) 107, per Dahiru Musdapher, JSC.

[3] Julie A. Oseid, The Power of Brevity: Adopt Abraham Lincoln's Habits (2009) 6 *JAWD*: 28; Jerry J. Phillips, Uncommon Predicates: Notes on Lincoln's Second Inaugural Address (2005) 72 *Tenn. L. Rev.* 807.

[4] Rewriting however must not be linear, but rather should be recursive. See Richard K. Neumann, Jr., *Legal Reasoning and Legal Writing: Structure, Strategy, and Style,* 5th ed., Aspen Publishers 2005, 63 & 65 (where the writer states that the first draft is actually the least important part of the writing process, because it is only in subsequent drafts [that] the focus shifts to the reader); Patricia G. Montana, Better Revision: Encouraging Student Writers to See Through the Eyes of the Reader (2008) 14 *J. Leg. Writing* 291 (an article that shows why most don't do a good job at revision or rewriting because they adopt the linear, narrow approach as to what revision entails. They equate revision with polishing-adding topic sentences or conclusions, changing words, editing grammar, and fixing citation, which prevents proper analysis of stepping into the readers shoes. It encourages recursive writing that takes the reader into account and manages the back and forth motion of the composition process n revising the substance, organization, and other parts of the writing); Christopher M. Anzidei, The Revision Process in Legal Writing: Seeing Better to Write Better (2002) 8 *J. Leg. Writing* 23.

experience points the other way-brevity that persuades is the product of conscious painstaking effort to excel in the art of persuasion. It is said that Lincoln did not possess special skills of musing, but that he rather worked hard to compose. He was known to also rehears his speeches by reading aloud. Lawyers can therefore further their skills of brevity by adopting his habits of writing in advance, visualizing their audience and ruthlessly editing to improve their presentation.[5]

(ii) He thought through his presentations

It is also important in developing the skills of brevity to think through the presentation. A good way to this is to start early. Some lawyers never get down to drafting their presentation until it is dangerously close to time for presentation. This forces them to hurriedly prepare and turn out never scarps and imperfect presentations. This explains why some lawyers are ever paying court penalty fees for late filing of briefs and are accordingly clogging court lists with motions for extension of time to comply with rules stipulating time.

Lincoln had the virtue of starting early. Starting out early to prepare comes with the added advantages of giving the persuader to deeply reflect on the facts, law and logic of presentation, and understanding of the case, especially in identifying strengths and weaknesses. With the hindsight of a case theory, early preparation is crucial to developing critical lawyering skills congruent with client's case theory.[6] Aside keeping the window open to edit presentation, early preparation gives the opportunity to craft an organized structure of presentation, thereby enabling the lawyer to draw a tight frame on her presentation.

(iii) He visualized his audience

Great presenter who have mastered brevity have often demonstrated the quality by visualizing their audience. For example, if a lawyer were to argue an application before a judge seeking the court to reverse its actions, say to stay execution of judgment pending appeal to a higher court, the lawyer in moving the terms of her application should be mindful to be more respectful and circumspect in her presentation. In presenting argument before the judge, the lawyer may find it helpful to visualize general human frailty which is reluctant to personally "undo" what a person has done, especially when the essence of the application slips on

---

[5]Oseid, above n. 3, 46.

[6] Case theory generally links the case to the client's experience of the world, enabling the counsel to use "the meaning of what happened" to bridge the gap between "what happened" and "what will happen." See, Kimberly A. Thomas, Sentencing: Where Case Theory and the Client Meet (2008) 15 (1) *Clinical L. Rev.* 187 at 189; Binny Miller, Teaching Case Theory (2002) 9 *Clinical L. Rev.* 293; Jessica A. Rose, Rebellious or Regnant: Police Brutality Lawyering in New York City (2000) 28 *Fordham Urban L.J.* 619; Lucie White, Mobilization on the Margins of the Lawsuit: Making Space for Clients to Speak (1987) 16 *N.Y.U. Rev. L &Soc. Change* 535; Edward D. Ohlbaum, Basic Instinct: Case Theory and Court Performance (1993) 66 *Temp. L. Rev.* 1.

subtle question of the rationale for the judgment appeal against. By simply visualizing general reluctance of the judge to reception of argument for stay, the lawyer would readily arrange and structure her argument to be more compelling and persuasive to overcome general initial reluctance of the judge. This may require the employment of proper voice modulation, volume control and mannerism that eases the court thereby predisposing it to favourable and more dispassionately considering the merit of the lawyer's application.

Visualizing the audience of presentation is also material in the choice of length of presentation. Children for example have a short attention span. So, any material presented to them which is lengthy would likely lose their attention. That explains why they learn more in pictures and their learning materials are often short, like the usual short stories children are fond of. But adults also can be susceptible to attention challenges. This would be the case if there are competing activities demanding their attention.

(iv) Edit for brevity

Some make the mistake that editing should be to correct spelling errors.[7] It is advised that if there is one thing only to edit for, it should be for brevity.[8] But brevity should not be sacrificed for clarity.[9]

(v) Use short sentences

Great writers and presenters always use short speeches, short sentences, or short words.[10] That was the style employed by Abraham Lincoln.[11]So too was Lord Denning.[12] That has been the conceptual driving force of the "plain English

---

7 Even though the real purpose to edit should not be to merely correct spelling errors, it is important to "pay attention to the minute details in a written product. A document that contains misspelled words and typographical errors sends readers the message that the writer is not detail-oriented." See, Smith, above n. 9, 186

8Oseid, above n. 3, 52. A very good English text for writers is the work of Strunk & White, originally written by Strunk in 1919. See, William Strunk Jr. & E.B. White, *The Element of Style*, 4th ed." ("vigorous writing is concise. A sentence should contain no unnecessary words, a paragraph no unnecessary sentence ... This requires not that the writer make all sentences short or avoid all detail and treat the subject only in outline, but that every word tell") Id. Introduction by E.B. White. See also, Patricia G. Montana, Better Revision: Encouraging Students Writers to See Through the Eyes of the Reader (2008) 14 Leg. Writing 291 (The purposes of a rewrite in legal writing, as with other writing, are to resolve any inconsistencies and fill in gaps, strengthen the analysis and reasoning, and present the in- formation in the clearest way possible).

9Strunk& White, above n. 11.

10Strunk& White, above n. 11, 28.as Rule 17 gives a list of common expressions that violate the principle of concise writing. For example, the phase "the question as to whether" can be simply stated as "whether." So also, is the expression "he is a man who" can just be stated as "he."

11Ibid.

12 Lord Denning, *The Family Story*, 1981, 216 ("if it [writing] is presented in a lively and attractive setting, they will sit up and take notice. They will listen as if spellbound. They will read with

movement."[13] Words should be used carefully and precisely.

Abraham Lincoln persuading

engrossment). See also, Bryan A. Garner, *Garner on Language and Writing*, 2009; Phillip Frost, Plain Language in Transition (2005) 84 Mich. B.J. 46 at 46 (good writing sings). A good example of how good writing has an aliveness that keeps the reader reading paragraph after paragraph is the lead judgment by Kayode Eso, JSC in *Military Governor, Lagos State* v. *Ojukwu* [1986] All NLR 233; (1986) NWLR (pt. 18) 621; (1986) LPELR-SC. 241/1985, where His Lordship said "I think it is a very serious matter for anyone to flout a positive order of a court and proceed to taunt the court further by seeking a remedy in a higher court while still in contempt of the lower court. It is more serious when the act of flouting the order of the court, the contempt of court, is by the executive. Under the Constitution of the Federal Republic of Nigeria, 1979, the executive, the legislative (while it lasts) and the judiciary are equal partners in the running of a successful government. ... The organs wield those powers and one must never exist in sabotage of the other or else there is chaos. Indeed there will be no Federal Government. I think, for one organ, and more especially the executive, which holds all the physical powers, to put up itself in sabotage or deliberate contempt of the order is to stage an executive subversion of the Constitution it is to uphold. Executive lawlessness is tantamount to a deliberate violation of the Constitution. When the executive is the Military Government which blends both the Executive and the Legislature together and which permits the Judiciary to co-exist with it in the administration of the country, then it is more serious than imagined."

[13]See, International Plain Language Federation, *What Is Plain Language?* Plain Language Association International, available in http://plainlanguagenetwork.org/plain-language/what-is-plain-language (last visited March 10, 2017 ("A communication is in plain language if the language, structure, and design are so clear that the intended audience can easily find what they need, understand what they find, and use that information."). See also Joseph Kimble, A Curious Criticism of Plain Language (2016) 13 *Leg. Comm. & Rhetoric: JALWD* 181; Joseph Kimble, You Think the Law Requires Legalese? (2013) Mich. Bar J. Nov. 2013, 48; Joseph Kimble, *Writing for Dollars, Writing to Please: The Case for Plain English in Business, Government, and Law,* 2012 (a discussion on why plain language is not subverted by the need to use technical terms); Martin Cutts, *Oxford Guide to Plain English*, 4th ed. 2013. But cf. Soha Turfler, Language Ideology and the Plain-Language Movement (2015) 12 *Leg. Comm. & Rhetoric: JALWD* 195 (an article that identifies three ideologies from the plain English, showing how each ideology perpetuates discriminatory norms and practices. It suggests that advocates of the movement erroneously promote a prescriptive style, by trying to standardize language, and by thinking that plain language is morally superior to traditional legal style.

Why Brevity Is Essential for Brief Writing

By the very nature of their function judges are busy people. They have to go through heaps of documents filed by litigants as court processes and exhibits. It is therefore to be expected why they would appreciate succinct, brief, straight to the point presentations. They are therefore not likely to be persuaded by lengthy, verbose briefs.[14] Visualizing the workload of judges compel brevity of presentation by lawyers.

According to an appellate judge in the United States he read about 3,500 pages of brief monthly.[15] That was far back in the early 1990s. By modest count, that number would have tripled today. The position in Ghana and Nigeria is likely to be worse on volume judges have to read. In Nigeria, for example, with an average of twenty cases per day for trial judges who sit in metropolis like Lagos, Accra, Ibadan, Kumasi, Port-Harcourt, Warri, Onitsha, Enugu, Kaduna, to mention just a few cities, it is expected that a judge would read about 6,000 to 7,000 pages of briefs (excluding law reports and statutes referred to in lawyers argument) a month. This does not include pages of statute, law reports, learned publications and other materials referred to by counsel or necessary research judges make to arrive at reasoned decision. Also, recent rules of court demanding what is popularly called "frontloading" of documents, brief and evidence would likely increase the volume of text writing judges are expected to read. I have had the advantage of attending courts in Accra and Kumasi, where I also find the court list of cases rather lengthy.

By usual count, appellate judges should have more to read than trial judges. They are saddled with records of proceedings from lower courts, which are often bulky in volume, the parties' briefs of argument, interlocutory applications and the like, all documentary.

An average textbook has 300 to 500 pages, and one can almost win a bet that many lawyers do not read more than a book monthly. If an active lawyer reads two books a month that will translate to a modest 1,000 pages monthly.

A look at the court cause list of new matters filed in a not-too-busy (state) judicial division in Nigeria shows that they receive about 1,000 new cases annually. Going by the average of 20 judges in a state judicial division, that will invariably translate to 50 new cases a year per judge. The document volume this can generate, in addition to existing caseload is best imagined. To therefore demand underpaid judges to read six or more times what lawyers generally read and not pay the necessary attention to brevity would be smack of insensibility.

---

[14] Cite Nigerian cases of annoyance with lengthy briefs.

[15] Alex Kozinski, The Wrong Stuff (1992) 1992 *BYU L. Rev.* 325.

To suggest then that judges are busy would be an understatement. Brief reading competes with other demands on judges' time. Brief writer should therefore contemplate and visualize the environment that their briefs would be read. This is what ordinarily should compel brevity and pointedness. Working as judges do, under time competition, it is expected that they would prefer simple, straight to the point written briefs.

Presentation that is persuasive must follow the preference of its audience or reader. Children book writers have long master this catch. They design short lessons laden with pictures to catch children's attention. The lawyer brief writer must also do the same by visualizing judges preference for brevity in presentation.

Some lawyers make the mistake of thinking that if the facts of a case are complex and complicated, then the accompanying brief should necessarily be lengthy to explain and make clear understandable to the audience. That is sure mistaken assumption. Good brief writers suggest the other way. Brevity in such a situation may even be more helpful in persuasion because it would be of little help to complicate understanding of a complex case by "using unnecessary complex sentence structure and complicated wordings."[16]

Conclusion

We recommend the concluding words of Oseid as mantra for lawyers who seek to persuade: "brevity is a virtue like many other virtues. Common wisdom advises that practising virtues makes them easier. This is true of the virtue of writing with brevity. In the beginning, it is painful to delete unnecessary pages, arguments, and words. But one day you will find yourself noticing and valuing brevity."[17]

---

[16]Michael R. Smith, *Advanced Legal Writing: Theories and Strategies in Persuasive Writing,* 3rd ed. Aspen Law & Bus. 2013, 164.155–56 ( ).

[17]Oseid, above n. 3 @ 54.

Chapter 13

Grammar Rules

Introduction

Errors in grammar and punctuation create interference with communication and persuasion, if not an unbridgeable gulf between legal author and audience.[1]Understanding grammar rules is an essential skill of lawyering because the proper use of grammar is a pathway to persuasion and communication.[2] Unquestionably, error in grammar interferes with clear understanding. This explains why a lawyer must be precise in her writing and oral argument. Grammar or language is the tool of the lawyer's business. A command of language is a must for her. According to Lord Denning, "words are the lawyer's tools of trade."[3]

The pervading use of words or grammar in the practice of law underscores the importance of a good command of language in communication. Lawyers address judges; interpret statutes; analyse words for meaning; draw up contracts;

---

[1] Laurel Currie Oates & Anne Enquist, *The Legal Writing Handbook,* 5th ed. 2010 @ 607 (noting that effective and correct writing "depends on understanding the grammar of an English sentence."); Richard K Neumann, *Legal Reasoning and Legal Writing,* 6th ed. 2009 @ 55 (correct punctuation and grammar make writing clearer and easier to understand); Martha Kolln, *Rhetorical Grammar: Grammatical Choices, Rhetorical Effects,* 5th ed. Pearson Educ. 2007; Anne Enquist& Laurel Currie Oates, *Just Writing: Grammar, Punctuation, and Style for the Legal Writer,* 2nd ed. Aspen 2005; Lillian Hardwick, Classical Persuasion through Grammar and Punctuation (2006) 3 *JALWD* 75. But cf. John Bronsteen, *Writing A Legal Memo,* 2006 @ 35-37 (arguing that conforming to grammatical rules is frequently "an enormous waste of time" and that "in many cases a thought can be expressed most clearly by violating a traditional grammar rule."). See also Williams & Colomb, *Styles: Lessons In Clarity and Grace,* 10th ed. 2010 @ 13-23 (distinguishing "Real Rules" of grammar that affect meaning from essentially arbitrary "Invented Rules" that grammarians think writers should follow).

[2]Bryan A. Garner, *The Legal Writing Skills Test,* (1994-95) 5 *Scribes J. Leg. Writing* 107; Bryan A. Garner, Take this Quiz to Gauge Your Grammar Skills, *Student Lawyer* 10 Feb. 2002. For much as classic rhetoricians like Aristotle used the triangle of logos (logical argument), ethos (credibility of speaker) and pathos (attitude created in the audience) to describe persuasion oral pathway, their analysis applies with equal force to writing. See George Kennedy, *The Art of Persuasion in Greece,* Princeton U. Press, 1963 @ 4-5; David S. Coale, Classical Citation, (2001) 3 *J. App. Prac. & Process* 733; Steven D. Jamar, Aristotle Teaches Persuasion: The Psychic Connection (2001-02) 8 *Scribes J. Leg. Writing* 61 ("Although Aristotle wrote about the spoken word, most of his teachings on style apply to writing as well.") In fact, the key word for classic rhetoric is persuasion. See Kenneth Burke, Rhetoric - Old and New (1951) *V.J Gen. Educ.* 202 @ 203 citing in Hardwick, above n. 1 @ ft. 3.

[3] Lord Denning, *The Discipline of Law,* Oxford Univ. Press1979 @ 5.

and many more, all requiring the use of good grammar. Words are very important in lawyering because they are the vehicle of thought. Lawyers, like most other think and communicate in words, not in symbols or numbers.

Grammar refers to the structure of a language, whether oral or written. Pieces of the structure have assigned names (noun, verb, adjective) that conveniently describe how the various pieces fit together.

Idiom is a grammatical term for the knowledge that dictates that particular words can fit into the structural slots. For example, "live" and "leave" are both transitive verbs, which mean they can take direct objects. However, they are not interchangeable in the same structure for all sentences. We can say "leave me", but it is not idiomatic to say "live me." In this sense, word choice is a part of grammar. Otherwise, word choice is generally a matter of stylistic choice, not grammatical rules.

Poor writing challenge of a lawyer does not simply arise from inability to communicate. It often is a problem with clear thinking. That is why writing professors suggest that developing the skills of good grammar usage requires addressing thinking and an understanding of rhetorical tradition from which legal argument derives. Classic rhetorician Quintilian in fact instructed: "Let no man look down on the elements of grammar as small matter."[4]Connecting grammar to the triangle of persuasion indicates that without proficiency in grammar a lawyer can hardly persuade.

Let us see now the rhetoric triangle fits into persuasion using proper grammar.

Persuasion and Grammar

What has been generally described as the rhetoric triangle involves logos, ethos and pathos.

Logos essentially mean the logical, rational argument deployed for persuading the audience. Ethos describes the credibility relationship between the speaker and the audience. Pathos is emotional element the speaker uses to move her audience to belief or act.[5] Much as logos may not directly impact and meld with grammar as persuasion tool, ethos and pathos are directly implicated with grammar. Ethos can be particularly potent in persuasion for the view taken of a speaker may well be all that her audience need to belief.[6] Orators know so and great speech person have exploited this aspect of persuasion over the years.

---

[4]*Quintilian's Institutes of Oratory* vol. 1 @ 30 (Rev. John Selby Watson trans. George Bell & Sons 1910).

[5]Michael R. Smith, *Advanced Legal Writing: Theories & Strategies in Persuasive Writing,* Aspen L. & Bus. 2002 @ 164.

[6] Acknowledging this Aristotle said "[i]t is not true, as some writers on the art maintain, that the

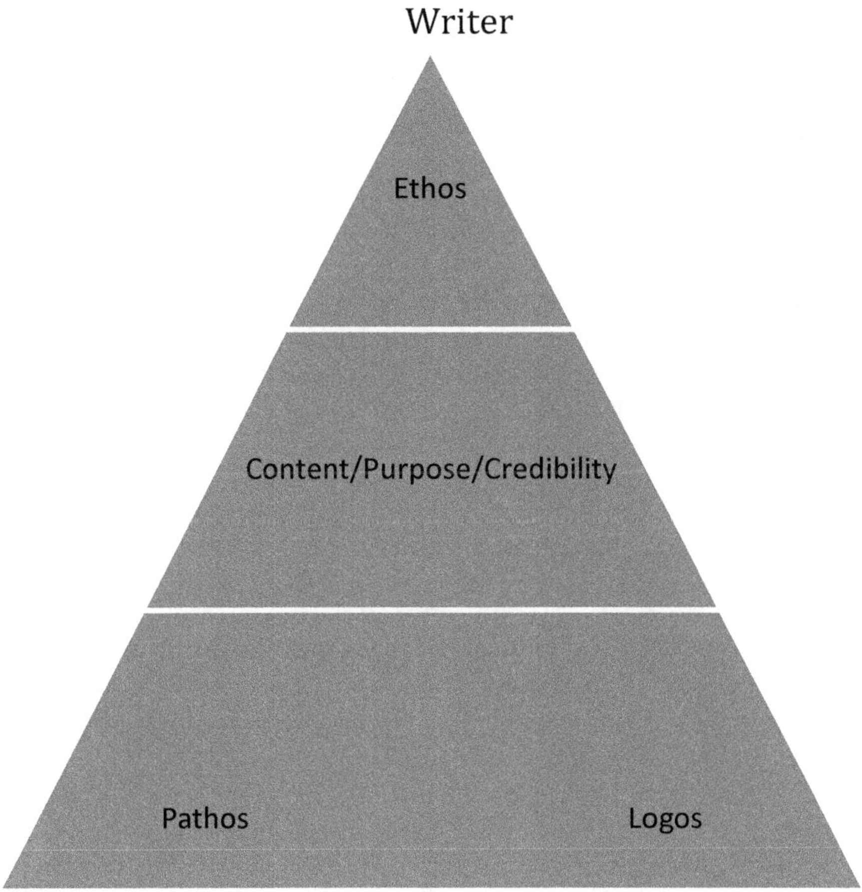

Audiences have been moved to believe or take action sometimes by merely hearing the voice of some speakers, their intonation, diction, word choice without really paying close attention to the specific content of the speaker's message.

The lesson can be potent for lawyering. Impression can be it. Similarly, a lawyer who introduces herself in writing conveys an impression. Her grammar in documents introduces her professionalism, eloquence, education and other qualities. Judges are susceptible to think that a written prose brief has substance. In contrast a brief riddled with grammar errors would likely be discounted in substance. It is natural. It is in this way that grammar resembles ethos in rhetoric.[7]

probity of the speaker contributes nothing to his persuasiveness; on the contrary, we might almost affirm that his character [*ethos*] is the most potent of all the means to persuasion." See Aristotle, *The Rhetoric of Aristotle* 7 (Lane Cooper trans. D. Appleton & Co. 1932) (bracketed language is from the translator) @ 9.

[7] Smith, above n. 4 @ 98; Kristen K. Robbins, The Inside Scoop: What Federal Judges Really Think

Also just as pathos involves causing positive affection in the audience, the legal writer can create positive or negative emotions in the reader with the use of proper grammar. This is so because grammar affects the ease and effect of information that support an argument. If it hinders ease of reading then it could likely detract from the believability of what is written.[8]

First impression matters. A lawyer usually cannot determine whether a particular judge or clerk will have a high or low tolerance for grammatical and punctuation errors; that is, the lawyer will not know in advance whether such errors will prejudice the reader before the reader ever reaches the subject of the pleading. The reaction many people have to typographical errors illustrates the point. Because first impression matters, lawyers should consider the effect of grammar error on the reader.

Unquestionably, typographic errors and imprecision in use of language conveys a picture of carelessness and lack of understanding.

How to Eliminate Grammar Errors

There are certainly many ways a lawyer can minimize grammar error and misspelling in documents. Modern computers have proved useful in proof reading. But even then care must be exercised in using the computer to spell check. For example, spell check cannot detect and correct personal typing idiosyncrasies, such as typing "that" when the writer wishes to type "this." "This" is certainly a correct word and so the spell checker would not correct it to "that" or the other way around, as the case may be.

About the Way Lawyers Write (2002) 8 *Leg. Writing: J. Leg. Writing Inst.* 257 @ 278 ("The care with which an advocate proofreads a brief is usually indicative of the care with which he has made his argument"). See also Howard Bashman, How Appealing's Twenty Questions for the Appellate Judge, http://howappealing.law.com/20q/ (follow "Tenth Circuit Judge Paul J. Kelly, Jr." hyperlink) (accessed 30 June 2018) (quoting the Hon. Paul J. Kelly, Jr. of the U.S. Court of Appeals for the Tenth Circuit: "'We review hundreds and hundreds of briefs every year; you don't want us distracted from the merits by missing verbs, misspelled names, incorrect citations, improper grammar or sentences that run for pages.'")

[8] It is in this sense that some writers suggest that grammar and punctuation differs from style. See Hardwick, above n. 1 @ 78 ("Writing style reflects the author's choices among different words meaning roughly similar things, the length of sentences, the use of active or passive voice, and the complexity of the sentence structure. Depending on the audience, two writers may communicate equally well although one uses short, simple sentences and the other prefers long, compound, complex, or compound-complex sentences. Through style, a writer may make a certain ethical appeal, presenting the writer as a straight shooter or as a complex thinker. Unlike stylistic choices, grammar and standard punctuation rarely reflect equally good choices; instead, they are requirements for communication. ... Deviations from the grammatical rules in speech often occur purposely, for emphasis or to suggest a certain personality trait or background. Few writers of legal documents, especially those filed with a court, violate grammatical guidelines or standard punctuation rules for emphasis or effect. Such violations are not stylistic choices, but rather errors that potentially undermine the ethical, logical, and emotional appeals of the writer.")

Chances are that even the writer in doing grammar and spell check would vocalize "this" as "that" as the writer reads on for correction. It is therefore advised that grammar proof should immediately precede writing as the tendency of reading what is intended rather what is actually written is taken for what is written. Writers must allow some time to pass between typing and proofreading so they do not merely read what they recall typing but rather what they actually typed.[9]If it is possible the writer of a document should seek a second reader for proofreading. The second reader is more likely to detect slips that passes the writer's eyes.

Grammar errors are more fundamental than misspellings. The reason for this is that while a reader of a spelling error document may quickly realize that "Jon" should actually read "John," grammatical error is often difficult for the reader to understand what is the writer's intention. Grammar slips confuses and offends the reader. Error-filled writing discounts the lawyer's credibility with anyone who recognize the errors.

Lawyers who make grammar mistakes often say the reader knows what is intended to be communicated. Some of us are familiar with lawyers who repeatedly say in court "what I mean…" But would it not make sense to be precise to "say what is meant" than always explaining again "what I mean?" the truth is that even though bad grammar lawyers think the reader or audience knows what they intend, the audience does not know their intended meaning. That anyway is why the writer keeps starting "what I mean." rather than is the point, or a big part of it.

Grammar rules can be tricky and that is why every skilled lawyer should be conversant with the basics of grammar rule. Hardwick article for example, gives a whole range of some of these common mistakes traceable to foundational deficiency in English language.[10]

One common grammar error is the substitution of "that" and "which" and vice versa. Both convey different meanings. "That" introduces a restrictive clause (one that limits meaning) and "which" introduces a non-restrictive clause (one that merely adds information and can be omitted from the sentence). That being so the use of one when the other meaning is intended can interfere with communication. To drive home the point he gives the following illustration:

"Joe gave me jewellery which I liked."

And

---

[9]Hardwick, above n. 1 @ 82.

[10] Ibid.

"Joe gave me jewellery that I liked."

In the former the statement implies that she liked the jewellery giver her by Joe, the primary information being that she receiving jewellery. But the latter says that she liked the particular jewellery given her by Joe, even though she isn't fond of the jewellery selection by Joe.

There are many good texts in English language usage. The rules are many and can sometimes be confusing, even conflicting. Yes, a lawyer may have good reason sometimes to override the standard rules of grammar (including punctuation) but it is first important for the lawyer to know precisely what the standard rules are. This underscores why the skilled lawyer should get familiar with standard rules, observe a couple of them to write better. For example, it will be helpful to note how split infinities such as "I" are to used properly. Rather than say correctly "between you and me" most will say "between you and I." Also common is the mistaken use of "who" in the objective position (as in "I know who I like" instead of "I know whom I like").[11]

It is important to watch one's grammar and as much as possible a lawyer should avoid misspellings as it suggests that the lawyer lacks education or has failed to read properly. The court would negatively react to lawyers who are not thorough thereby passing their mistakes to others in the work environment, increasing their work loads. Judges have been known to resent lawyers who seek amendment for lack of preparation, particularly when they are forced to read something not clear and concise.[12]

Vocalizing what is written has proved helpful in writing well. Good writers practice it, a practice more commonly used in group writing. It is therefore a suggested good practice to "hash" out as by loud reading out to oneself the language used in a document to determine appropriateness. Hashing out words for correctness is certainly very appropriate for group writing.

Pathos and Good Grammar

Lawyers are communicators. But communicators of a special class and every skilled lawyer must recognize the fact. Unlike other communicators, lawyers are constantly writing for hostile audience, particularly judges who will compare their works with that of the opponent.[13] It is therefore compelling for legal writers not to detract from an appearance of competence, carefulness and goodwill to their reading audience. According to Hardwick "a lawyer who sacrifices *ethos* and *logos*

---

[11] See Hardwick, above n. 1 @ 84.

[12] Judith D. Fischer, Bareheaded and Barefaced Counsel: Courts React to Unprofessionalism in Lawyers' Papers (1997) 31 *Suffolk U. L. Rev.* 1.

[13] George D. Gopen, The State of Legal Writing: Res Ipsa Loquitur (1987) 86 *Mich. L. Rev.* 333 @ 340.

through grammatical and punctuation errors may wind up with *pathos*, but not the kind he counted on, as he risks drawing a negative emotional response from his audience."[14]

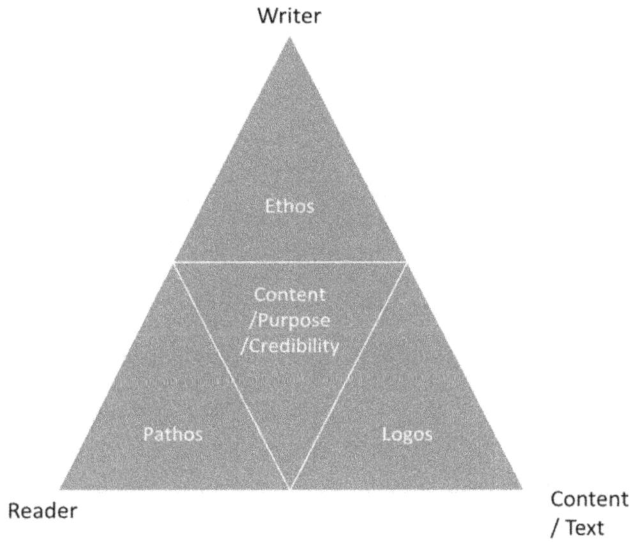

Conclusion

There are a few tips for learning and mastering grammar – the structure of language and its corresponding terminology. To hone skills in writing is important to prevent lawyers writing documents that confuse and alienate their audience or possibly leads to litigation.

Without instruction in law school, these lawyers will continue to create writing that at best will confuse and alienate their audience and at worst will lead to litigation.

Legal writing courses as part of legal methods should be given prominence by faculties.

Continuing legal education for practising lawyers is also beneficial.

[14]Hardwick, above n. 1 @ 99.

Chapter 14

Writing Style: Referencing Citation, Parenthetical and Punctuation

1. Referencing citation

Introduction

Citation literacy is the ability to read and write legal citation in legal documents.[1]It is a skill usually taught in first year legal method class as part of the curriculum.[2] To learn citation law students are required to learn the citation style of a standard legal common to legal writing. Most faculties use the English guide known as The Oxford Standard for Citation of Legal Authorities (OSCOLA).[3] American law schools generally use The Bluebook: A Uniform System of Citation. [4] Two basic rules inform these writing citation guides: need for

---

[1]Alexa Z. Chew, Citation Literacy (2018) 70 *Ark. L. Rev.* 869; Alexa Z. Chew & Kate R. G. Pryal, *The Complete Legal Writer II*, 2016 @ 11. Bryan A. Garner, *Legal Writing in Plain English: A Text With Exercises*, 2001 @ 77 (describing in-line citations as "thought-interrupters" and comparing reading them to driving over speed bumps on a highway).

[2] See BMAS curriculum for faculties of law in Nigeria. It is also so in the United States. See Ian Gallacher, Cite Unseen: How Neutral Citation and America's Law Schools Can Cure Our Strange Devotion to Bibliographical Orthodoxy and the Constriction of Open and Equal Access to the Law (2007) 70 *Alb. L. Rev.* 491 (describing legal citation as a skill primarily taught in the legal writing curriculum).

[3]OSCOLA was first devised by Professor Peter Birks in 2000, in consultation with law students and faculty at Oxford University, and with Oxford University Press and Hart Publishing. It is used by the *Oxford University Commonwealth Law Journal*, and the editors of that journal have also played an important role in its development . Subsequent editions of OSCOLA were produced in 2002 (by Professor Birks) and in 2004 (revised 2006, both by Timothy Endicott and Sandra Meredith). This latest revision of OSCOLA provides more detailed coverage of domestic legal sources, and in particular the treatment of Welsh, Scottish and Northern Irish sources has been considerably expanded. See Sandra Meredith & Donald Nolan, OSCOLA, 4th ed. 2010, 1 (introduction)

[4]*The Bluebook: A Uniform System of Citation* (Columbia Law Review Ass'n. et al. eds. 20th ed. 2015) [hereinafter Bluebook]. Robert Berring, *Introduction to the Bluebook: A Sixty-Five Years Retrospective,* 1998 @ v; (observing that the *Bluebook* "has inflicted more pain on more law students than any other publication in legal history.");Maureen B. Collins, Bluebook Blues: Changes in the Seventeenth Edition (2000) 88 *Ill. B.J.* 663 ("I hate the Bluebook. I view it as a necessary evil in a cruel world."); More inclusive statements of distaste also abound. Kris Franklin, *". . . See Erie."*: Critical Study of Legal Authority (2008) 31 *Univ. Ark. Little Rock L. Rev.* 109 ("[E]verybody knows that everybody *hates* blue booking. Law students hate to learn it, lawyers hate to do it, and law faculty hate to teach it."). But see Bret D. Asbury & Thomas J.B. Cole, Why The Bluebook Matters: The Virtues Judge Posner and Other Critics Overlook (2011) 79 *Tenn. L. Rev.* 95 ("*The Bluebook's*

consistency in legal writing; and consideration for the reader of legal documents. They are formulated under the operating assumption that because legal writing must be persuasive when the author cites a legal source it must be in a clear, consistent and familiar way to the reader; and that when it is easy to identify and to find the author's sources, it becomes easier for the reader to follow the legal argument. Conforming to citation style guides can be challenging for most legal writers (experienced and novice) because the rules are often cumbersome, especially in keeping to the standards of OSCOLA and the Bluebook. For example, the Bluebook consisting of 560 pages is in its twentieth edition. Reading it from cover to cover can be taxing, talk more of conforming to its style, which requires meticulous observance of its dictates.[5] OSCOLA, though 58-page is by no mean also easy to grasp.[6]

It is therefore not unexpected that some attempts have been made to replace the dominance of the OSCOLA and the Bluebook with different citation system.[7]They complement or are used in substitution of the other mentioned above.

---

much-maligned strictures and level of detail are both meaningful and useful for fledgling lawyers in at least two ways.") Id. @ 97. Mary Whisner, The Dreaded Bluebook (2008) 100 *Law Libr. J.* 393, 394 (describing "the core purposes of citation" as enabling the reader to evaluate the cited authority and locate the cited authority). Frederick Schauer, Authority and Authorities, (2008) 94 *Va. L. Rev.* 1931 ("Citation is not just a pathway to precedent; it is the language the law uses to embody its precedential character.") Id. @ 1955 n. 75; Robert Berring, On Not Throwing Out the Baby: Planning the Future of Legal Information (1995) 83 *Cal. L. Rev. 615* ("The Uniform System of Citation has assumed such significance in law that, for some, proper citation form is almost a fetish.") Id. @ 629.

5 See for example the frustration experienced by legal writer trying to conform with the Bluebook guide in Berring, above n. 4. But cf. Ashbury & Cole, above n. 4.

6 Observing the style guides is particularly difficult because some reader (especially academic editors) see them as inflexible rules of citation when they ought to be treated as general principle to guide good citation. See Meredith & Nolan, above n. 3 ("OSCOLA does not purport to be comprehensive, but gives rules and examples for the main UK legal primary sources, and for many types of secondary sources. As far as possible, the guidelines in OSCOLA are based on common practice in UK legal citation, but with a minimum of punctuation. When citing materials not mentioned in OSCOLA, use the general principles in OSCOLA as a guide, and try to maintain consistency. OSCOLA is a guide to legal citation, not a style guide.") Id. 1-2. So, it is not designed for grammar and style of writing, like how to use punctuation and the like.

7 For new citation material in the United States, see The Maroonbook, 2nd ed. Chi. L. Rev. 1989 (The University of Chicago Manual of Legal Citation); Sprigman et al., *The Indigo Book: A Manual of Legal Citation*, Public Resource, 2016 (compiled by a team of students at the New York University School of Law, working under the direction of Professor Christopher Jon Sprigman); Bryan Garner, *The Redbook: A Manual on Legal Style,* 3rd ed. 2013 [hereinafter "The Redbook"]; Adobe Legal Department Style Guide, 2015; Ass'n. of Legal Writing Directors & Coleen M. Barger, *Ass'n. Legal Writing Director Guide to Legal Citation,* 5th ed. 2014 [hereinafter "ALWD Guide"]. For Nigeria, see The Nationally Approved Uniformed Format and Citation Guides for Legal Research in Law Faculties/Institutions in Nigeria, approved by NALT, June 2015 (hereinafter referred to as "*NALTUF-CGs.*").

The importance of citation literacy derives from the professions adherence to logic that all conclusions ought to derive from reason. Legal citation is constitutive of reason as it aid an understanding to reason furnished to reach conclusion. Since any set of claims that form part of an argument requires understanding the information conveyed, to the extent that legal citation makes understanding clearer, it is a skill lawyer should possess.[8]Mastering the skill of understanding citation (reading and writing) could be difficult for some lawyers because it demands as prerequisite knowledge a significant understanding of matters like - sources of law, jurisdiction of court, history of court system, knowledge of precedent, court hierarchy, and many more – especially matters generally interrogated in legal methods and the legal system curriculum. This is not matter that should challenge an experienced lawyer. Expert readers can tell from a legal citation in a judicial opinion whether the court is an appellate or trial court, whether the authority cited is recent or not and the like. For example, an expert reader can tell instantly that the citation [2018] 1 SC 1 is a recent judicial opinion delivered in 2018 by the Supreme Court of Nigeria. So an expert reader recognizes that whenever she cites an authority the purpose is to communicate valuable information to its reader about the precedent used to build a legal argument. Since all readers do not possess the skill of citation literacy, this chapter is designed to build the skill in legal readers and writers. It would also discuss the "what" and "how" to cite legal authorities.

What to cite as legal authority

Legal citations are usually replete in legal documents, particularly those connected with the two main forms of lawyers writing, objective memorandum and brief. They are also found in judicial writing. Skilled lawyers give conscious thought to what authorities to cite and how to cite them because they recognize that legal citation goes to the root of reasoning – readers assess the merits of a legal analysis by reading the cited authority.[9]

How to cite legal authority

There are different generally two ways to cite legal authorities in a document: in-line and footnote citation. An in-line citation is one where the reference is contained in the same line as the text of the document, while a footnote citation is contained below the text of the document. This is an example of in-line citation:

---

[8]Alexa Z. Chew & Katie Rose Guest Pryal, *The Complete Writer,* 2016 @ 11 (stating that "citation literacy simply means the ability to fluently read and write legal citations.").

[9]Antonin Scalia & Bryan Garner, *Making Your Case: The Art of Persuading Judges,* 2008 @ 125-128 (describing how to choose which authorities to cite and how those choices impact the reader).

> According to the California Supreme Court, every time the police effectuate one of these arrests and searches, officers may not only seize and secure any smart phone the arrestee is carrying but also may rummage through the digital contents of the device. See *People* v. *Diaz*, 244 P.3d 501 (Cal. 2011) (reprinted at Pet. App. 25a-65a). Furthermore, the police may undertake such warrantless examinations not only briefly at the scene of arrest but also later at the police station after booking the arrestee. *Diaz*, Pet. App. 33a.[10]

The statement of the law applicable is supported by citation of the legal authority. In the context of citation, the sentence of the text is referred to as the "proposition." The style of legal citation immediately following proposition is usually contained in legal documents (memorandum and brief) and judicial writing. Legal writings of this genre customarily use in-line citation.

By contrast, footnote citation is common for academic writings. The style puts the reference at the bottom of the page where the proposition appears – usually below a horizontal line that separates the text from the footnote. This is the style employed in this book you are reading.

In-line citation is suitable for practical writing, while footnote is appropriate for academic writing. While the lines between both can sometimes be blurred, as when an academic article is cited in a memorandum or judicial, the genre remains practical writing. In that case it would still be preferred to use the practical style of in-line citation.

There are good reasons why the citation styles for practical and academic writing are different. Readers of practical writing want to quickly make sense of what they read to reach decisions. This is what makes in-line citation appropriate for the audience.[11] This type of readers, in-line citation allows them read smoothly without having to make their eyes go down the page looking for a footnotes citation. So, information is conveyed almost subliminally to them. What is more, in-line citation can transfer a lot of information from the text to because the reader is not distracted by going somewhere else to check reference, say the bottom of a page to check for footnote references. The citation is just next to the legal proposition it supports. Like people would say 'the reader does have to go to Sokoto (a faraway town in North-West Nigeria), because what is looked for is in the reader's "*shokoto*" (a Yoruba word for trouser).' However, the transferability

---

[10] Taken from the Supreme Court of the United States petitioner's brief in No. 13-132 (*David Leon Riley* v. *State of California*), Respondent. See appendix 1.

[11] Scalia & Garner, above n. 9 (stating that "lawyers must evaluate statements not on the basis of whether they make sense but on the basis of whether some governing authority said so.") Id. @ 134.

of a high degree of information using in-line citation has the drawback of lower readability in the sense that the reader's speed is slowed down by reason of having to note the in-line citation in the reading process. This is because in-line citation intersperse bibliographic passages in the text, which would not be the case if footnote were used.[12]

The writer can minimize the lower readability but reducing the amount of bibliographic materials included in the citation and using abbreviation. That is exactly what the California brief writer did using the in-line citation above. While the petitioner's lawyer uses [*People* v. *Diaz*, 244 P.3d 501 (Cal. 2011) (reprinted at Pet. App. 25a-65a] as support citation for the proposition that 'every time the police effectuate one of these arrests and searches, officers may not only seize and secure any smart phone the arrestee is carrying but also may rummage through the digital contents of the device,' the writer only uses citation abbreviation later when using the same authority to support the proposition that 'the police may undertake such warrantless examinations not only briefly at the scene of arrest but also later at the police station after booking the arrestee.' The full citation of [*People* v. *Diaz*, 244 P.3d 501 (Cal. 2011) (reprinted at Pet. App. 25a-65a] was merely abbreviated to read "*Diaz*, Pet. App. 33a."

Although in-line citation in practical writing could slow novice readers initially as unwelcome interruption to flow of reading, they would get over the challenge as they grow to become ardent, experienced readers. In-line citation communicates to the reader essential information about the cited authority, which in turn allows the reader to judge the strength of the writer's propositions without first looking at the cited authority.

Is important to note that legal writing is referenced writing, and so readers should expect frequent citation. In order however not to unnecessarily slow the reading process; the writer may use short citation forms and effective sentence structures to keep the document readable. Such short citation could be represented in the "id" or "ibid" or "supra" form. This notwithstanding the writer must include citations whenever a legal proposition is cited.

Purpose of in-line citation

In-line citation is best for practical writing as it quickly guides the reader. This form of citation serves the following purposes: (i) helps the reader to locate without delay the source of the cited authority – locative purpose; (ii) it communicates information about the relevance and weight of the authority cited – attributive purpose; (iii) to demonstrate the writer's credibility through

[12] Chew, above n. 1 @ 879.

impeccably formatted citations and (iv) to avoid plagiarism through proper attribution.[13]

Some writers suggest that of the four purposes, the locative purpose (being (i)) is the primary reason for use of in-line citation.[14]Generally, the first two purposes (locative and attributive) above apply to writing across academic disciplines (all writings), but the purposes enumerated in (iii) and (iv) apply particularly to legal writing. The basis for this is the thinking that all citation across disciplines usually include bibliographic information to help readers locate the source of reference and to attribute words to the writer as well as the ideas to the writer. This is a given. So, the requirements of (i) and (ii) apply to all in-line citations across disciplines.

But for practical legal writings, the purpose of credibility and avoiding plagiarism are particularly strong. In-line citation goes to credibility because legal readers are critical readers who are concerned about the weight of an authority cited. The form of citation chosen must inform the reader whether the writing is generally credible for it to receive attention. First the reader is concerned about form - whether the writer has taken the necessary care to follow a proper citation guide like OSCOLA and rules of grammar interrogated in writing.[15] If yes, the

---

[13] Ibid. @ 880

[14]Donna M. Bergsgaard & William H. Lindberg, Citation Formats in the United States: Is A Radical New Approach Needed?(1995) 23 *Int'l. J. Legal Info.* 53 @ 56 (stating that "[l]egal citations serve one overriding purpose: to lead the reader directly to the cited source accurately and efficiently, without enforced recourse to any other source of information."); Susie Salmon, Shedding the Uniform: Beyond a "Uniform System of Citation" to a More Efficient Fit (2016) 99 *Marquette L. Rev.* 763 @ 769 (stating that "[t]he second purpose is often equally or more important: effective legal citation efficiently communicates to the reader the weight and vintage of that support."). But cf. Chew, above n. 1 @ 881 where the earned writer argues that the communicative purpose is primary purpose of in-line citation, with the credibility purpose flowing mostly as a consequence of the communicative purpose, @ 884 (stating that "[a]ll of this suggests that the convention of in-line citation persists, despite some drawbacks, in order to communicate information to the reader. Communication is the only purpose that the very strong convention of in-line citations is reasonably serving. First, locating cited sources is often as easy as clicking a hyperlink or typing (or copy-and-pasting) the words of a citation into a search bar. Footnotes serve the locating purpose as well as in-line citations do. Second, the credibility purpose is no more served by in-line citations than footnoted citations—indeed, it might be better served by footnoted citations because they're all grouped together on the page for judgment. And finally, the attribution purpose overlaps somewhat with the communicative purpose, but it seems to be mainly concerned with avoiding plagiarism, which can be done without in-line citations.").

[15]Susie Salmon, Shedding the Uniform: Beyond a "Uniform System of Citation" to a More Efficient Fit (2016) 99 *Marquette L. Rev.* 763 @ 769 (stating that "[at a glance, a trained legal reader learns whether the source cited is law at all, whether it is binding authority in a given jurisdiction, when a case was decided, and whether the cited authority remains good law."). See also, Bryan Garner, *The Redbook: A Manual on Legal Style,* 3rd ed. 2013 @ 147 [hereinafter "The Redbook"] (stating that "[I]ncorrect citations can impair your credibility and call an argument's validity into question—they may even lead to sanctions. Correct citations, on the other hand, can enhance your credibility by reflecting the care and attention to detail that went into preparing the document.").

reader starts to give the writing a measure of credence. But that's not the end of the matter. The weight of the authority goes to the substance of credibility. The reader begins to interrogate how to assess the authority cited. This is so because "weight of authority" is a legal concept, central to the discipline of law. Legal readers assess weight of authority. For example, it is not enough for an in-line citation to simply state: "Justice Tabai, JSC 2014." Such a citation has specific source detail to guide a legal reader who often wants to place the appropriate weight to the writing of Justice Tabai, JSC. So, the reader begins to wonder is the cited reference about Justice Tabai in a judgment delivered at the Supreme Court. If so, was it a lead judgment or a concurring one or a dissenting judgment? If the citation is not a judgement, the reader continues to wonder, could it perhaps be a statement extra-judicial? If so, on what occasion was it issued? Was it in a book authored by the learned justice or what? All of these details matter to the legal reader because it affects how authoritative (or weighty or persuasive) depending the reader will make of the cited source. In all this, the reader is concerned and draws on previous knowledge about hierarchy, jurisdiction of courts, distinction between primary and secondary sources of law, and the like. For example, the reader thinks through the citation to determine how to classify it. If it is, is it a judgment referred to delivered at the Supreme Court, then the reader drawing on skills of legal reasoning is quick to assign it as primary source. But if it is a statement extra-judicial, it gets classified as secondary source. The lists of questions to ask when assessing the weight of a cited authority are many when an unclear legal citation as "Justice Tabai, JSC, 2014" is used in a document.[16]

Indirect citation

By contrast to the in-line citation, indirect citation systems require readers to leave the text and go elsewhere in the document to see the citation's bibliographic summary. It is usually more appropriate for academic writings. The reader has to flick the eyes from the text to the bottom of the page to read a footnote or flipping (or scrolling) to the back of a document to read an endnote. Thus indirect citation systems transfer less information at the reader's point of need.

However, it is a citation system that transfers much more information elsewhere in the document, than in-line citation. If the reader chooses to look for at the footnote or endnote, the reader gets a lot more information. For when a reader follows the marker in a document using an indirect citation system, she makes the decision to leave the text because she is motivated to learn additional

[16]David J.S. Ziff, The Worst System of Citation Except for All the Others, (2017) 66 *J. Legal Educ.* 668 @ 683 (an article criticizing the Bluebook as not being functional in approach to legal citation, @ 683 it tells why clear citation contributes to credibility).

information. The indirect citation system advances also the writer's desire to meet the need of the reader who requires more information in that the writer is less constrained by space in the text gives the detail information indirectly as footnote or endnote. The writer isn't forced to squeeze the bibliographic summary into the text, leaving her free to elaborate in the bibliographic summary without worrying about interrupting the flow of the text. Those engaged in academic writing need to master the rules for proper indirect citation.[17]

Place of citation

There is no question about it; the communicative purpose of legal citation is important to legal readers. Some scholars are however of the view that citation can constitute itself into obstacles between the writer and the reader.[18] However it must be emphasized that more important than citation style is for the lawyer to master the skill understanding how to write and read legal citation. This is what interrogates a deeper understanding of the purpose of legal citation and how readers make meaning from legal documents.

Legal citations play an integral role in legal analysis and legal documents, communicating important information from writer to reader about the support for the writer's claims. Skilled legal readers incorporate that information into their understanding of the legal texts they read, making meaning from them and using them to assess the quality of legal arguments. Lawyers need to be able to both read and write legal citations - to be citation literate. By learning more the skills of citation literacy over citation formatting, the lawyer might even reduce the misery associated with lack of deep understanding of legal citation.[19]

---

[17] See for example, The Nationally Approved Uniformed Format and Citation Guides for Legal Research in Law Faculties/Institutions in Nigeria, approved by NALT, June 2015 (hereinafter referred to as "*NALTUF-CGs*.")

[18] Bryan Garner, above n. 7 encourages writers to override The Bluebook where on a few points, such as when to spell out numbers, when to use a section symbol, and when to underline (Id. @ 149); to ignore any suggestion or prescription about placing citations in text in court papers. It advice instead that if a court rules otherwise allow footnoting citations, the writer should use footnote because using in-line text does clutters the document making it numerical pollution. (Id. @ 149. See similar views in Wayne Schiess, *Writing for the Legal Audience,* 2003 ("But often, including a lot of authority means the text won't flow; instead, the reader can get bogged down in citations. That's typical of legal writing—we lawyers often insert long, hard-to-read legal citations into our text, unintentionally creating 'hiccups' for our readers.") Id. @ 7-8; and @ 45–51 (suggesting reduced citations in writings to clients); Mark E. Steiner, Without Precedent: Footnotes in Judicial Opinions (1999) 12 *App. Advoc.* 3 @ 94 ("Put simply, footnotes are interruptions."); Linda H. Edwards, *Legal Writing: Process, Analysis and Organization,* 5th 2010); Bryan Garner, above n. 7@ 196.

[19] Chew, above n.1 @ 912.

2. Explanatory parentheticals

Introduction

Explanatory parentheticals are tools of persuasion used in legal documents when citing authority in memorandum and briefs. They usually follow a citation and show the relevance of the cited authority by providing substantive information about the authority.[20] Their use goes to credibility of the writing. This is so because if a lawyer cites an authority and fails to show the relevance of cited authorities, she implies that the authority is not carefully reviewed. So, parenthetical inform a court why the authority is cited and how the authority supports the legal proposition, thus bolstering the persuasive punch of the legal document.

Use of parentheticals

Lawyers primarily use parenthetical for two reasons: to make their writing clear and concise; and to establish the credibility of the writer.[21] Good legal writing must be clear and concise.[22] It does so by explaining the relationship between the cited legal proposition and the cited authority, showing that the cited authority supports the stated proposition. It thus focuses the reader or court on the portions of the cited authority that are relevant to the proposition – doing so in limited space. If contained in a brief it helps to focus the judge's attention prevent the judge from wondering how a cited authority melds with the stated proposition. Two good examples are contained in the petitioner's brief of argument in our sample brief – they are highlighted in bold typeface.

The first of them states:

> In the decision that dictated the outcome below, the California Supreme Court asserted that "binding precedent" from the pre-digital age left it no choice but to treat searches of smart phones seized at the time of arrests identically to searches of purely physical objects. *People* v. *Diaz*, 244 P.3d 501, 511 (Cal. 2011) (reprinted at Pet. App. 25a, 47a); see also id. 51a (Kennard, acting C.J., concurring) **(agreeing with the majority's approval of**

---

[20]Eric P. Voigt, Explanatory Parentheticals Can Pack a Persuasive Punch (2013) 45 *McGeorge L. Rev.* 269 @ 269 (stating that "[T]he parenthetical is a powerful tool of persuasion in a litigator's arsenal. Indeed, judges and top advocates want explanatory parentheticals to accompany citations in motions and briefs.")

[21]Richard A. Posner, Judicial Opinions and Appellate Advocacy in Federal Courts–One Judge's Views (2013) 51 *Duq. L. Rev.* 3 @ 36 (explaining that an "advocate should make his brief, as far as possible, self-contained").

[22] See discussion in chapters 11 and 13 - on good writing and grammar.

> **unrestricted cell phone searches "[u]nder the compulsion of directly applicable United States Supreme Court precedent")**.[23]

The second like it states:

> [E]very case addressing the reasonableness of a warrantless search [begins] with the basic rule that 'searches conducted outside the judicial process, without prior approval by judge or magistrate, are per se unreasonable under the Fourth Amendment – subject only to a few specifically established and well- delineated exceptions.' "*Arizona* v. *Gant*, 556 U.S. 332, 338 (2009) (quoting Katz, 389 U.S. at 357); see also Acton, 515 U.S. at 653 **("stating that where a search is undertaken by law enforcement officials to discover evidence of criminal wrongdoing, this Court has said that reasonableness generally requires the obtaining of a judicial warrant.**"). "Among the exceptions to the warrant requirement is a search incident to a lawful arrest.[24]

The reader of both passages above is not in any doubt as to why the cases are cited to support the propositions of law. The parenthetical contributes to the credibility of the writer. Not only does it present the material in a clear, understandable and concise form, its use demonstrates clear thinking of the writer. For to come up with the parenthetical which is more a less a summary of the ratio of the case cited, the lawyer must have read the cited case, understands it, think about it, and understand its rules and reasoning informing it to draw up the parenthetical.[25]

Drafting a parenthetical that illustrates the application of a rule, for instance, requires the writer to understand why a court held a certain way and to describe the case to an unfamiliar reader in a short amount of space. The lawyer not skilled in the use of parenthetical would simply have copied and pasted a quote of the authority without understanding properly its governing principle.

Parenthetical power in fact derives from its ability to prove or illustrate rules in short form without diminishing its persuasiveness. It enables the lawyer to

---

[23] Posner, above n. 21 @ 13

[24] Ibid @ 15

[25] Laurie A. Lewis, The Stellar Parenthetical Illustration: A Tool to Open Doors in a Tight Job Market (2010) 19 *Perspectives Teaching Legal Res. & Writing* 35 @ 40 (stating "[W]ithout clear thinking, there can be no clear legal analysis.").

explain how rules apply to a set of facts without having to fully describe each case in the text. For example, in the brief above (second example) the lawyer did not need to discuss the facts of *Arizona* v. *Gant*, to establish and ground the proposition stating that "where a search is undertaken by law enforcement officials to discover evidence of criminal wrongdoing, reasonableness requires the police to obtain a judicial warrant."

Fall of that would be difficult for the lawyer who is unskilled in the use of parenthetical. The unskilled would have had to discuss the case in the text to illustrate the search rule. But a parenthetical used by the skilled lawyer would have saved space without sacrificing persuasiveness because it would focus the reader only on the relevant portions of the case – for search to be reasonable a judicial warrant is required – illustrating how the court should treat the search of a defendant arrested by the police.

Parenthetical also advances the credibility of the writer in the eyes of the reader.[26] The lawyer can gain credibility in her writing if she accurately represents the facts and law, state the precise holdings of cases, address adverse authority, raise only the strongest arguments, and not overstate the arguments.

Parentheticals greatly contribute to the credibility equation in that their use demonstrates that the lawyer is intelligent and has mastery of the law. For instance, explaining the holding and reasoning of a case in just a few lines in a parenthetical requires strong analytical skills. Thus, stating the holding and reasoning of a case in a parenthetical conveys to a judge that the lawyer fully understands the case and how it relates to the stated proposition cited. As a result, the judge is unlikely to question the rule or the lawyer's analysis of the case. For example, if the passage above did not contain the parenthetical, the judge would question whether reasonableness requires a judicial warrant. And if the first is the case, whether the equivalence should be drawn between telephone search and searches of purely physical objects, the addition of the parenthetical clears the doubt out of the reader's mind. The reason for this is simple. Readers trust information that is specific. Not general information. Parentheticals are specific. The more specific information provided about an authority, the more likely the reader would trust the information. What is more, the specifics of parentheticals are assuring to the reader that the writer is unlike to misrepresent the authority. It is assumed that before including an effective parenthetical, the lawyer must have read, analysed, and understands the cited authority. As a result, the likelihood that the litigator will misrepresent the authority diminishes.

---

[26]Michael R. Smith, *Advanced Legal Writing: Theories and Strategies in Persuasive Writing,* 3rd ed. 2013 @ 127 ('the three qualities that helps to win the confidence of the reader are intelligence, character and good will.").

How to distil parenthetical

This is a skill that has to be learned. Before the lawyer chooses to employ parenthetical she must give conscious thought to three questions: (i) should the parenthetical follow the cited authority? The answer to the question would depend on the content and context of the presentation. No parenthetical would be necessary when the rule or argument is sufficiently explained in the sentence preceding the citation. Also, if the rule is well-known, such as the standard for proof for criminal cases, a parenthetical would be unnecessary to support the rule. Where however, the fate of the case rest on its application it might be necessary to use explanatory parenthetical. The more significant the authority and the more complex the issue, the more likely the authority should be fully described in the legal document. In fact, in such a case, it would be advisable to explain the authority rather than use a parenthetical.

If the choice is to use a parenthetical, the lawyer should use as guide the following rule: the substance of a parenthetical depends on the text preceding the cited authority and the purpose for including the parenthetical. Although the purpose of a parenthetical is an important factor, the text preceding the parenthetical is the most important factor that determines the substance of a parenthetical.[27] It is what determines whether a parenthetical should contain a complete sentence or one or two clauses or a short phrase, or one word only. It should also determine whether a parenthetical should be full or partial quotation, or should contain the procedural posture and outcome of a case, the holding and reasoning of a case, or only the facts of a case. Moreover, both the preceding text and the substance of a parenthetical must provide enough detail so that a reader or judge will understand the cited authority without having to read the actual case or statute.

Let us consider an example of the text preceding the parenthetical – one where the preceding text provides the outcome and reasoning of a case – making it one suitable for the parenthetical to state only the relevant facts.

> The Supreme Court has held in several cases that it is a very serious matter for anyone to flout a positive order of a court and proceed to taunt the court further by seeking a remedy from the court while still in contempt. *Military Governor, Lagos State* v. *Ojukwu* (1986) (pt. 18) 621; (1986) All N.L.R 233 (applying contempt of lower court's order); but cf. *Group Danone* v. *Voltic Nig*

[27] Smith, above n. 26 @ 59-62.

> *Ltd* [2008] 3-4 SC 32 (challenging the validity of an order by way of appeal is not contempt).

But if the preceding text lacks those details, the parenthetical may contain the outcome, relevant facts, and reasoning of the case. An example of this could be this: "Where a defendant challenges the validity of an order directed against her either by way of appeal or other application, she cannot be treated as being in contempt until the issue of the legality of the order is settled one way or the other." See *Group Danone* v. *Voltic Nig Ltd* [2008] 3-4 SC 32 (stating that where the order disobeyed is one issued without jurisdiction or where the party in disobedience is challenging the validity of the order, the principle that a contemptnor shall not be heard does not apply.)

To further illustrate, if the preceding text states that a court has concluded or determined something, the parenthetical may specify what the court did and at what stage of litigation it did the action. Using the Group *Danone* v. *Voltic Nig Ltd* [2008] 3-4 SC 32 the parenthetical could read like this:

> The court has concluded that a party for contempt who is challenging the validity of a lower court's order on appeal is improper because pending the determination of the validity of the order to punish the applicant could well turn out to be for an order without legal basis. See Group *Danone* v. *Voltic Nig Ltd* [2008] 3-4 SC 32.

If, however, the preceding text provides those details, the parenthetical should contain different information, such as the reasoning of a case. This can be as follows:

> This Court has concluded that contempt is based on acts that somehow affect the dignity of court in the administration of justice. See *Odu* v. *Jolaoso* [2005] 3-4 SC 116.

Parenthetical should be consciously used. When the lawyer fails to consider the text preceding a parenthetical explanation, the reader may not understand the substance of the parenthetical. The short phrases in the parentheticals below do not make sense because the preceding text provides no context. For example just stating "the court should dismiss the application for contempt. See *Group Danone* v. *Voltic Nig Ltd* [2008] 3-4 SC 32 (appeal on order pending)" says nothing. There is no context to give life to the parenthetical used here. Such a short phrase as "appeal on order pending" would only make sense if the preceding text had provided sufficient and necessary context.

The bottom-line is that parenthetical should be used only to provide information that is necessary for the reader to understand and possibly be persuaded to accept the proposition or argument it supports.[28]

Additionally, parenthetical may be used to (i) proving a rule from a single authority; (ii) to illustrate a rule from a single authority; (iii) to prove a rule that is synthesized from multiple authorities; (iv) to prove or illustrate a significant rule or argument with more than one authority; (v) to show the outcome and procedural posture of cases; (vi) to counter and distinguish adverse authorities; and (vii) to apply the rules to facts.[29]

Guideline for effective parenthetical

Like most rules for persuasive writing, there is no dogmatic formula for drafting effective parentheticals. The rules are mere suggestions that can advance effective parenthetical. The guidelines are seven.[30]

(i) Begin with a present participle and a lowercase letter and end without punctuation.[31]

Present participles often end with "ing". So, it should contain words like "providing", "affirming," stating," etc. If the parenthetical is employed for a statute it would be proper to begin with the word "providing." If it is about a case, it could be styled "reversing," or "affirming," or "granting," or "holding," etc. Present participle is used for effect. For in just one word the reader is informed of specific action of the cited authority. For example, the mere mention of the word "reversing" brings to the reader's mind what the court did. The absence of present participle gives a wrong signal to the reader. It makes the parenthetical appear to be the thoughts of the writer, not the cited authority. That is how most readers would consider a passage like this:

> [E]very case addressing the reasonableness of a warrantless search [begins] with the basic rule that 'searches conducted outside the judicial process, without prior approval by judge or magistrate, are per se unreasonable under the Fourth Amendment – subject only to a few specifically established and well-delineated exceptions.'

[28] Smith above n. 26 @ 57.
[29] Voigt, above n. 20.
[30] Ibid., @ 281.
[31] Smith above n. 26 @ 57; Ross Guberman, *Point Made: How to Write Like the Nation's Top Advocates,* 2011 @ 134.

> "*Arizona* v. *Gant*, 556 U.S. 332, 338 (2009) (quoting Katz, 389 U.S. at 357); see also Acton, 515 U.S. at 653 **("where a search is undertaken by law enforcement officials to discover evidence of criminal wrongdoing, this Court has said that reasonableness generally requires the obtaining of a judicial warrant.**).

But by simply adding the words *"stating that"* the parenthetical appears to be the holding of the court, not the writer's thought.[32]

It is important for the lawyer to know and use appropriately the words "holding", "stated", "determined", "decided" and the like. These are not loose word to be conflated. Often lawyers use the word "holding" when in fact that is not what the court did in the cited authority. In this respect, a refreshing of some skills of legal method would not be out of place. A world of difference exists between ratio and obiter. A court must have actually decided a disputed issue for the result to be the holding of the case. If the lawyer is in doubt on what the court decided it would be better to simply substitute holding with words like "concluding" or "determining" or "stated".[33]

(ii) Exception to rule to begin with present participle

Some parentheticals need to begin with present participle. They are exception to the rule. One, if the parenthetical is a quotation from a statute or case it need not begin with present participle. Also, parentheticals with a full quotation should start with a capital letter and end with closing punctuation. A parenthetical containing only a partial quotation, however, may start with a lowercase letter and end with no closing punctuation.

Example of statutory example is: "Section 3 of Criminal Procedure Act ("In making an arrest, the police officer or other person making the same shall actually touch or confine the body of the person to be arrested, unless there be submission to the custody by word or action.")

Case example is: See *Attorney-General of Bendel State* v. *Aideyan* [1989] 9 SC 127 ("It is that such expropriatory statutes which encroach on a person's proprietary right must be construed fortissimo contra preferences, that is strictly

[32]Eric P. Voigt, A Company's Voluntary Refund Program for Consumers Can Be a Fair and Efficient Alternative to a Class Action (2012) 31 *Rev. Litig.*617 @ 637.

[33] Glanville William, *Learning the Law*, 16th ed. London: Sweet & Maxwell, 2016; Akintunde O. Obilade, *The Nigeria Legal System*, London: Sweet & Maxwell, 1979; Judge Pierre N. Leval, Judging Under the Constitution: Dicta About Dicta (2006) 81 *N.Y.U. L. Rev.* 1249 @ 1257-58 (stating that the distinction between a holding and dictum "requires recognition of what was the question before the court upon which the judgment depended").

against the acquiring authority but sympathetically in favour of the citizen whose property rights are being deprived.")

Second, a parenthetical could start with something other than a present participle when it contains one word or a short phrase, such as when citing several cases to illustrate a synthesized rule. In the example below, the text preceding the parentheticals states a concise synthesized rule from two cases; therefore, the short phrases in the parentheticals are necessary to inform the reader which parts of the rule came from which cases. An example would be: "Only a person who is a party to a contract can sue or be sued on it. See *Ezeafulukwe* v. *John Holt* [1996] 2 SCNJ 104 (contracting with the wrong name); *Alfotrin Ltd* v. *A-G Federation* (1996) 9 NWLR (pt. 475) 634 (contracting with a third party)."

Also, a parenthetical may contain one or two words when the cited authority sets forth examples of the same thing. An example of parenthetical containing one or two words when cited as authority for the same thing could be like this: "*Ezeafulukwe* v. *John Holt* [1996] 2 SCNJ 104 (determining that no privity of contract arises where the claimant contracts with the wrong defendant); *Alfotrin Ltd* v. *A-G Federation* (1996) 9 NWLR (pt. 475) 634 (concluding that only the parties to a contract can benefit from it and that even if the contract was made for the benefit of a stranger and purports to give him the right to sue or to make him liable upon it, there will still be no privity of contract to ground the plaintiff's claim.") (same).

By using the word "same" the judge reading the second parenthetical is forced to see that the second authority amplifies the proposition.

(iii) Parentheticals may begin with a present participle and include quoted material

Starting a parenthetical with a present participle and quoting language from a statute or case are not mutually exclusive. An effective parenthetical often starts with a present participle and quotes key legal terms from a statute or case.

Statutory Examples: "Section 3 of Criminal Procedure Act ("providing that the person making an arrest shall actually touch or confine the body of the person to be arrested").

Case Examples: *Attorney-General Rivers State* v. *Attorney-General Akwa Ibom & Anor* [2011] 3 SC 1; (2011) 8 NWLR (pt.1248) 31 (stating that the court will give effect to the plain intention of the parties as revealed in their document"); *Yadis Nig. Ltd* v. *Great Nigeria Insurance Co. Ltd* [(2007) 14 NWLR (pt.1055) 584, [2007] 4-5 SC 236, [2007] 7 SCNJ 86 ("determining that once the terms of a contract are certain the business of the court will be to give effect to it")
.

In the above examples, the present participles keep the parentheticals concise while highlighting the legally significant terms. In addition, because the clauses in those examples are not complete sentences, the parentheticals start with a lowercase participle and end with no closing punctuation, even though the parentheticals contain quoted material.[34]

Lawyers are however advised not to start a parenthetical with a present participle and include a full quotation of a sentence. One such bad example would be this: "*Alfotrin Ltd* v. *A-G Federation* (1996) 9 NWLR (pt. 475) 634 at 657 ("affirming the privity of contract rule, "If the terms are unsettled, uncertain or vague that they cannot be ascertained with reasonable degree of certainty, there will be no valid contract enforceable.").

This could however be reversed to it pointed by including only the full quotation or integrating the first clause with the quotation (e.g., affirming the privity rule the court stated that rejecting a probable cause test and stating that "If the terms are unsettled, uncertain or vague that they cannot be ascertained with reasonable degree of certainty, there will be no valid contract enforceable.").

(iv) Parenthetical may contain two clauses

Although parentheticals generally contain only one clause or sentence, they may contain two clauses that address related or separate points. The two clauses may start with a present participle or something else, and they may be separated by a conjunction or semicolon. The semicolon is useful to create a pause to emphasize the second clause or to make the parenthetical more concise.[35] Here are two examples.

Example with semicolon: *Ezeafulukwe* v. *John Holt* (1996) 2 NWLR (pt. 432) 511, [1996] 2 SCNJ 104, [1996] LPELR 1196, (stating that It is a fundamental principle in the law that only a person who is a party to a contract can sue on it and if a person with whom a contract not under seal has been made is to be able to enforce it; the issue is . . . whether the parties are privies or not").

Example with conjunction: *Ogida* v. *Oliha* (1986) 1 NWLR (pt. 19) 786, [1986] 2 SC 406, [1986] All NLR 303, (1986) 1 NSCC 353 (applying agency rules and requiring plaintiff to show "the capacity in which a person makes a contract").

(v.) Parentheticals should not contain hidden rules

A lawyer must recognize that parenthetical are only explanatory of rules. So, the proposition must be in the text, not hidden as parenthetical. Propositions or rules

[34] Voigt, above n. 20 @ 285
[35] Ibid. @ 286

belong in the text preceding the parentheticals.[36] Parenthetical is meant to illustrate or prove the rule, not the other way around. So, if the rule is hidden in the parenthetical the reader is forced to seek for the rule, thereby diminishing the force of the rule, clogging reasoning of the reader, thereby making the argument presented less forceful.

An example of the bad practice is this: "A court relies on evidence. *Ivienagbor* v. *Bazuaye* (1999) 9 NWLR (pt. 620) 552, [1999] 6 SCNJ 240 (deciding that a court cannot decide issues on speculation no matter how close what it relies on may see to be on the facts. Speculation is not an aspect of inference that may be drawn from facts that are laid before the court).

The writer above states the relevant rules in the preceding text but then mistakenly introduced new rules in the parentheticals. Instead, the rules in the parentheticals should have been stated in the text preceding the citations. The parenthetical is not needed.

(vi) Parentheticals should not be redundant

The content of the parenthetical must not repeat the preceding text. It is not a restatement of what has been stated in the text. For it merely repeats it, then it is redundant, superfluous, adding nothing by way of analysis or something new.[37]

Such bad example would be: "Once the terms of a contract are certain the business of the court will be to give effect to it. No more. This is because the honourable court's duty is not to rewrite contract for the parties. *Yadis Nig. Ltd* v. *Great Nigeria Insurance Co. Ltd* [(2007) 14 NWLR (pt.1055) 584, [2007] 4-5 SC 236, [2007] 7 SCNJ 86 (concluding that the plaintiff did not show that the terms are not certain).

The parenthetical above is simply pointless. It adds nothing to understanding the authority. The rule in the text has said it all. The parenthetical simply repeats it. At best it makes the reader confused or angry. It does not persuade. If anything it diminishes persuasion.

(vii) Parentheticals should not ramble

The information in a parenthetical should be focused and should not ramble. The parenthetical is not the place to discuss interesting nuggets from a case or fine points of law. A rambling parenthetical distracts the reader, making her question the writer's understanding of the cited authority, thereby undermining the writer's credibility. If a parenthetical exceeds one complete sentence or has more

---

[36] Smith, above n. 26 @ 59 ("parenthetical should supplement the rule by illustrating how the rule was applied in specific factual context.")

[37] Smith, above n. 26 @ 59; Voigt, above n. 20 @ 287.

than two separate clauses, it is probably too long.[38] The purpose for using parenthetical must be consciously kept in mind when employing it as persuasion strategy.

A bad example could look like this: *Ezeafulukwe* v. *John Holt* (1996) 2 NWLR (pt. 432) 511, [1996] 2 SCNJ 104, [1996] LPELR 1196, (the plaintiff sought damages for breach of contract against the defendant for the purchase of tinned geisha mackerel fish in tomato sauce, the court stated that the court not having resolved identity question and the confusion between the name "Mich" and "Leonard" Ezeafulukwe as party that contracted with the defendant, there could be no privity of contract to ground the plaintiff's claim).

The parenthetical above is not concise; neither does it explain the relevance of the cited authority. The impression a reader gets from it is that the writer does not understand the governing rules and the relevance of the authority to the factual situation of her case. For she does, she would first state the relevant rules in the text preceding the citation and then draft a parenthetical that proves or illustrates the rule.

Parentheticals are useful to paraphrase express rules from statutes and cases; to prove a rule where the cited case does not expressly state the rule but its outcome, facts, and reasoning (or some combination) supporting the rule; to prove a rule that is synthesized from several authorities; to explain several authorities supporting a stated proposition and explain their relevance to the proposition without having pages of full case descriptions; to show the weight of an authority cited showing that a court applied the rule to the facts before it(as opposed to merely quoting the rule from a prior case); to show the importance of the cited authority to the factual issue before the reader; to counter and distinguish adverse authorities; and to apply the rules to the particular facts being interrogated.

Conclusion

The explanatory parenthetical - if properly crafted and incorporated effectively - can be a very effective persuasive tool in the hands of the lawyer. Its use enables the lawyer to cite authorities that clearly support each proposition, while avoid lengthy discussions of multiple cases. Parentheticals also demonstrates the lawyer's knowledge of the cited authority and how it supports her argument, thereby advancing clear, concise writing, and the credibility of the writer. Drafting effective parentheticals requires paying careful attention to its governing principle:

---

[38]Voigt, above n. 20 @ 289.

the substance of a parenthetical depends on both the content of the text preceding the citation and the purpose for including the parenthetical.

3. Legal punctuation

Introduction

Legal punctuation refers to symbols that organize and give structure to writing. Punctuation lets a document change the inflection of voice and give meaning to words of the writer.[39] Punctuation rule applies only to written language. This is understandable. One can only talk of punctuation in oral communication in writing. Its purpose is to simulate the pauses, inflection, and emphasis that clarify meanings in a document.

The importance of punctuation was recently heightened in a decision of the United States Court of Appeals for the First Circuit in Oakhurst Dairy.[40] The small-scale dispute gained global notoriety over the missing comma in a state legislation sufficient to create enough uncertainty to side for the drivers' request for the payment of overtime arrears. The case began in 2014 when two dairy drivers (in a class-action) sued the dairy company for four years overtime pay the company denied them. The State of Maine legislation requires time-and-a half pay for each hour worked after 40 hours. It however made exception for "the canning, processing, preserving, freezing, drying, marketing, storing, packing for shipment or distribution of: (i) agricultural produce; (ii) meat and fish products; and (iii) perishable foods." The dispute revolved around what followed the last comma in the sentence: "packing for shipment or distribution of." The court ruled that it was unclear from the construction of the legislation whether the law exempted the distribution of the three categories that followed, or if it exempted *packing* for the shipment or distribution of them. Had there been a comma after "shipment" the meaning would have been clear.[41]

---

[39] Gerald Lebovits, Do's, Don'ts and Maybes: Legal Writing Punctuation (2008) 80 (2) *New York Bar Ass'n. J.* 64; Lillian B. Hardwick, Classical Persuasion through Grammar and Punctuation (2006) JAWLD 75 (an article stating that grammar and punctuation are rhetorical avenues).

[40] *O'Connor* v. *Oakhurst Dairy*, No. 16-1901 (1st Cir. 2017) delivered on March 17, 2017. Available at Justia Law http//www/law.justia.com.cases/federal accessed on 30 June 2019.

[41] To clarify the law the Maine Legislature amended the law to now read "the canning; processing; preserving; freezing; drying; marketing; storing; packing for shipment; or distribution of: (i) agricultural produce; (ii) meat and fish products; and (iii) perishable foods." The dispute revolved around what followed the last comma in the sentence: " So, while the law is re-enacted with same words, it replaced the Oxford comma pedantry with the semicolon pedantry. By so doing, the intention of the legislature is made clear, that the distribution of certain products is exempt from the provisions governing overtime payment. Note, some stylist notably The Times stylebook discourages the use of serial comma, such as "A, B, and C" – often called the Oxford comma because it was traditionally used by Oxford University Press.

The case simply illustrates that though debate over punctuation such as comma is often inconsequential, it can be decisive in some cases. For in the list of serial sentence such as "rice, beans and eggs" some would insert a comma after "beans" and some would not. But as shown in the Dairy case the use of punctuation can be decisive. The dairy case reveals that it is difficult to know if the law intends to exempt the distribution of the three categories that follow or not. If there was a comma after "shipment" it might have been clear that the law exempted the distribution of perishable goods. So, the absence of the comma made it possible to side with the drivers. By the court ruling, Oxford comma defenders won the debate.[42]

It is important to remember that punctuation applies only to written language. Even so, the pathway to persuasion (rooted in logos, ethos and pathos) employed by classic rhetoricians like Aristotle also apply with equal force to rules of grammar and punctuation for none of Aristotle's persuasive means can reliably be achieved without proficiency in grammar and punctuation. That explains why legal writing professors connect a "strong command of the rules of grammar, usage, and punctuation" to classical rhetoric.

The rules of punctuation are designed to permit a level of understanding as similar as possible to spoken language. These rules have changed very little over time. Although minor modifications have appeared from time to time, it is not difficult to describe a uniform set of consistent punctuation rules with reliable explanations.

Let us examples of how punctuation gives structure and meaning to the words used by the writer.

(i) It can help speed up or slow down language.

Example of speeding up language: "Please note the court sits at the hour of 9 o'clock in the forenoon." In this example, the reader of the document does not pause in her reading. She reads to the end of the sentence without stopping for any punctuation. The period (of full stop at the end of the sentence) tells her when to rest.

(ii) It can slow down language

Example of slowing down language: "Please note, the court sits at the hour of 9 o'clock in the forenoon." In this example, the reader of the document slows down

[42]A recent survey in 2014 shows that 57 per cent Americans favour the use of Oxford comma and 43 percent oppose it. The Chicago Manual of Style uses the comma because it states that "the last comma can serve to resolve ambiguity." See http//www.bostonglobe.com accessed on 30 June 2019.

immediately after the comma. It is the comma that tells the reader when to breathe, slow down before reaching the end of the sentence. In effect, comma not only slows the reader, it tells her when to breathe.

(iii) It is used for emphasis or de-emphasis

Punctuation serves the writer's purpose of telling the reader what is emphasized or de-emphasized.

Example: "Mr. Dambo, SAN – the diligent lawyer – argued the motion on behalf of the applicant for stay of proceeding."

But this could be rephrased to read like "Mr. Dambo, SAN argued the applicant's motion for stay. (He is a diligent lawyer.)

The reader of both sentences above can feel the writer's pause – what is being emphasized. The first tells the reader whom the lawyer is that argued the case. It emphasizes the fact of the hearing or argument before the court, diminishing the relevance of diligence. But the second while giving the gist of the hearing emphasizes the diligence of the lawyer.

(iv) Punctuation conveys emotion

A simple example is the use of the word "great." The reader immediately gets to feel the emotion of the writer – that she is pleased. "Wonderful!"

(v) Punctuation can serve as attention-getter

For example the question "when is she coming?" quickly catches the reader's attention to give attention.

(vi) Punctuation clarifies

One unconfirmed source tells of an English language professor who wrote these words: "A woman without her man is nothing," on the board and asked the students to punctuate it correctly. All the male in the class wrote: "A woman, without her man, is nothing." On the other hand, all the female in the class wrote: "A woman: without her, man is nothing."[43]

Unquestionably, both sentence reconstructed by the students give different meanings. The punctuation by the male gives the impression that a woman needs a man to be it. But the punctuation by the female students says the opposite. It impresses that a man without a woman is nothing. The punctuation the writer uses and where it is put can alter how the reader will interpret what is written. It can clarify the writer's intention.

All the examples above illustrate that good punctuation makes it possible for the reader to feel, hear, and understand the language of the writer. Bad

---

[43]WhatsApp message received from Mrs. Chika Lasu on August 18, 2018. See a similar allusion to the example in Lebovits, above n. 39.

punctuation confuses and puts off the reader. This explains why good punctuation advances clarity and communication.

Rules of punctuation have over the years evolved as a convention so that the writer can give the reader reliable cues for communication. The rules of punctuation are designed to permit a level of understanding as similar as possible to spoken language. These rules have changed very little over time. Although minor modifications have appeared from time to time, it is not difficult to describe a uniform set of consistent punctuation rules with reliable explanations. Violating the rules of punctuation isn't considered mere stylistic choice violation as such errors can undermine the ethical, logical, and emotional appeals of the writer before the reader. In fact, good punctuation makes it possible for the reader to feel, hear, and understand language of the writer. Bad punctuation confuses and puts off the reader.

Punctuation types used in legal writing that will engage us are: periods; question marks; exclamation points; colons; semicolons; parentheses; comma; and brackets.[44]

Period

As a general rule of grammar, three punctuation marks are used at the end of a sentence. They are periods, question marks, and exclamation points. Legal writing sparingly uses enough periods. A peep at many transaction agreements confirms it. Most conveyancing and land transfer drafts hard use enough periods. A period is a full stop.

It is to be used at the end of a declarative sentence. A declarative sentence states an argument, fact, or idea. It doesn't require the reader to take action or answer.

Example: "Please note the court sits at the hour of 9 o'clock in the forenoon."

Periods should also be used at the end of commands.

Examples: "You must appear before the honourable court at the hour of 9 o'clock in the forenoon on September 23, 2018."

In addition periods are to be used at the end of a citation before a new sentence.

---

[44] Discussion on the rules of punctuation are mere guides for good writing and no one is prescribing that minor deviations are prohibited because the rules are sometimes lengthy, convoluted and unsettled. What this book advises it that the lawyer should substantially deviate from them if she desires communication to be clear and easily understandable.

Correct example: "*Military Governor, Lagos State* v. *Ojukwu* (1986) (pt. 18) 621; (1986) All N.L.R 233. In *Ojukwu*, the Supreme Court held that it is a very serious matter for anyone to flout a positive order of a court and proceed to taunt the court further by seeking a remedy from the court while still in contempt."

But it is incorrect to write: "*Military Governor, Lagos State* v. *Ojukwu* (1986) (pt. 18) 621; (1986) All N.L.R 233, In *Ojukwu*, the Supreme Court held that it is a very serious matter for anyone to flout a positive order of a court and proceed to taunt the court further by seeking a remedy from the court while still in contempt."

Periods, not question marks, are to be used after indirect questions.

Example: "The judge asked me if I was ready to call my witness."

Only one period, not two, should be used if the sentence ends in an abbreviation.

Incorrect: ": "Please note the court sits at 9.00 a.m."

This is incorrect because "a.m." is an abbreviation for before noon or for forenoon (taken from Latin *ante meridiem*)

Correct example: "Please note the court sits at 9.00 a.m."

However, if the sentence ends in a question mark or an exclamation point, a period should be used after the abbreviation.

Examples: "Were you in the court at 9.00 a.m.?" or "Please note the court sits at 9.00 a.m.!"

Most English weights and measures end with abbreviation. For example, "m." for metre, "pt." for pint, etc. Some writers advise that periods should not be used after degrees and metric abbreviations.[45]

Examples: "C" for "centigrade," "cm" for "centimetre," "cms" for "centimetres," and "F" for "Fahrenheit."

Writers are not agreed as to whether a period should be put at the end of an abbreviated title, even if the title isn't a true abbreviation. For instance, while American English will write "Dr. Eboibi," British deems "Dr Eboibi" correct.

There should be no space between periods when using initials.

Incorrect: "O. F. Emiri"

Correct: "O.F. Emiri."

This however a matter of style preference. So, if the person prefers to be addressed as O. F. Emiri, the writer should follow the preference of the named person.

---

[45]Lebovits, above n. 39.

Periods should not be used for an acronym. For example the writer should write "IRAC" for "issue, rule, application and conclusion," – an acronym can be pronounced as words.

The above rule does not apply to abbreviations. So, use periods for abbreviations. Abbreviations are different from acronyms because the speaker pronounces each individual letter in an abbreviation. Examples: N.L.C., N.J.C., I.N.E.C., F.B.I., K.G.B., etc. though most newspapers and magazines omit the periods from common abbreviations to save space. If your readers are familiar with the abbreviation, there will be no need to use periods.

It is proper to put periods inside the quotation marks, not outside it.

Incorrect: Justice Ajuwa said, "I want order in the courtroom."

Correct: Justice Ajuwa said, "I want order in the courtroom."

Question mark

Question marks are to be used at the end of a direct question, or one to which an answer is expected. Examples: "When will you get to the courthouse?" They are inappropriate for indirect question or declaration. Example of indirect question: "I wonder when you will get to the courthouse." Example of declaration: "Yenagoa is Bayelsa State capital."

A question mark should be used at the end of a sentence if a question is embedded in the sentence. Examples: "We reach the courthouse at 8.30 a.m. if we take the short-cut, should we?"

Question mark should not be used for a polite request. Examples: "Would everyone in the courtroom please rise."

So too, it should be avoided for a command, such as "could you help me with that book, please."

Question marks should not be used at the end of a sentence that begins with "whether" – particularly in brief writing, because the word "whether" is a statement, not a question.

Question mark should be inserted inside quotation marks if the question is contained in the original document cited. But it is to be put outside if it is not in the original.

Example of a question mark in the original: The judge asked, "Where is your next witness?"

Example of a question mark not in the original: Does the judge always say, "Counsel where is your next witness?"

If the sentence and the quoted material are questions, don't use two question marks. Only one should be used at the end of the sentence.

Incorrect: Did the judge say, "When will you call your next witness?"

Correct: Did the judge say, "When will you call your next witness?"

When a question ends with a series of brief questions that are follow-up questions to the main question, each follow-up question should begin with a lowercased letter and end with a question mark.

Example: "Who could have done this terrible thing? the lawyer? or the litigant? or someone else?"

Question marks are sometimes used in writing to denote uncertainty: "Justice Tobi delivered two (?) rulings today."

Place question marks inside parentheses when asking a question: "Justice Boufini's opinion (when did she learn to write so well?) is stellar."

Rhetorical questions, or questions a writer asks for which the writer doesn't expect an answer, should end with a question mark. Example: "What else should we expect of a brief written by Mr. Dambo, SAN?

Remember however that good brief writers don't ask questions, but offer answers to question in their brief. Notwithstanding, it may be strategic to ask questions in a brief if the purpose is make graphic the answers furnished in the brief.

The guiding principle on question mark is that the lawyer should generally avoid using question marks unless when asking question or quoting.

Exclamation point

An exclamation is a sudden cry or remark expressing surprise, strong emotion, or pain. So its use in writing often expresses the emotion of the writer. As a rule, it should be used at the end of a command, emphatic declaration, or interjection.

Examples of commands: "Stop!" "Quiet!"

Examples of emphatic declarations: "Wow!"

Examples of interjections: "Excuse me!" "Cheers!"

It should put inside the quotation mark if the exclamation point is in the original, but outside if the exclamation point is not in the original.

Exclamation points may accompany mimetically produced sounds: "All night long, I heard the frogs croaking!"

It is suggested that legal writer avoid exclamation points in legal writing because it could give the veiled impression of exaggeration or pointed screaming at the reader.[46]The lawyer who intends to give emotions to the fore in legal writing could instead use an intensive form of writing to convey the point, using concrete nouns and, even better, vigorous verbs, to accomplish what exclamation could do. Exclamation's place is instead for informal writing.

---

[46]Lebovits, above n. 39 @ 56.

Colon

Colons press the readers forward.

It should be used after a salutation in formal writing. Example: "Dear Ms. Tiwwa:"

If the salutation is for informal writing, the writer should use a comma instead of colon. It would therefore be inappropriate to salute as "Dear Ms. Tiwwa:" if the reader is a friend of the writer. Instead of using colon, the writer should use a comma, which should read like "Dear Ms. Tiwwa,"

Colon should be used to separate time, book titles, chapter from verse.

Correct examples: "1.15 p.m." "Legal Writing: Process, Analysis and Organization" "Proverbs 3: 5"

Use a colon to introduce a definition. Example: "Gipsy: an itinerant people."

Colon can serve as a good replacement for "is" or "are."

Example: "The book: fantastic."

Use a colon after an independent clause (i.e. a clause that has a subject, a verb, and can stand on its own as a sentence) to (i) introduce lists,
(ii) introduce an illustrative quotation, or
(iii) show that something will follow.

Good examples:

Introductory lists - "The defendant raised three defences: estoppel, laches and acquiescence, bona fide right of claim."

This can be rewritten to use the word "included" in which case the need to colon would disappear. So, if written as "The defendant raised three defences which included estoppel, laches and acquiescence, bona fide right of claim." The insertion of "included" dispenses with the need for colon because the preceding clause is no longer an independent clause.

Illustrative quotation - The court ruled against the claimant: Military Governor of Lagos State is in contempt."

Something follows - "The court established a new rule: no one in contempt can seek the court's remedy."

The three examples above show that colons signal that clarifying information will follow.

Unless what follows is a quotation, a colon may not follow a dependent clause, (i.e. a clause that cannot stand on its own as a sentence).

Incorrect example: "The phone numbers she calls most often are: (111), (222), (333), and (444)."

Correct example: "The phone numbers she calls most often are (111), (222), (333), and (444)."

Uppercase words should be used if the first word after a colon when an independent clause follows the colon.

Good example: “The court stated: It is improper not to separate a statement of defence from a counter-claim in a document.”

If more than one independent clause follows the colon, the lawyer should begin each independent clause with a capital letter:

Example: “The court refuses to lend a contemptnor its remedies for two reasons: First to protect the integrity of the judiciary. Second, to prevent a contemptnor foisting on it a state of hopelessness.”

Don’t capitalize after a colon when a dependent clause follows the colon. Examples: “The court gave a useful suggestion: to evaluate the merits of joining the statement of defence with a counter-claim in ne document.”

Colons always go outside quotation marks. Example: She described her legal career as a “roller-coaster ride”: some successes, some failures, and everything in between.[47]

Semicolon

Colons and semicolons are different. Colons press readers forward. Semicolons slow readers down. They function differently.

Semicolon is used to connect closely related independent clauses.

Example: “For simply applications, the judge delivers a bench ruling immediately; for complex, complicated applications, may in 30 days.”

If the statement is used to connect dependent clauses to independent clauses, comma rather than semi-colon is appropriate.[48]

Incorrect: “While we were waiting to hear the bench ruling; the judge adjourned hearing.”

Use semicolons to avoid run-on sentences. Use semicolons, not commas, to separate two independent clauses if the second independent clause begins with a conjunctive adverb (“accordingly”, “again”, “also”, “besides”, “consequently”, “finally”, “for example”, “furthermore”, “hence”, “how-ever”, “moreover”, “nevertheless”, “on the other hand”, “otherwise”, “rather”, “similarly”, “then”, “therefore”, “thus”).

Example: “In straightforward cases, the judge issues a decision in three days; therefore, litigants don’t have to wait for justice.”

Use a semicolon to separate two independent clauses if the second independent clause has a conjunctive adverb somewhere in the sentence, usually after the subject.

---

[47] Ibid.

[48] William Strunk, Jr. & E.B. White, *The Element of Style,* 4th ed. @ 14-15.

Example: "The judge told his law clerk to evaluate the merits of the case; he therefore told his law clerk to prefer logic to emotion."

Semicolon should be used in lists that contain internal commas or an "and" or "or".

Example of a list with an internal comma: "The legal representation for the defendant were Lawyer A of Queens, Lagos; Lawyer B of DF Legal, Lagos; Lawyer C of ODLA, Kumasi."

Example of a list containing "and": "For the firm's holiday party, please buy roast beef and turkey sandwiches; red and white wine; and diet and regular soda." Example of a list containing "or": "Check-in at 9:30 a.m. in Parts A or B; at11:30a.m. in Parts C or D; or at 2:15 p.m. in Parts E or F." It's acceptable in lists to use two or more semicolons in the same sentence.[49]

Use semicolons to replace commas and coordinating conjunctions ("and," "but", "for", "nor", "or", "yet"). Example (replacing "but"): "The respondent didn't agree with paragraph seven of the stipulation; he agreed with everything else." Example (replacing "or"): "Arrive at the courthouse by 9:30 a.m.; your case will be dismissed at 10:30 a.m."

The first letter after a semicolon should be lowercased, unless the word is a proper noun, e.g. a name.

Examples: "The legal representations for the defendant were Lawyer Akpofure of Queens, Lagos; Lawyer Bassa of DF Legal, Lagos; Lawyer Kwame of ODLA, Kumasi."

String citations should be separated with semi colon, not comma.

Example of academic reference: Wayne Schiess, *Writing for the Legal Audience,* 2003; Richard A. Posner, Judicial Opinions and Appellate Advocacy in Federal Courts–One Judge' s Views (2013) 51 *Duq. L. Rev.* 3 Mark E. Steiner, Without Precedent: Footnotes in Judicial Opinions (1999) 12 *App. Advoc.* 3; Linda H. Edwards, *Legal Writing: Process, Analysis and Organization,* 5th 2010.

Example of case reference: "*Ezeafulukwe* v. *John Holt* (1996) 2 NWLR (pt. 432) 511;

Ogida v. *Oliha* (1986) 1 NWLR (pt. 19) 786; *Ivienagbor* v. *Bazuaye* (1999) 9 NWLR (pt. 620) 552."

Semicolon should be used after and outside parentheses.

Example: "Manchester United lost the match (their third loss in 2 months); this season the player will get no match bonus."

When a semicolon follows an abbreviation with a period it is acceptable to put a semicolon after the period.

---

[49] Lebovits, above n. 39 @ 56.

Example: "The witness testified that in 2000 he received his B.A.; he graduated from KNUST Kumasi."

Semicolons always go outside the quotation mark.

Example: The judge told the defendant, "I want to make sure you never get out of jail"; thus, he sentenced the defendant to life without parole."

One space should be put after a semi-colon.

Parentheses

Parentheses are used in legal writing to direct readers to additional and slightly different information. They also set off explanations, interruptions, or phrases that obscure the main text.

Example: "Settle this case (trust me!)."

They are also used to introduce abbreviations and acronyms.

Example: "The Issue, Rule, Application and Conclusion organizational scheme (IRAC)."

Parentheses should be properly enclosed. Unenclosed parentheses are difficult to read.

Incorrect example: "1)."

Correct example:"(1)."

If the parentheses appear at the end of a sentence, punctuate after the final parenthesis. If the parentheses contain an independent clause, punctuate inside the final parenthesis.

Example of parentheses at the end of a sentence: "Lawyers must read carefully (and write carefully)."

Example of an independent clause inside parentheses: "Lawyers must read carefully. (They must also write carefully.)"

Use double parentheses in a sentence or sentence citation.

Correct example: "(*Group Danone* v. *Voltic Nig Ltd* [2008] 3-4 SC 32 (citing *Military Governor, Lagos State* v. *Ojukwu* (1986) (pt. 18) 621; (1986) All N.L.R 233))."

Parentheses de-emphasize. To emphasize, use "em" dashes ("-").[50]

Bracket

If a quotation contains a factual, spelling, or usage error, the legal writer should use "[sic]," meaning "thus," after the error. However, if the context makes it clear that the mistake was in the original, "[sic]" should not be added to the sentence. Correct example: "The defendant counsel subjected [sic] to the exhibit being admitted in evidence." In this case it is clear that the author meant to write

[50]Ibid. @ 57.

"objected," not "subjected," so "[sic] is used to give the reader a correct understanding of the document.

It is important to note that "[sic]"should be used sparingly, because its overuse could give a veiled impression that the writer is insulting or embarrassing the original quotation's author. It may therefore be proper to use brackets to correct the quotation rather than "[sic]."

Such brackets used in a quotation thus show alterations or additions to a letter or letters in a word.

Examples: "Clearly" becomes "Clear[]." "Proof" becomes "Pro[ve]." "Clearly" becomes "[c]learly". "Clerly" becomes "Cle[a]rly."

Consider the following original text in a judicial opinion: "For the above-mentioned reasons, the court finds that Defendant has no proof to substantiate her affirmative defence."

Alteration example (end of a word): The court determined that Defendant did not "pro[ve] . . . her affirmative defence."

Alteration example (capitalizing): The court made the following finding: "[T] he court finds that Defendant has no proof to substantiate her affirmative defence." Addition and alteration example: "[T]he court f[ou]nd[] that Defendant ha[d] no [documentary or testimonial] proof to substantiate her affirmative defence."

The lawyer should never add within quotation marks long bracketed text after a quotation.

Incorrect example: The court found that Defendant failed "to substantiate her affirmative defence [by a preponderance of the credible evidence]."

A space should be added between parentheses and brackets.

Example of spacing between parentheses: "*Group Danone* v. *Voltic Nig Ltd* [2008] 3-4 SC 32 (finding that challenging an order of court by appeal is not contempt)."

Example of spacing between a parentheses and a bracket: "Lucie E. White, Subordination, Rhetorical Survival Skills and Sunday Shoes: Notes on the Hearing of Mrs. G (1990) 38 *Buffalo L. Rev.* 1 (hereinafter referred to as "Sunday Shoes.")"

Example of spacing between two brackets: "(*Group Danone* v. *Voltic Nig Ltd* [2008] 3-4 SC 32 [finding that challenging an order of court by appeal is not contempt])."

Comma

The book, *Element of Style,* contains useful reading on how to use commas.[51] In a series of three or more terms with a single conjunction, comma should be used after each term except the last.

Good examples: "red, white, and blue." "He opened the letter, read it, and made a note of its contents." This comma is often referred to as the "serial" comma.

However, in describing the names of business firms the last comma is usually omitted.

Good example: "Finpong, Dafe and Company" or "Kwasi, Nkoyo & Tiwwa"

The legal writer is advised to enclose parenthetic expressions between commas. Application of the rule is sometimes difficult to apply because it is frequently hard to decide whether a single word, such as "however," or a brief phrase is or is not parenthetic. If the interruption to the flow of the sentence is but slight, the commas may be safely omitted. But whether the interruption is slight or considerable, the writer must never omit one comma and leave the other.[52]

Incorrect example: "My brother you will be pleased to hear, is now in perfect health."

Correct example: "My brother, you will be pleased to hear, is now in perfect health."

Dates usually contain parenthetic words or figures. They should be punctuated with commas correctly.

Good example: "February to September, 2000", "April 1, 2000", "Wednesday, November 1, 2000."

Note that it is customary to omit the comma in "1 April 2000"

The last form is an excellent way to write a date; the figures are separated by a word and are, for that reason, quickly grasped.

The abbreviations "etc.", "i.e." and "e.g." the abbreviations for academic degrees, and titles that follow a name are parenthetic and should be punctuated with commas accordingly.

Good examples: "Letters, packages, etc., should be received here.""Remi Jacobs, Ph.D., presides."

No comma, however, should separate a noun from a restrictive term of identification. Although "Junior," with its abbreviation "Jr.," has commonly been regarded as parenthetic, logic suggests that it is, in fact, restrictive and therefore not in need of a comma.[53]

---

[51] William Strunk, Jr. & E.B. White, *The Element of Style,* 4th ed. @ 11-16, particularly rule 1.4 & 1.5.
[52]Ibid. @ 12.
[53]Ibid. @ 13. See also, detail rule on the use of commas in rule 1.3-1.5 in *Element of Style.*

Conclusion

There is no question about it that punctuation rules can be technical and annoying to follow in some cases. But we cannot run away from the fact that grammar and punctuation are rhetorical avenues that lead to or away from communication and persuasion. Much as the lawyer must give attention to learning how to write well, she must also endeavour to master rules of grammar and punctuation because they are part of fundamental abilities that any legal writer is expected to possess. There is no better time than now for lawyers to devote attention to the technical aspects of clear writing, which advances communication and persuasion. Honing the skill can be useful in equipping the legal writer to become quicker drafters, able to adopt and implement a persuasive yet personal writing style to a variety of audiences and occasions. Continuing legal education courses in this area would transform many legal writers to writers who write legal document with requisite clarity through grammar and standard punctuation.

PART IV

Chapter 15

Case Theory

Introduction

The typical life of a life is busy. Lawyers are busy doing transactions, crafting documents for clients and defending cases in court. So, for them developing compelling stories for judges is a staple diet. It is simple. But by no means is it easy. Typically when trial lawyers are asked about their case theory before a trial, they give no conscious thought to it. They simple tell you 'we just got a case, or we have to win this case or we're working hard to win this case,' and the like. They hardly think of a case theory as important strategy in litigation. This isn't surprising. Legal education and even every practice do not teach the lawyer the necessity to develop theories of litigation as strategy for persuasion. The only strategy legal education gives the mint lawyer is some dose of adjectival law in the form of evidence and procedure law. The legal academy gives little or no attention to techniques and strategies for effective persuasion. So, law students do not cross the fact-law divide until after graduation. For example, typical evidence law teaches little about case theory because it narrowly skewed to focus on the assumption that facts leap from the testimony of witnesses and exhibits tendered in hearing, and that should be sufficient to teach strategy.[1]

The case theory deficiency is made more in practice. If anything, the mere mention of "theory" is annoying to practice lawyers who generally deride theory as opposed to the emphasis on "practice" and the "concrete" – considered the real business of lawyering. The practising bar and judiciary is largely contemptuous of theory.[2]This, no doubt, is mistaken thinking because theory is just another name for thinking, for deciding and appropriate argument.[3]And case theory actually lies

---

[1] Scott W. Howe, Untangling Competing Conception of Evidence (1997) 30 *Loy. L.A. Rev.* 1230.

[2] See C. Veljanovski, comment that "the English legal fraternity is wary of theory, contemptuous of experts and academics, and reluctant to accept the idea that other disciplines have something valuable to say about law;" and P.S. Atiyah – "Most English judges are emphatically neither intellectuals nor theorists; few are ever given to doubting their own first principles, at least in public, and most are deeply sceptical of the value of theory. . . Very few have more than the faintest glimmering of the vast jurisprudential literature concerning the nature of the judicial process. Most would pride themselves on being pragmatists, not theorists."

[3]Ruthann Robson, *Lesbian (Out)law: Survival Under the Rule of Law*, 1992 @ 15 ("The most important criticism of theory, it seems to me, is that it is useless. And theory can be useless: meditation at its

in the heart of lawyering, especially the techniques and strategies of effective persuasion.[4]

Case theory is the common theme projected in a case used to develop its narrative. It is useful for all trials, whether the lawyer is conducting a dry patent case or scandalous white-collar case. All must be built consciously around a strong narrative. It is what all great lawyers do. Unfortunately, many lawyers either skip the step or procrastinate on it and wait too long to full develop it.[5]It is a concept associate with storytelling and client narrative voice in the lawyering process.[6]Case theory's heighten importance is made manifest by the way human value stories. We are natural storytellers. Everything – faith, science, love and many more – all need stories for people to find them plausible. For example, even in the litigation process, lawyers can readily see that without a story no one will side with a case.

This chapter is about case theory, its implications for incorporating it in the lawyering process and essentially how it activates effective persuasion.[7]

What is case theory?

Case theory plays a prominent role in trials. It provides the framework for trial preparation and ultimately for trial.[8] Despite its importance, case theory isn't taken serious by many lawyers. They think it is all about case planning, strategy

---

most abstract and inapplicable. Yet theory is also just another name for thinking, for deciding, for arguing and examining one's own beliefs and principles as well as the beliefs and principles we have been taught. Theorizing is something we all do.").

[4] See Binny Miller, Give Them Back Their Lives: Recognizing Client Narrative in Case Theory (1994-1995) 93 *Mich. L. Rev.* 485 @ 487 ("Despite the view of many lawyers that case theory is central to the task of lawyering, and despite its prominence in highly publicized trials, most account of lawyering do not explore the richness of case theory.")

[5]*A2L Storytelling for Litigators: Building a Great Narrative for Judges and Juries*, 3rd ed. 2014 @ 19.

[6] See for example, Gerald P. Lopez, *Rebellious Lawyering: One Chicano Vision of Progressive Law Practice*, 1992; William Twining, Taking Facts Seriously- Again (2005) 55 *J. Leg. Educ.* 360 (an article that posits that storytelling plays a significant role in legal discourse and lawyering - in investigation, mediation, negotiation, appellate advocacy, and sentencing); Symposium, Lawyers As Storytellers and Storytellers As Lawyers: An Interdisciplinary Symposium Exploring the Use of Storytelling in the Practice of Law (1994) 18 *Vt. L. Rev.* 565; Kim L. Scheppele, Forward: Telling Stories (1989) 87 *Mich. L. Rev.* 2073; See William Twining, Taking Facts Seriously (1984) 34 *J. Leg. Educ.* 22.

[7] See especially, Lucie E. White, Subordination, Rhetorical Survival Skills and Sunday Shoes: Notes on the Hearing of Mrs. G (1990) 38 *Buffalo L. Rev.* 1 (hereinafter referred to as "Sunday Shoes") (an article that explores case theory by telling the deep emotional story of enforced silence , rhetorical survival of a poor woman engaged in administrative hearing at a welfare office). See also Robert M. Bastrees& Joseph D. Harbaugh, *Interviewing, Counselling and Negotiating: Skills for Effective Representation,* 1990 (a book illustrating that case theory applies to trial and non-trial lawyering); Clark D. Cunningham, Lawyer as Translator Representation as Text: Towards an Ethnography of Legal Discourse (1992) 77 *Cornell L. Rev.* 1298.

[8] Gary Bellow & Bea Moulton, *The Lawyering Process: Materials for Clinical Instruction in Advocacy,* 1978.

and analysis, without exploring the idea or its nuances in detail.[9] Case theory is an imprecise word of art, challenging to define but less difficult to explain, especially its function.

Traditionally, case theory is "the basic underlying idea that explains not only the legal theory and factual background, but also ties as much of the evidence as possible into a coherent and credible whole"[10] or put in another way it is "a view of how facts, law and circumstances can be put together to produce the outcome you and your client seek."[11]It is therefore not simply a statement of the applicable law or the facts supporting its legal interpretation. It is more. It is in fact, the anchor of the case – the basic concept around which everything about the case rest and revolves. Once it is consciously chosen, it serves as the centrepiece for all strategic and tactical decisions in the case. It is primarily incorporated and shapes the pleadings and any other application or process, such as those for discoveries, pre-trial, motions and the like. And even when trial begins, it shapes examination of witnesses and address by counsel.[12] The theory should be explicitly stated in the opening statement and reiterated in the closing argument.[13] In effect, a trial becomes a contest between competing theories of the case – that of the plaintiff and the defendant.[14]

Some scholars divide the universe of case theory into two categories: the affirmative theory and the rebuttal theory.[15] This is to be expected of legal controversy. It often involves adversaries at law, one affirming while the other rebuts. The affirming party states her theory of what happened, while the rebuttal theory responds to the version by probing weakness of the affirmative version but

---

[9] See Oputa, Trial Lawyer, Niki Tobi, all making tangential reference to case theory, treating it as it as a piece of case planning and strategy without exploring its deep roots.

[10] James W. McElhaney, *Trial Notebook*, 3rd ed. 1994 @ 78, cited in Miller, above n. 4 @ 492 ft. nt. 38.

[11] Bellow & Moulton, above n. 8 @ 305.

[12] Miller, above n. 4 @ 495 ("Case theory remains an elusive concept, beyond the seemingly simple statement that case theory is the legal and factual framework for organizing and presenting a case. Lawyers often mistake case theory for narrow tactical decisions, and this confusion is compounded by the use of other terms that closely approximate the idea of case theory but are not identical. While the term theory of the case and theme are sometimes used interchangeably, they seem to mean different things. Theory implies a linear, rational concept that drives the fact finder inexorably to a favourable result, theme, while geared to the same end, instead suggest a potent mixture of facts and emotion."). But cf. A2L, above n. 5 @ 57 where case theory is equated with the theme of the case ("An authority on jury persuasion says the first three or four sentences, the first 30 seconds, are what will "hook" the jury and grab its attention. You need to press your theme, your theory of the case, and your most important facts. That's what belongs in the hook and is critical to persuasion.").

[13] Marilyn J. Berger, John B. Mitchell & Ronald H. Clark, *Pretrial Advocacy: Planning, Analysis and Strategy*, 5th ed. Aspen Casebook, 2015 @ 33.

[14] Miller, above n. 4 @ 495.

[15] Marilyn J. Berger, et al, above n. 13 @ 17-51; David A Binder & Paul Bergman, *Fact Investigation: From Hypothesis to Proof*, 1984 @ 162.

need not offer an independent version of the event.[16] The defendant may however choose to offer affirmative or rebuttal stories, or both. For example, in an assault case, the State asserting affirmative theory would present evidence that the defendant stabs the victim. In response, the defendant could assert the affirmative defence that she is not guilty by reason of provocation or insanity, or present a rebuttal theory that attacks the credibility of the evidence.

There are two strands to case theory: the legal theory and the factual theory. The legal theory is the legal framework developed by the lawyer for interpretation, analysis and expansion of legal rules and standards.[17] On the other hand, the factual theory is the party's story justifying why relief ought to be granted under the legal theory.

Case theory or the theory of the case is the "explanatory statement linking the case to the client's experience of the world. It serves as the lens for shaping reality, in the light of the law, to explain the facts, relationships, and circumstances of the client and other parties in the way that can best achieve the client's goals. The relevant reality combines the perspectives of the lawyer and the client with an eye toward the ultimate audience-the trier of facts."[18] Case theory provides the framework for trial preparation and ultimately the trial. It generally consists of two separate theories, a legal theory and a factual theory. The former is the 'legal framework developed by the lawyer from interpretation, analysis, and expansion of legal rules and standards,' while the latter is 'the party's story justifying relief under the legal theory.'[19]

This traditional understanding of case theory is coming under criticism by lawyers who consider it too simplistic and atomistic, in that it "ignores context and misconceives the power of important facts – especially the client's life facts."[20]

---

[16] See rules on proof for criminal and civil cases, sections 134-136 of the Evidence Act.

[17] Marilyn J. Berger, et al, above n. 13

[18] Miller, above n. 17 @ 487.

[19] Marilyn J. Berger, et al, above n. 13. The factual theory often contains three main components: (i) explaining the party's version of the facts, (ii) the unfavourable facts, (iii) and the disputed facts. It is also to be measured against its sufficiency and in terms of how well it responds to the likely theory of the opponent. See Miller, above n. 4 @ 492-493.

[20] Miller, above n. 4 @ 498-499 (the writer for example states that the omission of the client's life realities renders the traditional concept of case theory a closed universe for critical lawyering – an unfortunate restriction that critical lawyering picks up). For other basis for criticizing the traditional conception of case theory, see Miller, above n. 4 @ 500-502. For some articles discussing creating reality through the lens of the client, see Miller, above n. 4; White, above n. 7; Jessica A. Rose, Rebellious or Regnant: Police Brutality Lawyering In New York City (2000) 28 *Fordham Urban L.J.* 619 (an article that encourages progressive lawyers of New York City to adopt a more rebellious form of practice to combat police brutality while empowering the client and community); Patricia J. Williams, *The Alchemy of Race and Rights*, 1991 (literary and legal theory); Kathryn Abrams, Hearing the Call of Stories (1991) 79 *Cal. L. Rev.* 971 (feminist theory); Clark D. Cunningham, above n. 7 @ 1331(ethnography discourse explaining the dynamic relationship

Traditionalists are criticized for expressing too much objectivity about facts thereby shutting away the useful insight client's life realities can infuse in the construction of knowledge, even ignoring the possibility that clients could have other noble goals for case theory other than winning litigation.[21] Unquestionably, tradition understanding of case theory lays out the contours and essential ingredients of case theory, but omits to account for the identity and reality of the client whose voice should not be muted in the lawyering process. Infusing client-centred lawyering into the process advances a robust thinking of case theory.[22]

In summary it can be said that case for practical purposes is the theory that explains and incorporates into "what happened" and "what will happen," the "meaning of what happened."[23]

Illustration of case theory

Kim Lane Schepple gives us a classic example of how to understand case theory from the imaginary story.[24] It is the story of Elmer Davis. It tells what is case

---

between knowledge and experience); Derrick Bell, *And We Are Not Saved*, 1987 (for critical race theory perspective); Katherine Bartlett, Feminist Legal Method (1990) 103 *Harv. L. Rev.* 829 (explaining the dynamic relationship between experience and knowledge in feminist epistemology).

[21] For how stories create facts fault-lines in perception, see Festus Emiri, Legal Storytelling and Perception (2004) 1 *Annual of Nigeria Law* 131 (an article that agues that just as there is legal indeterminacy, there is also facts indeterminacy; and so it is mistaken to think that facts are objective out there in the world, not susceptible to perceptive fault line). That facts when they arise in the context of disputes can be indeterminate in an epistemological (not ontological) sense, see Ernst Cassirer, (trans. Ralph Manheim) *Philosophy of Symbolic Forms,* 1953; Steven L. Winter, The Cognitive Dimension of the *Agon* Between Legal Power and Narrative Meaning (1989) 87 *Mich. L. Rev.* 2225; Steven L. Winter, Transcendental Nonsense, Metaphoric Reasoning, the Cognitive Stakes for Law (1989) *U. Pa. L. Rev.* 1105.

[22] Client-centred lawyering is generally rooted in the principle of client's autonomy and the idea that the client is in a better position than the lawyer to evaluate alternatives and consequences. See Miller, above n. 4 @ 503-506; and Id. @ 506-514 for professional responsibility standards negotiated in client-centred lawyering. the word "client" derives from the Latin verb "cluere," meaning "to be named, hear oneself named." In ancient Rome, persons under the patronage of patricians were called "clientem" because they were known by the name of their patron.' White therefore explains that because, even for the most enlightened modem day lawyers, "advocacy is a practice of speaking for [the client,]...the advocate...inevitably replays the drama of subordination in her own work. Lucie E. White, *Goldberg v. Kelly*on the Paradox of Lawyering for the Poor (1990) 56 *Brook L. Rev.* 861 – support for the autonomy hypothesis.

[23] Carl J. Hosticka, We Don't Care About What Happened, We Only Care About What Is Going To Happen: Lawyer-Client Negotiation of Reality (1979) 26 *Soc. Probs.* 599. See Cunningham, above n. 7 (an article that uses the metaphor of lawyering as translation, positing that lawyers mute clients voices because they fail to recognize and implement the art and ethic of the good translator - a translator who shows conscious awareness of shifts in meaning and who collaborates with the speaker in managing these changes. It therefore suggests as remedy a methodology, drawn from anthropology and sociolinguistics to make lawyers aware of how meaning is changes when stories translated, a methodology, termed the ethnography of legal discourse. See also Festus Emiri & Ayuba Giwa, Metaphoric Thinking About Law As Language And Lawyering As Translation [] ESUT.

[24] Kim Lane Scheppele, Forward: Telling Stories (1989) 87 *Michigan L.Rev.*2073 (discussing "point of

theory, how stories can reveal perceptive fault-lines – are indeterminate, in what sense lawyers not just hearers but also tellers of stories, but importantly why lawyers must pay close attention to construct stories, clearly revealing that where a story start or end impacts on persuasion, how do all of these explicate case theory, and importantly, why does good lawyering demand conscious, intentional choices as to how to client's stories should be told.

Elmer Davis, is an African-American, who confesses to rape of a white woman in North Carolina in 1958. Let us focus attention on one particular area of interest - the voluntariness or otherwise of his confessional statement. The evidence goes like this:

Prosecutor (P): Who is in charge of overseeing the interrogation of Mr. Davis?

Witness (W): I was.

P: Is there a Department protocol for interrogating prisoners?

W: Yes.

P: Describe that protocol to the judge.

W: We limit interrogation to twice daily, once in the morning and once later in the day.

P: What procedure did you follow for the interrogation of Mr. Davis?

W: We followed the Departmental protocol. I typically interrogated Mr. Davis in the morning, and another officer questioned him later in the day.

P: Did the procedure vary?

W: No, we followed that procedure the entire time Mr. Davis was in custody, up until the time he confessed.

With evidence like this, can we identify the state's theory of the case? Certainly, it is constructed to tilt in favour of voluntariness of Mr. Davis confession. It is revealed in evidence that the Departmental protocol was followed, a policy in place against around-the-clock interrogation. The prosecution kept faith with (what seemed) good police practice, which should ordinarily satisfy the judge.

But this is only side of the coin. Let us see how the defence can also construct its theory of the client's case to raise presumption of involuntariness.

---

viewlessness" The story describes two cases that ended up in the U.S. Supreme Court, one involving the rape of a woman, the other involving the allegedly coerced confession of a black man. She contrasts the appellate court decisions in both cases with the Supreme Court opinions, illustrating points about language and framing as important tools of persuasive storytelling.). The story originally appeared in Kim Lane Scheppele's forward to the Michigan Law Symposium on Storytelling. See (1989) *Mich. L. Rev.* For purposes of this paper we would adopt the scenario played out of the story by Carolyn Grose. See Carolyn Grose, in Storytelling Across the Curriculum (2010) *7 J. Asso. Legal Writing Directors* 37 @ 39.

Defence Attorney (DA): Mr. Davis, how long were you in jail before you gave the statement to the police?

Defendant (D): Sixteen days.

DA: Please describe the cell where you were being held?

D: It was a small cell in the back of the jail, with a bed and a chair. There was a little window out into the jail yard.

DA: Was there a clock in the cell?

D: No.

DA: Did you have a wristwatch?

D: No, they took my watch away from me when they put me in jail.

DA: During the sixteen days, how often did the police question you?

D: Pretty much all the time.

DA: When you say "pretty much all the time," what do you mean?

D: After I woke up in the morning, one of them would come and start asking me questions. That would go on all morning and then he'd leave. Then after a little while another one would come in and start up all over again.

DA: Was it light out while you were being questioned?

D: Sometimes it was.

DA: And was it ever dark out while you were being questioned?

D: Sure it was.

DA: How long did the questioning go on?

D: Every single day until they got me to sign this statement.

The client's theory of the case is radically different from the state's theory. It is all about the involuntariness of the confessional statement. Yes, the defendant was of the considered view that the interrogation was persistent, constant harassment, especially from the perspective that he didn't know what time it was and the questioning took place while it was light and while it was dark.

Thinking about the case theories (affirmative and rebuttal) constructed reveals that the two stories are true constructed of the facts, but from different viewpoints. It is true that the prosecution adhered to its protocol on questioning prisoners-twice a day between 7.30 a.m. and 11.30 p.m. Yes, the prosecution followed the protocol. However, remembering that the defendant's only sense of time was based on the changing light outside his window. It is equally true that from the defendant's sense of time based on the changing light from the little window, the interrogation was sporadic. While the prosecution can argue that the circumstances were not sufficient to constitute coerced confession, the defence could argue that the repeated nature of the interrogation created a kind of duress that should vitiate the confession.

One thing the story teaches us is to encourage us to learn first-hand how the lawyer is a constructor of stories and eventual legal reality, and that reality is not fixed, as though cast in steel. What happened is nothing near objective. What position gets vindicated as fact may just turn out to be the story adopted by the decision-maker. We can thus begin to appreciate experimenting with choices about how to use facts, frame examination of witnesses, how to structure facts, choose where a story should start and end, what evidence to highlight and the like in build our theory of the case.

The fact about voluntariness is therefore not an objective reality out there for capture. Both the prosecution and the defendant sure have their different case theories all stepped in facts that are true. It is expected that the prosecution will be happy to sustain the charge by showing the voluntariness of the defendant's confessional statement, a thing the defendant would challenge.

Persuasion and case theory

Good lawyering must persuade. A traditional model of legal argumentation based on formal or informal models of logic (though constituting the fulcrum of reasoning in law) has proved inadequate to fully describe persuasiveness of legal argumentation.[25] Ancient rhetoricians unpacked the goal of persuasion as following three paths: the concept of *logos*, *pathos*, and *ethos*.[26] *Logos* (persuasion

---

[25] Classical rhetoric reputed to begin in the fifth century B.C.E. continued for nearly 1,000 years of the Greco-Roman history. It started with scholars like Socrates, followed by Plato, Aristotle, Cicero and Quintilian. See Aristotle, *The Rhetoric* (trans. W. Rhys Roberts, 1965) available at htpp://www.iastate.edu/honey1/Rhetoric/ (accessed Sep, 2016); Marcus Tullius Cicero, *De Inventione* (trans. H.M. Hubbell, 1949); Marcus Tullius Cicero, *De Oratore* (trans. E.W. Sutton, 1942); Marcus Fabius Quintilian, *Institutio Oratoria* (H.E. Butler, 1954). See Michael Frost, Introduction to Classical Rhetoric: A Lost Heritage (1999) 8 *S. Cal. Interdisc. L.J.* 613 (tracing the history of rhetoric and argumentation to Corax of Syracuse). See also, Robert Burns, *A Theory of the Trial*, Princeton Univ. Press, 1999; Walter R. Fisher, *Human Communication as Narrative: Towards a Philosophy of Reason, Value, and Action*, U.S.C. 1989; Bernard Jackson, *Law, Fact and Narrative Coherence*, Deborah Charles Pub., 1988.

[26] Michael R. Smith, *Advanced Legal Writing: Theories and Strategies in Persuasive Writing*, 3rd ed. Aspen Law & Bus., 2013 @ 22; Aristotle, *On Rhetoric* (transl. George A. Kennedy, Oxford Univ. Press, 1991); George A. Kennedy, *A New History of Classical Rhetoric*, Princeton Univ. Press, 1998; Stephen Toulmin, *The Use of Argument*, Cambridge Univ. Press, 1958. For detail discussion on a theory of persuasion, see J. Christopher Rideout, Storytelling, Narrative Rationality, and Legal Persuasion (2008) 14 *J. Legal Writing Inst.* 53 (in answer to the question 'what is it about narratives that make them persuasive in the law,' he stated that (1) narratives are innate ways of understanding and structuring human experience; this makes them inherently persuasive; (2) narrative models go beyond models of persuasion based on formal or informal logic, to encompass 'narrative rationality; ' (3) narratives embody several properties that are psychologically persuasive: (a) coherence (a formal property); correspondence (a formal property); (c) fidelity (a substantive property) Id at 55. See also the interesting read, W. Lance Bennett & Martha S. Feldman, *Reconstructing Reality in the Courtroom: Justice and Judgment in American Culture*, Rutgers Univ. Press, 1981 (the social science researchers states that American criminal trial is organized around storytelling).

accompanied through logical reasoning embodied in the content of the communication) is the process of persuading using substance and logical argument, such as statute law, case-law and policy. *Pathos* (persuasion accomplished through the emotional response of the audience to the communication) on the other hand is persuasion through emotive argument. *Ethos* (persuasion accomplished through the perceived character or reputation of the speaker) refers to establishing and maintaining credibility in the eyes of the audience by showing intelligence, character and good will.[27] The three paths are often depicted as the "rhetorical triangle:" the three paths leading into one another.

Stories advance case-theory. This is expected because the connection between storytelling, narrative, communication, understanding and experience is an old one. Nothing better reveals this than the connection between narrative and knowledge. Dictionary meaning of narrative associates it with the process of telling a story. Etymological narrative derives from two Latin words, *narrare* and *gnarus. Narrare* means 'to tell,' and *gnarus* means 'to have knowledge or experience.'[28] Clearly therefore, narrative constitute a basic form by which we communicate social reality or experience to others with possible view that they acquire insight or knowledge about the object or subject of the story. Deepening the connection, it has been suggested that both Latin words *narrare* and *gnarus* came to the Romans from the Indo-European word *gnd* (to know), a word which is the root of both the Greek *gignoskein* and the Latin *cognoscere*, which yield the English words 'know' and 'cognition.'[29] Therefore, if the essence of lawyering is captured at a level of generality in the descriptiveness of 'representation' as in the case of a lawyer taking stand to present her client's case and interest in court, tribunal, or in negotiating on behalf of a client, then narrative being the means by which it is demonstrated to others would certainly be primary in the legal process. That being so, stories are the very foundation that gives voices to the often voiceless, mute clients, grounding better understanding of their case theory.

Since case theory describes how the lawyer would want the trier of facts to view the case, the theory must be based on the equities that appeal to the trier's sense of what constitutes fair or right. Creating the felt connection would be easier if the theory is based on strong facts and inferences, which can be fairly drawn by ordinary people from the facts presented. Since most person can intuitively reason

---

[27]Smith, above n. 26.

[28]*Oxford Latin Dictionary* 768, 1155 (P. Glare ed. 1985) cited in Steven L. Winter, The Cognitive Dimension of the *Agon*: Between Legal Power and Narrative Meaning (1989) 87 *Mich. L. Rev.* 2223 @ 2230, n. 18.

[29]Winter, above, n. 23.

from cause to effect, a theory based on such premise is like to be persuasive to the trier. It presents a scenario that is clear, understandable without more.

A case theory based on easy to imagine scenario by the trier, not one needing her to stretch imagination advances persuasion. It is therefore important for the facts to be grounded in common sense experience, especially of the trier.[30] This can be challenging for the lawyer, especially for those who practice poverty law or represent non-mainstream litigants. From the very way judges are selected, they are likely to belong to the middle-class, conservative segment of society. Therefore, drawing a felt connection between their experience and those from a different economic and social background can pose challenge. But skilled lawyers recognize that it is doable, by employing the narrative style of advocacy, paying attention to strategies of persuasion and the use of critical lawyering skills.[31]

The lawyer can also advance the persuasiveness of the chosen case theory if it builds on facts not subject to much, or any dispute. Case theory is made more compelling to believe if it is not inconsistent with incontestable facts. In addition, whatever case theory is chosen, it must be good enough to explain away unfavourable facts. This is material because it is rare to find a case where all the facts just sit in support of the client. So, if there are unfavourable facts, as there are bound to be, the theory must explain them their existence and show why they do should not trump over the client's story.

---

[30] On imagination see, James Boyd White, *Legal Imagination*, Boston: Little, Brown, 1973 ("Think of or read a law case, imagine the characters freed from the page and live in a storyland, and ask what their story would be like. You are familiar for example, with the ubiquitous personage of the law of torts, the Reasonable Man, and could write a story about him, I suppose: A Day in the Life of the Reasonable Man. ... If you cannot imagine that a novel built around characters defined in this way would have any interest for you, how can legal talk about such characters, the same events, have any interest?")

[31] For narrative strategies in creating felt connection, see Ruth A. Robbins, An Introduction to Applied Storytelling and to this Symposium (2008) 14 *J. Legal Writing Institute* 3; Kim Lane Scheppele, Forward: Telling Stories (1989) 87 *Michigan L.Rev.*2073; Steven L. Winter, The Cognitive Dimension of the *Agon*: Between Legal Power and Narrative Meaning (1989) 87 *Mich. L. Rev.* 2223. For persuasion strategies employing logos, pathos and ethos see, Michael R. Smith, *Advanced Legal Writing: Theories and Strategies in Persuasive Writing,* 3rd ed. Aspen Law & Bus. 2013; Aristotle, *On Rhetoric* (transl. George A. Kennedy, Oxford Univ. Press, 1991); George A. Kennedy, *A New History of Classical Rhetoric,* Princeton Univ. Press, 1998; Stephen Toulmin, *The Use of Argument,* Cambridge Univ. Press, 1958; Linda Levine & Kurt M. Saunders, Thinking Like a Rhetor (1993) 43 *J. Legal Educ.* 108; Michael Frost, Ethos, Pathos and Legal Audience (1994) 99 *Dick L. Rev.* 85; Michael Frost, Justice Scalia's Rhetoric of Dissent: A Greco-Roman Analysis of Scalia's Advocacy in the VMI Case (2002) 91 *KY. L.J.* 167. For reading on critical lawyering, see above n. 2. See also, Anthony V. Alfieri, The Antinomies of Poverty Law and a Theory of Dialogic Empowerment (1987-88) 16 *N.Y.U. Rev. L & Soc. Change* 659; Anthony V. Alfieri, Speak Out of Turn: The Story of Josephine V (1991) 4 *Geo. J. Legal Ethics* 619. Clark D. Cunningham, Lawyer as Translator Representation as Text: Towards an Ethnography of Legal Discourse (1992) 77 *Cornell L. Rev.* 1298; Lucie E. White, *Goldberg v Kelly* on the Paradox of Lawyering for the Poor (1990) 56 *Brook. L. Rev.*

Two visuals on case theory

How lawyers can learn to develop case theory

Developing skills of consciously crafting case theory is important for lawyering. Ability to do so enables the lawyer to convert the facts in dispute into legal problems soluble in the client's favour. The skill can be honed if the lawyer recognizes that lawyers are not just hearing of stories – what happened, but is also a creator of stories – particularly in the ability to shape reality. Learning by studying Lucie White's "Sunday Shoes" piece and Binny Miller's "Give Them Back Their Lives" can be useful in developing the skill.[32]

The lawyer must learn to think about the practice of law as a practice of storytelling, which gives the lawyer an opportunity to look behind and between and over and under the black letter rules that comprise "the law". It is in those interstices that the lawyer will find the facts, language, structure and ideas that go well beyond the holding of judicial opinion or the mandate of a statute – things not overt to the senses without deep reflection.[33] It is only by this consciousness that the lawyer comes to realize through the storytelling lens not only "how law is found but how it is made.

[32] See Miller above n. 4; White, above n. 7; Ruggero J. Aldisert, *Winning on Appeal: Better Briefs and Oral Argument,* 2nd ed. Natl. Inst. Tr. Advoc. 2003 @ 197 ("Visualize the whole before you begin. What overriding message is the document going to convey? What facts are essential to the argument? How does the argument take off from the facts? How do different arguments blend together? Better still, if it's a brief, visualize the way the judge's opinion should read if it goes your way.").

[33] Paul Gewirtz, Narrative and Rhetoric in the Law, in Peter Brooks & Paul Gewirtz eds. *Law's Stories: Narrative and Rhetoric in the Law,* Yale U. Press 1996 @ 2.

The process informs the lawyer that as a maker of legal arguments, she is on the driver's seat to decide what story to tell and how to tell it "guided by some vision of what matters and what will happen: the "what" and "how" of what happened. In arriving at the decision of the "what" - what matters and what will happen, the lawyer is obligated to figure out what story to tell and how to tell it. That invariably interrogates weighing three substantive factors – in fact, the same factors that make up the case theory: (i) the law, (ii) the facts, and (iii) the client's goals.[34]In addition, of course, the lawyer must consider contextual factors, e.g., the audience, the forum, the availability of resources, and the personalities of the client and other potential supporting or detracting characters in the story. The lawyer must also consider particular cultural norms and values in deciding among different stories and ways of telling them. And finally, the lawyer must consider factors personal to himself in determining what story to tell and how to tell it.[35]

Learning the skill brings a conscious realization that the full gamut of lawyering is underpinned in case theory. For example, when the lawyer drafts a statement of facts (statement of claim, defence or counter-claim), she does not simply record the known universe of "relevant" facts in an interesting way. Case theory consciousness tells the lawyer that there is no such thing as an absolutely neutral description of the facts. So right from when the client walks into the lawyer's office to tell what happened, she realizes that the fact-gathering process begins – legal research, anticipation of the other side's argument - and then the picking and choosing from the available facts to present a picture of what happened that most accurately reflects the lawyer's sense of what matters. And the other lawyers involved do exactly the same thing, with exactly the same pool of facts, but emphasizing different details, drawing different inferences, and thus drawing quite a different picture.[36]

This, however, is not the end of the crafting techniques for the lawyer. Having completed the selection of the "what" it is time for the lawyer to engage the "how". Case theory consciousness informs the lawyer that though the law define what is relevant – say as prescribed by rules of practice or statute like the Evidence Act, it cannot define how the relevant facts in a particular case, are to be

---

[34]Miller, above n. 4 @ 487.

[35] See for example, matters connected with professional responsibility. Jeanne M. Kaiser, When the Truth and the Story Collide: What Legal Writers Can Learn From the Experience of Non-Fiction Writers About the Limits of Legal Storytelling (2010) 16 *J. Legal Writing* 163 (an article that draws attention to the danger of a too-enthusiastic embrace of the power of storytelling capable of causing the profession to walk too close to the line between brief writing and fiction). See also Miller, above n .4 @ 506-514.

[36]Richard Delgado, Storytelling for Oppositionists and Others: A Plea for Narrative (1988) 87 *Mich. L. Rev.* 2411 @ 2421.

expressed.[37] It is up to the lawyer to figure out what words to use, with what emphasis. A lawyer's statement of facts thus reflects - by its inclusions and exclusions, the emphasis of its sentence construction, and the structures of its argumentation choices. This includes choices about the other technical elements of a story as well: when the story should begin and when it should end, how quickly or slowly the action should move, how fleshed out each character should be.

Thus, the statement of facts crafted by the skilled lawyer is not just a recipe for stringing together a set of hard facts, but is rather a bundle of construct and selection of "what" and "how" happened. The lawyer using skills of storytelling first construct the facts and then construct the stories by sorting through what is out there and figuring out both what to say and how to say it, based on her perspective about "what matters". The process is not a linear framework structure into which events are simply slotted. Instead it is a process where events (what happened) are organized into alternative narratives depending on perspective, circumstances, and interpretive frameworks. And those choices are governed by what the lawyer cares about. So, figuring out "what matters" is a complex and nuanced process. When she chooses what story to tell and how to tell it, she must work thoughtfully and responsibly to reconcile and balance various facets of "what matters".

Understanding storytelling as a way to craft the case theory is a way to understand persuasion. Using narrative theory in legal practice is therefore not a suggestion that lawyers do anything radically different, just that they harness what they're already doing in some systematic and intentional way.[38] So, as the lawyer listens to her clients to find out that something doesn't make sense, or she finds herself wondering about the absence or presence of a particular character, or she imagines how she might feel in a similar situation, narrative theory suggests that she should recognize those reactions as important clues. These clues will in turn help to guide on-going pursuit of the client's narrative and to work with the client to construct a story that will engage the decision maker's curiosity and compassion without triggering disbelief or dismissal.[39] The advice therefore is that

---

[37]Bernard Jackson, *Narrative Theories and Legal Discourse* in *Narrative in Culture: The Uses of Storytelling in the Sciences, Philosophy, and Literature,* 1994 @ 27. See also Grose, above n. 24 @ 45.

[38]Grose, above n. 24 @ 46.

[39] Ibid. ("This approach is distinct from letting a lawyer's own values and judgment guide the story construction process. Instead, narrative theory helps lawyers harness our natural curiosity and scepticism. Although imagination and common sense are valuable tools for listeners and storytellers, such tools need to be used carefully. If they are used with intention and awareness of the choices underlying story construction, then they will be used in ways that do not allow the lawyers' voice to dominate or overwhelm the client's and that do not lead to the making of law that

to hone the skill of crafting persuasive case theory, the lawyer must intentionally learn how to use the narrative theory to persuade the decision maker to act in a way the ultimate benefit of the client, or future clients. Yes, using narrative theory is a way to understand that lawyers are making these choices, and it helps us to make them intentionally, which in turn leads us to become better lawyers.[40]

Case theory and theme of the case

Some writers are of the view that both are distinct principles leading to effective persuasion.[41]While the controversy is neither here nor there, one thing stands out, critical lawyering or client-centred lawyering both have emotion at its heart. The rhetoric triangle accords a place for emotion in persuasion.[42] Cognitive psychology is replete with literature of about cognitive bias – the tendency to interpret new evidence as confirmation of one's existing beliefs or theories - and its place in decision-making. In fact, there appears to be substance in the thinking that decision-makers find few facts very interesting and important and they base their entire decisions on those few facts. Invariably, judges like other decision-makers tend to decide the outcome of a case after reading the statement of facts and thereafter in the first few minutes of the opening statement, then simply use the facts to fit their version of the case as reasoning in deliberation. In fact, there is a tendency for judges to closely listen long enough to confirm what they already believe. This is why the lawyer must recognize this fact and develop a theory of the case around the key facts onto which the decision-maker will tend to latch.[43]This is what makes it imperative for us to discuss how the theme of the case possible shades into the theory of the case and why and how it should not be conflated with the narrative and storytelling strategy and techniques.[44]

Unquestionably the theme of a case resembles the theory of the case. The term "theory" has been associated with a general scientifically acceptable general principle or body of principles offered to explain phenomena.[45]Since theory is another name for thinking as basis for examining beliefs and principles, then

---

the lawyer did not anticipate or intend through the adoption of misconstructed stories"). See also Miller, above n. 4 @ 503-506 (discussing client's autonomy)

[40] See chapter – on narrative and storytelling.

[41]Miller, above n. 4 @ 495. See also n. 12; Susan Kos- se & David Butle Ritchie, How Judges, Practitioners and Legal Writing Teachers Assess the Writing Skills of New Law Graduates: A Comparative Study (2003) 53 *J. Leg. Educ.* 80 @ 85 (a survey that found that "lack of focus" and "failure to develop overall theme or theory of case" were the two most common errors found in legal memo writing).

[42] See above n. 25 & 26.

[43]A2L, above n. 5 @ 7.

[44] See discussion in chapter – on opening statement (chapter 10), particularly section on case theme (chapter 15).

[45] Merriam Webster Dictionary @ .

transposed to lawyering as in formulating the theory of the case, it is the akin to the framework that ties the case, making it a believable story.[46] Both function to resonate a philosophy for understanding the case presented by the lawyer. In fact, reading through the interesting cases illustrating the case theory, particularly those by Miller and White, one comes off with an impression that the two are poles apart but pulling together.[47]This explains how it shades (even if it is not equivalent) with the theme of the case.

What is the theme of a case and how does it contribute to persuasiveness of the case presented? It is very easy for the lawyer to get so engrossed with the facts of a case and ignore building a convincing theme and story during litigation. That's understandable. Legal education only teaches the mint lawyer how to build a case around the law.[48] It hardly teaches persuasion. But the skilled lawyer knows that the essence of lawyering is persuasion of decision-makers. Recognizing the difficulty decision-makers could face dealing with mass of facts, sometimes complex in nature, the skilled lawyer strives to make the job of the judge easier by tying the disparate pieces of evidence to a theme or theory as explanatory basis for the human story told in court.[49] It is the theme that then focuses and keeps the decision-maker engaged and interested in the narrative evidence in court. Every skilled lawyer employs the-track procedure (law and persuasion track) in every trial – one for weaving the case facts around the controlling precedent, and the other, focusing on developing a convincing story that the decision-maker can instinctively relate to. Recognizing this strategy, the lawyer from the very beginning of a brief should immediately develop the case theme around the key facts of the case. In developing the story, she keeps in mind the theme that ties it together. It is the theme that then serves as the organizing principle around which the facts of the case is built. The goal of a theme therefore serves to give the decision-maker an organizing principle to fit the evidence into neatly.[50] It is important to keep close in mind that the theme of a case is different from the story of the case, though both are related.

A case theme can be thought of as a case's tag line, somewhat similar to corporate slogans like "the difference is clear" or "the ultimate driving machine." It is nothing but a shorthand version of the case designed to connect with the life

---

[46] See Robson, above n. 3.

[47] See Miller, above n. 4; White, above n. 7.

[48] A2L, above n. 5 @ 6-7 refers to this as the single track litigation strategy as the "law track" – one which focuses on identifying what the controlling precedent states and then using it as basis to tailor and build up the facts of the case around the precedent.

[49] A2L, above n. 5 @ 7 refers to this as the "persuasion track" – the building of a case to satisfy a jury in a "real life," non-legal sense. The skilled lawyer employs both the law and persuasion track in the litigation process.

[50]A2L, above n. 5 @ 55.

experiences of the trier or decision-maker. Many lawyers do not use either a theme or story in crafting statement of facts. We also have seen many cases where the litigators have a story but no theme; and others with a theme but no story. But the reality is that to be effective in persuasion, the lawyer must use both a theme and a story. Once a theme is chosen it must be emphasized in the opening statement and closing argument before the fact-finder. This is crucial because it is estimated that a number of decision-makers make up their mind just after reading the statement of facts and listening to the opening statement, thereafter merely confirming the bias as reasoned decision. Getting the right "theme-story combo" right is the sure path to being persuasive.[51]

We shall do a list of the fundamental differences between theme and stories. The differences are as follows:

Theme is attention getters, story is attention keepers: Think for once the corporate slogan like "the difference is clear" as an advert for a soft drink. It immediately gets the attention of the hearer. She thinks of the product as a rarity from the other competing brands in the market – a rarity attributed to its difference. So, it is what gets the audience to listen or pay attention to the advertisement. What follows after the slogan, likened to a story keeps the attention of the hearer. The same thing plays out in legal practice – whether in legal writing (memorandum and brief) or advocacy. The theme for example, gets the reader or decision-maker's attention, while the story (or content of the document as the case may be) sustains the interest to read on or hear more.

Theme provides reason for interest, story provide the emotional connection required to care: If a judge does not care about your case, she likely would not side with the lawyer and could well just be daydreaming even while making eye contact.

Theme explains, story motivates: Theme serves to tie together disparate facts with a label easy for the fact-finder to connect with, but it is the story that creates the necessary emotional connect with the document or advocacy. Yes, it is the felt connection of pathos in an argument.

Theme sounds like speaking as a lawyer, story sounds like speaking as a being human: theme is often a synthesis of reasoning on the facts to make out a unifying concept of explanation. It therefore comes out of what would resemble the product of "thinking like a lawyer." That is what makes appear as speaking as a lawyer. On the other hand, because a story is a narrative that connects with the emotions of the fact-finder, it comes out like the lawyer is speaking no longer as a professional, but as one who is also human.

---

[51]Ibid. @ 50. See chapter – on narrative and storytelling.

Theme provides a smidgen structure, story the broad framework: The essence of a theme is to provide the fact-finder a "spark" for thinking about the case. On the other hand, a story provides the trier a broad framework to reach a decision.

Theme primes, story finishes: A primer is either a small book for teaching children to read or a small introductory book on a subject or a short informative piece of writing.[52] Essentially with it does is primary in nature, leaving the finishing for a later date, method or device. A theme is like the primer. It introduces the case as being important enough to demand the adjudicating time of the trier. That is why skilled lawyers often use as persuasion tool for the opening statement; and fortifying the position in closing argument. The story is unlike it. Because it builds on the theme couched for the case, it is incorporated throughout the trial.

Judges will hardly mention the theme, but judges will mention the story and often adopt them as their own: Very few judges would mention the theme unifying the story of a case in their decision. On the other hand, they will mention the story told by the parties, especially if it is the version believed, even stating it as reason for their decision.

Theme contains no character, story contains character:[53] Stories are supposed to be interesting and to some degree entertaining. They are generally structured to have a beginning, a climax, and an ending. They have a theme, a setting, and fully developed characters.[54] Since an effective story provides the relationship between the facts and the characters – their motives or intention – for

---

[52] See Merriam Webster Dictionary @.

[53]An effective story provides relationships between the facts and the characters. It addresses the characters' motives or intentions. It puts this information into a context, a physical and psychological environment – the setting.

[54] For the structure of a story see Jerome Bruner, *Making Stories: Law, Literature, Life,* Harv. Univ. Press, 2002 @ 20; Anthony G. Amsterdam & Jerome S. Bruner, *Minding The Law,* Harv. Univ. Press, 2000 @ 133-134 (showing that stories are composed of the following elements: a steady state - that is, a state grounded in the legitimate ordinariness of things; the "trouble"—that is, something that happened to disrupt the "legitimate ordinariness of things; followed by efforts at redress, to cope or come to terms with the disruption; leading to an outcome or resolution; ending with a coda or moral - a retrospective evaluation of what it all might mean - which returns the audience from the "then-and-there" of the narrative to the "here-and-now of the telling."). See also, a similar plot of a story in Thomas M. Leitch, *What Stories Are: Narrative Theory and Interpretation,* Penn. St. U. Press 1986 @ 148. ; A2L above n. 5 @ 20 (describing that the structure of a story is like a drama, it states that a story is often split into five parts: "the introduction (also called exposition) is where characters are introduced, the scene is set and the plot is introduced; rising action is where the hero is revealed, the conflict is identified and our hero finds the solution to the conflict; the third act is the climax where our hero's situation is either clearly improved or worsened; falling action is where we see the conflict diminishing and our hero is now clearly winning or losing; the resolution or denouement provides a transition toward the end of our story. Morals are revealed, tension is released and a sense of relief is given to the listeners.").

the roles they play in the story, it is understandable why stories contain characters with understandable motive that the theme does not contain.

A theme highlights, story persuades: A story is told to persuade, but a theme is used to highlight the substratum of the story.

Theme offers something quickly relatable, story offers something more: Stories are usually narrative in form so provide details of what happened.

Theme don't really persuade, story does: Stories persuade because that is why they are told in the first place. A theme does not. It is merely foundational, to get the attention of the reader or audience.

Theme don't need visuals, but stories does: Since a theme merely highlight the substance of a case, it may not need supporting visuals, but stories sure do as it is geared to persuade.

How to use case theory to tell the case story

Since the case theory is basic philosophy around which the case rest and revolves, serving as the centrepiece for all strategic and tactical decisions in the case, let us see how it can used to persuade. We shall draw examples from transactional lawyering (inclusive of memorandum and transactional drafting, say conveyance, contracts, etc.) and general advocacy.

Use of case theory in transactional lawyering

Client-centred lawyering requires the lawyer to draft client's transactional documents that meet with their client's goals, reflecting their lives in a way that the client feels familiar and comfortable with. For example, if an elderly client of say 80 years enters a lawyer office desirous of making a "durable power of attorney for health care," the lawyer will take time out to listen to why the elderly considers one important. The discussion could reveal many of her fears and how she wants them cared for. Assuming, from the client's interview the lawyer can discern that the client is a "control freak" who wants her legal document to anticipate and possible resolve every conceivable scenario that may arise, the lawyer with case theory skills would quickly recognize that the document required must be detailed enough to give the client the outcome desired – control of many details. Such a document to specify treatment decisions and possible health care attorney's would be significantly longer and more detailed than might be necessary to persuade some future doctor on how to act. First case theory likely informs the lawyer that the document should be framed more like a will – a "living will" – with the necessary compliance with the formalities prescribed in the Wills Act.[55]The requirement of form compliance is chosen to allay the fears of the "control freak" client. If the client makes treatment choice decisions, the lawyer thinking intuitive would ask details of the choices and probably probe further whether the agent should be permitted to override the client's choices. If no, the reason. If yes, in the circumstances. The mental exercise of crafting the client's theory of the case which would inform how the document is later crafted informs the lawyer deep contours in the law and lawyering process. She comes to see that all durable powers of attorney for clients do not require mere use of "standard form" drafting. What the 80-year freak needs can be more extensive and elaborate. It could also give her the confidence to wrestle with the law to have it fit into her clients' lived realities, rather than funnelling the client's (future clients) lived realities into what she or they understand the law to require.[56]

With hindsight the document drafted can thus read:

"Durable Power of Attorney for Health Care

1. I --------------------- of ------------------ (hereinafter called the donor) set forth in this document my treatment instructions and appoint ----------------- of --------- to be my health care agent in case of my incapacity.

2. I am (describe the motive or goals of the donor) and I direct that NO TRANSFUSION of (detail name and description of prohibited treatment decision) be administered or given to me UNDER ANY CIRCUMSTANCE, even if health-care providers believe that such are necessary to preserve my life.

3. Regarding end-of-life matters I make the following choices: (i) I want my life to be prolonged as long as possible within the limits of generally accepted medical standards; (i) However I do not want my life to be prolonged if my situation is hopeless.

4. Regarding other health-care maters, I direct that (list of medical problems, current routine-medication, allergies, etc. and a further list of medical directions)

5. I give no one, including my agent any authority to disregard or override my instructions set forth in this document.

---

[55] Section of the Wills Act requires a will to be executed by the testator in the presence of two competent persons who witness the testator sign and who also in the testator's presence also witness the will.

[56]Grose, above n. 24 @ 58; Carolyn Grose, Of Victims, Villains and Fairy Godmothers: Regnant Tales of Predatory Lending (2010) 2 *Northeastern U.L. J.* 97.

Family members and friends may disagree with my choices but that does not diminish my resolve to stand by my treatment choice set out in this document.

6. Apart from the matters covered above, I appoint my agent to make health-care decisions for me.

7. I give my agent full power and authority to consent to or refuse treatment (including artificial nutrition and hydration) on my behalf, to consult with my doctors and receive copies of my medical records, and to take legal action to ensure my wishes are honoured.

8. If my first agent appointed is unavailable, unable or unwilling to serve, I appoint ------ of ------------- as my alternative agent to serve with the same power and authority.

(Attestation part attached)"

There is no question about it. Anyone reading the document like this would recognize that deep thinking goes to its crafting. The freaky old client is likely leaving the lawyer's chambers happy that she got a document reflecting her goals. That is how case theory informs the drafting process.

Let us consider a second example of how case theory advances the client's goals as the lawyer takes conscious effort to contextualising transactional documents in areas where "stock" perception is.[57] The existence of adverse stock story should discourage linear drafting style without effort to customize the document to reflect the client's specific goals. One such area highlighted by Chesler and Sneddon, is premarital (prenuptial) agreement.[58]

Medieval history tells us that these were agreements specifically designed for protection of women at a time when they enjoyed no property rights. They were essentially conceived to detail financial and non-financial responsibilities in the economic alliances between families created by marriage. Courts were however reluctant in enforcing them because they were thought of as encouraging divorces.

---

[57] Stock stories are conventional story type stripped of essential details but they carry cognitive models easily inferred by those who hear or perceive them. For example, it is easy to stereotype a man on dreadlocks wearing jean as a Rastafarian. Such automatic identification may prevent audience engagement with contrary narrative experience. For reading on stock story and cognition see, Vicki Schultz, Telling Stories About Women and Work: Judicial Interpretation of Sex Segregation in the Workplace in Title VII Cases Raising the Lack of Interest Argument (1990) 103 *Harv. L. Rev.* 1749; Mary Chiarella, Silence in Court: The Devaluation of the Stories of Nurses in the Narratives of Health Law (2000) 7 *Nursing Inquiry* 191 (the stock story of nurses as caregivers to patients, handmaiden of doctors or ministering angels, undermines the status of nurses which translated to a framework that devalues their professional opinion); Stephen Paskey, The Law Is Made of Stories (2014) 11 *Legal Comm. & Rhetoric: JALWD* 51 at 69.

[58] Susan M. Chesler& Karen J. Sneddon, Once Upon a Transaction: Narrative Techniques and Drafting (2016) 68 *Okla. L. Rev.* 263.

That is the stock story behind premarital agreements.[59] It is also the thinking that since most premarital agreements were widely used by the rich, then such agreements is limited to high-net-worth individuals or families. That is the stock character of ante nuptial agreements.

Faced with this stock position, how would the lawyer skilled in crafting case theory draft an agreement for a client desirous of such an agreement but a different purpose than that generally perceived about premarital agreement? The natural drafting technique after receiving client's instruction would be to take a precedent book, copy and paste with a few modifications. That being the case, the lawyer would have done nothing to thinker the stock story surrounding the type of agreement. In the event of litigation arising from the document, the interpreting authority is deprived the narrative benefits the client's specific needs so its implementation, interpretation, and the ultimate enforceability of the transaction document may just well follow the usual run of reluctance by the court to enforce.

All of that can change by the lawyer simply paying attention to how best to draft a document that reflects the client's aspirations. This pushes the lawyer to find ways to wrestle with the stock perception. This informs the lawyer that the best way to go about it is to employ a recursive, storytelling writing technique that tells the client's story – particularly mentioning the client's intention for wanting a premarital agreement. Employing such a technique (narrative technique) borne out of the theory constructed then enables the drafter to take deliberate steps to thinker and reframe the document in a way that can supplant stock position. The lawyer now begins to see how she can be a constructor of meaning in the context of the client's requirements. She reasons, after all, "what is wrong to clarify financial aspects of marriage." Don't even happy marriages all end on way or the other – if not by divorce, eventually end in death? So, why should people think that premarital agreements are designed to end marriages? She now chooses to wrestle with the stock conception, rather than funnel the client's realities into the mould. So, she decides to draw up a premarital agreement that is contextualized to displace stock story misunderstandings. The decision then is to modify the standard "acontextual" premarital recital. The standard draft that precipitates such thinking has a recital like this:

A. Marriage is intended soon between the parties.

---

[59] For a history and jurisprudence of premarital agreements, see Baker, History of English Law, *Snell's Equity*; Judith Younger, Perspectives on Ante-nuptial Agreements (1988) 40 *Rutgers L. Rev.* 1059; Brian Bix, Bargaining in the Shadow of Love: The Enforcement of Premarital Agreements and How We Think About Marriage (1998) 40 *WM & Mary L. Rev.* 145; J. Thomas Oldman, With All My Worldly Goods I Thee Endow, or Maybe Not: A Re-evaluation of the Uniform Premarital Agreement Act After Three Decades (2001) 19 *Duke J. Gender L. &Pol'y* 83.

B. Each party desires, before entering into the marriage, to know just what the rights of property are to be in each other's estate.

No question about it. The recital is though accurate can be cannon folder to the stock position. But it misses out necessary context that could reflect the client's aspiration.[60] So it falls within the mould of stock story surrounding premarital agreements. To avoid the stock-position label, the recital by the incisive lawyer skilled in the craft of using case theory meld with the narrative technique would reframe the recital this way:

A. Each party acknowledges and stipulates the purpose of this Agreement is not to promote or procure a divorce or dissolution of marriage, but to provide for marital tranquillity by agreeing on the property and support rights of each other at the commencement of marriage.

B. The parties have determined that the marriage between then shall have a better chance of success if the rights and claims that accrue to each of them as a result of their marriage are determined and finalized by this Agreement.

This later writing technique says it all. It contextualizes the party's intention, supplants the stock position, eliminate ambiguities, and reframe the narrative by highlighting the party's specific goals. Deliberate use of this narrative non-linear writing style, puts the client on the centre-burner of lawyering, leveraging on the client's intention to shape the "meaning" of what happened, even in the drafting sense.[61]

Case theory and litigation

Let us use two examples to illustrate how case theory proves useful in litigation: in oral advocacy and in drafting statement of facts.

The examination (examination-in-chief and cross-examination) of Elmer Davis (earlier stated) would be our roadmap.[62] (The reader is encouraged to please re-read the story to follow the analysis here played out on case theory). The theory of the case pressed by the prosecution in direct examination is that the confession was not coerced, supported by the facts that there was a policy against around-the-clock questioning and that the policy was followed.

---

[60] Chesler & Sneddon, above n. 58 @ 273.

[61] On furthering narrative techniques in transactional drafting, see also Frank L McGuane, Jr. & Kathleen A. Hogan, Drafting the Agreement Not to Encourage Dissolution, in *Colorado Prac., Family Law & Practice*, chapter 39; Joseph M. Williams & Gregory G. Colomb, Telling Clear Stories: A Principle of Revision that Demands a Good Character (1996) 5 *Persp. Teaching Legal Res. & Writing* 14 (on descriptive information about the parties in the background or recital section of agreements to provide three dimensional reference to the parties, such as on which includes (i) the human character of the parties, say (ii) seller and (iii) buyer rather than the two-dimensional reference of only seller and buyer).

[62] See above n. 24.

On the other hand, the defendant's theory of the case is that the confession was coerced because the defendant felt that he was being subjected to constant interrogation. The facts that support that theory are that he didn't know what time it was and that he was questioned while it was light and while it was dark.

Unquestionably, stories are "true" - there was a protocol observed during the interrogations (twice a day, between 7:30 a.m. and 11:30 p.m.), and the officers in this case followed that protocol; and the defendant's only sense of time was based on the changing light outside his window, and he was questioned while it was light and while it was dark. The prosecutor can therefore argue that the interrogation was "repeated" or "sporadic," and not coerced; therefore, it should be admitted into evidence in the trial. The defence, however, can argue that the interrogation was "constant" and therefore created a kind of duress that resulted in the defendant's confession. Thus coerced, the confession should be suppressed.

Because all the "facts" are "true," it illustrates the point both parties have choices to make about what facts to select to persuade the judge. The exercise further demonstrates that the "true story" - "what really happened" - is not something objective and static, waiting to be "found" by a good investigative lawyer. On the contrary, "what really happened" is determined by the decision maker's adoption of one or the other of the stories the lawyers have offered. And those stories are, in turn, constructed by the lawyer with the goal of persuading the decision maker. The law is made by the choices the lawyers make – yes, case theory is at the heart of this suppression hearing, and so in all litigation.[63]

Grose further illustrates how case theory can be used to drive the suppression hearing a bit further. It informs for example, he strategy on where and when to start the stories of the respective parties. If in the exercise as laid out, the judge at the suppression hearing allowed the confession to come in as admitted piece of evidence, then the prosecution would simply frame a linear story to back its theory. This would take this path: Davis murder X, he was arrested, he made the confession and so please convict as prescribed by law. End of story that fits the theory! The story is starts with the legal description of Davis, alleged murderer, his subsequent arrest, and the examination should end with his confession.[64]Period!

---

[63] See Grose, above n. 24 @ 52.

[64] Davis would no doubt have been described in the label of a murderer and no more. On interesting reading on how law talks about people, see James Boyd White, *Legal Imagination* (Abridged Edition), Chicago: Univ. Chicago Press, 1985 @ 114 (law – especially in its basic form...is a literature of caricature; it pares away all that can be said about a person's life until nothing is left except the rule and label. . . a narrative made up of the elements of the crime or cause of action, and this story tells us all we need to know about the person involved – either he did it, or he did not, and everything else is irrelevant.")

A very tightly framed story: Davis did this horrible thing. How do we know? Because he told us.

But a good defence can yet advance its own theory after the confession is admitted. Grose in her clinical class tells how she and her colleague in simulation exercises can keep the theory as strategy throughout the trial of Davis. It follows by leading evidence about not just "what happened," but the "meaning of what happened." It goes like this:

Defence Counsel: Mr. Davis, where did you grow up?

Defendant: Here in Alabama in Jefferson, just five miles from here.

Defence Counsel: Do you remember the first time a policeman ever talked with you?

Defendant: Yes.

Defence Counsel: Tell the jury about that, please.

Prosecutor: Objection, relevance?

Even when the role-play ends, the message sent out is clear. The line of questioning will lead to relevant information about the "meaning of what happened." The questions are directed to further the case theory that the defendant's confession was coerced (even if the jury doesn't buy this argument, the defence attorney is laying the groundwork here for appealing the judge's ruling at the suppression hearing).

The defence is seeking to make relevant the defendant's first contact with the police - the story of the defendant as a poor black kid in the south at the dawn of the civil rights movement, a young man who is afraid of the police due to frequent and intimidating questioning. All of these are designed to provide context and support for the case theory. The background story helps the decision-maker to more readily make the leap to coercion and duress. Again, the defence lawyer has made choices about how to frame and structure the story she is telling to persuade the decision maker to adopt the client's particular story and make law that takes that story into account.[65]

Case theory informs every strategy of the case - experimenting with choices about how to use particular facts; choices about how to frame the examination, where and when it should begin and when it should end; choices about what

---

[65] See how to prosecute critical lawyer for the oppressed Lucie E. White, Subordination, Rhetorical Survival Skills and Sunday Shoes: Notes on the Hearing of Mrs. G (1990) 38 *Buffalo L. Rev.* 1 (hereinafter referred to as "Sunday Shoes"); Clark D. Cunningham, Lawyer as Translator Representation as Text: Towards an Ethnography of Legal Discourse (1992) 77 *Cornell L. Rev.* 1298; Jessica A. Rose, Rebellious or Regnant: Police Brutality Lawyering In New York City (2000) 28 *Fordham Urban L.J.* 619; Binny Miller, Give Them Back Their Lives: Recognizing Client Narrative in Case Theory (1994-1995) 93 *Mich. L. Rev.* 485 @ 487; Kenneth D. Chestek, The Plot Thickens: The Appellate Brief as Story (2008) 14 *J. Legal Writing Inst.* 127.

language to use, and what evidence to of telling a persuasive story, and more. The crafting of the theory of a case is a practice that takes place in a particularized (and often stilted) way, yes, but one that requires intentional and consistent choices to construct a persuasive and compelling story for the decision maker. As in this case scenario it is clear that examination of a witness is not just about following legal prescriptions (rules of examination of witnesses) –not asking non-leading questions or annoying questions or indecent questions.[66] Case theory is rather a well thought strategy for persuasion and winning cases.

Let us now see how case theory informs drafting statement of facts.

We shall unashamedly use the scenario of Chestek to navigate the richness of crafting a case theory, which informs how to draw up statement of facts.. We have chosen to use the case to navigate the theory because it draws on the "meaning of what happened" to transform "what really happened," thereby determining the outcome of "what will happen."[67]

The essence of the appellate brief is a moot court story of adoption by a homosexual parent resisted by the state.[68] It is the story of Margaret Rubin, who is devastated by the loss of her homosexual partner, Francie Kohler, and the attempt of the legal system to take away her son from her, on the grounds that the marriage is not recognized by the *lex fori,* Old York, the residence of the parties. The gist of the matter is that both couple married of ten years and had a son, Johnnie, through *in vitro* fertilization (IVF). The marriage was entered into in Vermont, a state that permits the union of gay and lesbian couples. So what Margaret and Francie did was to leave Old York, a state that does not approve of lesbian marriage to marry in Vermont, a state that recognizes lesbian marriages. In fact, the Old York Supreme Court refuses to recognize the validity of Vermont gay marriages.

After the death of Francie, Margaret wants to adopt Johnnie and continue to raise him. But Margaret's mother who has always been opposed to the lesbian marriage resisted the adoption. She asked the Old York State to declare Johnnie a dependent child and place him in a foster home because under the law Margaret has no legal claim to guardianship. The law does not recognize lesbian marriages. What is more, the state adoption prohibits homosexuals from adoption. That is the stage plotted in the story.

Faced with this fact-intensive situation the skilled lawyer must develop a theory that can explain the narrative of Margaret to the trier. To succeed before

---

[66] See for example, some of the prescribed rules set out in ss. 214-239.

[67] Kenneth D. Chestek, The Plot Thickens: The Appellate Brief as Story (2008) 14 *J. Legal Writing Inst.* 127.

[68] This story is fictional, product of a modified moot court problem from Indianapolis School of Law, Indiana University in 2004. See Chestek, above n. 67 128 n. 1.

the trier requires drafting a statement of the facts that can draw the trier to empathize with the client's perspectives – reconstruct "what happened" to be seen from the perspective of the "meaning of what happened." Unquestionably, having favourable law helps, but having favourable facts is always a better bet. Where however the facts and law are unfavourable the task takes on more challenge. This is sure one such. The law is unfavourable. Old York law prohibits lesbian marriage. Its Supreme Court even refuses to recognize the validity of Vermont gay marriages. The facts are not any better. Lesbians are not the best of the society, nether are "court friends." If anything the Supreme Court of Old York refuses to recognize even lesbian marriage celebrated outside its jurisdiction.

Crafting the theory of the case no doubt would require ingenuity of the lawyer going against the uphill task of unfavourable law and facts. The lawyer must consciously design a theory that can sell the elements of a narrative with a strong plot in which "genuine" conflict is revealed, and the protagonist struggles to resolve the conflict. In formulating the theory the lawyer must thinking incisively on how to use the double helix to persuade.[69]

A theory that merely draws on the rule-based strand will meet the brick wall. Such a theory would simply not persuade. Its argument would follow a linear path like this: attack the law. The prohibition is unconstitutional under the substantive components of say the Due Process Clause; or the Equal Protection Clause; or that failure to recognize the lesbian marriage is against the Full Faith and Credit Clause, and the like. All of these grounds are likely to be dismissed because the court would be reluctant to create new rights not properly defined.[70]You can imagine it going this way: a review of the constitutionality of the Old York State adoption law. It will be dry and simply abstract with little or no power to convince. The technique will leave little room to dramatize the humanness of Margaret.

Thinking through all of this the lawyer would most likely choose a theme that draws on law and facts, giving the trier background details to aid the reader's understanding of why the dispute happened in the first place and why it is important o exclude distracting details. Thinking through the law also, the lawyer

---

[69]Robert P. Burns, Studying Evidence Law in the Context of Trial Practices (2006) 50 *St. Louis U. L.J.* 1155 @ 1171 (the lawyer should "construct their case from a double helix of norms. One of those strands is constituted by the law of rules. The other strand is constituted by the norms that find their natural home within the life-world of the judge and jury. These common sense norms are embedded primarily in the different sorts of narratives that the trial lawyer may employ at trial, from the fully characterized storytelling of the opening statement to the more Spartan narratives of direct examination."); see also J. Christopher Rideout, Storytelling, Narrative Rationality, and Legal Persuasion, 14 *Leg. Writing* 53 (2008).

[70] Most judges are of the opinion that the creation of new rights is a legislative, as opposed to a judicial power. Cite authority.

would need to show why the standard of controlling precedent requires detail analysis from say the historical and social setting.

Thinking about the theory of the case, the lawyer probes what should the "moral of the story be, what lesson(s) do I want the reader to learn from the writing, and ultimately what story will do the job? Choosing the right theory can mean success or failure I a brief of this nature where both law and facts are at odd with the client. The lawyer must therefore visualize the whole before you begin and carefully choose the theory. Choosing a wrong one risk alienates the extremely conservative ones. It just polarizes the court if it is an appellate court (as in this moot court exercise). The polarization would leave Johnnie's rights out of the picture entirely. But choosing a theme around the concept that over-generalizations can create terrible injustice in specific cases and then contextualizing it to the particular facts before the trier can just work the magic. So, a theme that plays up that the over-generalization that gays and lesbians are unfit parents posed a huge risk to the emotional well-being of a vulnerable three year-old child – in this case Johnnie.

With this overriding theme selected see how the brief is then written.

1. *Section on Introduction*

This is an application by Margaret Rubin to adopt Johnnie, her son, against the wish of Francie Kohler's mother asking that Johnnie be declared a dependent child, placing him in a foster home. Margaret married Francie in 2000, ten year ago in Vermont, a state that permits gay and lesbian marriages. In the couple desire to mature and raise a child, they decided to go through IVF, which help give birth to Johnnie in 2003.

The couple and their son lived happily thereafter in Old York until Francie was killed in a car-pedestrian accident, necessitating the present application by Margaret to adopt Johnnie with a view of continuing his care under her superintendence. It is this application that Francie's mother is opposed to.

2. *Section on Issue(s) for Determination*

The main issue that arises for determination in this case is whether it is constitutional for the Old York statute to deny Margaret adoption rights over Johnnie, her child or put otherwise, whether Margaret should be entitled to succeed in her application for adoption under the adoption statute of Old York State.

3. *Section on Rule*

Section 19-67-2 provides that the following persons are eligible to adopt: (1) a husband and wife together, or (2) an adult who is not married. Subsection (B) however states, 'homosexuals are not eligible to adopt under the statute.'

Noteworthy of mention, subsection (B) was not in the original legislation. It was only added after a highly publicized incident of a prominent musician was convicted for sexually abusing an adopted child. See *State* v. *Smith* (1985) 489 O.Y. 142.

This said prohibition violates the constitution of the United States, especially the protected rights to privacy; right to family integrity; due process right and it discriminates homosexual rights to equal treatment.

(The remaining part of the section would then go on to relate how it does in specifics of say the Fourteenth Amendment, Due Process Clause (Amend. XIV, cl.3), Equal Protection Clause (Amend XIV, cl. 4) and the like)

It will end by asking the court to declare the Old York statute unconstitutional, especially when it is not narrowly tailored to serve a "compelling state interest."

4. *Section on Application of Rules*

This section would ordinarily synthesize the facts of the case with the rules asking the court to scrutinize the state legislation in the context of the constitution and the peculiar facts of Margaret.

5. *Section on Conclusion*

This section will pray the court to overturn the state legislation and declare Margaret eligible for adoption of Johnnie.

So, the statement of facts plays the human drama of the case. By the lawyer consciously thinking about the case as one requiring human elements of character, conflict, theme, and point of view the plot truly thickens. Employing the style of fictional writing can do the magic.[71] The transformational appellant brief written to the Supreme Court of Old York State is compelling that we have chosen to highlight some material sections of the brief to illustrated the

[71] Fiction writer and film producers often plot stories using the structure of setting, conflict, character, point of view/voice, theme, plot, introduction/exposition, complicated incidents/rising action, climax, resolution/falling action, denouement and conclusion. See Anthony G. Amsterdam & Jerome S. Bruner, *Minding the Law*, Harv. Univ. Press, 2000, 20; Chestek, above n. 87; Elyse Pepper, The Case for Thinking Like a Filmmaker: Using Lars von Trier's Dogville as a Model for Writing a Statement of Facts (2008) 14 *J. Legal Writing Inst.* 171; James P. Eyster, Lawyer as Artist: Using Significant Moments and Obtuse Objects to Enhance Advocacy (2008) 14 *J. Legal Writing Inst.* 87.

persuasiveness of how theory informs the narrative structure of writing - brief in especially facts-intensive situations.

How does it all play out in the narrative constructed?

Let us do an excerpt of a few personalization highlighted by the learned writer. The facts section is very revealing. It goes like this:

> Margaret and Francie only wanted a child.
> Having committed themselves to each other emotionally and legally, they decided, as do many committed couples, that they wanted to raise a family. But the state of Old York told them that they were unfit parents, simply because they loved each other. Without knowing anything about the depth and sincerity of Margaret and Francie commitment to each other, and without any individualized investigation into their fitness as parents, the state categorically declared that they, along with all other gay and lesbian citizens, were unfit to adopt and raise children.

It then goes on to narrate how the couple devoted to their dream travelled to Vermont to legalize their relationship; how they attempted without success to seek agencies approval to adopt; how they then resorted to IVF which eventually produced Johnnie; what adjustment they made in their personal lives to create a happy family life and conducive environment for raising their child; how Francie got killed in an accident; the bond between Margaret and Johnnie; etc.

This narrative plot brings to fore the human elements of character (the story of a loving family, the kind law should promote, the hurdle erected by the state which prevents them to marry and raise a family, how they as protagonist scaled the pillars of hurdle erected by the state as antagonist, by the couple resort to travel to Vermont for their marriage and modern reproductive technology to raise a family). This is no doubt a great introduction preluding the beginning of the "rising action" of the story plot.

The rising action is the sudden intestate death of Francie, the couple not having planed and arranged their affairs. This absence is what introduces another antagonist to the scene, the mother of Francie, who now seeks a custodial regime over Johnnie. The rising action is part of the facts section, which provides the setting for a discussion of the legal section, the relevant rules that govern the resolution of the facts situation.

Since the statute prohibits lesbian adoption, the strategy most likely to persuade will be to create at least a plausible reason to preserve the stable family life for Margaret and Johnnie, by showing the irrationality of disrupting a stable, loving home, and putting Johnnie in a state facility most probably devoid of love and attention. Here the writer gives a history of the unreasonableness of the prohibition, showing that it is adopted out of animus towards homosexuals without individualization perspective and consideration of the "best interest" of the child analysis and further that it is not one within the protected state legitimate interest.

No question about it. This narrative structure is more persuasive and compelling for being client-centred. The article happily tells that the brief written in the narrative form was successful as the Supreme Court of Old York held in favour of Margaret. The lesson from the narrative brief is that thinking about lawyering through the lens of a theme which informs the plot of the story gives the lawyer an opportunity to look behind and between black letter rules, which possibly reveals facts, language, structure and ideas that go beyond abstract stipulations of statute and opinion of courts.[72] It also illustrates how playing conscious attention to developing a case theory empowers the client to say more within the conscripted legal space. Narrative style briefs help lawyers to wrestle with the law, to have it fit into their client's lived realities and experience, rather than funnelling their realities into what they think law requires. This is a hallmark of good legal writing and advocacy.[73]

Conclusion

The theory of the case advances client-centred lawyering and persuasion. To be effective professionals, lawyers need to master the skill of how to synthesis the gist of what make their case persuasive by asking themselves probing questions like what is the "bottom line" point to be prove? Why is my client's cause *just*, or why is the other side's cause *unjust?* Lawyers should spend a great deal of time discussing how to develop a theme, or theory, of their case to be effective persuaders, remembering always that the chosen theory should convert the facts into legal problems soluble to their clients favour.

[72] Carolyn Grose, Storytelling Across the Curriculum: From Margin to Centre, from Clinic to Classroom (2010) 7 *J. Ass'n Legal Writing Directors* 37. On the need to develop case theory with the client at the centre.

[73] Carolyn Grose, Of Victims, Villains and Fairy Godmothers: Regnant Tales of Predatory Lending (2010) 2 *Northeastern Univ. L.J.* 97.

Chapter 16

Narratives and Storytelling Skills

Introduction

Every trial is a competition between two narratives – that told by the plaintiff, who affirms a claim, and the defendant who makes rebuttal. Lawyers work with stories - those of their clients, those they tell in the courtroom, and those contained in judgment of courts (although the stories in judicial opinions are often better disguised and when not disguised, poorly or awkwardly told).[1] In fact, the common law legal system is addicted to stories. For once think of a judgment of court without facts; without character, no details, and no stories. Would lawyers understand *Lagos State* v. *Ojukwu* as establishing authority that a contemnor cannot seek judicial remedy without the facts, stories and details of the parties? Hardly! Unquestionably then, facts are central to the business of lawyering.

Law comes down to the legal community in cases; cases come with facts; and facts in turn are arranged in stories. So, law ultimately rest and is constantly mixed up with and on stories. Even our understanding of what law is in a given situation is constrained by how the facts limit the application of the rule in hypothetical future case. The obsession with stories is simply revealed with how law is culturally laced with facts. We name our cases after people; the gladiators on both sides of the divide are by the word "versus". Litigation is the controversy that arises from some form of relationship between the parties, and in prosecuting vindication each party comes with a story to tell.[2]

It is therefore clear that stories however singular, however challenged, are central to the way all think about the practice of law. For instance, it will be impossible to explain what the claim of fundamental rights means without the stories or facts that inform the facts about the fight for freedom? Any description of it without its history and story would turn out abstract and uninteresting to the reader or the lawyer. In fact, denying that stories inhere with law would be

---

[1]J. Christopher Rideout, Storytelling, Narrative Rationality and Legal Persuasion (2008) 14 *J. Leg.Writing* 53.

[2]Kim Lane Scheppele, Narrative Resistance and the Struggle for Stories (1996) 20 *Legal Studies Forum* 84 ("We can no more do law without stories than we can fly without mechanical devices").

tantamount to denying that our belief system has no bearing with our thinking about abstract legal concepts, such as an "ideal free market", "law and economics" etc. For it only if one can think and imagine what an ideal free market story is all about that one can think appropriately about the rules that regulate commerce.

The position is not any different in even areas of the law where facts are less overt. Even in those limited areas, our abstract analysis is often a product of the imagined facts and collective stories our brains make sense of them before we pronounce our analysis sound and scientific. So, it matters what constitute our collection of stories, which we use in the rationalization process.

Village story setting

Law, Stories and Imagination

Most lawyers, especially those training under the Anglo-American common law system view law as rule-based: law is seen as a system of rules from a sovereign to a people bound by it. The privilege positivist posture of law ("law as machine") however overlooks the perspective of viewing law as a social and linguistic endeavour ("law as rhetoric").[3] While not discounting law as machine, lawyers need to understand how law is an activity of speech and imagination occurring in the social world.

[3] James Boyd White, Imagining the Law in Austin Sarat & Thomas R. Kearns, eds. *The Rhetoric of Law*, Ann Arbor: Michigan Univ. Press, 1996 @ 29 [hereinafter referred to as "imagining"].

Lawyers by virtue of their profession read and write legal documents all of which require elements of imagination. They read legal documents, texts, the constitution and many other legal materials. The process of reading legal documents can be likened to reading literature. Both involve envisioning the world the writer creates. In doing so, the reader engages in a process of imagining. Just as the literary writer imagines the world in a certain way, and she wants to "think of the flower...the bird...the butterfly...as being like him, as actors with feelings with which he can identify—feelings of safety, danger, sympathy with others, feelings that will confirm the reality and importance of his own: imagining nature as a world of fellow feeling, the legal writer or advocate also imagines her world. It is therefore a proper skill for lawyers to hone legal imagination: to see lawyering is both a culture of argument and an inherently rhetorical enterprise.[4]Both the rhetoric of writing and reading law interrogates lawyering as imagining.[5]

Origin of Imaginative Theory

Over the years law and literature developed the storytelling movement. The real beneficiary of the storytelling movement is the creation of legal imagination skills for lawyers.[6] Storytelling as scholarship is rooted in law and literature. Even though some think law and literature is a recent phenomenon, it must be recognized that the field is ancient. Nineteenth-century English lawyers wrote about depictions of the legal system by Shakespeare, Dickens, and other famous writers.[7] Wigmore, the great American evidence law writer thought lawyers to read about great writers, to learn from them about human nature.[8] Far back in the 1940s Justice Cardozo's paper analysed the literary style of judicial opinions of his time.[9]1973 however witnessed the exponential growth of law and literature with the publication of James Boyd White *Legal Imagination.*[10]White (probably the

[4]Ibid @ 31. See also John C. Gooch, Reading, Writing, and Imagining the Law: Using James Boyd White's Theories as an Approach to Analysing Legal Rhetoric (2011) 4 *J. Canadian Society for the Study of Rhetoric* 1.

[5] James Boyd White, *When Words Lose Their Meaning: Constitutions and Reconstitutions of Language, Character, and Community*, Chicago: The University of Chicago Press, 1984.

[6] Ruth A. Robbins, An Introduction to Applied Storytelling (2008) 14 *J. Legal Writing* 4. See also Thomas D. Eisele, The Legal Imagination and Language: A Philosophical Criticism (1976) 47 *Univ. Colo. L. Rev.*

[7]C.Davis, *The Law in Shakespeare*, 1883; Stephen, The License of Modern Novelists (1857) 106 *Edinburgh Rev.* 124, both cited in Richard A. Posner, Law and Literature: A Relation Reargued (1986) 72 *Virginia L. Rev.* 1351.

[8]See Wigmore, Introduction, inJ. Gest, *The Lawyer in Literature*, 1913 @ ix-xii.

[9]Benjamin Cardozo, Law and Literature in M. Hall, ed.*Selected Writings of Benjamin Nathan Cardozo*, 1947 @ 339.

[10]James Boyd White, *The Legal Imagination: Studies in the Nature of Legal Thought and Expression*, 1973. See also James Boyd White, Reading Law and Reading Literature: Law as Language." *Heracles*

most committed advocate of law and literature) theories book gave birth to the law and literature movement: a movement now described as either "law in literature" or "law as literature."[11] Over the years, scholars in the Law and Literature movement have continued to interrogate the uses of literature to help lawyers stay connected to their imaginations, to their creativity, and to their humanity. Each of these scholarly movements has led to, or grown out of experiments with the use of narrative theory and storytelling strategies and techniques in legal practice and education.

Stories and Human Nature

Unquestionably, stories are essential ingredients in human interaction. They connect law with human experience and imagination. A lawyer interested in accomplishing the goals of effective legal communication and legal persuasion must learn to persuade like a rhetorician – a narrator and storyteller. Humans instinctively respond to stories and are persuaded by it because:

(i) Stories are response-shaping

Stories create or shape new knowledge. The common example is that of teaching a child how to behave in adult society or teaching an adult how to react in a new culture or setting.

(ii) Stories are response-reinforcing

This is the primary reason why people tell stories. We do so to reinforce responses we attempt to persuade our audience to buy or sustain. This is often done by reasoning through stories that suggest that our existing world view or knowledge is the correct knowledge. For example, religious stories are told to reinforce belief in the particular religious system. Lawyers do so by using precedent to persuade.

(iii) Stories are response-changing

This is what most people think when they say "I am trying to persuade you," though in reality this is the hardest response to achieve. Response-changing is what attorneys seek when they argue to change existing knowledge or beliefs.[12]

Bow: Essays on the Rhetoric and Poetics of the Law. Madison: The University of Wisconsin Press, 1985 @ 77; James Boyd White, Telling Stories in the Law and in Ordinary Life: The *Oresteia* and 'Noon Wine.'"*Heracles Bow: Essays on the Rhetoric and Poetics of the Law*. Madison: The University of Wisconsin Press, 1985 @ 168; Ian Ward, *Law and Literature: Possibilities and Perspectives*. Cambridge: Cambridge University Press, 1995.

[11] While law *in* literature considers the potential or possible relevance of literary texts, especially those texts telling a legal story as artefacts worthy of legal scholars' attention; law *as* literature, on the other hand, is the application of the techniques of literary criticism to legal texts. See Gooch, above n. 3.

[12]Robbins, above n. 6.

Metaphor and narrative constitute the frameworks for the construction of meaning. They both shape our perceptions and reasoning processes, often unconsciously, and we consciously use them to frame arguments and agreements. Because of the way the mind works and the way culture is constructed, metaphor and narrative are essential, and unavoidable, for persuasion and understanding. Law benefits from the full use of our imaginations that storytelling requires. Lawyering is a form of rhetoric, and so is socially constitutive nature of language. It is therefore proper to view law not so much as a set of rules and doctrines or as a bureaucratic system or as an instrument for societal control but also as a culture, most part of which is constitutive of argumentation.

Stories and Cognition

Storytelling skill for lawyers is a product of recognizing the structure of human "meaning-making." Cognitivist theorists' reveals that stories are effective tools for leading us from the familiar to the unfamiliar in that they expand our schema – organized pattern of thought - to accommodate new information effectively. Storytelling owes much of its origin to the "law and literature movement,"- a movement dedicated to exploring the use of literature to aid lawyers stay connected to their creativity, imagination and humanity.[13]Stories (particularly in our time) occupy a pride of place in lawyering in the context of critical lawyering and in incorporating the voices of "outsiders" in the litigation process. They have been skilfully employed to make triers of facts think creatively and compassionately about the true conception of "what happened." White's "Sunday Shoes" piece and Miller's "Give Them Back Their Lives" are two great examples of

---

[13]Stacy Caplow, Putting the "I" in Writing: Drafting an A/Effective Personal Statement to Tell a Winning Refugee Story (2008) 14 *Leg. Writing* 249; Kenneth D. Chestek, The Plot Thickens: The Appellate Brief as Story (2008) 14 *Leg. Writing* 127; Gail Hammer, A Conversation Between Friends: Adventures in Collaborative Planning and Teaching Ethical Issues in Representation of Children (2007) 75 *UMKC L. Rev.* 1025; Margaret Moore Jackson, Confronting "Unwelcomeness" From the Outside: Using Case Theory to Tell the Stories of Sexually Harassed Women (2007) 14 *Cardozo J.L. & Gender* 61; Stephen D. Easton, 'Toto, I Have a Feeling We're Not in Kansas Anymore:' Using the Wizard of Oz to Introduce Students to the Skills of Witness Examination (2006) 12 *Clin. L. Rev.* 283; Jennifer Kruse Hanrahan, Truth in Action: Revitalizing Classical Rhetoric as a Tool for Teaching Oral Advocacy in American Law Schools (2003) *B.Y.U. Educ. & L.J.* 299; Paul L. Caron, Back to the Future: Teaching Law Through Stories (2002) 71 *U. Cin. L. Rev.* 405; Kathleen Magone& Steven I. Friedland, The Paradox of Creative Legal Analysis: Venturing into the Wilderness (2002) 79 *U. Det. Mercy L. Rev.* 571; Dana K. Cole, Psychodrama and the Training of Trial Lawyers: Finding the Story (2001) 21 *N. Ill. U. L. Rev.* 1 (2001); Brian J. Foley & Ruth Anne Robbins, Fiction 101: A Primer for Lawyers on How to Use Fiction Writing Techniques to Write Persuasive Facts Sections (2001) 32 *Rutgers L.J.* 459; Dena S. Davis, Tell Me a Story: Using Short Fiction in Teaching Law and Bioethics (1997) 47 *J. Leg. Educ.* 240.

narrative and storytelling practice that demonstrate how these tools can be effectively used in recreating reality and thus further persuasion.[14]

Despite its usefulness in the legal process, some lawyers remain dismissive of the place of narrative in persuasion, relegating it to the mundane. In their opinion stories carry too much emotion to the legal process, a system that generally accords less importance to stories than logic. Such a thinking is not surprising. Lawyers were once law students. As students they were accustomed to using logic and the IRAC syllogism as the way to reason in law. They therefore enter the profession discounting stories.[15]Legal training and practice thus consigns narrative to a distant corner.

But this is mistaken thinking. Narrative skills are an important component of good lawyering. The Carnegie report states:

> While lawyers certainly need to be skilled at analytic thinking, they also need to be skilled at narrative thinking, and this can only be developed by teaching in context. Law schools are familiar with the task of helping students develop analytic thinking skills. "Analytic thinking detaches things and events from the situations of everyday life and represents them in more abstract and systematic ways." The other mode of thinking is based on narrative. "Here, things and events acquire significance by being placed within a story, an on-going context of meaningful interaction. This mode of thinking integrates experience through metaphor and analogy. Actual legal

[14]Binny Miller, Give Them Back Their Lives: Recognizing Client Narrative in Case Theory (1994-1995) 93 *Mich. L. Rev.* 485; Lucie E. White, Subordination, Rhetorical Survival Skills and Sunday Shoes: Notes on the Hearing of Mrs. G (1990) 38 *Buffalo L. Rev.* 1 (hereinafter referred to as "Sunday Shoes") (an article exploring case theory by telling the deep emotional story of enforced silence, rhetorical survival of a poor woman engaged in administrative hearing at a welfare office). See also Clark D. Cunningham, Lawyer as Translator Representation as Text: Towards an Ethnography of Legal Discourse (1992) 77 *Cornell L. Rev.* 1298.

[15]Festus Emiri, Ayuba Giwa & Jonathan Ehusani, Revisiting the Traditional IRAC Organizational Structure for Legal Analysis: Towards a Multidisciplinary Approach (2015) 11 *Nig. L.J.* 34; Laura P. Graham, Why-RAC? Revisiting the Traditional Paradigm for Writing About Legal Analysis (2015) 63 *Kansas L. Rev.* 681 at 706. See also, Brian Garner, Judges on Briefing: A National Survey (2002) 8 *Scribes J. Leg. Writing* 1 @ 2-3 (stating that from a survey of 100 state and federal judges in the U.S. prefer brief written as "an essay with a clear train of thought" in the narrative form); The Plot Thickens @ 132 ("I do not contend that IRAC and its brethren are inherently bad. IRAC clearly has a place in legal writing; it is a very useful tool for explaining and examining logical pieces of the legal puzzle that every case presents. But its utility is limited to small-scale organization and legal reasoning; when used to create the super-structure of a brief, it can lead to formulaic writing devoid of the personal stories that form the conflict being presented to the court. In short, IRAC is a building block—merely one type of material that a writer can use to construct a solid brief. My premise here is that what the writer builds with those blocks, the client's story, should be organized as a narrative.")

practice is heavily dependent upon expertise in narrative modes of reasoning.[16]

Storytelling and Litigation

Legal storytelling has assumed a pride of place as tool to help lawyers stay connected with their imagination, creativity and humanness.[17]It lies at the heart of what lawyers do in litigation. As James White tell us, every case starts with a story—the client's stories —and it ends with a legal decision that, in effect, offers another version of that story, one cast into a legal framework. In between, the client's story and the court decision is the story that engages lawyers - the stories told at trial, since most trials contain competing narratives. It is this middle story skills that lawyers need to master – how to do it consciously and persuasively.[18]

Like cognitive metaphor theory, narrative theory reflects a shift away from formalism and toward agreement that what we see and think is always being filtered through and affected by interpretive frameworks. As a story unfolds, it filters and focuses, helping us make sense out of a series of chronological events that would otherwise lack coherence and consistency. Stories make it easier for us to communicate our experiences, and they also help us predict what will happen and what we will need to do when we find ourselves entangled in a particular plight. While metaphor serves as a template, narrative becomes a path; narrative forms can become "recipes for structuring experience itself, for laying down routes into memory, for not only guiding the life narrative up to the present but directing it into the future.

Unquestionably, narrative is vital to us because it is how we make sense of our world. Cognitivists say that narrative shapes the human understanding of the world. The theory is simple. We understand our world using schema – a shorthand for interpreting events that we see, hear, or experience from our past experience of them. For instance, through schema we know what it is to sleep, visit a friend, observe sun rise and sun set, etc. Once the stimuli we observe falls

---

[16] William M. Sullivan, et al. eds. *Carnegie Fund for the Advancement of Teaching, Educating Lawyers: Preparation for the Profession of Law,* 2007 (hereinafter called the *Carnegie Report*) Foundation for the Advancement of Teaching, Preparation for the Professions Programme (PPP) 2007 @ 110.

[17]Stacy Caplow, Putting the "I" in Wr*t*ng: Drafting an A/Effective Personal Statement to Tell a Winning Refugee Story (2008) 14 *Leg. Writing* 249; Lorie M. Graham & Stephen M. McJohn, Cognition, Law, Stories, (Suffolk U. Law Sch. Legal Studies Research Paper No. 08-14, 2008) (available at http://ssrn.com/abstract=1126400); Martha C. Nussbaum, Cultivating Humanity in Legal Education (2003) 70 *Univ. Chi. L. Rev.* 265 @ 277-79; Lynne N. Henderson, Legality and Empathy (1987) *85 Mich. L. Rev.* 1574.

[18]W. Lance Bennett & Martha S. Feldman, *Reconstructing Reality in the Courtroom: Justice and Judgment in American* Culture, Rutgers U. Press, 1981 (a sociological survey of the U.S. criminal trial system reaching the conclusion that it is organized around storytelling.")

within a category we have experienced or within our pre-conceived expectation, we can quickly identify it unconsciously. Our schemas enable us to process what it is.[19] Schemas are useful in that without them we would have had to re-learn everything in our world when we see, hear or experience them. That would have been horrible to say the least.

Because there is a community of shared-schema we can understand and predict what others in our society are doing or thinking. In fact, the more schemas we understand, the better we are able to understand our world. This explains (probably) why an educated voter better understands democracy issues than the uneducated.

These schemas are the soils that grow the power of narrative in law. Some schemas or stock structures are actually stories, plots of events that take the shape of a beginning, middle and end- all congruent with our experience or culture.[20] This process of narrative construction of matching our experience to a schema happens automatic and unconscious.

There are certain stories peculiar in our environment and which are archetypes with respect to which we carry the blueprint of the archetype situations. So once an event activates the archetype we automatically create a mental outline of a story through which we understand the event.[21] So what happens is that over time, through these schemas we use narratives to tell and re-tell our tradition, culture, received-wisdom, values etc. using them to understand and interpret our world. That is how narrative helps us make sense of our world.

Because of its order of events, narrative creates with it a sense of causation. This causative sense is powerful as it suggests appropriateness, normality. Thus, bringing a collection of events into narrative form normalizes the events, making it plausible. That way narrative becomes natural, inviting and shared. As an audience receives the narrative, it becomes part of the telling, and may use their schema to understand the story or may learn a new way to understand the story.

---

[19] Linda H. Edwards, Where Do The Prophets Stand? Hamdi, Myth and Master's Tools (2013) 13 *Conn. Pub.Int'l. L.J.* 43 @ 51; Linda L. Berger, The Lady Or The Tiger? A Field Guide to Metaphor and Narrative (2011) 50 *Washburn L.J.* 275.

[20] Rideout, above n. 1.

[21] Berger, above n. 19 @ ("Stories embedded in our experience provide mental blueprints and cognitive shortcuts . . . Stories also make it easier to communicate our experiences, help us predict what will happen, and sketch out what we will need to do when we find ourselves entangled in a typical plight.").

Once understanding is created, identification is enhanced and the narrative provokes active thinking and promotes problem solving.[22]

Culturally-shared stories are powerful in persuasion because they are shared by the community. For example, most lawyers share the primacy of the "rule of law" doctrine. So, it is a powerful thinking and acting of law almost fossilized as an inflexible doctrine underlying the legal system.[23] Noteworthy of mention however, is that much as culturally-shared narratives seem inflexible, they could be changed through counter telling and re-telling.

Rideout is of the view that stories are great persuasion tools because:

(i) Narratives are "innate" ways of understanding and structuring human experience; this makes them inherently persuasive;

(ii) Narrative models go beyond models of persuasion based on formal or informal logic, to encompass what he terms "narrative rationality;" and

(iii) Narratives embody several properties that make them psychologically persuasive – properties of coherence (a formal property); correspondence (a formal property); and fidelity (a substantive property).[24]

Let us explore each of connection between narrative and litigation, beginning with narratives being an "innate" ways of understanding and structuring human experience. First, every litigation is a struggle between the parties to recount human events in way that the trier understands to reach a favourable decision. Each party endeavours to provide a structure that is understandable to either vindicate or defeat a claim. Narrative is what provides the structure because it is our natural way of understanding human experience.

Psychologists are of the view that humans have a predisposition to organize experience in the narrative form.[25]Jerome Bruner states that the very concept of the self depends on having a narrative of one's own life.[26] It is said that the predisposition is linguistically or psychologically innate to human eyes rendering into figure what it see for comprehension purpose. Some have further investigated

---

[22] Anne E Ralph, Narrative-Erasing Procedure (2018) 18 *Nevada L. Rev.* 573 @ 581

[23] The persuasive influence of narrative renders it susceptible to manipulation. See Peter Brooks, Narrative in and of the Law in James Phelan & Peter J. Rabinowitz, eds. *A Companion to Narrative Theory*, 2005, 415 @ 416 ("Narrative is morally a chameleon that can be used to support the worse as well as the better cause."). It is reported that Socrates banned poets from his republic because their art influenced the heart rather than the mind. See Plato, *The Republic of Plato* (Allan Bloom ed. & trans. 2nd ed. 1991 (stating "such a soul will be like that banished poetry which contained images of vice as well as of virtue") cited in Ralph, above n 2 582 ft. nt. 62

[24]Rideout, above n. 1 @ 56.

[25]Jerome Bruner, *Acts of Meaning*, Harv. U. Press, 1990 @ 47 (quoted in Robert Burns, *A Theory of the* Trial, Princeton U. Press 1999 @159) (stating that narrative provides "an innate schema for the organization and interpretation of experience.")

[26]Jerome Bruner, Life as Narrative (1987) 54 *So.Res.* 11.

whether the innate nature of narrative is a feature of language or is psychologically fundamental in some pre-linguistic way; whether narrative structure is congruent with reality or are some form of Kantian category – a structure of the mind that pre-exists and shapes understanding of experience.

In this respect, the works of George Lakoff has been very enlightening as to how the human mind makes sense of experience.[27] In the view of Amsterdam and Bruner, while narrative structures could be innate to human experience either in the structure of the mind (psychological structure) or in the structure of language (linguistic structure), it could be outside both and therefore located in the ways we culturally-share human experience.[28] This thesis imply that narrative structures are a type of social or cultural construction constructed from our reality of the temporal nature of the human cycle of life which contains elements of narrative structure of a beginning, the middle and the end, to which we assign meaning.[29] Steven Winter argues for an endogenous theory of narrative. In the learned writer's view narratives are fundamental mental models formed from stock stories, such as idealized cognitive models from which we construct meaning.[30]

One thing is given, narrative theorists agree that narrative forms are not only immediately recognizable, but that they allow us to assign meaning to events through pre-given understandings of common events and concepts, configured into the particular pattern of story-meaning. Narratives are therefore natural way of understanding experience.[31] Narrative structure gives logical understanding to human action.

Second, narratives have proven powerful as a model of persuasion because it encompasses narrative rationality. Persuasion using logical reasoning is insufficient to make any argument persuasive. Classical rhetoricians long recognize the fact.[32] While logic provides the proposition that must be proved or disproved, it is narrative of the logic of events, actors, backgrounds, actions, and

---

[27]George Lakoff, *Women, Fire, and Dangerous Things: What Categories Reveal about the* Mind, Univ. Chi. Press, 1987 (examining the human cognition, viewing it in terms of the mental structures that underlie "rationality.)

[28]Anthony Amsterdam & Jerome Bruner, *Minding the* Law, Harv. U. Press, 2000 @ 115-119.

[29]Ibid @ 31.

[30]Steven L. Winter, Making the Familiar Conventional Again (2001) 99 *Mich. L. Rev.* 1607 @ 1630–1632.

[31]Rideout, above n. 1 @ 59.

[32]Steven J. Burton, *An Introduction to Law and Legal Reasoning*, Aspen Publishers 2007. For example, Aristotle is of the view that formal logic (based on analytical syllogism) and rhetorical logic (based on probabilistic conclusion) both meld to ground argumentation. See also, Linda H. Edwards, The Convergence of Analogical and Dialectic Imaginations in Legal Discourse (1996) 20 *Leg. Studies Forum* 1 @ 50 ("[l]egal reasoning is incomplete without the soil of narrative from which the reasoning grows and to which it will return.").

motives that tie to make the argument whole. It is in this way that narrative is central to the lawyer's theory of the case. It provides the trier with concrete reasons for deciding one way or another. Logic as one side of the double helix – primarily serves the formal function of rendering the argument legally reasonable. It is rhetorical logic which melds with formal logic that creates what can be termed 'rationality' that provides the structure of understanding the world, and all valid forms of argumentation and persuasion.[33]

Three, narratives embody several properties that make them psychologically persuasive – properties of coherence (a formal property); correspondence (a formal property); and fidelity (a substantive property). Narrative coherence is only one of two formal or structural properties that render narratives persuasive, the second being narrative correspondence. Narrative correspondence is a matter of a story's corresponding to what a judge or trier knows about what typically happens in the world. This correspondence is an important part of the story's plausibility and hence of its persuasiveness.[34] The story at trial must correspond to what "could" happen, or what "typically" happens, not necessarily to what actually happened. What "could" happen is determined, not by the decision makers' undertaking an empirical assessment of actual events, but rather by the trier looking to a store of background knowledge about these kinds of narratives—to a set of stock stories.

Narrative fidelity, on the other hand, has to do with "whether or not the stories the trier experience ring true with the stories she know to be true in her life. Narrative fidelity is a matter of assessing the substantive worth of a story, but not in terms of its appeal to abstract universals like the truth, and not in terms of its ability to translate into formal, logical propositions about social reality.

Narrative Theory and Storytelling

Even though the words (narrative and storytelling) are used as synonyms they are different.[35] The former is more akin to case theory in that it is the building blocks of the later. Narrative is the putting together of the elements that comprise the story. Narrative is concerned with the process of constructing the story, its elements, the choices the author makes about its elements, the process the author

---

[33]Walter R. Fisher, *Human Communication as Narration: Toward a Philosophy of Reason, Value, and Action,* U. S.C. 1989 @ 47.

[34]Nancy Pennington & Reid Hastie, A Cognitive Theory of Juror Decision Making: The Story Model (1991) 13 *Cardozo L. Rev.* 519 @ 528.

[35]Anne E Ralph, Narrative-Erasing Procedure (2018) 18 *Nevada L. Rev.* 573 @ 576. See also, Simon Stern, Narrative in the Legal Text: Judicial Opinion and Their Narratives in Michael Hanne & Robert Weisberg, eds. *Narratives and Metaphor in Law,* 2018, available in http://papers.ssrn.con/so13/papers.cfm?abstract id=2830904 (legal scholars often speak of narratives when they mean something else. . .)

goes through to make the choices, such as what should be part or left out of the story, the factors that influence the author to intentionally or reflectively make the choices. It interrogates the essential nature of stories and why storytelling inheres with law and persuades triers. It is the theory, which explores why stories are essential for persuasion. It is therefore an exploration of the distinct and identifiable elements – both substantive and technical – of stories. Storytelling on the other hand, is the craft of putting the narrative theory into practice.[36]

Narrative according to James Phelan is "somebody telling somebody else on some occasion and for some purposes that something happened."[37] It also can be described as the "representation of an event or a series of event."[38] Narrative is the representation of events that occur in a story (the story-events). While narrative is the representation of a series of events, story on the other hand, is the "action" – that is, the event or sequence of events that is being represented.

A good example of the difference is the variety of narratives created from the events of happenings at Birmingham, Alabama around Easter 1963. It had to do with the street marches and boycott of stores by people of colour led by Dr. Martin Luther King Jnr. He was arrested, tried and convicted for contempt of court for calling out civil disobedience in the face of injunction prohibiting the march. The events are recounted in a number of different narratives, including the U.S. Supreme Court opinions in *Walker* v. *City of Birmingham*[39] and *Shuttlesworth* v. *City of Birmingham.*[40] A reading of the cases shows the difference. The *Walker* majority opinion read by Justice Stewart and that of the dissent read by Justice Brennan create different narratives of the same events leading up to the case. The same is true of the *Shuttersworth* opinion. The majority opinion of Justice Stewart presents yet another narrative. So, the same story-events generate different narratives. In effect, the narrative is told on different occasions for different purposes: to justify or refute and explain a particular result. Story is therefore a component of narrative. Their difference is exacerbated from the narrative that emerges from narration.[41]

---

[36] Carolyn Grose, in Storytelling Across the Curriculum (2010) *7 J. Asso. Legal Writing Directors* [JALWD] 37.

[37] James Phelan, *Narratives in Contest; Or Another Twist in the Narrative Turn,* Pub. Mod. Language Ass'n.2008, 166 @ 167, cited in Ralph, above n. 25 ft. nt. 13.

[38] H. Porter Abbott, *The Cambridge Introduction to Narrative,* 2008 @ 12. See also, Amsterdam & Brunner, above n. 18 @ 113.

[39] (1967) 388 US 307 @ 308-309

[40] (1969) 394 US 147 @ 148-149. See, David B. Oppenheimer, Kennedy, King, Shuttlesworth and Walker: The Events Leading to the Introduction of Civil Rights Act of 1964 (1995) 29 *U.S.L. Rev.* 645 (describing the historical events leading to civil rights in America)

[41] Ralph, above n. 35 @ 577.

This notwithstanding our discussion here will not make a water-tight distinction between narrative and story. We shall rather use them interchangeably to refer to the same thing, even though they do not necessarily conflate.

Both skills of narrative and storytelling are core skills of lawyering. The reason for this is simple. First, thinking about the practice of law as a practice of storytelling embolden the lawyer "to look behind and between and over and under the black letter rules that comprise the law."[42] In those interstices the lawyer becomes conscious that more is embedded in judicial holdings. Every holding is itself a contest between stories and the ultimate holding is also like Ronald Dworkin states a "chain novel" – an artificial literary genre made up of a group of novelists writing a novel in succession.[43]In his thesis, all decisions of court can be likened to each contributing or writing a new chapter, all bound by a common integrity. Each judge like the chain novelist adds to the whole using the best material she has been given by her successors. The addition is constrained by integrity to build up the precedent laid down by previous decisions. It is in this way that the common law tradition of precedent is much a practice of narrative.

The implication of this for lawyering is that an excellent way to persuade a trier of fact would require presenting a case which matches to a stock or culturally-shared narrative. This is how narrative melds with reasoning to persuade.

As judges write, legal rules become refined through telling and re-telling against new sets of facts. And the stories told or retold become powerful fossilized cultural narratives. Every judicial opinion is therefore art of a community of opinion, all of them narratives about how the law operates in particular circumstances. This taken, then it is plausible to think that the litigation process is itself a contest between narratives "positive for the democratic function of the legal system."[44] Adjudication is the system of testing narratives.

Also, thinking of law as storytelling give the lawyer the confidence to wrestle with the law to have it fit the clients' lived realities, rather than just funnelling the clients' lived realities into what is generally understood to represent the law.[45]

What is more, recognizing that lawyering involves some kind of persuasion and that all persuasion involves some kind of storytelling compels the lawyer to master how to construct and tell stories. In fact, this recognition tells the lawyer

---

[42]Grose, above n. 36 @ 41.

[43] Ronald Dworkin, *Law's Empire,* 1986 @ 229.

[44]Ralph, above n. 35 @ 587.

[45] The articles in footnote 4 above are good examples of how to challenging received wisdom through counter narratives in law rather than just fitting clients lived reality into the prescribed law-jacket. See, White, above n. 4; Miller, above n. 4; Cunningham, above n. 4.

that she is not just a teller of stories, but importantly is a constructor of stories that can shape the future of not only the client, but of society.

Narrative theory in fact, provides useful insight into lawyering. It provides a compelling explanation of why narrative is a powerful persuasive device, thereby providing a useful way to think about the inherent contestable nature of narrative, particularly in the litigation process.[46]

Storytelling is not just a simple recitation of information and facts in chronological order. It is rather a moving narrative tale of character - rich events told to evoke an emotional response in the listener.

Acquiring Storytelling Skills

Since all lawyering interrogates storytelling, learning how to tell persuasive stories is a skill lawyers must master. This section will be concerned with how lawyers should craft stories, the choices involved, an exploration of both the narrative theory and the practice of storytelling. According to Grose, mastering the theory of narrative is the key to aiding the lawyer to acquire the skills of storytelling. This requires identifying the following two steps:

(i) identifying what are stories;
(ii) identifying what makes stories “good” (persuasive, compelling), in the substantial sense (the “what” of the story) and in the technical sense (the “how” of the story).

Narrative scholars generally classify the events that make up the story told in the narrative according to their relative importance. The classification follows two general categories: (i) “constituent events” – those events that are necessary for the story to be what it is; (ii) “supplementary events” – events that do not drive the story, are not necessary for the story to be what it is, but nonetheless provides the building blocks out of which all the more complex [narrative] forms are built.[47]

The lawyer should therefore master those events that are necessary for the story to be it - plausible and believable. It is also important for the lawyer to identify the elements of a story.

In this respect a story is like a drama often split into five parts or essential elements:

The essential elements of stories are:

(i) an introduction or “steady state”. This can also be described as the “exposition”– where characters are introduced, the scene is set and the plot is

---

[46] Ibid.

[47] Abbott, above n. 38 @ 22.

introduced. In legal storytelling, it is a state grounded in the legitimate ordinariness of things.

(ii) the rising action. This is where the hero in a drama is revealed, the conflict is identified and the hero finds the solution to the conflict. It is the section where the "trouble" is identified – something that happens to disrupt the legitimate ordinariness of things;

(iii) the third act is the climax where our hero's situation is either clearly improved or worsened. It can be described as the section on the "effort" to resolve the trouble;

(iv) the falling action is where we see the conflict diminishing and the hero is winning or losing leading to an outcome or resolution. The resolution or denouement provides a transition toward the end of the story.

(v) The "coda" is the end part where the morals are revealed, tension is released and a sense of relief is given to the audience or listeners. It is an evaluation of what it all might mean which returns the audience from the "then-and-there" of the narrative to the "here-and-now" of the telling.[48]

These five elements put together make up the plot of the story – telling "what happened and why" of the story. Plots generally fit into particular genre constructed from our schemas through which we understand our world. So, once being told the audience recognizes and expects resolution in a certain way.

A2L contains a graphic illustration of how these five parts of storytelling can structured in a litigation story.[49] Using a failed mortgage bank scenario, it is plotted like this:

Introduction: I like to start with belief or fundamental truth and introduction of the characters like,

> Banks survive on greed - it's how they make money. When they make good loans, they make money. When they make bad loans,

---

[48]Anthony G. Amsterdam & Jerome S. Bruner, *Minding The Law,* Harv. Univ. Press, 2000 @ 133-134 (a book the authors translate literary theory and rhetoric into terms understandable to the contemporary legal as opposed to literary scholar). See also*A2L Storytelling for Litigators: Building a Great Narrative for Judges and Juries*, 3rd ed. 2014 @ 20 (describing that the structure of a story is like a drama, it states that a story is often split into five parts: " the introduction (also called exposition) is where characters are introduced, the scene is set and the plot is introduced; rising action is where the hero is revealed, the conflict is identified and our hero finds the solution to the conflict; the third act is the climax where our hero's situation is either clearly improved or worsened; falling action is where we see the conflict diminishing and our hero is now clearly winning or losing; the resolution or denouement provides a transition toward the end of our story. Morals are revealed, tension is released and a sense of relief is given to the listeners."); Jerome Bruner, *Making Stories: Law, Literature, Life,* Harv. Univ. Press, 2002 @ 20; Thomas M. Leitch, *What Stories Are: Narrative Theory and Interpretation,* Penn. St. U. Press 1986 @ 148.

[49] See A2L @. 28.

they lose money. These bankers are essentially being accused of making bad loans, which to be true would have to mean they were not trying to make money. When is the last time you heard of bankers not trying to make money? It makes no sense.

Rising Action: Since it is essential in this section to keep a logical flow and keep the tenor rising until the conflict is identified, it could be stated that:

After years of lacklustre home sales, finally it looked like Miami was positioned to take off and it was these bankers' jobs to make sure their bank made money - and that meant, making loans. And that's just what they did. Month after month, loan applications were up, and month after month, the bank was making more and more money. These bankers were at the top of their game. They received awards for their actions. But a storm was brewing. A real estate collapse had begun, and these bankers had to face it head on, sometimes at great personal sacrifice.

Climax: Because this is where the heroes overcome or are instead defeated by the conflict, it could be expressed like this:

Our clients did their best to weather the storm, but the reality of the real estate environment was too great to overcome. Loans were not repaid, foreclosures occurred and our clients either lost their jobs or retired and the bank ultimately failed. It was a brave battle but just not one you can fight at the age of 70 after a 40-year career in banking. Even if they wanted to, the fight was not winnable.

Falling Action: Since this is where we see the conflict diminishing and the hero is winning or losing leading to an outcome or resolution, it could be expressed like this:

So they returned to their families. They lived modestly. They played with their grandkids. On a part-time basis, each helped to wind down bank operations. In the end, they saw much of their life's work blotted out by forces that were completely beyond their control. After all, they are just a couple of retirees who did their job well – they made loans, the bank made money until the unthinkable happened.

Resolution: Being the final part, which provides a transition toward the end of the story could be structured like this:

> Ultimately insurance protected all of the bank customers, so no money was lost. The stockholders lost money in their investment, but not all investments work out, right? Not all of the loans these bankers made worked out, and there's no redo for them. So would it make sense to reward stockholders for their investment that didn't work out by giving them an award of money? If Bank greed makes us squirm, the greed of those trying to recoup a lost investment in a bank should make you sick.

That is just how the lawyer can structure her statement of facts to tell a persuasive story. These five elements are what make up "the plot" of the story – the "what happened and why" of the story.

Stories, whether told in the manner above or differently narrated are easily recognizable or familiar to the audience intuitively from the outset. They either register to the mind as a comedy, tragedy, or drama because they fits into particular "genres" – the human mental models representing possible ways in which events in the human world can go.[50]

Moving the plot of stories are the characters – the heroes, villains, lovers, enemies, protagonists, antagonists, etc. - who engage in the "what happened" and the "why" of the story. Developing the character makes real the character to the reader. The reader can then empathize with the character. To do the projection of the character, the writer must both understand the characters-their needs, dreams, fears, weaknesses, experiences, circumstances-and know how to convey that understanding to the reader.

Character can be established directly, by describing a protagonist's thoughts or by describing physical "appearance, clothes, possessions, body language, etc. which act as indices of class, character, status and social milieu. So, in effect character is to be described in such a way as "speak so the person is seen."

In determining the "what happened" the lawyer must figure out consciously what story to tell and how to tell it. This would involve giving thought to three substantive factors - the theory of the case - the law, the facts, and the goals of the client. It is also important to consider contextual matters, such as the cultural-shared schema; the personalities of the client; professional responsibility ethics implicated in telling the "what happened".

---

[50]Grose, above n. 36 @ 43.

What this mean is that drawing up briefs or doing a statement of facts or a deposition must not be a routine of recording as it were the known universe of "relevant" facts in a case. Recognizing that there is no such thing as an absolutely neutral description of the facts, every skilled lawyer must learn to pick and choose from available facts to present a picture of "what happened" that most accurately reflects the client's sense of what matters. A lawyer should thus know how to draw from the available pool of facts the picture sought to be presented.

The conscious selection should go beyond "what happened" to include the substantive component of the story – the "how" of the story. This implicates decisions on technical stuff that make the story go, like when the story begins, when it ends, what gets fully described, what is left out, how quickly or slowly the action should move, how fleshed out each character should be, etc. This is important because while law (such as court rules or rules of evidence) defines relevance, they generally do not define how the relevant facts, in a particular case, are to be expressed.[51]It is therefore a choice matter for the lawyer to decide up what words to use, and with what emphasis.

Viewed from this critical lawyering perspective, stories are not just a recitation of relevant facts in a chronological form, as though a linear framework structure for recording relevant facts. Stories can and ought to be recursive. They can be organized into alternative narratives, depending on the perspective sought to be projected. Rather they are constructed from facts and then rearranged into persuasive stories – taking into consideration what can be said, how to say it, etc. from the perspective of what matters to drive the case theory.

Why stories are important

Stories no doubt are essential ingredients in human interaction.[52] Because stories align with how we generally construct knowledge, we instinctively understand how they work. Even though lawyering is said to be about logical reasoning divorce from stories (stories being concerned with humanness), the two are inseparable.[53] Stories guide logic, reasoning and communication in law. The

---

[51]Bernard Jackson, *Narrative Theories and Legal Discourse* in *Narrative in Culture: The Uses of Storytelling in the Sciences, Philosophy, and Literature*, (1994) @27, cited in Grose above n. 36 @ 45 ft. nt. 45.

[52]Walter R. Fisher, *Human Communication as Narration: Toward a Philosophy of Reason, Value, and Action*, (U. S.C. 1989) @64 ("Humans are essentially storytellers.")

[53]James Boyd White, *Heracles' Bow: Essays on the Rhetoric and the Poetics of the Law* 168 (Univ. Wis. Press 1985). ("[T]he law always begins in story: usually in the story the client tells, whether he or she comes in off the street for the first time or adds in a phone call another piece of information to a narrative with which the lawyer has been long, perhaps too long, familiar. It ends in story, too, with a decision by a court or jury, or an agreement between the parties, about what happened and what it means.")

importance of stories is tied to how the audience responds to it as a communication tool.[54]

Generally, the hearer of a story responds in the following ways:

(i) it creates and shapes new knowledge, such as is the case where stories are used to teach a person acceptable behaviour in a given society;

(ii) stories are also told to reinforce responses, as when it is told to reinforce received knowledge as properly grounded and correct. That is exactly what lawyers for example, do when they use precedent to reinforce the correctness of legal propositions;

(iii) stories are also told to create response-changes in thinking. For example, the lawyer may use stories to persuade the trier if sheer abstract appeal to legal doctrine proves challenging for the trier to change her mind-set or stock position.[55] The factory closure case is a good example of how stories can be used to bring about mind-set change.[56]

Let us recreate the story in context to illustrate the point.[57] It is a story we often use in teaching social justice across the curriculum. The story is this: a factory in a city has operated for over fifty years. The city has grown around it, relies on it for employment and most of the city's activities are connected with it. Yet the company appears to be unconcerned about the welfare of the city. Its managers operate on the shareholder maximizing philosophy. Ruled by a distant and seemingly unapproachable board of directors, the company closes the factory. The effect of this on the city is enormous. Many suffer financial reverses, drop in their living standard. All its workers are unable to put things, including family life.

The teacher can ask a property or business associations law class if the company actions amounts to a betrayal case. One where the workers trusted the company and depended on it? Should we think the company lived off the trust, took advantage of it, and abused it?

---

[54] Ruth Anne Robbins, An Introduction to Applied Storytelling and this Symposium (2008) 14 *J. Legal Writing Inst.* 3.

[55] For examples of stories told for response-changing see Scheppele, above n. 2 (an article on how shareholder, etc); Kim Lane Scheppele, Forward: Telling Stories (1989) 87 *Michigan L.Rev.*2073 (discussing "point of viewlessness" The story describes two cases that ended up in the U.S. Supreme Court, one involving the rape of a woman, the other involving the allegedly coerced confession of a black man. She contrasts the appellate court decisions in both cases with the Supreme Court opinions, illustrating points about language and framing as important tools of persuasive storytelling.). The story originally appeared in Kim Lane Scheppele's forward to the Michigan Law Symposium on Storytelling. See (1989) *Mich. L. Rev.* For purposes of this paper we would adopt the scenario played out of the story by Carolyn Grose. See Carolyn Grose, in Storytelling Across the Curriculum (2010) *7 J. Asso. Legal Writing Directors* 37 @ 39.

[56] Joseph W. Singer, Persuasion (1989) 87 *Michigan L. Rev.* 2442.

[57] The story is a recreation from Joseph Singer. See Singer, above n. 56.

This no doubt would be nonsensical argument by common count. Most of our students will think that such an argument is unlikely to persuade a court. It simply would not work. Instead, they may consider the fact of closure regrettable. Those with a knowledge of an economic analysis of law can write off the situation as one example of efficiency at work-the efficient restructuring of production through the invisible hand of the market.[58] Yes, market decisions should pay less regard to social expectations. No have no quarrel with these shades of reasoning. After all it is not the business of a company to provide welfare to people. That business rests squarely with government under chapter two of our Constitution.[59]

If this were a writing assignment we are sure how our students would answer. With hindsight of their IRAC model they likely will raise four pillars of argument against regulating factory closures. First, they recall from memory and apply what they know from property law. A necessary incident of property right is ability to treat owned *res* the way the owner wishes, subject to a few rules on use and enjoyment. The factory is property. The owners are the shareholders. So, they can choose to do what they want with it. Regulating closures would derogate on the right. For the purpose of our illustration, let us call such an argument the *property argument*.

Two, they apply their learning from company law. Quickly they remember that as a general rule company law is rooted in shareholder-maximizing principle. They are the one who hire managers to maximize profit. That being the case, if an investment decision is closure, so be it. Let me refer to this as the *market argument*.

Recalling further a fundamental doctrine of contract law (freedom of contract) they wonder why the workers think that the situation raises an abuse of trust argument. The foundation of contract they learnt in school makes central freedom of contract. The workers should have been smart when they took their job offers. It was a bargain relationship. If they now feel disappointed because their fortune nosedives, that is their fault. Freedom of contract should have moved them to negotiate severance payments to cushion the possible challenge that has now arisen. Let us call this the *freedom of contract argument.*

If they are good enough to recall lectures in constitutional and administrative law, then they may also question the legitimacy of the breach of trust workers position by arguing that what the workers are demanding in the circumstance is tantamount to asking the court to create and recognize new property rights. That they say should be the business of the legislature rather than the courts. Let us call this *deference to the legislature argument*.

---

[58] Richard Posner, *Economic Analysis of Law*, 8th ed. 2010.
[59] 1999 Constitution of the Federal Republic of Nigeria.

These answers are fine looked from the prism of IRAC. But certainly, flawed from a social justice dimension. They sure do *think* like lawyers. All that matter is legal logic derived from rules. But with little recognition of the social implications of their scientific solution. The students take a monolithic, atomistic, abstract and acontextual view of the problem. For them IRAC syllogism is the key to solve the factory closure case. Their reasoning is stewed with no fellow feeling, no humanity, no context, no story. They obviously cannot do a good job representing the miserable workers in this factory closure case. They side with deep-pocket shareholders and the framers of company law legislation and the wider middle-class architecture of law.

To teach social justice to the class a teacher can simply tell a story that interrogates the students shared-cultural schema. It goes this way. Imagine this scenario: All the students of the Nigerian Law School six campuses are to be in their campus auditoriums on the Monday, a week to the commencement of the Bar final examination. The purpose is to listen to an important satellite talk by the Director-General (DG) of the Nigerian Law School (NLS) on behalf of the Council of Legal Education (CLE). Accordingly, they are gathered. The DG opening speech is revealing. For some time now, the profession and the public are concerned about the competence and character of new wigs. Reports of scandals involving lawyers are on the increase. The Legal Practitioners Disciplinary Council (LPDC) is increasingly saddled with malpractice complains. As a result of this the CLE two years ago set up an advisory committee to help address the challenge. The committee members were drawn from the judiciary, inner and outer Bar, and the ministries of justice across the country. Their report is now out. In it they attribute the downslide in competence and character to the large number of people seeking to become lawyers in the faculties and the NLS and have recommended a 50 per cent reduction across board and that the pass mark for all law subjects will be 50 per cent no longer 40 per cent. They have also asked the CLE to increase the Bar vocational training from one year to two. It is also their recommendation that it be implemented immediately to prevent further slide.

The CLE at its last meeting a few days ago unanimously approved all the recommendations and have instructed the NLS to commence its implementation with you. So, ladies and gentlemen we have no choice but start with you. Please take a good look at your neighbour. He or she may never become a lawyer. Only 50 per cent of you can be lawyers. The minimum pass mark is 50 per cent. Even if more than 50 per cent of you score above the minimum 50 per cent pass mark in the five Bar vocational subject, we would have no choice but fail them because only half of you can be lawyers. Also, your programme of study with us is no longer one year. It is now two. Your exams will not be next week. It will be one year one week from today. We recognize that implementing this new policy can be disruptive to you, nonetheless these measures are to promote efficient delivery of legal services. Good morning Bar-aspirants. That ends my speech. You may now respond if you have anything to say.

You can imagine how charged all the auditoriums would be. The students are overwhelmed with anger. You cannot do this. It is totally unfair, a breach and abuse of trust by CLE. They insist the position of CLE is unsustainable. If you do not immediately reverse yourself, we shall seek redress in court. You cannot toy with our rights this way and get away with it. Our story ends.

The teacher can now play the devil's advocate, using the four-pillar argument against the students which they erected against the city workers in the closure case. Starting with the property argument the teacher could ask them, do the students have rights? The NLS is the property of CLE. Consult the law. Since an owner of property can do what she wants with it, that's what CLE has done change of policy.

Remember the market argument. The board of CLE is charged under the Act with regulating vocational training and continuing legal education for lawyers to improve legal service delivery. So, it is simply promoting market efficiency for legal services by the new rules. It is like an investment decision to gravitate resources to most valued person.[60]

The students may think this most unfair that CLE changes the rules in the middle of the game. Here again, the teacher can resort to the freedom of contract argument, by simply saying: "gentlemen, please take a good look at the NLS students' prospectus. It clearly states that CLE/NLS can change the rules of engagement at any time. That is exactly what they have done. If you didn't like it, you should have bargained out of it."

Finally, our teacher can refer to the deference to legislature argument. Suppose (without conceding) that you think it is a breach of trust to change the rules in the middle of the game, this still does not ground reason for a court to grant the students the injunctive or monetary reliefs. By litigating against CLE/NLS you are asking for a right to attend their school, participate in their programme and be sponsored by them for admission to the Nigerian Bar-all that against the better judgment of the owners-CLE who run the NLS. Is that something they promised you? Did you bargain for it? In the absence of contract giving you the right, your claim would effectively be seeking the creation of a new property right-an entitlement to a qualifying certificate for call to Bar. This is a business more appropriate for the legislature, not the court.

---

[60]Posner, above n. 58 @ 16.

At the end of this exercise and accompanying story, no doubt the students would begin to reason that the court should interpret contracts in the light of new social conditions and values in a way and manner that promotes reasonable reliance on contract to promote justice. They all begin to think that even in the absence of legislation to their aid, the court should create (new) rights that prevents the CLE from frustrating their reasonable expectations. They trusted the CLE, and that trust is abused. In one swoop they realize that rights should transcend explicit contracts terms. By creating a felt connection between them and the vulnerable factory workers they realize how narrow legal reasoning, especially that which subscribes to the IRAC model can be. They graphically see that lawyering must take account of real life experience and be interpreted in a manner that advances social justice. Their atomistic view of legal rules and principles suddenly get converted to energy, expressed in legal creativity and invention. They can now see that the prevailing factory closure rules translated into company law, property law and the like are mere superstructure of law constructed from the perspective of corporate managers who make investment decisions on behalf of shareholders, without outsider perspective.

They begin to appreciate that outsider perspective is muted by law. The CLE/NLS story is what gives them the insight. They recognize that free market argument and its *cousins* assume too much. In real live situations, the relative bargaining power of parties to contracts is often unequal. The factory closure scenario teaches the students to understand and experience both vulnerability and broken trust. They are forced to see what it is for the city workers to be at the absolute mercy of corporate managers in the absence of contract hedging their future. Yes, stories do have power and can be useful in teaching.[61]This is how stories can be told to change mind-set.

Stories have been employed as a veritable tool for improving the law, particularly in bringing to the front burner the stories of "outsiders," - people whose stories are often excluded in the law-making and adjudication.[62] Stories are also useful for changing settled law, especially in areas where the legal position is unsupported or unsupportable by logic or experience.

There can be no doubt that lawyering is more of facts than about the law. This is a sad truth lawyers must recognize. In fact, empirical evidence shows that judges decide cases on story model as opposed to logical, probabilistic models of

[61] Symposium: Law, Knowledge, and the Academy (2002) 115 *Harv. L. Rev.* 1278.

[62]Kevin Jon Heller, The Cognitive Psychology of Circumstantial Evidence (2006) 105 *Mich. L. Rev.* 241 (stating that the best criminal defence can be a good alternative narrative). See also, Stacy Caplow, Putting the "I" in Wr*t*ng: Drafting an A/Effective Personal Statement to Tell a Winning Story (2008) 14 *Leg. Writing* 249 (immigration case).

decision-making.[63]Unfortunately, stories that make up the facts of a case are indeterminate, even though some lawyers think that facts are objective, determinate, not subject to different interpretation.

Introspection reveals that when brought to basics, facts and their construction are fundamentally indeterminate in nature.[64]It is for this reason that Neumann states that a lawyer should be skilled in the art of legal construction of fact, because (i) every skilled lawyer is required to understand the separation of facts from other things; (ii) the separation of determinative facts from other kinds of facts; (iii) the separation of inferences from facts; and (iv) the purging analysis of hidden and unsupportable factual assumptions.[65]

Lawyers have long put in the corner facts controversy. It is not uncommon to hear some lawyers say, 'facts are stubborn. No good advocacy can change facts.' But this is gross misstatement and unrepresentative of what really happens in the litigation process.[66] Indeterminacy of facts(albeit overlooked by lawyers) is without argument the kernel of every litigation. Determined facts in any lawsuit determine how the law would be applied to arrive at legal conclusion. Yes, even if a case travels all the way to appeal, the decided facts bear an enormous influence on how judges apply the law.

Deciding what make up facts interrogates a whole gamut of things that render the objective determinacy of facts suspect. For instance, when a judge decides what the facts of a case are, she would in effect have chosen among competing stories told by the parties, multiply, competing inferences, some spoken, other not. Such a choice undoubtedly is coloured and influenced by the judge's use of say common sense, experience, logic, biases, prejudices, psychology, and many more, that colour what eventually is taken as the facts of the case. All of

---

[63]W. Lance Bennett & Martha S. Feldman, *Reconstructing Reality in the Courtroom: Justice and Judgment in American Culture,* Rutgers U. Press, 1981 (stating that the criminal trial is organized around storytelling) @ 3; John H. Blume *et al.,*Every Juror Wants a Story: Narrative Relevance, Third Party Guilt and the Right to Present a Defence (2006) 44 *Am. Crim. L. Rev.* 1069 @ 1087 cited in Brian J. Foley, Applied Legal Storytelling, Politics and Factual Realism (2008) 14 *Leg. Writing* 17 @ 34 n. 83; Ty Alper*et al.,* Stories Told and Untold: Lawyering Theory Analyses of the First Rodney King Assault Trial (2005) 12 *Clin. L. Rev.* 1.

[64]Kim Lane Scheppele, Foreword: Telling Stories (1989) 87 *Mich. L. Rev.* 2073 (examining how same facts situation can be perceived as "lightly choke" or "heavy caress.").

[65]Richard K. Neumann, *Legal Reasoning and Legal Writing: Structure, Strategy, and Style,* 5th ed., Aspen Publishers 2005 @ 207. See also Serenda Stier, Reframing Legal Skills: Relational Lawyering, (1992) 42 *J. Leg. Educ.* 303, 317 (an article that advocates teaching lawyers the skills of facts finding – teaching lawyers how to find tell stories, how to find facts, how to find within them the hidden assumptions, how to those aspects that can be exploited by the advocate).

[66]For general reading on indeterminacy see, see Brian Bix, *Law, Language and Legal Determinacy,* Oxford: Clarendon Press, 1993, Jules L. Coleman & Brian Leiter, Determinacy, Objectivity, and Authority (1992) 142 *Univ. Pa. L. Rev.* 549; Lawrence B. Solum, On the Indeterminacy Crisis: Critiquing Critical Dogma (1987) 54 *Univ. Chi. L. Rev.* 462.

these come to play in deciding what are the facts of a case, even though rules of evidence explicitly excludes them as non-objective parts of the fact-finding process.

The unfortunate use of non-objective facts is even accentuated by the facts that judges receive no formal or professional training on how to overcome facts indeterminacy. They may receive training on how to overcome indeterminacy of law, but certainly not for legal construction of facts. Worse still, facts indeterminacy can present itself in even legally clear cases, because the "indeterminacy may come from the indeterminacy of facts or moral, ethical, religious, traditional, or political indeterminacy."[67]This is visible in instances where judges bring to their decision biases and prejudice that they are obligated to loath consciously.

Storytelling is a powerful tool for exerting control over facts and indeterminacy of facts. This is not surprising because as a persuasion tool it helps the lawyer to organize a compelling narrative. Stories fit into the broad framework for persuasion unpacked into the triangle of logos, pathos and ethos.[68]So long as much of lawyering is about persuasion, the combination of pathos and ethos in legal argument puts storytelling in the heart of professional persuasion.

Narratives and Pleadings

Most texts on pleadings focus on tactical and instrumental aspects of pleadings.[69] Only a few acknowledge the place of narrative in pleadings. This is rather unfortunate, because "bare-bone" complaint pleading cannot fly anything. Good pleading must tell a complete, coherent story in a persuasive way to give the court the perspective on the case. Stories whether arranged in chronological or sequential order of events must be well crafted to tell the judge that something went wrong and requires redress. But lawyers somehow mistrust stories, and so characterize it as an aspect of the drafter's personal style or technique.

Even though the components of every narrative is stable (following the path of an initial steady state grounded in the ordinariness of things; trouble start; efforts to redress the trouble; a new steady state created; coda) the nature of the trouble or conflict varies. It may stem from conflict with another, from conflict within the self, or from conflict with society. Whatever nature it takes, trouble

---

[67]Brian J. Foley & Ruth Anne Robbins, Fiction 101: A Primer for Lawyers on How to Use Fiction Writing Techniques to Write Persuasive Facts Sections (2001) 32 *Rutgers L.J.* 459.

[68] See Michael R. Smith, *Advanced Legal Writing: Theories and Strategies in Persuasive Writing,* Aspen L. & Bus. 2002 @ 49.

[69] Elizabeth Fajans & Mary R. Falk, Old Stories: Restoring Narrative To Pleading Practice (2009) 15 *J. Leg. Writing* 3 @ 10.

arises from controversy between the "agent, act, purpose (goal) and the agency (or means) and the scene.[70]

It is the organization of events into meaningful progression from steady state to conflict and then resolution that make narrative a persuasive force.

Detail is crucial to effective narration. The reason is simple. Details elicit emotion, create mental pictures, stimulate and lend fidelity to narratives. Elizabeth Fajans and Mary Falk article contain three complaints filed in federal courts in the U.S. Two of them (slip-and-fall complaints) however would be selected by us to illustrate the difference between bare-bone and narrative style of pleading. Much as the two contrast non-narrative and narrative pleading styles, they are by no means models, but rather samples only. The first, *Breeden* v. *Hilton Hotel* (example 1) is non-narrative.[71] The second, *Bork* v. *Yale Club*, (example 2) is narrative.[72] The style in the *Breeden's* case follows regular pleadings. Basics sufficient to raise negligence. No character development. No scene. No visual detail save that the floor was dangerous with water on the tiles.

On the other hand, the second, *Bork*, goes beyond the stock story of basics. It is a compelling narrative, with character. It identifies the parties. Tells the gravitas of the plaintiff - a speaker at an event for elites at an elite venue. The plaintiff isn't referred to in the third person – simply as "plaintiff." He is identified rather throughout the pleadings as – Mr. Bork. He remains an individual throughout the pleading, being addressed in the first person language. The venue is visualized, putting the judge at the scene. The stable components of the narrative are maintained – a steady state and the state is disrupted. What next occurs as the injury of Bork is vividly depicted. The injury and treatment is described in material particulars. So, the Bork story is presented in a way that makes it vivid and real to the reader.

Conclusion

Unquestionable, credible stories carry great rhetorical power. The create and re-create legal reality. Lawyers will better serve their clients if they learn how to persuade through stories. Narrative isn't simply a persuasion tool and literary enhancer, it can also be skilfully used for tactical advantages, as it could trigger or foreclose disclosure or widen or narrow discovery in the pre-trial conferencing. It is a skill all lawyer must hone to be great pleaders and advocates.

---

[70]Ibid @ 18.
[71]2004 WL 3054743 (N.D. Ala. Mar. 19, 2004).
[72]2007 WL 1686504 (S.D.N.Y. June 1, 2007).

EXAMPLE 1
Bare-bone slip-and-fall complaint

United State District Court, Northern District, Alabama

Mary Sue Breeden, Plaintiff, v. Hilton Hotels Corp. a Delaware corporation; *et al.* Defendants.

<u>Complaint</u>

Plaintiff Mary Sue Breeden hereby complains of the defendants Hilton Hotel Corporation, a Delaware corporation, [and other named defendants] . . .

The claims, actions and causes of actions [sic] described herein arise out of a March 21, 2002, injury event occurring in Alexandria, Egypt.

<u>Jurisdiction</u>

[. . .]

<u>Identification of parties</u>

4. The plaintiff, Mary Sue Breeden, is a resident citizen of Morgan County, Alabama, residing at 2805 Lexington Avenue, SW, Decatur, Morgan County, Alabama 35603.

5. Defendant Hilton Hotel Corporation is a Delaware corporation whose principal place of business is located in the State of California (hereinafter "Hilton Hotels")- Hilton Hotels, however, conducts business in at least two locations within the Northern District of Alabama.

<u>Facts</u>

9. On March 21, 2002, the plaintiff was a business invitee on the premises of the Hilton Borg El Arab Resort, Matrouh Desert Road, Borg El Arab, Egypt, in or near Alexandria, Egypt (hereinafter, "the Premises").

10. At all times relevant hereto...[the Defendants] were the owners of; through their agents, the possessors of; and other- wise through such agents and employees, exercised control, maintenance, supervision and/or management over the Premises.

11. On March 21, 2002, the Defendants negligently and/or wantonly caused, permitted, allowed, or created a dangerous condition to exist on the Premises in the form of water on a tiled surface over which pedestrian traffic was allowed. The Defendants had actual notice and/or had constructive notice of this condition and/or failed to exercise reasonable care with respect to their maintenance of the Premises, thereby negligently and/or wantonly failing to discover and remove this condition.

12. As a proximate consequence of the aforesaid negligence and/or wantonness, the plaintiff was caused to slip and fall, and to incur the following injuries and damages:

She sustained personal injury, incurred hospital, doctor and medical expenses, and suffered physical pain, permanent disability and impairment, and mental anguish.

Wherefore........the plaintiff Mary Sue Breeden demands judgment against the Defendants, jointly and severally, in the amount of Five hundred thousand Dollars, plus costs.

EXAMPLE 2
"Slip-and-fall complaint as narrative

United States District Court Southern District of New York

Robert H. Bork Plaintiff, v. The Yale Club of New York City, Defendants.

Complaint

[. . .]

Nature of the action

1.This is a personal injury action brought against Defendant Yale Club of New York City (the "Yale Club") for its negligent and grossly negligent failure to maintain reasonably safe facilities.

Parties

2. Plaintiff Robert H. Bork is a resident and citizen of Virginia. He was injured while visiting the Yale Club in New York, New York, to give a speech at an event there on June 6, 2006.

3. Defendant Yale Club of New York City is a private club with its principal place of business at 50 Vanderbilt Avenue, New York, New York 10017. The Yale Club offers guestrooms, restaurants, athletic, banquet and meeting facilities for its members and their guests.

Venue and Jurisdiction

Factual allegations

6. On the evening of June 6, 2006,the New Criterion magazine held an event (the "New Criterion event") at the Yale Club. The New Criterion invited Mr. Bork, among other guests, to deliver remarks at the event.

7.The New Criterion hosted the event in a banquet room at the Yale Club. As the host of the event, the Yale Club provided tables and chairs where guests could sit during the reception and the evening's speeches. At the front of the room, the Yale Club provided a dais, atop which stood a lectern for speakers to address the audience.

8. Because of the height of this dais, the Yale Club's normal practice is to provide a set of stairs between the floor and the dais. At the New Criterion event, however, the Yale Club failed to provide any steps between the floor and the dais. Nor did the Yale Club provide a handrail or any other reasonable support feature to assist guests attempting to climb the dais.

9. When it was his turn to deliver remarks to the audience, Mr. Bork approached the dais. Because of the unreasonable height of the dais, without stairs or a handrail, Mr. Bork fell backwards as he attempted to mount the dais, striking his left leg on the side of the dais and striking his head on a heat register.

10. As a result of the fall, a large hematoma formed on Mr. Bork's lower left leg, which later burst. The injury required surgery, extended medical treatment, and months of physical therapy.

11. Mr. Bork suffered excruciating pain as a result of this injury and was largely immobile during the months in which he received

physical therapy, preventing him from working his typical schedule before the injury. The months of relative inactivity weakened Mr. Bork's legs so that he still requires a cane for stability. In addition, Mr. Bork continues to have a limp as a result of this injury.

<u>First cause of action</u>

[Negligence]

12. The allegations set forth in paragraphs 1 through 11 of this Complaint are re-alleged and incorporated by reference as if fully set forth herein.

13. The Yale Club had a duty to provide reasonably safe facilities in its reception and meeting rooms, including providing a safe dais of reasonable height and with stairs between the floor and the dais and a supporting hand-rail.

14. At the New Criterion event, the Yale Club breached its duty to provide reasonably safe facilities by failing to provide a safe dais and stairs between the floor and the dais, a supporting handrail, or any other reasonable support feature to protect its guests attempting to mount that dais.

15.It was reasonably foreseeable that, by failing to provide a safe dais and stairs between the floor and the dais, a supporting handrail, or any other reasonable support feature, a guest such as Mr. Bork attending the New. Criterion even would be injured while attempting to mount the dais.

16. The Yale Club's negligent failure to provide reasonably safe facilities, and in particular, its failure to provide a safe dais and stairs between the floor and the dais, a supporting handrail, or any other reasonable support feature to protect its guests at- tempting to mount the dais, caused Mr. Bork to fall while at- tempting to mount the dais and caused his extensive and continuing injuries.

17. As a result of the Yale Club's negligence in failing to provide reasonably safe facilities, Mr. Bork has suffered actual damages. These damages include pain and suffering, a continuing leg injury, medical bills and related costs of treatment, and lost work time and

income. The long-term effects of his injuries continue to manifest themselves.

<u>Second cause of action</u>

[Gross Negligence]

18. The allegations set forth in paragraphs 1 through 11 of this Complaint are re-alleged and incorporated by reference as if fully set forth herein.

19. The Yale Club had a duty to provide reasonably safe facilities in its reception and meeting rooms, including providing a safe dais of reasonable height and with stairs between the floor and the dais and a supporting handrail.

20. The Yale Club breached its duty to provide reasonably safe facilities by wantonly, wilfully, and recklessly failing to pro- vide a safe dais and stairs between the floor and the dais, a sup- porting handrail, or any other reasonable support feature to protect its guests attempting to mount that dais.

21. It was reasonably foreseeable that, by failing to provide a safe dais and stairs between the floor and the dais, a supporting handrail, or any other reasonable support feature, a guest such as Mr. Bork attending the New Criterion event would be injured while attempting to mount the dais.

22. The Yale Club's wanton, wilful and reckless disregard for the safety of its guests, and in particular, its failure to provide a safe dais and stairs between the floor and the dais, a supporting handrail, or any other reasonable support feature to protect its guests attempting to mount the dais, caused Mr. Bork to fall while attempting to mount the dais and caused his extensive and continuing injuries.

23. As a result of the Yale Club's gross negligence and wan- ton, wilful and reckless disregard for the safety of its guests, Mr. Bork has suffered actual damages. These damages include pain and suffering, a continuing leg injury, medical bills and related costs of treatment, and lost work time and income. The long-term effects of his injuries continue to manifest themselves.

24. Because the Yale Club's gross negligence was wanton, wilful and in reckless disregard for the safety of its guests, punitive damages should also be awarded against it in an amount to be determined at trial.

Prayer for relief

Wherefore, Plaintiff demands the following relief against Defendant:

A. Awarding actual damages resulting from Defendant's wrongdoing in excess of $1,000,000.

B. Punitive damages in an amount to be proven at trial;

C. Pre- and post-judgment costs, interest and attorney's fees;

D. Such other and further relief as this Court may deem appropriate and equitable to decree.

Chapter 17

Visual Legal Writing and Persuasion

Introduction

Legal literature has a mountain of brief and legal writing text on how to write good and better legal briefs. Most of them focus on subjects like structure, language, how to write more succinctly, clearer, logically and other typologies. Books, articles, and websites on style, grammar, and typography are replete in legal scholarship. They mostly focus on text-based writing because it is assumed that the only or basic tool of lawyer's communication is textual - in words.[1] Yes, words may be the lawyer's primary tool, but they are not the only tool. Graphics legal writing is generally not the norm in lawyer's writing. If anything, it is strange bedfellow in writing because legal communication is generally text-based.[2]

This is to be expected from the bunch of lawyers trained before the common use of computers. It is therefore not surprising that lawyers have been slow to integrate images into their written works. Like most profession, change comes slowly. Law has been a text-based profession for hundreds of years. What is more, unlike the physical sciences, law deals with abstract ideas, making it not readily susceptible to visual imaging.[3]What is more, lawyers may be quick to associate

---

[1]Lord Denning allusion to words. See for example Professor Charles Alan Wright foreword to Brian A. Garner, *The Element of Legal Style*, 2nd ed. Oxford Univ. Press, 2002, at xvi. ("the only tool of the lawyer is words)."

[2] Steve Johnson & Ruth A. Robbins, Art-Inculcating the Analysis: Systemizing the Decision to Use Visuals as Legal Reasoning (2015) 20 *J. Leg. Writing* 57. See also, Elizabeth Porter, Taking Images Seriously (2014) 114 *Colum. L. Rev.* 1687 (discussion focusing on the three foremost dangers of unregulated visual advocacy: the danger that implicit biases and naïve realism—the belief that an image represents a transparent window into a single truth—could infect judges' decisions; the risk that images will warp the allocation of decision-making power between the judge and jury, and between appellate courts and trial courts; and the risk that images could vitiate legal discourse by sacrificing depth for flash—turning legal arguments into memes); Adam L. Rosman, Visualizing the Law: Using Charts, Diagrams, and Other Images to Improve Legal Briefs, (2013) 63 *J. Legal Educ.* 70 (article discussion showing that a lawyer's primary tool isn't only words, but includes images, and showing how well- crafted images—charts, diagrams, photographs—can make briefs more interesting and persuasive. It further discusses how law schools would do well to incorporate instruction in visual presentation).

[3] For instance, while a medical professional could readily use anatomical diagram to make a point, a lawyer would rarely illustrate legal concept in anything but words. See Adam L. Rosman, above n. 2. Visualizing the Law: Using Charts, Diagrams, and Other Images to Improve Legal Briefs, (2013)

images with emotion and irrationality – a thing that should be eschewed in law. Not surprising, for most part, Lady Justice has remained blind.

But there is no reason why moderns should shy away from visual writing, such as the use of photographs, graphic designs and the like. Advances in computer are changing all that. Incorporating images in text writing is made easy with computer. Consumers of legal services and the courts welcome innovative displays of information that make for better understanding of the facts or issues of cases. In fact, many courts have reformed their practice rules in response to technology and other changes to accommodate advances in electronic recording, filing of processes, and other court-related activities. Thanks to technology and cultural transformation. Images are moving out the evidentiary margin to the centre of lawyering.[4]

It must be noted that while words may be a lawyer's primary tool for communication, it is by no means her only tool. Well and skilfully crafted images, such as charts, diagrams, photographs, can make a brief more appealing, interesting and persuasive. So, that lawyers are textual does not rule out image communication in law.

In fact, visual evidence has been with law for centuries since the discovery of the camera and printing technology. It has only been taken for granted in the litigation process. Photographs and maps and other visual evidence have been part of trial since the nineteenth century. But their influence on communication style of lawyers has been minimal.

Visual writing has its attraction. It is a great way to communicate and persuade. The reason isn't farfetched. Objects that appeal to the eyes get quickly transmitted to the senses and mind, which ultimately triggers emotive responses.

---

63 *J. Leg. Writing*. See also, Helen Anderson, Changing Fashions in Advocacy: 100 Years of Brief-Writing Advice (2010) 11 *J. Prac & Process* 1 @ 17 (survey of brief-writing advice).

[4] See for example the use of image in judicial writing by Judge Richard Posner in *Sandifer* v. *United States Steel Corp. Sandifer* v. *U.S. Steel Corp.* (Sandifer II), 134 S. Ct. 870 (2014). (A case involving interpretation of the Fair Labor Standards Act, to determine whether workers donning certain items—including a hardhat, wristlets, a "snood," earplugs, safety glasses, steel-toed boots, a respirator, and flame-retardant pants and top—were "changing clothes)." See also, Richard A. Posner, Judicial Opinions and Appellate Advocacy in Federal Courts— One Judge's Views (2013) 51 *Duq. L. Rev.* 3 (discussion criticizing typical legal writing as merely "serviceable" and particularly criticizes lawyers' "surprising reluctance to use pictures). Judge Posner in *Gonzalez-Servin* v. *Ford Motor Co.,* 662 F.3d 931, 934–35 (7th Cir. 2011) (Posner, J.) (provides illustrations comparing unprofessional attorney to ostrich). See also, Elizabeth G. Porter, Taking Images Seriously (2014) 114 *Colum. L. Rev.* 1687 @ 1699 ("From plausible pleadings to fractured Supreme Court opinions, from reams of discovery documents to piles of due diligence, text defines the profession. For the most part, the visual comes into the law only in the guise of metaphor, or in a textual description of a religious symbol, a sonogram image, or a picture at the heart of a copyright dispute."); Ronald K.L. Collins & David M. Skover, Paratexts (1992) 44 *Stan. L. Rev.* 509 @ 534 ("The model of contemporary law remains largely print-based. Accordingly, text typically is the starting and ending point.").

Cognitivists tell us that messages communicated through the eyes as in the form of visuals or graphics stick faster and remain remembered more that text-based communicated.[5] Lawyers therefore, need to learn how to persuade using visual writing.[6]

For example, a simple chart can persuasively show factual and legal points; a diagram can explain a case's procedural history, and a photograph can save five pages of your brief – all of which are difficult, if not impossible to do with textual writing.[7]

What Is Visual?

Visual tools are devices that allow the lawyer to engage the audience through their sense of sight. Visual tools include film graphs, maps, drawings, slides, videos, computer, etc.

Visual tools can be divided into two categories according to their primary uses: (i) those suitable for presenting graphics such as pictures, cartoons, diagrams, graphs, and charts, hand-outs, chalkboards, flipcharts, overhead transparencies, and slides. These form of visual presentations do not use structure other than the sentence or paragraph to illustrate or analyse facts or concepts before the trier of facts; (ii) those suitable to project real-life events to an audience or experience to them or for the audience to view performance. Films and videos come within this category.

Visual and Cognition

Cognitive research suggests that people learn and understand in different ways. Learning unquestionably leads to knowing. So as people learn they come to understand better. Learning is enhanced and reinforced when verbal communication is combined with visual. Visual includes but is not limited to pictures, PowerPoint (PP) presentation, hand-outs, blackboard, flipchart, slides,

---

[5] Johnson & Robbins, above n. 2 states that scientific and social research reveal that "the general population is approximately 65 per cent visual in learning and communication styles." Johnson & Robbins, above n. 1, 58. Some even have suggested that with oral presentation only 70% is retained of information after 3 hours and 10% is what can be recalled of it after 3 days. Whereas if it were visual presentation, 72% is retained after 3 hours and 20% after 3 days. Where both oral and visual presentation is employed, retention is as high as 85% after 3 hours and 65% recall after 3 days-see Weiss-McGrath study on retention and recall. Some research suggests that much of the brain cortex region is devoted to imagery and that image processing is the main brain function than words. See Lucile A. Jewel, Through a Glass Darkly: Using Brain Science and Visual Rhetoric to Gain a Professional Perspective on Visual Advocacy (2010) 19 *S. Cal. Interdisc. L.J.* 237.

[6] Ellie Margolis, Is the Medium the Message? Unleashing the Power of E-Communication in the Twenty-First Century (2015) 12 *Leg. Comm. & Rhetoric: JALWD* 1.

[7] Adam L. Rosman, Visualizing the Law: Using Charts, Diagrams, and Other Images to Improve Legal Briefs (2013) 63 *J. Leg. Educ.* 70

videos and computer. Some learn best auditorally (listening and speaking), some experientially (simulations and field work), and some visually (graphics and videos). Legal audience, particularly judges are used to auditorally learners.[8] This is understandable because most lawyers trained in textual writing environment in the law schools, rarely know how to make more than auditoral presentation before triers. Lawyers just write and write, advocate and advocate – before courts and tribunal in form or furtherance of motions, depositions, briefs, etc. The primal use of auditory presentation however does not discount or displace the other two ways of presentation. Experiential learning for triers of facts sometimes can comes from legally enjoined rules relating to visit to locus and innovative storytelling techniques skilled lawyers employ in advocacy. Doses of visual learning could also be gleaned from maps and drawing used in land and auto-accident litigation. Save for these rare instances, experiential and visual learning have little place in creating understanding for triers of facts in the legal process. This to say the least is unfortunate because visual representations of facts and concepts are more memorable than the spoken word – so too is experiential learning for judges. Research shows that visuals are more effective in creating understanding and leading to persuasion than textual writing and oral advocacy.

The human capacity to learn and understand facts and concepts has shown to be related to how the brain connects isolated materials with prior experience to make them meaningful. Even though the brain is only able to recall a small number of unconnected and unimportant items for a short time, it however has a large capacity to learn concepts that are organized and connected (schemata). Visuals have proved helpful in creating schemata, thereby furthering understanding and persuasion because it helps the trier to connect more readily with the reality of facts presented. For example, a simple artwork of patent design can depict the relationship between two things sought to be compared for mark infringement in such a way that textual writing cannot do. When the trier retrieves the drawing in her mind, the effect is enormous. The judge retrieves not just information contained in the artwork, but also organizes it in such a way that it is used to connection with reality and lived experience.[9] The information and

---

[8] Gerald Hess & Steven Friedland, *Techniques for Teaching Law*, Durham, North Carolina, Carolina Acad. Press, 1999 @ 80.

[9] Hess & Friedland, above n. 8 @ 103 (Research revealing "that the human mind structures information by relating it horizontally - e.g., in a sequence-and vertically-e.g., in a hierarchy. Thus, a constitutional law class on due process may include students linking due process horizontally with other rights such as equal protection and vertically with "lesser included" concepts such as basic due process or void for vagueness.")

organization is then used as the lens or formula to resolve the controversy presented before the court. This is how visuals persuade.[10]

Visuals are particularly useful persuasive device if a case is complex. Demonstrative evidence can be skilful used to teach triers and argue from the lawyers' comfort-zone as it provides the trier what is needed to really understand what is being argued and be persuaded by it. Visual importance is heightened by the fact that most people, including judges, are visual learners. They watch television and surf the internet. So using visual as persuasive device is simply playing litigation in a familiar field with appropriate instruments.

The *Apple* v. *Samsung* patent infringement trial is illustrative of the point.[11] Both companies fought over patent infringements. The cases were complex and confusing to the trier, Judge Koh who even thought that it was as dicey as a "coin toss." But the simple graphics used by Apple Inc. says it all, even without words.

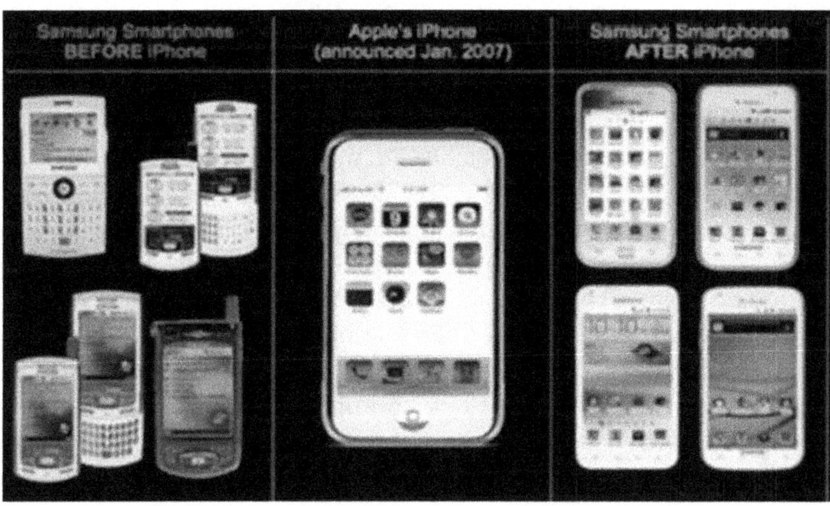

[10]Steve Johansen & Ruth Anne Robbins, Art-ticulating the Analysis: Systemizing the Decision to Use Visuals as Legal Reasoning(2015) 20 *J. Leg. Writing* 56 (an article examining visual presentation as component of legal reasoning); Adam L. Rosman, Visualizing the Law: Using Charts, Diagrams, and Other Images to Improve Legal Briefs (2013) 63 *J. Leg. Educ.* 70; Ruth Anne Robbins, Painting with print: Incorporating concepts of typographic and layout design into the text of legal writing documents (2004) 2 *J. ALWD* 108 (explaining why an "argument must be presented in a visually effective manner so the reader can more easily understand the argument and retain more of the material.").

[11]Ryan Flax, Demonstrative Evidence & Storytelling: Lessons from Apple v Samsung, A2L Consulting. See also *A2L Consultancy's Patent Litigation Toolkit*, 4th ed. @ 74-78.

Any trier of facts can see from the visual (even without accompanying textual writing) how Apple's iPhone design is pivotal to Samsung's mobile phone design in a simple "before" and "after" demonstrative. This certainly can persuade.

Why Visual Persuade

It is plausible for lawyers to worry about the admissibility of visual evidence and its use in brief writing. Scepticism about its use in legal-audience is expected in a community dominated by text-based communication. Not only would lawyers fear inadmissibility of visual writing, they may also fear if the audience would think them weird and unschooled in the ethos and style of the profession.

But these are less prevailing objections. No lawyer should fear innovation, even legal invention. Remember, the Brandeis brief changed the content and shape of legal writing in ways and manner hitherto unimagined.[12] Today the legal audience is becoming familiar with computers and e-communication as so would not think visual out of place in legal writing. What is more, visual writing has been part of lawyering for some time now. Lawyers use visual evidence daily without really given thought to it as a communication means. Those who do land litigation are conversant with dispute survey plans and maps. Also, drawings and graphics are not unfamiliar exhibits in motor accident trials. The advent of electronic filing, e-learning and more, all recreating legal reality certainly makes visual communication congenial to legal audience.

It is therefore not surprising that legal education and lawyering using visual is gathering steam. The American Judge Richard Posner in fact, invites lawyers to use visual in their brief.[13] There is no question about it-visual communication is here to stay and is a very incisive way to persuade. But for many lawyers trained in the days of blackboards, typewriters, and biro/ink writing, legal communication remains exclusively text-based. With the world going digital lawyers must learn to incorporate visual persuasion into their writings.

Visual tools are powerful for persuasion for many reasons:

(i) visuals focus the attention of the audience. For example, if a presenter puts a transparency on the overhead projector, shows a slide, the audience concentrates on the visual;

---

[12] Brandeis brief is reputed to be the pioneering legal brief in the United States history to rely more on scientific information and social science than legal argument. It contained 95 pages of scientific information and only 2 pages of law. See *Muller* v. *Oregon* (1908) 208 US 412.

[13] Richard A. Posner, Judicial Opinions and Appellate Advocacy in Federal Courts-One Judge's View (2013) 51 *Duq. L. Rev.* 3 @ 23, cited in Johnson & Robbins, above n. 2 @ 61. The legal practitioners and the academy appears poised to catch on the call for visual communication. See Elizabeth Porter, Taking Images Seriously (2014) 114 *Colum. L. Rev.* 1694; Adam L. Rosman, Visualizing the Law: Using Charts, Diagrams, and Other Images to Improve Legal Brief (2013) 63 *J. Leg. Educ.* 70. See also, Persuasion Litigation Blog at http://www.persuasivelitigator.com.

(ii) when the audience watches or perceives visual, it creates and encourages thinking and rethinking of the facts and concepts presented;
(iii) visual tools can help the presenter maintain high audience interest in the presentation;
(iv) research shows that an audience understanding and in fact motivation to know are enhanced when they experience a variety of knowing techniques (auditory, experiential and visual) for presentation.

Communication through the ear and also through the eyes (sight) increases the ability of an audience to grasp and retain information. The reason isn't farfetched. Objects that appeal to the eyes get quickly transmitted to the senses and mind, which ultimately triggers emotive responses. Cognitivists tell us that messages communicated through the eyes in for of visuals or graphics stick faster and remain remembered more that text-based or ear-based communication.[14]

As the demonstrative below shows in a 12-person jury trial of facts, 61% of them learn visually, 18.5% auditorally and 20% kinetically. This translates to 7 persons who learn visually, 2 auditorally and 3 kinetically. What this mean is that there are more persons who learn and come to know visually. It represents the better way to persuade than the style most lawyers use (auditorary) – in fact, it is the least avenue to knowledge and persuasion. If this survey is representative of judges as triers of facts (and there is no reason why it ought not be) then learning how to persuade using visual must be core skill to acquire. Something more is striking of the demonstrative below: a skilful combination of visuals, auditorary and kinetics can give a near 100 per cent persuasion grounding. Learning to combine all is thus advised.

Visuals in Modern Lawyering

But that has changed. Advances in computers make it relatively easy to integrate images with text, and there's every reason to think that courts (and other consumers of legal work) would welcome innovative displays of information. The legal brief itself, for example, has changed over time to reflect changes in the practice. The modern brief, with mandatory "procedural history", "facts" and

[14]Johnson & Robbins, above n. 2 @ 58 (stating that scientific and social research reveal that "the general population is approximately 65 per cent visual in learning and communication styles."). Some cognitive research suggest that much of the brain cortex region is devoted to imagery and that image processing is the main brain function than words. See David I.C. Thomson, *Law School 2.0: Legal Education for a Digital Age,* LexisNexis, 2009; Lucile A. Jewel, Through a Glass Darkly: Using Brain Science and Visual Rhetoric to Gain a Professional Perspective on Visual Advocacy (2010) 19 *S. Cal. Interdisc. L.J.* 237; Johnson & Robbins, above n. 3; Ellie Margolis, Is the Medium the Message? Unleashing the Power of E-Communication in the Twenty-First Century (2015) 12 *Leg. Comm. & Rhetoric: JALWD* 1.

The Court room Communication Gap

"legal argument" sections, is a "relatively recent invention, not an ancient legal tradition." And the federal courts have reformed their rules in response to technological and other changes, most recently to accommodate advances in electronic record collection and storage.

Resistance to the use of visuals in brief writing is waning. By the turn of the twenty-first century, lawyers started making spirited attempts to embrace visual form advocacy. Professor Joe Grundfest of Stanford is reputed to be the first lawyer to file such an innovative brief before the U.S. Supreme Court in a 1995 amicus brief. [15] He filed the first hyperlinked amicus brief on CD-ROM. Unfortunately, the court rejected the brief on the ground that it was not equipped to view it. That was the first volley. More were to come. Come, they did soon thereafter. Two year later, in 1997, the Court accepted its first CD-ROM brief—an amicus brief in *ACLU* v. *Reno* that linked to scientific and medical websites that would be caught up in the censoring web of the Communications Decency Act.[16] Since then, lawyers have introduced large scale visuals in U.S. court. Notable of them is Peter Bensinger, a Chicago litigator, probably "the most wired lawyer in America" known for filing what is termed "magazine briefs"—briefs on CD-

---

[15]Michael Whiteman, Appellate Court Briefs on the Web: Electronic Dynamos or Legal Quagmire? (2005) 97 Law Libr. J. 467 (describing early attempts to file non-traditional, technology-based briefs, including Professor Grundfest's CD-ROM amicus brief).

[16]*Reno* v.. *ACLU,* 521 U.S. 844 (1997) (No. 96-511), 1997 WL 74396

ROMs with full colour images, PowerPoint slides, and graphics seamlessly embedded into the text.[17] He is known for arguing that "showing why you are right, rather than just talking about it, builds credibility."

Despite these strides, the community remains sceptical of the use of images in brief writing. Most textd on brief writing contain little, if any, on use of visuals. They are rather replete with matters such as how to craft effective pleadings and briefs, etc. with no mention of demonstratives.[18]

In lieu of using images, judges and lawyer often resort to imagery – use of figures of speech such as metaphor to describe what ordinarily should be visualized.[19]

The longstanding barriers to visual persuasion in written advocacy is certainly now coming down with the availability of computers everywhere and the use of computer generated materials in our daily lives. We are gradually reaching a state where judges and lawyer are using images to drive arguments and—through explicit argument and implicit messaging—to compel conclusions. Lawyers and courts are harnessing the power of the new visual vernacular to market their views of a case.

Other civil litigants have harnessed the power of images to support their legal claims in a wide range of cases. Intellectual-property plaintiffs in particular have begun to unleash the full power of their copyrightable material in aid of their arguments. Given that copyright and trademark cases frequently depend on interpretation of visual material, it might seem surprising that this trend is so new. And indeed litigants have some- times included exhibits containing the material at issue. Despite the obvious attraction of using the material, however, even intellectual-property litigants have overlooked the persuasive power of images. As Judge Posner describes:

> Many years ago I was on the panel that heard an appeal in a trademark dispute between the Indianapolis Colts and the Baltimore CFL Colts. The briefs described the trademarked products (such as hats and T-shirts) but did not include pictures. At the oral argument, one of the judges (OK, I confess—it was I) asked the lawyer for the Indianapolis Colts whether he

---

[17]Peter B. Bensinger Jr., Magazine Briefs 2–15 (2000), available at http://www.bartlit-beck.com/media/news/10_article_92800.pdf (on file with the *Columbia Law Review*) (showing examples of embedded images, graphics, and informational sidebars, and providing specific instructions).

[18] Bryan Garner, *The Winning Brief*; Bryan Garner; *Garner's Redbook — A Manual on Legal Style*; Niki Tobi; Michael R. Smith, *Advanced Legal Writing: Theories and Strategies in Persuasive Writing*, 3rd ed. 2013; Antonin Scalia & Bryan A. Garner, *Making Your Case: The Art of Persuading Judges*, 2008.

[19] See however Judge Richard Posner in Ford Motor. See also *Scott* v.. *Harris* 550 U.S. 372 @ 386 (2007)(the court deleted the text of the two lower- court opinions, replacing those analyses with a link to the video and expressly inviting readers of the opinion to see for themselves)

> had any of the products with him. He was a little startled but went to his briefcase and pulled a pair of hats, one an Indianapolis Colt hat and the other a Baltimore CFL Colt hat. The hats looked identical. He won his case at that moment. He was lucky that he was asked that question. He would not have needed luck had he included a photograph in his brief.[20]

Much as images are useful persuasion tools, it is also fraught with dangers. There are potential dangers to quick-witted visual intelligence. Some think and feel it real—as if they are transparent windows onto reality, rather than curated, edited, visual arguments. As a result, "we tend to read images as representative of reality. Viewers may sometimes have an exaggerated confidence in visuals, reifying them, particularly of those that appear real. In this context, visual can be a double-edged sword for persuasion. It could create reality as well as mislead because they are tightly linked with emotion than is text. Seeing is said to be believing.

Visuals and Legal Education

It has been suggested that the prevalence of textual communication in law merely follows the blueprint of the scientific posture of law established by Christopher Columbus Langdell in the late 1800s – where law study was limited to black letter learning, dominated by blocks of texts. So today even though technology is changing the face of legal services, its efficiencies have served "primarily to reinforce, rather than revolutionize, long-established modes of text-centred legal discourse."[21] All the legal community is doing with technology is merely to harness it to create more and longer textual documents, rather than use it to communicate in a new, denser and potentially more powerful manner, using

---

[20]Richard A. Posner, Effective Appellate Brief Writing, App. Prac. J., Spring 2010, at 1, 16, available at http://apps.americanbar.org/litigation/litigationnews/trial_skills/appellate-brief-writing-posner.html (on file with the *Columbia Law Review*). See, *Grayson* v. *Schuler*, 666 F.3d 450, 452 (7th Cir. 2012) (embedding image of Bob Marley's dreadlocks to show a prisoner whose dreadlocks were forcibly sheared) per Judge Posner. This is how it looks.

[21]Porter, above n. 2 @ 1700. For example, Brian Leiter described Langdellian formalism as the law's "lingua franca,"which begins and ends with words. See Brian Leiter, American Legal Education: The First 150 Years, Huffington Post (Jan. 12, 2014, 9:35 AM), http://www.huffingtonpost.com/brian-leiter/american- legal-education-_b_4581672.html (on file with the *Columbia Law Review*) (observing despite significant developments in schools of legal scholarship, fundamental legal pedagogy remains rooted in Langdellian formalism).

visuals. In fact, the primacy of print over images in legal writing was reinforced by the invention of the type-writer, which swept through the legal profession in the 1870s. It is therefore not surprising that judicial opinions and legal documents were only in textual forms, eschewing visual communication.

Not surprisingly, lawyers have been slow to integrate images into their written work. Like any profession, change comes slowly—the law has been a text-only profession for hundreds of years. And unlike the physical sciences, the law usually deals in abstract ideas. A doctor can use an anatomical diagram to make a point, but it's difficult for a lawyer to explain a legal concept in anything but words. And until recently, it has been expensive and time-consuming to integrate images into a brief.

Visual literacy is not part of legal education or training. But the message from skilled professional, particularly best practice is that law schools need to reform legal education to provide more focus on training students in professionalism and practical skills.[22] The nature of legal practice and the job market today gives technology a central role in the reform of legal education. It would therefore be strange that law classrooms still look significantly the same as they were twenty or more years ago. Today's law classroom should look hi-tech because e-learning and other instructional methods that focus on developing skills will be more prevalent. Technology itself has become a core skill for effective law

[22] Roy Stuckey et. al., *Best Practices for Legal Education: A Vision and a Roadmap,* 2007 (hereinafter called *Best Practices*); William M. Sullivan, *et al.* eds. *Carnegie Fund for the Advancement of Teaching, Educating Lawyers: Preparation for the Profession of Law,* 2007 (hereinafter called the *Carnegie Report*).

practice.[23] It is thus imperative that legal education captures this component which will likely shape the structure of present curriculum. For instance, it is expected that legal text, learning and teaching should follow the lead of technology, particularly in incorporating visuals in the learning process.[24]

---

[23]Elizabeth G. Porter, Taking Images Seriously (2014) 114 *Colum. L. Rev.*1687 @ 1687 (an article that identifies and critiques the nascent phenomenon of multimedia written advocacy as a vital states that "[law] has been trapped in a stylistic straitjacket. The Internet has revolutionized media and communications, replacing text with a dizzying array of multimedia graphics and images. Facebook hosts more than 150 billion photos. Courts spend millions on trial technology. But those innovations have barely trickled into the black-and-white world of written law. Legal treatises continue to evoke Blackstone and Kent; most legal casebooks are facsimiles of Langdell's; and legal journals resemble the Harvard Law Review circa 1887. None of these influential forms of disseminating the law has embraced—or even nodded to— modern, image-saturated communication norms. Litigants, scholars, and courts have been rebooting the same formalist templates for over a century—templates that were formed before widespread use of the cam- era, never mind the computer. Outside of trial, where image-driven advocacy has a long history, legal practice begins and ends with text. But over the past five years, for the first time—unrecognized by scholars or courts—creative trial lawyers, receptive judges, and the iPhone camera are breaching these conservative bulwarks. Images are moving out of the evidentiary margins and are driving argument in litigation documents from pleadings to judicial opinions. If left unregulated, visual argument threatens fundamental premises of legal dis- course and decision-making. Yet in comparison with law's rich and detailed traditions for interpreting ambiguous text, lawyers and judges have few tools beyond common sense with which to ameliorate the interpretive risks of visual persuasion. "I know it when I see it" is not merely an aphorism; it is the reigning interpretive canon for images in law.").

[24]Stephen M. Johnson, Teaching for Tomorrow: Utilizing Technology to Implement the Reforms of MacCrate, Carnegie, and Best Practices (2013) 92 *Nebraska L. Rev.* 46 (an article which states that technology must play a pivotal role in legal education because: "(i) it provides a vital way to connect with the students from Generations X and Y that dominate the student body at most law schools; (ii) appropriate use of technology can relieve economic pressures in implementing [legal education] reforms; (iii) technology can facilitate access to new learning experiences for all students, regardless of disabilities or learning styles; and (iv) technology is itself a skill that must be mastered in order to practice law in the twenty-first century."); @ 54-5 ("However, it is not simply the facility with technology among Generations X and Y that should prompt law schools to focus on technology in transforming teaching and assessment methods. It is the impact technology has already had on the learning styles of Gen-Xers and Millennials that should be the driving force behind the focus on technology in the transformation. Computers and the Internet have been integrated into the educational experiences of students in Generations X and Y from their earliest days in primary school. Students are accustomed to having instant access to information. Accordingly, researchers suggest that they are less likely to have mastered previous learning primarily through books and "are more likely to be visual learners and holistic, right-brained thinkers, rather than sequential, logical thinkers. "Traditional law school pedagogy has predominantly targeted verbal learners, rather than visual learners. Research also suggests that students in Generations X and Y are less adept than previous generations at organizing and synthesizing information and have developed a passive relationship to information—a consumer mentality. In addition, research suggests that students in these generations are rabid multitaskers, even in the classroom. Since the learning styles of many of the students in Generations X and Y have been forged through technology, it would seem to be beneficial to incorporate technology more fully into law school pedagogy to fit those students' learning styles, rather than requiring students to try to modify their learning styles to fit the mould of the traditional law school pedagogy.")

Unfortunately, the legal academy is still unwelcoming to technology in the classroom. This is sad considering that most students today are more inclined to e-learning.[25] This explains why many students who eventually become lawyer remain basically textual communicators, without skills of visual communication. The present discounting of technology in the classroom harms demonstrative skills acquisition.[26]There is no question about it, technology is here to stay and will continue to inform and reform legal education and service delivery in law. The sooner technology skills are mastered the better for lawyers and lawyering.[27]

The emergence of critical lawyering and the calls for humanizing legal reasoning puts visual in the centre of lawyering as a core skill to acquire. Legal education should therefore respond appropriately to technology (and visuals) to train client-ready lawyers.[28]

Visual Typologies and Uses

One great way to use visual is the "flow charts." One flow-chat technique is "concept mapping." The technique is "the identification of concepts ... and the organization of those concepts into a hierarchical arrangement from the most general, most inclusive to the least general, most specific concept." (See, Novak,

---

[25] Johnson, above n. 6 @ 212-3 ("Seven-six per cent of the students surveyed indicated that bringing laptops to classes increased, or at least did not decrease, their participation in class."). See also, Karen Barton et al., Authentic Fictions: Simulation, Professionalism and Legal Learning (2007) 14 *Clin. L. Rev.* 143 @ 183–85; Paul Wangerin, Technology in the Service of Tradition: Electronic Lectures and Live-Class Teaching (2003)53 *J. Legal Educ.* 213. (technology in teaching).

[26]Johnson, above n. 6 @ 53 "[L]egal educators [who neglect technology in the classroom] are generally falling behind the legal profession itself. Modern trial lawyers regularly use display technology, such as computer animations, videotaped depositions, and PowerPoint presentations, to 'teach' and persuade juries, judges, and colleagues in a very effective way." Fred Galves, Will Video Kill the Radio Star? Visual Learning and the Use of Display Technology in the Law School Classroom (2004) *Univ. Ill. J.L. Tech. &Pol'y.*195 at 195-96 (discussing "visually enhanced communication in the practice of law).

[27]Richard Susskind, *The End of Lawyers? Rethinking the Nature of Legal Services*, 2009. See also, Thomas D. Morgan, *The Vanishing American Lawyer*, 2010; David I.C. Thomson, Law School 2.0: Legal Education for Digital Age, 2009; Michele R. Pistone & John J. Hoeffner, No Path But One: Law School Survival in an Age of Disruptive Technology (2013) 59 *Wayne L. Rev.* 193

[28]See for example, Richard A. Posner, Judicial Opinions and Appellate Advocacy in Federal Courts-One Judge's View (2013) 51 *Duq. L. Rev.* 3 (an article calling on lawyer to persuade adjudicators through visuals). See also *Gonzalez-Servin* v. *Ford Motor Co* 662 F.3d 931, 934 (7th Cir. 2011) @ 935, per Richard Posner J (where the learned judge used pictures to drive home his metaphoric comparison of a lawyer who ignored circuit precedent to an ostrich burying its head in the sand. "The ostrich is a noble animal," the opinion states, "but not a proper model for an appellate advocate."). The legal practitioners and the academy appears poised to catch on the call for visual communication. Also see *Sandifer* v. *U.S. Steel Corp.* (*Sandifer I*), 678 F.3d 590 @ 593-4 (7th Cir. 2012), per Posner J (using a picture of man in work clothing to interpret the Fair Labor Standards Act), aff'd, 134 S. Ct. 870 (image available at http://media.ca7.uscourts.gov /cgi-bin/ rssExec.pl? Submit=Display& Path=Y2012/D05-08/C:10-1821:J:Posner:aut:T:fnOp:N:917129:S:0 (on file with the *Columbia Law Review*); Elizabeth Porter, Taking Images Seriously (2014) 114 *Colum. L. Rev.* 1694; Adam L. Rosman, Visualizing the Law: Using Charts, Diagrams, and Other Images to Improve Legal Brief (2013) 63 *J. Leg. Educ.* 70.

1981 at 31, quoted in C. Rafferty and L. Fleschner, *Concept Mapping: A Viable Alternative to Objective and Essay Exams,* 1993 READING RESEARCH AND INSTRUCTION 25, 26.) "Concept mapping" promotes the use of diagrams, pictures, and maps to explain concepts. For example, the map of "due process", "freedom of speech", may be difficult to visualize, but could be made understandable by drawing and organizing a hierarchical picture to clarify the doctrinal area more than an oral or written explanation.

State how visuals can be shown all at once to convey the "big picture" of the case and the connections between concepts, e.g. how shareholders are connected with directors and the public.

Legal Status of Visuals

Documentary visuals are familiar to judges and lawyers, especially those related to maps, charts, survey plans and the like. It is hardly contested if they are admissible evidence. They are admitted once they meet the requirements of admissibility following the general division of evidence into basic classes: oral and documentary evidence, visual evidence of the sort described qualify as documentary evidence.[29]

Even outside court setting, lawyers use documentary visuals like photographs of accident sites, x-ray reports, etc.- all used to persuade, show rather than tell the reader the facts of the case. There is therefore, no reason why visuals cannot be used in pre-litigation and litigation writings. While it is admitted that rules of courts and evidence may vary from one jurisdiction to another, there is no court rule that actively disallows visuals in briefs or motions. Rather, survey maps, timelines, photographs, and maps regularly form court exhibits in cases.

Outside the use of the general, familiar visuals, analytical visuals that help to explain the connection between abstract rules and their application to facts can prove useful in problem-solving by identifying patterns, drawing inferences, clarifying legal concepts and helping to reach conclusions.[30] Analytical visuals often are shaped as flowcharts, graph, and photographs. They are employed to enhance reasoning on the facts of the case, how they tie with the law, and their policy or other evaluative parameters.

---

[29] See Evidence Act, s. 2, which defines document to "include books, maps, plans, drawings, photographs, and also includes any matter expressed or described upon any substance by means of letters, figures or marks or by more than one of these means, intended to be used or which may be used for the purpose of recording that matter." See LFN, 2004, Cap. E4.

[30] While much of pictorial visuals like x-rays, maps, etc. tell the reader what happened in a controversy, analytical visual is aimed at telling what happened, the meaning of what happened, and ultimately, what will happen.

Accordingly, it can be said that the era of magazine briefs has dawned.[31] Johnson and Robbins tell of the 2011 motion for summary judgment filed on behalf of Dallas Mavericks majority owner which completely relied on a photograph for its legal argument, and the proliferation of visual media experts now advising litigators, all making lawyers to pay more attention to visual impact in persuasion.[32]

Courts are enjoined to design formal rules ensuring that images are readable and fair. The legal status of visual briefs is challenging, so it seem. Since images can be a double-edge sword in the litigation process, some have been concerned if some form of protection is available to litigants from the influence embedded images can exert on judges. It is plausible to seek by motion the exclusion of images as redundant, immaterial, impertinent, or scandalous matter. American judges have generally been hostile to such motions, denying them "unless the challenged allegations have no possible relation or logical connection to the subject matter.[33]

Sincc rules of ethics prevent the presentation of falsehood, lawyers are enjoined not to present images that are prejudicial and false.

But such protections may be of limited use in situations where images have been edited in some way short of substantial alteration. After all, lawyers routinely edit their writing for clarity, persuasiveness, and emotional impact. Within the legal profession, there is widespread consensus about what constitutes appropriate editorial advocacy.

Beyond questions of tone—of propriety, collegiality, and sophistication—increased use of visual argument threatens to change the process by which judges and lawyers access information in legal documents. Side- bars, infographics, rollover states, and embedded video in briefs could draw the eye and the mind away from the nuanced and substantiated legal arguments that have characterized

---

[31]Michael Macaulay &IoannaPantazi, Material Difficulty and the Effectiveness of Multimedia in Learning (2006) 33 *Int'l. J. Instructional Media* 187 (states that multimedia presentation helps student learn difficult materials and boost long-term memory recollection). See also, Peter B. Bensinger, Jr., Magazine Briefs, A-Z Consultants at peter.bensinger@bartlit-beck.com ("when you learn something complicated, it is a lot easier to look at pictures. Often the most persuasive evidence in any jury trial is the demonstrative-the photo, the diagram, the blow up of the document with the key phrases highlighted. Yet when it comes to time to persuade a judge, the traditional legal brief is just words, no pictures. A picture is worth a thousand words. Even with a judge.)" this is said to be the "show, don't tell" approach to briefs. Please see Adobe in ipad on this section.

[32] Steve Johnson & Ruth A. Robbins, Art-Iculating the Analysis: Systemizing the Decision to Use Visuals as Legal Reasoning (2015) 20 *J. Leg. Writing* 57 at 65. See World Champion Dallas Mavericks & Radical Mavericks Management's Motion for Summary Judgment, Hillwood Inv. Props. Ill, Ltd. v. Radical Mavericks Mgmt., LLC, No. 10-05639, 2011 WL 2649590 (Tex. Dist. Ct. June 22, 2011).

[33]Porter, above n. 2 @ 1767.

legal writing until now. Where an image will do, perhaps readers will have less incentive to pore over detailed text. There is a real risk that visual advocacy will create more gloss but less substance in legal discourse.

Procedural rules seek to ensure that legal documents are readable and that litigants are treated equitably before a court. As parties increasingly rely on snapshots, maps, and other digital images in their legal documents, courts should include this form of legal argument within their regulatory umbrella. Courts may do this in several ways.

First, existing rules could be interpreted to apply to embedded images. For example, courts might construe Federal Rule of Civil Procedure 12(f), which allows motions to strike "redundant, immaterial, impertinent, or scandalous" material from a pleading, to apply to attempts by parties to embed graphic or highly gruesome images of a murder or accident scene into a complaint. Similarly, courts might analyse images in legal documents within the established framework of Federal Rule of Evidence 403 or its state analogues, barring images that are more prejudicial than they are probative, with sensitivity given to the context in which they are used. Yet these rules are blunt instruments for routine regulation of images in legal documents. Rule 12(f) has been used sparingly, and the rules of evidence are geared toward trial rather than toward early stages such as pleading. In addition, both Rule 12(f) and Rule 403 generally depend on one party moving to exclude material proffered by another—a cumbersome addition to the pleading or pre-trial briefing process.

Instead, courts may wish to develop multimedia-specific rules that put parties on advance notice of limits on embedding visuals into legal documents. To give a simple example, courts may take inspiration from the ethics rules governing photojournalists and prohibit parties from embedding into legal documents images that have been modified or edited. Courts that are willing to tolerate certain modifications to photographic images, such as cropping or colour adjustment, should specify as much. Courts should also consider whether and under what circumstances parties may stage photographs for use in legal argument, similar to what Judge Posner did in *Sandifer I*.

Relatedly, courts should consider requiring parties to state the source of any embedded image, the time and date the image was created, and any modification of the image by the party relying on it. Such a rule would serve two simultaneous purposes. First, it would minimize the risk associated with subtle but potentially prejudicial manipulation of images, such as that exemplified by *TIME*'s editing of O.J. Simpson's mug shot.

Second—and equally important—the requirement that parties identify the source of an image may act as a subtle but distinct reminder to courts that images advocate a viewpoint and are not mere neutral depictions of reality. Identifying information would "frame" images, revealing them as an artificial construct and "cu[ing] the reader that they are artefacts to be interpreted." This frame may reduce the pernicious but seductive effect of naпve realism, particularly but not only for photographic images.

Courts may also wish to promulgate rules that exclude certain categories of visual evidence as being more prejudicial than probative at the pleading and summary judgment stages. For example, it may be reasonable to exclude gruesome personal-injury or crime-scene photos, or personal snapshots like those in *Gordon* v. *DreamWorks Animation SKG, Inc.* This is not to argue that gruesome images are unpersuasive. To the contrary, in the words of several prominent historians, "[G]ruesome photographs have played a key role in influencing the great debates of the time . . . "Yet gruesome images do not add greatly to allegations of liability and raise the possibility of infecting the decision-making process with unnecessary and perhaps unconscious emotional bias.

B. Courts Should Develop Canons of Visual Interpretation

In addition to formal rules ensuring that images are readable and fair, courts should develop interpretive traditions for multimedia legal discourse. Canons of statutory interpretation provide a common, "off- the-rack" framework for giving meaning to ambiguous language. Analogously, canons of visual interpretation might provide agreed-upon departure points for analysing the meaning of images in legal discourse— "shared conventions for understanding [images] in context." Statutory canons also serve as explicit (if contested) recognition of the limits of courts' institutional competence in particular settings. In this context, too, visual canons will serve that purpose: They will provide an institutionalized reminder to courts of the risks inherent in visual advocacy and will provide a framework in which courts can openly acknowledge such risks. In their critique of *Scott* v. *Harris*, Kahan and colleagues argue that judges should "pause to consider whether what strikes them as an 'obvious' matter of fact might in fact be viewed otherwise by a discrete and identifiable sub-community." Courts use canons precisely to institutionalize such pauses—to nudge lawyers and courts into moments of heightened awareness about the limits of textual communication. Analogous canons may heighten institutional awareness about the limits of visual communication.

The first proposed canon of visual interpretation is the "non-plain- meaning rule." The traditional plain-meaning canon of statutory interpretation instructs courts to "follow the plain meaning of a text, except when doing so would require an absurd result." This plain meaning rule comes as close as possible to representing the current prevailing interpretive method for images in law, which is succinctly summarized by Justice Stewart's famous aphorism: "I know it when I see it." Modern textualism acknowledges another layer to the plain meaning rule, by requiring that interpreters seek to determine the assumptions—perhaps unstated—"shared by the speakers and the intended audience" of a communication when finding its plain meaning. But in the realm of the visual, where interpretation can seem largely or wholly organic, it is tempting to return to an unadorned, relatively naпve view of visual plain meaning—a view that does not acknowledge the unspoken arguments or narratives an image tells. The first canon of visual interpretation is thus simple but counterintuitive: Images lack plain meaning, and therefore courts should be explicit about the background source of any meaning with which they endow an image.

This Article's second proposed canon of visual interpretation addresses the interrelationship between multimedia advocacy and traditional decision-making structures. The second canon holds that the presence of visual media should not alter the standard of review or burdens of proof on a party. This is a simple rule, but again, it is a nudge toward complex interpretation of visuals. In the absence of such a canon, courts may believe that visual evidence obviates traditional structures. For example, the traditional rule is that when a court considers a motion for summary judgment, facts and reasonable inferences should be viewed in the light most favourable to the non-moving party.

C. Courts and Other Parties Should Consider Their Own Use of Images

While traditional court rules and canons might—rather simply— ameliorate risks of multimedia advocacy among litigants, there are few hard limits on the use of images by others, including by courts, legal databases, and scholarly journals. But these other institutions should also respond to the increasing use of images to disseminate the law.

As an initial matter, notwithstanding Judge Posner's colourful example of a more vibrant judicial discourse, there are good reasons for courts to exercise restraint in their use of images in judicial opinions. Courts, like litigants, should specify the origin of any image embedded into an opinion and explicitly state any modification made to an image. In that way, the parties to a case—as well as later litigants relying on precedent— would have a more complete understanding of the role that an image plays in a decision. For example, they would know whether the image came from the record, and, if it did, by which party it was introduced. They would also have an accurate sense of the court's involvement in the creation or editing of an image. Such a disclosure requirement might provide a healthy disincentive to judges to creating their own visual evidence, as Judge Posner did in *Sandifer I.* Such transparency may also assist appellate courts to review any staged visual argument with heightened scepticism.

Although there might be rare instances where it would be appropriate for a court to reach beyond the record to locate an image for a judicial opinion, judges should think carefully before embedding into opinions images that are only tangentially related to the subject matter of the case—particularly images that are not part of the record and that reflect pop-culture sensibilities as much as, or more than, legal principles. As isolated curiosities, judicial opinions containing images of Miss Wiggles or Bob Marley might be only mildly offensive. But such practices should not become the norm. There is, and should be, a line between respectful legal analysis and the cynical wit or celebrity fawning of a blog post. As it becomes ever easier to drop and drag an image into a legal document, judges—like litigants—should be wary of using images in opinions to garner publicity or merely a cheap laugh.

In addition to courts and litigants, legal scholars should also continue to expand their use of and access to visual argument both in their writing and in their teaching. form.

Other professions, from journalism to science, have embraced image-saturated communication. Outside of trial, however, law has largely turned inward in the face of the digital age, refining and reifying its typographic, formalist templates. Lawyers have harnessed new technology to cite more sources, draft longer documents, conduct more discoveries, and pay ever-more-detailed attention to precedent. None of these practices has harnessed the power of visual persuasion. To the contrary, whether in legal education, legal documents, or legal databases, law frequently deletes what few images do appear, treating them as irrelevant or as low-culture fodder for the (usually hypothetical) jury. Only now are image-saturated media challenging the hegemony of the written word in law. Images are seeping—unacknowledged and unregulated—into legal documents in a dizzying array of cases and courts. No longer confined to appendices, images are taking centre stage in legal argument and legal decisions, reinforcing textual arguments, and conveying implicit messages that support litigation narratives.

The Decision to Use Visuals

Choosing Visuals

In choosing whether to use visual, the lawyer should first consider the goals sought to be driven with its use.

Just as the choice and design of visual tools vary based on the class goals, the ways to use the visuals in class depend on the presenter's objectives. For example, visuals can be shown all at once to convey the "big picture" and the connections between facts and concepts presented.

Analytical visuals are particularly useful in the litigation process in enhancing legal reasoning and argumentation, and are very useful for lawyering. Johnson and Robbins provide a taxonomical guide for determining when and how to use analytical visuals. The steps are quite logical and self-explanatory. Step one, requires the lawyer to determine if she needs analytical visuals to further argumentation and reasoning. If the answer is yes, then the next step is to conceptualize the argument visually.

Once this is done, the lawyer would then take the three-path taxonomical steps of (i) identifying *what* kind of analytical visual would drive legal reasoning of the case, (ii) understanding *why* the selected visual is useful to the legal analysis, (iii) and understanding *how* the legal reasoning is shaped by the visual creation.

(i) Identifying What Type of Visual

The processing step begins with identifying the various kinds of visuals that exist. Even though visuals are known to cover an array of properties common in the genre of graphs, maps, charts, survey plans, x-rays, photographs, pictures, diagrams, etc., they can vary in their function and design. Functionally, they can generally be categorized as organizational, interpretive, and representative. This list is by no means exhaustive because, some visuals could shade into more than one class.

Organizational visuals present information in a hierarchical way. Examples of this are bullet points, organizational workplace flowcharts showing levels of relationship. This is a form common to lawyers, especially in use in legal brief of argument, often styled as page on table of contents, showing the content pages of the brief.

Interpretive visuals are designed to help the reader to better understand difficult phenomena. Examples of this can be infographics showing the progression of facts. The common weather forecast for the week is also an example of infographics. [34]

Representative visual presents textual information more in the form of pictorial or photographic presentations. As complement to text writing, its

---

[34]Jonathan Turley, Judge Posner Spices up Opinions with Web Photos, Res Ipsa Loquitur, Jan. 28, 2012,http://jonathantnrley.org/2012/01/28/jndge-posner-spices-np-opinions-with-weh-photos/; Debra Cassens Weiss, Posner Opinion Includes Ostrich Photo to Portray Lawyers Who Ignore Precedent, A.B.A. J., Nov. 28, 2011, http://www.ahajournal .com/news/article/posner opinion includes ostrich photo to portray lawyers who ignore precede/(showing how Richard Posner, uses pictures in judicial writing), both cited in Steve Johnson & Ruth A. Robbins, Art-Iculating the Analysis: Systemizing the Decision to Use Visuals as Legal Reasoning (2015) 20 *J. Leg. Writing* 57 @ 67.

educational purpose is styled dual-coding in cognition. A good way to do this is by incorporating photographs into briefs.

The functional classification is helpful in identifying what visual aid would aid reasoning or analysis for lawyering purposes.

Once the functional type is chosen, the lawyer would next decide how the chosen type advances the goals of persuasion in the three dimensions of classical rhetoric, *logos*, *pathos*, and *ethos.*[35] *Logos* (persuasion accompanied through logical reasoning embodied in the content of the communication) is the process of persuading using substance and logical argument, such as statute law, case-law and policy. *Pathos* (persuasion accomplished through the emotional response of the audience to the communication) on the other hand is persuasion through emotive argument. *Ethos* (persuasion accomplished through the perceived character or reputation of the speaker) refers to establishing and maintaining credibility in the eyes of the audience by showing intelligence, character and good will.[36] It is important to understand why a particular functional type is chosen because the goal is to find one that is useful to analysis the case.

For example, if the persuasive goal is to show say, how a material transmits heat to another object, an interpretive image such as a heat graph would be useful in showing the relationship between components of a factor test, whereas an organizational image would be useful as a table of content in brief writing to show the logic development of sections of the brief.

The bottom line in choosing is to access the effectiveness of visuals in the light of its ability to persuade. So, if visuals would not advance the goal of persuasion in the three dimensions it should be discarded. That being so, the

[35] Classical rhetoric started in the fifth century B.C.E. continued for nearly 1,000 years of the Greco-Roman history. It began with scholars like Socrates, followed by Plato, Aristotle, Cicero and Quintilian. See Aristotle, *The Rhetoric* (trans. W. Rhys Roberts, 1965) available at htpp://www.iastate.edu/honey1/Rhetoric/ (accessed September 23, 2016); Marcus Tullius Cicero, *De Inventione* (trans. H.M. Hubbell, 1949); Marcus Tullius Cicero, *De Oratore* (trans. E.W. Sutton, 1942); Marcus Fabius Quintilian, *Institutio Oratoria* (H.E. Butler, 1954). See Michael Frost, Introduction to Classical Rhetoric: A Lost Heritage (1999) 8 *S. Cal. Interdisc. L.J.* 613 (an article which traces the history of rhetoric and argumentation to Corax of Syracuse).

[36] Michael R. Smith, *Advanced Legal Writing: Theories and Strategies in Persuasive Writing,* 3rd ed. Aspen Law & Bus., 2013, 11; Aristotle, On Rhetoric (transl. George A. Kennedy, Oxford Univ. Press, 1991); George A. Kennedy, *A New History of Classical Rhetoric,* Princeton Univ. Press, 1998; Stephen Toulmin, *The Use of Argument,* Cambridge Univ. Press, 1958. For detail discussion on a theory of persuasion, see J. Christopher Rideout, Storytelling, Narrative Rationality, and Legal Persuasion (2008) 14 *J. Legal Writing Inst.* 53. See also the interesting read, W. Lance Bennett & Martha S. Feldman, *Reconstructing Reality in the Courtroom: Justice and Judgment in American Culture*, Rutgers Univ. Press, 1981 (the social science researchers stating that American criminal trial is organized around storytelling).

choice of visuals must depend on its transformative powers rather than its decorative use.[37]

Visuals acquire transformative power only when it enables the reader to create the necessary consciousness, as in introducing new perspective to knowledge and understanding of the reader or is one which aids the reader to understand the legal argumentation and reasoning of the presenter.[38]

Therefore, whether a particular visual is useful or non-useful is a matter of continuum on the scale of its persuasiveness requiring the presenter to use sound judgment and discernment. The diagram below is illustrative of the continuum between useful and limited useful/non-useful visuals.[39]

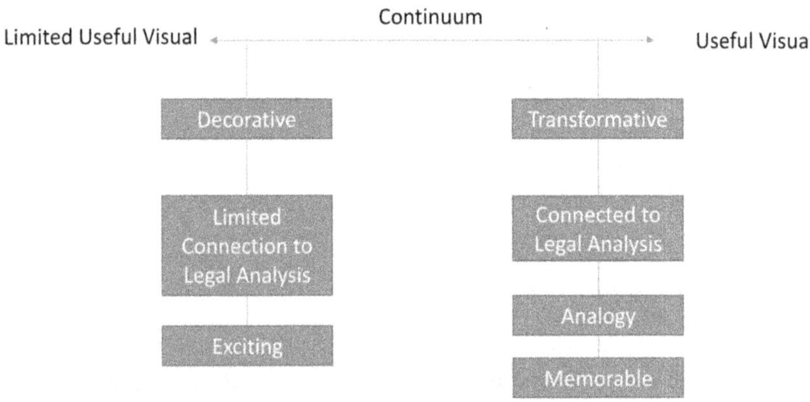

---

[37] While decorative visuals may be eye appealing, advancing pathos, in failing to interrogate the three paths of persuasion often depicted as the "rhetorical triangle" it does not significantly advance the goal of persuasion. On the rhetoric triangle, see Michael D. Murray, Classical Rhetoric, Explanatory Synthesis and the Treat Paradigm (Univ. Ill. L. & Econ. Working Paper No. 75, 2007), available at http://works.bepress.com/michael murray/9accessed September 23, 2016. See also Michael Frost, Justice Scalia's Rhetoric of Dissent: A Greco-Roman Analysis of Scalia's Advocacy in the VMI Case (2002) 91 KY. L.J. 167. Decorative visuals can be likened to secondary form of pathos, see Michael R. Smith, *Advanced Legal Writing: Theories and Strategies in Persuasive Writing*, 3rd ed. 2013, 14, cited in Johnson & Robbins @ 70.

[38] Linda Levine & Kurt M. Saunders, Thinking Like a Rhetor (1993) 43 *J. Legal Educ.* 108; Michael Frost, Ethos, Pathos and Legal Audience (1994) 99 *Dick L. Rev.* 85. See also Michael Frost, Justice Scalia's Rhetoric of Dissent: A Greco-Roman Analysis of Scalia's Advocacy in the VMI Case (2002) 91 *KY. L.J.* 167.

[39] See generally, James P. Eyster, Lawyer as Artist: Using Significant Moments and Obtuse Objects to Enhance Advocacy (2008) 14 *J. Legal Writing Inst.* 87 (discussing how to apply key techniques of the visual artists-the obtuse objet and significant moments to legal advocacy and their persuasive sting according to art history scholars, aestheticians, psychologists, and psycholinguists).

This being so, whether the choice is organization, representative or interpretive imaging, or a combination of any, the presenter must be mindful of choosing one that persuades in the light of the case facts. For example, an image that advances the case theory of the client creating deeper understanding of not just *what* happened, but also the *meaning* of what happened would be transformative in the process of explaining what *will* happen.[40]

Identifying what type of visual to choose also requires that the presenter accesses the design quality of the visual and the general gestalt of the document as a whole, which ultimately ought to influence the decision to use visual in the presentation. This can be particularly problematic a decision to take because the translation process of choosing and conceptualizing visual in the shadow of the presenter's chamber to its public presentation should be guided by different considerations. That a visual is thought good enough to explain, clarify and create better understand of legal analysis to the presenter does not automatically give it the same effect with the reader or third party or audience. How the reader could react or respond to it must be considered so that its transformative power is not weakened or distorted.

There does not appear a clear blueprint for the transition from shadow to public perception, but a few factors can be helpful if weighed properly. One useful hint for navigation is to gauge the usefulness of visual by first conceptualizing it as though it were metaphoric or literary legal writing. If it fits well, in the sense of

---

[40] For example, in using stories to recreate reality, critical theorist distinguishes 'what' happened from the 'meaning' of what happened, believing that by opening the client's world, the meaning of what happened can be better understood. See Binny Miller, Give Them Back Their Lives: Recognising Client Narrative in Case Theory (1994) 93 *Mich. L. Rev.* 485 (showing how the practice of lawyering should be reconstructed to embrace a greater role for clients in constructing case theories. In the article, the writer reveals how the narrative was expanded beyond 'what happened' scope of whether the $592 received by the defendant as damages benefit from an accident, spent by the defendant in buying Sunday shoes for her children, should count as money deductible from her social benefit. Her lawyer chose a narrative that concentrated on the meaning of what happened to vindicate and justify the receipt). See also, Lucie E. White, Subordination, Rhetorical Survival Skills, and Sunday Shoes: Notes on the Hearing of Mrs. G (1990) 38 *Buffalo L. Rev.* 1 (where the commentators using the story of Mrs. G welfare hearing application reveals that cultural images and long-established legal norms construct the subjectivity and speech of socially subordinate groups, like women, blacks etc., as inherently inferior to those of dominant groups). "Recognizing the importance of the client's life experience, critical lawyering involves clients in the choice of which story to tell and it expands the content of the narratives from 'what happened' to include the fabric of the client's life." Id. at 514; Peter Gabel & Paul Harris, Building Power and Breaking Images: Critical Theory and the Practice of Law (1982-83) 11 *N.Y.U. Rev. L &Soc. Change* 369; Lucie White, Mobilization on the Margins of the Lawsuit: Making Space for Clients to Speak (1987) 16 *N.Y.U. Rev. L &Soc. Change* 535; Jessica A. Rose, Rebellious or Regnant : Police Brutality Lawyering in New York City (2000) 28 *Fordham Urban L.J.* 619 (addresses current legal limitations in combating police brutality for subordinate groups and why and how the legal community must develop a more creative and rebellious methodology if it is to accomplish the goal of social transformation).

enhancing logical understanding of the legal analysis, then chances are that it would be accepted as visual public imaging that is persuasive and transformative.[41]

A second guide would be to consider if visual improves the overall design of the document or brief because the presenter's goal is to persuade and elicit positive responses from the reader rather than triggering negative reactions. That being so, the presenter should be mindful of things like whether visual images are too many and overwhelming by considering the whole configuration of the document to be presented.

It may prove useful to consider the cultural, social, religious and sometimes racial background of the reader.

Since the visual is intended as a legal document, whether as pre-litigation complaint or a brief, attention must be paid to matters of professional norms and responsibility law. For instance, it would be material for the lawyer to consider whether intended visuals would be ethical, promoting the interest of justice, and the like.

Importantly, an eye must be kept on the useful/non-useful dichotomy or continuum to determine persuasive relevance.

(ii) Understanding Why Select Visual is Useful

Having identified what type of visual would advance legal analysis, a conscious effort must next be turned to understanding why the selected visual is useful to the analysis. This *why* analysis also implicates much of the things the lawyer should consider in the *what* discussion above, such as assessing the design quality and gestalt of the document. But more importantly, it is the stage to consider the persuasive principles at play in the presentation. The *why* stage is time to give conscious attention to how the images meet the target; inform and persuade. If the image does not make the legal document more persuasive by making the legal arguments easier to understand, then it must be removed.

No doubt such assessment demands certain familiarity of what the audience already know and is capable of knowing if images can be used to generate clearer and better understanding. Thus, if the visual relies on an allusion, or cue, or cultural reference, the presenter must assess the background cognitive knowledge of the audience. In this respect, idealized cognitive models (ICMs) provides basis

---

[41] The literary test is recommended by Smith as touchstone for relevant transmission from shadow to public. See Michael R. Smith, *Advanced Legal Writing: Theories and Strategies in Persuasive Writing,* Aspen Law & Bus., 2002, chapters 9-14. For discussion on persuasion using narrative See Singer and the factory workers metaphor or literary narrative. Translating the narrative from shadow to public presentation in the form of visual would certain have force.

for common-ground knowledge for driving legal analysis and reasoning.[42] For if the audience know the referential image, then the visual simply taps into the pre-existing mental database that allows the reader or audience to draw the intended entailment or analogy between the reference and the legal argument. For example, a visual which relies on imaging of say how traffic congestion creates chaos and could delay the realization of beneficial transactions would make analogical sense to the Lagos audience than to an up-state or country-side reader or audience not readily familiar with the daily challenges of road traffic.

Knowing the peculiarities or background of the judge can be helpful in this regard. The lawyer can get an insight into the court by visiting the court prior to her hearing or presentation. Inquiries from colleagues can also supply hints on peculiarities. Goggle information about the judge can also be of assistance.

A useful gauge for knowing whether the reader or audience would likely be persuaded and informed about the legal argument with the aid of image would be for the lawyer to first determine the convincing properties of the visual personally. Chances are that if she finds it worthy in advancing legal analysis then the reader or audience may also do. The presenter's must first find it useful. It is only when the image advances the case-theory that it has probative value.

Asking the *so what* question is helpful in assessing the effectiveness of draft visual to advance persuasion. That an image may work does not mean it will work. There must be a close entailment between it and the case-theory, the substance of the case being advanced, such as a level of certainty that is compelling enough to transform cognition. For example, an otherwise useful visual that is tangential to the case-theory can be visually distracting. Also, one which is susceptible to challenge for inaccuracy should be avoided. That being so,

---

[42] See for example, the Sunday Shoe case the presenter constructed the client's reality into the case-theory. Joseph William Singer, Persuasion (1989) 87 *Mich. L. Rev.* 2442 (arguing that much of lawyering is persuading parties, juries, and judges to agree with one perspective rather than another. In this article, he explores how one persuades others about the values they should have. To illustrate his problem, he describes a property course in which he taught students about factory closings. While he expected students to identify the unfortunate social costs of closings on the surrounding towns and released employees, he repeatedly met with impersonal doctrinal arguments about managerial prerogatives, freedom of contract, and deference to the legislature. Concerned about the students' professional competence development, he developed a method of creating a relationship between the students and the people affected by factory closings. He constructed a hypothetical in which his law school decided to fail the lowest 33% of first-year students after their first-semester exams in an attempt to protect the public from unprepared lawyers in the future. Faced with similarly desperate and unfair circumstances, the students learned to appreciate the other side of factory closings cases. They felt empathy and connection with the released employees and were able to perceive the imbalance of bargaining power and breach of good faith where they had previously seen only market values. By creating a situation in which the students felt vulnerable and powerless, the author cultivated a relationship between the students and workers, thereby influencing the students' values)

the presenter should analyse the intended visual with the same rhetorical considerations as any other legal argument. That is why it is recommended that it may be helpful to hire professional visual law service firms especially for complex litigation.[43]

It should be remembered that visuals are best deployed to reinforce text-based writing, so they are more persuasive if they supplement and complement text writing on legal argument and analysis. Rarely should the presenter use them without text-based writing because visuals gather more force when introduced by text to demonstrate its place in reasoning and the inference desired to be drawn from them. Accordingly, "analytical visual cannot perform its persuasive purpose without the cognitive prime of an introductory thesis."[44]

Since visual imaging is closest to pathos in the rhetoric triangle, the presenter must take care to consider its design even when the image is effective in conveying the substantive idea of the argument. The gestalt should be carefully chosen, balancing professionalism, informative and sense-pleasing considerations. For example, I was in a workshop audience for legal teachers' training where the white presenter used visual image of a lorry filled on all sides with jerry cans leading for the United States White House as though conveying the President family from poor Africa to the United States. Though it was meant to convey with certain percentage of reality the undeveloped state of the African continent, the audience took offence at the visual depletion. Yes, the visual undoubtedly captured the argument of under development, but its gestalt did not consider the eye-displeasing and cultural background of the audience, who appropriately protested the use of the image. The lesson is simple: the pathos of the document should not be ignored even if its logos is appropriate.[45] It is important to check for the nuances of audience background, design layout, colour combination, complexity, and indeed all matters related to the visuals logos, pathos and ethos.

(iii) Understanding How the Legal Analysis is Shaped by Visual Imaging

Having decided the *what* and *why* of visual imaging selected, the presenter would next give attention to *how* the legal reasoning is shaped by the visual creation. Visuals can be created in a number of ways. But whatever style is used, it must shape better understanding of textual writing. Recognizing the persuasive goal of

---

[43] Robert Ambrogi, Vision Quest: Visual Law Services Are Worth a Thousand Words—and Big Money (2014) 100 *A.B.A. J.* 34 (May issue).

[44] Steve Johnson & Ruth A. Robbins, Art-Iculating the Analysis: Systemizing the Decision to Use Visuals as Legal Reasoning (2015) 20 *J. Leg. Writing* 57 @ 91.

[45] Michael R. Smith, *Advanced Legal Writing: Theories and Strategies in Persuasive Writing*, 3rd. ed. Aspen Law & Bus., 2013 @ 11.

imaging requires lawyers to spend some time thinking visually. At the stage of planning to write the presenter would need to think visually about how the images connect the substantive ideas of the client's case-theory. This is accomplished by putting the ideas in a shadow sketched visual, which is reviewed from stage to stage with the aim of making it strategic. Showing rather than telling is the way to think visually. Since it is not enough to have visual which nearly or may work, moving the image from shadow to the actual writing must be based on target-the visual should be precise in conveying an accurate and exacting analysis.

Empirical Examples of Visuals

Visuals may be used to strengthen text to illustrate the elements of a claim, to parse the relevance of statute or legal doctrine, and to capture the framework of legal analysis. For example, organizational visual, as in the form of simple bullet listing, can be used to identify elements of each claim or to show the controlling statute that governs the resolution of a controversy. Though text-based argument may explain the relevant statute, presenting it visually could make the explanation clearer and more accessible to the reader.

In a similar manner, interpretive visuals could be used to simplify the analysis structure for the reader. For instance, it could be used to illustrate relationship and relativity when the concepts are difficult or multi-dimensional. So too with representative visual. It can be used in the form of pictorial or photographic presentations to encode strong cognition.

This section will be used to illustrate how this can work with textual writing.

Example of Organizational Visual

A simple organizational visual can be bullet or table listing. For example, in a claim founded on negligence, the elements can be identified like this:

Proof of negligence	Controlling test
Duty of care	Neighbour or proximity
Breach of duty of care	Reasonable man
Damages arising from breach	Remoteness

What this does is that the bullet points serve as signpost showing the relationship between the elements and the controlling test governing them.

Example of Interpretive Visual

Infographics is a good example of interpretive imaging. So too is a heat map which displays data values between variables shown in colours.[46] Readers are often familiar with the different colour shades used illustrate them. A common example easily conceivable in geography map reading class depicts wet regions in green and dry region is patched colour of brown. Similarly, the blue and red colour mapping for Democratic Party and the Republican Party respectively as demography analysis of US election is another example of heat map.

These maps are generally interpretive in breaking down complex, multi-dimensional facts to easy understandable. That being so, heat maps can be useful interpretative visuals for illustrating between two or more seemingly independent ideas or concepts by showing their colour variation to demonstrate interrelationship for purposes of analysis or reasoning.

Rosman example of how unlawful disclosure affects stock price of a company shares is a good graphic example of an interpretive visual, and it is unashamedly copied hereunder to illustrate the point.[47]

Textual presentation: Moments after Defendant Frey disclosed the information, DynaCorp's stock dropped from $64.27 to $2.45.

Interpretative presentation: Moments after Defendant Frey disclosed the information, DynaCorp's stock dropped from $64.27 to $2.45.

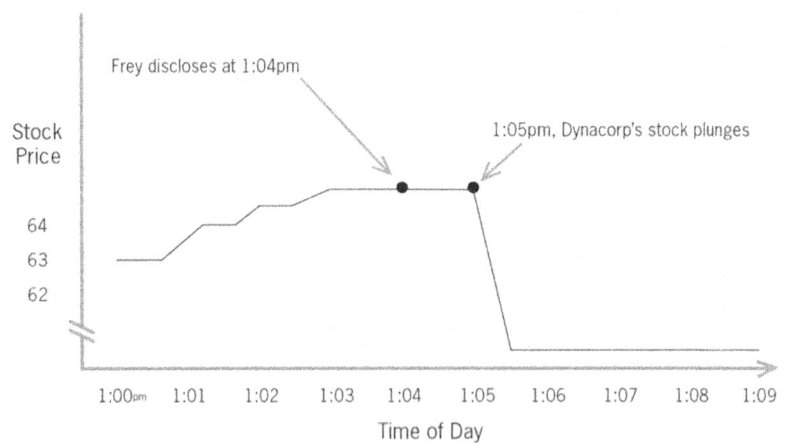

[46] The proper name for heat map is choropleth maps of which heat maps are a type. See Johnson & Robbins, above n. 2 @ 78.

[47] Adam L. Rosman, Visualizing the Law: Using Charts, Diagrams, and Other Images to Improve Legal Briefs, (2013) 63 *J. Legal Educ.* 70 @ 71.

This infograph is both informative and persuasive. It simply tell what happened to the stock of DynaCorp. It displays an important fact that text-based writing only might leave flat. From the infographic image the reader can see in one quick, convincing manner, how disclosure within a time frame of minutes, from 1.04pm to 1.05pm nose-dived DynaCorp stock from $64.7 to $2.45 in less than another minute, 1.06pm. The reader can thus see in one-go the grave, adverse consequences of disclosure.

Example of Representative Visual

Johnson and Robbins give a great example of a pictorial visual using the case of *Hillwood Investment Property* v. *Radical Mavericks Management*.[48] The minority owner of Dallas Mavericks basketball team through his corporation, Hillwood, sued the majority owner, Mark Cuban in 2011, alleging financial mismanagement and breach of fiduciary leading to financial reverses for the team. In response to this, Cuban filed a motion for summary judgment, essentially using pictorial images which looked like this:

"On June 12, 2011, the World Champion Dallas Mavericks defeated the Miami Heat to claim the franchise's NBA championship. A true and correct photo of one of the many victory celebration is incorporated herein:"

[48] Johnson & Robbins, above n. 2 @ 93.The full four-page motion is available at http://www.scribd.com/doc/58470086/ 2011-06- 22-WC-Mavs-and-Radical-Mavs-Mngt-MSJ or http//www.cbsdallas.files.wordpress.com, accessed September 23, 2016. It should however be noted that the brief by itself was a lousy legal document because it didn't answer pointedly the complain of the plaintiff. Realizing that simply stating that we won the championship, and therefore I could not have mismanaged the finances of the team failed to address any of the plaintiff's specific accusations, Cuban counsel sought and filed an Amended Motion for Summary Judgment that was far more traditional: 22 pages of specific arguments. The amended motion contained no visuals. Not surprisingly, the Amended Motion received virtually no publicity. It was, however, successful on a more important level—the court granted it and dismissed the case. But the point had been made the images could have been used by Cuban's counsel in the amended brief to draw attention to the fact that having a competitive team will attract more fans which invariably mean more money and increased value for the team. Creating effect on this as a teaching aid Johnson & Robbins show how they working their students insightfully added to the image graph showing that under Cuban the team maintained its longest sell-out streak in the NBA at over 400 games. The addition graph showing ownership structure, attendance and percentage win under Cuban makes the defendant's defence more solid.

Under Hillwood's ownership the team was deemed the worst franchise in professional sport. Under Mavericks stewardship the team has become one of the league's most successful team and are now NBA champions. Accordingly, there can be no genuine question that Hillwood's claims of mismanagement lack merit and Hillwood's claim be disposed of on summary judgment.

This powerful brief visual filed by Thomas M. Melsheimer of Fish & Richardson P.C. of the Texas State Bar received widespread publicity and lawyers and the popular press hailed it as a great piece of lawyering, even receiving award as a 'dagger brief.'[49]

The Future for Visuals

According to Porter "Unless courts specifically prohibit it, multimedia written advocacy will become the norm. To rising generations of young lawyers, images are the vernacular of modern communication. Even long-tenured judges—many of whom now rely on image-friendly tablets to read court papers—are newly receptive to visual written argument. In fact, embedded images are only the

---

[49]Brian Baxter, Fish & Richardson, Mark Cuban, and a Trash-Talking Summary Judgment Motion, Am La w Da il y , http://amlawdaily.typepad.mm/amlawdaily/20n/06/fish- richardson-cnhan.html (June 22, 2011, 6:19 p.m.); Debra Cassen Weiss, Are the Dallas Mavericks Mismanaged? Motion Uses Celebration Photo to Refute the Notion, A.B.A. J., June 23, 2011, http://www.abajournal.com/news/article/are the dallas mavericks mismanaged motion uses celebration photo to refute/. See also, Rachel M. Zahorsky, Texas Lawyer Honored for Unconventional Brief, A.B.A. J., Jan. 5, 2012, http://www.ahajonrnal.com/news/article/texas lawyer honored for unconventional brief/. The article reported that Green Bag Almanac & Reader would honor the Dallas attorney, Tom Melsheimer, for the motion. The honoree list can be seen at Exemplary Legal Writing: 2014 Honorees, http://www.greenbag.org/ green bag press/almanacs/almanacs.html. all cited in Johnson & Robbins at 95.

beginning: Technological advances have opened the door to integrating video, audio, and other technology into briefs or opinions."[50]

The digital age would undoubtedly transform legal discourse and trial-related technology.

Conclusion

Visuals should be readily used by lawyers in motions, in briefs, in depositions, in trials, in pre-trial hearings, in arbitration and alternative dispute resolution, in class certification hearing, in advocacy and lobbying presentations. It is the dagger presentation all lawyers must use as persuasion arsenal.

---

[50]Porter, above n. 7 @ 1693.

Chapter 18

Using Non-Legal Materials in Litigation

Introduction

Lawyer use legal materials (statute, case-law, regulations) in persuading courts and tribunals. Legal reasoning generally relies on legal resources as precedent for determining outcomes. Non-legal materials like scientific, economic or social data rarely find a place in legal discourse. This is to be expected of a profession that conservatively strive to remain an autonomous sphere. It is therefore not strange that the profession discounts non-legal materials and lawyers have found it challenging to use them even when relevant to litigation. The ability to use non-legal resources however must be a necessary skill to acquire in our time as the legal space increasingly admits of these resources. Materials outside law are beginning to have significant bearing on what shapes the law. A lawyer who desires to persuade effectively is now obliged to master the skill of using non-legal resources in the business of lawyering. The special language and tools of the profession now demands that law can no longer remain impervious of other disciplines.

For example, jurisprudence in the 1960s was dominated by debates between H.L.A. Hart positivism and Lord Patrick Devlin natural law disputation and the relationship between law and morals.[1] Some still understand the subject through that (false) dichotomy. That trend is now on the decline. The publication of Richard Posner's seminal text, *Economic Analysis of Law* in 1973 introduced a new lexicon to law.[2]Some scholars are even of the view that the ecological re-

[1] H.L.A. Hart, Law, *Liberty, and Morality* (OUP, Oxford, 1963), Patrick Devlin, *The Enforcement of Morals* (OUP, Oxford, 1965).

[2]Anthony T. Kronman, Remarks at the Second Driker Forum for Excellence in the Law (1995) 42 *Wayne L. Rev.* 115 @ 160 (a critic describing the book as "an enormous enlivening force in American legal thought" saying that it "continues and remains the single most influential jurisprudence school in the country); Jon Hanson & David Yosifson, The Situation: An Introduction to the Situational Character, Critical Realism, Power Economics, and Deep Capture (2003) 152 *Univ. Pa. L. Rev.* 129 @ 142. Jules L. Coleman, Markets, Morals and the Law, Cambridge Univ. Press, 1988 @ 67 (describing law-and-economics as the dominant theoretical paradigm for understanding and assessing law and policy); (Emerging as a trend in legal scholarship, law-and-economics constitutes (at least in the United States of America) the main discourse about law in our time, strong enough for Jules Coleman to state that it abysses (if for nothing, at least temporarily), analytical and all other philosophical thoughts promoted by great minds like Rawls and Nozick type of legal scholarship, introducing and welcoming scholars like Ronald Coase, Pigou, Calabresi and Richard Posner).

arrangement economics brings to law is an acting heeding the 1897 Holmes' occupational-call.[3]

The Brandies 1908 brief can be described as the greatest litigation brief that opens up law to the use of non-legal resources derived from other disciplines.[4] Today, the most conspicuous example of a changing attitude to the use of non-legal materials and citation practice comes from the social sciences. There is marked increase in the use and citation of non-legal sources in the last fifty years, and the phenomenon is not about to abate. Increasingly, virtually every discipline, scientific or non-scientific is becoming integrated to the lawyering process. Thus, even though most text explanations of what constitute "authority" do not typically include non-legal authority, the profession has long recognized the use of non-legal sources in actual practice.

This chapter will be concerned with how far lawyers can make use of non-legal ("Brandies-style brief") resources in argumentation.[5]

---

[3]Oliver Wendell Holmes, stated in 1897 that: 'for the rational study of law the black letter man may be the man of the present, but the man of the future is the man of statistics and the master of economics.' The Louis Brandies brief is an example of the normative power of economics and statistic in the legal process. See Robert D. Cooter, Law and the Imperialism of Economics: An Introduction to the Economic Analysis of Law and Review of the Major Books (1981-2) 29 *UCLA L. Rev.* 1260 (an article describing the extension of economics beyond its traditional precincts of the market to law, sociology, philosophy and political science as economic imperialism.)

[4]Ellie Margolis, Beyond Brandies: Exploring the Use of Non-Legal Materials in Appellate Briefs (2000) 34 *Univ. San Francesco L. Rev.* 197 (an article examining the scope of social science and empiricism in law). See also, Amy J. Griffin, Dethroning The Hierarchy of Authority (2018) 87 Oregon L. Rev. (an article describing the conventional view of legal authority centred on the judicial hierarchy, while proposing a re-orienting view of authority as a pluralistic practice rather than a fixed hierarchical list, accounting for a more nuanced and holistic account of legal authority); Frederick Schauer& Virginia J. Wise, Nonlegal Information and the Delegalization of Law (2000) 29 *J. Leg. Stud.* 495 (an article tracking and analysed the increase in use of "non-legal" authority, and questioning whether the distinction between legal and non-legal authority is itself breaking down).

[5] The term Brandies-brief is rooted in the brief submitted by Louis D. Brandies in *Muller v Oregon*, 208 U.S. 412 (1908) in which the attorney in defending the constitutionality of an Oregon statute limiting the number of hours women could work in a day, relied on existing social science research on the detrimental effect of long working hours on women. See also, John Monahan & Laurens Walker, Social Authority: Obtaining, Evaluating and Establishing Social Science in Law (1986) 134 *Univ. Pa. L. Rev.* 477; Laurens Walker & John Monahan, Social Frameworks: A New Us of Social Science in Law (1987) 73 *Va. L. Rev.* 559.

Visual non-autonomous nature of modern law

The Brandeis Brief Innovation

[Narrate the Brandies] *Muller* v. *Oregon* is a case in which Louis Brandeis prepared his famous Brandeis Brief for the State of Oregon.

The issue in *Muller* was whether Oregon could constitutionally restrict working hours for women based on a state interest in protecting women's health. The Brandeis brief' of 101 pages consisted almost entirely of non-legal information, such as statements by doctors, academics, anonymous government employees, and co-workers relating observations of and opinions about the lives of women workers. Virtually all of the named sources were men telling stories about women they had known. The brief includes page after page of entries such as these:

Mr. B, a foreman of a printing establishment:

"Girls must sit at the 'case.' I never knew but one woman, and she a strong, vigorous Irishwoman, of unusual height, who could stand at the case like a man. Female compositors, as a rule, are sickly, suffering much from backache, headache, weak limbs, and general 'female weakness."

Amale mule-spinner (a man who operated a spinning machine in a cotton mill), describing the women he worked beside:

"I have noticed that the hard, slavish overwork is driving those girls into the saloons, after they leave the mills evenings...good, respectable girls, but they come out so tired and so thirsty and so exhausted...Wherever you go...near the abodes of [overworked employees], you will always find the sign of the rumshop."

<u>An anonymous source quoted in a report from the Maine Bureau of</u>

Industrial and Labor Statistics

> Many saleswomen are so worn out, when their week's work is ended, that a good part of their Sundays is spent in bed, recuperating for the next week's demands. And one by one girls drop out and die, often from sheer overwork. This I know from observation and personal acquaintance.
>
> Another anonymous speaker at a legislative session
>
> "The woman wage-earner, gentlemen, does not always live at the mill-gates; she is therefore obliged to make a half or three-quarters' hour journey before she arrives; consequently she will leave home at half-past five in the morning, only to return at half-past eight or nine o'clock in the evening. Is that living? Under such circumstances can a woman truly care for her children and her home?"

Only two paragraphs quote a woman describing her own experience, her own health, her own family, or her own economic situation. The other101pages consist of quotations from anonymous speakers or from speakers whose expertise is absent or impossible to discern and whose reliability and neutrality are unknown.[6] Nearly all the quoted sources are speaking entirely out of their own subjectivity.

Even though after referring to the conspicuous social science materials in the brief, the court stated it 'may not be, technically speaking, authorities,' they nonetheless received it as 'judicial cognizance.' That was in 1908. About fifty years later in *Brown* v. *Board of Education*, the Court referred to the social science studies that supported the district court's finding that segregated public education harmed black children as 'modern authority'.[7]

---

[6]Linda H. Edwards, Telling Stories in the Supreme Court: Voices Briefs and the Role of Democracy in Constitutional Deliberation (2018) 29 *Yale J.L. & Feminism* 29 @ 50 ("On the question of reliability, the "social science" information in the iconic Brandeis Brief cannot be considered more reliable than the non-party stories of today's voices briefs.")

[7]347 U.S. 483 @ 494 (1954). For recent amicus briefs filed in the United States using non-legal materials, see, Brief of Amicus Curiae American Sociological Association in Support of Petitioners at 1, *Obergefell* v. *Hodges*, 135 S. Ct. *2584* (2015)(Nos. 14-556, 14-562, 14-571, 14-574), 2015 WL 1048442 (The *Obergefell* brief filed on behalf of the American Sociological Association (ASA), a professional organization of sociologists); Brief of the Institute for Justice as Amicus Curiae in Support of Appellant, Citizens United at 6-7, *Citizens United v. Fed. Election Comm'n*, 558 U.S. 310 (2010) (No. 08-205), 2009 WL 147860; Dick M. Carpenter *II, Disclosure Costs: Unintended Consequences of Campaign Finance Reform,* Inst. For Justice (Mar. 2007) @ 5-6, http://ij.org/wp-content/uploads/2015/03/DisclosureCosts.pdf, (all cited in Edwards, Linda H. (2018) "Telling Stories in the Supreme Court: Voices Briefs and the Role of Democracy in Constitutional Deliberation (2018) 29 *Yale J.L. & Feminism* 29 @ 51-52. For example judicial use of non-legal

The use of non-legal material has been commonly referred to as "legislative facts" (as opposed to adjudicative facts).[8] The legal status of legislative facts remains unclear. However, currently, social science-related information is now treated as another part of the vast realm of 'non-binding' authority.

Legal Argumentation

In argumentation, lawyers often cite as precedent cases, statute, regulations and other legal materials. The audience (judges) have no challenge in applying them. It is the staple of the profession. Much as this is what the profession employs for reasoning, legal resources can sometimes be challenging in providing adequate basis for resolution of controversy or for explaining legal direction. Such situations are conceivable if certain specialized information about a thing is helpful to clearly understand the phenomena. For instance, a judge may need non-legal information on how diseases get transmitted if communicable. So, to properly understand, say how AIDS gets transmitted from a carrier to the victim, the judge may require (scientific) information about causation of communicable diseases, such as tuberculosis, chicken-pox, etc., which information can be applied analogically to AIDS situation. Judges may also need sociological, psychological and economic data to reach decisions on regulatory matches or mismatches, and the like. Such information is not typically contained in or is part of legal resources found in book, statute or case-law. To get such information resort will be had to non-legal materials.

As a general rule, lawyers eschew non-legal materials in brief writing and advocacy. The reason for this is that lawyers are not trained in the use of non-legal materials. Some also believe that factual non-legal information will not meet the threshold of admissibility. And even if it does, may not be as reliable as legal precedent.

---

material, see: *Kumho Tire Co., Ltd. v. Carmichael,* 526 U.S. 137, 142-43 (1999) (where Justice Breyer described steel-belted radial tires at some length, even including a drawing of tire construction. In doing so, he relied on his 1998 softback book from Amazon Books; *Rowe* v. *Gibson*, 798 F 3d 622 @ 623-627 (7th Cir. 2015) (Judge Posner in analysing the medical condition of a prisoner cited internet sources such as the National Institutes of Health, the Mayo Clinic, WebMD and Wikipedia); *Grayson* v Schuler 666 F 3d 450 (7th Cir. 2012) (Judge Posner in a case arguing the right of a prisoner to wear dreadlocks included a web photograph of Bob Marley alongside the comment). In fact, in the seminal case of *Roe v Wade,*410 U.S. 113, 129-62 (1973)Justice Blackmun travelled to the Mayo Clinic to conduct his own medical research before writing his opinion. He wrote to the Mayo Clinic librarian to inquire whether "your well- equipped library [would] have anything about the history of abortion."

[8]Legislative facts have been described as "generalized facts about the world that are not limited to any specific case. See Allison O. Larsen, Trouble With Amicus Facts (2014) 100 *Va. L. Rev.* 1757 @ 1759; Kenneth C. Davis, An Approach to Problems of Evidence in the Administrative Process (1942) 55 *Harv. L. Rev.* 364 @ 404.

While all of these are genuine concerns, it must be admitted that non-legal materials have always been present in the litigation process without notice and fears expressed about them. Land litigation is often replete with evidence of surveyors and visual maps. Murder trials also calls in much of medical (scientific) information, with little eye-browsing. Non-legal materials are not rendered inadmissible by rules of court or evidence. There is no rule that prohibits the use of non-legal (factual) materials relevant in litigation. If anything, the doctrine of judicial notice opens a window for their use in many instances. Non-legal materials stating facts about the parties and facts bearing on law and policy are particularly helpful in persuasion and in helping judges to make correct policy decision.

Some lawyers suggest that the place of non-legal resources in law is insignificant because in their view courts only use empirical evidence to further an already taken position by the judges. While this is not seriously disputed, it fortifies the thinking that courts do use non-legal information. If so, then lawyers should hone their skills of presenting non-legal information to support their arguments. It is important that a lawyer does not miss the opportunity to make the presentation where appropriate. If she does, chances are that the judge may find it out on her own to draw conclusions, often unsupportable by brief or advocacy. Current use of non-legal information should therefore impel lawyers to take a more active role to understand when and how to present non-legal materials, if appropriate to the client's case.

Recognizing that traditional legal resources may not always provide adequate basis for certain forms of litigation, a lawyers should be quick to know when non-legal material would be helpful in aiding the court to reach a favourable decision. This should be especially so in cases where the court is invited to develop a new legal rule from unclear precedent. The lawyer can, for instance, use non-legal materials to illustrate the effect a legal rule.

Presenting factual effect information is a suggested way to providing court information on the prediction or effect of a legal rule or policy. Margolis provides a powerful example of it this way:

> For example, in a case in which the court is asked to impose tort liability on a mother for injury to a child caused by the mother's negligent conduct during pregnancy, the mother may argue that a duty to a foetus would be unduly intrusive because it would affect every moment of a woman's life, even before pregnancy (the policy argument). As support, she may provide medical information (legislative fact) about the many ways a woman's conduct before

> and during pregnancy, such as diet, physical activity and choice of work, could affect the health of a foetus. If medical information supports the contention that the mother's health even before pregnancy can affect the health of the foetus, the policy argument will be much more persuasive than the same assertion without any factual support.[9]

Unquestionably, the medical information about the many ways a woman's conduct can affect her foetus will one way or the other influence the decision the judge will reach on the question of imposing liability for pre-natal injuries. That is how non-legal information creates persuasive window in law.

Congenial Situations for Non-Legal Materials

Non-legal material will be particularly useful in cases requiring the resolution of a novel issue or new legal rule in the following three situations:
(i) first application of common law case;
(ii) constitutional law case raising novel application;
(iii) cases requiring statutory application.

The three areas are particularly interrogated because the common law reasoning technique creates gap-filling structures.[10] According to Pierre Legrand:

> the common law has not left the inductive stage of methodological development. The isomorphs used by common law lawyers were, and are, too descriptive to function as an abstract system of thought divorced from particular sets of facts. One cannot axiomatise English legal thought, for common law lawyers use discrete inductive ideas capable of functioning only within limited factual spheres. It is empirical (and often metaphorical) notions such as "neighbour" and "life in being", "proximity" and "frustration", and "the officious bystander" and "remedy" which underpin much of the case law. New developments are secured by way of analogies rather than through the application of a system of *jura in personam.*[11]

[9]Margolis, above n. 4.
[10]Cass R. Sunstein, Incomplete Theorised Arguments (1995) 108 *Harv. L. Rev.* 1733.
[11]Pierre Legrand, European Legal Systems Are Not Converging (1996)45 *Int'l. & Comp. L. Quarterly* 52 @ 64-65.

It functions as a system where legal rules develop from facts moving from one *res* to another.[12] In effect, every time a judge is faced with a case the court must decide whether an existing rule or precedent apply to the factual situation before it. This is what makes the common law judge an incremental legislator, of a sort, when filling gaps in legal reasoning. Judges ultimately must treat every case as somehow novel, requiring the deployment of law and policy arguments, which invariably invites a place for the use of non-legal materials. Constitutional law and statutory application to instant cases provide plenty such opportunity. Thus, courts applying the conventional common law reasoning techniques may have to resort to sources outside precedent to determine cases – reasoning from facts to facts – and then formulating the law. It is in this respect that non-legal materials skills are required of lawyers who must persuade judges, particularly in litigation where novel issues or new rules come up for decision-making in the first application of common law cases; constitutional law raising novel questions; and cases requiring statutory application.

Ethical Challenges of Use of Non-Legal Materials

Objection against the use of non-legal materials for persuasion fall into two broad categories.

(i) Evaluation of non-law information

The first is fear expressed about the use of non-law resource has been concern that judges and lawyers lack the competence to evaluate scientific and social science research. Legal players are generally not well-equipped to evaluate the authoritative value (or substantive merits) of non-legal sources. This invariably means such information is susceptible to abuse because the legal profession cannot use them appropriately. Few judges [or lawyers] are trained in economics, mathematics, statistics, demography, psychoanalysis, cognitive psychology, or whatever the relevant science or social science material may be.

(ii) Reliability of non-legal material

The second fear of misuse comes from distrust of the non-legal materials themselves. Not all non-legal materials are reliable. Scientific and social science information can be manipulated to achieve certain programmed outcome. Everyday experience informs us that non-legal information can range from those which are thorough and competently executed to those which are poorly designed

---

[12]Geoffrey Samuel, *The Foundations of Legal Reasoning* (1994) @ 195.

and incompetently executed. Researchers can manipulate data, or even doctor results in order to support desired results.

What this mean is that care must be taken to check the abuse of unethical use of non-legal material in the litigation process. The drawbacks notwithstanding, lawyers must not discount the value of non-legal information in driving persuasion. Let us consider ethical safeguards that could prevent its abuse.

Ethical Safeguard

There are several safeguards for preventing misuse of non-legal information in lawyering.

(i) First, lawyers and judges need not sheer from the use of non-legal material. Primer (working) knowledge of non-law information can be acquire through sufficient knowledge of research methods for the legal community to use them properly in making basic persuasive arguments about most research studies.

(ii) The filter of rules of professional ethics can remove impurities associated with likely cases of abuse of non-law information. Lawyers are enjoined not to perpetrate fraud on the court. A lawyer is therefore not expected to knowingly make a legal argument based on a false representation of law using non-legal information. Lawyers should not openly and knowingly misrepresent non-legal material such as statistical findings or economic theories in the context of making an argument in a brief. This should curb the most egregious misuses of non-legal materials.

(iii) Just as lawyers do not fear to use precedent to advance legal argument, any fear expressed of using non-legal material to perform the same function in supporting a policy argument must be considered sheer alarmism, objection without grounding.

(iv) A possible guard against bias concern for the use of non-legal material seems to be the adversarial design of the judicial system.

Conclusion

Since the advocate functions to present the client's case with the best of her ability and in the most favourable light, leaving it to the court to evaluate the information proffered in support of an argument, lawyers should hone their skill for using non-law information to persuade and to determine its reliability and persuasive value. That is what an adversarial legal system expects of a skilled lawyer persuading effectively with (even) non-legal materials can define and separate the expert lawyer from the novice.

The advice of a former federal judge Richard Posner, ought to summarize how the profession should treat non-legal evidence. He said: judges should be "relying more than they do on facts established to a reasonable degree of certainty by science, including the social sciences, and technology, including statistical tools for marshalling and analysing evidence."[13]

[13] Richard Posner, *Divergent Paths: The Academy and the Judiciary, 2016* @ 319.

Chapter 19

Brief Writing

Introduction

Brief writing is central to the lawyer's litigation work. Lawyers writes briefs for applications, motions, statement of facts, appeals, etc.[1] There is no question about it, the skilled lawyer recognizes the importance of explaining clearly and concisely to the judge what the applicable law is and how it applies to the specific facts of a particular case. But honing the skill of good brief writing can be challenging to the mint lawyer and the experienced lawyer for two reasons:

(i) most brief writers fail to recognize that judges have quite a heavy work load and would be pleased to find as quick as possible the points being pressed by counsel;[2]

(ii) and that unlike many lawyers who are specialist in their area of practice, often judges are generalists who regularly confront a wide variety of subjects. There is therefore a need by lawyers to explain in clear, understandable form their cases.

Judges appreciate effective brief because they are busy readers, often having to read as much as over 1,000 pages of court documents (briefs and processes) excluding reading law reports annually. They therefore value well-organized and concise legal analysis. This chapter will discuss tips for effective brief writing.

Preliminary Matters

We would like to address a few preliminary matters on brief writing. Brief writing is a core skill all lawyers must possess. According to Karon, "[God] gave us two ways to communicate: speaking and writing. And because our profession, these days, offers meagre opportunity for oral argument, we need to always be the better, brighter, tighter writer."[3]

---

[1] Sarah E. Ricks & Jane L. Istvan, Effective Brief Writing Despite High Volume Practice: Ten Misconception That Result In Bad Briefs [2007] 38 *Univ. Toledo L. Rev.* 1113

[2] Kristen K. Robbins, The Inside Scoop: What Federal Judges Really Think About the Way Lawyers Write (2002) 8 *J. Legal Writing* 257 @ 264 ("The judges seem to think that lawyers can find the law, but they are not doing enough with it; the legal analysis in their briefs is mediocre.").

[3] Daniel R. Karon, Simple Secrets for Writing a Killer Brief, March 1, 2019, Law360, (Portfolio Media, Inc. NY) available at www.law360.com, accessed on March 15, 2019.

Since writing is a necessary ingredient for good brief writing, lawyers must recognize the following fundamentals about the process.

(i) Writing requires a writer's tool box

All legal writers must possess a writer's tool box. All work people, such as artists, engineers, artisans, footballers, etc., have toolkit boxes. As professional writers too, lawyers must have toolboxes for their wordsmith since words are their stock in trade. Writing requires creating a modest but functioning writing library. Materials for the box should include books on English language usage,[4] English language dictionary,[5] dictionary of legalese,[6] good brief writing manuals and text,[7] electronic writing and storage equipment,[8] and a few essentials. Access to good prose writing materials, such as the Guardian and Punch Newspapers, "the classics — for delicious turns of phrase and inspiring syntactical gems that will make your heart stop because you'll never come close to replicating them — is essential, too." [9] Internet access to good prose writing tutors can be very useful.[10]More than anything else is recognizing that the best way to elevate a lawyer's prose writing is to study writing and to practice it every day.

---

[4]Strunk& White, *The Elements of Style* (of course); Bryan Garner, The Chicago Guide to Grammar, Usage, and Punctuation; Bryan A. Garner, *The Redbook: A Manual on Legal Style* § 23 (2d ed., Thomson/ West 2006) (In his book, Bryan Garner not only addresses legal writing style in terms of mechanics, grammar, usage, and editing, but also covers preparing legal documents such as judicial opinions). Bryan Garner, *Dictionary of Modern American Usage*; Matthew Butterick, *Typography for Lawyers*; Bryan A. Garner, *Garner's Modern English Usage*, 4th ed. 2016; Richard Wydick, *Plain English for Lawyers*, 5th ed. 2005; Joseph Kimble, Drafting Examples from the Proposed New Federal Rules of Evidence, *Mich. B.J.* Aug. 2009 @ 52; Sept. 2009 @ 46; Oct. 2009 @ 54; Nov. 2009 @ 50; Joseph Kimble, Lessons in Drafting from the New Federal Rules of Civil Procedure (2008-2009)12 *Scribes J. Legal Writing* 25. But cf. Soha Turfler, Language Ideology and the Plain-Language Movement (2015) 12 *Legal Comm. & Rhetoric: JALWD* 195 (an article where the learned writer describes the plain English movement as resting on three "ideologies" and she undertakes to "discuss how each ideology perpetuates discriminatory norms and practices). See reply to the criticism of the three ideologies by Joseph Kimble, A Curious Criticism of Plain Language (2016) 13 *Legal Comm. & Rhetoric: JALWD* 181. See also, Joseph Kimble, Answering the Critics of Plain Language (1994-95) 5 *Scribes J. Legal Writing* 51.

[5] Black's Law

[6] Chambers Dictionary

[7] Bryan Garner, The Winning Brief; Bryan Garner; Garner's Redbook — A Manual on Legal Style; Smith; Niki Tobi; Michael R. Smith, *Advanced Legal Writing: Theories and Strategies in Persuasive Writing*, 3rd ed. 2013; Antonin Scalia & Bryan A. Garner, *Making Your Case: The Art of Persuading Judges*, 2008.

[8]Laptop, desktop etc.

[9]Karon, above n. 3.

[10] For free subscription services to internet sites promoting daily content, including essential grammar and punctuation exercises, seedailywritingtips.com;lawprose.org; quickanddirtytips.com; and grammarbook.com.

(ii) Writing process is recursive, not linear

Good writing is a recursive process. Telling of the difference between a good writer and a novice writer, Susan Provenzano and Leslie Kagan states:

> [E]xpert legal writers adopt specific rhetorical strategies for producing well-organized, precise, and deep legal analysis. They use reflective writing techniques and approach the writing process recursively, moving from global to local concerns and back, and from parts to wholes and back. Expert legal writers are also able to step back from their writing and imagine audience needs and responses. The expert's written product is thus reader-centred, with a clear focus on the document's communicative purpose. Novice legal writers, on the other hand, tend to view the writing process as linear, cannot remove themselves from their writing, and concentrate on telling what they know irrespective of their audience's needs. The result is a "knowledge-telling" document that memorializes the writer's thought processes but is not of great use to the reader.[11]

An expert writer should therefore think about each element of IRAC in a recursive way rather than in the linear way suggested by IRAC. Since writing is recursive the process must involve pre- writing, writing, and revision as activities that overlap and intertwine. It is therefore not a clear-cut linear progression from beginning to end. Rather it is a process wherein the writer moves back and forth among planning, drafting, and revising.[12] It therefore requires a brief writer to engage recursively in re-reading previously written words; re-reading a particular keyword or topic information; and if possible, returning to see the sensation generated by what is written – yes, putting the writer in the reader's chair.[13]

---

[11]Susan E. Provenzano & Lesley S. Kagan, Teaching in Reverse: A Positive Approach to Analytical Errors in 1L Writing (2007) 39 *Loy. Univ. Chi. L.J.* 123; John C. Dernbach *et al., A Practical Guide to Legal Writing & Legal Method* 205 (3d ed., Aspen Publishers 2007) @168 ("Legal writing is too complex to be approached in a linear fashion and requires instead a recursive approach."); Patricia Grande Montana, Better Revision: Encouraging Writers to See Through the Eyes of the Reader (2008) 14 *J. Leg. Writing* 291 @ 292 ("Under a recursive model, writers continually revisit all aspects of their writing experience so that they can dis- cover the best way to organize and communicate their thoughts to the reader. This model presents an opportunity for law students to see their writing through the reader's eyes and thereby produce better revision.")

[12]Teresa Godwin Phelps, The New Legal Rhetoric (1986) 40 *Southwestern L.J.* 1089.

[13]Stacy Caplow, Putting the "I" in Wr*t*ng: Drafting an A/Effective Personal Statement to Tell a Winning Refugee Story (2008) 14 *Leg. Writing* 249 (an article that teaches how to draft recursive, persuasive affidavit for asylum seekers). See also, Cara Cunningham & Michelle Streicher, The Methodology of Persuasion: A Process-Based Approach to Persuasive Writing (2007) 13 J. Leg.

Good writers know the value of revising what has been written. Revision of documents can help spot ambiguities, mistakes, and other human errors that are removable or amended to make a document speak as intended. But some lawyers don't revise what they write. The purpose of revision is to resolve any inconsistencies and fill gaps in a document.

Skills teachers usually require students to rewrite their assignments to attain competent performance in legal writing classes. Same level of diligence should be exhibited by lawyers in drawing up document. Sadly however, the common plague noticeable in most rewriting is that rather than use the opportunity to resolve inconsistencies and do gap-filling, most who rewrite or review documents often consider the first draft as complete and so merely superficially edit for word choice, grammar, spelling, sentence structure, and citation only. Attention is hardly given to the substance of the writing. This typical revision habit is borne out of the view traditionally held that writing is fixed linear process and so revision is nothing but the end-product of the sequence.[14] Most who rewrite focus on surface changes rather than the substance which makes the writing reader-friendly and persuasive.

Thinking of writing as a recursive process can help combat the revision weakness and aid a writer to transform her document to meet reader needs. Conceiving writing as recursive requires the writer to revise documents more globally to persuade.

Writing 159 (an article examining the process of drafting statements of fact and arguments and a system of argument organization that is created to supplement the "learn by example" approach for legal writing). The author states that recursive process teaches students [the lawyer] that from the beginning conscious efforts should be deployed to work through the facts or an argument several times, and that it is not a punishment or an indication that she is a bad brief writer. It helps the good lawyer to recognize that much as it is hard to undo pre-existing ideas put down in writing, reviewing is rewarding because doing so increases the likelihood that she will create a persuasive end-product.

[14] Montana, above n. 11; Christopher M. Anzidei, The Revision Process in Legal Writing: Seeing Better to Write Better (2002) 8 *J. Leg. Writing* 23 & 43–45 ("The ability to effectively revise their own work is a skill that requires law students to set aside their perspectives as writers and review the text from the reader's standpoint. It is from the vantage point of the reader that writers are able to see whether they communicated the entire analysis and whether the presentation is clear. This allows them to make meaningful, rather than mere superficial, changes to their drafts. In my experience, most first-year legal writing students struggle with this transformation from writer to reader, especially in the fall semester when they have to revise a graded assignment for the very first time. They struggle because they mistakenly believe that a first draft is the most important part of the writing process when it is, in fact, only the beginning of the writer's journey.")

Tips for good brief writing

A: Organization of the brief

(i) Theme

Every brief should be organized around a theme or theory of the case.[15] The theme should permeate every section of the brief - the question presented, the statement of facts section, the headings, the introductory paragraph summarizing the argument, the explanation of the governing law, the key facts selected to support the legal argument. It should be logical and easy for the trier to relate with.

Every litigation requires a powerful theme to drive the client's story through the brief. Without a strong theme, there is no good story. Every book one reads has a theme. They range for example on justice, responsibility, perseverance, truth, etc., so all briefs should also have. A lawyer able to steer a compelling story through a potent theme would be very persuasive in presentation.

Some triers consider the most important element of a brief. It can be likened to the "slogan" of the case captured in one or two sentences.[16] For example, a brief where the plaintiff's property is seized by the defendant wrongfully in pursuance of a commercial debt could have as theme the following: "No person can resort of self-help to enforce an alleged breach of contract." Thereafter, all sections of the brief should be structured to support the theme.

(ii) Organizational schemata

Syllogism is the reasoning model used in legal analysis. Lawyers are generally familiar with the IRAC organizational scheme.[17] It provides an intellectual framework of synthesizing legal reasoning by making law's complexity more manageable as it allows lawyers to communicate with common vocabulary for discussing social realities in a manner, which produces principled, rational solutions. It can be termed the grammar structure of legal discourse.

Several shades of organizational structure for legal analysis are also used by lawyers, all invariably buying on the IRAC model raised to power two or the

---

[15] is the theme the same as theory. See articles. Linda H. Edwards, *Legal Writing And Analysis*, 2003 @ 186-187 (equates both). See discussion in chapter – on case theory.

[16] Susan H. Kosse & David T. Butle Ritchie, How Judges, Practitioners, and Legal Writing Teachers Assess the Writing Skills of New Law Graduates: A Comparative Study (2003) 53 *J. Legal Educ.* 80 @ 90.

[17] The precise origin of IRAC is largely unknown, but it as been suggested that it likely originated as a simple mnemonic for teaching legal analysis. It certainly was not intended as an organizational paradigm for legal writing. See Laura P. Graham, Why-RAC? Revisiting the Traditional Paradigm for Writing About Legal Analysis (2015) 63 *Kansas L. Rev.* 681 at 706. See Festus Emiri, *et al.*, Revisiting the Traditional IRAC Organizational Structure for Legal Analysis: Towards A Multidisciplinary Approach (2016) *NLJ* 1.

like.[18] Whatever, structure is adopted, the lawyer should make clear in her brief how she wants the trier to apply the law to the particular facts to arrive at a rational conclusion. It is therefore advisable to use the CRAC (conclusion, issue, rule, application and conclusion) structure if the facts of the case make it appropriate for use. It is a model, which begins with a conclusion and ends with another conclusion. This may seem repetitious but it is a good style in that the second conclusion simply fortifies and emphasizes the opening conclusion. In fact, the style is recommended because it generally follows the pattern of legal (and human) reasoning. It is a recognizable fact that the lawyer in trying to formulate the "issues" in an IRAC model is bound to engage in some preliminary analysis - preconceived knowledge of the question of law interrogated by the particular facts of the case, the entire relevant facts and rules applicable to the case and the rational conclusion the lawyer would want the court to reach. So, the "issue" itself is laced with conclusion about the case. This being so, the CRAC model can be useful as a model of legal analysis.

The analysis should therefore follow this pattern:

"Conclusion" – this is a summary of how the law applies to the facts, and a brief statement of the legal conclusion the lawyer wants the court to reach.

Example:

> The Applicant respectfully request the honourable court to protect her fundamental rights and preserve the purity of due process in the country because the undisputed facts demonstrates that the Respondent resorted to self-help and abused the fundamental rights of the Applicant.

"Issue" – this section states the question of law interrogated by facts. An issue is a legal question, answer to which dissolves the controversy between the parties.[19]

---

[18]Diane B. Kraft, CREAC in the Real World (2015) 63 *Clev. St. L. Rev.* 567; George D. Gopen, IRAC, REA, Where We Are Now, and Where We Should Be Going in the Teaching of Legal Writing (2011) 17 *J. Legal Writing Inst.* xvii (keynote address at Capital Area Legal Writing Conference, Feb. 26, 2011- "there is not and cannot be a single structure that is the right answer to the question of how argumentative thought is best conveyed from the mind of a writer to the mind of a reader. ... These organizational structures [CRAC, CREAC, MIRAT, IDAR, ILAC, TREACC, CruPAC, ISAAC, CRRACC, BARAC etc.] are both necessary and dangerous, both supporting and defeating. As with any good idea or good invention, they can all be used for harm as well as good," id xviii); Dennis R. Honabach, IRAC or (QfrFR)+IRAC, *The Second Draft* (Legal Writing Institute, Tacoma, Washington, Nov. 1995, 8.

[19] *Rogers' Estate* v. *Helvering*, 320 U.S. 410 @ 413 (1943), per Justice Felix Frankfurter ("[i]n law[,] the right answer usually depends on putting the right question.")

Example:

> Whether the Defendant can resort of self-help and the use of public criminal enforcement tactics to enforce alleged breach of pure, commercial agreement.

While most lawyers begin drafting the issue with the "whether" phrase, it is recommended that the practice should be discarded and replaced with phrases that are syllogistically drafted. The reason is simple. The right question triggers the right answer. This being so, the framed issue must be deep enough not only to engage the judge but also avoid the judge having to dig inside the brief to find the right answer. A syllogistically drafted deep issue framework delivers on both. A judge having to read a brief issue framed with "whether" can only find the answer by reading the brief. But a syllogistically drafted brief is quick to deliver, in fact, suggest the right answer quicker.

A syllogistically drafted question or issue section follows the general pattern of reasoning in syllogism. It is a three-sentence question style. The first sentence (the major premise or predicate of the conclusion) is the law. The second sentence (the minor premise or the subject of the conclusion) describes the facts. And the last sentence (the conclusion) expresses the necessary and desired outcome that naturally follows from feeding the facts through the law. It invites the judge to answer the issue in a way favourable to the lawyer's case. So, rather than ask the "whether" question drafted like: "whether the Defendant breached her contract with the Plaintiff" style, the syllogistic raft would look like this:

> The Defendant's contract with Plaintiff required Defendant to give Plaintiff one million Naira (₦1,000,000.00) for the supply of two thousand (2,000) widgets. The Plaintiff paid the said sum of one million Naira (₦1,000,000.00) for the supply of two thousand (2,000) widgets to the Defendant, but the Defendant only supplied one thousand five hundred (1,500) widget. Did Defendant breach its contract with Plaintiff?

The difference between the bare-framed issue and that syllogistically drafted is clear. The question drafted using syllogism follows the three steps for scientific reasoning.

(i) The major premise or predicate of the conclusion

"The Defendant's contract with Plaintiff required Defendant to give Plaintiff one million Naira (₦1,000,000.00) for the supply of two thousand (2,000) widgets."

(ii) The minor premise or the subject of the conclusion

"The Plaintiff paid the said sum of one million Naira (₦1,000,000.00) for the supply of two thousand (2,000) widgets to the Defendant, but the Defendant only supplied one thousand five hundred (1,500) widget."

(iii) The conclusion

"Did Defendant breach its contract with Plaintiff?"

Drafting issues this way is certainly more effective in triggering right answers. If the major and minor premise are correct, the judge will quickly reach a one irresistible conclusion. This is the better way to frame issues.

"Rule" - this section explains the legal proposition upon which the lawyer relies. It sets forth the legal precedent that should control the particular facts. For example, in the facts scenario of a defendant adopting self-help to manually seize the goods of the plaintiff, the lawyer would need to set out the binding case law that sets the standard for determining self-help and how the facts of the particular case comes within the bracket and the remedial measure the court would take to redress the wrong.

Example:

The honourable court has long insisted that no person must resort to self-help enforcement, no matter how noble the cause of the defendant may be. In *Agbor* v. *Metropolitan Police Commissioner* (1969) 1 WLR 703 the court held that self-help amounts to breach of due process. See also *Okotie-Eboh* v. *DPP* (1962) 1 All NLR.353 and *Military Governor of Lagos State* v. *Ojukwu* (1986) NWLR (pt. 18) 621; (1986) All N.L.R 233; *Attorney-General of Lagos State* v. *Attorney-General of the Federation* (2004) 9-12 SCM (pt. I) 82; *Saidu Garba* v. *FCSC* (1988) 7 SC (pt. II) 170. In *Prof. Ajibayo Akinkugbe* v. *Ewulum Holdings Nigeria Limited* (2008) 4 SCNJ 404 (deciding that a landlord who resorts to self-help runs foul of the law and is liable to be assessed for damages).

"Application" – this section is often fact laden. It explains how the legal proposition formulated applies to the facts of the case. Using our fact scenario above, it should describe how the facts establish that the defendant without recourse to due process sought to manually seize the plaintiff's goods in self-help in furtherance of enforcing (seeming) contractual rights. The lawyer should then repeat the legal test and apply it to the facts. It requires an explanation of how the legal principles from statute, case law, or both, are similar to the case compelling the court to reach a conclusion that the defendant's action is wrongful.

"Conclusion" – this section reiterates the legal conclusion. Most lawyers conclude a brief in the usual mundane way: "Based on the foregoing, Plaintiff's motion should be denied." Not only are the words used passive, it adds nothing to the brief. The judge of course knows that the brief is that of the defendant who should ordinarily oppose the motion. But a more effective conclusion should be like a closing statement, highlighting the brief's main points in only a few words, then wrapping it up with a stirring and committed pitch for truth and justice directed by the lawyer's position.[20]

Example:

> The oppressive use employment of self-help to humiliate responsible citizens is wrongful and it invites the honourable court to award exemplary damage against the defendant. The court is therefore respectfully urged to grant the reliefs sought in this suit.

It is advised that for each issue submitted to court, the lawyer should reach a conclusion on it before moving to the next argument.

(iii) Headings

The lawyer should use headings to set out the various segments of the brief. The use of headings makes it easy to follow the main points of an argument. It allows the main points to stand out for easy reading and clear understanding. Heading thus emphasizes the principal ideas of a brief and it helps the court to figure where the argument is going.[21] An effective heading must not be a general statement. Rather it should be an articulated statement of the legal argument. A good way to ensure that the judge understands the case is for the lawyer to use an organizational plan that is overt by using section headings, tabulation, and enumeration.[22]

---

[20]Karon, above n. 3.

[21]David R. Cohen, Writing Winning Briefs (2000) 26 *Litig.* 46 @ 48 ("Tell the reader where your argument is going. Briefs with few headings can seem disorganized; frequent headings make the brief seem more logical."); Bryan A. Garner, Judges on Briefing: A National Survey (2001-2002) 8 *Scribes J. Legal Writing* 1 @ 16 (quoting the advice of the Hon. Daniel M. Kolkey, California Court of Appeal, that "[s]ections and subsections should be *liberally* used to focus a busy court on the key components of the argument, and only one point per subsection should be made").

[22]Wayne Schiess, *Writing for the Legal Audience,* 2003 @ 87-90 (advising that the "best way to ensure that a trial judge will understand your case is to ... [m]ake your organizational plan overt" by using section headings, tabulation, and enumeration).

Weak Example:

"Kofi's Fundamental Rights Were Violated."

Good Example:

"Kofi's Fundamental Rights Were Violated When She Was Arrested And Detained Without Warrant."

Weak Example:

"Rule 12(b)(6) Standard"

Good Example:

"Rule 12(b)(6) promotes a forgiving standard that support this Court's order sustaining Plaintiff's complaint."

The difference between the weak and good examples is that both good examples tell the judge what arguments would follow the heading and the reason why it would be so. The judge is not left in doubt as to what and why follows a heading. The weak example is more of a general statement than an articulated one.

Headings include the use of a table of content. The table enables the reader to easily grasp the brief's logical structure. It helps the judge to see with a quick eye survey how the argument in the brief is organized. It is advised that even if the rules of court are silent on the use of headings, the lawyer should use one for briefs that exceed ten pages.[23]

Bullet and numbered list should also be used. But care should be taken to avoid its overuse, as overuse can make the brief clumsy to read. If the legal argument can be logically presented in an enumerated list, the lawyer should do so to help the judge appreciate the structure of the brief.

Example of enumeration:

The substratum of the plaintiff's case is located in the evidence of (1) the evidence of the plaintiff, PW1, (2) the evidence of the surveyor, PW4, and (3) the evidence of the head of family, PW7.

Example of enumeration and tabulation together:

[23] Ricks & Istvan, above n. 1 @ 1118

"The substratum of the plaintiff's case is located in the evidence of:

(1) the evidence of the plaintiff, PW1,

(2) the evidence of the surveyor, PW4, and

(3) the evidence of the head of family, PW7."

Use Transitions

(iv) Use of transitional words

Transitional words help to provide connection between what would ordinarily seem as disjointed ideas in a brief of argument. A good way to achieve it is to prepare the mind of the reader to the next idea to be emphasized in the brief. The lawyer should arrange the brief in a manner that makes clear how the arguments relate to one another and the conclusion. Ideas are easier to relate by the use of transitions, such as "in addition", "by contrast," or "in the alternative," or "so." Transition words are a must especially when arguing in the alternative, as it makes it easy for the court to tie the thread of the argument together. For example, if the brief attacks jurisdiction, but counsel yet argues on the merit of the case, the argument in alternative could state: "Even if this court has jurisdiction..." or "Regardless..." Words like this are helpful in alerting the reader as to a change in thought transition.

(v) Summarise argument before making details argument

It is best to summarize the argument in a concise form before making out detail argument. The advantage of this is that it gives the trier a peep at what the whole brief seeks to say. The summary should be like an executive summary paragraph memorandum, setting out the explicit outlines of the argument.[24]

(vi) Address threshold issues first

The most important issues should be addressed first in a brief, unless there is a strategic reason to do otherwise. Lawyers know from practice experience that matters going to jurisdiction are germane to every litigation. Jurisdiction is the bedrock on which every process lies. It is therefore strategic to argue on jurisdiction first (if it is an issue in a brief) before arguing on the merits of a case. The reason for this is that if the threshold argument persuades the court, it may not need to go into the merits of the case.

---

[24]Schiess, above n. 8 @ 84-87 (recommending that briefs should begin with "a bold synopsis," a "one- or two-sentence summary of your point, highlight[ed] with boldface text, and set ... off with indentations)." See also, Edwards, n.3 @ 71; Robbins, n. 2 @ 273.

(vii) Open with the strongest argument

Starting from the strongest argument is important because like is said in every day parlance, "first impression makes a lasting mark," by starting with the strongest argument, the lawyer leads from a position of maximum strength. The first pointed argument catches the judge's attention first and could define how the court considers the other arguments that follow the first.[25] It is important to lead from the front than from the back. Leading from the front gives the impression of the lawyer being "in-charge", and so advances credibility.

B: Factual and legal assertions

This section discusses how to make effective factual and legal assertions in a brief. The good lawyer recognizes that she is obligated to provide access to the facts and law that supports her argument easy for the judge easy to find. This can be advanced by:

(i) Pincite references

It is important to ensure exact and accurate citation of the references of cases, their precise pages and volume in a brief. If the reference is to a statute or regulation, the precise section of the statute or regulation. So, the lawyer must take care to double check the accuracy of her reference before filing a brief. Incorrect or misleading citation detracts from persuasiveness. It dampens credibility.[26] Error in citation forces the judge to wade through pages of say a law report to locate the legal principle on which a brief rest, making it difficult for the judge to evaluate the validity of the writer's argument.

(ii) Make only factual assertions

The lawyer must only make correct, supportable factual assertions. If the brief is an appellate one, the lawyer must only cite correct records of the trial court. If quotations are used, it must be the precise record quotation. This makes it easy for the judge to locate the specific fact that supports the argument. This is also good self-discipline. Like accurate pincites to the relevant law, precise record citations help ensure that the lawyer's recollection of the factual record is accurate, not wishful thinking.[27]

---

[25]Robbins, n. 2 @ 273. See also, Kathryn M. Stanchi, The Science of Persuasion: An Initial Exploration [2006] *Mich. St. L. Rev.* 411 @ 421 ("The persuasive writer wants to create an argument chain that leads the judge to start nodding 'yes' to her arguments."), cited in Ricks & Istvan, above n. 1 @ 1120.

[26] Garner, above n. 7 @ 127.

[27]Ricks & Istvan, above n. 1 @ 1121.

C: Explain relevance of reference

It is effective to provide the court not only with the case citation, but also to explain why the reference is relevant to the facts of the particular case. Persuasion is advanced when the lawyer quotes from the governing precedent and even highlights the relevant portions by using italics or caps. The strategy lightens the work for judges. To advance the goal of reference explanation, the lawyer should do or not do the following:

(i) Avoid string citation

As a general rule, the lawyer should avoid string citation. Legal readers, including judges are usually "critical readers". Critical readers are not susceptible to trusting what they read. Each point for them demands proper grounding. So, if the lawyer uses string citation, the judge is often not likely to trust the validity of the governing precedent used to establish the proposition of an argument. It is therefore the course of wisdom to prove to the court that each case cited is on point. Such a strategy tells the court why each case is cited. Parentheticals are a useful way to drive home the explanation of cases cited.[28]

(ii) Explain and discuss best cases in detail

Key cases or governing precedent on which the case hinges should be explained and discussed in detail. The discussion should highlight the key facts and reasoning of the governing precedent and show why it applies analogically to the particular case or is distinguishable from it, or controlled by the precedent case. For the brief's application of the law to persuade the court, the explanation of the law needs to lay the groundwork for the brief's later analogies and distinctions.

(iii) Quote the legal test if the court will parse the language

Quoting the legal test is both helpful to the court and the lawyer. It ensures that the memory of the lawyer of the legal test is not more favourable to her client than its reality. Summarizing the language of a legal test may gloss over nuance.[29]

(iv) Except for the legal test, rarely quote from cases

The lawyer should not make a practice of quoting from other cases, which does not state the legal test. Too many quotes in a brief makes it too flowery and there is danger that if too much is emphasized the main point or legal test would not be made to stand out. Block quotes should be avoided. They are not reader

---

[28] See discussion on parentheticals in chapter --.

[29] Richard K. Neumann, Jr. *Legal Reasoning and Legal Writing*, 4th ed. 2001 @ 248 (recommending quotation of words "that must be *interpreted* in order to resolve the issue").

friendly.[30] If used in a brief, it should be employed sparingly. It is advisable to only use them when: (i) the quote is completely on point; (ii) the quote sets forth a legal test; or (iii) to plug in the names of your litigants to demonstrate the quote's application to your case.[31]

(v) For long quotation, introduce the quote and highlight key passage

It is important for the lawyer to introduce her quote by explaining why it is in the brief. An effective introduction must arouse the interest of the reader to read the quotation. If it fails to do so, the reader may just simply skip it. If the quote is long, underline, *italicize*, or bold key short passages to pique interest. But this technique should be used sparingly, as special type is no substitute for forceful logic and overuse can annoy the reader.[32]

D: Relate the precedent to the case

The lawyer must recognize that the judge does not share familiarity with the client case. So, it is important that the lawyer does a good job of tying the law to the facts of her case to give the reader a clear understanding of the controversy and how and why it should be resolved as argued by the lawyer. This requires explaining how the facts of a particular case make it distinguishable, analogous, or controlling to the governing precedent.[33] Below are some tips to help you apply the law to the pending case more explicitly.

(i) Repeat the language of the legal test when applying the law

It is imperative for an effective brief to repeat the language of the legal test when applying the law to the particular facts of the case. For example if the governing precedent is *Military Governor of Lagos State* v. *Ojukwu* (1986) NWLR (pt. 18) 621; (1986) All N.L.R 233; a case of forceful ejection of tenant from possession, the example of applying the law to the facts could be like: "The defendant resorted to self-help *because* the defendant broke into the house of the plaintiff to recover

[30]Ruth A. Robbins, Painting With Print: Incorporating Concepts of Typographic and Layout Design into the Text of Legal Writing Documents (2004) 2 *J. Ass'n. Legal Writing Directors* 108 @ 123 (posits that readers dislike the visual impact of block quotes because block quotes interrupt the reader's rhythm by requiring them to switch to a shorter line length) (bold typeface is preferred to underline and all capital, as both slows down and annoys the reader) Id. @ 118. See also, Neumann, above n. 15 @ 249 (recommending block quotes be avoided because judges view them as evidence of laziness; busy readers "will skim over or refuse to read large quotations" because their experience tells them that it is not worth the effort to ferret out the important words)

[31]Ricks & Istvan, above n. 1 @ 1123.

[32] Garner, above n. 7 @ 69

[33]Kosse & Butle Ritchie, above. 4 @ 89 (a survey of federal judges in the United States reports that less than 20% of briefs use governing precedent in analogizing or distinguishing cases)

possession without recourse to the court or due process." The word "because" connects the precedent to the particular case.

(ii) Make the analogy or distinction easy to grasp

The analogy will be easy to grasp by use of connecting words, like "in this case," etc.[34]

Example:

> The defendant in *Military Governor of Lagos State* v. *Ojukwu* (1986) NWLR (pt. 18) 621; (1986) All N.L.R 233; who resorted to self-help by breaking into the house of the plaintiff, *in this case* the defendant broke into the house of the plaintiff to recover possession without recourse to the court or due process.

It is also useful to make distinction between the client's case and the facts of the decided case explicit for easy reading and understanding of the judge.

Example:

> *Unlike* the defendant (landlord) in *Military Governor of Lagos State* v. *Ojukwu* (1986) NWLR (pt. 18) 621; (1986) All N.L.R 233; who resorted to self-help by breaking into the house of the plaintiff (tenant), in this case the parties do share a tenancy relationship.

(iii) Show brief consistent with policy underlying the precedent

The lawyer should make it easy for the judge to see the result the brief advocates as consistent with the policy underlying the governing precedent.[35]

Example:

> The policy served by the ratio that no one no matter how highly placed shall not resort to self-help underlined in *Military Governor of Lagos State* v. *Ojukwu* (1986) NWLR (pt. 18) 621; (1986) All N.L.R 233; imposes an obligation on the defendant in this case to comply with due process for the recovery of possession from the plaintiff.

---

[34] Edwards, n. 3 @ 165-166 (advise that a brief should be explicit in stating the similarities between the client's case and facts of the precedent).

[35] See Ellie Margolis, Closing the Floodgates: Making Persuasive Policy Arguments in Appellate Briefs (2001) 62 *Mont. L. Rev.* 59 @ 71-83 (explaining that categories of policy arguments include judicial administration, normative, institutional competence, and economic; cautioning that each must be rooted in authority to be used persuasively) cited in Ricks & Istvan, above n. 1 @ 1124, n. 39.

E: Facts recited must be compelling

Many lawyers make the mistake to think that what matters in brief writing is the law. So, they give discussion of the law prominence, while sparingly evaluating and discussing facts. This is responsible for why some lawyers just make their facts as though sterile recitation of the court record or copied without context from books on pleadings.[36] This is a mistaken conception. Facts should rather be related in a story manner that is compelling, without distortion. A good story is one that focuses on people, telling the how and why things happen written from a sympathetic perspective. Any lawyer whose "skills do not go beyond bare-bones form-book pleading risk disserving their clients, because legal readers, judges included, are as responsive to the call of stories as other readers."[37]A lawyer should avoid minimalistic "boiler-plate" drafted briefs or pleadings. The facts of a brief should be story-like.

In doing so, a lawyer should emphasis the favourable facts supporting the case of the client, using concrete, easily visualized words. If need be, a lawyer should use word picture description and images to bring the facts to reality.[38]

Word pictures concertizes reality, making the audience think and feel the client's reality. It creates a graphic mental picture in the mind. When combined with strong subject-verb (communicating doctrines or facts) can have real favourable persuasive effect. Facts must be presented in a way that provokes imagination. For example, just saying that "the defendant sat in her car" does not provoke anything serious. But to say that "the defendant sat in the car of another person" provokes thinking and imagination. True the statement has a subject, a verb and a direct object, but it goes nowhere in provoking imagination. It could raise questions like, why did she do that, what is really particular about her sitting in another person's car, is the other person her friend, etc. This example simply tells why facts recitation should engage the mind. Story must move the reader forward. The judge should be made to experience the same as if she were reading an exciting novel. The story should evoke a good storyteller's response. One fine way to achieve it according to the great English language writers, Strunk & White, is to "omit needless words."[39]

We may be familiar with this joke: [professor and class]

---

36 Burley & Leake on Pleadings

37 Elizabeth Fajans & Mary R. Falk, Old Stories: Restoring Narrative To Pleading Practice (2009) 15 *J. Leg. Writing* 3 @ 4.

38 See discussion in chapter – on narratives and storytelling. See also Robin W. Slocum, *Legal Reasoning, Writing, and Persuasive Argument*, 2006 @ 462 ("To read a story from the client's perspective, the reader must be able to ... sense somehow what the people in the story must have heard, seen, tasted, smelled, felt and believed.") cited in Ricks & Istvan, above n. 1 @ 1125.

39 Strunk & White

Brief writers should both tighten and lighten the story.

Most lawyers have a penchant for "telling," rather than "showing" the facts.[40] Telling isn't as powerful as showing. What is told may be forgotten, but what one sees hardly gets forgotten.

An easy way to show is to avoid arguing by adjective and adverb.

Consider this sentence:

"Defendant blatantly disregards the order of this Court and continues to trespass on the property ignoring continually the rule of law."

What is the idea of stating so loud through adjective (blatantly and continually) and adverb (ignoring) the conduct of the defendant? If the sentence writer removes the adjectives and even the adverb, the meaning would remain the same. In fact, it would make the sentence more compelling.

Another great way to make the facts provocating is convey the facts using word-picture. This style drives home the writer's perspective and invokes appropriate reader response.

Karon provides a good example this way: suppose a lawyer is responding to a motion to dismiss a complaint in a gruesome case involving a high school principal who abuses his students, it would be useful to introduce the antagonist, say, Principal Jones this way: "Principal Jones was a monster who routinely molested Plaintiff and other students." Telling the judge that the antagonist is a monster does not show much. The judge must be made to see how monstrous he is. So, the facts can be told this way -

> Principal Jelly Fingers. That's what they called him — at least those whom he molested. One time, when Plaintiff needed a permission slip signed, he had to ask himself whether his absence from class was important enough that it was worth getting fondled.[41]

The word-picture here used invites the judge to see, feel, hear and even smell and taste what happened. Any one reading it gets to feel the terror regime of the Principal. This way of "showing" is very effective in persuading the judge, than "some thoughtless version of subject, verb and direct object."[42] Now you see what I mean when I say that this technique isn't easy. To do this requires a degree of introspection. But it is worth it to tell creative and thematic stories.

It is also important in reciting the facts to neutralize any unfavourable fact by juxtaposing it with other facts that explain, counterbalance, or justify it. Facts

---

[40] See discussion on visuals in chapter.

[41] Karon, above n. 3.

[42] Karon, above n. 3.

being presented should remain facts – stories. A lawyer should therefore limit the use of adjectives because it gives the impression of telling from a coloured perspective. Facts must also be presented in a manner that avoid legal conclusion. Much as the lawyer strives to keep facts telling and showing what happened, it should eschew overtly argumentative statements of facts. An effective fact section persuades without arguing. It does this primarily by story order.

Facts strategy is very important. It is recommended that the favourable facts should be presented first. Thereafter the unfavourable facts should be presented in a manner understood in the context of the favourable facts. It helps the trier to see the context of the unfavourable facts. The practice by some lawyers, particularly if they represent the defendant, first presenting the claimant's facts and thereafter relate the defendant's story is not strategic. Recognizing the value of "first impression" cognitive bias requires highlighting favourable facts before unfavourable facts. One technique for explaining unfavourable facts is to de-emphasize them, explain them in the context of favourable facts by introducing them using transitions signalling contrast, such as "despite," "although," etc. Some strategists advise that unfavourable facts should not be used to begin a paragraph, but rather should be placed in the middle of a paragraph, when readers pay less attention; and that a passive voice should be used in presenting them.

Make no mistake about it – "word counts". The choice of descriptive words used in relating the statement of facts matter to how an audience receives what is communicated. What a thing is called goes a long way to determine how the reader thinks of it. Whether what happened is a "slight choke" or "assault," or the dog that bites a plaintiff is a "pet" or "bull-dog" matters.[43] It is important to be sufficiently graphic with facts description. Some writing teachers recommend that lawyers learn to write like fiction-writers, using concepts, such as classic conflicts - (e.g., Man Against Institution, Man Against Leader, or Man Against Powerful Entity) to frame the facts and infuse the client's legal position with emotional force.[44]

One such example is the statement of facts filed by some indigenous farmers to answer a motion for dismissal of their complaint (against powerful institutions alleged to have expropriated their land under the doctrine of eminent domain) on grounds of procedural insufficiency.

The introductory statement of facts was presented this way:

---

[43]Brian J. Foley & Ruth Anne Robbins, Fiction 101: A Primer for Lawyers on How to Use Fiction Writing Techniques to Write Persuasive Facts Sections (2001) 32 *Rutgers L.J.* 459 @ 466; Kim L. Scheppele, Foreword: Telling Stories (1989) 87 *Mich. LR* 2073.

[44] Foley & Robbins, above n. 23 @ 469

Every day across the country hundreds of people (usually less powerful and disadvantaged) are subject to abuse of their fundamental rights by powerful persons who resort to means less than civilised and proper to breach rights of Nigerians. Sometimes, these powerful individuals and corporations act in conscious support and approval of state-actors/governments, who ordinarily should be right-protectors, and promoters of the people. What paradox!

While a vast majority of these right violations are glossed over and not vindicated by the right-holders for many reasons not unconnected with the size of many right-holders pocket, some are challenged, as in this case, before the honourable court.

In rare cases where right-holders have sought and even dared to challenge the oppression, right-violators often cloak their justification vide procedural landmines as protective cover.

Nearly everyone rightly disdains the approach. And yet, for a phenomenon decried, procedural-cloaking remains elusive for many reasons. Much as different people perceive procedural-cloaking as plausible defence for right-vindication claims, this honourable court is respectfully enjoined to make prevailing the overriding objectives of the *sui generis* nature of fundamental rights claims-to construe procedure as handmaiden of justice to secure fairness, eliminate expense and delay, and to effectively and efficiently dispense justice.

My Lord, this application concerns whether such tactics of procedural-cloaking will be allowed to trump genuine prayers for the enforcement of rights or whether the court will allow the Defendants prevent *in limine* the hearing of the substance of the Applicants grievances properly within the competence of this honourable court.

My Lord, the stakes in this case are heighten by the comparative net worth status of the Applicants to the Defendants, especially, the megalomaniac, grandiose powers of the 1st to 4th Defendant, state-actors, acting in consort with big-business Respondents. With hindsight of the purpose of rights guaranteed under the Constitution, we most humbly urge that, the honourable court should pay particular attention to the rights sought to be vindicated by the Applicants rather than superficially treating it as subsumed under covers of state powers as the 1st to 4th Defendants seek to say and do. My Lord, this is the heart of the application by the 1st to 4th Respondents and our opposition to it herein.

The Applicants early in 2018 instituted an action praying the enforcement of their fundamental rights intricately connected to their survival and cultural integrity against the various Defendants for acts of purported eminent domain and incompatible usage.

The Applicants are natives of Eyin-Osa, Epe, engaged in humble occupation of peasant farming, hunting, native brewing and the like peculiar to persons of African decent living in rural setting. Their claim for right-violation redress is against the Defendants who are mainly state-actors or high-net worth corporations.

In process against the 1st to 4th Defendants, the Applicants question the propriety of the purported exercise of eminent domain by the Defendants as constituting right abuses vindicatable under our Constitution.

These are the contending issues before the honourable court."

With facts description like the above, the reader can see and feel the classic conflicts between poor farmers against oppression by powerful entities and institutions, and their position is framed in a way that gives their legal position emotional force. This way the necessary empathy, felt-connection is triggered. The statement of facts begins by summarizing the rampancy of "right-violation" and why much of it goes unchallenged in the country – because most litigants in developing economies are simply poor to afford legal services. But in this case, even though the plaintiffs are poor, they think the present litigation important enough to spend their "all" in protecting their ancestral land, culture and artefacts from expropriation by the powerful, no matter how strong against them they might be. The statement makes pointedly important and highlights the relative status differences between the contending parties, thereby setting the stage for their favourable emotional force. The statement does not gloss on the unfavourable fact - that there could indeed be certain procedural slips by the plaintiffs, but they are explained in the context of favourable facts. The plaintiffs describe the motion to dismiss its complaint by the defendants as "procedural-cloaking" – which it urges the court to disregard for reasons - genuine grievances will not be trumped by matters of form that go to no substance. That way unfavourable facts are neutralized, particularly in the context of empathy.

F: Brief Must Be Concise

Some lawyers mistaken think that a brief must contain every conceivable argument they dream up. They are also wordy, use legalese and long sentences to create impression. All of these have no place in good brief writing. A good brief must be concise. If a brief is too long and complicated, chances are that the judge would not read it, and if it is read, it may not be understood. Judges are busy people and so will be happy to get the point being presented quickly. A concise brief is one that focuses the judge's attention on a few good arguments. A good lawyer will observe the basic rules of editing. Statements which add nothing to a brief should be removed. Failing to edit out weak arguments undercuts a brief's stronger arguments by suggesting the writer cannot be trusted.[45]

One such prominent prescription is that "a sentence should contain no unnecessary words, no unnecessary paragraph, for the same reason that a drawing should have no unnecessary lines and a machine no unnecessary parts.[46][Quote Strunk and state reason – it irritates and so implicates the rhetoric triangle.]

So too should be weak arguments. Their presence in a brief weakens the whole fabric of a brief. Weak arguments undermine credibility (ethos).

[10 Questions Young Ask illustration of a chain]

Judges will be happy to read briefs in plain English.[47] It is recommended that brief writers use short sentences – according to Wydick, sentences containing not more than twenty-five words.[48] This is because a brief with long sentence often

---

[45] Lillian Hardwick, Classical Persuasion through Grammar and Punctuation (2006) 3 *JALWD* 75; Judith D. Fischer, Bareheaded and Barefaced Counsel: Courts React to Unprofessionalism in Lawyers' Papers (1997) 31 *Suffolk U. L. Rev.* 1. (Editing involves trimming for conciseness. So "[s]it down and write," the late Supreme Court Justice Antonin Scalia and Bryan Garner instruct. "Then revise [and] revise again. Finally," they say, "revise.")

[46] William Strunk, *The Element of Style*;

[47] For plain English movement impact in law see, the seminal work of David Mellinkoff, *The Language of Law*, Boston: Little Brown & Co. 1963, which gives rise to the Plain Language Movement in law. See also, Joseph Kimble, *Lifting the Fog of Legalese: Essay on Plain Language,* 2006; Judith D. Fischer, Why George Orwell's Ideas About Language Still Matter for Lawyers (2007) 68 *Mont. L. Rev.* 129; Joseph Kimble, Writing for Dollars, Writing to Please (1996-97) 6 *Scribes J. Legal Writing* 1. Plain language movement is a movement led by an influential group of legal scholars, judges, and practitioners who seek to advance clarity in legal writing by purging it of cumbersome sentence constructions and empty legal jargon. Proponents of the movement apply this prescription broadly to legislative and transactional drafting, as well as to expository legal writing. For example of its use in expository text, see Wayne Schiess, The Art of Consumer Drafting (2007) 11 *Scribes J. Legal Writing* 1.

[48] Richard C. Wydick, *Plain English for Lawyers*, 1998 @ 9-24.

rambles. What is more, both the writer and reader are likely to lose track of the point.

G: Proofread Brief

A shoddy brief creates credibility challenges for the lawyer. A brief with missing verbs, misspelled names, incorrect citations, improper grammar or sentences that running through it gives the impression of a disrespectful lawyer.

H: Contextualize Your Brief

Brief banks are now available in Internet sites. Some lawyers would simply copy a brief from Westlaw and paste. This is dangerous to say the least. Any pasting from the Internet or another brief must be contextualized. The lawyer should make sure that the legal points in the brief fit and are accurate.

I: Writing Professionally

Facts should be drafted to speak for themselves without inflammatory characterizations. Legal writing must be professional.

J: Observe Candour

Rules of ethics require candour. A lawyer must not misrepresent facts. She must address adverse authorities. Failing to mention it gives the impression that the authority is fatal to the lawyer's case. By failing to mention contrary precedent in the opening brief, the advocate makes that precedent more weighty than it perhaps should be. A good lawyer would address it, explain it either as bad law or neutralize its impact. Failing to address contrary precedent can be dangerous as a lawyer who fails to address it may never have the opportunity to do so if the opponent mentions it and failure communicate to the court that the case or those facts are fatal to the client's position. What is more, chances are that a judge would view as less credible a lawyer who hides contrary precedent.

It is important to keep in mind that repute is a prized commodity. It is built over time. But it can be lost in a single moment. Likewise, a brief loses credibility the instant it starts to mislead the reader. "A brief can mislead by misrepresenting legal authority, exaggerating the facts, misquoting something, not providing a spot cite or mischaracterizing portions of the record. As a general matter, the reader's perception of the writer's credibility will affect how the brief is read."[49]

---

[49]Ricks & Istvan, above n. 1 @ 1134.

Conclusion

Brief writing is all about legal imagination. The lawyer imagining the facts and communicating it to the judge to imagine what happened. Effective briefs require the lawyer to imagine how the judge is likely to react to the unfamiliar legal and factual information set out in the brief. Recognizing some of the common misconceptions about brief writing can help the writer to appreciate the reader's position and help the writer tailor the brief to meet the reader's needs. Undoubtedly, briefs interrogates creativity and consumes time, but if a lawyer observe the outlined rules, she will write good, effective briefs that will persuade. The craft of good brief writing (which involves (grammar, syntax, usage, punctuation, organization, typography, and many more) can be mastered by everyday writing and paying attention to what makes brief writing persuasive. As lawyers learn to tell stories laced with law, doctrine and policy, they become better prose brief writers.

PART V

Chapter 20

Metaphor Reasoning

Introduction

Much as classic rhetoricians were concerned with the fundamental *process* of persuasion, they also recognized that the *means* of persuasion should not be discounted. Unquestionably, the substance of argument presented using the rhetoric triangle of logos, pathos and ethos requires communication in a style that transmits the logic, emotion and credibility in easily understandable form.[1] Much as the style of communication goes only to means and not the substance of communication, it contributes to persuasion in that it provides the audience clearer understanding of what is communicated. Style in this context gives eloquence and drama to what is communicated thereby making the presentation eloquent, graphic, pointed and experiential.

For example, metaphoric thinking structures influences the way that an audience reads and reacts to a legal argument. One example will do: If the audience accepts the metaphor that copyrights constitute "property" like real estate, then it becomes easy for it to transfer inferences and rules from one concept to the other with certain consequences, such as, like real estate, copyrights can be bought and sold, divided, leased, and even protected against trespass.[2]

Rhetorical techniques in the form of figures of speech such as rhetorical figures (metaphors) and other literary allusions as hyperboles, metonymic,[3] and

---

[1]Aristotle, The Rhetoric of Aristotle, Prentice-Hall, 1932 (trans. Lane Cooper) @ 182 ("it is not enough to know what to say- one must also know how to say it.")

[2]Linda L. Berger, Studying and Teaching Law as Rhetoric (2010) 16 *J. Leg. Writing* 3 @ 38. See also, George Lakoff& Mark Johnson, *Metaphors We Live By,* Univ. Chi. Press, 1980; George Lakoff & Mark Johnson, *Philosophy in the Flesh: The Embodied Mind and Its Challenge to Western Thought,* Basic Bks. 1999 @ 123; Linda L. Berger, What Is the Sound of a Corporation Speaking? How the Cognitive Theory of Metaphor Can Help Lawyers Shape the Law (2004) 2 J. ALWD 169.

[3]Linda L. Berger, Of Metaphor, Metonymy, and Corporate Money: Rhetorical Choices in Supreme Court Decisions on Campaign Finance Regulation (2007) 58 *Mercer L. Rev.* 949 (an article which examines metaphorical and metonymical perspectives on the use of corporate money to finance election campaigns.)

the likes have proved helpful in persuasion.[4] So too have been of images,[5] analogies,[6] metaphors,[7] stories,[8] symbols,[9] and emotive language.[10]

Visual of literary allusion – Aristotle in session

Images, analogies, metaphors, stories, symbols, and emotive language are all potent devices that help the lawyer to persuade the audience. Presentations using metaphor has proved useful as a way to better communicate the substance of

[4] See generally Michael R. Smith, *Advanced Legal Writing: Theories and Strategies in Persuasive Writing,* Aspen L. & Bus. 2002 @195-339.

[5] James Parry Eyster, Lawyer as Artist: Using Significant Moments and Obtuse Objects to Enhance Advocacy (2008) 14 *J. Leg. Writing* 87 (an article that examines how lawyers can attain greater clarity and power in their advocacy by taking on the artist's mantel and becoming verbal painters of significant moments in their clients' dramas, complete with the background and accessory objects that best display the righteousness of the client and the failings of the adversary. The learned writer urges lawyers to imitate the visual artist who faces the challenge of condensing a complex issue or rich life into a frozen glimpse of what was, what is, and what will be, exploring the techniques that have helped them to create powerful paintings, photos, and sculptures that reveal the souls and hearts of their subjects). (2008) 14 *J. Leg. Writing*105. See also Elyse Pepper, The Case of Thinking Like A Filmmaker: Using Lars Von Trier's *Dogville* As A Model For Writing A Statement of Facts (2008) 14 *J. Leg. Writing*171 (an article that discusses using a film as a model for fact writing).

[6] See discussion @ in this book

[7] See discussion @ in this book

[8] See J. Christopher Rideout, Storytelling, Narrative Rationality and Legal Persuasion (2008) 14 *J. Leg. Writing* 53 (an article that discusses the psychological persuasive properties of narratives and their relationship to legal persuasion). See also discussion @ in this book

[9] Eyster, above n. 4.

[10] See for example, Bret Rappaport, Using The Elements of Rhythm, Flow and Tone To Create Persuasive Acoustic Experience in Legal Writing 16 (2010) 10 *J. Leg. Writing* 67 (an article that explains how to write more persuasively by incorporating rhythm, flow, and tone into legal writing to attract and keep readers' interests—the innate connection between language and music). See also, Linda L. Berger, King Solomon: Narrative, Metaphor, and Trial Court Judges with Discretion, (Association for the Study of Law, Culture, and Humanities Conference, Suffolk University Law School, Boston, MA. 2 April 2009).

argument as it aids the audience to make the imaginative leap of seeing one thing "as" another in understanding new and unfamiliar concepts and abstractions.[11]

Metaphor is considered the most prominent figure of speech even by classic rhetoricians.[12] The reason for this is simply: it helps the audience to understand and experience one kind of thing in terms of another.[13] Metaphor, like narrative is a powerful tool for structuring experience and expression. It shapes our perceptions and reasoning processes, often unconsciously, and so we consciously use it to frame arguments. It is suggested that because the mind is quick to structure experience as real, metaphor is an essential tool for persuasion and understanding.[14]

A metaphor is a figure of speech that uses one thing to mean another and makes a comparison between the two. It is sometimes used in conjunction with analogy to achieve persuasive effect. For example, the lawyer can use the metaphor: "the stock market is a supermarket." In reality anyone conversant with the stock market knows it is no literal supermarket where we buy sugar and tea. So, the use of the metaphor "supermarket" tells the audience or make it see the similarity between a supermarket and the stock market, with the result that it can

---

[11]Michael R. Smith, *Advanced Legal Writing: Theories and Strategies in Persuasive Writing,* Aspen L. & Bus. 2002) @ 15-30 (discussing how presentation using metaphor is a good way to better communicate the substance of argument).

[12] Marius Fablus Quintilianus, *Institutio Oratoria,* (HB Butler, trans. Harvard Univ. Press, 1954) @ 3 (rhetoric is the "supreme ornament" of prose.). see also, Michael Frost, Greco-Roman Analysis of Metaphoric Reasoning (1996) 2 *J. Leg. Writing* 113.

[13]George Lakoff& Mark Johnson, *Metaphors We Live By,* Univ. Chi. Press, 1980 @ 162 ("The essence of metaphor is understanding and experiencing one kind of thing in terms of another. . . In order to understand the world and function in it, we have to categorize . . . the things and experiences that we encounter."). See also, Joseph M. Williams & Gregory G. Colomb, *Style: Lessons in Clarity and Grace,* 10th ed. 2010 @ 156-160 (discussing the role metaphor plays in elegant writing). Linda H. Edwards, "The Trouble with Categories: What Theory Can Teach Us about the Doctrine-Skills Divide" (2014) 20 *J. Legal Educ.* 181 (an articles that examines how the doctrine and skills divide in teaching law can be harmoniously bridged using history and metaphor theory to explain how it can be realized. ("Under the classical view, categories are metaphoric containers. Like containers, they operate according to a simple in/out structure. Each potential category member is evaluated according to at least one characteristic that defines category membership. If the potential category member possesses the necessary characteristic, category membership is granted. If not, the potential member is excluded. Classical category labels identify a characteristic shared by all category members.") @ 183.

[14]Linda L. Berger, How Embedded Knowledge Structures After Judicial Decision Making: A Rhetorical Analysis of Metaphor, Narrative, and Imagination in Child Custody Disputes (2009) 18 *S. Cal. Interdisciplinary LJ.* 259 (The article is a rhetorical analysis showing why the best interests of the child standard fails to explain child custody outcomes, and the analysis suggests that the cognitive setting for custody disputes—cluttered with outmoded metaphors, simplistic images, and unexamined narratives—interferes with the ability of judges to attend to complex and radical transformations of parent-child relationships. It therefore proposes that practicing lawyers and scholars use rhetorical analysis first to uncover the symbols and stories that affect judicial decision making and then to construct arguments that may overcome deeply rooted constraints, help individual clients, and persuade policy makers.).

begin to think of the stock market as a market and treat events in the trial that occurred in the stock market as if they occur in the market.

For instance, to make it graphic for the court to see why a patent should be protected, the lawyer can say: "every piece of land worthy of protection must have defined boundaries." Since the court would think there is something amiss with a property whose boundaries are unclear, it can imagine the same of an ill-defined patent.

Metaphor is the comparison of two things of unlike nature with a degree of commonness to create understanding.[15] Metaphors have three distinct characteristics. One such comparison that comes to mind is a scenario in a court. Counsel for the petitioner in her argument in closing submission insisted that the court should consider the exhibits admitted in evidence as material and that the defence discount of them goes not to relevance but weight of evidence to be attached to the exhibits. The defence counsel however said the following in pressing that the exhibits were useless to relevance:

> My Lords, the exhibits are irrelevant to the case before the court. They do not interrogate the issues for determination. Since they are irrelevant, they cannot be of any weight. Air has no weight. It only occupies space. That explains why a measuring scale is always zero reading even in the presence of air in the environment. It is only when an object is put on the scale that it reads. This notwithstanding, physics teaches us that air occupies space. That is why if an empty bottle is inserted or immersed in water it bubbles out air to let in water.

In a closing submission like this it is clear from the defence counsel language that she makes a comparison between two things: non relevance and air; but she isn't explicit to the court that two things are being compared – one thing is simply equated with another thing to create felt experience; and the comparison is symbolic as the two things being compared share no literal likeness. The language used here invites the judge to see that irrelevant evidence can have no weight as no properly functioning scale reads on it. It could also be helpful to the court in appreciating that even that which is irrelevant does occupy space – like an empty but air-filled bottle immersed in water. So the irrelevant exhibit could just have been the reason for a trial that takes up the business time of the court with no tangible benefit, save a waste of time.

From the example above three main characteristics are evident in the use of metaphor. One, it is language that involves making a comparison between two

---

[15]Smith, above n. 3 @ 197.

things in our example between irrelevance and air. Two, the comparison is not explicit with the use of words such as "like", "as", "in both cases", "akin", "identical", "equivalent" and like words. All the speaker or writer does is to equate by implication one thing with another and suggest that the two things are being compared.[16]Three, the comparison is figurative, in that two things compared are not literally alike, but are in symbolic ways – evidence and air.

Because of its importance in projecting experience and understanding in such graphic way this figure of speech can be described as a "lens" as a "map" as "conversation" as "grounded" and as "imagination."[17] It derives its potency from its ability to interact between the *source* thing which is an usually abstract, unfamiliar thing ("air" to court) and the *target* that is the concrete, familiar concept ("evidence" to the tribunal) by drawing attention to their properties to create perspective understanding and experience. It is thus a projection of the principal subject through a subsidiary thing.

Metaphor and Cognition

Cognitive psychology teaches that metaphor is grounded in understanding, in that it provides a way of seeing and saying, thinking and knowing in structuring reason. A mastery of its use can help the skilled lawyer shape law and persuade effectively. Since metaphor isn't simply a literary *device* but instead *creates* meaning, it follows that a dominant metaphor, as a stock-position can only be uncovered and surmounted by the skilful use of alternative metaphor to ground meaning and understanding.[18] This been so cognitive knowledge about

---

[16] This is what differentiates metaphor from simile. While both could meld they are not equivalent. Simile involves explicit comparison.

[17]Linda L. Berger, What Is the Sound of a Corporation Speaking? How the Cognitive Theory of Metaphor Can Help Lawyers Shape the Law (2004) 2 *J. ALWD* 169 (an article that applies metaphor theory to analyse the briefs filed in the Supreme Court in a case raising First Amendment corporate speech issues in which the author states that "a metaphor is like a lens because it focuses and filters. . . Metaphor is a map ..power to shape and direct your understanding by superimposing a known structure onto a new concept makes metaphor fundamental to thinking and learning. Metaphor is conversation . . .its meaning comes from an interaction between the target — an abstract or unfamiliar concept — and the source — something concrete and already known — and between the qualities and properties that each of these entails. The interaction emphasizes certain perspectives of the target and the source, and it expands your view of each. So, for example, the map metaphor draws your attention to the shaping and directing qualities of a map rather than to its depictions of distances and boundaries. The interaction of the word map with the word metaphor helps you see the map-like qualities of a metaphor: that it guides you along certain paths, that it points you toward particular landmarks, and that it imprints understood forms onto uncharted ideas. The interaction may cast light on the metaphor-like qualities of a map as well, revealing that maps shape our views as much as they direct our journeys. Metaphor is grounded . . . it grows out of our physical beings, our neural networks, and our experiences in the world. . . . Metaphor is imagination. It springs from our capacity to see one thing as another, giving us legs and eyes to make the leap from there to here.) @ 169-170.

[18]Berger, above n. 13.

perception, imagination, how the mind uses language to construct meaning must be a skill to learn.

Generally metaphor is connected with imagination. By stretching our understanding of the concrete, familiar concept trough imagination from the (target), new concept it enables us to perceive and understand the unfamiliar (the source). This is why psychologists and linguistics posit that metaphor is a powerful imaginative tool embodying experience in reflecting the way the mind works. "Growing out of our physical and mental experience, grounded in a cultural and social context, metaphor shapes thought by mapping onto the new experience the structures, inferences, and reasoning methods of the old."[19]

It helps us make the imaginative leap of seeing one thing "as" another. So, it is a necessary component in creating understanding of new and unfamiliar concepts and abstractions. For example, metaphor is used to classify and reason about AIDS as a sexually transmitted disease. Being transmittable, we can conceptualize it within the framework of communicable diseases such as ---.

According to cognitivists much of our knowledge and thinking is unconscious.[20] It is suggested that our conceptual system and knowledge is built

---

[19]Berger, above n. 13 @ 171 (Metaphoric thinking structures and influences the way that an audience reads and reacts to a legal argument. If the audience accepts the metaphor that copyrights constitute "property" like real estate, it will transfer inferences and rules from one concept to the other and certain consequences will follow: like real estate, copyrights can be bought and sold, divided, leased, and even protected against trespass.

By helping us make the imaginative leap of seeing one thing "as" another, metaphor is most obviously necessary to understand new and unfamiliar concepts and abstractions. For example, metaphor is used to classify and reason about technological advances; years after the introduction of the Internet, metaphor still pervades the way that we talk about it. Through the Internet, you receive electronic "mail" on your "desktop"; because of these images, it seems appropriate to treat a legal issue concerning the delivery of an e-mail the same way that you would analyze an issue involving a letter written on paper, deposited in a mailbox, and delivered to your physical desk. While using the Internet, you "browse" for information as you might in a bookstore, and you set "bookmarks" as you might keep your place in a book. Depending on the results they want, lawyers may characterize Internet providers of information as publishers or distributors or as newspapers, radio or television stations, and even bulletin boards. The choice of metaphor determines legal consequences.") @

[20] See George Lakoff& Mark Johnson, *Philosophy in the Flesh: The Embodied Mind and Its Challenge To Western Thought,* Basic Books, 1999 @ 128, cited in Berger, above n. 13 @ 263 ft. nt. 19. See also. Steven L. Winter, Transcendental Nonsense and Metaphoric Reasoning, And The Cognitive Stakes For Law (1989) 137 *Univ. Pa. L. Rev.* 1105 (an article that examines the ubiquity and necessity of metaphor in human thought explaining the use of metaphor in constructing a framework for both a more realistic concept of law and of rights. It shows that human knowledge is grounded in our direct physical and social experience with the world, but is elaborated *indirectly,* largely by means of metaphor and the extension of idealized cognitive models). For classical reading on how image-schemata shapes law, see Winter, The Metaphor of Standing and the Problem of Self-Governance (1988) 40 *Stanford L. Rev.* 1371. For general reading on the puzzling problems in semantics and construction of meaning, see S. Blackburn, *Spreading the Word: Groundings in the Philosophy of Language* (1984); R. Rorty, *Body and Mind*; M. Johnson, *The Body in the Mind: The Bodily Basis of*

from unexamined thought processes because we see a thought process as something else in order to talk understandingly of it. Metaphors derive from our interaction with social and physical environment. For example, from our bodies experience we can conceive motion from walking, balance for upright, more as up, etc. So too are concepts such as "knowing created from seeing" and "understanding as grasping." We learn then from the world through our senses of sight and touch. Because of the metaphoric process of transferring inferences from one domain to another, we are able to perceive and understand abstract concepts in the same way that we "see" and "grasp" physical ones.

In effect, much of what we describe as logical reasoning appears to be structured imagistically and metaphorically – in fact through unconscious processing. We only make sense out of new experiences by placing them into categories and cognitive frames constructed (schema) that emerge from our prior experience. Even the concept of categories is understandable only because we have encountered containers in our interactions with the environment. Because of that experience, we transfer our perceptions and inferences, and we are able to see categories "as" containers, with an interior, an exterior, and a boundary. But for the metaphor of the container, which allows us to gather them up, group them together, and "contain" them, ideas would have been disparate, difficult to understand.[21]So too, categories are artificial concepts created from experience not found in nature. Thus when the legal system chooses a category within which to classify a legal event or situation, the choice carries with it several implications. It is not just a process of matching what factual situations come within a category. It is not box-fitting but interpretative. For once a label is struck on a phenomena it carries with it legal conclusion that follows the categorization.

Understanding remains a lifelong process constructed from daily living.

For example, as we experience movement (birth and death) from a beginning along a path to the end, we create the "source-path-goal" image

---

Meaning, Imagination, and Reason (1987). For argument on that the process of social construction is interactive and multidimensional, see Winter, Transcendental Nonsense, Metaphoric Reasoning, and Cognitive Stakes for Law, (1989) *U. Pa. L. Rev.* 1105. Some commentators suggest that reality is intimately connected with beliefs and values, and to the extent that these do not exist in the world of pure abstraction, but with and on specific assumptions of the state of the world people differently situated in the social world see and name events in distinct and distintive ways. For reading on this form of social theory and perceptual fault lines in naming see, Scheppele, The Revision of Rape Law (1987) 54 *Univ. Chicago L. Rev.* 1095; A. Schutz & T. Luckmann, *The Structure of the Life-World* (1973); P. Berger & T. Luckmann, *The Social Construction of Reality* (1966), both cited in Kim L. Scheppele, Foreword: Telling Stories (1989) 87 *Mich. LR* 2073 at 2082 n. 29.

[21]Edwards, above n. 12. See also, Ronald Chen & Jon Hanson, Categorically Biased: The Influence of Knowledge Structures on Law and Legal Theory (2004) 77 *S. Cal. L. Rev.* 1106 @ 1131–1218 (an article describing how categories and schemas are critical building blocks of the human cognitive process).

schema, which in turn leads to more complex conceptual metaphors such as life as a journey. These mental blueprints are then used to sort and organize our experiences and acquired knowledge of the world, from which we assess new situations and ideas without having to interpret and construct a diagram of inferences and relationships from our experience.

At a more complex level, schemas are used to construct idealized cognitive model (ICM).[22] ICMs fossilize as 'folk' theory or cultural understanding that organizes knowledge of events, people, objects, and their characteristic relationships in a single gestalt structure that is experientially meaningful as a whole.[23] That explains why a restaurant owner would approach anyone who enters the premises and ask what sort of food or drink the fellow would like served for a price. ICMs are models not actually found in the world, but are based on what we have come to believe is natural through experience within a particular culture. They simply provide shortcuts and stereotypes, transforming new and unfamiliar situations into the normal and natural course of events.

This is how metaphor grows out of our physical and mental experience, stewed in culture and society, metaphor is thus able to shape our thinking by mapping onto new experience the structures, inferences and reasoning methods of the old.

Formalist and fundamentalists however disagree with the grounding of knowledge through metaphor. In their objective view metaphor is simply language used to create imprecision.[24] Experientialism since the 1980s however has exploded formalism this major thesis of formalism. Experientialism now establishes that the cognitive process uses a concrete, experienced source domain to structure and understand more abstract domain.[25]

It provides a way of understanding our world where knowledge is negotiated through our interaction and "constant negotiation with the environment and other people in society. That is what makes metaphor fundamental to both thought and expression. It requires us to be able to relate one thing to another, drawing on imagination. And because metaphor imaginatively projects one concept onto another and expands understanding of both, it can accommodate

---

[22]Steven L. Winter, *A Clearing in the Forest: Law, Life And Mind*, 2001.

[23]Winter, above n. 22.

[24]See Aristotle, *The Poetics* in the *Rhetoric and The Poetics of Aristotle* @ 223, 251(7457b lines8- 11) (Ingram Bywater trans., Random House 1954).

[25]Lakoff & Johnson, above n. 13. See also, I.A. Richards, *The Philosophy of Rhetoric*, Oxford U. Press, 1936 @ 92-94. According to cognitive metaphor theorists, conceptual metaphors grow out of our bodily experiences, the images we see in the world, and the stories we are told. They are learned so gradually and embedded so deeply that their application to a new experience or concept will appear seamless and unremarkable.

individual complexity far better than binary categories and rigid rule structures of formalism.

As a modern science, cognition concerns itself with investigating how we gather information and use them, all of which interrogates thinking, memory, learning, response to stimuli and thought process. Studies reveal that problem solving involves a process of recognizing patterns and retrieving solutions from a stored repertoire acquired by encountering similar problems in the past. We simply interpret the world from our reservoir of experience (schema) from which we apply to solve new, like challenges. These schemas are efficient basis for further decision making even in the absence of complete information. We are just wired to solve the complex from our prior knowledge of the simple. Like those schemas, metaphor is a stored structure that makes a new concept meaningful by mapping or transferring relationships and inferences from one concept to another without difficulty.

Metaphor shapes thinking. We think about abstract concepts embodied, often unconscious, and mostly metaphorical. Thinking is "embodied" because "the same neural and cognitive mechanisms that allow us to perceive and move around also create our conceptual systems and modes of reason. The mental structures we use are meaningful because they are connected to our bodies and our physical experiences. Basic-level concepts grow out of our "motor schemas and our capacities for gestalt perception and image formation" while primary metaphors projected by our brains allow us to "conceptualize abstract concepts on the basis of inferential patterns used in sensorimotor processes that are directly tied to the body.

That is why everyday reasoning is structured and moulded by a series of cognitive metaphors. These metaphors are cognitive because they organize thinking and are experiential because they arise out of physical experience. Conceptual metaphors are reflected in linguistic metaphors. There is, for example, a communal, cognitive, conceptual metaphor that argument is war; its structure is reflected in linguistic expressions. The metaphor shapes what we do and how we understand what we do; it structures the steps we talk when we argue.[26]That is why visualizing argument as war makes it possible to either win or loss arguments. The opposing parties are described as opponents who should attack the other's position. Conceptualizing requires that the parties plan and strategize as war. This is how metaphor creates understanding and shapes meaning.

---

[26]Linda L. Berger, What Is the Sound of a Corporation Speaking? How the Cognitive Theory of Metaphor Can Help Lawyers Shape the Law (2004) 2 *J. ALWD* 169 @ 173-4.

How Metaphor Persuades

Metaphor is a powerful persuasive tool. Etymologically it is rooted in the Greek expression for experience, suggesting the transmission of meaning from the target to the source. It was thus thought to carry-over meaning by substitution or comparison from one thing over to another – a position now discarded. This undoubtedly explains why some classic rhetorician discounted the usefulness of metaphor as a persuasion tool.[27] The restrictive view of metaphor as an indirect way of presenting an intended literal meaning, which is that target A is like source B, has long been abandoned by new cognitive learning grounded in experientialism.[28]

We now recognize that metaphor is primary to imagination as it is borne out of long, unconscious experience used to define reality. For as we live in the world we construct primary metaphors automatically from our interaction with our physical environment and society. Metaphors are thus imaginative rationality that enables us see one thing as another.

Metaphor is a powerful tool for persuasion because we "know" from experience and what we know we deeply believe since it is created through unavoidable, repeated experience. Thus, when seeking to understand a new concept we are simply happy to impose our received organizational structure (schema) to understand the new concept. This way metaphor operates to help us understand new concepts in our received structures and categories.

Metaphor also influences reasoning because it allows us to borrow patterns and inferences and methods of evaluation from the source to the target.

Metaphor derives its persuasive force from the quietness of its presence. Its position is often unannounced. It quietly makes comparison by implication. Once a metaphoric position is taken as "received wisdom" it is often difficult to question a position based on it. For example, metaphor such as "veil" of incorporation operate silently in law and can be difficult to displace because it is a position rooted in entrenched, but unconscious metaphor assumed to be correct legal maxims.

It is therefore important for the lawyer to master how to use metaphor in legal argument. Lawyers must learn to use it skilfully to shape imagination and received wisdom in law.[29] Since legal reasoning is a product of our basic human

---

[27] Aristotle for example considered metaphor to be false, dangerous, and suspect. See Aristotle, *The Poetics* in the *Rhetoric and The Poetics of Aristotle* @ 223, 251(7457b lines8- 11) (Ingram Bywater trans., Random House 1954). ("[m]etaphor consists in giving the thing a name that belongs to something else; the transference being either from genus to species, or from species to genus, or from species to species, or on grounds of analogy.")

[28] Lakoff & Johnson, above n. 13.

[29] See Berger, above n. 25. But cf. Mark Johnson, Introduction: Metaphor in the Philosophical

capacities, the cognitive theory of metaphor makes legal reasoning susceptible to comprehension. Legal rules are a product of mediation between complex matrix located in history, culture, society, institutions and practices. This being so, a good knowledge of how metaphor operates can help the lawyer refocus on the mediation between the two components of judicial decision making: the creation of categories and the interpretation of rules.

Categories are essential to meaningful living, thinking and reasoning. It has been suggested that categorization is the very process of reasoning itself.[30] But categories are not value free. Once adopted, they shape perception. Unfortunately, they can also obscure perception.[31] This is because most people subscribe to the objective view of categories. A thing is either within or outside a category. For them membership of a category is given from their checklist of membership of a category.

The simple, paradigmatic example of syllogism explains it: The category-(men) has a necessary condition for membership (mortality). Thus, if Socrates is within the category of men, he must be mortal.

This notwithstanding, empirical evidence suggest that categorizes are more of imagination and so they remain flexible particularly in penumbra cases. Much as a central core is knowable, extensions related to the core could also be generated by the rule. Because such extensions are derived from the core in different ways, the extensions may have little or nothing in common with each other beyond their shared connection to the central case.

Also, because all things do not necessarily come truly within the core some categories are marked by prototypes. Therefore some prototypes could be more core than others. For example, the word "lady" would more describe a prototype for Miss Nigeria, than say, a film actor. This should be so because the use of the word "lady" immediately conjures an ICM in which lady is a label or category of a proper unmarried woman than any spinster out there.

Tradition in Mark Johnson, ed. *Philosophical Perspectives on Metaphor*, Univ. Minn. Press, 1981 @ 3.

[30]Steven L. Winter, *A Clearing in the Forest: Law, Life And Mind*, 2001 @ 70. See also Lakoff & Johnson, above n. 13 @ 162.

[31]Anthony G. Amsterdam & Jerome Burner, *Minding the Law*, 2000 @ 19. ("[W]e are always at risk that our categories may lead us astray. Indispensable instruments, they are also inevitable beguilers. To interrogate their uses and their dangers is a necessary part of legal studies, as it is of any preparation for considered thought and action."). See also, Winter, above n. 30 @ xii ("It is common ground among many students of the philosophy of language, including Rorty, that there is no objective description of reality separate from our conceptual schemes. This is so because, as Hilary Putnam explains, there cannot be 'any inputs which are not in themselves to some extent shaped by our concepts, by the vocabulary we use to report and describe them, or any inputs which admit of only one description, independent of all conceptual choices.'")

What is more, all our constructed categories though created by rules are interpreted within the framework of ICMs – which are like stock, received wisdom – cultural model that are used to organize knowledge.

They are "idealized" because they do not exactly fit actual situations but they capture our normal expectations as they have been shaped by the environment and our cultural practices and conditions; they produce prototype effects. The model allows for inferential connections between many concepts by means of a single structure that is meaningful as a whole. That is why hearing words like "father" conjures so many things to the mind. From our model of family we can relate how the father should behave and care, and a whole range of societal invocations.

These sorts of modelling affect how we categorize and reason about categories. Because even the simplest rule makes sense only "against the backdrop of a massive cultural tableau that provides the tacit background assumptions that render it intelligible, models affect how we interpret rules. Yes, words like "father," "market," and the like matter in constructing and interpreting rules. They affect our understanding of the law, the analytical ability to critique arguments, and the imaginative ability to craft arguments. To the extent that metaphoric language helps both speaker/writers and audience to think differently about a subject, it aids understanding and clarification of argument. It helps the audience to see and feel resemblances and patterns and to make inferences where they might not otherwise be explicit.

Noteworthy of mention is that a metaphor is inherently open to varied interpretation. So it could be used to advance uncertain or contradictory ideas depending on the card sort to be played by the skilful lawyer. Such a cloaked imprecision is part of metaphor's appeal and its peril.[32]

Employing Metaphor in Argumentation

The cognitive theory of metaphor is a *lens* from which the skilful lawyer can analyse the brief of other lawyers and decisions of court. To do so the lawyer must understand metaphor and how it shapes and controls subsequent thinking about a subject. This is particularly true in metaphoric reading of authorities like *Lagos State Government* v. *Ojukwu* where "self-help" was used as a metaphor to prohibit resort to extra-judicial settlement of dispute.[33] The metaphor has created

[32] KK DuVivier, Misguided Metaphors, 22 Colo. Law. 507 (Mar. 1993). Justice Benjamin Cardozo in *Berkey* v. *Third Ave. Ry. Co.* (1926) 155 N.E. 58 ("[m]etaphors in law are to be narrowly watched, for starting as devices to liberate thought, they end often by enslaving it").

[33](1986) NWLR (pt. 18)621 (1986) All N.L.R 233; *Agbor* v. *Metropolitan Police Commissioner* (1969) 1 WLR. 703 the court held that self-help amounts to breach of due process. See also *Okotie-Eboh* v. *DPP* (1962) 1 All NLR.353; *Attorney-General of Lagos State* v. *Attorney-General of the Federation*

an assumed reality and mantra that shapes future actions that prototype "self-help" without the legal community seriously interrogating the real ambits of the metaphor.

But deep thinking should tell that that the metaphor is too widely applied without more for in law self-help is permitted in many situations. For example, the right of lien, etc. are legitimate self-help situations. To therefore blanket say that self-help is prohibited in law is to apply a metaphor beyond its legitimate application. This is the trouble with categorization and the use of metaphor as an umbrella to understand the world.[34] This notwithstanding every skilled lawyer must learn to master the use of metaphor and its cognitive effect to improve the lawyer's understanding of how to develop the metaphor or reconstruct to trigger change.

A keen awareness of the cognitive power of metaphor, particularly how one thing is projected as another can be helpful to aid the lawyer uncover the received wisdom, narratives, metaphors, and analogies that underlie many legal reasonings. Many of these imaginative maps for understanding are so deeply embedded in the development of the law and in our consciousness that we hardly realize they are there. If they go unnoticed, it is impossible to understand their impact or to counteract their effects in arguments that lawyers deploy to confirm or change judicial thinking.

(Give example of how the self-help metaphor was affected by --- case advocacy)

Lawyers must also recognize the cognitive power of metaphor to use it creatively and consciously for persuasion.[35] Since metaphor carries with it certain attributes, inferences and characteristics that it transports from one thing to another the lawyer must know how to make the leap (from one thing to another) and do it in such a way that makes it compelling and convincing. Metaphor must therefore be chosen consciously with great care to achieve the persuasion purpose.[36]

(2004) 9-12 SCM (pt. I) 82; *Saidu Garba* v. *FCSC* (1988) 7 SC (pt. II) 170; *Prof. Ajibayo Akinkugbe* v. *Ewulum Holdings Nigeria Limited* (2008) 4 SCNJ 404 (a landlord who resorts to self-help held to run foul of the law and liable to be assessed for damages).

[34] *Berkey* v. *Third Ave. Ry. Co.* (1926) 155 N.E. 58, per Benjamin Cardozo, J; Linda H. Edwards, "The Trouble with Categories: What Theory Can Teach Us about the Doctrine-Skills Divide" (2014) 20 *J. Legal Educ.* 181.

[35] Recognizing the value of being creative and conscious, Strunk & White in the section on figures of speech stated: When you use metaphor, do not mix it up. That is, don't start by calling something a swordfish and end by calling it an hourglass @ para 18. See Strunk & White

[36] The example of evolution of a metaphor of an artificial entity becoming a person protected by the First Amendment in *Nike, Inc.* v. *Kasky*, 539 U.S. 654, 123 S. Ct. 2554 (2003) discussed in Linda L. Berger, What Is the Sound of a Corporation Speaking? How the Cognitive Theory of Metaphor Can Help Lawyers Shape the Law (2004) 2 *J. ALWD* 169 @ 180-204 is a good illustration of how failing

In the *Nike* case[37] for example where the company Nike was besieged with allegations and responded to charges, the company participated the public debate as a good corporate citizen because the metaphor of "corporation-as-person" entailed many assumptions: a corporation can be somewhere; it can act and move, sue and be sued; it can see, hear, speak; it can perceive and understand; it can formulate ideas and adopt views; it can express those ideas and views. And because it can do all these human things, the corporation must be treated as an equal participant in the free market of ideas under the First Amendment.

The reason for this isn't far-fetched. The metaphoric grant of personhood to corporations reifies an otherwise abstraction to become real as though it is a person with natural, human motivations, characteristics, and activities. That is just how the human mind works in understanding metaphors. Metaphor allows us to comprehend unfamiliar experiences (say a corporation) in terms of familiar (natural person) and then make the leap from one thing to the other. Since the company was not different from person it could take advantage of the First Amendment and participate in a debate.

The lesson here is that the given metaphor was simply used to determine the legal outcome. A lawyer who seeks to change that outcome must therefore learn how to fight the "corporation-as-person" metaphor with another alternative metaphor – substituting one that is sensible and consistent with the attributes of a corporation. That's how to change the game.[38] An alternative metaphor such as "corporation-as-machine" could have discounted the Nike speech turning it to something analogous to commercial speech, thereby making its manufactured and distributing products fit within the mould of manufactured images, marketing tools, and cultivated commodities as a way to view Nike's corporate public relations products.[39] Such alternative metaphor could have shown that

---

to question the "corporation-as-a- person" metaphor can make it difficult to dispute that a corporation like Nike is indistinguishable from other competitors in the market or other participants in a debate under the First Amendment (protecting the speech) under the US Constitution. The article is about briefs filed in the U.S. Supreme Court in a lawsuit brought by a consumer activist against Nike, Inc., alleging violation of California's false advertising and unfair competition statutes.

[37](2003) 539 U.S. 654, 123 S. Ct. 2554.

[38]Meir Dan-Cohen, *Rights, Persons, and Organizations: A Legal Theory for Bureaucratic Society,* Univ. Cal. Press 1986) @ 42; Mark Johnson, *Introduction: Metaphor in the Philosophical Tradition*, in *Philosophical Perspectives on Metaphor* 3, 3-4 (Mark Johnson ed., U. of Minn. Press 1981) @ 318-322; both cited in Berger, above n. 35 ft. nt. 257. See also, Michael R. Smith, *Advanced Legal Writing: Theories and Strategies in Persuasive Writing,* Aspen L. & Bus. 2002) @ 217-221. For instance, it is conceivable to use as alternative metaphor the "corporation-as-machine" metaphor to illustrate that unlike a natural person the motivations and activities of a corporation can only be triggered by human force as it has no independent will of its own. For such alternative metaphoric analysis and argument, see Dan-Cohen @ 44-51.

[39] Berger, above n. 35 @ 207.

Nike's products could not one of such things interrogatable under the First Amendment. It could reveal why the products isn't different from other products viewed as mere fungibles and that Nike's public relations products are made by corporate employees who are not expressing their own ideas or views but instead are responding to corporate designs and directions; the content of the product is influenced not by self-expression or enhancement of knowledge but by sales potential. Like other products, their manufacture, distribution, and sale should be subject to state regulation to protect the public.

What is more, the alternative metaphor carries with it implications that the marketing of Nike's public relations image should be viewed as the marketing of an investment opportunity and so subject to state regulation as representations that are designed to pique interest in the investment. Just as regulation of statements made in connection with investments is necessary to assure that investors do not make purchases based on inaccurate or misleading information, regulation of statements made in connection with sales of a particular public relations image is necessary to assure that listeners do not buy the image without accurate information.[40]

The scenario above therefore teaches why the lawyer must be a master in the use of metaphor using it to create and consciously persuade, particularly if desired to use it to present counter cognition in further of counter-intuitiveness and counter-hegemonistic thinking in law.[41]

Furthermore, recognizing the cognitive power of metaphor is helpful to the lawyer to gauge in a calibrated way her ability, chance and opportunity to overturn a longstanding or dominant metaphor and the desirability of sidestepping it if need be. The Nike "corporation-as-person" metaphor is illustrative enough on this point. For much as the personification metaphor is helpful in making the necessary leap from one thing to another, uncovering it will allow the lawyer to make informed decision to counter, confront and reject it by using alternative metaphor. The new metaphor could itself create new understanding allowing us see things in another light. Doing so could invite the lawyer to create a new metaphor to highlight certain aspects of the target and suppressing other, interrogating specific aspects of the source concept. As the *Nike* example, the lawyer using the alternative metaphor of "corporation-as-machine" could give the target new meaning leading to different understanding of corporation by simply highlighting the inability of a corporation to act with

---

[40] Ibid.

[41] See for instance Linda L. Berger, How Embedded Knowledge Structures After Judicial Decision Making: A Rhetorical Analysis of Metaphor, Narrative, and Imagination in Child Custody Disputes (2009) 18 *S. Cal. Interdisciplinary LJ.* 259.

human mind and force. When the force comes into being, the corporation then mirrors the human mind thereby justifying the (alternative) metaphor of a machine with accompanying inferences of why it should be depersonalized in a world increasingly scientific. In effect, the skilful recognition of the cognitive implications of metaphor and mastery of its use makes the lawyer not only a cannon folder of meaning and reality but also a creator of it. Unquestionably, thinking metaphorically is an inescapable and fundamental method of increasing understanding.

Metaphor and Legal Writing

Generally, lawyers are textual writers, hardly incorporating visuals in their writing. It is therefore uncommon to see image-driven written argument used by lawyers and judges even though cognitive science justifies its use as a rhetorical flourish.[42] In fact, the only rare cases lawyers use visuals in legal writing has been limited to their use. In those rare occurrences images have served as powerful metaphoric tools for persuasion.[43]

---

[42]Elizabeth G. Potter, Taking Images Seriously, (2014) 114 *Columbia L. Rev.* 1687; Stephen R. Miller, The Visual and the Law of Cities (2013) 33 *Pace L. Rev.* 183 (describing influence of visual persuasion on urban development law). But cf. Rebecca Tushnet, Worth a Thousand Words: The Images of Copyright, (2012) 125 *Harv. L. Rev.* 683 (an article which criticizes the use of images in copyrights litigation) ("[C]ourts don't like to think about images, and have few tools to deal with them . . . .") @ 684–85, ("Images seem especially dangerous because their power is irrational.") @ 694. See also, Robert H. Jackson, Advocacy before the Supreme Court: Suggestions for Effective Case Presentations (1951) 37*Am. Bar Ass. J.* 801 @ 803 (1951) ("[M]ost contentions of law are won or lost on the facts."); Alex Kozinski, The Wrong Stuff, (1992) *B.Y.U. L. Rev.* 325 @ 330 ("There is a quaint notion out there that the facts don't matter on appeal—that's where you argue about the law; facts are for sissies and trial courts. The truth is much different. The law doesn't matter a bit, except as it applies to a particular set of facts.").

[43]Elizabeth G. Potter, Taking Images Seriously, (2014) 114 *Columbia L. Rev.* 1687 ("People now see more images in a day than our ancestors would have seen in their lives; over 3.5 trillion photos have been taken, and there are ubiquitous tools for sharing such photos. Few of those images come from or end up in legal documents, however. Words, not images, are a lawyer's most essential tool. From plausible pleadings to fractured Supreme Court opinions, from reams of discovery documents to piles of due diligence, text defines the profession. For the most part, the visual comes into the law only in the guise of metaphor, or in a textual description of a religious symbol, a sonogram image, or a picture at the heart of a copyright dispute. But that does not mean text must be the sole medium for disseminating legal ideas. Visual evidence has been a "taken- for-granted form of proof" in trial practice for well over a century, and extensive research has proven its capacity to efficiently and powerfully convey even complex information.") @ 1699.See also, Bernard J. Hibbitts, Making Sense of Metaphors: Visuality, Aurality, and the Reconfiguration of American Legal Discourse, 16 *Cardozo L. Rev.* 229, 230 (1994) (listing host of visual metaphors for describing legal concepts, including "bright-line" tests, constitutional "penumbras," and "bundle of sticks" in property rights). (describing role of metaphor in legal discourse); Jonathan H. Blavin& I. Glenn Cohen, Gore, Gibson, and Goldsmith: The Evolution of Internet Metaphors in Law and Commentary (2002)16 *Harv. J.L. & Tech.* 265 @ 267 ("When courts encounter new technologies not yet anticipated by the law, their reliance on analogical reasoning plays a profoundly important role in the application of proper legal rules.")

One such example is Judge Posner judicial opinion in *Gonzalez-Servin* v. *Ford Motor Co.,*[44] where the learned judge used pictures to drive home his metaphoric comparison of a lawyer who ignored circuit precedent to an ostrich burying its head in the sand. "The ostrich is a noble animal," the opinion states, "but not a proper model for an appellate advocate."

The textual metaphor is followed by not one but two images placed one over the other. The first is of an ostrich with its head in the sand; the second is of a suited man in an identical pose:

[44] *Gonzalez-Servin* v. *Ford Motor Co.*, 662 F.3d 931, 934 (7th Cir. 2011) @ 935.

Although the opinion of brilliant Judge Richard Posner is only five pages long, its message is loud and clear. Its triple overkill—two images and a textual metaphor—effectively conveys the court's disdain for wilfully ignorant lawyers.[45]

Unquestionably, such metaphoric images are powerful because images not only "tell" but "show" in graphic ways that textual writing can hardly do. Skilled lawyers should learn and effectively use images to persuade.

Metaphoric Allusion in Legal Writing

Metaphoric allusions are generally used in four levels of legal writing: (i) at doctrinal level; (ii) at legal methods level; (iii) as stylistic metaphors; (iv) as inherent metaphor.[46]

1. Doctrinal Metaphor

Doctrinal metaphors are metaphors that refer to doctrinal aspects of law – governing principles of law. It is common to hear lawyers say for example the following:

It is the "covering the field" principle in constitutional law;

The "veil of incorporation" theory of company law;

The "ring" doctrine of conspiracy;

The concept of "apprenticeship" in professional legal education;

These and other short cut metaphors used to summarize legal doctrine are taken as given by the profession. Much as they are powerful and helpful hints on how to understand law, they can be potentially dangerous road maps to understanding doctrines. For much as they are descriptive of abstract principles of law, used to name nameless things (expressing the abstract in the concrete) they truly cannot capture all the nuances of the abstract and loyalty to them can mislead.[47]

A skilled lawyer must therefore know when and how it is appropriate to confront established doctrine metaphor to create change. The Nike discussion is

---

[45] See Elizabeth G. Potter, Taking Images Seriously, (2014) 114 *Columbia L. Rev.* 1687 @ 1773-4. (Some commentators characterized the opinion as disrespectful, and the Houston lawyer who was the target of the attack stated, "I think it takes some dignity away from the court.")

[46] Smith, above n. 3 @ 205-216.

[47] See *Berkey* v. *Third Ave. Ry. Co.* (1926) 155 N.E. 58 @ 61; 244 NY 84 @ 94, per Benjamin Cardozo, J ("metaphors in law are to be watched, for starting as device to liberate thought, they end often by enslaving it."). See also, Linda H. Edwards, "The Trouble with Categories: What Theory Can Teach Us about the Doctrine-Skills Divide" (2014) 20 *J. Legal Educ.* 181 (an article that examines how categories can imprison useful commonality, particularly in the doctrine/skills divide in the teaching of law). The example of evolution of a metaphor of an artificial entity becoming a person protected by the First Amendment in *Nike, Inc.* v. *Kasky*, 539 U.S. 654, 123 S. Ct. 2554 (2003) discussed in Linda L. Berger, What Is the Sound of a Corporation Speaking? How the Cognitive Theory of Metaphor Can Help Lawyers Shape the Law (2004) 2 *J. ALWD* 169 @ 180-204 is a good illustration of how the doctrinal metaphor of "corporation-as-person" can affect legal interpretation.

useful in this regard.[48] For example, courts have had good reasons to replace some doctrinal metaphor with simple literal rules to prevent stock-positions defining legal consequences. In *Laya* v. *Erin Homes Inc.*[49] adopted a 19-factor test for determining whether to disregard the corporate entity metaphor. In disregarding the prevailing doctrinal metaphor and formulating the test the court stated:

"Examination of the numerous relevant factors in a "totality of the circumstances" test provides a more enlightening analysis than merely applying metaphors, like "simulacrum", "alter ego", "instrumentality", etc.. to describe the unity of shareholders and the corporation justifying, where equitable, the piercing of the corporation veil in the case."[50]

What this demonstrates is that establish doctrinal metaphors can be reassess them in the light of the facts of a case and so skilled legal actors must learn to assess whether a prevailing metaphor accurately reflects the reality of the legal issues being interrogated by a particular case.

2. Legal Method Metaphor

A legal method metaphor is one that expresses a concept of method and analysis in metaphoric term. For example, the following statements are legal method metaphors:

The operating "test" applicable to the rule is . . . ;"

The "ingredients" of the offence are . . .;"

The "narrow" construction makes applicable . . .;

A "breakdown" of the rule reveals . . .

Etc. are all legal method metaphors because they are not based on legal doctrines but an analysis of how the doctrines should be applied. Often lawyers use them unconsciously as part of everyday legal lexicon.

Because the metaphors interrogated as going to method is often used by lawyers reflexively and the legislature sometimes use the language (such as "reasonable", "elements", "spirit", "weight", etc.) in drawing up legislation, it is easy to confuse legal method and doctrinal metaphors. This notwithstanding, both are different. Legal method metaphor is different in that the rule itself is not metaphoric but tools used to analyse or apply the rule are metaphoric. This being so, legal method metaphors do not include court-established tests which ordinarily qualify as doctrinal metaphors. Thus it would be improper to treat as legal method metaphor say "reasonableness" as the operative negligence test for

---

[48]Berger, above n. 47.

[49] (1986) 177 W. Va. 343 @ 347-48; 352 S.E. 2d.93 @ 98-99 (Supreme Court of West Virginia). See Smith, above n. 3 @ 207.

[50]Ibid., @ 348; @ 99. See also, Engel v Vitale (1962) 370 US 421 @ 445-46, per Stewart, J (dissenting); *Wallace* v. *Jaffree* (1985) 472 US 38 @ 106-07 Rehnquist, J, dissenting.

medical malpractice, when such a test is already a court-acknowledge and recognized test.[51]

3. Stylistic Metaphor

This is metaphor used by the writer as a matter of style not going into the substantive (the *what*) but is rather strategy employed in doctrinal or legal method metaphor. Stylistic metaphor rather implicates the writing style strategy of *how* the writer uses her expression. Stylistic metaphor is however not synonymous with aesthetic or ornamental writing style.

Smith divides this type of writing into two categories: metaphoric themes and point-specific stylistic metaphors. Metaphoric theme style is one where the theme of a brief or writing is described metaphoric. While most legal themes are known to be simple smidgen statements summarizing narrative, such as "the ultimate driving machine," or "the difference is clear", and are often not legalese, they could sometimes be couched as metaphoric.[52] Since the theme organizes narrative, the theme metaphor should be such that runs through a brief and provide an organizational structure to understand what the lawyer is driving at.

A good way to do so is to employ word picture as the theme of a brief. For example, in a sex abuse brief, the lawyer can use the metaphoric phrase of "Megalomaniac Defendant" to introduce and describe the antagonist defendant who thinks he has a right to molest unrestrained his employees. Such a metaphor has the effect of showing (not simply telling) the audience who the defendant is. It creates a word picture that invited the reader to see, feel, hear and even smell and taste how the defendant treats employees.

Such a recurring metaphoric theme is certainly unrelated to doctrine rule governing the analysis of how to treat sex molestation cases. But it is thematic enough to invite the audience to see, feel and if possible smell the principles that underlies the lawyer's position on the issue before the court.

Point-specific stylistic metaphor involves using the metaphor to drive home a single, specific point in argument. For example, the following would qualify as point-specific stylistic metaphors:

---

[51] For discussion on the judicially recognized test for medical malpractice see, *Okonkwo* v. *Medical & Dental Practitioners Disciplinary Tribunal*1996) 6 NWLR (pt. 786) 1 (SC); *Bolam* v. *Friern Hospital Management Committee* [1957] 2 All ER 118 @ 121, [1957] 1 WLR 582 @ 586, per McNair, J [hereinafter referred to as the "Bolam" test]. But cf. *Montgomery* v. *Lanarkshire Health Board* [2015] UKSC 1 (recent extension of the *Bolam* test in England).

[52] A theme is like a "case-tag" designed as the organizing principle around which the facts of the case is built. The goal being to give the decision-maker an organizing principle to fit the evidence into neatly. See *A2L Storytelling for Litigators: Building a Great Narrative for Judges and Juries*, 3rd ed. 2014 @ 19.

"There are two visual ways to gain knowledge of a country with which one is completely unfamiliar. One is to purchase a map and to study the landscapes and towns, not just in themselves, but in terms of the relationships between them. Distances and heights can be precisely measured; names of areas, regions, villages, and cities can be carefully located; and, of course, considerable quantities of agricultural, industrial, climatic, and other information can be gleaned by inductive, deductive, and (or) hermeneutical reasoning by the learned map-reader from the signs and signifiers used by professional cartographers. There is a science of mapping.

A second means of gaining information, however, is to obtain a series of photographs of the country in question. A typical city centre, a range of landscapes, an industrial zone, several coastal scenes, and so on will give the viewer literally a snapshot understanding of the country in question. And while such an approach may not be scientific in its geographical precision, it will have the great advantage of allowing the viewer to form an in-depth and three-dimensional understanding of some precise areas of the country in which the photographs were taken.

In some ways these two approaches act...for the understanding of legal knowledge in Europe. Codes, at least as originally conceived in the era of the *mosgeometricus*, might be likened to the mapping approach, while the forms of action, which so dominated English law thinking until relatively recently, might be compared to knowledge by photographs. Yet the difference of approach goes beyond the dichotomy between legal traditions; those, whether civilian or common lawyer, who yearn for conceptual precision in legal thinking and reasoning . . ."[53]

In the above excerpt, the learned writer uses the metaphor of "mapping" and "photograph" to make implicit comparison between the civil and common law traditions, showing that both yield important perspectives to how the legal systems work without necessarily being fully revelatory. The writer uses the precision of the science of cartography is an ideal metaphor for logical ordering of law and photograph for a less logical but detailed reasoning technique system. The point-specific stylist metaphor is cleverly used to draw attention to a single, specific point – how the civil and common law legal systems work.

Point-specific metaphor is the most common form of stylistic metaphor used in legal writing.

[53] Geoffrey Samuel, Can the Common Law Be Mapped? (2005) 55 *Univ. Toronto LJ* 271.

4. Inherent Metaphor

This is the type of metaphor that inheres to us as given created by our interaction with our environment and society. These are metaphors created by us from making sense and interacting with the world.[54] We therefore create such metaphoric language unconsciously from the way we come to understand our world. Such metaphors are all around us. For instance, the word "up" and "down" are used by us to describe our spatial understanding of things away or close to the centre of the earth. So, we are used to describing pleasant feeling as though "up". Hence, we could say: "I feel *good* today", "I'm in *high* spirit", "I'm *depressed* today." In all of this we associate "up' with a feeling of happy and "down" with a feeling of sadness.

Our languages thus are full of metaphoric words and concepts that we employ in communication without us giving conscious attention to them. Many of these inherent metaphors are used in everyday legal writing and advocacy. For example we say *"advance* your argument", "*move* your motion", "*merge* your grounds of appeal", "*lower* court", *grounds* of appeal", "*burden* of proof" and many others as though they are literal words when in fact they are metaphoric. We however (erroneously) think them literal when they are not because they have virtually become commonplace.

They are automatic part of language and so do not implicate specific rhetorical strategies for lawyers as do the other types (1-3) discussed preceding this.

Learning the Craft of Metaphor

All lawyers can learn to master the skills of crafting effective metaphor. While some may be more gifted in doing so, all certainly can learn to become master crafters.[55]

The necessary steps in learning follow these basic steps in descending order:[56]

(i) identify the main point of argument to be expressed through metaphor;
(ii) the point should be conceptualized from a generalized term;
(iii) constructive think and reflect of the tangible (source) image that can express

---

[54] George Lakoff & Mark Johnson, *Metaphors We Live By*, Univ. Chicago Press, 1980.

[55]Mastery learning philosophy teaches that the majority of learners, if not all can be trained to be competent performers, debunking the notion that different capacities is the reason for sorting of large numbers of students according to their ability. See Benjamin Bloom, *Our Children Learning*, 1981; J. Block & L. Anderson, *Mastery Learning in Classroom Instruction*, 1975; Benjamin Bloom, *Mastery Learning: Theory and Practice* in J. Block, ed. 1971; Jay Feinman & Marc Feldman, Pedagogy and Politics (1984-1985) 73 Geo. L. J. 876. See also Benjamin Bloom, *Human Characteristics and School Learning*, 1976.

[56] See Smith, above n. 3 @ 242.

the broad concept of the target;

(iv) draft the metaphor that expresses the figurative analogy;

(v) vocalize the metaphor for appropriateness; and

(vi) avoid metaphoric usage pitfalls

Step (i) requires the lawyer to first think whether an argument will be advanced persuasively through the use of metaphor. If the answer is yes, then she must think reflectively about what point in the argument would best benefit from the use of the metaphor. What part of an argument will best benefit from the metaphor is a strategic decision which should be influenced by considerations such as what is the relevant issues before the court that should determine the outcome of the argument, is there a knotty point difficult to explain or grasp literally that demands simplification of the abstract to make it concrete, how would the hearer interpret the metaphor as applicable to the facts, and the like.

Step (ii) would demand of the writer to sort of step back a little and revise the narrow point sought to be highlighted in the argument in generalized term. The point of the target sought to be explicated must be expressed as generalized concept. For example, while "air" is certainly useful to use, there is acknowledge admission of its "no-weightiness," particularly when scaled for measure.

Step (iii) requires that the concrete source used to explicate the target be conceptualized in general terms to cover many features of the target to make the metaphor easily appreciated and understandable to the hearer. For example, the lawyer comparison of "no-evidence" to "air" possibly interrogates why the question of weight of evidence is inapplicable in the given facts situation, it also provides explanation for the wasted court time. The metaphor applies to ore than one feature of the trial, so, it is malleable to quickly draw similarities implicated by its use.

Step (iv) requires the writer to then craft (many) possible metaphors that graphically capture the broad concept of the target thing. the appropriateness of the chosen metaphor would be determined by such factors as the metaphor that drives better the substantive point; the concreteness of the source as explicative of the target; the resulting contribution it advances to logos, pathos and ethos.

Even after making the decision as to what metaphor to use, it may still be helpful to vocalize the metaphor to determine it is pungent enough to persuade – step (v). It is a good practice to vocalize writing for group writing and when we try to persuade others of our wording or sentence, particularly so with the use of metaphor where the writer seeks to make a leap from one thing to another that are dissimilar and latently unrelated until a felt connection is captured.

Step (vi) finally demands the crafter to sit back and analyse the crafted metaphor to determine appropriateness in it not suffering from metaphors pitfalls. The writer should analyse to avoid metaphoric overuse, avoid insulting or arcane metaphors, and the like.

These steps when mastered can be helpful in turning amateur writers to skilled persuaders through the use of metaphor.

Legal Imagination and Metaphor

Metaphor and narrative are linked; one provides background and foundation for the other. In one sense, all narrative is metaphor. Consider: when we tell a story, we invariably are inviting our listener to see one thing "as" another or, more often, to see a series of things as related events with a narrative arc or a plot. This "seeing [one thing] as [another]" is the essence of metaphor. Narrative also leads to the shorthand use of metaphors: once a story is embedded in tradition and culture, the die is cast and you no longer have to tell the tale, you can simply use the name of the character or the title of the story as a metaphor, and the plot, characters, and moral will follow, appearing to be logical entailments.[57]

Narratives contain and become metaphors, metaphors emerge from and engender stories, and legal concepts and categories are formed by and understood as both, separately and in combination. To take an example, the legal concept of malice aforethought can be structured and expressed as the story of an angry lover watching from a hiding spot with a weapon in hand, or it can be structured and expressed as the image of a mind as a container full of hate.

Metaphor advances persuasion because it provides a lens to see clearly an argument. It power to shape understanding derives from its capacity to enable the audience understand by superimposition a known structure onto a new concept. It builds from an interaction between the target (usually an abstract or unfamiliar concept) and the source (the concrete already known to the audience).[58]Metaphor is grounded in that its source is from our physical beings,

---

[57] See Linda L. Berger, How Embedded Knowledge Structures Affect Judicial Decision Making: A Rhetorical Analysis of Metaphor, Narrative, and Imagination in Child Custody Disputes (2009) 18 *South Cal. Interdisc. L.J.* 259.

[58]Linda L. Berger What is the sound of a corporation speaking? How the cognitive theory of metaphor can help lawyers shape the law (2004) 2 *Journal of the Association of Legal Writing Directors* 170. See also discussion in chapter ---. For reading about the cognitive power of metaphor, see George Lakoff, *Women, Fire, and Dangerous Things: What Categories Reveal About the Mind*, Univ. Chicago Press, 1987. Linda L. Berger, How Embedded Knowledge Structures Affect Judicial Decision Making: A Rhetorical Analysis of Metaphor, Narrative, and Imagination in Child Custody Disputes(2009) 18 *South Cal. Interdisc. L.J.* 259 (an article which examines how these embedded knowledge structures affect judicial decision making, showing that the best interests of the child standard fails to explain child custody outcomes because the cognitive setting for custody disputes is cluttered with outmoded metaphors, simplistic images, and unexamined narratives, all of which interferes with the ability of judges to attend to complex and radical transformations of parent-child relationships).

our neural networks, and our experiences in the world. But it is also a product of imagination. Yes, it springs from the users capacity to visualize one thing as another, and then to make the audience so see it so too.

Skilled lawyers recognize that metaphor can only be used as a persuasion tool if they are able to unravel it; to argue for a new metaphor by imagination.

The word metaphor is a metaphor derived from experience, coming from the Greek words that mean, "to carry over" and suggesting that the meanings and ideas associated with one thing are carried over to another. It is imaginative rationality because it brings together the reasoning processes of categorization and inference with the capacity to see one thing as another. It is a great persuasion tool because what we know from experience is more believable than what we learn or read about. Metaphor draws on tacit knowledge that has been embedded through unavoidable and repeated experience. Its great power is fortified by the quietness of its presence; unlike an announced position, it is hard to question a position based on assumptions that are rooted in entrenched, but unnoticed metaphors.

Metaphor matters to lawyers because they affect their understanding of the law, their analytical ability to critique arguments, and their imaginative ability to craft arguments. Metaphoric language helps both writers and readers think differently about a subject; it thus aids in invention as well as in clarifying an argument. Metaphor helps persuasion by leading an audience to see resemblances and patterns and to make inferences where they might not otherwise be revealed. Because a metaphor is inherently open to interpretation, metaphors can be used to advance uncertain or contradictory ideas. Such "cloaked imprecision" is part of metaphor's appeal and its peril.

Conclusion

Skilful mastery about use of metaphor in legal argument is a rhetorical tool for persuasion that should not be minimized. It implicates all aspects of classical rhetoric (logos, pathos and ethos).

Logos functions to communicate the logical substance of an argument. When a writer consciously uses effective metaphor it helps the audience to get the substance of the argument through analogy. In fact, substantive points are easier to communicate using metaphor than using literal terms. [59]in this regard, metaphors can be likened to African parables, they convey substantive, concrete ideas and concepts difficult to express literally in abstract form easier for the audience to grasp.

---

[59] Aristotle refers to it as "giv[ing] name to nameless things." See Aristotle, *The Rhetoric of Aristotle* (Lane Copper trans.) Prentice-Hall, 1932 @ 188.

Metaphors also implicate pathos – the process of persuasion through emotion. Undoubtedly, a well-crafted metaphor would generate favourable emotional appeal to the audience. Because metaphors make the leap from one thing to another, it is like riddle to be solved by its hearer. Solving it by making the necessary felt connection between the target and source – two ordinary dissimilar things is pleasing to the hearer, thus creating pleasant emotional appeal. In fact, in cases where the hearer is in suspense as to the relation between the target and source because they at first appear dissimilar, and then comes unexpectedly to appreciate the symbolic similarity can entertain the hearer. Thus, metaphor can serve to "charm" he hearer or reader. Once that positive mood is triggered, the writer substantive argument will be more welcomed.

Additionally, metaphor carries with it ethos function – persuasion by establishing credibility in the eyes of the reader. The effective use of metaphor conveys to the hearer intelligence of the writer.[60]

Useful as metaphors are in crafting legal arguments the lawyer must avoid its pitfalls: not overuse them, use offensive metaphors, arcane or far-fetched metaphors or those that trivializes legal issues being interrogated.

---

[60] Aristotle states that the skill of constructing effective metaphors "is, in itself, a sign of genius." See Aristotle, Aristotle's Poetics: A Translation and Commentary for Students of Literature (Leon Golden trans.) quoted in Michael Frost, Greco-Roman Analysis of Metaphoric Reasoning (1996) 2 *J. Leg. Writing* 113 @ 127.

Chapter 21

Figures of Speech in Persuasion

What is truth? a mobile army of metaphors, metonyms, anthropomorphisms, in short, a sum of human relations which were poetically and rhetorically heightened, transferred, and adorned, and after long use seem solid, canonical, and binding to a nation. - *Friedrich Nietzsche, On Truth and Lying in Friedrich NietzscheOn Rhetoric and Language (Sander L. Gilman et al. eds. & trans., 1989) @ 250.*

Introduction

In the view of Aristotle, rhetoric is "the faculty of observing in any given case the available means of persuasion."[1] It is therefore helpful for the lawyer to explore the role of rhetoric as an available means of persuasion.[2]

---

[1]Aristotle, *The Rhetoric of Aristotle*, book I, chapter I @ 1355b, line 26 (Lane Cooper trans., D. Appleton & Co. 1932) @ 224. The Rhetoric continues:

"It is clear, then, that rhetoric is not bound up with a single definite class of subjects, but is as universal as dialectic; it is clear, also, that it is useful. It is clear, further, that its function is not simply to succeed in persuading, but rather to discover the means of coming as near such success as the circumstances of each particular case allow. In this it resembles all other arts. For example, it is not the function of medicine simply to make a man quite healthy, but to put him as far as may be on the road to health; it is possible to give excellent treatment even to those who can never enjoy sound health. Furthermore, it is plain that it is the function of one and the same art to discern the real and the apparent means of persuasion, just as it is the function of dialectic to discern the real and the apparent syllogism. What makes a man a "sophist" is not his faculty, but his moral purpose."

[2]Rhetoric examines how the law works by exploring a meaning-making process, one in which law is "constituted" as human beings located within particular historical and cultural communities write, read, argue about, and decide legal issues. So, from the rhetorical point of view lawyers are human actors whose work makes a difference because they are the readers, writers, and members of interpretive and compositional communities who together "constitute the law. See Linda L. Berger, Studying and Teaching Law as Rhetoric: A Place to Stand (2010) 16 *J. Leg. Writing* 3 @ 6 (an article that treats law as rhetoric rather than just a tool or technique, or art or craft of persuasion, but instead as an interactive process of persuasion and argumentation that is used to resolve uncertain questions. It makes the bold assertion that rhetoric is not all about literary device that glosses legal reasoning, but is in fact central to perception, understanding and expression). For general reading on rhetoric, see Stanley Fish, Rhetoric, in Doing What Comes Naturally: Change, *Rhetoric, and the Practice of Theory in Literary and Legal Studies,* Duke Univ. Press 1989; Richard K. Sherwin, The Narrative Construction of Legal Reality (1994)18 *Vt. L. Rev.* 681; Gerald Wetlaufer, Rhetoric and Its

Literary allusions are important to persuasion because once the lawyer's arguments are invented, selected, and arranged, they must put into words or writing. Cognitive linguistics are of the view that speakers put ideas or meaning (objects) into words (containers) which is transferred through a kind of conduit to the hearer. The process follows a pattern of extracting ideas from the words used in communication. [3] Since the communicator invariably has a more sophisticated understanding of the idea she seeks to relate than does the hearer and because "we tend to understand abstract phenomena in terms of more concrete things" the communicator would often we use metaphors and metonyms as tools for transferring an idea using objects that represent, and also characterize, the ideas.[4]

Generally, the function of figures of speech is to create impression and emphasis points. The writer or speaker by using figures of speech not customary seeks to draw the audience attention to the memorable specific important point in a discourse.

Classical rhetoricians identified a number of figures of speech, schemes which are deviation from the ordinary pattern of words but are used for purposes of persuasion. [5] These figures of speech can be divided into schemes and tropes.[6]Schemes refer to deviation from grammatical structure or arrangement of words. In using them the writer arranges words in a way different from their ordinary structure. Smith gives a classical anastrophe illustrative example stating:

"how Sunday into Monday melts!"

This is certainly a deviation from customary arrangement that should read:

"how Sunday melts into Monday."

Denial in Legal Discourse(1990)76 *Va. L. Rev.* 1545 @ 1549 (discussing a range of ideas related to the "epistemological consequences of rhetoric").

[3]Johan Vanparys, *A Survey of Metalinguistic Metaphors*, in *By Word of Mouth: Metaphor, Metonymy, and Linguistic Action in a Cognitive Perspective* 1, 2 (Louis Goossens *et al.*, eds., John Benjamin's Pub. Co. 1995); James Parry Eyster, Lawyer as Artist: Using Significant Moments and Obtuse Objects to Enhance Advocacy (2008) 14 *J. Leg. Writing* 87.

[4]Carl Jung, *On the Relation of Analytical Psychology to Poetry*, in *The Portable Jung* 301, 307 (Joseph Campbell ed., R.F.C. Hull trans., Viking Press, Inc. 1971); Friedrich Nietzsche, On Truth and Lying in *Friedrich Nietzsche On Rhetoric and Language* (Sander L. Gilman et al. eds. & trans., 1989) @ 250 (where figures of speech is considered a device for creating truth in society, the writer states: "What is truth? a mobile army of metaphors, metonyms, anthropomorphisms, in short, a sum of human relations which were poetically and rhetorically heightened, transferred, and adorned, and after long use seem solid, canonical, and binding to a nation.").

[5]Edward P. J. Corbett & Robert J. Connors, *Classical Rhetoric for the Modern Student*, 4th ed. Oxford U. Press 1999) @ 1.

[6]Scheme denotes a figure of speech taken from Latin *schema*, which in early sense designated 'diagram or outline, while tropes refer to figurative words. See Corbett & Connors, above n. 3 @

In employing anastrophe, the writer intentionally inverts the verb "melts" and the proposition "into Monday" by adding flair and style to the statement.

Tropes, on the other hand, are a deviation in the meaning or significance of words. It is the use of words to mean something other than their traditional meaning. Metaphor, simile, hyperbole are good example of tropes.

Much as the classical rhetoricians division if schemes and tropes can be helpful in understanding figures of speech, this chapter however will only discuss a few of the various sub-division considered particularly connected with modern writing and advocacy.

Schemes include:

(i) schemes of balance, such as parallelism and antithesis;

(ii) schemes of unusual or inverted word order, such as anastrophe (inversion of the natural or usual word order), parenthesis, and apposition;

(iii) schemes of omission, such as ellipsis, asyndeton (deliberate omission of conjunctions), and polysyndeton (deliberate use of many conjunctions); and

(iv) schemes of repetition, such as alliteration, assonance, anaphora (repetition of the same word or group of words at the beginning of successive clauses), epistrophe (same but at the end of successive clauses), climax (arrangement in order of increasing importance), antimetibole (repetition of words, in successive clauses, in reverse grammatical order).[7]

And tropes include:

(i) related tropes of metaphor, simile, synecdoche, and metonymy;

(ii) puns;

(iii) antanaclasis (or repetition of a word in two different senses); paronomasia (use of words that sound alike but have different meanings);

(iv) periphrasis (substitution of a descriptive word for a proper name or of a proper name for a quality associated with the name);

(v) personification;

(vi) hyperbole;

(vii) litotes (deliberate use of understatement);

(viii) rhetorical question;

(ix) irony;

(x) onomatopoeia;

(xi) oxymoron; and

(xii) paradox.[8]

---

[7] Corbett & Robert J. Connors, above n. 3 @ 377-395.

[8] Ibid @ 395-409.

Schemes and Tropes Figures of Speech

Schemes are various ways a speaker or writer could arranges words different from their ordinary structure to create effect. Tropes, on the other hand, are a deviation in the meaning or significance of words. Both could be classified under contemporary heads to include the following:

A. Specific Figures of Speech

(i) Alliteration

Alliteration involves the use of two or more similar words producing some rhythm. Its use emphasizes because it is melodious. It is commonly used in poetic writing, particularly verse writing.

One such is the poem on "the other room." Its verses read thus:

"The other room
Where a woman pretends
To be weak
So that a man
Can believe he is strong . . .
The other room
Where the gods of men
Become worshiper of women. . .
The other room . . ."

Modern politicians are known to use alliterative speech. The great rhetorician Martin Luther King made good use of it in persuasion. His "I have a dream" alliteration is common place. The speech is replete with the alliteration of "I have a dream."

Alliteration is however discouraged as a writing style for prose because some consider it too fanciful and artistic. Whatever view one takes, it must be stated that it can be useful in legal writing particularly when used sparingly and strategically. F deemed fit for legal writing by the lawyer, she should consider its purpose – it must serve not only to be artistic but also relevant in driving the important point sought to be emphasized.

(State a few legal writings using alliteration.)

(ii) Allusion

Allusion is casual, indirect or subtle reference to a person, event or thing which is wrapped in the memory of the audience. It is generally a clever device of omit the mention of a thing directly. Allusion of this sort is effective in writing only when the audience can draw the necessary connection to the thing being alluded to.

(iii) Anastrophe
Anastrophe is the inversion of the natural or usual word order. It is sometimes referred to as inversion because words in a sentence are deliberately placed out of their traditional order. It actually involves deliberate breaking of grammar rules for purpose of emphasis. So, it must only be used where the audience establishes the credibility of the writer or speaker as to her general grammatical skills.

Examples of anastrophe are:

"""How Sunday into Monday melts!"

(iv) Antithesis
Antitheses are words (ideas) in a sentence that are juxtaposed to create effect. While the two ideas are technically antithetical, antithesis as a figure of speech here is rather concerned with placing the seeming contrasting ideas side by side in parallel structure. This is the type that is effective in rhetoric.

Examples include:

"We know what we are today, but we don't know what we may be tomorrow."

"No one knows tomorrow, but we can plan for tomorrow."

Antithesis figure of speech is generally powerful because it presents contrasting ideas; the seeming contrasting ideas are presented side by side; it uses similar wordings and parallel grammatical structure. In example one "know" is common and the ideas about tomorrow as placed as parallels.

(v) Antonomasia
Antonomasia the use of a proper name to express a general idea (e.g. a Scrooge for a miser or Shylock for a greed person).

(vi) Aporia
Aporia occurs where a writer expresses difficulty as how to determine where to begin a task or what to do I the light of the magnitude of a task. Its use in writing is to create dramatic effect, thereby attracting the attention of the reader.

Example:

"The task ahead is enormous. Where do we start from?"

"The errors in this brief are so numerous, that it is simply difficult to know where to start."

(vii) Apostrophe

Apostrophe an exclamatory passage in a speech or poem addressed to a person (typically one who is dead or absent) or thing (typically one that is personified). It often employed when a writer turns away from the regular discussion to address an absent person or a personified abstraction.[9]

Example:

"How else can a defendant exhibit greed!"

(Give examples)

It is generally very dramatic, for what reason some suggest that it is inappropriate for legal writing.[10]

(viii) Iconicity

Iconicity sometimes referred to as bulk is the matching of composition style with substantive ideas being expressed. For example, when stating that a thing is small or insignificant, the writer may small words, letters, sentences or paragraphs. The converse is the case.

Example:

It was fun. We laughed and laughed and laughed and laughed.

The length of the sentence and of course the repetition describes the effect of the fun. It was real fun. Plenty of it.

B. Conjunctive Deviation

(ix) Asyndeton

Asyndeton is a scheme of omission which omits the conjunctive word simply to emphasis, create dramatic and rhythm effects. It is a deliberate omission between words or phrases in a series.

Examples:

The boy, the man, the girl, the woman all fled for their dear lives.

By deliberately omitting the conjunctive "and" the writer achieves emphasis, drama and rhythm.

---

[9]Smith @ 318.

[10] Ibid @ 319 ("lawyers. . .would probably be better off leaving apostrophe to the worlds of drama and poetry.")

(x) Polysyndeton

Polysyndeton is the opposite of asyndeton. It involves the use of excessive conjunctions. The Bible (Genesis) account of creation is a good example of polysyndeton. It reads:

> And God said, Let there be light, and there came to be light. And God saw that the light was good, and he separated the light from the darkness."

Undoubtedly, the many "and" creates effect. It emphasizes. It is dramatic. It is all rhythmic. Here also our use of "it" can be subtle polysyndeton.

C. Correction

Correction is to recall statement and correct it. It is used to amend a statement, usually by restating it more forcefully. True a writer can easy delete the incorrect statement. So, if a writer uses correction, all the writer says to the audience is that I am intentional in not deleting the incorrect statement but I am restating the correct position more forcefully so that the audience knows what I mean and what I do not mean. It reveals that the writer chooses his words consciously and deliberately to show her strong feeling and precision of thought. The ultimate aim being for the audience to place the same quantity of emphasis the writer puts on the correct statement.

Example:

> This is the point all are making - excuse me, reasonable people are making.

D. Ellipsis

Ellipsis the omission from speech or writing of a word or words that are superfluous or that can be understood from contextual clues.it is very rare for an ellipsis to occur without a linguistic antecedent.

Example: is "a set of dots (…) indicating an ellipsis. So, it is used when words otherwise necessary for the complete grammatical construction of a sentence is deliberately omitted without undermining the sentence coherence and understanding.

Example:

> He is tall, huge, intimidating in size.

If written without ellipsis the sentence would read: "He is tall. He is huge. He is intimidating." Ellipsis omits the "he", yet the reader understands that all the adjectives refer to the same person.

Ellipsis is thus better created with the use of two parallel clauses by omitting the second or subsequent clause. The structure of the first clause supplies the context to understand subsequent clauses.

Example:

To err is human, to forgive is divine.

E. Hyperbole

Hyperbole is the use of exaggeration in expressing thought. We daily use it in everyday speaking. Such as "I'm damn hungry I can eat a cow."

Hyperbole is not advisable in legal writing because our code of ethics demand truthfulness and precision.

F. Irony

Irony is used to describe the very opposite of the literal meaning. Like hyperbole it is common in everyday communication. For example, a person suffering from harmattan cold could say "it's really warm here." The use of such a speech tell the hearer that what the speaker means is the very opposite of what is said.

Because it is susceptible to misinterpretation, irony is not advisable for use in legal writing.

G. Litotes

Litotes is like hyperbole, but whereas hyperbole is deliberate exaggeration, litotes is deliberate understatement. For example, a quack scientist can be described as "a genius."

H. Paralepsis

Paralepsis is emphasizing something by pretending to pass over it. For example, one can say "his evidence is full of contradictions and many at times weird to imagine, *to say nothing of her outright admission of crime.* In truth the speaker has by the statement indicted her of committing crime. Phases often used as paralepsis include expressions like "not to mention", "say nothing of", etc.

I. Personification

Personification is a figure of speech which ascribes human qualities to inanimate objects, abstraction and animals.

For example, "trust is a slow runner, but gets the upper hand with time."

J. Puns

Pun is a joke exploiting the different possible meanings of a word or the fact that there are words which sound alike but have different meanings. For example: "the Railway Society reception was an informal party of people of all stations (excuse the pun) in life." Puns are witty plays on words.

K. Repetition

Repetition is used to emphasis points. The types of repetition identified by rhetoricians include anadipolis, anaphora, antimetibole, and epistrophe.

Anadipolis

Anadipolis is the use of same word or phrase at the end of one clause and at the beginning of a subsequent clause. For example: "all of them act as animals - animals, they truly are."

Anaphora

Anaphora is the repetition of the same word or group of words at the beginning of successive clauses. In it the writer uses the same words or group of words at the beginning of successive clauses.

Example:

> The young as so strong, so exuberant, so energetic, so full of life.

Antimetibole

Antimetibole is the repetition of words, in successive clauses, in reverse grammatical order or inverted order.

Example:

> Fellow citizen, ask not what you country can do for you, but what you can do for her.
>
> Let no man live in fear, but we must fear not to fear.

Epistrophe

Epistrophe is the use of same words or group of words at the end of successive clauses. For example: "democracy is the government of the people, by the people, for the people."

"The sovereign is the uncommandable commander who commands all backing it with sanction."

L. Metonym

Metonym usual function to clarify an idea by transmitting an object to the mind of the listener, particularly in describing an (unpleasant or embarrassing)target by presenting it through a vehicle that mystifies or ostentatiously hides the target. For example, one could simply use the metonym "Aso Rock" to describe the Nigerian presidency or using the metonym "downsize" rather than the harsh, unpleasant literal word "sack". In the later example, while "downsizing" is the firing of employees, the use of the metonym does not directly describe the unpleasant event of the workers dismissal. The safety of the mystifying, or obscuring, metonym is a characteristic that makes it useful in describing a disturbing target.[11]

It involves referring to a thing not by its literal name, but by a word suggestive of or associated with it. We often in everyday speech use "pen for writing", "bottle for alcoholic beverage", etc.

Psycholinguists consider metonyms are equally as powerful as metaphors in communicating abstract ideas. While the metaphor reminds us of something else because of its similarity, a metonym on the other hand, brings an association because it is part of something else (such a particular necklace could remind us of a particular woman). But more than such a poetic tool, a metonym is "recognized as a particular type of mental mapping" presented to call to mind "an entire person, object, or event."[12]

A metonym is designed to allow the use of one idea as a vehicle to reach a "target" idea. Sometimes however there are several targets to choose interrogated by a metonym. Much as this can be confusing to the hearer, research suggests that the listener will usually choose the clearest and the most relevant interpretation of a metonym. For example, if a communicator uses the phrase at a marriage ceremony such as "who gives the hand of this lady in marriage," listeners could either think the question demands to know who literally is giving the lady's hand or who is betrothing her for marriage. Most in the audience of course will give the metonym its clearest meaning – associating the question with betrothing.

---

[11]Eyster, above n. 4 @ 111-112 (the safety of the mystifying process through metonym in describing a disturbing target is suggested to be at the core of its obtuse object's power).

[12]Raymond W. Gibbs, Jr., *Speaking and Thinking with Metonymy,* in *Metonymy in Language and Thought* (Klaus-Uwe Panther & Günter Radden eds., John Benjamin's Pub. Co. 1999) @ 61, 66..See also, Linda L. Berger, Of Metaphor, Metonymy, and Corporate Money: Rhetorical Choices in Supreme Court Decisions on Campaign Finance Regulation (2007) 58 *Mercer L. Rev.* 949 (an analysis of *McConnell* v. *Federal Election Commission,* 540 U.S. 93 (2003) containing metaphorical and metonymical perspectives on the use of corporate money to finance election campaigns).

M. Rhetorical Question

A rhetoric question is one asked by a speaker not designed to elicit hope or expectation of answer from the audience. It could be either by a transitional or substantive rhetorical question.

For the former the speaker uses a self-imposed question to set an immediate answer or to transit on a new point of discussion. For example: what is the heart of this appeal? Simple! That the defendant must respect the rule of law."

The primary function of the transitional rhetoric question is to put the audience in a mould that gets it ready to listen or read further discussion by the writer or speaker. It draws the reader's attention by announcing that a question that has become apparent by the preceding discussion is about to be answered.

On the other hand, substantive rhetorical question is the making of substantive point by stating it in the form of a self-answering question. The question merely suggests an irresistible answer. For example, a lawyer could state: "of what use would the rights guaranteed under the Constitution be if the defendant can go on in disobedience of court orders??

I this context the writer's point is made, albeit, obliquely, rather than directly. The point comes out not through direct assertion but from obvious context.

Conclusion

Figures of speech as tools of persuasion. They assist the writer to elicit strong emotional responses from the audience. They often make presentation dramatic and emphasis point of discussion. This is how they perform pathos function. The audience is kept in a receptive mood to receive and understand the presentation.

Also, it performs ethos function in that the audience is often inspired and admires effective presentations that are delightful. This creates the necessary credibility in the eyes of the audience.[13]

[13]Marius FablusQuintilianus, *Institutio Oratoria,* (HB Butler, trans. Harvard Univ. Press, 1954) @ 211-213 (" by the employment of skilful ornament the [advocate] commends himself at the same time [that he commends his argument.")

PART VI

Chapter 22

Persuasion and Professional Responsibility

Introduction

Professionalism implicates the appropriate behaviours and integrity of a lawyer in a range of situations; which includes the capacity to deal sensitively and effectively with clients, colleagues, and others from a range of social, economic, and ethnic backgrounds, identifying and responding positively and appropriately to issues of culture and disability that might affect communication techniques and influence a client's objectives.[1]Professional responsibility therefore generally understood, it refers to conduct consistent with the tenets of the legal profession as demonstrated by a lawyer's civility, honesty, integrity, character, fairness, competence, ethical conduct, public service, and respect for the rule of law, the courts, clients, other lawyers, witnesses, and unrepresented parties.

Our society expects lawyers to provide competent legal services that achieve their clients' goals. In providing such services, a professional lawyer will comply with the law as well as with the rules and values of the legal profession. A professional lawyer will be trustworthy and honest, work cooperatively with opposing counsel, judges, colleagues, and clients, perform on schedule, keep promises, respond promptly to telephone calls, answer questions courteously, and charge a fair price. A professional lawyer will be accountable for the quality of his or her work.

[1]The Law Society, Qualifying as a Solicitor – A Framework for the Future: A Consultation Paper 6 (March 2005) [hereinafter Law Society Framework], available athttp://www.lawsociety.org.uk /documents/downloads/becomingtfr05consultppr. pdf. (last visited May 23, 2018). See also, Wash. State Ct. A.P.R. 11 Regulation 101(n) (Supreme Court of Washington and the Washington State Bar) ("Professionalism" is no more, and no less, than conducting one's self at all times in such a manner as to demonstrate complete candour, honesty, courtesy and avoidance of unnecessary conflict in all relationships with clients, associates, courts and the general public. It is the personification of the accepted standard of conduct that a lawyer's word is his or her bond. It includes respectful behaviour towards others, including sensitivity to substance abuse prevention, anti-bias or diversity concerns. It encompasses the fundamental belief that a lawyer's primary obligation is to serve his or her clients' interests faithfully and completely, with compensation only a secondary concern, acknowledging the need for a balance between the role of advocate and the role of an officer of the court, and with ultimate justice at a reasonable cost as the final goal.").

The MacCrate Report for example, described four "fundamental values of the profession:" (i) provision of competent representation; (ii) striving to promote justice, fairness, and morality; (iii) contributing to the profession's fulfilment of its responsibility to enhance the capacity of law and legal institutions to do justice; and (iv) professional self- development.[2]

In chapter however we will focus on the two fundamental values (ii) and (iii) as those more intricately connected with the lawyering skills of persuasion.

Truth as Fundamental Professional Value

No serious lawyer will question the place of professional responsibility in the practice of law. This is what makes questionable whether the rhetorical techniques and strategies discussed in this book interrogate good, moral and ethical lawyering.[3] Some consider legal rhetoric as merely manipulative use of language, devoid of ethics and intellect.[4] As a result, they have become prejudicial of persuasion techniques. In fact, rules of professional conduct prohibit falsehood and unethical conduct in advocacy.[5]

Of all the values implicated in professional responsibility and ethics, truth is paramount. According to Burke much as all professional values deserve attention, truth and justice should be accorded primacy. He stated:

---

[2] American Bar Association, Section of Legal Education and Admissions to the Bar, Legal Education and Professional Development - an Educational Continuum, Report of the Task Force on Law Schools and the Profession: Narrowing the Gap [hereinafter referred to as *MacCrate Report*]. But cf. Russell G. Pearce, MacCrate's Missed Opportunity: The MacCrate Report's Failure to Advance Professional Values (2003) 22 *Pace L. Rev.* 575 (an article that suggest that complained that the MacCrate Report did not give first priority to values over skills and that the Report inadequately describes and explains professional values).

[3] L. Lerman& P. Schrag *Ethical Problems in the Practice of Law*, 2nd ed. NY: Wolters Kluver, 2004; D. Nicholson & J. Webb *Professional Legal Ethics: Critical Interrogations*, Oxford: Oxford Univ. Press,1999; Kurt M. Saunders, Law as Rhetoric, Rhetoric as Argument (2006) 3 *J. ALWD* 164; Jeanne Kaiser, When The Truth and The Stories Collide: What Legal Writer Can Learn From The Experience of Non-Fictional Writers About The Limits of Storytelling (2010) 16 *J. Leg. Writing* 163.

[4] *Aristotle's Nicomachean Ethics*, Book VII; *Aristotle, the Ethics of Aristotle: The Nicomachean Ethics*, Book VI, @ 177 (J.A.K. Thomson, trans., 1953) (Aristotle perceives the study of rhetoric as deep activity - referring to it as "a habit of the mind."); Kristen Konrad Robbins, Philosophy v. Rhetoric in Legal Education: Understanding the Schism between Doctrinal and Legal Writing Faculty (2006) 3 *J. ALWD* 108 @ 112. See also, Laurie C. Kadoch, *So Help Me God: Reflections on Language, Thought and the Rules of Evidence Remembered*, 9 *Rutgers J.L. &Relig.* 2 (forthcoming Fall 2007) (available at http://org.law.rutgers.edu/publications/law-religion/forthcoming.shtml), both cited in Laurie C. Kadoch, The Third Paradigm: Bringing Legal Writing Out of the Box And Into the Mainstream: A Marriage of Doctrinal Subject Matter and Legal Writing Doctrine (2007) 13 *J. Leg. Writing* 55 @ 57 ft. nt. 10.

[5] Rules of Professional Conduct for Legal Practitioners, 2007 [hereinafter referred to as RPC] s. 1 (providing that a lawyer shall foster the cause of justice); s. 32 (3) (providing that a lawyer may not knowingly make a false statement of fact to a tribunal); s. 19 (2) (providing that in the course of representing a client, a lawyer shall not knowingly make a false statement of fact to a third party).

> First, we should say that truth and justice are our goals; that, though we may never find totally objective truth or achieve perfect justice, we will seek and strive for them to the best of our professional ability. Second, we should make clear that this quest for truth and justice is a professional responsibility upon which rests the reliability and integrity of the entire legal system. Hence, an individual client's desires and objectives must be subordinate to that quest. Third, our rules of conduct should specifically prohibit lawyers participation in lying, falsification, misrepresentation, or deception in every aspect of practice from courtroom advocacy to office consultation and practice.[6]

While law finds its strength in justice, justice is not synonymous with legality. A lawyer should therefore pursue justice as well as consider herself as an officer of court.

Rhetoric interrogates the basic understanding of the structure and process of legal argumentation.[7] It is the failure to appreciate the heuristics of argumentation that is responsible for why some consider persuasion as unethical lawyering. Argument traditional follows two patterns for validity: (i) the normative and (ii) descriptive correctness. It is therefore not a product of sheer formal logic (norm-giving), but a combination of it heuristics of description created from practice and culture (norm-descriptive). [8] In fact, Aristotle considers argumentation as dialectical reasoning and argument are practical in nature, not merely rigorous systems of logical and mathematical proof, as they are inadequate to explain how people actually make arguments in the real world.[9]

---

[6]Richard K. Burke, "Truth in Lawyering:" An Essay on Lying and Deceit in the Practice of Law, (1984) 38 *Ark. L. Rev.* 1 @ 3-4' @ 22 ("Truth, justice, and fairness, both in means and ends, are paramount on the scale of legal values, and when those are at stake, the other values must yield.")

[7]Anthony G. Amsterdam & Jerome Bruner, *Minding the Law,* Harv. U. Press, 2002 @ 14 (Rhetoric encompasses "ways of winning others over to our views, and of justifying those views to ourselves as well as others, when the question of how things in the world ought to work is contested or contestable."); Gerald Wetlaufer, Rhetoric and Its Denial in Legal Discourse (1990) 76 *Va. L. Rev.* 1545 @ 1546 ("By 'rhetoric,' I mean the discipline . . . in which the objects of formal study are the conventions of discourse and argument."); James Boyd White, Law as Rhetoric, Rhetoric as Law: The Arts of Cultural and Communal Life (1985) 52 *U. Chi. L. Rev.* 684 @ 684 (rhetoric establishes, maintains, and transforms the community and the culture), all cited in Linda L. Berger, Studying and Teaching Law as Rhetoric: A Place to Stand (2010) 16 *J. Leg. Writing* 3 @ 5 ft. nt. 9. For a bibliography highlighting numerous articles that explain "how rhetoric theory applies to the discipline of legal writing, see Michael R. Smith, Rhetoric Theory and Legal Writing: An Annotated Bibliography (2006)3 *J. ALWD*129.

[8]Toulmin in Stephen Toulmin *et al., An Introduction to Reasoning*, 2nd ed. NY 1984; F. Van Eemerenet. al. ,*The Study of Argumentation*, NY, 1984. See also, Linda Levin & Kurt M. Saunders, Thinking Like a Rhetor (1993) 48 *J. Legal Educ.* 108.

[9]Aristotle, On Rhetoric: A Theory of Civic Discourse (George A. Kennedy trans. Oxford Univ. Press 2nd ed. 2007) @ 112-113 (states that the most persuasive arguments are those that appeal, at least in part, to the audience's emotions.); Linda L. Berger, Studying and Teaching Law as Rhetoric: A Place to Stand (2010) 16 *J. Leg. Writing* 3 @ 50 (the learned writer states that Stephen Toulmin

As we all know, in the real world argument does not just proceed on logic grounds for it to be valid and persuasively convincing. For while logical arguments are designed to produce conclusions that are universal and absolute in their proof, practical arguments on the other hand, are designed to establish the probability or reasonableness of an assertion. Transposed into how lawyers prove facts in courts, it follows that legal argument is not concerned with proof of absolute truths, but the reasonability of legal assertions.[10]

This is what makes it plausible to say there is no bad argument in law. It is always possible to argue on two (sometimes) good positions in law- for or against a legal assertion. An argument which supports one claim would not entirely exclude those supporting opposite assertions. Thus, strict logos without the input of pathos and ethos cannot guarantee validity of an argument, because arguments depend upon language, and language admits of ambiguity and multiple interpretations.[11]

A legal argument is resolved when the audience is convinced of the logic and the reasonableness of the position canvassed by the lawyer - yes, that it is more reasonable than another rather than as objectively and inherently valid. Thus, the persuasiveness of an argument or assertion depends upon what the audience regards as persuasive. It is the audience ultimately that decides when and to what extent an assertion is justified by argument.

---

distinguishes between theoretical and practical arguments. While a practical argument requires an inferential leap from data or evidence to reach a reasonable conclusion, and the leap must be justified by claims that fit the context of a specific situation, theoretical argument on the other hand, requires no such inferences because the conclusion is certain; it goes no farther than the data in the premises and is based on universal principles. Since theoretical arguments were rare, it follows that for the subjects of arguments are rarely governed by a single principle, knowledge changes over time, and probabilities are more frequent than certainties.). See also, Paul T. Wangerin, A Multidisciplinary Analysis of the Structure of Persuasive Arguments (1993) 16 *Harv. J.L. & Pub. Policy* 195 @ 203; Saunders, above n. 1 @ 165.

[10] Aristotle, above n. 9 @ 113 ("Arguments that support one claim never entirely exclude those supporting the opposing claim. Strict logical consequence and certainty are never the result, because arguments depend upon language, and language always admits of ambiguity, equivocality, and multiple interpretation."). See also Pierre Schlag, Hiding the Ball (1996) 71 *NY Univ. L. Rev.* 1681 (an article that states that the multitude of meanings ascribed to the authoritative legal sources goes to ontological question that the legal community have constantly resisted, turning such ontological questions to epistemic questions). W.S. Merwin, *Asian Figures* (1973) 65 ("A judge decides for ten reasons nine of which nobody knows") (Chinese proverb) cited by S.I. Winter, The Cognitive Dimension of the Agon: Between Legal Power and Narrative Meaning (1988-89) 87 *Mich. L. Rev.* 2225 n. l. According to Winter, of the ten reasons only one is revealed in the judicial opinion and so for those who experience legal doctrine as manipulable, it is plausible to think that the doctrinal surface of judicial decisions merely conceals it subjective purposes looking more like the 'wheel [thrust] inside a wheel' in Ezekiel's vision of the chariot, see *Ezekiel* 1: 16,17.

[11] Kadoch, above n. 4 (an article describing how language shapes the way humans conceive of and structure reality); Jane B. Baron, Language Matters (2000) 34 *John Marshall L. Rev.* 163; Raymond W. Gibbs, Jr., Speaking and Thinking with Metonymy in Klaus-Uwe Panther & Gunter Radden eds. *Metonymy in Language and Thought*, John Benjamin's Pub. Co. 1999, 61 @ 66.

When the lawyer skilfully employs rhetoric and persuasion tools in an effective story, she undoubtedly empowers the fact-finder to choose the most satisfying resolution to the controversy. The fundamental principle espoused by rhetorically lawyering is that it carries persuasive power that lawyers should harness in their advocacy. Lawyers are therefore encouraged to present the facts from their clients' point of view; to emphasize positive facts; and to make an emotional appeal where appropriate for fact-triers to reach favourable conclusion on their behalf. In fact, legal writing professionals encourage lawyers to even employ sophisticated literary techniques in their efforts to persuade. [12] The suggestion that a lawyer should supplement logos with pathos and ethos to manipulate the subconscious impulses of a judge is an interesting one, and it is perhaps debatable whether lawyers should even make the attempt. It implicates the question whether a lawyer can weave these techniques into writing and advocacy without sacrificing professional responsibility.

Ethical Conundrum

The ethical challenges of rhetoric are well illustrated by the challenge posed by an imagined Socrates in James Boyd White's *A Dialogue on the Ethics of Argument.*[13] Speaking as Socrates, White tells two young lawyers that:

> by reason of your training and natural capacities you have what is commonly called a great power, the power of persuading those who have power of a different kind, political and economic power, to do what you wish them to do...
>
> Your professional aim is to present your case, whatever its merits, so that those with control over economic and political forces will decide for your client, and you most succeed when you most prevail. You use your mind, as we used to say of the Sophists, to make the weaker argument appear the stronger...[But] neither the power of money nor the power of persuasion is a good thing of itself; that depends upon whether it is used to advance or injure

[12] See Michael R. Smith, *Advanced Legal Writing: Theories and Strategies in Persuasive Writing,* Aspen L. & Bus. 2002) @ 193-303 (for instance, the learned writer urges the use of metaphor and literary allusion as persuasion techniques.)

[13] James Boyd White, *Reading Law and Reading Literature: Law as Language,* in *Heracles' Bow: Essays on the Rhetoric and Poetics of the Law,* Univ. Wis. Press, 1985 (an imaginary dialogue between Socrates and two modern lawyers examining the morality of advocacy invented by White). See also, White, above n. 7.

one's interest, and that is no concern of yours, with respect to your client or apparently to yourself.

You say you are your client's friend, but you do not serve his interests; in truth you are not his friend...Likewise, you are no friend to the law...

In all of this you are least of all friend to yourself...You never ask yourself in a serious way what fairness and justice require in a particular case, for to do that would not leave time for what you do."[14]

Socrates in the imaginary dialogue continues saying:

The art of rhetoric is in fact the art of ministration of the pleasures of another, really a specie of prostitution. As the sexual responses and energies of a prostitute are debased and debasing by the way they are employed, so also are your intellectual energies and responses, your ways of seeing things and describing them, your ways of making appeals and claims and argument, the very workings of your mind and the feelings of your heart. When you represent an unjust client, you are in the position of wanting an unjust result. And what do you get in return? A prostitute's pay. Like other flatters you tend to become like the object of your flattery, but since you have so many and various objects of attention, what you really give yourself is the character of none but that of a chameleon, who appears to whatever suits the moment.

Interestingly, White's dialogue contains what makes the lawyers' responses. First, that Socrates misunderstands the lawyers' enterprise, which is to "preserve and improve a language of description, value, and reason—a culture of argument—without which it would be impossible even to ask the questions that you think are most important, questions about the nature of justice in general or about what is required in a particular case.[15] Then it goes on to make the case that practicing law has a tendency not to injure but to improve the character, a tendency greatly affected by the nature of the ethical community that one establishes both with one's clients and with other lawyers and judges.[16]

---

[14]White, above n. 13 @ 215-119. See Berger, above n. 3 @ 57-58.
[15]White, above n. 13 @ 225.
[16]White, above n. 13 @ 227.

It thus requires an understanding of the process in which the lawyer makes her argument and why such arguments are ethically justified:

> the lawyer's task will always be to make the best case he can out of the materials of his culture in addressing an ideal judge. By its very nature, this is to improve his materials, both by ensuring their congruence with the world of facts outside the law and by moving them toward greater coherence, fairness, and the like.[17]

The view provides an answer as well to ethical questions:

> while I am in a sense "insincere" when I say to a judge, for example, that "justice requires" or "the law requires" such and such result, this insincerity is a highly artificial one, for no one is deceived by it...But at the same time I am implicitly saying something else, with respect to which I am by any standard being sincere: that the argument I make is the best one that my capacities and resources permit me to make on this side of the case.[18]

There is therefore nothing unethical in rhetoric techniques lawyers employ in persuasion.

Visual of Socrates

[17]Ibid. @ 227.
[18]Ibid. @ 225.

Ethical Justification of Rhetoric

Persuasion techniques and strategies in law can further be justified on the following grounds:

(i) The adversary system and truth seeking

In the common law countries, the arguments for the two sides in a dispute are made exclusively by their lawyers, and the judge is not supposed to direct a line of questioning or develop an argument. In this adversarial process, the judge acts more or less as a neutral referee who makes the lawyers follow the rules of procedure and evidence. The principle underlying the adversarial system is that the truth will emerge from a vigorous debate by the two sides.[19]Rhetoric therefore is simply a tool for pursuing truth under the adversarial system.

(ii) Lawyering skills are deployed to promote just cause

While it is a strong argument that lawyers deploy their skills of "rhetoric" (in the sense of making the weaker argument seem the stronger), some lawyers can argue that they are not necessarily indifferent to justice and the promotion of just cause. The argument however seem dubious on grounds that even where a just cause is pursued, the fact of representation itself projects a feeling of belief in the client's matter that can colour the lawyer's ability to be objective about what is fair and just in the matter. It is suggested that the psychological phenomena of projection, identity and transference could make a lawyer become overtly sympathetic to the client's cause and to exaggerate even the injustice represented by the opposing side.[20]

(iii) Skills are used to protect the architecture of modern democracy

This undoubtedly is a given. Without the profession of law and the deployment of its skills to protect individuals and groups against oppression and the Leviathan state and the powerful in society, modern democracy would be a mirage. In fact, lawyers have deployed advocacy in many cases to address social and economic injustice by using skills of persuasion to serve public good.

(iv) Rules and regulation constrains unethical lawyering

Advocacy operates within the constraints of rules that prevent lawyers representing clients from employing unethical persuasive strategies for victory. These constraints exist either the form of formal rules (such those on evidence

---

[19] Robert Cooter & Thomas Ulen, *Law and Economics,* 6th ed. MA: Boston, Addison-Wesley, 2016 @ 57-58

[20] Smith, above n. 12 @ 348-349.

and procedure) and rules of professional conduct for lawyers which constrains the limits of strategies that can be employed in pursuit of victory.[21]

(v) Social and professional roles of lawyers

Lawyers recognize the value of practical arguments in the real world. To know that machinelike alone is insufficient to persuade in the real world.[22]In other words, lawyers in engaging in rhetoric are simply thinking of law not as a social machine or a technical system of regulations applying its rules in a mechanical way, but are reflecting upon the law as an interaction of authoritative texts and as a process of legal thought and argument.[23] So, in deploying rhetoric, lawyers are bringing to play the socially constitutive nature of language – law as rhetoric.[24]

(vi) Legal morality is internal and peculiar to the profession

Whether law is autonomous in its analysis of morality invites an inquiry into whether it has its own peculiar parameters for judging right and wrong - especially in the sense of having an independent system of evaluation divorced from outside externalities.[25] Law has its exclusive legal standards for measuring legal right and wrong devoid of morals. This is not to deny that morality is a primary means of

---

[21] Jack L. Sammons, The Radical Ethics of Legal Rhetoricians (1997) 32 *Val. Univ. L. Rev.* 93 @ 98 ("Why is a rhetorical conception of the practice of law not to be so feared? . . . To begin, legal advocacy is not unbridled rhetoric. . . .If you think of lawyering as a game . . . you will know that the objective of lawyering is not winning *per se*, but winning in the way consistent with the playing of the game and the maintenance of it.")

[22]James Boyd White, Imagining the Law in Austin Sarat & Thomas R. Kearns, eds. *The Rhetoric of Law,* Univ. Mich. Press,1996 (a book on an interdisciplinary critique of the relationship between words and the law) @ 35 (where White distinguishes between "law as machine" and "law as rhetoric," by arguing that the legal profession has privileged the former thereby overlooking the law as first a social and linguistic endeavour. While the article does not necessarily seek to displace "law as machine" with "law as rhetoric," it encourages lawyers to consider law as an activity of speech and imagination occurring in a social world.)

[23]White above n. 22 @ 55.

[24] James Boyd, White, *When Words Lose Their Meaning: Constitutions and Reconstitution of Language, Character and Community,* Univ. Chi. Press, 1985 @ 267 (makes this point that "the law is best regarded not so much as a set of rules and doctrines or as a bureaucratic system or as an instrument for societal control but as a culture, for the most part a culture of argument. It is a way of making a world with a life and a value of its own.").

[25] Brian Leiter, Law and Objectivity in Jules Coleman and Scott Shapiro, *The Oxford Handbook of Jurisprudence and Philosophy of* Law, Oxford Univ. Press, 2002, 990, Andrei Marmor, An Essay on the Objectivity of Law in Brain Bix (ed.) *Analysing Law: New Essays in Legal theory* (Oxford, Clarendon Press, 2000)1; Festus Emiri & Felicia Eimunjeze, Law, Objectivity and Truth: A Cathedral View (2011) 10 *Nig. L. Prac. J.* 1. For example, Sir Edward Coke is quoted to have said: 'then the king said, that he thought the law was founded upon reason, and that he and others had reason, as well as Judges: to which it was answered to me....but His Majesty is not learned in the laws of his realm of England, and causes which concern the life, or inheritance, or goods, or fortunes of his subjects which are not to be decided by natural reason but by the artificial reason and judgment of law. Law is an act which requires long study and experience. [Prohibitions Del Roy, 6 Coke Rep. 280, 286(1608)] cited in Richard A. Posner, The Decline of Law as an Autonomous Discipline: 1962-1887 (1987) 100 *Harv. L. Rev.* 761 @ 762 fn. 1.

evaluating legal morals, but it is misleading to subsume all evaluation on the basis of morality alone. That being the case, an evaluation that proceeds on the platform that if morals are subjective then law in the final analysis must also be is misleading. Rather, rhetoric is in itself a legal norms measured objectively from a largely legal inner perspective that admits of certain externalities of which moral is one without necessarily being subjective. In effect, it is ethical for lawyers to deploy rhetoric as tool for persuasion by measuring its propriety by an exclusive legal standard of autonomy in appraising legal rightness and wrongness.

(vii) Improve a culture of argument as way to social justice

Lawyers in deploying rhetoric in argumentation teach society to resolve disputes through dialogue and dispute resolution mechanism.

Conclusion

All persuasion techniques does is to remind the lawyer that pathos and ethos must not be ignored for the sake of emphasis on logic and reason, as constitute part of the process of practical argumentation from which the audience justifies the reasonability of any argument. All arguments involve flesh and blood, real people, their society, and their language. It is the lawyer's job to make them come alive in the construction of reality. To the extent that persuasion relies on logic and an interactive heuristic of practical argumentation, it is the job of the good lawyer to bring both to the table.[26]

[26]Robert Burns, *A Theory of the Trial,* Princeton Univ. Press, 1999 @ 36-38 (P]ersuasion . . . relies on two strands—one strand of narrative and one of logical argument— related to each other like a twisting double helix that forms a lawyer's theory of the case).

Index

www.ingramcontent.com/pod-product-compliance
Lightning Source LLC
Chambersburg PA
CBHW050519240926
51846CB00003B/624
9789785764352